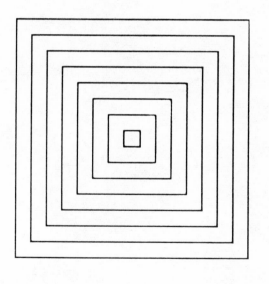

Principles of Educational and Psychological Testing

Frederick G. Brown
IOWA STATE UNIVERSITY

THE DRYDEN PRESS INC./HINSDALE, ILLINOIS

Profile and descriptive list on pages 382 and 383 reprinted from MANUAL FOR STRONG VOCATIONAL
INTEREST BLANKS, 1969 Supplement, by David P. Campbell, with the permission of the publishers, Stanford University Press. © 1969 by the Board of Trustees of the Leland Stanford Junior University.

Preface

Like many other books, this one was written because I had a particular approach, a point of view, regarding teaching educational and psychological testing which I thought to be better than other approaches. This approach, which I have tried to stress in the book, is to emphasize the logic of psychological measurement. By "the logic of measurement" I mean the consideration of why psychological measurement proceeds as it does.

This approach implies that we must ask, and answer, such questions as: Why do we measure psychological characteristics? What is being measured by psychological tests? Why is the determination of the degree of consistency of measurement essential? Why is validity a central concept in testing? What assumptions are made when achievement, aptitudes, or personality characteristics are measured? Consideration of the *why* leads directly to the *how*, the techniques of measurement, and makes discussion of the latter more meaningful.

Another orientation, the emphasis on the applied and practical aspects of psychological testing, also probably shows through. I am an applied psychologist, and most of the readers of this book, if they become psychologists or educators, will use tests in applied situations. Thus, rather than emphasize the esoteric refinements of statistical aspects of psychological measurement, I have chosen to stress the advantages and disadvantages of tests as aids in decision making.

My goal in the book, as in my courses in psychological measurement, is to provide the student with the necessary background so that he can make an intelligent evaluation of a test when the need arises. Because each situation in which a test is used is unique, one cannot say that a given test is good or bad. But one can combine his knowledge of the situation with his knowledge of the principles of psychological measurement to make an intelligent estimate of the usefulness of a particular test in a given situation. Stated differently, my goal is to teach the student what questions he should ask when evaluating a test.

The potential user may justifiably ask how this book differs from other comparable books. To me, the major differences can be summarized as follows:

(1) The emphasis on the logic of psychological measurement, the consideration of the why's of psychological testing.

(2) The avoidance of the cataloging approach. Rather than discussing a large number of tests I have cited specific tests primarily to illustrate certain principles. This approach follows from my emphasis on the logic of measurement, on principles rather than specific techniques. It also reflects my observation that students find such cataloging both boring and of little value in understanding the principles of testing. Third, it allows the instructor flexibility in choosing examples and illustrations that are particularly appropriate to his class.

(3) The sequential development of topics, particularly the relationship of consistency, validity, and scores and norms. Consistency is considered first, as without consistency of measurement we cannot relate test scores to other variables. Validity is considered before scores and norms because unless a test is valid, unless we know what the scores actually measure, any score is no more than a point in a distribution and thus psychologically meaningless. Norms are then considered as a method of meaningfully expressing validity data.

(4) The treatment of homogeneity as a distinct property of tests. Most psychologists classify internal consistency measures under reliability and factor analysis as a method of determining validity. I have found it a useful conceptual and pedagogical device to classify these two areas as homogeneity and treat it as a separate property of tests.

(5) The emphasis on certain concepts and techniques that are considered only briefly in most other texts but which are crucial to a full comprehension of testing. Examples include incremental validity, base rates, homogeneity, and techniques for determining selection efficiency and decision-making accuracy.

A problem that arises in courses in educational and psychological measurement is the amount of background knowledge in statistics to presume. Ideally, perhaps, every student should have had a course in elementary statistics before taking a course in psychological measurement. Realistically this is not feasible in many situations. Also, the students with weak statistical backgrounds, frequently the prospective teachers and counselors, are often the ones who could benefit most from a course in psychological measurement.

I have assumed that some of the readers of the book have had little or no previous work in statistics. Thus I have done several things. First, I have reduced statistical formulas and manipulations to the minimum needed for comprehension of the basic concepts. Second, whenever feasible, I have separated examples of data manipulation from the text. Third, a brief explanation of fundamental statistics is included in Chapter 1. The purpose of these procedures is to provide for continuity in the discussion of concepts and problems, without interruption for statistical presentations, and yet provide convenient references for students who need to clarify their statistical thinking.

Several other points regarding the content and the organization of the book should be mentioned. First, as it is not possible, without producing an enormous tome, to discuss all aspects of educational and psychological measurement, I have omitted, or given only fleeting reference to ratings, attitude scales, questionnaires, and environmental measures, to cite but a few examples. In addition, certain specific types of tests — for example, reading tests — have been discussed only briefly; however, the principles that govern their construction are discussed in a broader context.

Second, I had originally planned to include a section on the uses of tests in education, counseling, business and industry, and in research. But I soon found that these topics could not be treated with justice in the space available; thus this section has been eliminated.

Third, as the reader will note, many of my illustrations involve tests or testing procedures most directly applicable to college settings and college age students. This choice was deliberate. As my experience has been primarily in a college setting, I feel more competent to talk about testing practices in these settings. But more importantly, these examples should have more immediate relevance to the reader and thus should provide a better basis for learning.

I would like to express my gratitude to all the people who helped in the preparation of the book. Sue Robson, Penny Jacobson, Agnes Page, and Judy Dodds all transformed my sometimes illegible scrawls into neatly typed manuscript pages. Drs. William B. Michael, Dale Harris, Philip Jackson, and Jack Merwin all read portions of the manuscript and contributed valuable suggestions for improving the manuscript. Karen Schroder and my wife, Barbara, had the onerous task of checking references.

Although the book was started at Iowa State University, it probably would not have been completed had it not been for the opportunity to spend a year as a Fellow at the Center for Advanced Study in the Behavioral Sciences at Stanford, California. Not only did the Director, Dr. O. Meredith Wilson, and his assistant, Jane Kielsmeier, provide for the necessary secretarial and library assistance, discussions with my colleagues at the Center — most notably, Sandy Astin, Dave Peizer, Ira Steinberg, and Merlin Wittrock — served to sharpen my thinking and clarify my ideas. This year was partially financed by a post-doctoral fellowship in educational research, sponsored by the U.S. Office of Education.

Finally, the biggest vote of thanks must go to the students in my courses in Psychological Measurement at Iowa State, who not only suffered through the problems involved in using duplicated earlier revisions of the book, but also contributed many valuable comments regarding ways to make the manuscript a better teaching tool.

Frederick G. Brown

Ames, Iowa
September 1969

Contents

The nature of psychological measurement

Chapter 1

INTRODUCTION

One common perception of a psychologist is that he is a person who administers and interprets tests. And certainly many psychologists do spend a significant portion of their time using tests for some purpose—to help decide which applicants should be admitted to college, to aid individuals in selecting appropriate careers, to help an employer decide which applicant for a position is to be hired, to determine whether a child doing poor school work might profit from a special class, and to study the structure of personality.

Attitudes toward psychological tests

Paradoxically, many people hold either of two extreme views regarding the efficacy of psychological tests. On one hand, there are a large number of people who overestimate the accuracy of tests. They see test scores as providing almost perfect, unchanging indications of a person's abilities or personality characteristics. These people think that if a test shows Johnny to have an IQ of 135 then he is more intelligent and should obtain better grades than Sam, whose IQ is only 127. Or, if Jake's score on a mechanical comprehension test is relatively low, these people would discourage him from becoming a mechanic, neglecting the fact that he rebuilt the engine on his car. This view of tests is comforting because it provides an easy way to make decisions—there is no need to weigh a variety of factors, only to do what the test scores indicate.

On the other hand there is another large group who feels that psychological tests are essentially useless. These people argue that relying on tests will, in some cases, result in making wrong decisions; thus tests should be eliminated. This argument is buttressed with examples—the boy who was told that he did not have the ability to complete college and later became a successful physician, the company president who "failed" the employment test of his own company, the sullen "genius" who obtained a low score on the intelligence test because he rebelled against being asked to submit to the test.

A related view is that tests are undemocratic and an invasion of privacy. Proponents of this view argue that certain characteristics, usually some aspect of personality, should not be considered in making decisions about individuals. Their argument is frequently in terms of "what ought to be" rather than "what is"—that is, they assume that certain personality characteristics ought not to be related to success and that if the empirical evidence indicates such a relationship exists it is only because some component of the situation produces a spurious relationship. Besides, they argue, in a democracy a person's personality is his own business and to consider personality factors in practical decision making is an invasion of privacy.

As is usual in many controversies, neither extreme view accurately represents the situation. Psychological tests are by no means perfect and no reputable psychologist will say they are. Yet, even though tests do make mistakes in individual cases, there is a body of evidence that shows that in a variety of situations tests do a better job than other available evaluation methods. This point is often overlooked. In making decisions for practical purposes the question is not a black-white, accurate-inaccurate distinction, but rather which procedure makes the most correct decisions.

DEFINITION OF A TEST

The word "test" is one of those common words that everyone feels he understands and therefore seldom takes time to define precisely. Yet, as most of the basic concepts discussed in this book derive from the definition, one must be attempted. *A test will be defined as a systematic procedure for measuring a sample of an individual's behavior*. This definition can best be understood by considering the implications of its various components.

The inclusion of the phrase "systematic procedure" indicates that a test has been constructed and is administered and scored according to certain prescribed rules. A test is systematic in three areas: its content, procedures for administration, and scoring. Not only is the item content systematically chosen from the domain to be measured, but also the same items or tasks are administered to all persons taking the test. The administration procedure is *standardized* in that specific instructions are developed with respect to what directions will be given the person taking the test, how answers are to be recorded, time limits, and other relevant procedural matters. Scoring is *objective* in that there are predetermined rules for recording and evaluating responses. Although the minimum essential for objective scoring is agreement between competent scorers, many tests allow for routine scoring by a clerk or electronic scoring machine. The reason for these systematic procedures is, of course, to minimize the influence of irrelevant personal and environmental variables on test scores.

In the strictest sense, any test is restricted to measuring only test-taking behavior, i.e., to measuring the responses the person makes to the test items. Thus any statements about the intellectual or personality structure of the individual made on the basis of the test scores necessarily will be inferential. That is, we do not measure a person's characteristics (traits) directly; we only infer them from his responses to the test items. To the extent that the test adequately mirrors the trait (or our construct of it) the test will provide useful information. If the test behavior does not adequately reflect the underlying characteristic, inferences made from the test scores will be in error.

Not only does a test measure only behavior, rather than some construct, but also it measures only a sample of the possible behaviors. No test is so comprehensive that it measures every possible aspect of a given behavior domain. Because of the necessity for sampling, two problems arise. First, one must insure that the items chosen for inclusion on the test actually are a representative sample of the universe of possible behaviors. This is the question of *content validity*. A second problem involves determining whether the person would obtain the same score if he responded to a different sample of items from the same behavior domain. This is the question of *reliability*, specifically reliability as the equivalence between forms of a test.

Implied in the concept of measurement (discussed in the next section) is the idea that a test compares two or more persons. An index of the performance of one individual on a test (his score) would be meaningless unless there were some standard of comparison. In psychological testing this standard of comparison almost universally is the performance of other people who, in some relevant way, can be classified as similar to the test taker. In other words, psychological measurement is relativistic; there are few, if any, absolute standards of performance. Although comparison is involved at many stages of test development, it is most obvious when the person's test score is compared to that of a relevant group, the *norm group* (see Chapter 7).

It might be noted in passing that nothing in the definition of a test requires that one specific format (e.g., paper-and-pencil) be used, that the test taker make specific preparations for the test, or that the test taker even be aware that he is being tested. Although the majority of tests are of the paper-and-pencil variety and the test taker is aware he is being evaluated, and often specific advance preparations such as studying or review are made prior to the administration of the test, these are not necessary conditions. In fact, in situations where one wants an estimate of the test taker's typical performance, as contrasted to his maximal performance, preparation and awareness of the testing may be undesirable, serving to reduce the effectiveness of the testing.

Measurement

Central to the definition of a psychological test is the idea that a test is a measuring instrument. But what is meant by measurement? In simplest terms, measurement is the description of data in terms of numbers (Guilford, 1954).[1] More precisely, *measurement has been defined as the assignment of numerals to objects or events according to rules* (Stevens, 1951). Therefore, in order to measure some object or event, one must go through certain procedures (operations), according to certain rules, which compare the object or event to some defined standard or scale.

With physical dimensions measurement is relatively straightforward.[2] Consider how to measure the length of an object. We have a defined standard or scale, in our country, of feet and inches. There also is an operation available for determining the length of the object in question—to superimpose the object on a device calibrated as to length, say, a yardstick—and certain rules to follow in doing the measurement (e.g., place one end of the object exactly at one end, the zero point, of the scale and read the scale to the nearest, say, quarter inch). Going through this set of operations gives a reading of the length of the object in scale units (feet and inches).

Measurement of psychological characteristics, unfortunately, is not so straightforward or simple. However, the same steps are followed as with physical measurement. We define a dimension or trait to be measured, determine the measurement operations, specify the rules, and have a certain scale of units to express the measurement.

Suppose, for example, that we are interested in the rate at which people read. We could define reading speed in terms of a scale measuring in "words-read-per-minute." In other words, the dimension is reading speed, the scale units words-read-per-minute. The problem now becomes to specify a procedure (operation) for determining reading rate. One obvious method is to allow each person to read a standard passage for a set amount of time. By having each person start at the same place, read for the same amount of time, and indicate how far he had read when the time limit expired, one can count the number of words read. Then by dividing the number of words read by the number of minutes spent reading, we obtain the rate of reading in words-read-per-minute. The procedure is directly analogous to that used in measuring length.

There are further aspects, however, that must be considered in psychological measurement. As you probably realize, the difficulty of the reading passage will

[1] Literature references are to the bibliography at the end of this book.

[2] The description of the process of measurement given here will necessarily be brief and simplified. For a more detailed discussion consult the references in the section "Suggestions for further reading" at the end of the chapter.[Readings listed in these sections will be ones that treat specific topics in more detail or illustrate a particular point made in the chapter.] For a relatively nontechnical discussion of the process of measuring physical dimensions, the reader may wish to consult the articles by Astin (1968) and Faller (1967) cited in the bibliography.

affect the reading rate. Thus the obtained rate will be meaningless without some specification of the nature and difficulty of the material read. The length of the reading period may also be important. For example, if it is so long that fatigue factors enter, the rate will be reduced. The conditions under which the test was conducted may also have an effect—e.g., reading rate might be lower in a noisy bus than in a quiet room. In addition, what is meant by "reading" would have to be defined clearly. The point being, of course, that although physical and psychological measurement may involve the same basic processes, there are more variables to be defined and controlled in psychological measurement before meaningful measurement can occur.

Scales

To understand the preciseness of psychological measurement, one must consider the nature of the scale on which the characteristic is being measured. Measurement can exist at several scale levels, depending on the mathematical and logical assumptions that are fulfilled. These scales are hierarchical in that the higher level scales meet all the assumptions of the lower order scales plus additional ones characteristic of their particular level. From lower to higher order, from simpler to more complex, the scales are labeled *nominal, ordinal, interval,* and *ratio.*

NOMINAL SCALE. At the simplest level is the nominal scale. Measurement on a nominal scale involves only assignment to qualitatively different categories. What is involved is determining if two objects or events are members of the same category or class. For example, people can be classified as male or female; voters as Republican, Democrat, or independent; college students as enrolled in engineering, home economics, agriculture, liberal arts, medicine, or some other curriculum. The fundamental operation is the determination of equality, the determination that all members of the class possess some common characteristic that nonmembers do not possess.

Measurement on a nominal scale is of limited usefulness in psychology, since it allows for only broad classification without any indication of magnitude, while in most instances we are interested in some estimation of magnitude. In addition, the only statistical operation that can be performed on nominal data is that of counting, e.g., determining how many people fall into each category. Because nominal scales indicate only qualitative differences and not quantitative ones, some people do not consider nominal scales as representing measurement, but only as enumeration. However, as nominal scales do meet the requirements of our definition, the assignment of numerals to objects or events according to rules, we shall consider nominal scales as an example of measurement.

ORDINAL SCALE. The next level of measurement, the ordinal scale, allows not only grouping by category, as in a nominal scale, but also an indication of magnitude, of greater or lesser amounts. That is, an ordinal scale allows us to rank people in order of magnitude on some dimension. For example, we could line up every child in a schoolroom in a descending order according to their height, from tallest to shortest. If Charles was the tallest, followed by Eric, and then by George, we can not only say that Charles is taller than Eric, and Eric taller than George, but also that Charles is taller than George. However, we cannot say how much taller one child is than another; we can only say which one is taller.

In many situations ranking is sufficient. If we want to select the five tallest boys in a class we need only to rank all boys in the class by height to make our choice. Similarly, if we want to choose the top 25 students out of a class of 100 for a special section of a course, we have only to give some measure (test) that will identify the 25 highest scorers. We do not need to know how much higher they scored than the rest of the class, only that they obtained the 25 highest scores. In general, when we are selecting only the top (or bottom) number or percent of people, an ordinal rating will suffice.

An ordinal scale allows for computation of some useful statistics. We can compute the *median* (the score that divides the distribution into halves), *percentiles* (the percent of the people scoring below a given individual or score point), and *rank order* correlations. What we cannot do is say that a difference of a certain magnitude means the same thing at all points along the scale.

INTERVAL SCALE.   Only when the score units can be shown to be equivalent at all points on a scale can it be said that, say, a 5-point difference in scores in one segment of the scale is equivalent to any other 5-point difference. This type of scale is called an *interval scale*. On an interval scale there can be determinations of equality, of greater or less, and of equality of units. All that is lacking is a true zero point, i.e., an absolute zero. (Scales with true zero points, called *ratio scales*, are nonexistent in psychological testing and so will not be considered in detail here.[3])

The crucial operation in the development of an interval scale is the establishment of equality of units, which is called *additivity* and must be established empirically. That is, we must be able to show that a given interval on the scale, say the 10-point difference between scores of 60 and 70, is, in fact, equivalent in magnitude to any other 10-point interval at any other place on the scale. In a test composed of a number of items, each carrying a unit weight, this requirement would demand that we could establish empirically that each item measured an equivalent amount or degree of the characteristic being measured.

On an interval scale scores can be transformed in any linear manner. That is, we can add, subtract, multiply, or divide the scores on an interval scale by a

---

[3]A new approach to test construction, which seems to include a definition of a meaningful zero point in the scaling process, has been described by Rasch (1966) and Wright (1968).

TABLE 1.1 Characteristics of types of measurement scales

Scale	Operation	Description
Nominal	Equality	Mutually exclusive categories; objects or events fall into one class only; all members of same class considered equal; categories differ qualitatively, not quantitatively.
Ordinal	Equality Ranking	Idea of magnitude enters; object is larger or smaller than another (but not both); any monotonic transformation permissible.
Interval	Equality Ranking Equal-sized units	Additivity; all units of equal size; can establish equivalent distances along scale; any linear transformation permissible.
Ratio	Equality Ranking Equal-sized units True (absolute) zero	True or absolute zero point can be defined; meaningful ratios can be derived.

constant without destroying the relationship between scores. Expressed as a formula:

$$X' = aX + b \tag{1.1}$$

where X' = transformed score; X = original score; a,b = constants. Scores on one scale can thus be converted to a scale employing different units through multiplying by a constant (a) and/or adding a constant (b). The main advantage of transforming scores in psychological testing is that it allows for scores on two or more tests to be compared directly. The more common statistics, such as means, standard deviations, correlations, and significance tests can also be used with interval scales.

What level is psychological measurement?

In one sense, measurement is a game we play with objects and events and numerals, a game with certain rules. (cf. Kerlinger, 1965, Chapter 23). The object of the game is to produce an isomorphism between the measurement procedure and number system and reality, i.e., the objects and events being measured. The greater the isomorphism, the better the measurement. From this view, whether psychological measurement, as exhibited in tests, represents measurement on an ordinal or interval scale is an open question. The critical consideration is, of course, whether the assumption of equality of units is more isomorphic to "reality" than is not assuming equal units. If the units are equal at all score levels, measurement is on an interval scale; if not, it is on an ordinal scale.

AN EXAMPLE.   The problem can best be illustrated by an example. Suppose that we are interested in an individual's ability as a bowler. The obvious index of his ability is the score he makes when he bowls. From one point of view, one pin is always one pin and a 10-point difference in scores between two bowlers, or between one bowler's scores at two different times, would always be a 10-point difference. Thus the difference between scores of 210 and 200 would be the same as the difference between scores of 100 and 110. Measurement could then be considered to be on an interval scale.

A little reflection, however, might lead one to conclude that the increment in ability needed to improve one's score from 100 to 110 is not as great as the increment needed to raise one's score from 200 to 210. Thus we do not have equality of units (i.e., the 10 pin improvement between 100 and 110 is not equivalent to the 10 pin improvement from 200 to 210) and, therefore, we do not have an interval scale. Since we can agree that a score of 210 indicates more skill than a score of 200 or, more generally, the higher the score the greater the skill, without question we do have an ordinal scale.

The basic distinction between these two interpretations is whether any inference is made over and above the operations of computing an index of ability from the number of pins knocked down. The first approach, often called *operational*, makes no inferences beyond the actual score. The second approach suggests that considering scores alone is not enough, that the scores are not meaningful without considering the psychological difficulty of improvement at each level. The isomorphism in this latter case involves a "reality" that includes psychological components.

OBTAINING AN INTERVAL SCALE.   Because an interval scale possesses distinct advantages over an ordinal scale when statistical analyses of test scores are to be made, most psychologists prefer that test scores be expressed on an interval scale. Fortunately there are several ways to circumvent the ordinal versus interval scale dilemma and proceed as if the assumptions of an interval scale have been met.

One procedure uses the first approach of the bowling example, defining variables solely in terms of test scores. Thus we hear that intelligence is what an intelligence test measures and rigidity is what a test of rigidity measures. This approach makes no inferences about postulated underlying abilities and thus has a certain mathematical purity. However, it can lead to some psychological absurdities.

A second approach involves statistically transforming the raw scores on a test (the scores derived directly from the test—e.g., number of items correct, time to completion) into some sort of derived score scale having equal units. The most common transformation is to standard scores—scores expressed in standard deviation units (see Chapter 7). This approach is, in some ways, analogous to pulling oneself up by one's own bootstraps.

The third, and probably most common approach (Ghiselli, 1964; Guilford, 1954; Kerlinger, 1965) is a pragmatic one. Although the details of each author's argument vary, the general argument has two facets: (1) although our test construction procedures do not guarantee an interval scale they at least approximate one, and (2) treating test scores as if they are on an interval scale produces useful results. In short, we assume an interval scale and act as if we had one. Since the results of analyses assuming an interval scale make sense (i.e., seem to preserve the isomorphism), we have added confidence that the assumptions could not have been far off base.

What is being measured?

Up to this point we have not specified what we are measuring, only how we are attempting to measure whatever it is that we are measuring. Our definition of measurement indicated that we were measuring objects or events. Actually we measure the properties and characteristics of objects or events, or, even more precisely, we measure indicants of these properties and characteristics of objects and events. Test scores are the indicants and from these we make inferences about the characteristics of the object.

In psychological testing, these characteristics are generally referred to as *traits*. A trait is a construct, a summary or synthesizing of a variety of elements or specific behaviors, a descriptive label applied to a group of interrelated behaviors. These behaviors may be inherited or acquired. The trait name (e.g., intelligence, aggressiveness, rigidity) is a shorthand notation. Most psychologists use the word "trait" in an operational sense, referring to a cluster of empirically interrelated behaviors. However, some psychologists will use "trait" to refer to some presumed underlying factor that determines the behaviors. In this book we shall subscribe to the former definition.

PURPOSES AND USES OF TESTS

In the most general sense, tests are used to measure the nature and extent of individual differences. If a test measuring a given trait is administered to a number of persons we can determine how they rank on that trait. If the same person takes several tests, we can describe his performance on several dimensions (traits). If a group of people take a variety of tests we can study how people differ from each other and how traits are interrelated in the population. This last approach, when extended to many tests administered under a variety of conditions to a variety of persons, provides one method for studying the nature and range of human abilities and personality characteristics and furnishes some necessary normative data for the development of psychological theories. (See, e.g., Cattell, 1965; Guilford, 1959; Vernon, 1961.)

More frequently tests are administered to supply data that will aid in decision making. The decision may involve an individual, a group, or some hypothesis. The adequacy of the decision reached will depend not only on the quality of the measurement instrument (the test), but also on other considerations, such as how adequately the problem has been formulated, how much of the relevant variation is measured by the test, and how the data are used. Thus, when tests are used as decision-making aids, accurate test information will be a necessary, but not sufficient, condition for reaching an adequate decision.

There are several types of situations where tests are often used as aids in decision making. One of the most common is in *selection*, either in academic settings or in business and industry. In the selection situation there are more applicants than can be accepted or hired, and a decision has to be made as to which applicants will be accepted. The role of the test data is to aid in selecting the most promising applicants, those with the greatest probability of success. In the simplest case, the decision is either accept or reject, but in certain situations there may be more than two possible decisions. For example, a college may accept a student unconditionally, accept him on probation or with the stipulation that he meet certain other requirements, or reject him. Commonly, the organization doing the selection is interested only in those accepted. It wants to maximize the number of selected persons who will succeed. They are less interested, or not at all interested, in those persons who are rejected.

Another common use of tests is for *placement*. In placement we have one or more individuals and several alternative courses of action—for example, several academic tracks, several training programs, or several jobs. Each person is to be assigned to one alternative with the goal of the placement procedure being to match the individuals and alternatives in an optimal manner. Examples include using tests to assign persons to occupational specialities in the armed services or to assign college freshmen to the various levels within a sequence of French courses.

A third use is in *diagnosis*, the comparing of an individual's strengths and weaknesses in several areas in order to determine why he is having difficulty in certain functions. The implication is that once the areas of disability are identified a program of remediation can be undertaken. Thus a diagnostic reading test might provide scores in areas such as vocabulary, paragraph meaning, sentence meaning, and reading rate with a goal of identifying the student's particular weaknesses and strengths. Or a personality inventory might have subareas of home and family relationships, social relationships, and emotional stability in order to try to identify (diagnose) the area of conflict. Once the area is identified, a program of counseling or remedial help can be arranged.

In psychological research tests are often used for *hypothesis testing*. One might hypothesize, as Sarason et al. (1960) have, that anxiety would have a detrimental effect on performance on intellectual tasks. By using standard measures (tests) of anxiety, studies can be conducted that test the hypothesis. Studies of this nature have, in fact, demonstrated that under certain conditions anxiety does have a detrimental effect on intellectual performance.

Though less frequently considered as a possibility, tests can also be used for *hypothesis building*. This use can be illustrated by surveys and by the use of tests in counseling. Suppose that a survey shows that persons living in a certain part of the United States score lower on intelligence and achievement tests than persons of comparable age and education in other states. Why? Several hypotheses can be developed. One is that the people living in the particular area are innately less intelligent. Another is that the results reflect differences in the quality of education. A third hypothesis might attribute the effects to socioeconomic and cultural differences. These hypotheses, and others, could then be checked by further studies.

The counselor or psychotherapist often builds hypotheses about his clients on the basis of test scores. Suppose tests show that Clarence, whose father is an engineer, has excellent scholastic aptitude, is interested in literary and artistic activities, is submissive, and has conflicts with authority figures and a problem with family relationships. He is now enrolled in engineering and is failing. From the test data the counselor might build a hypothesis that Clarence is in engineering because of parental pressure and, being unable to directly confront his parents with his dislike for engineering, he has decided on the indirect method of choosing to fail his courses. This hypothesis could then be checked through further interviews.

Another use of tests is in *evaluation*, as exemplified by classroom examinations, a procedure that everyone is familiar with. Although classroom examinations and other academic achievement tests are usually used to evaluate students, they may also be used to evaluate the course of instruction or even the teacher. Properly utilized, the achievement test will not only give an accurate indication of the differences between students, but will also indicate to the instructor which areas the students understood and which areas they had difficulty comprehending. If the student has the opportunity to review his examination, he can also determine his strengths and weaknesses and evaluate the effectiveness of his own preparation.

All of these uses involve some decision. In selection, the decision is whether to accept or reject an applicant; in placement, which alternative course of action to instigate; in diagnosis, which remedial treatment; in hypothesis testing, the accuracy of the theoretical formulation; in hypothesis building, which further testing or information is needed; and in evaluation, what grade or mark to assign to a student or procedure. The prime question whenever tests are used is whether use of psychological tests results in better decision making than a procedure in which tests are not used. The question is not whether tests are accurate or inaccurate, useful or worthless, but how their accuracy and decision-making ability compares to other available techniques.

In addition to serving as decision-making aids, psychological tests can also serve as *instruments of psychological and educational theory.* Theories in psychology and education, like those in other disciplines, involve both laws and constructs. One common way of defining these constructs, and measuring their magnitude, is through the use of tests. Thus if our theory involved a construct called intelligence, this construct could be measured by an intelligence test; if the theory involved a construct called anxiety, this too might be measured by a psychological test; if the theory implied that under certain conditions learning would occur, an achievement test could be used to measure the amount of learning. This use of tests is similar to our discussion of tests as hypothesis-testing aids, with the additional stipulation that the test defines the construct of interest, either wholly or partially. This topic will be treated in much greater detail in Chapter 6 when we discuss construct validity.

Summary

A psychological test may be defined as a systematic procedure for measuring a sample of an individual's behavior. A test is systematic in that it is constructed, administered, and scored according to set procedures. Scores on tests represent only responses to the items and any statements made about underlying characteristics are necessarily inferential. Interpretation of test scores is further complicated by the fact that tests only sample relevant behavior and cannot include all manifestations of the behavior. Psychological measurement is also relativistic in that the meaning of an individual's score generally is determined by comparing his performance with that of other persons who have taken the test.

A psychological test is a measuring instrument. By "measurement" is meant the assigning of numerals to objects or events according to certain rules. Measurement can be at various levels: nominal scales require only the determination of qualitative equality, ordinal scales allow ranking, and interval scales possess equal units. There is some debate as to whether psychological measurement is on an ordinal or interval scale, but there are several procedures that allow test scores to meet the assumptions of an interval scale. The characteristics measured by tests are called traits.

The major use of psychological tests is to aid in decision making; thus tests should be evaluated in terms of their contribution to increased accuracy in decision making. Common uses include selection, placement, diagnosis, hypothesis testing, hypothesis building, and evaluation. Tests may also serve to define constructs in psychological and educational theories.

Suggestions for further reading

Ghiselli, E. E. *Theory of psychological measurement*. New York: McGraw-Hill, Inc., 1964. Chaps. 1–3 discuss test scores as measures of individual differences and some fundamental aspects of psychological measurement such as types of scales, score distributions, and descriptive statistics; a relatively nontechnical presentation.

Guilford, J. P. *Psychometric methods* (2nd ed.). New York: McGraw-Hill, Inc., 1954. Chap. 1 presents a general theory of psychological measurement with emphasis on the postulates and theorems underlying the various types of measurement scales.

Kerlinger, F. N. *Foundations of behavioral research*. New York: Holt, Rinehart and Winston, Inc., 1965. Chap. 23 discusses the foundations of measurement using set theory concepts and considers a question of what is being measured; brief and nontechnical.

Lorge, I. The fundamental nature of measurement. Pp. 533–559 in E. F. Lindquist (Ed.), *Educational measurement*. Washington, D. C.: American Council on Education, 1951. Another relatively nontechnical discussion with emphasis on educational measurement.

Stevens, S. S. Mathematics, measurement, and psychophysics. Pp. 1–49 in S. S. Stevens (Ed.), *Handbook of experimental psychology*. New York: John Wiley & Sons, Inc., 1951. A longer and more technical presentation of the nature of psychological measurement, mathematical models, measurement scales, and psychophysics; a classic statement on measurement in psychology.

Some basic statistics

Appendix to chapter 1

In order to understand many of the fundamental principles of educational and psychological testing, it is necessary to have an understanding of some basic statistical concepts. The statistical concepts which will underlie our discussion are primarily descriptive statistics, those statistics that summarize and precisely describe a set of data. The following paragraphs briefly explain and illustrate these basic statistical concepts; all other statistical concepts presented in the book will be variations of, or derivations from, the concepts presented in this section. For a more detailed discussion of any of these concepts, consult an elementary statistics text, e.g., Edwards (1969) or Hays (1963).

Types of scores

Scores which are obtained directly from test performance—e.g., the number of items answered correctly, the number of errors, the time taken to complete the test—are called *raw scores* (and denoted by the symbol X). Sometimes these raw scores are used in test analysis and interpretation; usually raw scores are transformed to another scale and thus become *derived or transformed scores*. For example, raw scores are often transformed to percentile ranks, a scale which expresses scores as a relative ranking within a group of people (see Chapter 7).

As adding or subtracting a constant does not affect the relationship between scores on an ordinal or interval scale, many transformations involve the addition (or subtraction) of a constant:

$$X' = X + K \qquad (1.1a)$$

where X = the raw score, K = a constant value, and X' = the transformed score. Similarly, scores can be multiplied (or divided) by a constant without affecting their interrelations:

$$X'' = XK \qquad (1.1b)$$

where X'' is the transformed score and X and K are defined above.

Another important distinction is between discrete and continuous
scales. On a *discrete scale*, scores can fall only at distinct points along the
scale. The number of persons in a room and the number of points scored
in a football game are both discrete scores, as fractional scores are in-
admissible. On a *continuous scale*, however, scores theoretically can fall
at any point along the scale, the only limitations being the precision which
the measurement techniques allow and/or the precision desired from the
measurement. Thus, the dimensions of a room might be described in
feet, in feet and inches, or even in fractions of inches, depending on the
purpose of the measurement and the measuring tools available. Although scores on psychological tests may appear to be discrete, they
are usually treated as if on a continuous scale, the assumption being
that more precise distinctions could be made if deemed necessary.

Frequency distributions

Suppose that scores on a classroom quiz were as follows:

4 8 3 0 8 2 4 5 5 6 7 4 3 5 2 3 6 7 1 5 6 7 6 4 5 9 4 5 1 6

This arrangement tells little except that the range of scores was from 0 to
9 and that there are 30 scores. However, if the scores are regrouped into
a table showing how many people obtained each score, a clearer picture
of the distribution of scores appears. Such a table is called a *frequency
distribution*, as it indicates the frequency of occurrence of each score in
the distribution. For example:

X	0	1	2	3	4	5	6	7	8	9	Σ
f	1	2	2	3	5	6	5	3	2	1	30

In the table f = the frequency of each score, and Σ means "the sum of."
Thus $\Sigma f = 30 = n$, where n = the total number of scores.

This distribution can also be shown graphically by plotting the frequencies, f, of each score, X. The graph, illustrated in Figure 1.1, is a
frequency polygon.

Although the distribution of test scores often approximates the normal
(bell-shaped) curve, or is at least symmetrical, a variety of other distributions are occasionally encountered. For example, if a test is very easy,
scores will bunch at the high end of the scale and tail off toward the low

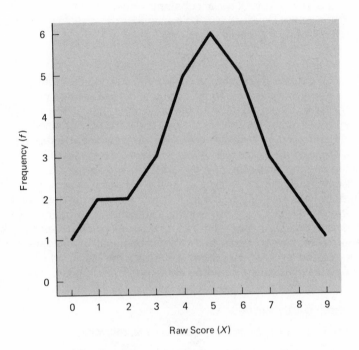

Figure 1.1 Example of a frequency polygon.

end. Conversely, on a difficult test, scores will bunch at the low end. These two distributions are called *negative skewed* and *positive skewed*, respectively. These, and other common distribution shapes, are depicted in Figure 1.2.

Central tendency

It is often desirable to have one number which represents the average score of the group. This score is a measure of *central tendency*. The three measures of central tendency in common use—the *mode*, the *median* and the *mean*—are appropriate to measurement on a nominal, ordinal, and interval scale, respectively. Hence, the mean is generally the most useful measure. The median, however, may be more useful in certain circumstances, e.g., when the score distribution is skewed.

The *mode* is the score that occurs most frequently. In the example the mode is 5, as 5 is the score which occurs with the highest frequency.

The *median* is the score that divides the distribution into halves, the score above and below which 50 percent of the scores fall. In the example, the median is 5 because the point that divides the distribution into halves, the point between the fifteenth and sixteenth score, is a score of 5. (There

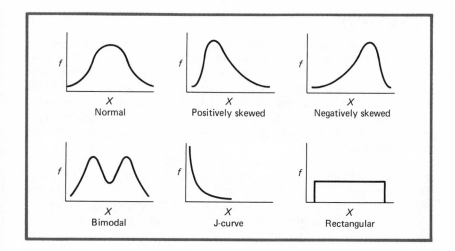

Figure 1.2 Common shapes of statistical distributions.

are methods for establishing a more exact median by dividing the scores within the category containing the middle score; these will not be discussed here.)

The *mean* is nothing more than the arithmetic average and can be found from the formula:

$$\overline{X} = \Sigma X/n \qquad \text{where } \overline{X} = \text{the mean} \qquad (1.2)$$

To compute the mean, sum all the scores and divide by the number of scores, *n*. In the example:

$$\Sigma X = 4 + 8 + 3 + \cdots + 1 + 6 = 141$$

and $\qquad \overline{X} = \Sigma X/n = 141/30 = 4.7$

The mean can also be computed from the frequency distribution using the formula:

$$\overline{X} = \Sigma f_i X_i/n \qquad (1.2a)$$

where f_i = the number of scores in a particular class, X_i. That is, multiply each score by its frequency, sum the products and divide by *n*. In the example:

$$\Sigma f_i X_i = (1)(0) + (2)(1) + (2)(2) + \cdots + (1)(9) = 141$$

And, of course, the mean will be 4.7 (141/30), the same value as obtained using the alternative formula.

Variability

Two score distributions may have the same mean but in one distribution the scores may be bunched around the mean while in the other the scores vary widely, as shown in (a) in Figure 1.3. Conversely, two distributions may have the same degree of variability but differing means. See (b) in Figure 1.3. Thus to completely describe a distribution, a measure of variability or dispersion, as well as a measure of central tendency, is needed. Of the various measures of dispersion only one, the standard deviation, is widely used.

A measure of dispersion must indicate the variability of scores around a given point; in the case of the standard deviation, this point is the mean of the score distribution. The *standard deviation* (or *s*) is defined as the square root of the average squared deviation of the scores from the mean. To compute *s* it is first necessary to find the deviation of each score from the mean of the distribution:

$$x = X - \overline{X} \tag{1.3}$$

to square these deviation scores (x^2), sum the squares, divide the sum of squares (Σx^2) by the *n* and take the square root of the quantity:

$$s = \sqrt{\Sigma x^2/n} \tag{1.4}$$

Because transforming raw scores, *X*, into deviation scores, *x*, can be rather cumbersome, an equivalent raw score formula is usually used in any computations. A common one is:

$$s = \frac{1}{n}\sqrt{n\Sigma X^2 - (\Sigma X)^2} \tag{1.4a}$$

Other formulas can be found in a book on statistics.

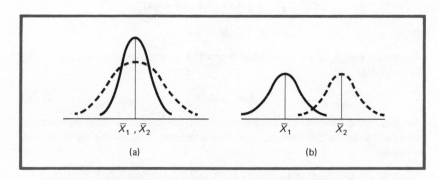

$\overline{X}_1 , \overline{X}_2$ $\overline{X}_1$ $\overline{X}_2$

(a)   (b)

Figure 1.3 Examples showing need for measure of dispersion as well as of central tendency: (a) same mean, different dispersion; (b) same dispersion, different means.

Applying this latter formula to our example we find:

$\Sigma X = 141 \quad n = 30$

and $\Sigma X^2 = (4)^2 + (8)^2 + (3)^2 + \cdots + (6)^2 = 803$

and substituting in the formula:

$$s = \frac{1}{30}\sqrt{(30)(803) - (141)^2} = 2.2$$

A practical and intuitive knowledge of the meaning of s can be attained by reference to the normal curve. In a normal distribution, there is a specifiable relation between the proportion of cases falling within certain score limits and the standard deviation. Some major benchmarks are presented in Figure 1.4; a complete set of relationships can be found in a Table of Areas of the Normal Curve (see Appendix).

Figure 1.4 shows that 34 percent of the scores fall between the mean and plus one standard deviation (+1s) and another 34 percent fall between the mean and minus one standard deviation (−1s). Thus 68 percent of the scores fall within plus or minus one s of the mean. The range ±2s includes approximately 95 percent of the scores and ±3s includes almost all scores (99.8+ percent). A third way of looking at the relationship is that 84 percent of the scores will fall below the point +1s and 97.5 percent of the scores will fall below the point +2s. Thus knowing where the person's score falls, in standard deviation units from the mean, one can tell what proportion of the sample his scores surpass.

Although test score distributions are not normal—and, in fact, cannot be because the normal curve is a mathematical and not an empirical

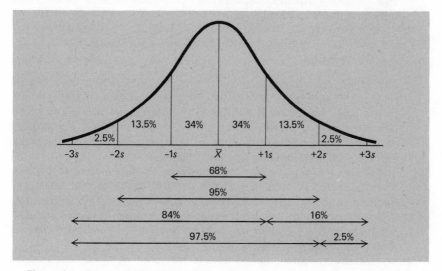

Figure 1.4 Some of the main relationships in a normal distribution curve.

concept—score distributions frequently approach normality and, therefore, the normal curve can be adopted as a working model. Applying the relationships shown above to the example (which had $\overline{X} = 4.7$ and $s = 2.2$), the following relations would be expected to hold:

68 percent of the scores will fall between 2.5 and 6.9 $(\overline{X} \pm 1s = 4.7 \pm 2.2)$;

95 percent of the scores will fall between 0.3 and 9.1 $(\overline{X} \pm 2s$
$$= 4.7 \pm 2 \times 2.2);$$

84 percent of the scores will be lower than 6.9 (lower than the point
$$\overline{X} + 1s \text{ or } 4.7 + 2.2)$$

and so on. Comparing the obtained frequencies to the expected frequencies will indicate if the distribution (in the example) does, in fact, approach a normal distribution.

The square of the standard deviation (s^2) is called the *variance:*

$$s^2 = \frac{\Sigma x^2}{n} = \Sigma X^2 - \frac{(\Sigma X)^2}{n}\left[\frac{1}{n}\right] \qquad (1.5)$$

The variance is a measure of the total amount of variability in a set of test scores. The variance has the important property of additivity that allows the proportion of variability in a set of test scores which is attributable to each of several variables (and their interactions) to be determined. This property forms the basis of several important statistical techniques (e.g., analysis of variance) and also enables meaningful statements to be made about the relative influence of each variable. In essence, the total variability (s^2) can be broken down and distributed among several effects. The variability attributable to these component effects, when summed, will equal the total variability.

Correlation

The other important concept is *correlation*, which is a measure of the relationship (literally the "co-relation") between two parallel sets of data. In the uses discussed in this book, the correlation will generally be between two sets of scores collected on the same persons, e.g., the scores obtained on two administrations of the same test, scores on a college entrance examination and grades in college.

There are many different measures of the degree of correlation. The one which is most frequently used in psychological testing is the Pearson product-moment correlation coefficient, r. This coefficient is a measure of linear relationship, linear meaning that the relationship between the two variables can best be described by a straight line rather than a curve, as indicated in Figure 1.5.

Other correlation measures are based on nonlinear models. But if one uses a linear model, such as r, and the relationship is actually better

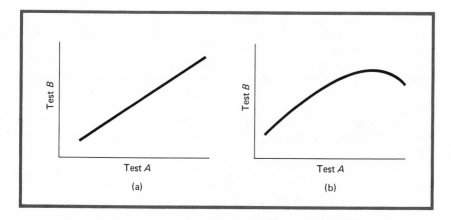

Figure 1.5 Linear relationship (a) and curvilinear relationship (b) between two variables.

described by a nonlinear model, the correlation coefficient will underestimate the degree of relationship present.

The logic of the correlation coefficient can best be seen if scores are expressed in *standard score* form, in which the deviation of a raw score from the mean is expressed in standard deviation units:

$$z = \frac{X - \bar{X}}{s} = \frac{x}{s} \qquad (1.6)$$

where z is a standard score and the other terms have been defined previously. If the two variables being correlated are designated a and b, and the corresponding standard scores as z_a and z_b, then the correlation between a and b will be:

$$r = \frac{\Sigma z_a z_b}{n} \qquad (1.7)$$

where $n =$ the number of *pairs* of scores (each pair being derived from a different individual). It can be seen that if z_a and z_b are both large and have the same sign (both deviate in the same direction from the mean), r will be large and positive; if both are large but have opposite signs, r will be large but negative; if both are small or some ($z_a z_b$) pairs have positive signs and others negative signs, the value of r will approach zero.

The value of r can range from +1.00 to −1.00. The absolute value of the coefficient tells the strength of the relationship, the higher the value the greater the correspondence between the two sets of scores. Thus when $r = 1.00$ there is complete correspondence and scores on b are completely predictable, knowing scores on a. If $r = 0.00$ there is no relationship and prediction is no better than chance. The sign of the coefficient tells only the direction of the relationship. Thus $r = +.68$ and $r = -.68$ represent equal degrees of predictability.

The relationship summarized by the correlation coefficient can also be shown by scatterplots of the test scores in Figure 1.6. If there is a high correlation, the scores should cluster around a straight line (in an elliptical pattern if scores on both variables are distributed normally); if there is no relationship, the pattern will be circular. The orientation of the plot in relation to the axes indicates whether the coefficient is positive or negative.

There are a number of alternative formulas for r. One formula that aids the conceptualization of r, but is infrequently used computationally, is:

$$r = \frac{\Sigma x_a x_b}{n s_a s_b} \tag{1.7a}$$

where all terms have been previously defined. Two raw score formulas that have certain computational advantages are (adopting the common notation of letting X stand for predictor scores and Y for criterion scores):

$$r = \frac{n\Sigma XY - (\Sigma X)(\Sigma Y)}{\sqrt{n\Sigma X^2 - (\Sigma X)^2}\sqrt{n\Sigma Y^2 - (\Sigma Y)^2}} \tag{1.7b}$$

and
$$r = \frac{\Sigma XY/n - (\bar{X})(\bar{Y})}{s_x s_y} \tag{1.7c}$$

Other formulas for r and formulas for other types of correlation coefficients may be found in statistics textbooks.

INTERPRETATION.   There are a number of ways to interpret r—in terms of the strength of the relationship between the two variables, in terms of the accuracy of predicting one variable from another, in terms of common elements, and so on. Perhaps the simplest and most broadly applicable way is to interpret r^2 as the proportion of variability in one set of scores that can be attributable to, or is shared in common with, the other variable. Thus if $r = .50$, r^2 will equal .25, and 25 percent of the variability in one measure can be said to be associated with (attributable to) variation in the other measure.

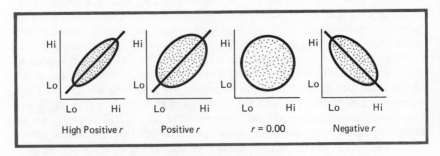

Figure 1.6 Scatterplots of test scores, indicating degree of correlation.

It cannot be overemphasized that r only indicates the degree of relationship between two variables and does *not* indicate causation. If variables *a* and *b* are highly correlated, there are at least three possible explanations: (1) *a* causes *b* and thus changes in *a* will result in changes in *b*; (2) *b* causes *a* and thus the changes in *a* reflect changes in *b*; and (3) both variables may be influenced by some other variable or set of variables. In other words, a correlation coefficient is never a sufficient basis for inferring causation.

A COMPUTATIONAL EXAMPLE. Suppose that two forms (X and Y) of an arithmetic test are administered to ten students. (In practice we generally would not compute r for this small a group but it will suffice for illustrative purposes.) The scores were as follows.

Individual	a b c d e f g h i j		
Form X	9 6 5 2 5 7 1 5 8 6	$\Sigma X = 54$	$\Sigma X^2 = 346$
Form Y	8 7 5 4 6 5 3 4 8 7	$\Sigma Y = 57$	$\Sigma Y^2 = 353$

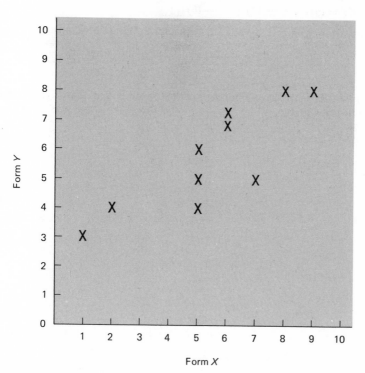

Figure 1.7 Scatterplot showing relationship between scores on tests X and Y (see text).

The table indicates that individual a obtained a score of 9 on form and X 8 on form Y, individual b scored 6 on X and 7 on Y, and so on. The scatterplot of the scores is shown in Figure 1.7. As the scores fall close to a straight line and high scores on one test are associated with high scores on the other, a high positive value of r will be expected.

Using the fourth formula (1.7c) for r (to provide another example of the computations of means and standard deviations), it is necessary to find $\bar{X}$, $\bar{Y}$, s_x, s_y and the sum of the cross-products (ΣXY):

$$\bar{X} = \Sigma X/n = \frac{54}{10} = 5.40$$

$$s = \frac{1}{n}\sqrt{n\Sigma X^2 - (\Sigma X)^2} = \frac{1}{10}\sqrt{10(346) - (54)^2} = 2.33$$

$$\bar{Y} = \frac{\Sigma Y}{n} = \frac{57}{10} = 5.70$$

$$s = \frac{1}{n}\sqrt{n\Sigma Y^2 - (\Sigma Y)^2} = \frac{1}{10}\sqrt{10(353) - (57)^2} = 1.68$$

$$\Sigma XY = (9)(8) + (6)(7) + \cdots + (6)(7) = 341$$

Substituting in the formula for the correlation coefficient:

$$r = \frac{\Sigma XY/n - (\bar{X})(\bar{Y})}{s_x s_y} = \frac{341/10 - (5.40)(5.70)}{(2.33)(1.68)} = 0.85$$

Thus approximately 72 percent of the variability in scores ($.85^2$) is common to the two tests.

Test development:
An overview

Chapter 2

INTRODUCTION

The procedures and methods used in constructing a test have been developed to connect the measuring device (the test) in a logical way to the desired goals and purposes of the measurement. The construction is accomplished through the application of the principles of measurement discussed in Chapter 1. Although the construction procedure will vary depending upon the type and purpose of the test, certain general steps can be identified. These steps include: specifying the purpose of the test, translating the purpose into operational terms, constructing the items, pretesting and item analysis, assembling the final form of the test, standardizing, and obtaining technical data about the test. In the construction of any specific test some of the steps may be omitted, the order of carrying out the various steps may change, or several steps may be in process simultaneously. Yet a general sequence can be identified.

This chapter will present an overview of the process of test development, showing in broad outline how the pieces fit together. Several of the most important individual steps and concepts will then be considered in detail in following chapters. Throughout the discussion the reader should keep in mind that the process of test development is both a science and an art, uses both statistical and logical reasoning, and balances practical with theoretical considerations. The goal is to develop an instrument that psychometrically is as sophisticated as possible within the practical limitations imposed by its content and proposed use.

The reader should also constantly be aware of the fact that, in many situations and for many uses, a psychological test is only one among several methods of obtaining the desired information. For example, if we want an indication of a high school student's level of achievement in mathematics we might administer a test to him; but we might instead check his grades in mathematics courses or ask his teacher for a rating of his knowledge of the subject. Therefore, if at any point it becomes clear that constructing a test to obtain the desired information is not feasible, or some other method of obtaining the information is more accurate or practical, the process of test construction should be terminated and the other procedure used in its place. And, as a corollary to the last statement, if at any place in the test construction process it becomes apparent that the approach being followed is nonproductive, the test builder should back up several steps in the process and start anew.

Although our discussion will be limited to test construction, the reader should not conclude that the only alternative is to construct a new test. The test user can, of course, use an extant test if one fits his requirements. Our purpose in this chapter is to illustrate the process of test construction rather than to discuss test selection; the latter problem will be discussed in Chapter 9.

THE TEST PURPOSE

From a pragmatic viewpoint, the test constructor has two major decisions—he has to determine the content of his test and its format. That is, he must determine what areas of knowledge or experience the test will cover and in what form items covering these content areas will be presented to the test taker. Before he can make these decisions, however, he must ask two prior questions: What are the purposes and intended uses of the test? What are the composition and characteristics of the groups to which the test will be applied? The answers to these two questions will both set constraints on the test construction process and give indications of how to proceed.

The question of purpose is the pre-eminent one. Most commonly a test is developed, not for a single purpose or use, but for some combination of purposes and uses. Although the purpose of most tests is at least implicitly defined, an explicit and comprehensive statement of the purpose is highly desirable, if not essential. For example, the College Entrance Examination Board, in describing its Scholastic Aptitude Test (SAT), states:

> College admissions officers sometimes need a common measure of ability that applies to all students. The SAT meets this need by providing a standard measure of academic ability, a measure that enables colleges to make a fair comparison of your performance with the performance of applicants from other schools.

The purpose is even further explicated by another statement:

> The [SAT] is . . . designed to measure how well you have developed your verbal and mathematical skills. The verbal sections of the SAT mea-

sure your ability to understand the relationships among words and ideas and to comprehend what you read. The mathematical sections measure your ability to understand and reason with mathematical symbols and to use them in solving problems.[1]

Note that these statements not only explain the purpose of the test but also delineate the content and format of the test.

The other major consideration is the composition and characteristics of the group for which the test is intended. Here the test constructor must take into account such variables as the subjects' age, intellectual level, education, socioeconomic and cultural background, and reading level. Which of these variables, or other variables, will be relevant in a specific circumstance will, of course, depend upon the type and purposes of the test. For example, the SAT is designed for applicants to American colleges and universities. Thus the large majority of the persons taking the test will be of approximately the same age (17–18 years old, the age of high school seniors) and will have been exposed to a common core of educational experiences. They are also more homogeneous than the general population in their level of intellectual development. Thus, the items in the SAT are written to be of appropriate difficulty and coverage for this group.

The test as representing or predicting

The purpose and function of psychological tests can be viewed from several angles. In Chapter 1, we made a distinction on the basis of usage—for selection, placement, and so forth. We have also incidentally mentioned a distinction based on content area—achievement, ability, and personality. A third classification, one that will aid in the conceptualization of the test construction process, distinguishes between tests that represent a particular behavior domain and tests that predict extratest behavior. In this approach, the test is a representation when the test items involve the same behaviors as those we are interested in measuring; the test is a predictor when the focus is on some nontest behavior that the test scores predict, rather than on the test itself.

THE TEST AS REPRESENTING.   Suppose, for example, that we want to measure a child's ability to add pairs of three-digit numbers. We could ask him to solve every possible problem involving the addition of two three-digit numbers. However, this would result in an extremely lengthy test. So we select a sample of problems and have him solve these selected problems. On the basis of his performance on these problems, the sample, we infer how well he would have done on the entire range of possible problems (the domain). The accuracy

---

[1]From *A Description of the College Board Scholastic Aptitude Test*, 1967, p. 4. Reprinted with permission from the College Entrance Examination Board, New York.

of our inference will depend, primarily, on how well we sampled from the potential pool of items. If by some quirk of sampling we selected many easy items we would overestimate his ability; if hard problems are over-represented on the test his ability will be underestimated. The method of item selection, however, is clear—we sample in some systematic way from the pool, or universe, of potential items. The sample of items on the test, therefore, represents the universe of possible items.

Although achievement tests, such as arithmetic and vocabulary, give the clearest example of a test as representing, the sampling concept can be applied to other areas of testing. Suppose that we wanted to measure the honesty of grade school children. One possible way would be to select a sample of situations where a child had an opportunity to demonstrate his honesty, or lack of it, and observe whether in these situations he was, in fact, honest. We might allow the child to correct his own test paper, place a copy of an upcoming examination in a place where he could readily observe it, allow him to make his own change, or provide him an opportunity to smuggle a valuable object out of the classroom. From observing his behavior in this sample of situations we could make inferences about his honesty in a variety of stiuations.

These two examples illustrate two distinct manifestations of the idea of a test as representing. In the arithmetic example the items were chosen to represent a particular content area, that of adding two three-digit numbers. The second example, that of measuring honesty, exemplifies sampling behaviors that are presumed to reflect a postulated psychological trait, honesty. Thus they start from different points, the fomer from a delineation of a content area, the latter from a definition of a psychological trait. However, given the initial domain, the process of sampling is essentially similar.

TESTS AS SIGNS.   Several authors make further distinctions within the general class of tests that represent. Goodenough (1949) distinguished between tests as samples and tests as *signs*, with a primary basis of distinction being the clarity with which the universe sampled can be defined. A test is a sample when the items are drawn from a clearly, but probably arbitrarily, defined universe; a test is a sign when the universe is openended and not completely defined. The implication of the term "sign", in her definition, is that the test points to, or "signals," the nature of the universe being sampled. Thorndike and Hagen (1961) distinguished between validity as representing, as predicting, and as signifying. The first two concepts are similar to the terms used in this book, and the third is analogous to the Goodenough idea of a test as a sign.

THE TEST AS PREDICTING.   In many situations, however, we are not interested in how the individual responds to the test items per se but are interested in the test because responses or scores enable us to predict performance in another, qualitatively different, situation. For example, a college admissions test may include many vocabulary items but we are not primarily interested in the student's vocabulary; rather we are interested in his vocabulary score because it predicts how well he will do in college. The focus is on what is predicted, not on the predictor. We are concerned with the test only in that it is a predictor of another behavior or characteristic—the criterion.

The essential element in developing a test for use as a predictor is that the test can be shown to relate to the behavior of concern. That is, does the test demonstrate predictive validity (see Chapter 5)? Because the selection of items for such a test is based upon the accuracy with which the item predicts the nontest behavior, items are frequently included on predictor tests that seem to have no logical relationship to the behavior under consideration. For example, interest inventories include items such as asking the person if he likes to play golf. Logically this item might seem to have little relationship to any vocational choice, except possibly that of a professional golfer. However, because liking golf can be shown empirically to be related to an interest in certain occupations, this item can serve to predict interest in these occupations. A test used as a predictor is still a sample of behavior, as considered in our definition of a test, because not all possible items, or behaviors, are included. The test items are thus only a portion of all the possible items.

SAMPLE VERSUS PREDICTOR. The distinction being made regarding a test as representing or predicting refers to whether the test items and the relevant nontest behavior (criterion) are similar or different. If the test and nontest behavior are essentially similar, the test is a sample (representation) of the relevant behavior; if they are different, the purpose of the test items is to signal (predict) the nontest behavior. The process of test development will, in part, vary depending upon whether the test is to function as a sample or a signal. Particularly, the process of item selection and validation will vary. When the test is constructed as a sample, items will be chosen by systematically sampling from a defined universe, and evaluation will consist of determining the adequacy of sampling. On the other hand, if the test serves as a predictor, different methods of item selection will be used and the crucial step will be to establish an empirical relationship between the item and behavior being predicted.

The distinction between tests as samples and predictors is not a clear dichotomy because the same test can be both a sample and a predictor. For example, a mathematics test, developed by sampling from concepts taught in high school, may predict academic success in an engineering curriculum when administered to entering college freshmen. Thus the test is both a sample of achievement in high school mathematics and a predictor of success in engineering. However, the process of test construction will vary depending on the test's primary function. If the primary goal is to develop a test that measures mathematics achievement, representative sampling from the universe of mathematics problems will be the *sine qua non* for item selection; if predictive accuracy is primary, sampling representativeness will be subsidiary to predictive power as a basis of item selection. Thus, even though the test may serve both purposes, one or the other will probably be stressed in the test construction process.

Translating the purpose into operational terms

The purpose of the test is usually stated in fairly general terms as aims to be accomplished or functions to be measured. Although the statement of the purpose may imply some limits on content and format, as illustrated in the SAT example, this statement usually is not explicit enough to allow the test constructor to move directly into the process of item construction. Rather, the test constructor, in order to proceed with the building of the test, must translate the purpose into operational terms. That is, he must phrase his purpose in terms that will specify the operations he must go through in constructing the test. This specification will cover two major areas—content and format. As with other aspects of test construction, this step will vary depending on the type of test. (See Figure 2.1.)

TESTS THAT REPRESENT.   In achievement testing operationalization takes the form of delineating the content and skills to be covered by the test. Thus a test might be developed to cover the sonnets of Shakespeare, the laws of permutations, the social and economic factors in the rise of the Nazi party, or the principles of achievement test construction. The content is further specified by reference to particular materials; for example, in the typical classroom examination the content would be defined in terms of the required reading assignments and the material covered in class discussions. Along with the specification of content to be covered, the skills to be tested (e.g., memory of facts, application of facts, evaluation) would be indicated. After giving these limiting conditions, the content to be covered and the skills to be tested, one can proceed to the next step —item construction.

If the test is being developed to measure a particular psychological trait or characteristic, the test constructor's job is somewhat more difficult. First he must define, as explicitly as possible, the trait being measured. He must then indicate the behaviors through which this trait will be manifested. In many cases this will involve making certain predictions about the relationship of scores on this test to other variables and as to how scores will vary with certain experimental manipulations. (See Chapter 6 on construct validity.) The essential step is defining the trait in behavioral terms.

TESTS THAT PREDICT.   When a test is being developed to serve as a predictor, the situation becomes even more complex. The first step is to make a thorough and systematic analysis of the situation in which the prediction will be made, with particular emphasis on the performance that we are attempting to predict.

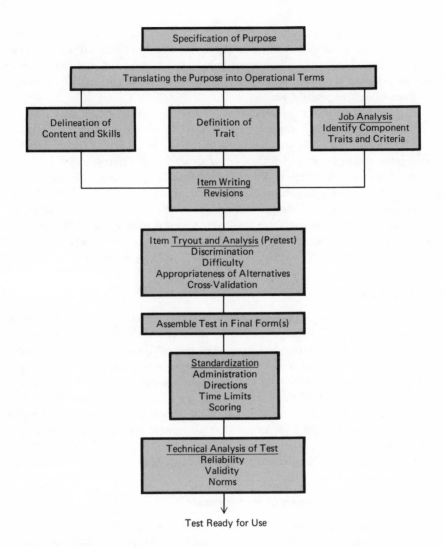

Figure 2.1 Steps in test construction.

In other words, a job analysis is conducted. The goal of this analysis is twofold: (1) to determine the criteria and (2) to identify traits or behaviors that appear to be necessary for satisfactory performance of the task.

A *criterion* is a measure of success on the performance being predicted. It is the behavior the test will predict. If the test is designed to predict successful performance in an area, what constitutes successful performance must be defined and a measurable index of success, the *criterion measure*, identified. For example, success as a relay assembler might be defined as the number of units assembled per hour, success as a salesman as the net value of sales, success as a student as the grade-point-average. Criteria will be discussed in detail in Chapter 5. At this point we will stress only that an adequate criterion measure must be relevant (i.e., that it actually measure successful performance), stable, free from bias, and readily available.

The other goal of the job analysis is to identify the behaviors, and thus the psychological traits, that appear to be related to success on the job. Thus, if the job involves installing small springs in the mechanism of a watch, the test constructor might hypothesize that finger dexterity is a necessary ability. If a job component is keeping inventory, he might hypothesize that arithmetic reasoning is a prerequisite ability. If the job is cutting floor tiles to fit irregularly shaped floor areas, spatial visualization might be involved. Having hypothesized what abilities, skills, or traits are involved in performing the job, the test constructor then proceeds to build or select items that measure these abilities and skills.

Test format

Besides the content to be covered by the test, the test constructor must also be concerned with item format, that is, the manner in which the items are presented. Will this be a paper-and-pencil test or will it involve some sort of apparatus? Will the test taker have only to recognize the correct response, as in multiple-choice examinations, or will he have to recall the correct response, as in completion items? Will the test emphasize speed of response, or will speed be only a secondary consideration? Some of the common dimensions of test formats are listed below. It should be noted that any single test will combine several of these dimensions, i.e., the test may be a speeded, paper-and-pencil achievement test with recognition items.

Common dimensions of test formats

1. *Recognition versus free response.* In a recognition item, the test taker chooses from among available responses as in multiple-choice, true–false, or matching items; in free response items, the test takers supply the response as in completion, short answer, or essay questions.

2. *Speed versus power test.* In a speed test the items are very simple, there is a time limit, speed of response is paramount, and the score is an index of speed of response. A power test is composed of items of varying difficulty, has no time limit or a limit which allows individuals to complete all the items they can do correctly, and the score reflects the level of difficulty of item the test taker can answer correctly.

3. *Maximum performance versus typical performance.* Distinction made by Cronbach (1949). On a test of maximal performance the goal is for the test

taker to attain the highest, or best, score he possibly can; on a test of typical performance we are interested in his usual performance. The set for maximal or typical performance is controlled mainly by directions to test takers. Achievement and ability tests generally are maximum performance measures, personality tests are typical performance measures.

4. *Objective versus subjective test.* Refers to scoring. In an objective test there are rules to insure agreement between scores (see pp. 42–43); on a subjective test the scorers' judgments enter.

5. *Paper-and-pencil versus performance versus oral.* Differences in way test stimuli are presented and responses made. Performance tests involve manipulation of some object or apparatus.

6. *Group versus individual.* The reference is to mode of administration. Group tests (usually paper-and-pencil) can be administered to more than one individual at a time; individual tests can be administered to only one person at a time. Group tests can always be administered individually but the converse is not true.

7. *Individual versus group solution.* There are a few testing situations where a group of subjects work together to produce one solution. Each individual in the group is assigned the score made by the group as a whole.

8. *Language versus nonlanguage.* The latter make no use of language or only minimal use in the directions. Nonlanguage tests are used with persons with language deficits, such as young children, the mentally retarded, and persons whose native language is not that of the tester.

9. *Structured versus projective.* In a structured test the stimuli and subject's task are clearly specified; in a projective test the stimuli and task are somewhat ambiguous.

10. *Product versus process.* In a product test the interest is in the test taker's response or what he makes or accomplishes; in a process test the interest is in some aspect of how he attacks and solves the problem presented.

11. *External observation versus self-report.* In a self-report test (e.g., personality and interest inventories) the subject reports on his own behavior; in the external observation test an outside observer rates the subject's performance on the task.

The format, content, and purpose of the test can be related in various ways. In all cases the format must be consistent with the purposes; in most instances, the purpose will limit the available formats; and in some cases, the format may almost be dictated by the purpose (and content) of the testing. These same relationships hold between the purpose and content of the test and between the content and format. For example, if the purpose of the testing is to assess the student's ability to compare, contrast, and evaluate the platforms of the Republican and Democratic parties in the 1968 election, it is difficult to conceive of any format other than an essay exam that would adequately serve this purpose.

In many instances, several formats will be consistent with the purpose and content of the test, and the problem is to select the best format. Two considerations aid in making a decision between appropriate formats: the composition of the group to be tested and practical considerations. The latter are undoubtedly less important than the former. The role of the composition of the group tested can be illustrated by (1) the practice of giving oral, instead of paper-and-pencil, tests to young children and persons with reading deficits and (2) providing tests with no or minimal verbal content to persons who are taking tests in a country where the language is not their native tongue. Practical consideration are exemplified by the use of multiple-choice exams in college admissions testing, and other national testing programs, where the volume of tests administered is so great that the only feasible method of scoring is with electronic scoring machines, the use of which requires that responses be of the recognition (e.g., multiple-choice) mode.

Finally, it should be noted that a test or test battery is not restricted to one format. As students we have all had the experience of taking a test that contains both objective (multiple-choice, true-false) items and essay questions. If the test purpose and content suggest multiple formats, then multiple formats should be used.

CONSTRUCTING THE TEST

After the goals and purposes have been specified and then translated into operational terms, the test developer is ready to start constructing the items for the test. Again, he has several options as to how to proceed, the exact process being determined, and limited, by the format and content specifications developed previously. Consider the sources used in developing ideas for individual items. For the typical classroom examination the teacher will refer to the textbook assignments, supplemental reading lists, lecture outlines, and class discussions as sources of items. For achievement tests developed by test publishers for use in a variety of schools and communities, item writers will consider not one text but the most commonly used texts and the materials covered, not by one teacher, but by a variety of teachers and subject matter experts. Personality inventory items, in contrast, are usually developed as derivatives from personality theories, from terms or phrases used to describe personality, from statements in clinic records, from statements people use to describe themselves, and even from items on other personality inventories.

The variety of sources and methods used will be considered in detail in Chapters 10–12. To illustrate the process of test development, we shall use as an example the construction of a standardized achievement test. This example was chosen because, in many ways, the procedures are more straightforward than in other areas of educational and psychological testing and because almost all of the steps used in test construction are present. It also represents a type of test that

most readers have taken and thus have some familiarity with its content, procedures, and format. When appropriate, comments on construction of other
types of tests will be interspersed.

Item writing

The process of obtaining the final form of an item is one of writing, tryout,
revision, tryout, revision—alternating until a satisfactory product is developed.
The number of tryouts and revisions will, of course, depend upon the skill of the
item writer, the care which he invests in item construction, and the standards of
accuracy desired for the test.

The construction of a standardized achievement test is a joint venture of
teachers and other subject matter experts and test construction specialists. From
the test specifications (purpose, content, format) this group develops a test plan,
the essential elements of which are the subject matter areas to be covered, the
skills to be tested, and the relative emphasis on each content-skill category. (See
Chapters 6 and 10 for more detailed discussions of the test plan.) Items are then
written to cover the designated content-skill areas. On standardized achievement tests the items are usually written in a multiple-choice format. The individual items may be written by subject matter experts, by test construction
experts and/or submitted by other item writers. Many more items are written
initially than will be included in the final form of the test because many items
will be eliminated in succeeding steps of the analysis.

The first drafts of items are then reviewed, criticized, and revised. This
review may be made by the same group that wrote the items or by an independent group of subject matter and test construction specialists. Most of the revisions will involve eliminating ambiguities, clarifying wordings, and strengthening weak alternatives. Although a skillful and experienced item writer can avoid
many common pitfalls, most items can be improved by this editing process. This
editing step also eliminates duplicate and obviously unusable items.

Item tryout and analysis

The items that survive this initial screening are then combined into one or more
forms of a *pretest*. These pretests are then administered to samples of persons who
are similar to the persons who will take the final form of the test. In the case of a
standardized achievement test, these groups will be students of the same grade
level and subject matter background (e.g., high school juniors who have taken
three years of mathematics) as those the test is designed for and will, ideally,
consist of groups displaying a wide variation on certain relevant dimensions—
e.g., academic ability, geographic area, and cultural background. The goal of
pretesting is to obtain information on students' reactions to the items. This
evidence will be both qualitative—comments on techniques used in solving the

items, ambiguities present in the items, etc.—and quantitative—evidence of the difficulty and discrimination power of the items.

ITEM DIFFICULTY. One aspect of the analysis is to determine item difficulty, i.e., the percentage of people that choose the correct response to each item. Knowing the difficulty of each item enables the test constructor to compose a test of a given level of difficulty, or a test that consists of items of a desired distribution of difficulties. For example, if the test is being designed to identify students with the greatest degree of knowledge, say, to select students for advanced sections of a course, then a difficult test might be desired. If, on the other hand, the purpose of the test is to identify students in need of additional or remedial help, a test of low difficulty would be preferable.

The concept of difficulty makes sense with achievement tests and ability tests, tests with definite correct responses and where students are attempting to make a maximum score (i.e., tests of maximal performance). The meaning of difficulty is not so clear with personality inventories, where there is no "correct" answer. With the latter type of test, however, we may desire tests having various patterns of response (e.g., percent agreement and disagreement with a statement). The procedures for obtaining tests having given item-response patterns are analogous to obtaining tests with given patterns of item difficulty. (See Chapter 12 for further discussion of this topic.)

ITEM DISCRIMINATION. The most crucial index is the validity, or discrimination power, of the item—the extent to which the test item measures what it is designed to measure. Ideally, an outside criterion would be available, such as grades on a final course examination, against which the item responses could be compared. In this situation it could be determined empirically whether the people who correctly answered the item were the same ones who obtained high scores on the criterion measure. If they were, the item would be considered valid. If not, the item would not be measuring what is desired and would need revision.

In practice such outside measures are frequently not readily available. As a substitute procedure, the pretest answer sheets are divided into groups on the basis of the total score on all items and the responses to individual items compared to determine if more of the persons obtaining high scores (on the total test) answered the item correctly than do persons obtaining lower scores. This procedure gives an index of item discrimination which, though not as desirable as a validity index, is frequently the only available index. In personality tests, and other tests with no "correct" answers, analogous procedures are used. (See Chapter 12.)

APPROPRIATENESS OF ALTERNATIVES. In determining the discrimination power of an item, an added bit of data is obtained—the number of persons choosing each alternative response to each item. If certain alternatives are very infrequently, or never, chosen, these alternatives should be revised because they are not contributing to the item, i.e., they draw no responses and thus cannot discriminate between persons with various degrees of knowledge. Obviously, items where all, or almost all, respondents choose the same alternative also lack discrimination power.

OTHER ANALYSES. In specific situations certain other analyses may be performed. If the test is designed to measure a single, homogeneous trait some measure of internal consistency, of the interrelationships between items, will be needed. (See Chapter 4.) If we are concerned with the stability of individual items, the extent to which the individual will make the same response to the item on two separate occasions, some measure of reliability (Chapter 3) will have to be obtained. If speed of completion is important, analyses of the effect of various time limits will need to be made.

Because statistics derived from one sample will vary, due to sampling errors, from those derived from another sample, the entire process of item analysis should be conducted on two independent samples. In technical terms, the items should be *cross-validated*. Only items that meet the minimal technical requirements in both samples are retained. This cross-validation procedure decreases the probability of including an item which appears valid but actually is reflecting only chance fluctuations.

Assembling the test

Using the results of the pretest analyses, the test construction staff selects for the final form of the test those items that best meet the technical and practical requirements. That is, they select those items that provide the best coverage of content and skills, which provide the best discrimination and appropriate difficulty, and do not have any practical limitations, such as requiring inordinate amounts of time for completion. This selection is a balancing and compromising procedure in that it may be necessary, for example, to include items of lower technical merit in order to insure the desired subject matter balance. If two or more equivalent forms of the test are being built from the same item pool, as is frequently the case when developing standardized tests, the test constructor has the further task of equating these forms in coverage, difficulty, discrimination power, and along any other relevant dimension.

After this tentative final form of the test is assembled, the items are once more reviewed. Changes at this point are likely to be minor but do occur. When all changes have been made, the test is printed in booklet form, and for the first time in the construction process the test exists as a separate, distinct entity. At this point, we have a collection of good items but not necessarily a good test. Whether the test will be excellent or mediocre will depend on the quality of its standardization and the provision of technical information regarding the meaning of the test scores.

STANDARDIZATION

The goal of psychological testing is to obtain as accurate an estimate of the test taker's performance as is possible. Accurate estimation in psychological testing, as in other scientific procedures, depends on the control of errors, that is, on minimizing the influence of factors irrelevant to the purpose of the testing. This control is established by developing procedures designed to make the test-taking situation the same, or as similar as possible, for all individuals. The process of developing these controls is called *standardization*.

The term "standardization" means different things to different authors. There is general agreement that standardization implies that the same content (items) be presented to each test taker and that there be rules specified for administering and scoring the test. Other authors would add the requirement that performance norms be available and another group would add the further requirement that reliability and validity data be provided. The definition of standardization adopted in this book will include only the requirements of standard content, standard procedures for administration, and scoring. The provision of adequate normative, reliability, and validity data, though essential, will be considered separately. In short, standardization will refer to procedures for obtaining scores, not for provision of data necessary to interpret the scores.

Content

The first essential element is the provision of a common set of items (stimuli) to which all test takers respond. Unless all persons are exposed to the same items, or items of demonstrated equivalence, their performance cannot be directly compared. As the major portion of the previous discussion in this chapter has illustrated how a standard set of items is developed and combined to form a test, no further comments regarding content would seem necessary at this point.

Administration

Even though the same items are administered to all test takers, the results will not be directly comparable unless the tests are administered under the same conditions. Exact comparability is, of course, impossible because the test will be administered to different persons or groups at various times and places and by different examiners. However, much of the irrelevant variability can be controlled by following prescribed directions for administering the test, by having all persons take the test under the same time restrictions, and by providing scoring methods that insure a high degree of objectivity.

DIRECTIONS.   Two sets of directions are usually necessary—one for the test taker and one for the test administrator. The purpose of the directions for the test taker is to explain, as clearly and simply as possible, what he must do in responding to the items. These directions are printed at the beginning of the test, preferably on a separate cover page, and may range from the simple, one-sentence directions on a classroom examination to a page or more on standard-ized examinations, as illustrated in Figure 2.2. Directions to the test taker should cover the purpose of the test, how to choose a response, how to make the response (e.g., by marking in the test booklet or on a separate answer sheet), time limits, and any other special procedures. In many cases the directions will include a statement about guessing or how to respond when uncertain. It may also be desirable to include sample items, particularly if the item format is likely to be unfamiliar to the test takers.

Directions to the test administrator include a wider variety of topics and are printed in a separate test manual. These directions will include not only those given to the test taker, with a further explanation of their ramifications, but also details such as the arrangement of the testing room, seating, timing, procedures, scoring, and so forth. These directions should also give detailed instructions on how to handle emergencies and questions arising during the testing session.

TIME LIMITS.   One salient aspect of the directions is time limits. In many instances, particularly testing in public schools, time limits are partially dictated by the length of the class period and consequently tests, or sections of the test, are constructed to fit into one or two class periods. Preferably, however, the de-termination of time limits should be based on the purpose and content of the test. Most measures of typical performance—including interests and personality—are administered without a time limit, thus allowing the test taker to proceed at his own pace. If any directions are given, test takers are to work as rapidly as possible and not spend too much time on any one item.

However, when abilities or achievement are being measured, speed of response is often a factor of concern. We can establish a continuum for describing tests based on the role that speed plays in determining the individual's score. At one end is a pure *power test*, defined as a test where the individual is given unlimited time to respond to a series of items of increasing difficulty. His score, therefore, depends solely on the number of items he can answer or, stated somewhat differently, on how difficult an item he can correctly answer. At the other extreme is a pure *speed*, or *time limit*, *test*, one in which the items are so simple that anyone taking the test could correctly answer all items, given sufficient time, but which has stringent time limits. Scores on a pure speed test reflect differences in speed of response, not in difficulty.

Figure 2.2 Examples of test directions.

A. *Directions for a classroom exam (college level course)*

Directions: On each of the following items choose the alternative that is correct and mark its letter in the appropriate place on the answer sheet.

B. *General directions for a test having several subtests*

GENERAL DIRECTIONS

This test consists of ten parts measuring different aptitudes and abilities. Each part has its own time limit. The time limits are short. *Work on each part only during the time allowed for it.* If you finish a part before time is called, go back and check your work on that part. *Do not* return to a previous part, or go ahead to a later part. Work *rapidly* on each part, but try not to make mistakes.

Each part has its own special directions, and one or two examples, correctly marked. Be sure you understand the directions for each part *before* you start to work on it. The examiner will *not* answer any questions after the starting signal for a part has been given.

C. *Directions for a subtest within an aptitude battery*

I. VOCABULARY

Each test word, in capital letters, is followed by five possible answers. The correct answer is the word which *means most nearly the same* as the test word. Make a *heavy* line with your pencil between the pair of dotted lines at the right which are lettered the same as the correct answer. EXAMPLE:

FREQUENT: A) always   B) often   A   B   C   D   E
        C) never   D) very   E) soon

"Often" means most nearly the same as "frequent," so a heavy line has been made between the dotted lines at the right under B.

Figure 2-2 (continued)

Mark an answer for every word. If you don't know the meaning of a word, make the best choice you can.

You will have *three minutes* to work on this test.

DO NOT TURN THE PAGE UNTIL YOU ARE TOLD TO DO SO.

D. *Directions for an interest inventory*

Minnesota Vocational Interest Inventory
Kenneth E. Clark

In the booklet, you will find many activities listed—they are arranged in groups of three. In each group, you should choose the one thing that you would most LIKE to do, and the one thing that you would most DISLIKE to do. For the item you like best, fill in the oval in the row marked L, <u>above</u> the letter which is the same as that of the item. For the item you dislike most (or like the least), fill in the oval in the row marked D, <u>below</u> the letter of the item. Leave the ovals for the other item blank.

Now look at the Example below. The marks indicate that item c, "Study welding" is liked most, and item a, "Study carpentry" is disliked most, or liked least. The other item is then left blank.

Example X: a. Study carpentry.
b. Study first aid.
c. Study welding.

Most tests fall somewhere on the continuum between these two extremes. A common rule of thumb, used with most achievement and ability tests, is to set time limits that allow approximately 90 percent of the persons to finish the test within the time allowed. If, in addition, the items are arranged in order of increasing difficulty, practically all the persons will be able to complete the items that they can solve. The administrative advantages of this procedure are obvious. The relative weight given to speed and power will, of course, depend on the purpose of the testing and the empirical evidence as to the validity of the test in various situations and under various time limits.

SCORING.   The third element in standardization is the provision of directions and procedures for objective scoring. Objectivity, in scoring, means agreement between two or more competent (trained) scorers. Ideally the agreement between scorers should be perfect; in practice, especially in scoring free response items, agreement will be less than complete. In no case, however, should we consider the scoring procedure to be objective unless the agreement between scorers exceeds 90 percent. In all cases, the goal of objective scoring is to reduce variability due to scoring differences so that differences between scores may be attributed solely to differences between test takers.

Although a myriad of scoring techniques are available, from hand scoring to the use of high speed electronic scoring machines, the basic requirements for insuring objectivity in scoring can be reduced to a few basic steps. The first essential is immediate and unambiguous recording of responses. Whether the test taker makes a mark on an IBM answer sheet, writes a letter, word, phrase, or essay, or speaks an answer to an examiner who records it (as in most individual intelligence tests), the response should be recorded immediately and completely. This permanent record avoids distortion due to memory loss and provides the basis for classifying responses.

The second requirement is a list of standard or correct responses. This list is commonly called a *scoring key*. In a multiple-choice examination this key would be the number or letter of the correct response to each item. In a short-answer (completion) item it would be a list of the correct responses and acceptable variations. In an essay exam, it would be an outline of the points to be covered. In a personality inventory, the key will designate which responses are indicative of the presence or absence of the trait or characteristic being measured. If various responses are to receive different weights, the weight to be assigned to each response, and variation of response, should also be included with the key.

The final requirement is specification of a procedure for comparing the key to the actual responses, a procedure for objective classification of responses. In items that require only a choice among alternatives, such as multiple-choice items, the procedure is straightforward and obvious. In instances where the scorer's judgment may enter, as in grading essay exams, he will need to develop rather complete directions for assigning scores. An excellent example of specifications for scoring is provided in the manual for the Wechsler Adult Intelligence Scale (Figure 2.3). This key provides a listing of acceptable responses, variations of responses, and scoring weights, by giving illustrations of potential responses. The scorer compares the response in question to the examples provided in the scoring manual and assigns to the response the weight of the most nearly comparable example. Although this procedure does not yield perfect agreement between scorers, it does restrict variation to tolerable limits.

Standardization applied to the achievement test example

The administrative considerations for a standardized achievement examination, such as our illustration, are basically those discussed in the previous paragraphs. A time limit would be set that would allow 90 percent or more of the test takers to finish in the allotted time. The directions to the test taker would include a statement of the purpose and possible uses of the test, and directions for responding. Because the test is in a multiple-choice format, there would be a statement about guessing. Since the test would involve use of a separate answer sheet, there would be statements telling how to record answers on the sheet. Even though test takers would probably be familiar with the multiple-choice format, unless the test were designed for use with the lower elementary grades, several practice examples would need to be developed and included with the directions. Because standardized achievement tests are frequently administered by classroom teachers, or other persons without extensive training in psychological testing, rather complete and specific directions to the test administrator will need to be developed.

Scoring procedures for a standardized achievement test which uses a separate, electronically scored answer sheet are straightforward. The correct answers to the items are put on a scoring stencil that the scoring machine can read, the stencil is fed into the scoring machine, the machine programed to derive total or part scores, then the answer sheets are fed into the scoring machine and scores derived automatically. The test could also be handscored by use of an appropriate stencil, but this procedure is much slower and less accurate. Either approach involves only a counting operation.

TECHNICAL REQUIREMENTS

The procedures discussed so far insure but one thing—that the score an individual receives on a test will reflect, to the degree that we were stringent in applying the principles of test construction, his performance on the designated sample of material covered by the test and will not reflect peculiarities and vicissitudes of the testing situation. They do not answer the larger questions: What do the test scores mean? What is the appropriate interpretation to be placed on any score? What inferences can be drawn from the score?

Figure 2.3 Example of a scoring manual: Wechsler Adult Intelligence Scale.

SCORING CRITERIA AND SAMPLE ANSWERS: VOCABULARY

In general, any recognized meaning of the word is acceptable, disregarding elegance of expression. However, *poverty of content* is penalized to some extent; indication of only a vague knowledge of what the word means does not earn full credit. Responses to words 1-3 are scored 2 or 0, while all the other words are scored 2, 1 or 0. The following are general principles for scoring responses to the Vocabulary items.

2 Points

1. A good synonym.
2. A major use.
3. One or more definitive or primary features.
4. General classification to which word belongs.
5. Several correct descriptive features which are not precisely definitive but which cumulatively indicate understanding of the word.
6. For verbs, definitive example of action or causal relation.

1 Point

1. A response that is not incorrect but which shows poverty of content.
2. A vague or inexact synonym.
3. A minor use, not elaborated.
4. Attributes which are correct but not definitive or not distinguishing features.
5. Example using the word itself, not elaborated.
6. Correct definition of a related form of the word, e.g., "haste" instead of "hasten," "obstruction" instead of "obstruct."

0 Points

1. Obviously wrong answers.
2. Verbalisms, e.g., "Repair a car," when no real understanding is shown after inquiry.
3. Responses which show great poverty of content or are very vague even after questioning.

For the specific items, a general criterion for scoring is shown for every word at the 2-point level, followed by several sample answers. In some instances, a general criterion is given for 1-point and 0-point responses together with examples. For other items there is no appropriate generalization at these levels of credit beyond those provided by the general scoring principles, and only sample answers are given. Of course, these lists contain only a few of the many responses that are possible or that subjects will give. They are intended, however, to supplement dictionary definitions and the general scoring principles in such a way as to facilitate the task of scoring this test accurately.

Figure 2.3 (continued)

SAMPLE ANSWERS; VOCABULARY*

1. Chair

   2 points — a piece of furniture to sit in; to conduct a meeting
   to sit in . . . to sit on . . . sit on when eating
   1 point — furniture made of wood
   0 points — sitting down . . . soft object . . . be at a meeting

2. January

   2 points — first month of the year
   a month . . . first month . . . cold winter month
   1 point — after December . . . starts year . . . New Year's is January 1
   0 points — a Roman God

3. Construct

   2 points — to build or devise something; something built systematically
   to build . . . erect something . . . put together using a plan
   1 point — construct a building . . . make . . . process of building
   0 points — divide . . . tighten, draw together . . . helpful

   *To preserve the security of the test actual WAIS items were not used. The hypothetical items used are similar to the WAIS vocabulary items and the format of the scoring manual identical to the WAIS manual.

These questions can be answered only from further data. In particular, we need three types of data: on the consistency or reliability of the measurement, on the validity of the test, and on the performance of various norm groups. These data are all essential for an adequate interpretation of the meaning of a test score. Each will be mentioned only briefly below. Their importance is indicated not by the space devoted to them in this chapter but by the fact that one or two of the succeeding chapters are devoted to each of the topics.

Consistency

Unless a test measures consistently, that is, unless an individual would obtain the same, or almost the same, score on repeated administrations of a test, little faith can be placed in the results obtained. Without consistency, testing would be analogous to measuring with a rubber ruler, with different results being obtained on each application, depending on the amount of stretching of the ruler present during each measurement. The estimation of the degree of consistency of measurement, called the reliability of the test, can be done in several ways: by administering the same form of the test twice, by administering equivalent forms of the test to the same sample of people, or by artificially splitting the test into two subtests and comparing performance on the two portions. The exact method used will depend upon the type of test and its proposed uses.

As a practical matter this requirement means that the test constructor must obtain a sample of subjects, similar in composition to the groups the test is designed for, apply one or more of the procedures mentioned in the previous paragraph, and calculate a reliability coefficient. Methods of determining reliability, as well as the theory of reliability, will be discussed in detail in the next chapter.

Validity

The single most paramount characteristic of a psychological test is its validity, the extent to which it measures whatever it is designed to measure. Without empirical data regarding the validity of a test, we have no evidence, conclusive or persuasive, as to what the test actually measures. Without this evidence we cannot give meaning to or interpret the test scores.

Because the individual items comprising the test were selected partially on the basis of their validity (discrimination power), we have some assurance that the test scores will have a degree of validity. Since the test as a whole may be something different than just a sum of its parts (items), it is necessary to collect validity data utilizing the test in its final form. This means administering the test in several situations, with a variety of groups, and determining its effectiveness. Because validity is specific to the situation and sample of subjects, collecting validity data is essentially an endless process. The test constructor's obligation is to provide sufficient data on the test's validity, based on studies in a great enough variety of situations, so that it is clear that the test is succeeding, in some significant measure, in attaining its purposes.

A detailed discussion of the theory and methods of establishing validity is presented in Chapters 5 and 6.

Normative data

Test scores by themselves have little, if any, meaning. They attain meaning only when: (1) validity data is available, and (2) an individual's score is compared to scores of other persons taking the test. By comparing the individual's score to scores of other persons in a specific, well-defined population, called the *norm group*, we can get an indication of his relative position on that test in that population. By combining this normative information with validity data from the same population, we are able to interpret the meaning of the score as we know what the test measures and the individual's ranking in some relevant population.

The test constructor, thus, must present evidence on the performance of a relevant group of persons on the test. As, in most instances, we will wish to compare the individual's scores to several diverse groups, the test developer will have to provide data for various groups, i.e., he will have to provide various norm groups. Since this book takes the view that normative data is worthless without validity data, the norm groups will coincide with groups used to establish the validity of the test, or at least of groups so similar to those used to establish the validity of the test that we can be confident in making inferences from the validity group to the norm group.

Scores on psychological tests are generally expressed in forms and on scales other than those derived directly from scoring the test. That is, when the test is first scored we obtain a score, called the *raw score*, which is usually expressed as number of items correct, time needed to complete the test, or other similar units. For these scores to be interpreted, they must be compared to the performance of the norm group, a procedure that usually involves developing scoring scales (such as percentiles and standard scores) based on the performance of the norm groups. Thus the test constructor not only has to collect normative data, he also has to develop appropriate scales for expressing the test scores. The procedures followed will be discussed in Chapter 7.

Summary

In order to understand what is measured by psychological tests it is necessary first to know how measurement of psychological characteristics proceeds. This chapter gave a brief overview of the test construction process, from the beginning step of specifying the purpose of the testing to the point where the test is ready for widespread use. The process was illustrated by an example, the construction of a standardized achievement test.

Constructing a test is basically a process of defining what is to be measured and then developing operations that measure the desired behavior. Thus the first step in test construction is to define the purpose of the test. This purpose must then be translated into operational terms, the translation process varying depending on whether the test is designed to represent a given universe or predict a nontest behavior. Specification of the test purpose will also delineate the test content and format.

The test constructor then writes the items for the test. Obtaining the final, polished form of an item is a continual process of writing, evaluation, and revision. Evaluation is both qualitative and quantitative. Qualitative evaluation takes the form of review by subject matter and test construction experts, with emphasis on the content and wording of the item. Quantitative evaluation is obtained by an item analyses of the pretest and includes item difficulty, item discrimination, appropriateness of alternatives, and other relevant analyses.

The items surviving these evaluations are then combined into the final form, or forms, of the test. The test is then standardized, that is, procedures are developed for insuring that the test will be administered in the same way to all test takers (e.g., with the same instructions and time limits) and for objective scoring. Finally, the test constructor provides information on the reliability and validity of the test and provides normative data to aid in the interpretation of the test scores.

Suggestions for further reading

Goodenough, F. L. *Mental testing*. New York: Holt, Rinehart and Winston, Inc., 1949. Chap. 7 presents her distinction between tests as signs and as samples and the bearing of this distinction on the meaning and interpretation of test scores.

Katz, M. (Ed.). *ETS builds a test*. Princeton, N.J.: Educational Testing Service, 1965. A pamphlet providing a broad overview of the process that a test publisher goes through in developing a standardized test.

Smedslund, J. Concrete reasoning: a study of intellectual development. *Society for Research in Child Development Monograph*, 1964, 29 (2, Whole No. 93). Includes an excellent discussion of the process of building a series of test items for use in an experimental study.

Super, D. E., and J. O. Crites. *Appraising vocational fitness* (rev. ed.). New York: Harper & Row, 1962. Chap. 3 gives an overview of the methods of constructing, standardizing, and validating a test with emphasis on tests used in vocational selection and placement.

Consistency I: Reliability

Chapter 3

INTRODUCTION

The problem of consistency of measurement has been likened to the money problem: it is only the lack of it that causes any trouble (Kerlinger, 1965). If we could be assured that our tests would measure consistently, we would have no cause for concern. But since scores on psychological tests are derived from human responses, and one characteristic of human beings is that their behavior tends to fluctuate from time to time and from situation to situation, we have to be concerned with consistency in test scores. Furthermore, any test contains only a sample of all possible items and is administered at a particular time, one of many possible times. Thus the sampling of items, the circumstances of a particular administration, and the characteristics of the test taker may introduce inconsistency (error) into the measurement.

The need for consistency of measurement may be so obvious that you have never thought about it, or at least not have thought about it in the terms that we are concerned with in psychological testing. Most of the dimensions that we measure in everyday life, being of physical characteristics (e.g., length, weight, speed, volume), are ones that can be measured with great precision and with little variation from occasion to occasion. True, your height may occasionally be measured as 5 feet, 10 inches instead of your usual 5 feet, 10½ inches, but you are likely to attribute this slight variation to rounding errors, to viewing the measuring device from a slightly different angle, or to some other specifiable cause. Your weight may fluctuate more widely but here also you do not question the measuring technique; rather, you attribute the fluctuations to true changes in weight due to a specific reason—e.g., you are just back from Christmas vacation during which time you overate, or you have had the flu for a week and lost weight.

Such a high degree of consistency cannot be ascribed to psychological measurement because test scores are readily influenced by extraneous conditions. For example, you probably have had the experience of getting a high mark on an exam because it just happened to stress the areas that you had studied most thoroughly. Or you might have obtained a lower mark because there was a heavy emphasis on material that you had skimmed over. At other times you might have felt that your performance was adversely affected because you were not feeling well on the day of the test. In each of these cases you may have felt, and probably rightly so, that the test was not a fair measure of your true ability; the implication being that if the test were revised, or given under different circumstances, your score would have been different. It is just such concerns, and other related ones, that have caused psychologists to study the consistency of their measurements.

THE THEORY OF RELIABILITY

The generic term given to the problem of consistency of measurement is *reliability*. When studying reliability we are basically interested in two sets of questions. The first set involves the degree of consistency of test scores: What is the degree of relationship between scores obtained under varying testing conditions? How many points would a person's score change upon retesting? How close is an individual's obtained score to this "true score"? Is the test measuring consistently enough so that it can be applied in practical situations? The second set of questions revolves around the causes of discrepancies among test scores: What factors produce inconsistent scores? What is the relative magnitude of their effects? How do they operate? Traditionally, the study of reliability has emphasized the first set of questions, concentrating on the development of methods for making more precise estimates of the degree of consistency of measurement. Only recently have there been concentrated attacks on the second set of questions.

The basic equation

The fundamental conception of reliability can best be presented by introducing the idea of a true score. A *true score* is the score that a person would obtain if the measuring instrument (test) were perfect, if the test could measure a given characteristic without error.[1] However, no psychological test yet devised mea-

---

[1]An alternative definition is that a true score is the average score the individual would make over an infinite number of repeated administrations of the test. This definition assumes that no learning, fatigue, or practice effects are present on repeated testing—an untenable assumption in a practical situation.

sures without error, so the score a person actually obtains on a test is a function of both his true score and the error involved in the measurement. Expressed as an equation,

$$X_t = X_T + E \qquad\qquad (3.1)$$

where X_t = the obtained score on the test

X_T = the true score on the test

E = the error involved in the measurement

The *error* term (E) represents the contribution of any variable(s) that are irrelevant to the purposes of the test and produce inconsistencies in measurement. The error component can be either positive or negative—if it is positive, the person's true score will be overestimated by his obtained score; if negative, his true score will be underestimated. Error represents unsystematic variation; thus E and X_T are uncorrelated.

Reliability defined

Equation (3.1) shows the relationship between obtained scores, true scores, and error but it does not define reliability. *Reliability* may be defined as *the ratio of the true variance in a set of test scores to the total, or obtained, variance*, i.e.,

$$r_{tt} = \frac{s_T{}^2}{s_t{}^2} \qquad\qquad (3.2)$$

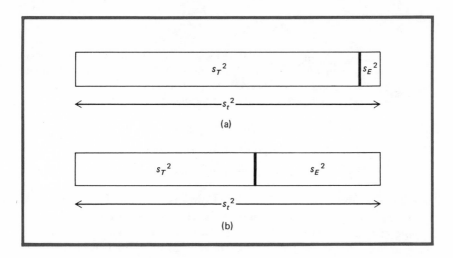

Figure 3.1 Reliability as the proportion of true variance: (a) a highly reliable test (small $s_E{}^2$); (b) an unreliable test (large $s_E{}^2$).

TABLE 3.1 Relation of the basic equation to the definition of reliability

(1) The basic equation, Equation 3.1, is:

$$X_t = X_T + E$$

(2) This equation, when applied to a set of test scores, rather than an individual's scores, can also be written in terms of variances (recall that variances are additive, see p. 20):

$$s_t^2 = s_T^2 + s_E^2$$

Or, the variance of the obtained scores (s_t^2) equals the variance of the true scores (s_T^2) plus the error variance (s_E^2).

(3) We can divide both sides of the equation by s_t^2 to give:

$$\frac{s_t^2}{s_t^2} = \frac{s_T^2}{s_t^2} + \frac{s_E^2}{s_t^2} = 1.00$$

(4) And as reliability was defined as:

$$r_{tt} = \frac{s_T^2}{s_t^2}$$

(5) We can also define reliability as:

$$r_{tt} = 1 - \frac{s_E^2}{s_t^2}$$

or

$$r_{tt} = \frac{s_t^2 - s_E^2}{s_t^2}$$

Because s_t^2 can be calculated from the distribution of test scores and s_E^2 can be calculated from the distribution of discrepancies between pairs of test scores, these formulas provide a basis for estimating r_{tt} from the obtained test scores.

where r_{tt} = the reliability of the test

s_T^2 = the variance of the true scores

s_t^2 = the variance of the obtained scores

The relation of this equation to Equation (3.1) is shown in Table 3.1, and the idea of reliability as the proportion of variance is shown in Figure 3.1.

Note that in Equation (3.2), in contrast to Equation (3.1), we are now talking about a set of test scores, not scores of an individual. Reliability, as a concept of psychological measurement, refers to consistency within a set of measurements. From our knowledge of the degree of inconsistency (the reliability) of a set of test scores, we can infer the extent to which an individual's score will vary. However, reliability is a property of the total set of test scores, not of an individual's score.

The reader who completely understands the equations and definitions is probably now saying, "Fine—but since you can never know a person's true score or precisely define the error component, what have you?" And he has put his finger on an important point—one can never determine reliability precisely—one can only estimate it from a set of obtained data. Certain of the concepts in the equations—e.g., true score, error, true variance, error variance—cannot be directly measured, they can only be estimated. Thus reliability is a construct, a hypothesized property of test scores. Certain procedures, described below, have been developed to estimate the reliability of a test. Before considering these procedures, however, we will discuss some of the factors that produce inconsistencies in test scores and show how their effects are minimized or controlled.

CONTROLLING ERROR

The goal in psychological testing is to have the obtained scores reflect the true scores with as little error as possible. In order for the obtained scores to approximate the true scores, irrelevant factors that influence the obtained scores, but not the true scores, must be controlled and their influence minimized. In this way we attempt to minimize error. And, because reliability is defined as the proportion of true variance in test scores, we are in essence trying to maximize reliability.

Error defined

Error can be a rather elusive concept to define. As indicated above, we will define error as *any variable that is irrelevant to the purposes of the testing and results in inconsistencies in measurement.* Thus if there are differences in John's scores on two administrations of the same mechanical aptitude test taken two months apart, and mechanical aptitude is assumed to be quite consistent over such short periods of time, then some factor has introduced error into the measurement. Again, if Ellen obtains different scores on two (supposedly) comparable spelling tests taken the same day, then the particular sample of items on the two forms can be seen as introducing error into the measurement of her spelling ability.

The definition of error is two-pronged: it indicates that a variable can be considered as introducing error if it (1) is irrelevant to the purpose of the testing and (2) produces inconsistencies in scores from one administration of the test to another. The former half of the definition (the relevancy aspect) is also a question of validity and will be discussed in detail in Chapters 5 and 6. Suffice to say, at this point, that if an irrelevant variable produces a constant or systematic change in test scores, its effect will not be detected in a reliability analysis because it produces no inconsistencies in scores. Yet it is still a type of measurement error. To illustrate, the responding rate on most verbal tests will be a function of both reading speed and knowledge of the material covered by the test. As the test is usually designed to tap only the latter aspect, across testings reading speed will produce an irrelevant, albeit systematic, effect. In studying reliability we are concerned with a second type of error, variable errors—factors that produce discrepancies between scores on repeated administrations of the test. The primary concern is with stability, not relevance.

Although the particular error factors present in a given situation will vary depending upon the group being tested, the type of test and the conditions of the testing session, certain common sources of error can be identified (Thorndike, 1951). One class of error variables will relate to changes within the test taker. These may be long-term changes resulting from education, training, or changes in environment, or they may be relatively short-term fluctuations in variables such as mood, health, attention, and fatigue. A second group includes variations due to the test itself—primarily variations resulting from the particular sampling of items included on the test. A third class of error variables involves the particular test administration, e.g., the physical situation, directions, subtle helps, distracting factors, and errors in timing.

Errors within the test

The entire process of test construction is designed to minimize errors attributable to the test itself. However, any aspect of an item that causes the test taker to respond to that item on bases other than knowledge of the "correct" or appropriate response may introduce error. Ambiguity in the wording of an item or in specifying the procedures for responding may thus produce unstable responses. Difficult items that require the test taker to guess frequently introduce errors. At a more gross level, the length of the test influences reliability, longer tests generally being more reliable. And restrictive time limits, which encourage hasty reading, responding, and recording of answers, frequently produce unstable performance.

Error may also be introduced in the scoring of the test. As mentioned in Chapter 2, scoring errors are best minimized by providing objective scoring methods, such as the utilization of electronic scoring machines to score multiple-choice examinations. Under these conditions scoring errors should be negligible. In free-response tests, especially essay examinations, scoring can produce larger error effects and a check on interscorer agreement (reliability) is essential.

Because consistency over various samples of items is one index of reliability, the problem of developing equivalent forms of a test becomes central. In order to have truly equivalent forms, the test forms must be matched, preferably item by item, on content and function. In addition the forms must be equally difficult and the distributions of test scores similar. These requirements are straightforward, but in practice such equivalence is difficult to attain, coming only as a result of exceedingly careful item construction and analysis. To the extent that the several forms of the test do not yield equivalent scores, error has been introduced into the measurement, because the test taker would obtain different scores depending upon the sample of items (i.e., form of the test) he was administered.

The test administration

As psychological tests have become more common, and administrative procedures have become more standardized, errors attributable to the conditions of the particular test administration have probably decreased. However, because misunderstanding of directions, mismarking of answer sheets, mistakes in timing, unforeseen interruptions, and other distractions do occur, it is essential that the test administrator be alert to conditions that might result in inaccurate scores. These errors are most likely to occur in tests with complex procedures or directions, when testing very large groups, in individual testing where the test administrator has more leeway in setting the testing conditions, and when testing young children or other persons who are unfamiliar with testing procedures.

Some examples of disruptions of administrative procedures that the author has experienced include: failure of the watch used to time the test during a timed section of the test; failure of the air conditioning, followed by intolerable ventilation; use of the testing room by the custodian as a passageway when emptying trash cans; failure of the microphone used for giving directions; misprinted test booklets and answer sheets; students caught cheating on the test; and, in one case, an epileptic seizure by a test taker. In each such instance the test administrator must decide how to handle the immediate situation so as to produce the minimal inconvenience and distraction to the other persons taking the test, estimate whether the disturbance was deemed serious enough to result in inaccurate scores, and, if the disturbance was deemed serious, make plans for retesting.

Of the three sources of error—those within the test, the test administration, and errors attributable to the test taker—those concerned with the test administration are probably easiest to control or minimize. This is true because experience with testing has resulted in the development of detailed instructions for administering and scoring the tests, instructions that minimize the variability between test administrators by outlining specific procedures to follow, thereby reducing irrelevant variability. Unless there is some compelling reason for alteration, the test administrator should always follow the instructions exactly as printed in the manual.

The test taker

The most difficult sources of error to evaluate and control are those which are inherent in the test taker. Even if we could build several equivalent forms of a test that perfectly sampled the universe of possible items, and if we could completely standardize the rules for administering and scoring tests, and if the physical arrangements for testing were always ideal—in short, if we could provide model testing conditions—there would still be errors in test scores, inconsistencies attributable to the test taker. Some of these fluctuations would result from rather pervasive and long standing characteristics of the individual—his motivation, experience with tests, his learning history and education. Others would reflect more transient factors: coaching for a specific test, fatigue, illness, or temporary lapses in attention. Although it is relatively obvious how specific short-term influences (such as illness on the testing date) will affect reliability, it is not always clear whether the more pervasive characteristics introduce variable or constant errors.

MOTIVATION.   Tests can be divided into two categories: tests of maximal performance and tests of typical performance (Cronbach, 1949). On a test of maximal performance the goal is to obtain an estimate of the upper limits of a person's capabilities, to determine what is the maximum performance he can attain. This type of approach is illustrated by a classroom examination. In general, all achievement, aptitude, and ability tests will fall into this category. On a test of typical performance, however, the interest is not in the person's maximum output but rather in how he typically responds. This approach is utilized in personality and interest inventories.

The distinction between typical performance and maximal performance is made by the test constructor, not the test taker. The test constructor, if he wishes to obtain the type of performance that he desires, must communicate this emphasis to the test taker through the test directions. Directions on aptitude and achievement tests thus generally stress trying one's best, choosing the correct answer, and answering as many questions as possible, while personality and interest inventories stress that there are "no correct answers" and that the person should respond according to his own feelings and typical behaviors, not on the basis of what he thinks is correct behavior or how he thinks other people would react to the item.

Knowing the purpose of the test also influences the person's approach to the test. The purposes for which achievement tests are usually given (e.g., assigning grades, testing mastery, placement) are those which most people consider calling for one's best performance, i.e., as being a situation where a high score is desirable. The same is true of aptitude tests, which usually are administered to indicate, directly or indirectly, whether the person will be eligible for a certain class, school, or job. In the typical performance realm, the idea of personality inventory having "no correct answers" is becoming ingrained in many people's experience and thus influences their approach to these tests.

The problem for the psychologist occurs when a particular person, or group of persons, has a different motivation for taking the test than do the majority of the test takers. Whenever this happens there is a question as to whether the test results of the minority group are comparable to those of the others, or in terms of consistency of measurement, as to whether similar results would be obtained under different testing conditions.

Examples can illustrate the effects of motivation. As mentioned above, most children and adults view an achievement test as a situation calling for maximal performance, for a commonly held value in our society is to do one's best. However, psychologists, sociologists, and educators have found that in certain segments of our population, particularly the lower socioeconomic classes, this value or drive for achievement does not operate with the intensity that it does in middle- and upper-class children. Thus, even though the test is considered one of maximal performance by the test constructor, the child may have little motivation to do well. The person interpreting the test scores then has the complex task of determining, in each individual situation, what the child's motivation was when taking the test and how this motivation affected his scores.

An analogous situation occurs when a personality inventory is given as an aid in selection. Although the person using the test to make the decision may be interested in the employee's typical performance, the employee (test taker) may feel that it is to his advantage to try to make a good impression. For him, the testing situation thus becomes a maximal performance situation (i.e., showing his best possible profile or his knowledge of what is desirable) rather than presenting a picture of his typical behavior.

Or consider, as a third example, a star high school athlete who has little interest in academic work. This disinterest also manifests itself on tests. When taking a college admissions test he treats it as a joke, responding haphazardly, and feeling that his athletic ability will insure his admission to college. However, he then learns that he will not be awarded an athletic scholarship unless he attains a higher test score. He then takes the test again, this time approaching it seriously and attempting to obtain his maximal score.

Atypical motivational patterns may manifest themselves in several ways. In the second example, a systematic bias is introduced, a bias that would operate in a constant manner on repeated testings. This would invalidate the scores but would not necessarily produce any inconsistency. In the first example, however, it is highly probable that the person's response to the test items will be somewhat haphazard and erratic. In this situation, there will be a systematic effect (underestimation of the person's ability) plus a variable error producing decreased reliability. In the third example, the test-retest relation (reliability) will be lowered because of the differential motivation during the two administrations.

LEARNING AND EDUCATION.   Every test measures what the test taker has learned throughout his lifetime; in fact, the purpose of testing generally is to assess the level of developed skills in a certain area. Thus variations in test scores due to specific or general learning experiences are, for the most part, reflections of constant errors and are of little direct concern in determining reliability. There are, however, several situations where learning experiences are important. One instance is when an individual or subgroup has received specific coaching for a test, while the other test takers have undergone no special preparation. This problem is discussed in the section on coaching. The second case occurs when the two administrations of the test, from which the reliability estimates are derived, are separated in time and, in the time period intervening between testings, some of the group receive special education and training and part of the group does not have this experience. In these circumstances the scores on the second administration of the test will reflect both what was tested on the first administration and what was learned between administrations. Because the test takers received varying amounts of relevant training, their scores will be affected differentially and the correlation between scores on the two administrations will decrease.

EXPERIENCE WITH TESTS.   Another fundamental assumption of psychological testing is that the persons taking a test have had equal exposure, at least within broad limits, both to the materials covered by the test and to the procedures and skills involved in taking the test. Although knowledge of the extent of each person's exposure to the material covered by the test is vital for an accurate interpretation of any test score, from the point of view of consistency of measurement the question of familiarity with the procedure and skills of testing is more crucial. We are concerned with consistency of performance, whether this be consistently good or consistently poor performance, and wish to know whether the test scores are accurate indices of the trait measured or are distorted by the test takers' inability to fathom the format of the test.

Any time a new format for a question or new procedure for responding (e.g., a different type of answer sheet) is introduced, there is the possibility of misunderstanding and consequently of introducing error into the measurement. ("New," in this circumstance, means new to the person taking the test.) To reduce the possibility of misinterpretation, practice problems and illustrations should be included whenever a new, or uncommon, test format or response mode is used. In most circumstances, this small amount of exposure and practice will be sufficient to insure that the item format does not produce extraneous variability. However, the test administrator should always ascertain that everyone understands the test procedures before the test is started.

A reverse phenomenon also occurs. Some persons have developed their test-taking skills into a fine art. These people, who are said to be *test sophisticated*, are experts in understanding the subtler aspects of testing—in seeing through devices used to disguise the true purpose of items, in detecting nuances that indicate the correct answers, in knowing how to make the optimal use of the time allowed to complete an exam. Through application of these skills, they, of course, frequently receive higher scores on tests than their true score would suggest.

TEST ANXIETY.   A related problem is that of test anxiety. Some people get very tense, nervous, and upset at the prospect of taking a test or examination. Frequently these are people who do not have an adequate understanding of testing procedures and/or are unsure of their own abilities. Because excess anxiety has a detrimental effect on the level of performance and often produces erratic performance, test anxiety can contribute to measurement error. Minor cases of test anxiety can often be alleviated by a thorough explanation of the purposes of the testing and the uses of the test scores, and by insuring that the subject is familiar with the testing procedures. The latter goal can be accomplished by extensive practice on problems similar to those to be found on the test. Both approaches decrease anxiety by reducing unknown conditions. In more severe cases, special testing arrangements or counseling might be needed.

COACHING.   The effect of coaching on test scores is frequently misunderstood. Many people feel that test scores can be fairly readily altered by coaching. However, in a series of studies (summarized by the College Entrance Examination Board, 1965), it has been found that coaching results in negligible improvement in scores on college entrance examinations. These and other studies show that coaching is likely to be ineffective unless the person is naïve regarding test procedures (i.e., if he lacks test sophistication) or has very little knowledge of the subject matter, or if the coaching reduces test anxiety. Even under these conditions, and in spite of the claims of operators of coaching schools, coaching does not necessarily produce significant increases in scores, nor even produce increases greater than the practice effect usually found when a test is taken a second time.

From the point of view of measurement accuracy, the crucial question is whether coaching increases the person's knowledge of the area covered by the test or only increases his test score. The former outcome should both increase the person's test score and provide long term benefits to the individual; the latter only results in inaccurate measurements.

PHYSIOLOGICAL VARIABLES.   We all have bad days, or at least feel we do, and tests taken on these days may not give the same results as tests taken on days when our mood is better. Tests taken when we are ill or fatigued may yield different results from tests taken when we are healthy and alert. In a long testing session, the test taker may become fatigued, bored, and suffer momentary lapses of attention, thus decreasing his performance. Although the evidence tends to indicate that fatigue and illness may not influence test performance significantly, especially when motivation remains high, the test administrator should be alert to the potential effect of these variables. If there is any indication that performance may have been affected by physiological or psychological disturbances, the safest procedure is to readminister the test under more favorable conditions.

ESTIMATION OF RELIABILITY

Having identified and briefly discussed some of the variables that can produce inconsistencies in test scores, we now return to the problem of measuring the magnitude of their influence. Ideally we would obtain an estimate of each individual's consistency by retesting him a large number of times (theoretically, an infinite number) on equivalent forms of the test. This procedure, however, is obviously infeasible both in terms of testing time and test construction problems and because the person's performance would change (because of learning, shifts in motivation, fatigue, etc.) with continual retesting. Thus an alternative procedure has been adopted. Instead of each individual being tested several times, many are tested twice and the difference between their performance on the two administrations used to estimate reliability. This approach assumes that measurement errors occur randomly, and therefore the distribution of differences between pairs of scores for a group of individuals tested twice will be similar to the distribution of differences of the various pairs of scores for the same individual if he were tested a large number of times.

Reliability coefficients

Since we are concerned with the distribution of pairs of scores for a group of individuals, the appropriate measure of consistency (reliability) is the correlation coefficient. Most indicators of reliability are thus expressed as a correlation coefficient, in this situation called a *reliability coefficient*, which is nothing more than the correlation between two sets of scores, obtained at two testing sessions, and used as an index of consistency of measurement. It can be shown (see, e.g., Guilford, 1954) furthermore, that the reliability coefficient derived in this manner is equivalent to reliability as defined earlier in the chapter, i.e.,

$$r_{tt} = r_{tT}^2 \tag{3.3}$$

where r_{tt} = the reliability coefficient

r_{tT} = the correlation between true and obtained scores

Because the square of a correlation coefficient indicates the proportion of variance in one measure attributable to the other, Equation (3.3) states that the reliability coefficient indicates the proportion of true variance in the test scores. This, of course, is the definition of reliability.

The particular value obtained for the reliability coefficient will depend upon the specific conditions under which the data were obtained, the composition of the group being tested, and the sources of error that influence the scores. Thus there will never be only one reliability coefficient for a test; rather, there will be as many reliability coefficients (estimates of reliability) as there are conditions for computing the reliability coefficient. Theoretically, each test would have an infinite number of possible reliability coefficients associated with it.

It should also be reiterated that a reliability coefficient is only a measure of the amount, or magnitude, of inconsistency. It does not indicate the causes of inconsistent measurement. It tells how much the scores may be expected to vary, not why they vary. Thus, if we have reliability coefficients for two tests, obtained under similar conditions, we can tell which of the two tests measures more consistently under these conditions. To determine which factors influence the consistency of measurement on the two tests would involve further comparisons and analyses.

VARIETIES OF RELIABILITY COEFFICIENTS. Because of the myriad of factors that may influence reliability, any classification of types of reliability will necessarily be an oversimplification. However, there are three methods of estimating reliability that are in such common use that it is useful, pedagogically, to consider them as classes of reliability estimates. (Cf. Cronbach, 1960.)

Because many psychological characteristics are assumed to be quite stable over time, any test designed to measure these characteristics should give stable results upon retesting. Therefore one type of reliability coefficient, called a *coefficient of stability*, is obtained by repeated measures over time. A second category arises from the fact that any test contains only a sample of all possible items. We can thus determine how consistent scores are from one sample of items to another sample, that is, the consistency in performance on equivalent forms of a test. This index is referred to as a *coefficient of equivalence*.

The third class of estimates usually assumed under reliability are measures of *internal consistency*. These indices indicate if all the items in the test are measuring one common characteristic (whether the test is homogeneous) or if the test measures several characteristics (that is, is heterogeneous in content). Because there is some logic in considering homogeneity as a separate property of tests, distinct from reliability, measures of internal consistency will be discussed in the following chapter.

STABILITY. For those psychological traits that are assumed to be relatively stable over time (e.g., aptitudes, personality, and temperament dispositions) and for those variables that are used to make decisions involving long-term plans (e.g., aptitudes and interests) some measure of the stability of the test scores over time is essential. Even for characteristics known to vary with time, knowledge of the degree of stability of test scores over short periods is desirable for seldom, if ever, is a test given and a decision made that will be applicable only at that particular point in time.

The paradigm for determining the coefficient of stability is quite simple.

$$\text{TEST} \xrightarrow{\text{time}} \text{RETEST}$$

The test is administered, a period of time passes, and the same test is administered again. Because the procedure consists of a test followed by a retest, stability is often referred to as *test-retest reliability*. To determine the coefficient of stability we merely correlate the two sets of scores, test and retest. (See Table 3.2.)

Because the time interval between tests can vary from a day or two to several years, different values of the reliability coefficient will be obtained, depending on the time elapsed between testings. Thus there will be at least as many estimates of reliability as there are time periods. In general, if we were to plot the relationship between the magnitude of the reliability coefficient and the time elapsed between administrations of the test, we would find that the magnitude of the correlation decreased over time. Of course, it is not time per se that causes the changes in scores but the experiences of the individual within the time period.

Several assumptions are made when a coefficient of stability is computed. The first, and most crucial, assumption is that the characteristic being measured by the test is stable over time. If the trait is not stable, an index of stability is meaningless. This assumption leads to a certain ambiguity and circularity for, if the trait is assumed stable but the test-retest reliability estimate is low, we cannot determine whether our assumption of the trait's stability was in error or whether extraneous conditions instead produced the lack of consistency. Conversely, if we assume that the trait is unstable but our reliability estimate is high, we do not know whether the assumption was in error or whether some systematic bias was producing a spuriously high correlation. The meaning of a coefficient of stability thus can only be interpreted within the context of our full range of knowledge of the trait being measured by the test. For a further discussion of this problem see the section on construct validity in Chapter 6.

Second, we must assume no differential practice effects. If a test is repeated, some people may remember their responses to certain items, especially when the test is readministered after a short interval, or else they may have learned something about the technique of taking the test. In either case, if one person's score is influenced to a different degree than another person's score, reliability will be decreased. Third, no differential learning should occur between the two administrations. For example, if the same test is given as a pretest before a unit in a course and as a post-test after the unit is completed, and if students learn different amounts during the unit, a pretest/post-test correlation will reflect differential learning effects, not stability.

As calculation of a coefficient of stability involves two administrations of the test, any variable that influences performance on one administration and not on the other will serve to reduce the correlation between scores, that is, will reduce reliability. Thus any errors associated with the specific administration of the test will affect the test-retest reliability. So, also, will day-to-day fluctuations in mood, health, motivation, and other personal variables. If the time between testings is relatively long, then factors with longer term effects—e.g., differential training or learning—may become involved; with shorter intertest intervals only more transient variations will have a significant impact. Item sampling will not affect the coefficient of stability because the same form of the tests is used on both administrations.

EQUIVALENCE. Because any test contains only a sample of the possible items, it is theoretically possible to construct a number of parallel forms of the test (each covering the same content areas) using the same type of items and being of the same difficulty. Such parallel forms are desirable in many instances when retesting with the same test is not feasible. For example, you have all probably worked on "logic" problems—the type involving deducing how a person could be murdered in a sealed room. These problems are complex, but once you find the solution you remember both the solution and the method of obtaining the solution. If the same problem is presented again you immediately know the answer and do not have to repeat the deductive steps. A particular test using this type of problem could obviously not be administered more than once because performance on the second administration would involve memory, not problem-solving abilities. Analogously, many mathematics and science test problems that are useful because they present a new situation upon repetition present only a routine calculation exercise. For these and other reasons, alternative forms of tests are desirable.

In these situations the reliability question becomes: How consistent are scores from one form of the test to another form of the same test? To determine the equivalent forms reliability we would administer Form A of the test and then, with a minimum time lag,[2] administer Form B. Correlating the scores on the two forms gives a coefficient of equivalence. (See Table 3.2.) Diagrammatically the procedure would be:

minimal
time
FORM A————————→FORM B

[2]Theoretically, the two forms would be administered simultaneously. Because this is impossible, the two forms are administered as close together in time as is feasible—generally within a few days of each other.

TABLE 3.2 Calculation of the coefficients of stability, equivalence, and stability and equivalence

(1) Assume that two (equivalent) forms of a 16-item test were adminis-
    tered to a group of 20 persons on a total of three occasions—Form
    A on March 1, Form B also on March 1, and Form A again on May 1.
    These administrations will be referred to as A_1, B_1, and A_2, respec-
    tively. Scores were as follows:

Subject number

	1	2	3	4	5	6	7	8	9	10	11	12	13	14	15	16	17	18	19	20
Test																				
A_1	15	14	13	12	12	11	11	10	10	10	10	10	9	9	9	8	8	7	6	5
B_1	16	14	14	12	13	10	11	11	10	10	9	10	8	9	9	8	7	7	6	6
A_2	15	14	16	15	13	12	11	13	12	12	10	11	11	11	10	9	10	7	8	8

The summary statistics are:

Test	ΣX	ΣX^2	$\overline{X}$	s	Cross-products (ΣXY) A_1	B_1	A_2
A_1	199	2101	9.95	2.46	—	2118	2381
B_1	200	2144	10.00	2.68	2118	—	2403
A_2	229	2731	11.45	2.33	2381	2403	—

(2) *Coefficient of stability.* The coefficient of stability is the correla-
    tion between scores on two administrations of the same form of
    the test, separated by a time period—in this example the correla-
    tion between A_1 and A_2. Using as the formula for a correlation
    coefficient,

$$r = \frac{\Sigma XY/N - (\overline{X})(\overline{Y})}{s_x \, s_y}$$

Or, in terms of the reliability problem

$$r_{tt} = r_{(A1)(A2)} = \frac{\Sigma(X_{A1})(X_{A2})/N - (\overline{X}_{A1})(\overline{X}_{A2})}{(s_{A1})(s_{A2})}$$

Substituting in the data from the example and solving,

$$r_{(A1)(A2)} = \frac{2381/20 - (9.95)(11.45)}{(2.46)(2.33)} = .894$$

Table 3.2 (continued)

This value ($r = .894$) is the coefficient of stability.

(3) *Coefficient of equivalence.* The coefficient of equivalence is the correlation between scores on parallel forms of the test, administered with a minimal time lag between testing—in the example, the correlation between A_1 and B_1.

Stated as an equation:

$$r_{tt} = r_{(A1)(B1)} = \frac{\Sigma(X_{A1})(X_{B1})/N - (\bar{X}_{A1})(\bar{X}_{B1})}{(s_{A1})(s_{B1})}$$

Substituting in the data and solving,

$$r_{(A1)(B1)} = \frac{2118/20 - (9.95)(10.00)}{(2.46)(2.68)} = .971$$

(4) *Coefficient of equivalence and stability.* This coefficient is the correlation between two parallel forms of the test administered at different times—in the example, the correlation between B_1 and A_2.

Stated in equation form

$$r_{tt} = r_{(B1)(A2)} = \frac{\Sigma(X_{B1})(X_{A2})/N - (\bar{X}_{B1})(\bar{X}_{A2})}{(s_{B1})(s_{A2})}$$

Subtituting in the data and solving:

$$r_{(B1)(A2)} = \frac{2403/20 - (10.00)(11.45)}{(2.68)(2.33)} = .905$$

(5) *Interpretation of the coefficients.* The very high value ($r = .97$) obtained for the coefficient of equivalence, plus the similarities in means and standard deviations, indicate that forms A and B, are, in fact, parallel forms. As both stability indices were also high ($r \sim .90$), the trait tested evidently is quite stable, at least over a period of two months. However, as the retest coefficients were lower than the equivalent forms coefficients, it appears that there is some instability over time and thus further data on retest reliability should be collected. Note also that there is some practice effect operating (i.e., the mean on A_2 is higher than the mean on A_1).

In practice, to counterbalance any effects due to order of administration, half of the group would be administered Form A followed by Form B, the other half, Form B followed by Form A. Because the procedure involves use of equivalent, or parallel, forms of the test, it is often referred to as *parallel forms reliability.*

The primary assumption in computing a coefficient of equivalence is that the forms are, in fact, equivalent. This means that they are equivalent in content, format, length, difficulty, and have the same mean and standard deviation. To the extent that these conditions are not met, the coefficient of equivalence will give a distorted estimate of reliability.

Using this paradigm, inconsistencies in scores can be attributed primarily to differences in item sampling. As the two forms of the test are given close together in time, long term fluctuations are eliminated. However, short term fluctuations in the test taker's mood or differences in administration of the two forms are not entirely eliminated. Thus, a pure measure of equivalence is not obtainable. The major source of variance, however, is the difference between items on the two forms of the test.

STABILITY AND EQUIVALENCE. Given alternative forms of a test, it is possible to determine reliability by a combination of the two previously discussed methods. The procedure would be to administer Form A, allow a period of time to pass, then administer Form B:

time

FORM A————————→FORM B

(As with equivalent forms reliability, the experimental design would involve some people taking Form A first, others taking Form B first.) The *coefficient of stability and equivalence* would be the correlation between the two sets of scores. (See Table 3.2.) Because all the factors that operate to produce inconsistency in scores in the test-retest paradigm plus all the factors that produce inconsistency in the parallel forms design can operate in this design, we would expect the greatest inconsistency in scores, i.e., the lowest reliability coefficients, using this method of estimating reliability. Thus the coefficient of stability and equivalence will provide the most rigorous test and will give the lower bound (lowest estimate) of reliability.

SPLIT-HALF RELIABILITY. In many situations it is not possible to calculate either equivalent form or stability indices of reliability. For example, in the typical classroom exam the teacher will not wish to give alternative forms of a test (even if she had time to construct them) or repeat the examination at a later date. Nevertheless, some estimate of reliability may be needed. Fortunately several methods are available for estimating reliability in these situations. One common method involves splitting the test into two equivalent halves—hence the designation *split-half reliability*. This is a statistical split, not an actual split, and is done after the test is given. To satisfy the assumptions of a coefficient of equivalence two independent halves are needed—halves that are equal in content, difficulty, means, and standard deviations. Unless there is some systematic bias in test format, such as alternating two distinct types of items or having the response to one item depend on the response to a previous item, this split can usually be accomplished by using the odd items as one form, the even items as the other. In other words, for each test paper you would obtain separate scores for the odd and even numbered items. If the odd-even split does not produce equivalent forms, another method of obtaining a split must be used. This method may be based on theoretical considerations or may involve empirical combinations that produce the desired distributions of item characteristics. The correlation between these two scores gives an estimate of reliability. (See Table 3.3.)

One problem with this procedure is that you end up with two "tests," each half as long as the original test. Since reliability is dependent on test length (see below), the reliability as estimated from the halves of the test will be lower than that which would have been obtained from a test of the original length. To estimate the reliability of a test of the original length from the split-half correlation we can use the *Spearman-Brown formula:*

$$r_{tt} = \frac{2r_{hh}}{1 + r_{hh}} \tag{3.4}$$

where r_{hh} = the split-half reliability coefficient and r_{tt} is the estimate of the reliability of the test of the original length. The general Spearman-Brown formula can be expressed as:

$$r_{nn} = \frac{nr_{tt}}{1 + (n - 1)r_{tt}} \tag{3.5}$$

where n = the factor that the test length is increased by (increased length/actual length); r_{tt} is the reliability of the original test; and r_{nn} is the estimated reliability of the test n times as long. This formula not only allows an estimate of the reliability of a longer, or even a shorter, test but also can indicate, by solving for n, how much a test would have to be lengthened to reach a desired level of reliability.

The Spearman-Brown formula assumes that the variability of the two halves of the test are equal. An alternative formula (Guttman, 1945) enables a reliability estimate to be made without this assumption, i.e.:

$$r_{tt} = 2 \left[1 - \frac{s_a^2 + s_b^2}{s_t^2} \right] \tag{3.6}$$

where s_a and s_b are the standard deviations of the two-part scores and s_t is the standard deviation of the total score. This procedure has the advantage of not requiring computation of the correlation between the parts, as well as not requiring the assumption of equal variability of the two subparts. Other formulas are presented by Thorndike (1951) and Stanley (1969).

TABLE 3.3 Calculation of split-half reliability

(1) Form B of the test described in Table 3.2 was split into two halves—
odd and even numbered items—and each half scored separately.
Scores were as follows:

Subject	1	2	3	4	5	6	7	8	9	10	11	12	13	14	15	16	17	18	19	20
Odds	8	8	7	6	6	5	6	5	5	5	4	6	4	4	5	4	3	4	3	3
Evens	8	6	7	6	7	5	5	6	5	5	5	4	4	5	4	4	4	3	3	3
Total	16	14	14	12	13	10	11	11	10	10	9	10	8	9	9	8	7	7	6	6

The summary data were:

	ΣX	ΣX^2	$\overline{X}$	s	
Odds	101	553	5.05	1.47	$\Sigma X_o X_e = 532$
Evens	99	527	4.95	1.36	
Total	200	2144	10.00	2.68	

(2) The split-half reliability is computed by correlating scores on the
odd-numbered items (o) with scores on the even-numbered
items (e):

$$r_{tt} = r_{oe} = \frac{\Sigma X_o X_e/N - (\overline{X}_o)(\overline{X}_e)}{(s_o)(s_e)}$$

Substituting in the data and solving

$$r_{oe} = \frac{532/20 - (5.05)(4.95)}{(1.47)(1.36)} = .802$$

The value, $r = .802$, is the uncorrected split-half reliability coefficient.

(3) As each half of the test contained only eight items, and the full
test contained 16, we can use the Spearman-Brown formula to
estimate the reliability of a 16 item test:

$$r_{tt} = \frac{2r_{oe}}{1 + r_{oe}} = \frac{2(.802)}{1 + .802} = .890$$

The value, $r_{tt} = .890$, is the *corrected* split-half reliability coefficient.

(4) We could also estimate the split-half reliability using the alternative formula:

$$r_{tt} = 2\left[1 - \frac{s_a^2 + s_b^2}{s_t^2}\right] = 2\left[1 - \frac{s_o^2 + s_e^2}{s_t^2}\right]$$

$$= 2\left[1 - \frac{(1.47)^2 + (1.36)^2}{(2.68)^2}\right] = .883$$

Note that the two formulas produce essentially the same value
for r_{tt} (.88 and .89) and that these values approximate the value
found for the coefficient of equivalence.

A split-half reliability estimate is interpreted in a manner similar to the interpretation of a coefficient of equivalence. However, as the two forms (halves) are, in essence, administered simultaneously, only fluctuations that are of such a short term that they effect only one item will influence reliability. An application of the Spearman-Brown correction is shown in Table 3.3.

Other factors influencing the reliability coefficient

In discussing the various methods of computing a reliability coefficient we have considered a number of sources of error that influence the magnitude of the obtained correlation. We have noted that the coefficient of stability and equivalence gives the lowest estimate of reliability because more factors have a chance to influence the scores and, conversely, that the corrected split-half correlation generally gives the highest estimate because the least number of factors have a chance to operate. However, there are still other factors that influence the magnitude of the obtained correlation and which must be considered in interpreting a reliability coefficient (Thorndike, 1951).

RANGE OF INDIVIDUAL DIFFERENCES. Correlation coefficients, of which a reliability coefficient is just one example, are influenced by the distribution of scores within the sample used to calculate the coefficient. As the variability (standard deviation) of the scores decreases, the correlation coefficient generally decreases; as the variability increases, that is, the scores become more heterogeneous, the coefficient will increase. This relationship occurs because with a greater range of scores, cross-products (XY) can assume larger values and, because the cross-products are in the numerator of the correlation formula, larger sums of cross-products (ΣXY) will yield a higher correlation coefficient.

As an example of how this consideration becomes important to reliability, assume that you want a reliable estimate of spelling ability for third-grade students. The manual for a test you are considering gives the retest reliability based on a sample of third, fourth, fifth, and sixth graders. The reliability coefficient obtained using the combined group is likely to be higher than the reliability coefficient that would be obtained using only third-grade students, as a change of x points in scores will be relatively larger when compared to the distribution of scores within one grade than when compared to the distribution of the combined group, because the range of scores in the combined group will be much wider. Reliability coefficients calculated from the more heterogeneous combined group will be an overestimate of the actual reliability for the more homogeneous group of third-grade students. A much better indication of the reliability for your purposes would be obtained by calculating the reliability coefficient on a sample of third-grade students. In general, whenever the reliability reported is for a group more heterogeneous than the group of direct concern, it is likely to be an overestimate.

TEST DIFFICULTY. There is no simple relationship between (1) the difficulty of the test and reliability or (2) between the level of performance of the group tested and reliability. Because of the effect of range of individual differences on reliability, any time the range of scores is reduced the reliability estimate will also probably be reduced. Thus if the test is too difficult or too easy for a group, the range of scores will be reduced and the reliability affected. This implies that, to maximize reliability, the level of difficulty of a test should be such as to produce a wide distribution of scores.

A specific problem occurs when the test is so difficult that testees can respond only in a chance, or random, manner. When a person responds randomly we cannot place any confidence in the consistency of his scores, especially scores on individual items. If only a few people respond at the chance level, or for some other reason respond randomly, their scores will be low on both tests (i.e., on test and retest or on both forms) and reliability will not be seriously overestimated. However, if a test is so difficult that many people are essentially guessing or responding randomly, differences from test to retest or between forms will be attributable primarily to randomly distributed error factors, and the value of the reliability coefficient will approach zero.

LENGTH OF THE TEST. A third factor influencing the reliability coefficient is the length of the test. In general, adding more items, providing they are reliable items, will increase the reliability of the test. The effect of the increase in length can be determined by the Spearman-Brown formula. An unreliable test thus can often be made more useful by increasing its length. A point of diminishing returns occurs fairly rapidly, however, and adding large numbers of items will not automatically produce large increases in reliability. One can also understand the operation of the increased length by considering it a method of producing a wider range of scores.

SPEEDEDNESS. Speed is a fourth factor that influences reliability. In fact, the effect of speed is such as to render the computation of a (split-half) odd-even reliability coefficient inappropriate when speed is a major factor in test performance. To illustrate, assume that you give a 100-item test of multiplication to fourth graders. The problems are ones they have studied and understand and thus, with sufficient time, most of the students would get almost all of the items correct. However, by setting a time limit such that not everyone can finish, we can produce a speeded test. Under these circumstances, a person who completes 90 items will get 90 correct, 45 even and 45 odd; a person who finishes 80 items will get 80 correct, 40 even and 40 odd, and so forth. Thus each student will get the same score (with the exception of a few errors) on both parts and the split-half coefficient will be spuriously inflated.

An analogous situation occurs whenever speed plays a part in determining scores on a test. One way to minimize the problem is to use methods for determining reliability that are less influenced by speed—for example, equivalent forms. If alternative methods are not feasible, one can try to estimate the proportion of variance due to speed. At this point let it suffice to warn you that reliability coefficients obtained from one administration of a highly speeded test are overestimates and should be taken with a grain of salt.

Interpretation of a reliability coefficient

Having discussed the potential sources of inconsistency in test scores and the methods for estimating reliability, we must now face two complex and interrelated questions: How is a reliability coefficient interpreted? And, what constitutes an acceptable level of reliability? In attempting to answer these questions, three considerations must be kept in mind. First, as has been stressed, there will be as many reliability estimates for a test as there are samples and procedures used to determine the reliability coefficient. Consequently the reliability of a test, as estimated by one technique in one situation with one sample, may not be the same as an estimate obtained with a different technique, in a different situation, or with a different sample. Thus, we will always be interpreting a specific reliability coefficient instead of making statements about *the* reliability of the test. Second, a reliability coefficient is only an estimate, and a rather gross one at that, of the magnitude of inconsistency in test scores. It does not indicate, except indirectly, the causes of the inconsistency. Third, reliability is not the be-all and end-all of psychological measurement; it is not an end in itself but rather a step on a way to a goal. That is, unless test scores are consistent, they cannot be related to other variables with any degree of confidence. Reliability can be seen as placing limits on validity, and the crucial question thus becomes whether reliability is high enough to allow satisfactory validity.

With these considerations in mind, we will briefly discuss four possible ways of interpreting reliability coefficients: (1) as the correlation between obtained scores and true scores, (2) by comparing the reliability of a given test to the reliability attained by other tests of the same type, (3) as the percentage of persons who would change their rank or classification, and (4) as an index of the amount of error in individual scores.

CORRELATION BETWEEN TRUE AND OBTAINED SCORES. Earlier in the chapter, reliability was defined as the ratio of true score variance to the variance in the obtained scores (Equation 3.2) and it was shown that the reliability coefficient was equal to the squared correlation between obtained and true scores (Equation 3.3). Thus a reliability coefficient can be interpreted in terms of the proportion of variance in the obtained scores that represents variation in true scores. For example, if $r_{tt} = .90$, we can say that 90% of the variability in obtained scores is due to differences in the true scores and only 10% is due to errors of measurement. At the extremes, if $r_{tt} = 1.00$, there is no error of measurement, all variability being true score variance; if $r_{tt} = .00$, all variability reflects errors of measurement. In short, the reliability coefficient tells us directly the proportion of variance that is due to variance in true scores and the proportion that is measurement error. More precisely, since reliability is specific to the testing situation, a reliability coefficient indicates the extent of measurement error obtained when a given form of a test is administered to a particular sample of people under certain conditions.

COMPARATIVE RELIABILITY.   If we are concerned with empirical evidence, the actual state of affairs, we have a second method of interpretation—one which uses the reliability of existing tests as guidelines or standards. Using this criterion, we find that many measures of aptitudes, achievement, skills, and abilities have reliabilities of .90 or higher, and often as high as .95 under certain conditions. Tests in these areas can be expected to have at least this degree of reliability. Measures of personality, interest, values, and other less objective characteristics generally have reliabilities of .80–.85 or higher, at least over short time periods. Many experimental or short tests have slightly lower reliabilities. From this point of view, interpretation consists of comparing the reliability of the test in question with the range of reliabilities attained by similar tests. The danger of this approach is, of course, that attainment of the present norm becomes the final goal, rather than being viewed as a minimum standard.

CHANGES IN RANKING OR CLASSIFICATION.   If the test measured without error (i.e., if $r_{tt} = 1.00$) then every individual would have the same ranking on each administration of the test. However, if the reliability coefficient is less than 1.00, there will be some changing of ranks between the testings. In the same way, if scores are grouped in classes and, if the reliability is less than perfect, then there will be changing between classes. One way to explain the meaning of a reliability coefficient would be to show the pattern of category changes or changes in ranks with different levels of reliability. Figure 3.2 shows this relationship graphically. The graph shows the percent of time that the order of two individuals scoring at the 75th and 50th percentile (i.e., scoring higher than 75 and 50% of the group, respectively) would be reversed on retesting when the reliability of the test assumes various values. The graph shows that when $r_{tt} = .60$ there is about one chance in three (32%) that individuals falling at the 50th and 75th percentiles would reverse positions on retesting; but when $r_{tt} = .95$, there is only one chance in 50 (2%) of a reversal.

A weakness of this approach is that the number of changes in classification depends not only on the reliability, but also on the number and size of the classes used. For example, with constant reliability, there will be more shifts in classification with a larger number and/or narrower categories. It does have the

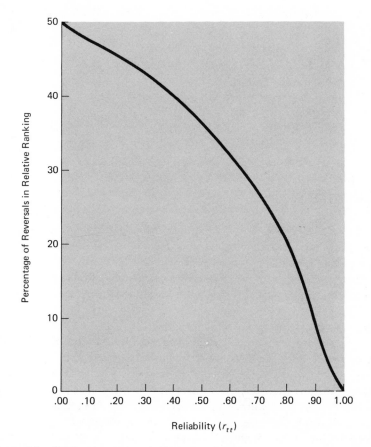

Figure 3.2 Changes in relative rankings as a function of test reliability. (Graph adapted from Table 7-7, p. 190, Thorndike & Hagen, 1961).

advantage of showing the effects of increasing (or decreasing) reliability in graphic, readily understandable terms.

ERROR IN INDIVIDUAL SCORES. When interpreting the test score of an individual, the most important question regarding consistency is: How many points will this score be expected to vary upon retesting? In other words, what is the magnitude of the error of measurement for this particular individual? It can be shown that the magnitude of this error is directly proportional to the reliability of the test. This topic, that of errors in individual scores, will be treated in detail in the next chapter.

Our discussion of the interpretation of a reliability coefficient can be summarized by answering three questions: (1) What is an acceptable level of reliability for a test? Ideally, tests would have perfect reliability ($r_{tt} = 1.00$); in practice, we should insist on reliability coefficients at least as high as those found for other similar tests and hopefully improve on this standard. (2) Can we speak of "the reliability" of a test? Only as a hypothetical concept as a reliability coefficient is specific to the test, the sample being tested, the testing situation, and the method used to calculate the reliability coefficient. (3) Is there any meaningful way of comparing the reliabilities of various tests, of referring to one test as being more reliable than another? Only if by "more reliable" we mean that one of the tests has demonstrated higher reliability in a variety of testing situations.

Summary

Reliability is the generic term given to the estimation of the consistency of measurement attained by psychological tests. Reliability can be defined as the proportion of true variability in a set of test scores. This definition assumes that a person's performance (obtained score) on a given test is a function of his true score (the score he would obtain if the test measured without error) and an error component.

Error, in the estimation of reliability, refers to any factor that is irrelevant to the purposes of the testing and which produces instability in performance. The major classes of error are those inherent in the test itself, primarily in the item sampling; those which are a function of the person taking the test; and those which are attributable to the circumstances of the particular test administration. Of these, the errors associated with the test taker—e.g., his motivation, attitudes, and physical condition—are the most difficult to control.

An estimate of the magnitude of inconsistency in a set of test scores is obtained by the reliability coefficient, which is the correlation between individuals' performance on two sets of test scores. Reliability estimates can be classed as measures of stability (consistency over time), equivalence (consistency over test forms), or split-half estimates. Reliability coefficients are influenced by the range of test scores and the length, difficulty, and speededness of the test.

Reliability coefficients can be interpreted in several ways: as the correlation between true and obtained scores, as the proportion of persons who would change classification on retesting, as an index of the amount of error in scores, or by comparing a given reliability coefficient to coefficients attained by other similar tests. As reliability coefficients are specific to the test, the testing situation, the sample being tested, and the method used to compute the coefficient, interpretation of a reliability coefficient will always be specific to the particular testing circumstances; the idea of "the reliability" of a test is only a summarizing fiction.

Suggestions for further reading

Ghiselli, E. E. *Theory of psychological measurement*. New York: McGraw-Hill, Inc., 1964. Chaps. 8 and 9 present a mathematical treatment of the concept of the reliability of measurement, factors affecting reliability coefficients, and empirical methods for estimating reliability.

Helmstadter, G. C. *Principles of psychological measurement*. New York: Appleton-Century-Crofts, 1964. In Chap. 2 he presents a discussion of the types of errors involved in psychological measurement and in Chap. 3 applies this classification to the problem of the estimation of reliability; a relatively nonmathematical discussion.

Kerlinger, F. N. *Foundations of behavioral research*. New York: Holt, Rinehart and Winston, Inc., 1965. Chap. 24 is a brief presentation of the concept of reliability using an approach similar to that used in this book.

Magnusson, D. *Test theory*. Reading, Mass.: Addison-Wesley Publishing Company, 1967. Chap. 5 presents a mathematically based discussion of the concepts of true score and error as they relate to the basic reliability equation.

Stanley, J. C. Reliability. In R. L. Thorndike (Ed.), *Educational measurement* (rev. ed.). Washington, D. C.: American Council on Education, 1969. A comprehensive statement of the theory and measurement of reliability in educational testing.

Thorndike, R. L. Reliability. In E. F. Lindquist (Ed.), *Educational measurement*. Washington, D. C.: American Council on Education, 1951 (pp. 560–620). Another comprehensive discussion of the problem of reliability with particular emphasis devoted to the errors that influence the various estimates of reliability.

Wesman, A. G. Reliability and confidence. New York: The Psychological Corporation, Test Service Bulletin No. 44, 1952. Practical considerations and common misconceptions in interpreting reliability data; written for the test user.

Consistency II: Homogeneity and error in scores

Chapter 4

INTRODUCTION

In this chapter we will continue our discussion of the consistency of psychological measurement and we will focus on four additional areas. First we will consider the concept of homogeneity, the degree to which the items on a test are interrelated and measure a single trait or characteristic. This discussion is pursued separately from that of other methods of estimating reliability so that we can emphasize the distinction between the concept of homogeneity and other approaches to measuring consistency. We shall then discuss the question of error in individual test scores, the basic concept discussed here being the *standard error of measurement*. After this section, we will move to problems that arise when more than one test score is available—the reliability of subtest and difference scores, and the measurement of change. Finally, we shall briefly consider several alternative approaches to consistency and the problem of obtaining information on the relative influence of various error sources.

HOMOGENEITY

In the previous chapter we discussed the concept of reliability, that is, whether the test measured some variable consistently. Reliability was considered in several senses: as consistency on the same material over time (stability), as consistency over different forms of the test (equivalence), and as consistency over both forms and time (stability and equivalence). We did not consider the internal consistency of the test, that is, the interrelationships among the various items that comprise the test. True, split-half reliability can be considered as a measure of within-test consistency but, as typically used, it is a measure of equivalence, differing from other measures of equivalence in that the designation of the two forms occurred after the administration of the test. That is, when split-half reliability estimates are used, the test items are administered as one form of the test, while in the typical equivalence paradigm two distinct forms of the test are administered separately.

Homogeneity defined

In analyses of the internal consistency of educational and psychological tests the basic question is the degree to which the items on the test are interrelated. In operational terms, are the scores on the items intercorrelated positively? If the scores on the various items are positively intercorrelated the test is homogeneous; if not, the test is heterogeneous. *Homogeneity can thus be defined in terms of consistency of performance over all items on a test.* (Loevinger, 1947; Anastasi, 1968). A corollary is, of course, that in a homogeneous test, knowing the person's performance on one item will allow us to make better-than-chance predictions of his performance on other items within the test.

Although we have defined homogeneity as consistency over all items on a test, the concept could be applied to subtests or clusters of items within the test. The appropriate level of analysis will depend on the structure of the test and the purposes of the analysis. Thus, it is possible to have a test which, considered as a whole, is heterogeneous but is composed of a number of subtests or clusters of items that are, within themselves, highly homogeneous.

Note that the emphasis is on performance (scores) and not on the format or style of the items. Thus, even if a test consisted of several different types of items, if the responses to these items were positively intercorrelated, the test would be homogeneous. Conversely, if the items were all of the same format or within the same content area but were not positively intercorrelated, the test would be heterogeneous. The homogeneous-heterogeneous distinction is not a dichotomy but, as will be illustrated below, a continuum ranging from complete homogeneity, where all items intercorrelate perfectly, to complete heterogeneity, where there are only chance relations between items.

The concept of homogeneity has a further implication—that of *unidimensionality*—that the test measures only one variable (trait) rather than some combination of variables. If a test is homogeneous, it might be inferred that it is measuring only one trait. This inference would seem to follow from the fact that if a test is homogeneous all items are positively intercorrelated and thus presumably measure a common characteristic. It is conceivable, however, that all items on a test might be complex (i.e., measure more than one variable or trait) yet still be highly intercorrelated. As an example, consider the typical word problem in algebra:

Two motor boats travel along the same route but beginning from opposite ends of a lake 25 miles long. They start at the same time and one travels eastward at 15 miles per hour, the other travels westward at 10 miles per hour. How many minutes will it be before they meet?

If a test were composed entirely of items of this nature it is possible, and quite probable, that responses to the various items would be highly intercorrelated. Yet more detailed analyses would undoubtedly show the test was complex and that at least two abilities were measured by the test—the ability to read and comprehend the meaning of the problem (reading comprehension) and the ability to perform the algebraic manipulations necessary to arrive at the correct answer (algebraic manipulation).

Thus, if homogeneity is defined as consistency of performance over the items composing the test, a high degree of homogeneity does not necessarily insure that the test measures only one trait; it may be that all items measure the same combination of traits. Conversely, if the test does not possess a high degree of homogeneity, it is obvious that the items, or subgroups of items, measure different characteristics. Therefore, homogeneity is a necessary, but not sufficient, characteristic of a test designed to measure a unitary trait.

Measures of homogeneity

A reliability coefficient gives an index of consistency over time or forms of a test; an index of homogeneity will give an index of interitem, or intratest, consistency by indicating the degree to which the various items on a test are positively intercorrelated. Because the typical test consists of a relatively large number of items, this index, like the reliability coefficient, will be a summary statement, an index of the average degree of relationship between various pairs of items, or between scores on items and the total score on the test.

KUDER-RICHARDSON FORMULAS. Probably the most widely used indices of the homogeneity are the several Kuder-Richardson formulas (Kuder & Richardson, 1937; Richardson & Kuder, 1939). These formulas are usually classed as measures of reliability, specifically measures of the internal consistency of a test, as they measure the consistency of measurement of a test—the consistency over items within the test. But because they are measures of the interrelations of the items composing the test, they can as readily be interpreted as measures of homogeneity. The latter classification will be used in this book.

One basic assumption of the Kuder-Richardson formulas is that the items on the test are measuring one common trait or factor, i.e., that the test is homogeneous. Although Kuder and Richardson developed several formulas, the most useful is their formula 20 (K-R 20):

$$r_{tt} = \frac{k}{k-1}\left(\frac{s_t^2 - \Sigma p_i q_i}{s_t^2}\right) \tag{4.1}$$

where $\qquad$ k = the number of items on the test

$\qquad$ s_t^2 = the variance of the total scores on the test

$\qquad$ p_i = the proportion of the group passing an item

$\qquad$ $q_i = 1 - p_i$ = the proportion failing an item.

An example of the application of this formula is given in Table 4.1.

To the degree that the test items are heterogeneous the value of r_{tt}, as computed by K-R 20, will be lowered. Hence, K-R 20 can serve as a measure of test homogeneity. The formula is inappropriate for speeded tests as values of p (and q) can only be computed if each item has been attempted by all persons. Because the data are obtained from a single administration of a test, all error sources associated with the circumstances of the test administration are not operative, nor are any attributable to other than exceedingly short term (i.e., item to item) fluctuations in the individual. Thus the primary error source is noncomparability of items. However, because unreliability within a single item is not entirely controlled in this analysis, we do not have a pure measure of homogeneity (Thorndike, 1951).

FACTOR ANALYSIS. A second approach to determining the homogeneity of a test, and one considered by some writers (e.g., Lumsden, 1961; Keats, 1967) to be the best method, is *factor analysis*, which is essentially a statistical technique for determining the minimum number of constructs (factors) necessary to account for the interrelations among a group of variables. In terms of homogeneity, if a factor analysis indicates that one factor is sufficient to account for the variation in performance on all items, then the test is homogeneous in composition; if more than one factor is necessary to account for performance, then the test is heterogeneous. As the process of factor analysis is complex, and there are a variety of computational approaches to the analysis, we will only consider the general logic of the procedure here. The reader who wishes to study the technique in more detail may consult any of several excellent sources (e.g., Cattell, 1952; Guilford, 1954, Chapter 16; Harman, 1967; Kerlinger, 1965, Chapter 36; or Thurstone, 1947).

When using factor analysis to investigate the homogeneity of a test, the input data are the scores of each individual on each item of the test. The intercorrelations between *items* (not people) are computed and these intercorrelations subjected to the factor analysis procedures. In this specific case (establishing homogeneity) we are interested in determining whether one factor, called a *common factor*, underlies performance on all the items in the test. If one common factor will suffice to account for performance on all items, the test may be said to be homogeneous; if more than one common factor is needed to account for performance, the test is heterogeneous. One common factor will account for

TABLE 4.1 Computation of an index of internal consistency using Kuder-Richardson formula 20

(1) Suppose that a ten-item test was administered to ten persons. Each item was scored either 1 or 0; 1 for a correct response, 0 for an incorrect response. The results were:

					Item							
Subject	1	2	3	4	5	6	7	8	9	10	X_t	X_t^2
A	1	1	1	1	1	1	1	1	1	1	10	100
B	1	1	1	1	1	1	1	1	1	0	9	81
C	1	1	1	1	1	1	1	0	1	0	8	64
D	1	1	1	1	1	1	1	1	0	0	8	64
E	1	1	1	1	1	0	1	0	0	1	7	49
F	1	1	1	1	1	1	0	1	0	0	7	49
G	1	1	1	1	1	0	0	1	0	0	6	36
H	1	1	1	1	1	0	0	0	1	0	6	36
I	1	1	1	1	0	1	0	0	0	0	5	25
J	1	1	1	0	0	1	0	0	0	0	4	16
Σ	10	10	10	9	8	7	5	5	4	2	70	520

(2) To compute the index using Kuder-Richardson formula 20 we need to know the variance of the test scores (s_t^2) and the sum of the proportions passing and failing each item ($\Sigma p_i q_i$):

$$s_t^2 = \frac{\Sigma X^2}{N} - \left(\frac{\Sigma X}{N}\right)^2 = \frac{520}{10} - \left(\frac{70}{10}\right)^2 = 3.00$$

Table 4.1 (continued)

(3) The proportion passing each item (p_i) is simply the number of people passing the item (n_{p_i}) divided by the total number in the sample ($n_t = 10$). The number failing the item (q_i) equals $1 - p_i$. These data are shown below:

Item	1	2	3	4	5	6	7	8	9	10
n_{p_i}	10	10	10	9	8	7	5	5	4	2
p_i	1.0	1.0	1.0	0.9	0.8	0.7	0.5	0.5	0.4	0.2
q_i	0.0	0.0	0.0	0.1	0.2	0.3	0.5	0.5	0.6	0.8
$p_i q_i$	.00	.00	.00	.09	.16	.21	.25	.25	.24	.16

The figure needed for the formula, $\Sigma p_i q_i$, is the product $p_i q_i$ summed over all ten items:

$$\Sigma p_i q_i = 0.00 + 0.00 + 0.00 + 0.09 + \cdots + 0.16 = 1.36$$

(4) Substituting in the formula

$$r_{tt} = \frac{k}{k-1}\left(\frac{s_t^2 - \Sigma p_i q_i}{s_t^2}\right) = \frac{10}{9}\left(\frac{3.00 - 1.36}{3.00}\right) = .607$$

(5) $r_{tt} = .61$ is an index of the internal consistency of the test.

performance only if scores on all items on the test are highly intercorrelated.

The relationship of factor analysis to reliability is straightforward. In Chapter 3 we indicated that the score on a test (or an item) was a function of two components—true score and error, that the total variance in test scores (or item scores) was the sum of the true variance and the error variance, and that the proportion of true variance defined the reliability of the test. Factor analysis allows us to further subdivide the true variance component into two segments: common factor variance, and specific variance, that which is specific or unique to the given test. This relationship is shown in Figure 4.1 and by

$$s_t^2 = s_{co}^2 + s_{sp}^2 + s_e^2 \tag{4.2}$$

where

s_t^2 = the total variance of a measure

s_{co}^2 = common factor variance

s_{sp}^2 = specific variance

s_e^2 = error variance

This equation can be applied to individual item scores as well as test scores and, as can be seen, indicates that reliability will always be greater than homogeneity.

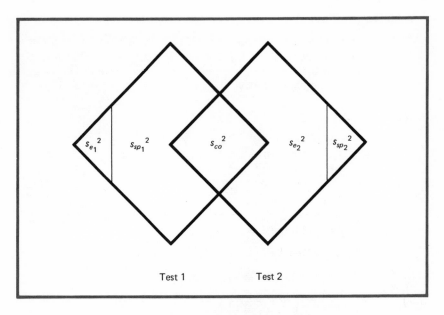

Figure 4.1 Distribution of variance components in test scores.

OTHER MEASURES OF HOMOGENEITY. A number of other measures of homogeneity have been developed (see, e.g., Lumsden, 1961; Loevinger, 1947; Horst, 1966; Magnusson, 1966) but no single measure seems to be in common use. One reason, no doubt, is the divergence of opinion as to an exact definition of homogeneity. As mentioned above, some authors consider a test homogeneous if the items are highly intercorrelated, while others add the requirement that the test must measure one factor and thus make implications about the nature of mental organization. Still others (for example, Loevinger, 1947; Keats, 1967) make further restrictions regarding the difficulty of items and do not consider a test homogeneous unless the item's difficulties can be scaled in such a manner as to produce a true interval scale of measurement. With such a divergence of definitions and conditions, it is no wonder that homogeneity is often relegated to limbo in discussions of the application of concepts of measurement to testing.

Homogeneity and psychological theory

With the lack of agreement on the definition of homogeneity and on the appropriate index of homogeneity, and with the neglect of the concept by most writers and test constructors, the reader might well ask why the emphasis is placed here on the concept of homogeneity. The answer is quite simple: homogeneous tests are necessary in order to develop an adequate psychological theory.

What constitutes a theory is a matter of considerable debate among philosophers of science, the technicalities of which will not be discussed here. We will adopt a view similar to Kerlinger's:

> A theory is a set of interrelated constructs (concepts), definitions, and propositions that present a systematic view of phenomena by specifying relations among variables, with the purpose of explaining and predicting the phenomena (Kerlinger 1965, p. 11).

The aspect of this definition that is central to our discussion is that a theory includes defined constructs. In psychological research these constructs are frequently defined by, or inferred from, scores on psychological tests. If the tests used in developing the theory are not homogeneous (i.e., if they are factorially complex) we will have an endless number of complex constructs and never have "pure" measures of the constructs. If, however, homogeneous tests were developed to measure these constructs, making inferences from test scores would be simpler because each test would measure only one construct. An added consequence of the development of homogeneous tests would probably be a reduction in the numbers of constructs, or at least the number of measures (tests) used, a desirable consequence in that it would preserve parsimony. Thus the development of psychological theory could proceed more rapidly.

ERROR IN INDIVIDUAL SCORES

The reliability coefficient is an index of the consistency of a set of test scores over time or test forms; an index of homogeneity informs us about the internal consistency of the test. Thus both types of evidence are essential to evaluate the *test*. Neither, however, gives a direct indication of the amount of variability or error that can be expected in an individual test score.

The counselor, teacher, employer, or anyone else using an individual's test score in a decision-making situation is interested in the amount of error in the test score and the degree to which the individual's score will vary on retesting. For example, suppose that a school psychologist administers the Wechsler Intelligence Scale for Children (WISC) to a child who obtains an IQ of 116. Since tests never measure with perfect consistency (i.e., $r_{tt} \neq 1.00$), he knows that the child would not obtain exactly the same score on retesting; the question is how much variation can be expected. Or an employer may administer a selection test to a prospective employee and find that he obtains a score of 50. Like the school psychologist, he wants to know the extent to which the score would vary on retesting, to determine whether the obtained score is a relatively stable indication of the person's performance or not much better than a random guess.

The standard error of measurement

The problem, expressed in more technical terms, is to estimate the person's true score and the magnitude of the error component. Classical measurement theory postulated [see Equation (3.1)] that an obtained score is a function of the true score plus error: $X_t = X_T + E$. On some occasions the obtained score will thus exceed the true score $(X_t > X_T)$, sometimes the true score will exceed the obtained score $(X_T > X_t)$, and on some occasions the two scores will be equal $(X_t = X_T)$. In other words, the obtained score may overestimate, underestimate, or equal the true score.

In the theoretical case we would test the person an infinite number of times, determine the distribution of his obtained scores, and compute the mean and standard deviation of this distribution. In this hypothetical situation the mean would be the individual's true score and the standard deviation would be a measure of the variation of obtained scores around the true score. This standard deviation would be an index of the magnitude of the error of measurement.

The theoretical procedure is obviously infeasible. An estimate of the variability can be made, however, by using the performance of a group of subjects on two administrations of the test as a substitute for repeated testing of the same individual. The assumption made is that the distribution of differences between the performance of individuals on two tests will be similar to the distribution of differences between one individual's performance on various pairs of tests. These discrepancies represent the errors of measurement. The standard deviation of this distribution of errors of measurement is called the *standard error of measurement*. (For a further discussion see Magnusson, 1966, Chapter 6.)

The standard error of measurement is the standard deviation of the distribution of error scores and is computed:

$$s_m = s_x\sqrt{1 - r_{tt}} \tag{4.3}$$

where s_m = the standard error of measurement

s_x = the standard deviation of the distribution of obtained scores, and

r_{tt} = the reliability coefficient for the test

Knowing the standard deviation of the obtained scores for a group of which the individual is a member, and the reliability of the test, we can thus estimate the magnitude of error in individual scores. (Table 4.2 shows an example of the computation and interpretation of s_m.)

There are several pesky problems with using s_m as an estimate of error in individual scores. First, as there are many possible estimates of the reliability of the test there will also be many estimates of s_m. This problem can be alleviated by using the reliability estimate appropriate for the situation for which you are making the estimate of variability. That is, if you are interested in the stability of the individual's score over a six months period you would use as the reliability estimate a coefficient of stability computed with a six months interval between testings. Second, the estimate assumes that s_m is of the same magnitude at all score levels—that is, that s_m is the same for very high scores as very low scores. This, however, if often not the case. If an indication of the average error of measurement is sufficient, s_m computed as above will suffice, because it is an index of the average error of measurement throughout the score range. If more precise estimates are needed, more complicated procedures are needed (see Lord, 1957; Magnusson, 1966).

Interpretation of s_m

As s_m is a standard deviation (the standard deviation of errors of measurement), it can be interpreted as any other standard deviation; in this situation the mean will be X_T and the standard deviation, s_m. Reference to the Table of Areas of the Normal Curve (Appendix A) shows that X_t will fall within $\pm 1\ s_m$ of X_T on approximately 68 percent of the test administrations, within $\pm 2\ s_m$ of X_T on approximately 95.4 percent of the administrations, and within $\pm 3\ s_m$ of X_T on approximately 99.7 percent of the administrations. Thus the standard error of measurement is a useful index of the expected variability of obtained scores around the true score and, as a corollary, an estimate of the magnitude of variability in scores to be expected on retesting.

The test user, however, must approach the problem of estimation from the other direction—he knows the obtained score (X_t) and wants to estimate the true score (X_T). In essence, he wants to know the estimated range of score values that will, with a given probability, include the true score. He may select any probability level that is accurate enough for his purposes but will generally choose the 95 or 99 percent confidence level, the level that will insure that the range of scores will include the true score on 95 or 99 percent of the instances, respectively.

It can be shown (e.g., Hays, 1963, p. 288) that the probability is .95 that the true score falls within the range:

$$X_t - 1.96\ s_m \leq X_T \leq X_t + 1.96\ s_m \qquad (4.4a)$$

and that the probability is approximately .99 that:

$$X_t - 2.58\ s_m \leq X_T \leq X_t + 2.58\ s_m \qquad (4.4b)$$

---

[1]Although some statisticians would claim that it is not completely accurate to make such statements when estimating X_T from X_t, McHugh (1957) has shown that doing so generally will not introduce any large amounts of error.

TABLE 4.2 Computation and interpretation of the standard error of measurement

(1) For illustrative purposes we will use data from the reliability example presented in Table 3.2. We will use scores on the first administration of Form A and use the coefficient of stability as our reliability estimate. The mean ($\bar{X}_{A1}$), standard deviation (s_{A1}), and reliability coefficient (r_{A1A2}) were:

$$\bar{X} = 9.95 \qquad s_x = 2.46 \qquad r_{tt} = .894$$

(2) To compute the standard error of measurement (s_m) for this example use Equation (4.3):

$$s_m = s_x \sqrt{1 - r_{tt}}$$

Substituting the appropriate values into the equation and solving for s_m:

$$s_m = 2.46 \sqrt{1 - .894} = .80$$

(3) Suppose that an individual scored 12 on Form A of the test and we want to know the 95% confidence limits for his true score. Knowing, from the table of the normal curve (see explanation in the text), that the limits are:

$$X_t \pm 1.96 \, s_m$$

and substituting in the values from the example:

$$12 \pm (1.96)(.80) = 12 \pm 1.57 = 10.43 - 13.57$$

we can say that the probability is .95 that the true score for an individual with $X_t = 12$ is between 10.4 and 13.6 points.

(4) Analogously we could use more strict or lenient confidence limits: Using the 68% confidence limits:

$$12 \pm (1.00)(.80) = 12 \pm .80 = 11.20 - 12.80$$

Or, using the 99% confidence limits:

$$12 \pm (2.58)(.80) = 12 \pm 2.06 = 9.94 - 14.06$$

Rounding off, we would say that the probability is .68 that his true score is between 11 and 13, and .99 that it is between 10 and 14.

Or, in other words, the probability is approximately .95 that X_T falls within $\pm 1.96 \, s_m$ of X_t and .99 that X_T falls within $\pm 2.58 \, s_m$ of X_t.[1] The range of values thus obtained is called the *confidence interval* and the boundaries of the interval are called the *confidence limits*. Confidence intervals and confidence limits have an attached probability level; thus the range of scores $X_t \pm 1.96 \, s_m$ would be referred to as the 95 percent confidence interval for X_T and the two boundaries of the range, $X_t + 1.96 \ s_m$ and $X_t - 1.96 \ s_m$, would be called the 95 percent confidence limits.

Application of these relationships will tell the test user two things: the amount of variability (difference in scores) to be expected on retesting and the range within which the true score will probably fall. The former can be accomplished by using s_m directly as an index of variability, the latter by applying formula (4.4a) or (4.4b). To illustrate, consider the example given above of the child who obtained an I.Q. = 116 on the WISC and assume $s_m = 5$ IQ points on the WISC. Using the 95 percent confidence level, we would expect that his score on retesting would be within approximately 10 points (1.96 $s_m = 1.96$ $\times 5 = 9.80$) of his original score. Similarly, by adopting the 95 percent confidence level and applying Equation (4.4a), we could say that his true score probably lies between 106 and 126 (i.e., $X_t \pm 1.96 \ s_m = 116 \pm 1.96 \times 5$ = 106.2-125.8, or rounded off, 106-126). We say probably as we have used the 95 percent confidence interval and thus our estimate will be in error in approximately 5 percent of the instances. (For another example see Table 4.2.)

EXACT SCORES VERSUS RANGES. The standard error of measurement has another advantage beyond telling the user the amount of error involved in a test score—it forces him to think of test scores not as exact points but as ranges of scores. The obtained score on the test (X_t) will be the best available estimate of the person's true score (X_T), but, because of errors of measurement, it is not an exact indicator. How precise an estimate of X_T any given X_t will be is indicated by the magnitude of s_m and, indirectly, by the reliability of the test. As r_{tt} never is 1.00, *test scores must be thought of as ranges of scores, not as precise points.* The larger the s_m (and lower the reliability) the more imprecise is the measurement and the wider the range. If the test interpreter constantly thinks of scores as ranges rather than points, he will avoid the habit of overinterpreting small differences between scores.

CONSISTENCY WITH MULTIPLE SCORES

Having discussed the sources of error in test scores, the estimation of reliability, the concept of homogeneity and errors in individual scores, we now turn to three more minor, but nevertheless important, problems. The first two, the reliability of subtests and the reliability of differences, arise out of the fact that we seldom deal with only a single test score but usually consider several scores simultaneously. The third, the measurement of change, deals with the situation where the focus is not on consistency but on changing performance.

Reliability of subtests

Although many tests provide only one score, others have procedures for determining scores on a variety of parts or subtests. Scores on these subtests may be combined to obtain a total score or they may be treated separately. For example, the College Entrance Examination Board's Scholastic Aptitude Test is composed of two separate subtests, a verbal test and a mathematical test. The American College Testing Program test, in contrast, consists of four distinct parts—English, Mathematics, Natural Sciences, and Social Sciences—but also yields a Composite score based on the average of the four part scores. The Wechsler Adult Intelligence Scale has eleven distinct subtests, which can be combined into a Verbal Scale (six subtests), a Performance Scale (five subtests), and a Full Scale (all 11 subtests). In each of these tests, a given item appears on only one subtest, each subtest is administered with separate directions and time limits, and the test taker is aware of the individual subtests.

The concern regarding reliability occurs when tests are composed of subtests whose scores are summed to yield a composite score, but when interpretations are made and inferences drawn from individual subtest scores. If the test publisher provides data on the reliability of each subtest there is no cause for concern as the evidence needed to evaluate the consistency of measurement of the subtests is available. However, it is not an unfrequent occurrence to find reliability data available for the composite scores but not for the subtest scores, with the implication being that the subtests are equally as reliable as the composite score. But as the subtests necessarily contain fewer items than the total test, and reliability is partially dependent on test length (see Chapter 3) the reliability of the subtest scores will almost certainly be lower than that of the composite score.[2] Thus the test user should always check to see if reliability estimates are reported for each subtest for which a score is derived; if no estimate is available he cannot be sure that the subtest possesses acceptable reliability.

Reliability of differences

In many circumstances the test user may want to compare an individual's performance on two different tests or on two parts of the same test. For example, after a standardized achievement battery has been administered in an elementary school class the teacher may want to know if one of her students scored higher in arithmetic or language usage. Or a counselor may want to know if the aptitude of his client is higher in quantitative areas than in verbal areas. In both examples, two scores would need to be compared.

Because every individual score is unreliable, the difference between scores

---

[2]In contrast, because a subtest is generally composed of items of similar format and content, and the vaious subtests will differ among themselves in format and content, the homogeneity (internal consistency) of a subtest will probably be higher than that of the total test. One should also note that the reliability of any composite score, be it a composite of several subtests or several individual tests, will generally be higher than the reliability of its component measures.

will also be unreliable. A formula (Mosier, 1951) for the reliability of the difference between two test scores is:

$$r_{dd} = \frac{r_{jj} + r_{kk} - 2r_{jk}}{2(1 - r_{jk})} \tag{4.5}$$

where r_{dd} = the reliability of the difference $X_j - X_k$

r_{jj}, r_{kk} = the reliabilities of test j and test k, respectively

r_{jk} = the intercorrelation of j and k.

Because the reliability of a difference score will be lower than the average of the two subtest reliabilities, the standard error of measurement will consequently be relatively larger [see formula (4.3)]. This fact, coupled with the fact that the range of difference scores will probably be less than the range of scores on either test, means that the error of measurement will encompass a relatively greater range of the possible scores, and a relatively large difference in scores on the two tests will be necessary before the difference can be attributable to factors other than chance errors of measurement. Extreme caution must thus be used in interpreting difference scores, especially when, as is often the case, an index of the reliability of the difference is not readily available.

Measurement of change

Throughout this and the previous chapter we have emphasized the need for consistency in measurement, and inconsistencies, or changes in performance, have been considered as error. The goal of test construction was seen as the production of measurement techniques that yielded consistent results.

In many situations, however, we are more interested in changes in performance than in consistency. The goal of any educational program, be it a specific unit or lesson or an entire curriculum, is to produce certain defined changes in the students' repertoire of knowledge and skills. Or when studying changes in attitudes and values as a consequence of college experiences or personality changes that occur as the result of counseling or psychotherapy, we are more interested in the changes than in stability. In fact, in these instances stability of performance would be an indication of the failure of the treatment or experience.

When psychological tests are employed to study change, many problems arise—some from the fact that change scores are difference scores and thus possess the properties of difference scores, and others from the idiosyncrasies of the change situation. Most of these problems are exceedingly complex and well beyond the scope of this book, revolving around questions such as the appropriate corrections to make in formulas, the appropriate score scale to use, and whether to measure change directly or as the difference between two test scores.

The general flavor of the problems will be illustrated by one specific problem, one which has been labeled *the unreliability-invalidity dilemma* (Bereiter, 1963).

Briefly, the problem is as follows. When we use a test to measure change the paradigm is similar to that for the measurement of stability, or test-retest reliability—one test (the pretest) is administered, a time period elapses and then a second test (the post-test) is administered. In measuring change, however, there are two distinct differences from the stability paradigm. First, some specific treatment is usually interposed in the period between tests, a treatment designed to produce change. Second, the variable of major interest is the actual magnitude of change in performance, the change score, rather than the differences in rankings of individuals on the two test administrations.

In this situation, as a test becomes more sensitive to identifying changes in performance on the two administrations, the test-retest correlation will consequently decrease. That is, as the test becomes more valid in identifying change, the difference scores will become less reliable. Thus high reliability and high validity, both requirements of a good test, seem to be incompatible in this situation. If in constructing a test or manipulating the experimental conditions, we attempt to increase validity (i.e., sensitivity to changes), reliability will decrease; if we increase the test-retest correlation (i.e., increase reliability), the test will become less sensitive to change. Hence, the unreliability-invalidity dilemma.[3]

A related question is that of the processes used by the test taker in responding to the test items and the relation of these processes to the validity of the change score. In order to legitimately talk about change, the measures given prior to the treatment (the pretest) and the measure given after the treatment (the post-test) should be comparable, preferably two forms of the same test. Yet, as a result of the treatment intervening between the pre- and post-test, the latter might have a different meaning for the test taker than did the pretest and/or the process used in responding to the items might differ. For example, suppose we ask a student how many different combinations of faces can appear when tossing two dice. Before he has been exposed to the laws of combinations and permutations he might arrive at the correct answer empirically by listing all possible combinations. After a lesson on combinations and permutations, however, he might attack and solve the same problem by applying the appropriate formula. The item has remained unchanged but the process of solving it has shifted.

Bereiter (1963) has attempted to show that the unreliability-invalidity dilemma is a pseudodilemma by arguing that the requirement that the pretest and post-test measure the same thing is an unnecessary assumption. Whether his

---

[3]The statistical basis of the dilemma can be seen by studying Equation (4.5). The problem is further complicated by the fact that all persons in the group may change by approximately the same amount, giving high reliability with high validity. In most situations, however, there will be differential changes from pretest to post-test, thus giving rise to the unreliability-invalidity dilemma.

analysis will hold up remains to be seen because the concentrated study of change scores is relatively recent in psychological testing and many of the issues are far from resolved. The dilemma does, however, illustrate the complexity of the problems that must be dealt with when studying change. It also hints that the traditional views of consistency and reliability may need to be expanded or altered to handle new problem areas. The reader who is interested in further study in this area should consult the book by Harris (1963).

SOME THEORETICAL AND EMPIRICAL PROBLEMS

In our discussion of consistency we have, for the most part, followed the traditional view. That is, we have conceptualized reliability in terms of a model that involved three components: a true score, an obtained score, and an error factor. Reliability was defined in terms of the relation between true and obtained scores, and a reliability coefficient was computed by estimating the magnitude of the error component. Actually it would be more correct to say that we have considered two parallel models: a theoretical model involving the true score—obtained score (X_T, X_t) relationship and an empirical model based on obtained scores. As the two models were, to a large degree, isomorphic we could move back and forth between them with few problems.

The major divergence between the presentation in this book and in the traditional view was the treatment of the internal consistency of a test. The traditional view classes internal consistency measures as an aspect of reliability closely allied to the notion of equivalent forms reliability. That is, there is a continuum ranging from consistency over rather large samples of items as represented by alternative forms of the test, through consistency across subgroups of items, to consistency over items considered individually. The computational parallels would be the coefficient of equivalence, split-half reliability, and internal consistency measures, respectively.[4] However, as measures of internal consistency seem, logically, to be directed at a different question—that of the homogeneity of the test, rather than consistency over forms or situations—we have emphasized their distinctiveness rather than their similarity to other approaches to estimating reliability.

Alternative approaches to reliability

By referring to a traditional view of reliability, we have implied that there are alternative approaches to the study of consistency of measurement. One alternative approach (the one used in this book) is that of considering homogeneity as distinct from reliability. In the succeeding paragraphs we shall briefly discuss

[4]The statistical relationship between the various formulas for reliability and internal consistency can be found in a book on test theory, e.g., Gulliksen (1950), Horst (1966), or Lord and Novick (1968), and in the article by Cronbach (1951).

two other conceptions of the consistency problem. Because the traditional approach has worked quite successfully, both as a conceptual tool and as a guide to the development of computational procedures, it still dominates most discussions of the consistency of psychological measurement. However, because certain problems such as the question of change scores discussed above appear to present difficulties to the traditional view, reformulations are constantly being proposed.

CATTELL. Recently Cattell (1964) proposed what he considers to be a more basic set of concepts which he groups under the generic term consistency. In his view "consistency" covers three major areas, which are distinguished by the sources of error involved. He proposes that the term "reliability" be restricted to consistency over time, "homogeneity" be used to refer to consistency over items, and "transferability" be used to refer to consistency over people. The third aspect, transferability, refers to the idea that a test score should have the same meaning when obtained from various groups, for example, for subjects of different ages or socioeconomic levels. That is, a test of reading comprehension could be said to measure consistently only if it actually measures reading comprehension in diverse groups of subjects; if it measures reading comprehension in one group, intelligence in another, and recall of learned materials in another, the scores are not transferable.

Cattell further subdivides these main categories. For example, he distinguishes between types of reliability coefficients depending upon whether the major sources of error can be attributed to different test administrators or administrations, differences in scoring, differences in the way subjects react to the test, or various combinations of these factors. Believing that there is no justification for a concept unless there is an operational procedure for identifying the concept, Cattell provides formulas and procedures for calculating coefficients for each estimate of consistency.

RELIABILITY AS GENERALIZABILITY. A second reformulation is that of Cronbach and his colleagues (Cronbach, Rajaratnam & Gleser, 1963; Gleser, Cronbach & Rajaratnam, 1965). Their approach considers any observation (test) as being only one sample from a universe of possible observations. The conditions under which one observation is obtained can vary along many dimensions—e.g., a test is given at only one of many possible times, it involves a particular sample of items, it is administered and scored by one of many possible administrators or scorers, and so forth. The major problems are to determine what effects these various sources of variation have on the specific observation and how accurately the universe score (ideal score or true score) can be inferred from the observation (obtained score). Because the basic concern is with making inferences about the universe from a particular observation, one that represents only one of an infinite number of possible observations, the problem of consistency is viewed as one of the generalizability of the meaning of an observation.

In their papers the authors derive formulas and consider experimental designs for various types of studies, both of generalizability (i.e., reliability or consistency) and also of decision making (validity). The designs they present have the important advantage of allowing computation of the magnitude of the effect of the various error sources as well as providing an index of the accuracy of generalizability. This index, which is the ratio of the expected universe score variance to the expected observed score variance, is shown to be directly related to r_{tT}, i.e., to reliability as it is traditionally defined. Their approach also serves to emphasize the fact that there is no one reliability for a test, that reliability is situation specific, and provides a unifying framework by viewing the varying approaches to reliability as aspects of the problem of generalizability across observations.

Error components

The feature that all conceptualizations of the consistency problem share is that they are based on a classification of error sources. While consistency, as an area of study, is concerned with variable errors, as contrasted to constant or systematic errors (cf. Helmstadter, 1964), there are, as can be seen in the alternative approaches, various possible subclassifications of variable errors. How these subclassifications are organized is the basic differentiation between the various approaches to consistency.

There is, however, another aspect of the error components problem, one that we mentioned in the first pages of our discussion of consistency at the beginning of this chapter, but which has been only tangentially referred to in the succeeding discussion. That is, the question of the relative magnitude of the effect of the various error sources in determining the (obtained) score on a test. We have mentioned that error may be introduced by the particular examiner, by the circumstances of the test administration, by the sample of items constituting the test, by scoring unreliability, by fluctuations in the test taker's attention, and by a myriad of other factors. What has not been discussed is the relative contribution of each of these factors to the error in scores in a particular testing situation or in certain types of situations.

Although test constructors and test users have been aware of these sources of error, there has been relatively little systematic study of the magnitude of their effects. Partially, no doubt, this has been due to the complexity of the problem, the fact that in any testing situation a variety of sources of error enter. Furthermore, the various sources of error interact with each other, further complicating the analysis and necessitating a highly sophisticated experimental design to partial out the effects of the various error sources. Here designs such as those presented by Cronbach et al. would seem to be a particularly appropriate and valuable tool.

Another reason for the relative scarcity of experimental studies is the fact that test constructors have succeeded quite well, at least in the areas of achievement and ability tests, in developing tests that have controlled the error sources effectively enough so that the tests measure with high degrees of consistency. By using item selection and standardization methods designed to eliminate or control the major apparent sources of error, tests with $r_{tt} \geq .90$ have been developed. Thus, as a pragmatic matter, investment of time and resources in detailed studies of the magnitude of error effects might be an unprofitable undertaking.

However, there has been intensive study in certain areas, for example, on the effects of varying time limits, the effects of guessing, the effect of the administrator in individual tests, and the reliability of scorers and scoring procedures. There have even been studies on such specific problems as the design of answer sheets (e.g., color, layout, and the use of right- or left-handed answer sheets). Personal characteristics of the test taker have also come under study as, for example, the previously mentioned studies of test anxiety. In recent years systematic biases in responding when the test taker is unsure of the correct response (called *response sets*) and systematic response tendencies that occur in spite of item content (*response styles*), have been extensively studied. These studies, by and large, have shown that each of these variables do affect test scores, at least in certain types of circumstances. Because of the design of the studies, the relative contribution of each of several error-producing factors or the absolute magnitude of effect on any single factor has generally not been determined. How serious a shortcoming this is depends on one's point of view. If the goal of these studies is seen as identifying the sources of error and the conditions under which they operate, so that control procedures can be built into the tests, the studies have been productive. On the other hand, if the goal is to obtain a precise specification of all variables affecting test scores, with an estimation of the magnitude of their effects, these studies leave much to be desired. This divergence of views does, however, illustrate a fundamental dichotomy in thinking about psychological tests—the view of tests as being practical, decision-making aids versus tests being seen as instruments of psychological theory. This dichotomy will reappear repeatedly throughout the book.

These studies have also pointed up another problem—it is not always easy, in practice, to classify the effects of certain variables as producing constant or variable errors. Certain events, such as mistiming, improper directions, and distractions occurring during the testing session, occur only on one administration of the test, are not repeated, and thus introduce only variable errors. Other variables, such as the person's level of knowledge or skill in the relevant content area, usually produce only constant effects, at least when there is a minimum time lag between tests. Yet, when the testings are separated in time there will be differential learning and/or forgetting, because of both incidental learning by the test taker and any manipulation by the examiner or an outside person or agency, such as formal instruction or coaching, that occurs between the testing sessions. This differential learning causes instability in scores, thus producing variable error, but may also indicate a relatively permanent change within the individual.

When personality characteristics of the test taker are considered the water becomes even murkier. For example, should test anxiety be considered as producing only random variability and thus be classed as variable error, or does it constitute a relatively long-lasting and pervasive influence that will affect performance in a predictable way, operating as a constant error? Or perhaps individuals vary in a cyclical fashion on some personality and temperamental dimensions. If so, we could identify at least three components in test scores: a constant component (responses that remain unchanged over repeated administrations of the test), systematic variation (responses that vary but in a systematic, predictable manner) and random variation (error). The typical reliability study, involving at most two administrations of the test, does not allow this systematic variation to be isolated.

Even the stable variance in test scores is complex. We have mentioned that in the view of the factor analysts, non-error variance is composed of common factor variance plus specific variance. Earlier we mentioned that the constant component is composed of information relevant to the purposes of the testing and other information which, though stable, is irrelevant. The next two chapters will focus on the meaning and interpretation of stable, non-error portions of the test score variance; that is, they will discuss the validity of test scores.

Summary

The present chapter continues the discussion, begun in Chapter 3, of the consistency of measurement with focus on the concept of homogeneity, estimation of the amount of error in individual test scores, and some theoretical and practical problem areas.

Homogeneity was defined as consistency in performance over items on the test. Thus, a test can be said to be homogeneous only if all items are positively interrelated. It was pointed out that some approaches to homogeneity (1) also infer that the test measures one underlying trait or ability and/or (2) further restrict the definition by imposing additional requirements, e.g., as to the difficulty of items. Two approaches to the measurement of homogeneity, the Kuder-Richardson formulas and factor analysis, were discussed. The former was classed as a measure of homogeneity, rather than internal consistency reliability, because it answers the question, "To what degree are the items on the test interrelated?" which is the basic question in homogeneity. The importance of the concept of homogeneity was seen in its relation to the construction of psychological theories.

The question of error in individual scores was approached through a discussion of the standard error of measurement, a statistic that can be interpreted as the standard deviation of the errors of measurement. Methods for estimating the expected variation in obtained scores and for determining the confidence limits for the true score were illustrated.

Three specific problems that arise when multiple scores are available—the reliability of subtests, the reliability of difference scores, and the measurement of change—were then discussed. It was pointed out that subtest scores are generally less reliable, but frequently more homogeneous, than composite scores and that difference scores were notoriously unreliable. The problems inherent when using one important type of difference score, i.e., change scores, were discussed in some detail.

Several alternative conceptions of the consistency of measurement by psychological tests, those of Cattell and Cronbach, were presented. It was then emphasized, again, that the majority of the work on consistency has been devoted to the improvement of tests designed for practical use (through identification and control of error sources) and that little precise data concerning the magnitude of the effects of specific error-producing factors in specific situations are available. Finally, the difficulty in distinguishing between constant and error-producing variables was reviewed.

Suggestions for further reading

Bereiter, C. Some persistent dilemmas in the measurement of change. Chap. 1 (pp. 3–20), in C. W. Harris (Ed.), *Problems in measuring change*. Madison: The University of Wisconsin Press, 1963. A discussion of some of the problems encountered when attempting to measure change.

Cattell, R. B. Validity and reliability: a proposed more basic set of concepts. *Journal of Educational Psychology*, 1964, 55, 1–22. Cattell's presentation of his restructuring of the classes of reliability and validity estimates; a relatively technical and involved paper.

Cronbach, L. J., N. Rajaratnam, & G. C. Gleser. Theory of generalizability: a liberalization of reliability theory. *British Journal of Statistical Psychology*, 1963, 16, part 2, 137–163. A discussion of another proposed revision of reliability theory; again a very technical paper.

Doppelt, J. E. How accurate is a test score? New York: The Psychological Corporation, Test Service Bulletin No. 50, 1956. A discussion, in simple terms, of the standard error of measurement written for the test user.

Lumsden, J. The construction of unidimensional tests. *Psychological Bulletin*, 1961, 58, 122–131. Discussion of the various approaches to constructing unidimensional and homogeneous tests; quite complex.

Magnuson, D. *Test theory*. Reading, Mass.: Addison-Wesley Publishing Company, 1967. Chap. 6 presents a brief mathematical treatment of the standard error of measurement.

Validity: I
Criterion-related validity

Chapter 5

INTRODUCTION

Test scores have meaning only as they are related to other, psychologically meaningful variables. It would be possible, at least theoretically, to develop a test that measured with perfect consistency ($r_{tt} = 1.00$) but whose scores were not correlated with any other variable. Such a test would be of no practical value, nor could its scores be meaningfully interpreted, because the scores on the test would be related to nothing other than scores on another administration of the test. Such a test would measure with high consistency but would have no validity.

The previous two chapters have focused on the consistency of measurement, the precision with which a test measures. The basic problems were to identify error-producing variables, to estimate the magnitude of their effects, and to institute methods of control of error that would result in tests that will measure more consistently, i.e., with less error and variability. We now turn to the questions of (1) what the test measures and (2) how well the test measures. These two questions are the fundamental issues of validity.

VALIDITY DEFINED

Like consistency, validity is a generic term given to a class of closely related ideas, concepts, and procedures. Validity can thus be defined at various levels and in various ways. The flavor of the concept can be conveyed by the types of questions that validity analyses seek to answer: How well does the test do the job it is employed to do? What traits are being measured by the test? Is the test actually measuring what it was designed to measure? Does the test supply information that can be used in making decisions? What interpretation can be given to scores on the test? What can be predicted from the test scores? What percent of the variance in the test score is attributable to the variable that the test measures?

Since the determination of validity may involve diverse questions and procedures, validity, as consistency, will always be situation-specific. That is, under differing conditions, using various samples and/or methods of analysis, other results will be obtained. Thus one can legitimately speak only of the validity of the test under certain specified conditions. To say that one test is more valid than another is meaningful only if the statement means that the test has been found to be valid in a wider variety of situations or for a greater number of purposes.

Whereas reliability was defined by the proportions of true and error variance, *validity is determined by the proportion of true variance that is relevant to the purposes of the testing.* Relevant, as used here, means attributable to the variable[1] that the test measures. That variable, in turn, may be a trait or attribute or some independently observed criterion. Therefore, *the validity of a test is defined either by (1) the extent to which the test measures the hypothesized underlying trait, construct, or factor, or (2) the relationship between test scores and some extra-test criterion measure.*

Relationship of reliability and validity

The relationship between reliability and validity can best be shown through the use of equations. In Table 3.1 we showed that the total variance in a set of test scores equaled the sum of the true variance plus the error variance:

$$s_t^2 = s_T^2 + s_E^2 \tag{5.1}$$

This formula provided the basis for the definition of reliability as the proportion of true variance in a set of test scores. Defining validity as the proportion of relevant variance, as discussed in the previous paragraph, implies that true variance can be divided into two components—relevant variance and other reliable, but irrelevant, variance:

$$s_T^2 = s_V^2 + s_I^2 \tag{5.2}$$

where s_V^2 = relevant, or valid, variance

s_I^2 = irrelevant but reliable variance

In other words, the stable (reliable or true) variance in test scores can be divided into two components: that attributable to the variable being measured (relevant

---

[1]To avoid repeating the awkward phrase "variable or variables" we will use only the word "variable", realizing that a test may measure more than one variable; that is, it may be heterogeneous.

or valid variance) and that attributable to other sources (irrelevant reliable variance). Both sources represent systematic influences that produce stability in scores but they differ in their relation to the purposes of the testing.

If Equation (5.2) is substituted into Equation (5.1), we obtain:

$$s_t^2 = s_V^2 + s_I^2 + s_E^2 \tag{5.3}$$

or, the variability in a set of test scores is determined by the valid variance, variance attributable to reliable but irrelevant sources, and error variance.[2] Equation (5.3) indicates that as the error variance decreases (i.e., the test becomes more reliable), the proportion of potentially valid variance increases. However, as the remaining systematic variance may be either relevant or irrelevant, low error variance does not guarantee high validity (see Figure 5.1); thus low error variance is a necessary but not sufficient condition for high validity.

The validity-reliability relationship can also be shown by formulas involving the *correction for attenuation*, the correction to take into account the fact that psychological measures are not completely reliable. Given certain assumptions it can be shown (see Guilford, 1954 or Hays, 1963) that:

$$r_{xy} \leq \sqrt{r_{tt}} \tag{5.4}$$

where r_{xy} is the validity coefficient. Equation (5.4) states that the validity coefficient cannot exceed the square root of the reliability coefficient. Or, in more general terms, the validity of a test will be limited by the reliability of the test.

Types of validity

Although there are many possible classifications of types of validity, we will follow the Standards for Educational and Psychological Tests and Manuals (APA, 1966) and treat validity as falling into three major classes: criterion-related validity, content validity, and construct validity. Other types of validity will be subsumed under one of these three classes. Before discussing each type extensively, we will briefly describe each type.

CRITERION-RELATED VALIDITY. One frequent use of psychological tests is to predict an individual's future performance or standing on some significant nontest variable (the criterion). For example, to predict the grade average of a prospective college student or the job tenure or performance of a worker. The basic validity question in these situations is: How well do scores on the test predict status or performance on the independent, nontest behavior? An index of this predictive accuracy will be a measure of the validity of the test.

[2] Compare formula (5.3) to formula (4.2). If one were to look at validity solely in factor analytic terms, the two formulas would be equivalent with $s_V^2 = s_{co}^2$ and $s_I^2 = s_{sp}^2$.

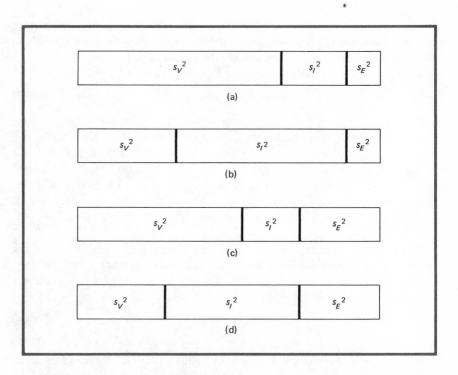

Figure 5.1 Relationship of reliability and validity: (a) high reliability, high validity; (b) high reliability, low validity; (c) low reliability, relatively high validity; (d) low reliability, low validity. In each diagram, s_V^2 refers to the valid variance, and s_I^2 refers to nonvalid but stable variance.

Note that the most important aspect of the situation is the *criterion,* hence the classification criterion-related validity. What is of ultimate interest is the individual's performance on the criterion variable; the test score is important only in that it predicts the criterion. Thus the content of the test is essentially irrelevant, the major concern in developing the test being to select items that will predict the criterion. Thus the test operates as a predictor, rather than as a representation or sample.

CONTENT VALIDITY.   In other situations, the test user wants to know: How would the individual perform in the universe of situations of which the test is but a sample? For example, the typical classroom examination samples an individual's knowledge in a variety of areas, and scores on this sample of items are then used to make inferences about the student's knowledge of the total universe of content covered by the examination. Or a person's ethnocentrism could be inferred from his reactions to a sample of different types of persons. Here the emphasis is on the test content *per se* and the test represents a fairly well-defined universe. The test content will thus closely parallel the tasks constituting the universe under study and performance on individual items—both the accuracy of the response and the process used to solve the item—will be of primary interest.

Because this type of test requires making inferences from a sample to a population, evaluation of the validity of the test will be made in terms of the adequacy of the sampling. Because no quantitative index of sampling adequacy is available, evaluation will necessarily be a rational, judgmental process.

CONSTRUCT VALIDITY. A third use of psychological tests is in the study of psychological traits and their manifestations. Here the basic question is: What trait does the test measure? When we know what trait, or traits, a test measures we may then use the test for studies of individual differences and for the development of theories of psychological trait organization. The focus of construct validity, therefore, might be on the individual, the test, or the trait; the trait emphasis, however, is pre-eminent.

Validation in this situation proceeds by an accumulation of evidence as to what trait the test does, in fact, measure. Evidence is accumulated in various ways and comes from various sources including studies of content and criterion-related validity. As evidence accumulates, the trait-test relationship is clarified and the trait definition becomes sharper. As with content validity there is no quantitative index of the construct validity of a test, evaluation being a judgmental process.

The essential characteristics of the three classes are summarized in the following list. In the discussion that follows we will treat each class separately although they are, as has been indicated and will be amplified later, interrelated, and evidence on all three types of validity will generally be appropriate in evaluating any test.

Summary of differences between content, criterion-related, and construct validity

CONTENT VALIDITY

Question asked: How would the individual perform in the universe of situations of which the test items are a sample?

Evaluation: By estimating the adequacy of sampling. No quantitative index available.

Orientation: Toward the task or behavior, the test process.

Examples: A classroom examination sampling the content of a given unit of the course; a personality scale measuring ethnocentrism by sampling persons' reactions to different classes of people.

CRITERION-RELATED VALIDITY

Question asked: How well do scores on the test predict status or performance on some independent measure?

Evaluation: By comparing scores on the test with scores on the independent (qualitatively different) measure. Various quantitative indices possible with the correlation coefficient being the most frequently used.

Orientation: Toward the criterion, the predicted variable.

Examples: Using a scholastic aptitude test to predict college grade average; using a mechanical aptitude test to predict success as an automobile mechanic; using a personality inventory to predict which automobile drivers will have accidents.

CONSTRUCT VALIDITY

Question asked: What trait does the test measure?

Evaluation: By accumulation of evidence as to what the test does and does not measure. No one quantitative index possible.

Orientation: Toward the trait being measured by the test.

Examples: Developing a test to define a trait such as intelligence or creativity.

CRITERION-RELATED VALIDITY

Probably the most common use of tests, other than classroom examinations, is for the prediction of some future behavior. Scholastic aptitude tests are used to predict academic success in college and professional schools, interest inventories are used in counseling to predict the occupations in which a person will find satisfaction, personality inventories are used to determine who will develop psychiatric problems or even who will become involved in an automobile accident, achievement tests are used to place students in various class sections (i.e., to predict the section in which the student will do optimal work), and measures of aptitudes and skills are used to predict tenure or performance on a job. In each of these situations the function of the test is to predict performance on a variable that involves a type of performance qualitatively different from that required by the test and which is, generally, of some social relevance. The variable which is predicted by the test is called the criterion, hence the designation criterion-related validity.

The paradigm

A basic paradigm for investigating criterion-related validity can be identified, regardless of the nature of the test and criterion. The procedure involves establishing the relationship between scores on the test and the criterion:

$$\text{TEST} \xrightarrow{\text{(measure of relation)}} \text{CRITERION}$$

Because the test is used to predict the criterion, criterion-related validity is sometimes referred to as *predictive validity*. And, because determination of criterion-related validity always involves collection of empirical data on the relationship between test scores and the criterion measure, some writers refer to it as *empirical validity*.

The designation "criterion-related validity" emphasizes the fact that the fundamental concern is with the criterion performance. We are not interested in the test scores per se, but are interested in the test because it predicts some important criterion behavior. The content of the test is thus relatively unimportant and the items comprising the test need bear no apparent relation to the criterion. What is vital is that the test demonstrate empirical validity—that the test scores can, in fact, be shown to predict criterion performance.

One further distinction should be made—that between predictive and concurrent validity. In the earlier edition of the standards for psychological tests (APA, 1954) these two concepts were considered separate classes of validity, while in the more recent edition (APA, 1966) both are considered varieties of criterion-related validity. In the earlier publication *predictive validity* referred to the situation where the criterion data are collected in some future time, that is, at some time distinctly later than the time the test was administered:

$$\text{TEST} \xrightarrow{\text{time}} \text{CRITERION}$$

Hence, the test scores were actually used to predict the criterion scores. In *concurrent validity* studies, however, the test and criterion data are collected at essentially the same point in time. Thus, the purpose of the test is not to predict the criterion, since the criterion scores are available at the same point in time, but rather to substitute for actually collecting the criterion data. For example, could scores on a personality inventory, administered by a clerk, be used in place of an examination by a psychiatrist to determine the presence of psychopathy? Obviously such a substitution would be valuable only if (1) there were a high degree of relationship between test scores and criterion measures—in our example, between a diagnosis made from the test and a diagnosis made by the psychiatrist—and (2) if the use of the test is more efficient, in time and/or money, than actually collecting the criterion data. Hence, concurrent validity is, in some ways, logically different from predictive validity in that it involves a substitution of the test for the criterion rather than a prediction of the criterion from the test. However, because both are basically concerned with the empirical relationship between test scores and the criterion, they may both be considered as aspects of criterion-related validity.

Predictive validity and decision making

Implicit in the concept of criterion-related validity is the idea that tests are used as part of a decision-making process. In using a scholastic aptitude test to predict college grades, the decision, from the college's point of view, is whether to admit the prospective student; when a test is given to a job applicant to predict his expected tenure or job performance, the decision is whether he is a good employment risk and should be hired; when an achievement test is used to aid in sectioning students into classes, the decision concerns the section in which the student should be placed to maximize learning. In each situation, there is some decision to be made, a decision that will be influenced by the score the individual makes on the test. The test is valid to the degree that it increases the effectiveness of the decision making.

There are several aspects of the decision-making situation that merit specific attention. First, and most important for the present discussion, a decision has to be made regarding the treatment of individuals, a decision that will be made partially, or wholly, on the basis of the individual's test scores. If each individual were to undergo the same treatment (i.e., if all students were allowed to enter college or all applicants were hired), no decision would need to be made and consequently there would be no need for the testing. It is only when a decision must be made, be it accept-reject, as in the selection situation, or which of the various treatments to assign the individual to, as in the placement problem, that the test can provide any useful information.

Second, the relative weight or influence of the test scores, as contrasted to other sources of information, in determining the course of action may vary tremendously. In certain types of situations, decisions may be made solely on the basis of test scores; in other situations test scores may be invoked only when a decision cannot be reached using other types of data. The relative weight given to test data in the decision-making process should be determined empirically by gathering evidence regarding the unique contribution test scores make to increasing decision-making accuracy. In fact, the point of view taken by this book is that *the proper measure of a test's criterion-related validity, and thus its usefulness, is an index of its relative contribution, over and above that of other measures and sources of information, to increased decision-making accuracy.* This topic will be treated in more detail below and in Chapter 8.

Third, in each situation there is an outcome or outcomes (the criteria), specified or implicit, that is regarded as the "desirable" outcome. For example, in industrial settings the goal may be increased productivity; in academic situations it may be the attainment of higher grades. The goal of the decision-making process is to select or assign individuals so as to maximize performance on the criteria. Because the validation process attempts to maximize the relationship between the criteria and the test, any limitations of the criterion measures will limit overall decision-making effectiveness. In other words, the validity of the test is judged only by its relationship to the criteria, and to the extent that the criterion measures do not adequately reflect the desired outcome, the decision-making process will be less effective, but this decreased effectiveness is attributable to the deficiencies in the criteria, not in the test. For example, consider the use of grades as a criterion of success in college. Even if a test could be found that predicted grades with absolute accuracy, the admissions office still might not be able to identify the type of student they would want to admit. Using the test to decide who should be admitted would only increase the proportion of students who would obtain high grades. The test would not select students with other desirable characteristics, unless these characteristics were highly correlated with grade-getting ability.

Finally, the problem is most adequately viewed as one of making decisions about groups of persons, rather than about individuals. Validity data, as we shall see below, are always collected on groups and thus, logically, *statements about the validity of a test always refer to the validity for sets of scores, not for an individual score*. Athough some inferences can be made about individual scores, the manner of collection of validity data and the error (unreliability) in individual scores makes such inferences exceedingly risky. But inferences can be made with a reasonable degree of accuracy regarding the effectiveness of a test for groups of persons.

Criteria

In most studies of criterion-related validity it is the criterion, or *criteria*, not the test, that is of ultimate interest. The test is of concern only to the extent that it is related to the criteria. In fact, as mentioned previously, the adequacy of the entire decision-making process hinges more on the adequacy of the criteria than on any other single aspect of the situation. If, however, our primary interest is in evaluating a test, criteria are important because they indicate the types of behavior the test can predict, thus providing a basis for inferring what traits the test measures and for giving an indication of the practical usefulness of the test.

If a test is designed to measure performance in an area, some standard of success or measure of performance must be identified. This standard is the criterion. For instance, what is the criterion of success as a student? The most common approach is to use grade-point-average but most authorities, including students, would argue that grade averages are only one, and not necessarily the best, criterion of academic success. Other criteria are also possible—for example, the amount of knowledge possessed, the amount learned (which is not necessarily the same as the amount possessed at the end of a given course), the ability to integrate and organize material, the ability to evaluate knowledge critically, the ability to learn without outside direction, or the development of positive attitudes towards education and learning.

Talking about *the* criterion is thus an oversimplification, as many writers have pointed out (see, e.g., Dunette, 1963; Ghiselli, 1956; Weitz, 1961). In most, if not all, situations multiple criteria are necessary. Although choosing one criterion might be simpler, this approach neglects much valuable information. Combining the various criteria into a meaningful composite, however, becomes a knotty problem. If the various criteria are highly related, the use of a combination of criteria will not add greatly to the use of a single measure because all criteria are essentially measuring the same behavior. Conversely, if the various criteria are not highly inter-related it is not legitimate, statistically, to combine them, since they measure different things.

Ghiselli has also pointed out two other problems besides the problem of combining criteria (which he calls the static dimensionality of criteria). A second problem (called dynamic dimensionality) revolves around the fact that the meaningful criteria may change over time. What is a good measure of success at the present time may not be a good measure at some time in the future, even though the job and worker remain the same. That is, the components of successful performance may change over time (see MacKinney, 1967).

A third problem, which Ghiselli has labeled dimensionality of the individual, relates to individual differences. Two persons may perform the same job in quite different ways yet still be rated as equally successful. For example, two salesmen may attain the same volume of sales, one by contacting a large number of customers but having a low percentage of sales, the other by contacting fewer customers but having a higher sales ratio; or, in professional football, one wide receiver may depend primarily on his speed to get open, while another receiver may depend primarily upon his faking ability. The psychologist studying job performance is thus faced with the dilemma of accepting two methods of performance as being equally valid, thus complicating his methodology, or choosing one method and ignoring other possibilities.

CRITERION MEASURES.   Strictly speaking, a distinction can be made between a criterion and a criterion measure (see, e.g., Astin, 1964). The criterion is the global concept of successful performance, what Astin calls the *conceptual criterion*. But, as in all measurement, this concept must be translated into operational terms, into a measure that can actually be utilized in determining the validity of a test. Thus the conceptual criterion might be success in college, the criterion measure being grade-point-average; the conceptual criterion success as a salesman, the criterion measure being dollar volume of sales. As all empirical relationships studied will involve a criterion measure, even an ideal conceptual criterion will be useless unless an adequate measure of the criterion behavior can be found.

ESSENTIAL CHARACTERISTICS OF A CRITERION MEASURE.   The most important characteristic of a criterion measure is its *relevance* or validity. The criterion measure must actually reflect and measure the important facets of the conceptual criterion. Thus grade-point-average will be a relevant measure of college success (the conceptual criterion) only if it can be shown that the characteristics that are considered indications of college success are reflected in the student's grade-point-average; output will be a relevant criterion measure of job performance only if it directly reflects the individual's skill, rather than some characteristic of the work situation. Determining the relevance of a criterion measure is, of course, a rational judgmental procedure, not a quantitative one, and involves establishing that all relevant dimensions of the conceptual criterion are represented in the criterion measure.

A second characteristic desired in a criterion measure is *reliability*, or consistency of measurement. Unless the criterion measure is consistent over time and circumstances, or varies in some predictable way, it will not provide useable data. The reason is obvious; if a person's criterion score varies from time to time we cannot consistently relate it to another measure, including a predictor. With an unreliable measure, if we caught the worker on a good day, when his production is high, we would overestimate his output; if the criterion data were collected during a slump, or slack period, we would underestimate his output. In either case we would not obtain an accurate measure of his production. The implications for the selection of a criterion measure are twofold: (1) the factors that introduce measurement error—those discussed in Chapters 3 and 4—must be controlled, for they influence criterion measures as well as predictors; and (2) if control of relevant error producing factors does not produce a stable criterion measure, reliability can usually be increased by obtaining a larger sample of criterion behavior and/or sampling over several occasions.

A third essential is *freedom from bias or contamination*. Criterion data must be collected under circumstances where irrelevant factors do not influence the score assigned. This problem is particularly crucial when the criterion measure is a rating. For example, if the rater assigns a criterion score on the basis of some characteristic other than actual performance, such as his general opinion of the worker, the score will be biased and will possess less relevance. If judgmental criterion measures must be used, the best control against bias is to provide specific, concrete directions and descriptions of the characteristics to be rated, in short, to make the rating procedure as objective as possible.

A specific problem is *criterion contamination*, which refers to the situation where a person's criterion score is influenced by the rater's knowledge of his predictor score. Suppose that we want to determine if a vocabulary test predicts grades in English and the criterion measure is the grade received in an English class. If the teacher assigning the grade knows the students' scores on the predictor (vocabulary test) her evaluation of the students' performance may be changed. The most frequent bias probably occurs when the student scores high on the test but does not perform well in class. In this case the teacher may be tempted to raise the student's grade, feeling that she was underestimating his performance because a student with his ability certainly should be able to do well in class. The opposite possibility may also occur—a student may be graded down because the teacher thinks, on the basis of his test score, that he should have done better, that he probably didn't try hard in class and thus should be reprimanded by a poorer grade.

Criterion contamination can be avoided by not allowing the person making the criterion rating to see the predictor scores. Under this procedure the scores on the predictor test are collected and filed away—the treatment (e.g., course, training program, or job experience) takes place—criterion ratings are collected, and then the predictor scores are related to the criterion. This procedure insures independence of predictor and criterion scores.

Finally, other things being equal, the best criterion measure is the one which has the most *practical advantages*, the one that is the simplest to use, is readily available, and costs least to obtain. It should be emphasized that this is the least important consideration—relevance, reliability, and freedom from bias are much more crucial determiners of the adequacy of a criterion measure.

TYPES OF CRITERION MEASURES.   A wide variety of variables are used as criterion measures in studies of criterion-related validity. One class is the direct measure of output, performance, or persistence. In industrial and business settings criterion measures may be volume of sales, production per unit time, salary received, advancement, number of customers serviced, or tenure on the job; in academic settings the criterion measure might be grade average, level of education attained, or graduation from a specific program. In another class of situations the criterion measure is performance on a test. Examples would include tests given at the end of training programs, course examinations, and tests given for certification of competency in certain professions (e.g., CPA examinations and medical specialties). Where objective measures of output or performance are unavailable or inappropriate, ratings by supervisors or peers are often used as criterion measures. These classes are not mutually exclusive—college grades, for example, could be considered as direct measures of performance, as a reflection of test scores, or as a type of rating. The classes do, however, represent distinct emphasis.

Other types of criterion measures are less familiar. In certain types of situations, the criterion measure is membership in a defined group. For example, intelligence tests and other tests of characteristics presumed to change with age frequently use an age differentiation criteria—i.e., items are considered valid if the proportion of individuals passing the item increases with age. Interest inventories are considered valid if they differentiate between persons in different occupations; personality tests if they differentiate between people with various syndromes; aptitude tests if they differentiate between workers judged successful and unsuccessful. Finally, as will be emphasized in the discussion of construct validity, the criterion measure is sometimes a statistical one—factor loadings or internal consistency indices.

A NOTE OF CAUTION.   It is a truism that a test will be no better than the criteria used to establish its validity. Because the items used on a test, or the tests included in a test battery, are selected and validated primarily on the basis of their relationship to the criterion measures, any weaknesses or limitations in the criteria will be reflected in the test and will limit its usefulness. The problem seems to be not one of selecting an adequate criterion measure, but rather of a failure to appreciate the fact that, for most tests and situations, there is no such thing as *the* criteria; multiple criteria are needed and the validation process should thus relate the test scores to a variety of criteria. The caveat to the test user, therefore, is to consider carefully the nature of the criteria used in validating the test and to be aware of the limitations that these particular criteria impose on the interpretation of the test scores.

METHODS OF DETERMINING CRITERION-RELATED VALIDITY

Having discussed the paradigm for studies of criterion-related validity and the role of criteria, we now turn to a discussion of methods for assessing criterion-related validity. Four methods will be presented in detail—validity coefficients, indices of group separation, decision-making accuracy, and utility indices. These methods have been chosen for discussion because they are widely used and/or possess certain distinctive advantages. All provide a quantitative index of the relationship between the test and the criterion.

In the discussion of the various techniques we will use as an illustration the selection situation where only one predictor is used. Although this is a simplified and somewhat unnatural situation, e.g., several predictors used jointly being the more common case, the use of illustrations involving one predictor simplifies the exposition and clarifies the logic of the methodological approach. The more complex multiple-prediction situation will be considered in detail in Chapter 8.

Validity coefficients

The method most frequently used to establish the validity of a test is to correlate test scores with criterion scores. The procedure involves five steps: (1) selecting an appropriate group to serve as subjects in the study, (2) administering the test to the designated group, (3) applying the relevant treatment, (4) collecting the criterion data, and (5) correlating the test scores with the criterion scores. In diagrammatic form, given the experimental group,

TEST⟶TREATMENT⟶CRITERION

the resultant correlation is called a *validity coefficient*. The validity coefficient, r_{xy}, is the correlation between test, or predictor, scores (the X variable) and the outcome, or criterion scores (the Y variable).

Because a validity coefficient is a correlation coefficient, the data used must meet the assumptions necessary for the computation of any correlation coefficient. Also, any factor that influences a correlation coefficient will necessarily influence the validity coefficient. Two factors are particularly relevant here. First, the type of correlation coefficient most frequently used in validity studies, the Pearson product-moment correlation coefficient (r), requires that the two variables being correlated are related in a linear manner (see pp. 20-21). If the two variables are not linearly related, the magnitude of the correlation will be underestimated. Although most variables used in criterion-related validity studies will be linearly related, there will be some exceptions. Thus it is always necessary to determine if the relationship is linear before computing r_{xy}; if the relationship is not linear, scores must be transformed to another scale or other correlation methods (ones that do not involve the assumption of linearity) must be used.

The second important consideration is the range of individual differences. As mentioned in the discussion of reliability, a reduction in the variability of scores will limit the correlation. This problem is important in validity studies because there are several different groups of persons that potentially could be used in a validity study (Cronbach, 1969). One extreme would be to use all persons who applied for the position or treatment—for example, all persons applying for the particular job. This group is generally not used since some of the applicants are deemed to be obviously unqualified and/or it is infeasible to let them enter the treatment. This group, however, does present the widest range of individual differences and thus represents, in many respects, the most desirable group for establishing validity. At the other extreme is a group composed of persons who have persisted and completed the treatment. If there is any relation between test scores and persistence, this group will display a restricted range of talent, and the validity coefficient will be lowered. Between these two groups is a group of "screened applicants," the group that would be allowed to enter treatment under normal selection procedures. Because this group represents a reasonably wide range of ability (unless unduly restrictive screening procedures are operating), is comparable to persons the test will be applied to, and has certain practical advantages, it is most often the choice for validity studies. Validity coefficients obtained from this group will generally fall between those obtained using the other two groups.

INTERPRETATION OF r_{xy}.   A validity coefficient can be interpreted in several ways. Probably the most common method is comparative, to choose the test with the highest validity coefficient in a given situation. Thus, if in situation S, using group G and criterion Y, the validity coefficient for test A is .40 and for test B .50, test B would be adopted for future use, as it is more valid under these circumstances.

Validity coefficients can also be interpreted in terms of percent of variance. The percent of variance accounted for is obtained by squaring the obtained correlation coefficient. Thus if, in a given situation, $r_{xy} = .50$ one can say that 25 percent of the variance (i.e., $.50^2 = .25 = 25\%$) is shared by the two measures, or that 25 percent of the variance in the criterion measure is attributable to variations in predictor scores. Note that r_{xy} must be .71, a value higher than usually attained in validity studies, before half of the variance in the criterion is accounted for by the variance in predictor scores.

Brogden (1946) has presented a third method of interpretation. He feels that the approach based on the proportion of variance accounted for (discussed in the previous paragraph), though valuable, tells nothing of the quality of the group that would be selected if the test were used to make the selection decision. He shows, given certain assumptions, that r_{xy} can be interpreted directly as a measure of predictive efficiency, i.e., as the ratio of the average criterion score made by persons selected by the test, to the average criterion score made by selecting the same number of persons on the basis of their criterion scores.

To illustrate, consider the following example. Suppose we have 100 applicants for 40 positions and wish to choose the 40 best workers. The ideal procedure would be to allow all 100 to work for a period of time, collect a performance measure (criterion data), and retain the 40 best workers, "best" meaning those obtaining the highest criterion score. The average criterion score of these 40 workers would be, obviously, the highest average obtainable by any combination of 40 workers. But as such a selection method is usually infeasible, instead we administer a selection test and choose the 40 applicants who score highest on the test. Brogden showed that if performance is expressed in the appropriate units,[3] the validity coefficient will equal the ratio of the average criterion performance of the 40 persons selected by the test to the average performance of the 40 who would have been selected, had the criterion performance itself been used as the basis of selection. Thus if $r_{xy} = .50$, the group selected by the test will have an average criterion score half that of a group selected on the basis of criterion scores. If $r_{xy} = 1.00$, the two groups would be identical.

A fourth method of interpretation involves prediction errors. This approach will be discussed below, but first we will introduce an example showing the computation of a validity coefficient.

AN EXAMPLE. A sample computation of a validity coefficient is given in Table 5.1, which shows the selection test scores and job performance rating (criterion scores) of 100 workers. The data represent a situation where all applicants were hired and given a two-week trial; supervisors' ratings at the end

---

[3]Both predictor and criterion scores must be expressed as standard scores. Their derivation is discussed in Chapter 7.

TABLE 5.1 Calculation of a validity coefficient

(1) A group of 100 applicants was given a selection test, hired, and given a two-week trial. At the end of two weeks supervisors rated each worker. These ratings served as a criterion measure. The scatterplot of the results was as follows:

Test Scores (X)

Performance Rating (Y)	0	1	2	3	4	5	6	7	8	9	10	Σ
8										1		1
7							1	2	2			5
6					1	2	4	3	2			12
5				1	4	6	5	3	1			20
4			2	2	6	5	4	1				20
3		1	4	5	6	4	1					21
2		1	3	3	3	3	1					14
1	1	2	1	2	1							7
Σ	1	3	5	11	12	20	18	15	9	5	1	100

(2) The summary statistics were:

$$\Sigma X = 534 \quad \Sigma X^2 = 3278 \quad \Sigma Y = 393 \quad \Sigma Y^2 = 1813 \quad \Sigma XY = 2366$$

$$\bar{X} = 5.3 \quad s_x = 2.1 \quad \bar{Y} = 3.9 \quad s_y = 1.6$$

(3) The validity coefficient is the correlation between predictor (test) scores and performance ratings (criterion scores). Using the raw score formula;

$$r_{xy} = \frac{N(\Sigma XY) - (\Sigma X)(\Sigma Y)}{\sqrt{N\Sigma X^2 - (\Sigma X)^2} \sqrt{N\Sigma Y^2 - (\Sigma Y)^2}}$$

$$= \frac{100(2366) - (534)(393)}{\sqrt{100(3278) - (534)^2} \sqrt{100(1813) - (393)^2}} = .79$$

(4) The validity coefficient is .79 for this group of applicants. One interpretation of the data is that 62 percent of the variance ($.79^2 = .62 = 62\%$) in the criterion scores is associated with variability in the predictor scores. Other interpretations are also possible (see text).

of the two-week period were used as the criterion measure. On both variables, higher scores represent better performance.

A glance at the scatterplot shows that the relationship between test and criterion scores is linear, so a validity coefficient can be computed using Pearson's r as an index. The obtained value, $r_{xy} = .79$, can be interpreted as indicating that 62 percent of the variance in the criterion scores is associated with variability in the predictor (test) scores. The magnitude of r_{xy}, which is higher than is obtained in most validity studies, is partially attributable to the fact that r_{xy} was computed on a group that included all applicants. With no preselection or screening, the score range on the predictor variable was at a maximum, thus introducing no restriction on the value of the correlation. Also the data are based on a validation, rather than a cross-validation sample, and so may be spuriously high.

PREDICTED CRITERION SCORES. One of the major advantages of the correlational approach to validity is that, knowing an individual's test score and the validity coefficient, a prediction of an individual's expected criterion score can be made. The procedure, shown in detail in Table 5.2, is based on the fact that the relationship summarized by the validity coefficient (or any correlation coefficient) can also be described by a line, called the *regression line*, that best fits the data points. Such a line can be described by a formula of the form:

$$Y' = a + b_{yx}X \tag{5.5}$$

where Y' is the predicted criterion score; a is a constant to correct for the difference in $\bar{X}$ and $\bar{Y}$; b_{yx} is the regression constant; and X is the score on the predictor variable. Such an equation is called a *regression equation*. (For a discussion of the derivations of the formulas involved see Hays, 1963, Chapter 15.)

Such an equation can be calculated from a given set of data and then applied to individuals who are similar, in relevant ways, to the group used to derive the equation. For example, if X were high school grades and Y college grades, the regression equation could be computed from data on one freshman class and applied to future classes. Thus, when the high school grades of a prospective freshman are known, his potential college performance could be predicted, thus enabling both the prospective student and the admissions officer to make a more appropriate decision.

One further clarification is needed. What is predicted (Y') is the average criterion score made by persons with the same predictor score (X). But, unless $r_{xy} = 1.00$, the relationship between predictor and criterion scores will not be perfect and there will be some error in each prediction. That is, the actual criterion scores of the group of people with the same predictor score will vary over a range, with Y' being the average score; some people will obtain criterion scores higher than the average, some lower, and some will have exactly the predicted score. The discrepancy between actual and predicted criterion scores will be *prediction error*.

PREDICTION ERRORS. The magnitude of the prediction errors is indicated by the *standard error of estimate* (s_{est}), s_{est} being the standard deviation of the distribution of prediction errors. This statistic is computed as

$$s_{est} = s_y\sqrt{1 - r_{xy}^2} \tag{5.6}$$

TABLE 5.2 Illustration of the use of a regression equation to predict an expected criterion score

(1) The basic format of the regression equation with one predictor is:

$$Y' = a + b_{yx}X$$

This equation, as it stands, is in raw score form; that is, the predictor score (X) and the predicted criterion score (Y') both are expressed as raw scores.

(2) The regression equation is an equation for a straight line and as such contains two constants—a slope constant (b_{yx}) and an intercept constant (a). The slope constant indicates the rate of change of Y as a function of changes in X; the intercept constant indicates the point where the regression line intercepts the Y axis, the value of Y when $X = 0$. We will not derive the equations here (see e.g., Hays, 1963, Chapter 15 for a derivation), but only give the relevant equations:

$$b_{yx} = r_{xy}\frac{(s_y)}{(s_x)}$$

and

$$a = \bar{Y} - \bar{X}(b_{yx})$$

(3) Using data from the example in Table 5.1, we can calculate the values of the constants. The necessary values are:

    Mean predictor score $= \bar{X} = 5.3$
    Standard deviation of predictor scores $= s_x = 2.1$
    Mean criterion score $= \bar{Y} = 3.9$
    Standard deviation of criterion scores $= s_y = 1.6$
    Validity coefficient $= r_{xy} = .79$

Substituting these values into the equations and solving:

$$b_{yx} = r_{xy}\frac{(s_y)}{(s_x)} = (.79)\frac{(1.6)}{(2.1)} = .60$$

$$a = \bar{Y} - \bar{X}(b_{yx}) = 3.9 - 5.3(.60) = 3.9 - 3.2 = .7$$

(N.B.: Usually the calculations are carried out to 3–5 decimal places; for illustrative purposes we have rounded the figures off to one decimal place.)

(4) Substituting the values of a and b_{yx} into the regression equation:

$$Y' = .7 + .6X$$

This equation can be used to obtain a predicted criterion score (Y') for any value of the predictor score.

Table 5.2 (continued)

(5) For example, suppose that an applicant attains a score of 6 on the predictor test. His expected criterion rating is:

$$Y' = .7 + .6\,(6) = 4.3$$

That is, the most probable criterion rating for an applicant with a predictor score of 6 is 4.3 points.

(6) Applying formula (5.6) we find

$$s_{\text{est}} = 1.6\,\sqrt{1 - (.79)^2} = 1.0$$

Knowing that the $s_{\text{est}} = 1.0$, and Y' for $X = 6$ is 4.3, we can say that 95 percent of the persons having a test score of 6 will have a criterion score between 2.3 and 6.3 $(4.3 \pm 1.96 + 1.0 = 4.3 \pm 2.0 = 2.3\text{–}6.3)$ or, considering an individual's score, the probability is .95 that, if his predictor score were 6, his ranking on the criterion would be between 2.3 and 6.3. The best estimate of his criterion score is 4.3, the average criterion score made by individuals with a predictor score of 6.

where s_y is the standard deviation of the criterion scores and r_{xy} is the validity coefficient. If, on the basis of an equation derived from past experience, one obtained a predicted criterion score for each person in a group (Y_i'), then obtained their actual criterion score (Y_i), subtracted the predicted score from the actual score to get an error measure $(E = Y_i - Y_i')$, plotted a distribution of these error scores, the standard deviation of the resulting distribution would be the standard error of estimate.

Interpretation of the standard error of estimate is the same as the interpretation of any standard deviation. Thus in 68 cases out of 100 the actual criterion score will fall within $\pm 1\,s_{\text{est}}$ of the predicted criterion score and 95 times out of 100 the actual criterion score will fall within $\pm 1.96\,s_{\text{est}}$ of the predicted criterion score.

The value $1 - r_{xy}^2$, the ratio of s_{est}/s_y, or some variation of these (e.g., $1 - \sqrt{1 - r_{xy}^2}$) provide another method of interpreting the meaning of a validity coefficient. These indices all give an estimate of the proportional reduction in prediction errors that results from knowledge of the validity coefficient. Although these indices often are referred to as showing the degree of improvement over chance prediction, they actually show the degree of improvement over predicting the mean criterion value for all persons regardless of their test performance.

EVALUATION. The correlational approach to validity has several advantages. It provides an index, the validity coefficient, that summarizes the relationship between the predictor and criterion over the entire range of scores. It allows for the prediction of an expected criterion score for each individual through use of the regression equation, a prediction that is on a continuum rather than being an either-or, accept-reject decision. Validity coefficients are in widespread use, providing some degree of comparability to other studies and data. There are several methods of interpreting r_{xy}. Many of the complex analyses involving multiple scores are based on the correlational model.

There are also some distinct disadvantages. If the predictor-criterion relationship is not linear, special correlational methods must be applied. A great disadvantage, however, is that, with the exception of Brogden's procedure, there is no direct index of the effectiveness of the decision making that would occur if the test were used as the basis for making the decision, because the usefulness of a test with any given validity will vary depending on the proportion of people to be selected in a group of applicants and the proportion of persons judged successful. In short, the major limitation is that no direct index of decision-making accuracy is directly obtained from the validity coefficient.

Group Separation

A second method of determining validity is to compare two or more criterion-defined groups to see if the average test score differentiates the groups; that is, identify groups by their criterion performance (e.g., acceptable and unacceptable workers, students who graduate versus those that drop out), then compare the groups on the predictor test. As an illustration, consider the data in Table 5.2 and assume that a performance rating of 4 or above indicates that the worker is judged "acceptable" and a rating of 1–3 indicates that he is judged "unacceptable." This procedure divides the total group into two subgroups: acceptable and unacceptable workers. Next compare the test scores of these two groups (see Table 5.3). The acceptable group has an average test score of 6.5 and the unacceptable group an average of 3.8, a statistically significant difference ($p < .01$). In other words, workers judged successful obtained significantly higher test scores than those judged unacceptable.

The main problem with using measures of group separation as indicators of validity is that the significance of the difference between groups is related to the size of the groups. As the size of the groups increases, smaller absolute differences in average scores will become statistically significant. With very large groups small differences between average scores will be statistically significant, but the test may be of little practical value in discriminating between groups.

To get an indication of the ability of the test to separate the two groups, one can also determine the amount of overlap between the two distributions. One possible index is the percent of scores in one group that exceeds the mean score of the other group. Using the data from the example (see Figure 5.2) we find that only 1 of 30 persons whose test score was above the mean of the acceptable group was ruled unacceptable; conversely, only 2 of the 20 persons with scores

**TABLE 5.3 Computation of the statistical significance
of the difference in performance of two groups of employees**

(1) Using the data in Table 5.1 and considering any performance rating of 4 or above as acceptable performance, and a rating of 1–3 as unacceptable performance, the total group can be divided into two subgroups. The relevant summary statistics are:

Acceptable	$N = 58$	Unacceptable	$N = 42$
(a)	$\Sigma X_a = 376$	(u)	$\Sigma X_u = 158$
	$\Sigma X_a^2 = 2576$		$\Sigma X_u^2 = 702$
	$\bar{X}_a = 6.5$		$\bar{X}_u = 3.8$
	$s_a = 1.5$		$s_u = 1.6$

(2) To compute the statistical significance of the difference in means, we can use the t ratio, the ratio of the difference in means to the standard error of the mean difference:

$$ t = \frac{\bar{X}_a - \bar{X}_u}{\sqrt{\dfrac{s_a^2}{n_a} + \dfrac{s_u^2}{n_u}}} = \frac{6.5 - 3.8}{\sqrt{\dfrac{(1.5)^2}{58} + \dfrac{(1.6)^2}{42}}} = 8.44 $$

(3) To determine the significance of the difference we refer to any table of the t distribution (e.g., Table II, Appendix C, in Hays, 1963). This table shows that the probability of a difference this large occurring by chance is less than one in 100 ($p < .01$). Thus, statistically, the means of the groups are significantly different; workers rated successful having higher predictor test scores than workers later rated unsuccessful.

below the average of the unsuccessful group were later judged successful. Thus the test scores do separate the two groups, at least at the extremes. Note, however, that unambiguous classification is possible on only 24 of the 100 cases, those scoring ≤ 2 and ≥ 8 on the test. The procedure described in the previous paragraph thus tends to give an overly optimistic picture of the degree of separation. An alternative procedure (Tilton, 1937) defines overlap as the percentage of area common to the two distributions, i.e., the percentage of scores made by one group that could be matched by scores in the other group. Applied to the data in our example, the overlap would be 38 percent using Tilton's index and 3 percent using the prior index (percent exceeding the mean of the other distribution.)

To summarize, data from studies of group separation can be very misleading. To avoid misinterpretation, the group means, standard deviations, and

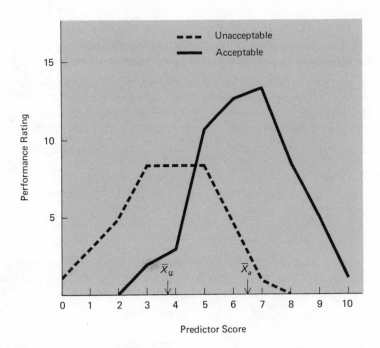

Figure 5.2 Overlap of groups designated acceptable and unacceptable.

an indication of amount of overlap should be reported as well as the statistical significance of the difference in average scores. A statistically significant mean difference may or may not indicate a sufficiently large difference to be of practical value to the decision maker. However, failure of test scores to discriminate between criterion-defined groups does indicate the invalidity of the test.

Decision-making accuracy

The decision maker is always interested in the accuracy of the decisions. He strives to increase the proportion of correct decisions and decrease the proportion of incorrect decisions. Therefore, one possible way to evaluate a decision maker's performance is to determine the proportion of his decisions that are accurate or correct. Analogously, when psychological tests are used as the basis for making a decision, an index of their effectiveness is the proportion of correct decisions made. The most effective (the most valid) test is the one that produces the greatest proportion of correct decisions. An index of the validity of the test would be the proportion of correct decisions made when test scores are used as the basis for making the decision.

The basic paradigm is quite simple, requiring only that we classify the decision recommended by the test into two or more independent (i.e., mutually exclusive) categories, that the criterion data be similarly classified, and the two sets of data compared. The simplest case, where both predictor and criterion data are dichotomized, is shown in Table 5.4. Here the decision, made on the basis of the test score, is either positive or negative (e.g., accept-reject, predict success-predict failure, hire-don't hire) and the criterion performance is also expressed as a positive-negative (e.g., acceptable-unacceptable performance) dichotomy. Therefore, there are four groups: those persons predicted to be successful and who were successful (cell B), those persons predicted to be successful who were unsuccessful (A), those persons predicted to be unsuccessful who succeeded (D), and those persons predicted to be unsuccessful who were, in fact, unsuccessful (C). Cells B and C represent correct decisions, or hits; cells A and D, incorrect decisions, or misses.[4]

TWO TYPES OF ACCURACY. One obvious index of decision-making accuracy is the proportion of the decisions made that are correct decisions, i.e., the ratio of correct decisions (hits) to total decisions:

$$P_{CTot} = \frac{B + C}{A + B + C + D} = \frac{B + C}{N} \qquad (5.7)$$

where P_{CTot} is the proportion of the total decisions that are correct (sometimes called *total hits*); A, B, C, and D are the numbers of persons classified in each cell

TABLE 5.4   Paradigm for evaluating decision-making accuracy

	Criterion performance	
Test decision	Negative (−) (unsuccessful, unacceptable, etc.)	Positive (+) (successful, acceptable, etc.)
Positive (+) (accept, hire, predict success, etc.)	A miss	B hit
Negative (−) (reject, do not hire, predict failure, etc.)	C hit	D miss

[4]Various terms are often applied to the categories, e.g., false positives, false negatives. But as these terms have been adopted from other fields where procedures differ, the use of such terms often confuse rather than clarify issues. Thus we will stick with letters as labels.

of the table; and N is the total number of decisions made. P_{CTot}, therefore, is an index of the validity of the test when validity is defined as the accuracy of decision making.

Two aspects of this index deserve special note. First, the index takes into account all decisions made. Thus it is comparable to a validity coefficient computed using all applicants for the positions, not some screened group. Second, both correct and incorrect decisions are weighted equally. If, for some reason, a premium is placed on certain types of decisions, differential weighting of categories must occur. For example, in selecting airlines pilots or munitions handlers, the consequences of accepting a person who will later fail to perform adequately are much more serious than failing to hire someone who might have succeeded. In such instances, the decision-making strategy must be designed to minimize cases in cell A, even at the cost of greatly increasing the number of cases that will fall in cell D, and the index of decision-making accuracy might involve placing a large (negative) weight on cases falling in cell A. Further discussion of this issue will be presented in the section on utility.

In some situations, another index of accuracy may be more appropriate. For example, the typical employment manager is more concerned with the success or failure of the applicants he hires than with the fate of persons whom he does not hire. The goal of the college admissions officer, too, is to select students so that a high proportion of the students he accepts will be successful. In these situations, a more appropriate index of decision-making effectiveness will be:

$$P_{CPos} = \frac{B}{A + B} \tag{5.8}$$

where P_{CPos} is the proportion of those selected who later are successful (*positive hits*), and B and A are the number selected who are successful and unsuccessful, respectively. In other words, the index of accuracy is the ratio of the number of persons selected who are successful to the total number selected. This index is the appropriate validity index when the goal of the selection procedure is to maximize the proportion of people selected who will be successful. While it is recognized that incorrect decisions are made by not accepting some people who would have been successful, this category of decisions is considered relatively unimportant and is given no weight in the computation of the index.

SETTING CUTTING SCORES. In our discussion we have assumed that the point on the test score scale that divided the acceptable (prediction = successful) and unacceptable (prediction = unsuccessful) groups was known. For purposes of determining the validity of a test, we could choose an arbitrary series of scores and determine the decision-making accuracy at each point. For the test user, however, a more important task may be to determine the optimal cutting point, the point on the test (predictor) scale that will separate the groups so as to produce the maximum number of correct decisions.

In setting a cutting score and determining its validity, three statistics are of particular relevance: the selection ratio, the total correct decisions, and the positive hits. The *selection ratio* is the proportion of applicants selected, i.e., the ratio of persons selected to applicants. As the selection requirements become more stringent (i.e., as a higher cutting score is used), the selection ratio becomes lower. The other two terms have been defined previously.

An illustration of the effects of using various cutting scores is shown in Table 5.5, the data being those first presented in Table 5.1 and used in all further examples in this chapter. Several trends can be noted from the data:

1. As the cutting score is set higher, the selection ratio decreases. This follows directly from the definition of the selection ratio.
2. As the cutting score is set higher, positive hits become greater. In other words, there is a negative correlation between the selection ratio and positive hits.
3. As the selection ratio decreases, total correct decisions increase, then decrease.

If the goal of the selection procedure is to maximize positive hits, the cutting score should be set as high as possible. Setting a stringent cutting score, however, results in a lower selection ratio and thus fewer persons are accepted. (In the example, perfect accuracy—$P_{CPos} = 1.0$—was attained with a cutting score of 8; however, use of this cutting score meant rejecting 85 out of every 100 applicants.) If no set number of persons are to be hired, the low selection ratio presents no problem. If, however, as is usually the case, there are a certain number of positions to be filled, there are two alternatives. The cutting score can be lowered, thereby increasing the selection ratio, but consequently also decreasing the validity of the selection procedure. Or one can attempt to create a larger pool of applicants, thus increasing the number of acceptable applicants without lowering the cutting score or decreasing validity. The alternative chosen will depend upon the exigencies of the situation.

The series of tables below shows the number of cases which would fall in each prediction-outcome category if various cutting scores were utilized to make the selection decision. The data are those from Table 5.1. Test scores are dichotomized at the cutting score; those applicants attaining the cutting score, or a higher score, on the predictor test are deemed acceptable (i.e., prediction = success) and would be selected; all others would be rejected. These two groups are coded ACC and REJ, respectively. Criterion performance is also dichotomized, those obtaining a rating of 4 or higher being judged successful (SUC), those rated 1-3 being classified unsuccessful (UNS).

Summary data reported include two measures of decision-making effectiveness—total correct decisions or total hits (P_{CTot}) and positive hits (P_{CPos})—and the selection ratio.

TABLE 5.5 Decision-making accuracy at various cutting score levels

Cutting Score $= 3$

		Criterion		
		UNS	SUC	
Test	ACC	33	58	Selection ratio $= 33 + 58/100 = .91$
	REJ	9	0	$P_{CTot} = (58 + 9)/100 = .67$
				$P_{CPos} = 58/(33 + 58) = .64$

Cutting Score $= 4$

		Criterion		
		UNS	SUC	
Test	ACC	24	56	Selection ratio $= .79$
	REJ	18	2	$P_{CTot} = .73$
				$P_{CPos} = .70$

Cutting Score $= 5$

		Criterion		
		UNS	SUC	
Test	ACC	15	53	Selection ratio $= .68$
	REJ	27	5	$P_{CTot} = .80$
				$P_{CPos} = .78$

Cutting Score $= 6$

		Criterion		
		UNS	SUC	
Test	ACC	6	42	Selection ratio $= .48$
	REJ	36	16	$P_{CTot} = .78$
				$P_{CPos} = .88$

Cutting Score $= 7$

		Criterion		
		UNS	SUC	
Test	ACC	1	29	Selection ratio $= .30$
	REJ	41	29	$P_{CTot} = .70$
				$P_{CPos} = .97$

Cutting Score $= 8$

		Criterion		
		UNS	SUC	
Test	ACC	0	15	Selection ratio $= 15$
	REJ	42	43	$P_{CTot} = .57$
				$P_{CPos} = 1.00$

If the goal of the selection process is to maximize the total number of correct decisions a different situation obtains. Here maximal validity occurs in the middle ranges of scores. The reason, of course, is that as the cutting score is raised, the number of persons who would be successful but who are rejected increases and, as the cutting score is lowered, the number of accepted persons who are unsuccessful increases. Only in the middle ranges of scores are these two outcomes balanced. In the example, the maximal number of correct decisions (80) occurs with a cutting score of 5 and a selection ratio of .68.

Needless to say, if the relation between predictor and criterion scores had been of a different shape or magnitude, the results would have been different. The point here was only to illustrate the procedure for setting cutting scores and for determining validity with a given cutting score. For further discussion of selection efficiency the reader is referred to the excellent paper by Meehl and Rosen (1955).

EVALUATION. The main advantage of the decision-making accuracy, or selection efficiency, approach is that it clearly reflects the type of evaluation the test user has to make. While the validity coefficient provides an index of the predictor/criterion score relationship throughout the entire range, the decision-making accuracy approach is concerned with the effectiveness of a particular cutting score in making a particular type of decision. Thus the latter model is a closer representation of "reality" than the correlational model. Other advantages include its computational simplicity and the ease with which the layman can understand the data.

A frequent criticism of this approach is that, due to the errors of measurement, use of a cutting score will do an injustice to some people, particularly those whose scores fall just below the cutting line. This criticism, which is really a criticism of the decision strategy rather than of the validity index, neglects the fact that any strategy involves drawing a select-reject line at some point. A more telling criticism of the index is that the use of groups (e.g., accept-reject) rather than a continuum of scores will reduce precision. The reply to this criticism would be that the precision of the regression approach is a false precision, because data from throughout the score range are used when the critical question is the accuracy in the area of the cutting score.

Utility

One further method of evaluating the usefulness of a test will be considered—that of ascertaining the utility of the test. An analysis of utility is essentially an analysis of the costs and benefits of various courses of action. Therefore, to use utility as an index of the validity of the test would involve a determination of the benefits attained and costs incurred by using the test.

To illustrate, consider a selection situation where there is no concern with persons who are not hired. In this situation there are three classes of costs and benefits that can be estimated: (1) the benefit to the company of hiring a successful worker, (2) the cost to the company of hiring a worker who later proves unsuccessful, and (3) the cost of the selection program. The calculation of each of these values is a complex cost-accounting procedure. For example, the benefits derived from hiring an applicant who proves to be a successful worker will be a function of his productivity minus the costs of his salary, fringe benefits, equipment needed to perform his job, training costs, and supervisory and overhead costs. A more thorough analysis would include such factors as expected job tenure, his influence on the productivity of other workers, and social costs and benefits associated with the employment of the worker.

Let us assume, however, that the direct benefits of hiring a successful worker and the costs of hiring a worker who later proves to be unsuccessful can be established. Then utility can be calculated from a formula of the form:

$$\text{Utility} = B(N_s) - C(N_u) - S \tag{5.9}$$

where B is the average benefit accrued by a successful worker, C the cost associated with hiring a worker who proves to be unsuccessful, N_s and N_u are the numbers of successful and unsuccessful workers hired, respectively, and S is the cost of the selection program. Equation (5.9) is a highly simplified version (cf. Cronbach and Gleser, 1957, 1965) but does show that for any selection program to have utility the gains obtained through testing must exceed the costs of the testing program.

In any situation where the costs and benefits can readily be translated into exact values, such as dollars, the utility analysis has the distinct advantage of translating validity into units that are meaningful to the decision maker. However, when exact values cannot be assigned to the various outcomes, the utility model may not be as applicable. For example, in most educational situations exact outcome values cannot be determined. Although attempts have been made to apply the model in educational situations, e.g., to determine the economic value of higher education or the utility of attending a particular college, these applications are open to the criticisms that they do not include the intangible values of an education (e.g., a more satisfying life) or that one must assign arbitrary values to certain costs and benefits.

INTERPRETING CRITERION-RELATED VALIDITY DATA

Having presented, in schematic fashion, four approaches to determining criterion-related validity, we now turn to the interpretation of these validity data. First we shall discuss some of the factors that influence the magnitude of the obtained validity index and, consequently, influence its interpretation. Then we shall consider the question of the generalizability of validity data—the extent to which data derived in one situation can be applied to other situations. Although both of these issues have been mentioned tangentially earlier in the chapter, their importance merits further discussion at this point.

Factors influencing validity indices

Any variable that affects the test scores or the criterion measure, or operates so as to alter the situation in which the validity data are collected, will influence the magnitude of a validity index. Many of these sources of error have been discussed earlier and therefore will not be considered here. However, three inter-related factors—the sample used to determine validity, the base rates, and the selection ratio—have a pervasive influence and so will be discussed in some detail.

THE SAMPLE. As has been indicated several times previously, the composition of the sample used in the validation study will have an effect on the magnitude of the obtained index. Two dimensions of the sample are most crucial: its size and representativeness. As the size of the sample increases, errors of measurement will tend to counterbalance each other and more stable results will be obtained. In addition, the larger the sample the more likely that the obtained results will be statistically significant. As indicated in the discussion of indices of group separation, this is not an unmixed blessing. Yet, other things being equal, large samples are preferable to smaller ones.

Of more importance is the representativeness of the group; that is, how the group was selected. The over-riding requirement is that the group used in the validity study be one to which the test might reasonably be applied. Thus, studies of the validity of college aptitude tests should be conducted using applicants for college; an achievement test in geometry should be evaluated using students who are in or have completed a geometry course; an industrial selection test should be applied to applicants for the relevant job; and an intelligence test for bilingual subjects should be evaluated using bilingual groups.

Using this general designation of an appropriate group, there still remain several alternative sampling strategies. One approach is to include all members of the group, or a random sample of the group, in the validity study. Thus, in an industrial situation the selection test would be administered to all applicants; all (or a random sample) would be hired, irrespective of their test scores, and allowed to work for a set period of time; criterion data would be collected; and the validity of the test determined. Needless to say, criterion contamination must be avoided.

Although this procedure is, in many ways, the most desirable one because it utilizes all applicants, allowing data to be collected along the entire range of predictor and criterion scores and permitting the maximal possible relationship between predictor and criterion, still it is often infeasible. Because employers might want immediate results from the selection procedure, or because space and cost considerations might not allow all applicants to be hired, some applicants are rejected. Since the persons screened out are generally those with less ability (those having lower predictor scores), the range of individual differences is reduced and there is no opportunity to determine validity at the lower end of the predictor scale.

A second design for ascertaining validity uses only the screened applicants—those who have survived the initial culling. This initial selection may be made on the basis of the predictor variable (the test being validated) or another variable. If the latter procedure is followed, the effects will depend on the relationship between the scores on the test being validated and the variable used for screening. If these two variables are positively correlated, as is generally the case, screening will reduce the range of individual differences on the predictor test; if they are independent, there will be no effect. Screening using the scores on the predictor test will, of course, reduce the range of scores used in computing the validity index. The most likely outcome, regardless of the basis of screening, is that the range of individual differences will be reduced, thereby reducing the potential magnitude of the validity index.

When viewed from the framework of decision-making effectiveness, this second design is appropriate when the concern is with positive hits, while the first design approximates when the concern is with total hits. While this second design does not allow determination of the predictor-criterion relationship throughout the entire score range, and thus has some disadvantages from a theoretical view, it probably most closely reflects the practical situation.

A third sampling procedure is, unfortunately, sometimes used. In this approach, presently employed workers are divided into groups on the basis of their criterion performance (e.g., more and less successful workers) and tests administered to see what variables differentiate the groups. This design has several major shortcomings. First, it provides no information about people who were screened out and not selected or who left before the criterion data were collected. The only persons included in the study will be those who survived all screening procedures and persisted until the criterion data were collected—certainly a group which heavily over-represents successful persons and under-represents the unsuccessful. Second, the skills or characteristics that differentiate the two groups might have developed on the job and might not have been present when the groups were hired. Third, the skills needed to perform the job may be common to everyone on the job but seldom found in other groups. The design does not allow for detection of these latter two possibilities. All of these shortcomings make it exceedingly difficult to draw inferences from this type of sample.

The third approach, using presently employed workers, therefore should be used only in preliminary investigations, and even then the results must be interpreted with extreme caution. Either of the first two sampling methods is preferable, the choice between them being made on the basis of the practical and theoretical goals of the investigator. Needless to say, regardless of what sampling design is chosen, the actual sampling of subjects for the study from among the pool of available subjects must be done in such a way as to introduce no further biases.

BASE RATES.   We previously stated that the most valid test was the one whose use resulted in the most correct decisions being made. However, the test that makes the largest number of correct decisions, or has the highest validity coefficient, still may not be a useful instrument. We have made this statement at least three previous times: (1) when contrasting practical and statistical significance in the discussion of measures of group separation, (2) in the discussion of utility, and (3) when emphasizing that validity is concerned with the ability of the test to provide additional evidence over and above that provided by other measures.

We shall now approach the problem from yet another angle—from a discussion of base rates. The *base rate* may be defined as the rate of occurrence of a phenomenon in an unselected population. Thus, the base rate would be the proportion of people who would be successful on a job or in an academic program if there were no selection. Actually, all groups probably are selected in some way, be it formally or informally, by an implicit or explicit method, or whether the selection is self-selection or made by an outside person or agency. Thus, in validity studies, the base rates more appropriately refer to the rate of occurrence of the phenomenon in the present, relatively unsystematically selected group.

To be of any use the test must improve on the base rates; that is, it must make more correct decisions than would be made from the base rates alone. To illustrate, in our example (see Table 5.6) 58 out of 100 workers were rated as successful—.58 thus being the base rates for successful performance. If the selection procedure adopted was to hire anyone with a test score of 8 or higher, correct decisions would have been made in only .57 of the cases ($P_{C\text{Tot}} = .57$). Thus, in this situation, using the test with a cutting score of 8 would have resulted in more errors than relying on the base rates.

The effect of base rates is particularly apparent when the phenomenon being predicted occurs either very frequently or very infrequently in the population. In these circumstances any prediction made on basis other than the base rates is likely to result in more errors than would predicting the most likely outcome. Suppose, for example, you wanted to identify people who will attempt to commit suicide. If the base rates are such that 5 persons in 1000 will attempt suicide, and if you predict that no one will attempt suicide, even knowing that some people will, your accuracy rate will be .995, or five errors per 1000. As no existing test will predict with that degree of accuracy, a test will not be useful in predicting suicide. Conversely, if you were to select persons for a job that was so simple that 95 percent of the persons could perform it adequately, the optimal

PRINCIPLES OF EDUCATIONAL AND PSYCHOLOGICAL TESTING

TABLE 5.6 The effect of the selection ratio on selection efficiency

| | Selection Ratio | | | | | | | | | | |
Validity	.05	.10	.20	.30	.40	.50	.60	.70	.80	.90	.95
.00	.60	.60	.60	.60	.60	.60	.60	.60	.60	.60	.60
.05	.64	.63	.63	.62	.62	.62	.61	.61	.61	.60	.60
.10	.68	.67	.65	.64	.64	.63	.63	.62	.61	.61	.60
.15	.71	.70	.68	.67	.66	.65	.64	.63	.62	.61	.61
.20	.75	.73	.71	.69	.67	.66	.65	.64	.63	.62	.61
.25	.78	.76	.73	.71	.69	.68	.66	.65	.63	.62	.61
.30	.82	.79	.76	.73	.71	.69	.68	.66	.64	.62	.61
.35	.85	.82	.78	.75	.73	.71	.69	.67	.65	.63	.62
.40	.88	.85	.81	.78	.75	.73	.70	.68	.66	.63	.62
.45	.90	.87	.83	.80	.77	.74	.72	.69	.66	.64	.62
.50	.93	.90	.86	.82	.79	.76	.73	.70	.67	.64	.62
.55	.95	.92	.88	.84	.81	.78	.75	.71	.68	.64	.62
.60	.96	.94	.90	.87	.83	.80	.76	.73	.69	.65	.63
.65	.98	.96	.92	.89	.85	.82	.78	.74	.70	.65	.63
.70	.99	.97	.94	.91	.87	.84	.80	.75	.71	.66	.63
.75	.99	.99	.96	.93	.90	.86	.81	.77	.71	.66	.63
.80	1.00	.99	.98	.95	.92	.88	.83	.78	.72	.66	.63
.85	1.00	1.00	.99	.97	.95	.91	.86	.80	.73	.66	.63
.90	1.00	1.00	1.00	.99	.97	.94	.88	.82	.74	.67	.63
.95	1.00	1.00	1.00	1.00	.99	.97	.92	.84	.75	.67	.63
1.00	1.00	1.00	1.00	1.00	1.00	1.00	1.00	.86	.75	.67	.63

The figures in the table show the proportions of persons who will be judged successful when selection is made on the basis of a test of given validity and the base rate is .60 (Table from Taylor and Russell, 1939, p. 576).

selection strategy will be to go with the base rates, to hire people as they apply, because no test will identify successful persons with greater than .95 accuracy, the accuracy obtained using the base rates. (For a further discussion, see Meehl and Rosen, 1955.)

SELECTION RATIO.   A third consideration is the selection ratio, the proportion of persons selected out of the number of applicants. If the predictor is positively related to the criterion, by being more and more selective we can increase the probability that any person selected will be successful. That is, we can select only from ranges of the population that have high probabilities of success; we can take the cream of the crop.

The effect of the selection ratio on selection effectiveness is illustrated in Table 5.6. This table shows that the effectiveness of the selection procedure (i.e., the proportion of selected applicants who will be successful) can be increased in two ways: by increasing the validity coefficient or decreasing the selection ratio. The former is shown by the increasing values as one goes down the columns, the latter by the increasing values as one goes across the rows from right to left. Thus even a relatively invalid test can be of value if the pool of applicants is large enough so that the selection ratio can be set at a stringent level.

Generalizability of validity data

Throughout this chapter we have continually emphasized that validity data are situation-specific, i.e., that the particular results obtained in any validity study are dependent upon the characteristics of the specific situation in which the data were collected. This approach has two important consequences. First, it means that a test will have not one, but many validities—at least as many validities as situations in which its validity is investigated. Second, even though the validity of a test has been established in one situation, it cannot be assumed uncritically that the test will be equally useful in another, presumably comparable, situation.

Such a view implies that, in any situation, the adoption of a test should always be tentative, that reliance on a test as a decision-making aid must wait until its validity has been established empirically. The need to evaluate the test independently for each specific use cannot be overstressed. In the author's opinion, using a test without evaluating its effectiveness is not only poor practice but also borders on the unethical. But where some immediate screening must be done, when narrowing the field to potentially useful tests, and to provide underpinnings for test construction practices, some basis of generalizing validity results must be found.

The first step is to establish that the index of validity obtained in a specific situation is, in fact, a good estimate of the degree of relationship between the test and the criterion in that situation. Although strict control of the variables possibly influencing test scores is an essential guard, spurious results may still be obtained because of the inherent instability (error) in psychological test scores (including criterion measures) and the possibility that some variable in the situation, which has been overlooked in the analysis, is influencing the results. Thus cross-validation and replication are needed.

CROSS-VALIDATION. Cross-validation and replication are related concepts, both referring to the process of determining a relationship, on data collected from two or more samples independently drawn from the same population. In validity studies this means establishing the predictor-criterion relationship on two separate samples drawn from the same population. Although computation of the relationship in two samples will not detect any systematic effects, it will detect variable errors, that is, it will establish the reliability of the validity data. Thus the magnitude of chance errors (those associated with one sample) can be estimated and the data corrected.

Cross-validation, in a single predictor situation, might proceed as follows. Test scores and criterion data are collected on one sample, the r_{xy} computed, and a regression equation derived. A second sample is then independently drawn from the same population. For each person in this second, cross-validation, group the regression equation is used to calculate a predicted criterion score. Actual criterion performance data are then collected and the correlation between predicted and actual criterion scores calculated. This correlation should not differ markedly from the validity coefficient established on data from the first sample. If it does, we know that the first correlation was spuriously inflated and is not a true estimate of the relationship. The coefficient calculated on the cross-validation sample will generally be slightly lower than the original correlation, because chance factors that tend to maximize the original correlation will not operate in the cross-validation sample. Thus the cross-validated correlation is a better estimate of the true degree of relationship.

VALIDITY GENERALIZATION.[5] Cross-validation involves only one very specific type of generalization—the generalization over various samples drawn from the same population. For a complete understanding of the meaning of test scores we must consider generalization on at least five dimensions: predictors, criteria, situations, samples or populations of subjects, and methods of establishing validity. Let us consider each dimension individually.

Up to this point our discussion of validity has been concerned with only one test or predictor. Thus the question of generalizability over tests (predictors) may seem unnecessary. Yet we might ask such questions as: Do tests supposedly measuring the same trait or ability have comparable validity in a particular situation? Would validity be the same with a different item format? Or, within a given test form, we might be concerned with the validity at different score levels: e.g., is the test as valid for persons scoring high as for persons obtaining low scores? Thus, on the predictor dimension, information is needed on generalization over comparable tests, over item formats, and over score levels.

We are also interested in generalizability over criteria. Earlier in the chapter we stressed that the idea of *the* criterion was a myth, that there are various possible criteria, but as a pragmatic matter one or a few criteria are selected for use in any specific study. The obvious question, then, is: Does the test predict the

---

[5]In contrast to the specific meaning given to "validity generalization" by some authors (validity across populations of subjects), we will use the term to refer to generalization along any of the relevant dimensions.

other possible criteria equally well? Because criteria involve a time dimension one might also ask about the comparative validity for predicting the immediate future versus validity for predictions over a longer time span. Or, analogous to the score level problem of predictors, what is the validity of the test at various criterion score levels? Can both good and poor performance be predicted?

The various permutations and combinations of testing situations are far too numerous to mention. A few relevant points include: What is the generalizability over different examiners? Over different administration conditions? Over different instructions or sets to take the test? This latter point is especially crucial because validity may very markedly depend on whether the test is structured as part of an experiment, as a standardization project, for counseling or advising purposes, or as part of a selection procedure for a position or an educational opportunity.

Of central importance is the generalizability over different groups of subjects. Here the important questions are: Over what age range is the test valid? For what educational levels? Socioeconomic levels? Is the test valid for both men and women? In different parts of the United States or different countries? Or even in different towns or schools? For what range of jobs or companies? Because there is such a diversity among groups (e.g., the applicants to Stanford or Harvard differ greatly from the applicants to South Siwash Tech), the limits of generalizability, or applicability, have to be established. Just because a test is designed for use with college freshmen does not mean that it will be valid at all colleges. The question is: In what types of colleges is the test valid?

Finally, by what method is the validity established? Unfortunately the results obtained from the various techniques of measuring validity do not always agree. For example, it is possible to have a high validity coefficient but poor decision-making effectiveness. Or, decision-making accuracy may be high but utility low. Thus one must also consider the method or index used when interpreting validity data.

At least three conclusions can be drawn from the comments on validity generalization. First, because validity is influenced by many variables, systematic collection of validity data is essential. Most of the validity studies reported in the literature have been conducted to justify use of a particular test (e.g., the data provided by the author and test publisher in the test manual) or represent the hit-or-miss, shotgun approach of many investigators, each pursuing his own interests and specific problems. Although attempts have been made to summarize available validity data (e.g., Ghiselli, 1966; Super & Crites, 1962), the underlying disorganization cannot be wholly overcome, even in a skillful review. More studies that deliberately and systematically vary the relevant parameters to establish the limits of the trans-situational validity of commonly used tests are needed.

Second, in addition to an increase in the number of studies, more adequate methods are needed for summarizing and interpreting the results. The development of a single summary index of trans-situational validity is probably not possible. But the variables influencing a particular test and the effects of manipulating each relevant parameter can be specified. This specification would not only aid the person using the test to solve practical problems by providing him with a more accurate estimate of the probable validity of the test, but would make it easier to draw inferences about the meaning of the test score. In essence, one would have a miniature theory for each test.

Third, the discussion shows the close relation between the data and concepts of validity and those of consistency. Many of the relevant variables in validity generalization are the same as, or parallel to, those which influence the consistency of test scores. And, as reliability was measured by consistency over forms and occasions, and homogeneity was measured by consistency over items, so too, consistency over tests and occasions—as well as over samples, criteria, and methods—is basic to validity. In both validity and consistency we are interested in generalizability; the difference occurs in the number and nature of the dimensions on which generalizations are made.

Two final points

We have avoided explicit discussion of the question that plagued the discussion of reliability—the question of how high is high, or, in more technical terms, what is an acceptable level of validity. Because of the situation-specific nature of validity, the variety of validity coefficients, and the multitude of factors that influence a validity coefficient, it is impossible to give one definite answer. At best one can set certain minimal requirements: (1) The cross-validated relationship between predictor and criterion scores must be statistically significant, that is, more than a chance relationship. (2) Using the test must result in more correct decisions than would be made by resorting to base rates alone. (3) The test must possess some utility; the net result of its use will result in a gain to the user, rather than a loss. (4) The effectiveness of the test must be greater than other available decision-making tools, that is, the test should provide some unique information. If these requirements are not met—at least the ones that can be evaluated in the situation—use of the test is not justified.

Finally, we also have not discussed the applicability of test results to individuals. Although test results are ultimately used to make decisions about individuals, the validity of a test is established by determining its effectiveness for a group of persons. Because there is no logical link that allows group results to be applied to an individual member of the group, the effectiveness of a test must always be evaluated in terms of decisions made regarding the group collectively, not the decision made in the case of John Jones. Although the decision made about John Jones is of utmost importance, with imperfect tests some errors will be made in individual cases. Our goal is to reduce the number of errors in individual cases to a minimum. Yet, until the day arrives, if it ever does, when tests with perfect prediction accuracy are available, some errors will be made in individual cases. When evaluating tests as aids to the decision maker the appropriate question is not "Will some errors be made in individual cases?" (a question that obviously can only be answered Yes) but rather, "Will fewer errors be made in individual cases using the test or using some other technique?"

Summary

Validity is a generic term applied to a class of methods, procedures, and techniques that attempt to determine (1) the nature of the variable(s) a test measures and (2) how well the test measures the variable(s) it was designed to measure. Validity can also be defined using the variance model, as the proportion of true variance (true meaning non-error variance) that is relevant, that is, reflects the variable the test is attempting to measure.

The various types of validity fall into three general classes: criterion-related validity, content validity, and construct validity. Criterion-related validity is investigated by determining the degree of relationship between test scores and a criterion measure. Content validity requires that the test represent the behavioral domain which the test items sample. Construct validity involves the accumulation of evidence to define more precisely the nature of the trait being measured by the test.

Criterion-related validity is appropriate in practical situations where the fundamental interest is in predicting some criterion behavior. In these instances, where the major interest is on the criterion, the test is useful to the extent that it predicts the criterion. The basic validation procedure, therefore, is to determine the relationship between test scores and the criterion measure in some relevant group. Since the goal is often to predict criterion scores from the test scores (such as when using the test as a selection device) this type of validity is frequently referred to as predictive validity.

Central to criterion-related validity is the notion of the criterion, an independent nontest standard of success. Actually, the idea of *the* criterion is misleading, because in any situation there are a variety of possible criteria. However, for reasons of economy, in any specific study, one or a few criteria are chosen for use from the range of possible criteria. A clear distinction must also be made between the conceptual criterion, the global concept of successful performance, and a criterion measure, an operationally defined variable used to measure the conceptual criterion. Criterion measures can be of various natures but must be relevant, reliable, free from bias, and must possess certain practical advantages.

Four major methods of determining criterion-related validity were discussed: (1) validity coefficients—the correlation between test scores and criterion measures—which have the advantage of allowing prediction equations to be developed and to enable predictions of an expected criterion score to be made for any individual having a predictor score; (2) indices of group separation, which tell how accurately two groups may be distinguished by their test scores; (3) decision-making accuracy, or indices of the selection efficiency using different cutting scores; and (4) utility measures which take into account the costs and benefits of the selection strategy. Illustrations of the computation of each type of index, using a common set of data, were given.

The considerations involved in interpreting validity data were discussed and the dependence of the empirical results and their interpretation on the sample, the base rates, and the selection ratio were pointed out. The need for cross-validation of all empirical relationships and the need for systematic data collection to provide the basis for generalizing results were stressed. Finally, the questions of the acceptable level of validity and interpretation of scores for groups and for individuals were discussed.

The point of view of the chapter could be summarized by saying that a test cannot be considered valid unless it improves upon the base rates, has utility, and does a better job (e.g., makes more correct decisions) than other available techniques.

Suggestions for further reading

Anastasi, A. The concept of validity in the interpretation of test scores. *Educational and Psychological Measurement*, 1950, 10, 67–78. A general discussion of some of the practical aspects of determining validity with emphasis on the need for obtaining evidence of the demonstrable correlates of test performance.

Cronbach, L. J. Validity. In R. L. Thorndike (Ed.), *Educational measurement* (rev. ed.). Washington D. C.: American Council on Education, 1969. A comprehensive treatment of the concept of validity and the methods of determining the validity of tests.

Cureton, E. E. Validity, reliability, and baloney. *Educational and Psychological Measurement*, 1950, 10, 94–96. A report of a study that demonstrates the need for cross-validation of item selection statistics.

Dunnette, M. D. A modified model for test validation and selection research. *Journal of Applied Psychology*, 1963, 47, 317–322. Dunnette's model emphasizes the need for considering situational factors and predicting specific components of performance rather than a single criteria.

Ghiselli, E. E. Dimensional problems of criteria. *Journal of Applied Psychology*, 1956, 40, 1–4. Discussion of some of the problems involved in choosing criterion measures.

Ghiselli, E. E. *Theory of psychological measurement*. New York: McGraw-Hill Inc., 1964. Chap. 11 presents a mathematical discussion of the concept of validity of measurement.

Kerlinger, F. N. *Foundations of behavioral research*. New York: Holt, Rinehart and Winston, Inc., 1965. A brief, relatively nontechnical discussion of validity emphasizing construct validity and the relationship of validity and reliability.

Validity II:
Content and construct validity

Chapter 6

INTRODUCTION

In Chapter 2 we made a distinction between tests that represent and those that predict. Chapter 5 discussed the latter type, tests that function as predictors. We now turn to the second type, tests that represent, a class which was in turn subdivided into two further classes—tests that sample and tests that serve as signs. A test is a *sample*, it will be recalled, when the items are drawn from a fairly well defined universe of content or behaviors; a test is a *sign* when the universe is openended and the test serves to point to the nature of the universe being sampled. This distinction has a parallel in the categories of validity, content validity being the analog of tests as samples and construct validity being analogous to a test as a sign. Content validity will thus involve a focus on the process of evaluating the adequacy with which the test items sample a content or behavioral universe, while in construct validity the focus will be on the definition of the trait being measured by the test, i.e., on the ability of the test to provide information concerning the nature of the trait of interest.

CONTENT VALIDITY

The classroom teacher is frequently confronted by the problem of assessing the degree of her students' knowledge in a certain, usually quite well-defined, content area. If time permitted, she would administer to each student individually an extensive examination covering all important aspects of the subject matter. Such an examination would require hours, if not days, and even then many questions would be left unasked. Obviously such a procedure, desirable as it may be, is unfeasible and some substitute procedure must be devised to permit a valid estimate of each student's knowledge in a reasonable amount of time. An achievement test is the usual solution.

In these circumstances the variable of direct concern is the students' knowledge of the subject matter domain. The test, being a sample of the content or behavior of immediate concern (subject matter achievement) thus serves as a representation of the behavioral domain. Scores on the test are used, not as ends in themselves, but rather to make inferences about performance in the wider domain. In other words, the purpose of the classroom examination is to provide an objective basis for making an inference about the students' knowledge of the material covered in the unit over which they are being examined. Because we cannot ask every possible question about the unit, we select a sample of the possible items, give this sample as a test, and, on the basis of the student's performance on this sample of items, infer his degree of knowledge of all the material in the unit. To the extent that the items are a good sample of the universe (i.e., the total pool of potential items) our inferences will be valid; to the extent that any bias is introduced in the selection of items, the inferences will be in error, and the test will be invalidated.

Definition of content validity

The basic question in content validity, therefore, is whether the items composing the test do, in fact, constitute a representative sample of the content area or behavioral domain of concern. Thus content validation involves the determination of the adequacy of the sampling of items from the universe of potential items, and content validity is a "measure" of the adequacy of sampling. "Measure" is placed in quotes because, as will be seen below, determination of content validity is a rational judgmental procedure rather than the establishment of a quantitative relationship.

Before considering the method used to establish content validity, however, we will consider some of the major implications of the definition.

CONTENT.   Content validity is, as its name indicates, concerned with the content of the test and the test items. Content here means the substantive constituents of the materials, the factual and informational components. Therefore, on achievement tests the emphasis will be on the subject matter covered (e.g., the laws of permutations and combinations, the novels of Charles Dickens, measures of central tendency, irregular French verbs), not on the processes used to solve the problems presented by the items. The mode of response, too, will be of less importance than the content of the item.

The appropriate role of the process dimension is an open question. Some experts feel that, because the same problem will be solved by different persons through the use of different processes (e.g., the item "multiply 11 by 12" might involve computation by one child and simple recall of a learned fact by another) and because several processes may be utilized in one problem, the process dimension can be ignored. They argue that inclusion of process factors introduces unnecessary ambiguity. Other experts, however, feel that failure to consider process dimensions is both sterile and dangerous. They would argue that the type of achievement test that is so widely criticized (e.g., tests composed solely of items testing factual recall) would never be developed if the test constructor considered process variables.

In addition to the more traditional emphasis on content and behaviors, one can also conceive of a test that would sample a universe of possible criteria or outcomes. That is, we could define instructional goals, not in terms of content covered, but in terms of the skills that an individual might be expected to possess at the end of the course. Using this approach, we would not sample, say, the content in Chapter 5 of this text; rather we would sample some of the desired outcomes produced by the study of Chapter 5—for example, the ability to calculate a validity coefficient, to design a validation study, or to interpret the standard error of estimate. But regardless of whether the domain is defined in terms of content, skills, behaviors or outcomes, it must be clearly specified so that the adequacy with which the test items sample the domain can be determined.

The definition also implies that the boundaries of the universe are well defined. Although some authorities would insist that content validity cannot be determined without an explicitly defined, finite universe of items (probably an impossible requirement), most people interpret this requirement to mean that the test constructor must specify what material the test is designed to cover as clearly and unambiguously as possible. In achievement testing, the content may be specified by the topic area (e.g., the theory of reliability, alcoholism among women) or by the actual assignments to be covered (e.g., Chapters 10–12 in the text and all the class lectures since the first of the month).

Although the concept of content validity is usually associated with achievement testing, there is no reason why it cannot be applied to other areas of psychological testing. For example, in Chapter 2 we used an example involving honesty, showing how one could observe students' honesty in various situations and use performance in this sample of situations to make inferences about a trait of honesty. We have also mentioned that a person's reactions to a sample of different types of persons could be used to estimate his ethnocentrism. No doubt one reason that content validity has been applied primarily to achievement tests is that in this area the boundaries of the universe can be most clearly specified.

REPRESENTATIVE SAMPLING. The definition of content validity states that the items on the test must be a representative sample of the universe of possible content or behaviors. Note that the definition specifies *representative sampling*, not random sampling. Representative sampling means "taking a sample that includes in due proportion or frequency every relevant or required characteristic of the whole" (English & English, 1958, p. 473). In test construction, the actual procedure of item sampling, which might appropriately be called proportionate stratified selection of items, proceeds as follows. First the content universe is divided into a number of subcategories representing the relevant content areas (stratification); the proportionate weight to be given to each category is determined; then items are sampled from within each category until the required numbers of items are attained in each category.[1] In practice, for various reasons the sampling in the last step is not truly random:

1. The items selected generally have to meet certain statistical requirements—for example, be of appropriate difficulty and discrimination level.
2. A balance of content within each category is desired. Thus if too many items covering a particular subtopic appeared in the first selection of items, some of these items would be rejected in favor of items covering a different subtopic.
3. Items sometimes are chosen to serve a specific function—for example, to be easy "warm up" items or to serve as buffers between critical items.

One further modification of the theoretical representative sampling design is usually made. Not all material in the content universe is considered equally appropriate for inclusion on the test. For example, in the typical classroom unit some of the material repeats what has been learned in previous units, some material is trivial or included as filler, and some material is otherwise inappropriate for test items. All these materials are not included on the test. Rather the test includes material that, in the judgment of the test constructor, is important material and covers important content and/or skill dimensions. The test items, therefore, need not be representative of the total content of the course or unit, but only of the material judged to be relevant and important.

Note also that there is nothing in the definition that requires the test to be homogeneous. In fact, categorization of the material into various strata would imply at least a certain degree of heterogeneity within the test. A high degree of homogeneity within content (or content-skill) areas may be desirable, but it is not necessary that the test as a whole be homogeneous. Considering that even the most limited course unit involves a variety of content and skills, a requirement of homogeneity would be both unrealistic and undesirable. Where one is interested in the content validity of a test designed to measure some psychological trait or construct, however, homogeneity may be both feasible and desirable.

Methods for determining content validity

The principal method of determining content validity involves comparing the coverage provided by the test items with the postulated universe of behaviors or

[1]For a more detailed description of the process of defining the domain, developing a test plan, and selecting items, see Chapter 10.

content the test is supposed to represent. If the test items appear, to the expert judge, to adequately represent the universe, the test can be said to possess content validity. This procedure is logical and rational, involving an evaluation of the correspondence between the test and the universe. As such, it has several drawbacks. First, there is no quantitative index, or even a set of agreed upon qualitative categories, that can be used to describe the degree of relationship. Second, lacking any more specific operational description of the process of establishing content validity, different judges may well arrive at different decisions regarding the content validity of the test. Third, any lack of clarity in the specification of the limits of the universe will introduce ambiguity into the judges' ratings.

Several procedures could be introduced to make the judgment of content validity more objective. As a starting point one would have to insist upon a well-specified definition of the content universe, one which would include the delineation of the domain, the relevant skills and content, and the source materials used (if an achievement examination). Relevant subcategories would then have to be defined and their proportionate emphasis specified. The test constructor would also specify, for each item, the content and skills being tested and the item's relative scoring weight. Finally, rating scales would be developed to measure the overall validity of the test and/or establish its rating along several relevant dimensions—e.g., coverage of skills, coverage of important materials, and appropriateness of item format to content. The judge rating the content validity of the test would then go through the test, item by item, and compare his categorization of each item with the test constructor's categorization. The judges would also make their ratings on the summary rating scales.

Besides standardizing the descriptive language, such procedures could also be analyzed statistically. Indices of interjudge agreement could be computed on the results of the ratings. Or an index of agreement between a reviewer's and the test constructor's, or between two independent reviewers', categorization of items could be calculated. In either case, the extent of agreement would be analogous to the reliability of the measure, the magnitude of the rating analogous to the validity.

In practice, several of these steps are now used. The content universe is usually spelled out in some detail, a test plan showing the relative emphases on various content and skill categories is available, and the number of items that fall in each category is given. The judge uses this information when studying the test and making his evaluation. This sort of evaluation occurs when the test is being developed, utilizing the test construction team as judges, when a potential user evaluates the test, and when a test is reviewed for a journal or a publication like the *Mental Measurements Yearbook* (see Chapter 9).

Other methods of obtaining information about content validity are theoretically possible. Recently Cronbach (1969) has proposed that content validity could be evaluated quantitatively by correlating scores of two forms of a test, independently constructed from the same content universe.[2] If the correlation were high both forms would have high content validity; if the correlation were low at least one form would lack content validity. An alternative method would involve pretesting a group that was naïve regarding the content area covered by the test, exposing the group to a course or training program covering the relevant material, and then administering a post-test. Although this procedure would not unambiguously establish content validity, it would indicate whether the test reflected achievement in the relevant content area. Procedures analogous to these two suggestions are currently used to establish the construct validity, as explained below.

FACE VALIDITY.   Content validity is not infrequently confused with face validity. A test is said to display face validity when the items look like they measure what the test is supposed to measure, that is, when the test taker looks at the items, he sees them as being relevant to the purpose of the test. Thus a test containing items that ask the individual's reactions to activities such as basketball games, solid geometry, selling as an occupation, and uncooperative people, would have face validity as an interest inventory but not as an intelligence test. In short, face validity is determined by a somewhat superficial examination of the test by the test taker and considers only obvious relevance. Content validity, on the other hand, is established by the thorough and systematic evaluation by a psychometrically sophisticated judge and considers both subtle and obvious aspects of relevance.

Face validity is an important variable to the extent that the apparent relevance of the items has any influence on the test taker's motivation. In some situations, particularly in employment testing, if the test lacks face validity the test taker may not be motivated to do well, feeling that the test can have no relevance to the decision being made. In other situations, such as measuring personality characteristics, a high degree of face validity may be undesirable as it may either threaten the test taker or encourage him to dissimulate. We can see that face validity, though not guaranteeing accurate measurement, may be an important influence on test-taking motivation and thus on the validity of the obtained scores.

SPECIFICITY OF CONTENT VALIDITY.   In one sense, content validity is general rather than situation-specific. That is, if the test constructor defines the content universe and selects items to represent this universe, he either succeeds or does not succeed (more precisely, succeeds in x degree) in attaining his goal.

---

[2] By "independently constructed," Cronbach means built by two separate test construction teams working from the same definition of the content universe and following some agreement on guidelines regarding time limits, format, etc. Such a procedure would obviously be feasible only where massive resources are devoted to the test construction, such as the national college entrance examinations or widely used standardized achievement tests.

Although we may disagree with his definition of the universe, we must evaluate the test in terms of how well the test constructor attained the goal he specified—by how well the test represents the universe as the test constructor defined it.

In another sense, however, content validity is situation-specific. The test user must apply the test in a specific situation, to measure certain behaviors that he, the user, has defined as important. If the universe as defined by the user and as defined by the test constructor are congruent there is no problem, because to the extent that the test accomplishes the test constructor's goal (possesses content validity) it will be appropriate (valid) for the user. If, however, the user construes the universe differently than did the test constructor, a conflict arises. Now the test is not a good representation of the universe, as the user defines it, and thus is less valid for his purposes. In this sense, content validity is situation-specific.

To illustrate, suppose that a standardized, nationally distributed test for grades 4–6 is constructed to measure achievement in mathematics as it has been traditionally taught in the upper elementary grades. Assume also that the test constructor has done an excellent job in constructing the test so that the important concepts are covered by well constructed items—in short, that we have a test that has very high content validity as a measure of mathematics as traditionally taught in the grades 4–6. If this test is used in a school system that teaches mathematics in the traditional manner it will have content validity. True, there will be some differences in emphasis and coverage because of the particular text used and teacher preferences in that district, but, by and large, these will be minor differences and the test will be a good measure of achievement. On the other hand, if the test is administered in a school system that teaches the "new" mathematics, some of the items on the test will cover materials not taught or emphasized in the new curriculum and some of the important concepts and materials emphasized by the new curriculum will not appear on the test. In this instance, the disparity in definitions of the content universe is so great as to render the test inappropriate—in essence, to destroy its validity.

This illustration also raises another point. Content validity, like other types of validity, must periodically be reviewed. Particularly in achievement areas where knowledge expands, teaching methods change, and subjects may be introduced at different points in the curriculum at different times, a periodic review of the appropriateness of a test is needed. What is taught in the sixth grade today, may be taught in the fourth grade tomorrow, or not taught at all!

Evaluation of content validity

Content validity, as a concept and as a method, has both its strong points and limitations. Its emphasis on the need for an evaluation of the correspondence between the items on the test and the stated content, skill, or behavioral domain sampled is unequivocably a positive contribution, both for insuring care in item selection and requiring careful specification of the domain that the test samples. Thus considerations of content validity are an essential aspect of test construction. Content validity is clearly the most appropriate method for evaluating the validity of achievement tests (unless, of course, the achievement test is used primarily as a predictor). And content validity, as a concept, emphasizes that the test user's major concern is not the test itself but the inferences which can be made from the test scores about performance in the domain sampled.

The major limitation, of course, is the lack of clearly specified methods for determining content validity and communicable standards that summarize the degree of content validity. Quantitative indices, although desireable in many respects, are not essential. Rather what is needed are clearly specified methods, techniques, and procedures for determining content validity and a scale, or set of standards, that can be used to summarize the degree of content validity. Such procedures and scales are, in principle, attainable; however, no acceptable ones are yet available.

CONSTRUCT VALIDITY

If psychology is to advance as a science it must provide some sort of theoretical framework to integrate and explain its data and provide direction for further work. As was mentioned earlier, one essential element of a theory is well-defined constructs. Frequently these constructs are operationally defined and measured by psychological tests. As neither criterion-related nor content validity have as their fundamental goal the understanding of the trait (construct) that a test measures, the original Technical Recommendation for Psychological Tests and Diagnostic Techniques (APA, 1954) put forth a new approach to validity, called *construct validity*, which focuses on this problem. This approach was further explicated in an article by Cronbach and Meehl (1955), who provided an extensive discussion of the logic and methods of construct validity.

In the revision of the Technical Recommendations construct validity is said to be appropriate when "The test user wishes to infer the degree to which the individual possesses some hypothetical trait or quality (construct) presumed to be reflected in the test performance." (APA, 1966, p. 12) Thus construct validity is important whenever a test is to be interpreted as a measure of some attribute or quality (construct) that people are presumed to possess. Construct validity studies attempt to answer the questions: (1) What is the psychological construct being measured by the test? and (2) How well does the test measure this construct? Thus the central concern is with the construct. The focus is on the characteristic being measured.

The definition implies something more—that the construct being measured may not be definable solely in operational terms. The definition of the construct may include more than purely operational terms and encompass statements which, though anchored in observable data, contain elements that go beyond the data and thus provide a broader, more significant definition than would be provided by a mere rephrasing of the empirical relationships.

Thus no single quantitative index of construct validity is possible. Construct validity is evaluated, rather, by the accumulation of evidence. To determine the construct validity of a test, one must examine the entire body of evidence surrounding the test—the variables its scores do or do not correlate with, the sort of items included on the test, the stability of the test scores under varying conditions, the homogeneity of the test, and any other data that cast light on the meaning of test scores. By evaluating, sifting, and refining the evidence about the test, a clearer definition of the construct measured by the test emerges.

The logic of construct validation

Before considering the specific methods used to establish the construct validity of a test, it would be well to discuss the philosophic and logical bases of the idea of construct validity. Here, as throughout our discussion of construct validity, we will rely heavily on the paper by Cronbach and Meehl (1955).

In many ways the logic of construct validity, as well as its processes, are essentially those of the scientific method. One starts with a theory which includes a construct presumably measured by the test in question. From this theory, certain predictions are made about the relationships between the test scores and other variables. These predictions are then tested empirically. Depending on the results of the empirical check, the theory is supported or revised. Continual prediction, empirical tests, and theory revision increase the precision of the definition of the construct. This, in short, is the process of construct validation. Let us now, however, be more specific.

THE NOMOLOGICAL NET. Any theory which attempts to explain a phenomenon is comprised of a series of interrelated concepts, propositions, and laws. This system of interlocking laws is called a nomological network (Cronbach & Meehl, 1955). The laws relate observable characteristics to other observables, observables to theoretical constructs, or one theoretical construct to another construct. The relationships in the laws may be either deterministic or statistical, that is, be all-or-none or probabilistic in nature. At some point, all laws and concepts must be tied to observable behaviors. However, a given law or concept may not directly involve observables, i.e., it may be derived from other laws and concepts that, themselves, are directly tied to observables. The essential requirement is that the definition of the concept (or formulation of the law) can be traced back to laws or concepts that are anchored in the observable data.

To clarify the meaning of any concept in the network we must elaborate the network (i.e., include more lawful relationships) or make the existing relationships more specific and definite. Thus many different, even qualitatively different, operations can be used to measure the concept if they can be shown to be related to the concept through the nomological network. Psychological tests are one, but only one, method of explicating the meaning of the pertinent construct.

There are several important implications of this metatheoretical position. First, at some stage in the process of inferring the meaning of a construct, there must be observable data. The psychological test may be used to supply these data. Second, the process of inference from the observable data to the meaning of the construct must be public and explicitly specified. Otherwise there is no means of checking the accuracy of the inference. Third, unless the various users of the construct adopt essentially the same network, communication and agreement among investigators are not possible. This point is especially relevant in psychological research where investigators frequently use the same construct label to refer to different constructs (e.g., different people mean different things by "intelligence") or use different labels to refer to the same construct (e.g., divergent thinking and creativity sometimes refer to the same construct).

VALIDATION PARADIGM.   The validation procedure implied by this view of theory has been mentioned previously. In essence it involves deducing testable hypotheses from the laws and constructs defined by the nomological network and then collecting observable data to test the hypothesis. When reporting validity data one must, therefore, clearly specify (1) the interpretation proposed—i.e., what construct one has in mind, how this construct is defined, and how the particular hypothesis tested in the study was derived from the relevant theory; (2) how adequately the interpretation was substantiated—i.e., give an evaluation of the over-all substantiation and specific segments where the hypotheses were particularly well supported and the areas where support is weak; and (3) tell why one believes he has substantiated his claims—i.e., give details of the experimental procedure and the line of reasoning taken in making inferences from the procedures to the meaning of the construct.

POSITIVE AND NEGATIVE RESULTS.   Suppose that the results of the empirical test give good reason to believe that our hypotheses have been substantiated. What do the results mean? Certainly they do not "validate" or "prove" the entire theory, the whole nomological network, because we were dealing with only a portion of that network. However, if the predictions are confirmed by the empirical results we can retain our belief that the test measures the construct and thus have more faith in our adoption[3] of the concept. And, of course, the particular relationships found in the study should both clarify the meaning of the construct and render the relevant laws more specific and definite.

What then of negative results, of the data failing to confirm the prediction? Here there are at least three possible interpretations. First, it could be that the

---

[3]Cronbach and Meehl used the term "adopt" because they believe that a construct can never be proved correct in some absolute sense but can only be adopted as the best working definition.

test does not measure the construct. Second, the theoretical framework may be in error, allowing for an incorrect inference. Third, it may be that the design of the experiment did not permit an appropriate test of the hypothesis. Unfortunately, it is not always clear which of these three possibilities is operating in a specific instance. The third, faulty experimental design, is probably easiest to detect; the other two are more likely to be confounded. Therefore, failure to obtain confirmation of one's predictions indicates that some revision is needed in the theoretical network or the experimental procedure, but the exact locus of the failure and the next step might not be clearly defined. This ambiguous interpretation of negative results is an obvious drawback of construct validity.

TESTS AS SIGNS. The picture we have presented of a formalized theory involving defined constructs and a set of specified laws is overly idealistic. Most psychological constructs and laws are vaguely and incompletely defined and nothing approaching the systematic structure implied by the nomological network is available. Yet attaining maturity as a science involves progress toward that ideal. Construct validation aids this progress because, in addition to clarifying extant constructs and laws, it may also point out relationships that henceforth went undetected. In this process the test serves as a sign (cf. Goodenough, 1949, and the introductory part of this chapter) by providing information that clarifies the nature of the behavioral domain of interest. This function of the test also explains why Thorndike and Hagen (1961) and others refer to construct validity as signifying—the test signifies the nature of the behavioral domain and thus the nature of the construct.

Methods of gathering information regarding construct validity

In construct validation, as we have described it, there is a simultaneous validation of both the construct and the theory surrounding the construct. Hence any evidence that bears on either the theory or the construct is admissible and relevant. Where content and criterion-related validity were investigated using several different techniques, construct validity can also be investigated by a wide variety of methods, including all the methods of content and criterion-related validity. These techniques can be classified in various ways (see, e.g., Cronbach & Meehl, 1955; Cronbach, 1969); in our discussion we shall group the techniques in five categories: intratest methods, intertest methods, criterion-related studies, studies involving experimental manipulation, and generalizability studies.

INTRATEST METHODS. The first class consists of techniques that study the internal structure of the test—its content, the inter-relationships between items and subtests, and the processes involved in responding to the items. Because these techniques are concerned solely with the internal structure of the test and do not consider external variables, by themselves they are not sufficient to establish the construct validity of a test. That is, they can tell us something about the nature of the construct but nothing about the relationships between the construct and other variables (i.e., about the laws in the nomological network).

One source of evidence regarding construct validity that falls within the category of intratest methods, is studies of the *content validity* of the test. The specification of the content or behavioral domain being sampled by the test, a necessary condition in content validity studies, also serves to define the nature of the construct that the test measures. For example, if in constructing a test of "verbal intelligence" (and determining its content validity), the test author defines the content universe as encompassing the ability to define the meaning of words, to reason by analogies involving verbal concepts, and to apply words in appropriate ways he has, in essence, defined his construct of "verbal intelligence." In this situation, the process of establishing the content validity of the test will also provide evidence regarding the construct validity of the test.

A second subclass of intratest methods would be studies of the *homogeneity* of the test. Here one might derive a measure of internal consistency (e.g., Kuder-Richardson coefficients), factor analyze the items, or compute some other measure of homogeneity. These homogeneity analyses aid in the definition of the construct primarily by indicating whether the test measures a single trait or is multifaceted.

On many tests we are interested not only in the content of the items but also in the processes individuals use in responding to the items. Any *process analysis* may clarify the meaning of the construct by identifying the skills, abilities, or reaction tendencies the person brings to bear in responding to the item. For example, in an algebraic word problem (such as the example given on page 78) one might find that solving the problem involved at least two steps: translating the word problem into an algebraic equation, and doing the algebraic and arithmetic manipulation necessary to solve the problem. Or, we might find that when responding to the personality inventory item "I frequently get angry when things do not go my way," many people consider both their actual behavior and the social desirability of responding positively to the item. Knowledge of the processes people use in responding to items may further clarify the nature of the construct that the test measures by indicating the variables that determine the responses to the test items. However, because it is likely that different people will have their responses determined by different variables, a process analysis may also introduce complicating elements into the picture.

INTERTEST METHODS.   In this classification we shall group all methods that consider several tests simultaneously but do not consider extratest variables. In general, these methods indicate the features that several tests share in common but do not allow direct inferences to be made regarding the relation of test scores to external variables.

The simplest method in this class, which is sometimes called *congruent validity*, is to correlate a new test with an established test For example, new intelligence tests are usually compared to the well-established individual measures, such as the Stanford-Binet or one of the Wechsler Intelligence Scales. If the correlation is high the two tests can be said to measure the same construct. Because the meaning of the older test has been established, at least tentatively, this meaning can also be attributed to scores on the newer test, and one can infer that scores on the new test will relate to other variables in the same manner as scores on the established test. The danger in this approach is that unless the two tests are highly correlated (i.e., their correlations are of the same magnitudes as their reliabilities) the factors that are operating to lower the correlation may be the relevant ones in determining the relationship between the test and the external variable and thus invalidate the inferences made on the basis of the intercorrelation between the tests.

A second approach is to perform a *factor analysis* on a group of tests. This analysis will provide several relevant bits of information. It will show which tests share common variance and thus measure the same construct. By investigating the common content of the tests loading on the same factor, one can infer the nature of the construct being tapped, and even possibly label the construct. A factor analysis will also show the extent to which each test is saturated by common factor variance and to what extent its scores depend upon specific variance. And, according to one common definition, the proportion of total variance in the test scores that is common variance is an index of construct validity.

Factor analysis is probably the most commonly used technique to establish construct validity. Many writers, in fact, designate *factorial validity*, defined as the loading of the test on the factor (construct) of concern, as a specific and major type of validity.

Closely related to the previous two approaches is Campbell's (Campbell, 1960; Campbell and Fiske, 1959) conception of *convergent validity* and *divergent validity*. According to Campbell, validation usually proceeds by convergent methods, that is, we attempt to establish that two different measurement techniques or instruments (tests) are, in fact, measuring the same construct. Factorial and congruent validity are good examples of convergent methods. But, adds Campbell, not only should a test be highly correlated with other tests purporting to measure the same construct, but it also should be uncorrelated with tests that measure distinctly different constructs. This latter point is the divergent aspect of the dichotomy. Thus, a test proposed as a measure of creativity could not be accepted as such unless scores of the test were uncorrelated with scores on an intelligence test. In other words, a valid test must measure a construct that is demonstrably independent of other established constructs. (A technique developed to investigate convergent and discriminant validity will be discussed later in the chapter.)

CRITERION-RELATED STUDIES. The nature and type of criteria that the test scores predict are another indication of the construct that the test measures. Thus data from criterion-related validity studies provide relevant information for establishing construct validity.

One common source of evidence is the ability of the test scores to separate naturally occurring or experimentally contrived groups (*group differentiation*). For example, items composing the Strong Vocational Interest Blank were selected by contrasting the responses of persons in specific occupations with a group of men-in-general. To construct a scale for physicians, Strong selected items that differentiated physicians from men-in-general; to construct a scale for real estate salesmen, he selected items that differentiated real estate salesmen from men-in-general. A scale so constructed, *ipso facto*, has concurrent validity. Or, to use a different illustration, a test proposed as a measure of creativity in art should differentiate between highly creative artists and persons whose art is stereotyped and mundane.

An alternative approach can also be used: groups can be constructed on the basis of their test scores (e.g., those scoring in the top quarter and those scoring in the bottom quarter) and the distinguishing characteristics of the groups identified. These characteristics serve to define the construct. For example, in a study using this approach Barron showed that graduate students who scored high on an Ego Strength scale were rated as being alert, adventuresome, determined, independent, [having] initiative, outspoken, persistent, reliable, resourceful, and responsible, while low scorers were rated as being affected, dependent, effeminate, mannerly, and mild. (Barron, 1963, pp. 125–126). These adjectival descriptions give the flavor of the construct being measured by the test, thus defining its nature.

Validity coefficients also provide relevant data. A test designed as a measure of scholastic aptitude should, of course, predict grades in academic subjects; a test of finger dexterity should predict success in an occupation, such as watch repairing, where fine movements are an essential job component; a test of sociopathic tendencies should predict delinquency. Confirmation or disconfirmation of these predictions would strengthen or weaken, respectively, our confidence in the test as a measure of the purported trait.

EXPERIMENTAL MANIPULATION. A fourth general class of methods involves experimentally manipulating some variable and then observing the effects on test scores. For example, suppose we define test-taking anxiety as the fear of failure on examinations, the results of which have significance for a person's self-concept. From this definition we could hypothesize that performance on an examination would be negatively related to test-taking anxiety (i.e., high anxiety produces poor performance) if the examination were structured as being important to the person—e.g., used to make some decision about his educational future—but that test-taking anxiety and examination scores would be unrelated if the test were structured so as to produce no threat to the individual (e.g., the test was presented as part of a standardization project with responses being anonymous). If such an experiment were conducted and scores on the anxiety test did have the predicted relationships with examination scores, we would have evidence that the test did, in fact, measure test-taking anxiety.

The category of experimental manipulation would also include evidence on variation resulting from naturally occurring events. For example, if the definition of the trait (construct) in question implies that the trait is exceedingly stable over time and highly resistant to environmental effects, one should obtain a high value if he computed a coefficient of stability. Here, reliability data is being used as validity evidence—another illustration of the close relationship between the two concepts. Or, if intelligence is defined so as to imply that under normal circumstances it will increase with increasing age, then a test that presumes to measure intelligence must show increasing scores as the age of the subjects taking the test increases.

GENERALIZABILITY STUDIES.   The fifth category is harder to delineate but can be referred to as studies of generalizability. Studies that fall into this category systematically study the test over a wide range of conditions or dimensions—e.g., they study the test in a variety of populations, with different administration methods, or over a variety of criteria. (cf. pp. 129-132) The systematization may be imposed through use of multivariate statistical techniques or through the data collection procedures.

Probably the clearest example of this approach is the *multitrait-multimethod matrix* proposed by Campbell and Fiske (1959). They pointed out that any test is really a trait-method unit, i.e., a test measures a given trait by a single method. Therefore, because we want to know the relative contributions of the trait and method components to the test score, we must study more than one trait and more than one method. In essence, we are studying convergent and discriminant validity—convergent validity being established by showing that the correlation between the same traits measured by different methods is high; discriminant validity being established by showing that the different traits are not highly intercorrelated, even when they are measured by the same method.

An example of a multitrait-multimethod matrix is shown in Table 6.1. This table shows the hypothetical correlations obtained when three traits (A,B,C) were measured by three different methods (1,2,3). The three traits might, for example, be independence of judgment, social sensitivity, and self-assurance as measured by three methods—self-report personality inventories, projective techniques, and peer ratings. Or the matrix might represent measures of verbal comprehension, numerical reasoning, and immediate recall as measured by a paper-and-pencil test, an individually administered test, and teacher's ratings. In short, the method can be used to study any number and variety of traits

TABLE 6.1 An example of a multitrait-multimethod matrix

	Traits	Method 1			Method 2			Method 3		
		A1	B1	C1	A2	B2	C2	A3	B3	C3
Method 1	A1	.89								
	B1	.51	.89							
	C1	.38	.37	.76						
Method 2	A2	.57	.22	.09	.93					
	B2	.22	.57	.10	.68	.94				
	C2	.11	.11	.46	.59	.58	.84			
Method 3	A3	.56	.22	.11	.67	.42	.33	.94		
	B3	.23	.58	.12	.43	.66	.34	.67	.92	
	C3	.11	.11	.45	.34	.32	.58	.58	.60	.85

Adapted from Table 1 of Campbell and Fiske, "Convergent and discriminant validation by the multitrait-multimethod matrix," Psychological Bulletin, 56, 1959, p. 82. Copyright 1959 by the American Psychological Association, and reproduced by permission.

measured by any method. Also, the number of traits and methods utilized can be any number greater than one, with the number of traits not necessarily being equal to the number of methods. The three traits and three methods used in the example are arbitrary choices.

The correlations in Table 6-1 can be divided into four categories. The correlations in the diagonal running from thet op left-hand corner to the lower right-hand corner are the reliabilities, monotrait-monomethod values representing the results of measuring the same trait by the same method. The triangles outlined by the broken lines are referred to as "heterotrait-heteromethod triangles" because they show the correlations between separate traits measured by different methods. The triangles outlined by solid lines are heterotrait-monomethod triangles, and the values within the triangles are the correlations across traits using a single method. Finally, the values in the diagonals between the heterotrait-heteromethod triangles are the validity coefficients. Validity, in this approach, means convergent validity, since the values show the correlation between the same trait measured by different methods.

Four lines of evidence from the matrix are relevant to validity. To be used as validity evidence the following requirements must be met: (1) The values in the validity diagonals, the validity coefficients, should be significantly larger than zero and high enough to encourage further study. These coefficients, of course, establish convergent validity. (2) The values of any validity coefficient should be greater than the values in the corresponding rows and columns of the adjacent heterotrait-heteromethod triangles. (3) A variable should correlate to a higher degree with an independent effort to measure the same trait than with measures of a different trait employing the same method. (4) In all heterotrait triangles, the same pattern of trait interrelationships should hold. While the first point was relevant to convergent validity, points 2-4 are directed toward discriminant validity, all showing that the interrelations between traits are not method artifacts.

Two aspects of the multitrait-multimethod matrix approach deserve further mention. First, notice that reliability is defined as the agreement between two measurements of the same trait using the same method, and validity is defined as the agreement between two measurements of the same trait using different methods. Thus the fundamental difference between reliability and validity is the similarity of the measurement methods. Second, this matrix gives evidence on the extent of the method bias by showing the degree of relationship between various traits measured using the same method. In the typical validity study it is logically impossible to separate the effects of the trait, the measurement method, and their interaction.

An example of construct validation

As construct validity is a relatively new concept, and the procedures utilized are not as familiar and direct as other methods discussed so far, it may be helpful to consider, in some detail, an example of how evidence on construct validity might be gathered. As an illustration we have chosen Barron's development of the Ego-strength Scale. This example was chosen because (1) a variety of types of evidence was utilized, (2) the development represented a blending of theory and empiricism, (3) the process illustrates how the test served as a sign to point out the nature of the behavioral domain, and (4) the process is described, in even greater detail, in an accessible source (Barron, 1963, Chapters 9 and 10) so that the reader who wishes can consult the original source.

Barron's original goal was to build a scale that would predict which psychoneurotic persons would respond favorably to psychotherapy. Thus he administered the Minnesota Multiphasic Personality Inventory (MMPI), a collection of 550 personality items, to a group of patients prior to therapy. After therapy the group was divided into two subgroups: those rated improved and those rated as unimproved. Using improvement as a criterion, an item analysis was conducted, and 68 items selected for the Scale. Odd-even reliability and a coefficient of stability were calculated and found to be of an acceptable level. Barron then classified the items into rational groups and attempted to summarize the content of the scale—in essence he performed a content analysis. On the basis of this analysis, and other data such as a study of adjectives rated descriptive of persons obtaining high and low scores on the Scale, Barron postulated that the test measured something broader than response to psychotherapy, that it measured Ego-strength. He also proposed a tentative description of Ego-strength.

Given that the test measured Ego-strength (Es), Barron predicted that scores on the Es scale would relate in certain ways to other variables. He tested these relationships in various groups and, in most instances, his predictions were confirmed. For example, he hypothesized that Es and measures of intellectual ability would be moderately positively correlated and found such relationships (r's = .35.-.50). He also correlated Es with characteristics exhibited in social interactions—self-confidence, drive, submissiveness—and found the correlation with variables such as tolerance (r = .40), ethnocentrism (r = $-.40$), and measures of psychopathology (r's = $-.50$ to $-.60$). These relationships were viewed as supporting his interpretation of the Es scale.

Barron also cross-validated the Es scale with three separate groups of psychotherapy patients, obtaining validity coefficients of .42, .54, and .38 in the three groups.

At this point Barron defined Ego-strength as a construct expressed in characteristics such as physiological stability and good health, a strong sense of reality, feelings of personal adequacy and vitality, permissive morality, lack of ethnic prejudice, emotional outgoingness and spontaneity, and intelligence.

From this definition certain implications and hypotheses were drawn and then tested in further studies using various groups of normal subjects. Es scores were related to a variety of variables, including intellectual performance, spatial orientation, ability to play Charades, performance in the Asch experiment, and courage under fire in the Korean war. A cluster analysis to determine the item groupings was also conducted.

Although far from exhausting the possible relationships and studies, and being collected in a somewhat unsystematic manner, these data all serve to clarify the meaning of the construct Ego-strength. In addition they provide the basis for a set of laws relating Ego-strength to other concepts. Thus they are a good beginning for the continual process of validating the Es scale as a measure of the construct "Ego-strength."

Evaluation of construct validity

Reactions to the concept of construct validity have ranged over the entire spectrum. Some writers (e.g., Loevinger 1957) feel that the construct validity is the essence of validity and that all other concepts of validity can be subsumed under construct validity. At the other extreme we find those who vigorously attack the notion (e.g., Bechtoldt, 1959; Ebel, 1961), primarily on the grounds that construct validity violates the canons of operationalism. In between are those who approve of the idea but suggest some modifications. For example,

Jessor and Hammond (1957) point out that the theory surrounding the construct plays an important part in test construction, and thus the concepts and methods of construct validity should be applied to test construction as well as validation. Campbell (1960) suggests that there are really two varieties of construct validity: *trait validity* and *nomological validity*, with the former focusing on the trait (construct) and the latter concerned with the test as representing a term in a formal theoretical network.

Probably the greatest contribution the concept of construct validity has made to psychological testing is to focus attention on psychological tests as instruments of psychological theory. Thus tests are viewed in broader perspective than solely as tools to aid in practical decision making. Even when no formal theory is involved, construct validity forces the investigator to precisely define the trait being measured and to specify the relationships expected between test scores and other variables. It has also placed an emphasis on collecting a variety of data to support one's claims, rather than to rely on only one technique. Finally, it has suggested a systematic way to proceed with validation when "hard" data that bear directly on the construct are not abundantly available.

Construct validity also has several disadvantages. One result of its introduction was that many persons have tried to pawn off sloppy evidence as indications of construct validity. This, however, is more a fault of the investigator than of the concept. Second, the necessary operational steps and procedures are sometimes rather hazy. For example, negative evidence has several possible interpretations, and no clear indication is presented of which way to proceed after obtaining negative evidence. Third, there is no summary statement or index to describe the degree of validity. Although the proportion of variance attributable to the trait being measured would appear to be a simple, quantitative index of construct validity, in reality such an index is unobtainable unless the permissible methods are limited to factor analytic techniques. Fourth, unless all parties agree upon the definition of the constructs and the theoretical structure, the results of various studies will not be comparable. In a field such as psychology, where terms are frequently only vaguely defined, it is not unusual for the same term to be applied to different concepts and the same construct to be given different names by different authors. Unless there is agreement on basic terms, the investigators will just talk past each other. And finally, the process of construct validation as proposed by Cronbach and Meehl (1955), with its stress on the nomological network, may be unnecessarily complex. It may be that something more akin to Campbell's (1960) concept of trait validity provides a more workable framework.

FIVE POINTS WORTH RE-EMPHASIS

We will end the discussion of validity by emphasizing several ideas which, though implied throughout the discussion, may not have emerged as independent points. First, for any given test, any or all of the types of validity may be relevant and desirable. For example, the typical achievement test is evaluated primarily in terms of its content validity. But as achievement tests usually also serve, at least implicitly, as predictors of success in the next unit or course in the sequence, their ability to demonstrate criterion-related (predictive) validity may also be required. Or a test of divergent thinking could be evaluated in terms of its sampling of the various facets of divergent thinking (content validity), its ability to predict success in occupations or academic curricula requiring divergent thinking (criterion-related validity), and its role as a defining construct in a theory of intellectual organization (construct validity). Two corollaries follow from this position: (1) validity will always be situation specific, and (2) any test will have many different validities.

Second, although the various concepts of validity can be classified or organized in numerous ways—for example, the tripartite division used in this book—there are basically two major questions asked in validity studies: (1) How effective is the test as an aid to decision making? and (2) What is the nature of the variable measured by the test? Criterion-related validity data are generally used to evaluate the test's effectiveness as a decision-making aid. The question of the nature of the variable measured by the test is answered by evidence from studies of construct validity. Content validity can, without too many difficulties, be subsumed under construct validity.

Third, although validity is usually discussed in connection with the final form of a test, the basic philosophy of validity plays an integral role in the test construction process. The pool of potential test items is composed of items that point to some important construct, sample some relevant content or behavioral domain, or are presumed to be predictive of the relevant criteria. Items included on the final form of the test are selected from this pool of potential items on the basis of their content or criterion-related validity. Items not meeting certain requirements dictated by the nature of the trait measured (e.g., ones which reduce homogeneity) are eliminated. Thus, in many ways, the concepts and procedures of validity enter into the test construction process.

Fourth, not all types of validity that have been proposed were included in our discussion. In particular, two types—synthetic validity and incremental validity—that are of some importance were not discussed. *Synthetic validity* (Balma, 1959) is the process of inferring validity in a specific situation from a logical analysis of job elements. The basic procedure involves three steps: identifying the essential elements in a job or groups of jobs, determining the validity of tests in measuring these elements, and combining the elemental validities into a composite validity. This procedure, which is most commonly used in industrial and business settings, would appear most valuable in the initial stages of developing a testing program, where one is interested in identifying relevant criteria and potential predictors. As the rational portion of the procedure lends itself to empirical confirmation, synthetic validity would seem to be an aspect of criterion-related validity.

Incremental validity (Sechrest, 1963) stresses the fact that the validity of a test is determined by its unique contribution to predictive efficiency, that a test is valid to the extent that it produces an increment in predictive accuracy. The idea of incremental validity is, of course, consistent with the philosophy of this book (cf. page 104). Because the concept of incremental validity is easier to illustrate with multiple measures, its introduction will be postponed until Chapter 8.

Fifth, and finally, we will once again emphasize the relationship between reliability, homogeneity, and validity. Reliability, of both the predictor and criterion, limits criterion-related validity. Reliability and homogeneity data both were relevant information in construct validity. Taking a broad view, one could place reliability, homogeneity, and validity all under the tent of measures of generalizability, the only difference between the concepts being the dimensions over which generalizations are made.

Summary

This chapter discussed the concepts of content validity and construct validity. Content validity is the extent to which the items included on a test are a representative sample of the important and relevant elements of a well-specified content or behavioral universe. It is relevant when one wishes to make inferences about a person's expected performance in a universe of situations of which the test is but a sample.

The adjective "content" refers to the fact that sampling typically is of content, the substantive constituents of the universe. The sampling from the universe is representative, not random; that is, the distribution of items on the test should parallel the emphasis on the various components in the universe. Although content validity is generally applied to achievement tests, it can appropriately be used in any domain where a well-defined universe of content, skills, or behaviors can be circumscribed.

The process of evaluating content validity is rational and judgmental, and attempts to rate the adequacy of sampling. Suggestions for improving the objectivity of the process were discussed. It was also pointed out that a test having high content validity, when judged according to the test constructor's definition of the content universe, may not be useful in a situation where the relevant universe is described differently.

Construct validity attempts to answer the questions: What variable(s) is the test measuring? How well does the test measure the pertinent variables? Thus the focus is on the trait (construct) that the test measures. Although no quantitative index of construct validity is available, the proportion of variance in test scores that is attributable to the trait measured by the test could be used as such an index.

A construct is conceptualized as a defining term in an interlocking network (the nomological network) of constructs and laws that constitute a psychological theory. The test is the operational measure of the construct. Thus the process of construct validation consists of: (1) making certain predictions on the basis of the definition of the construct and its related laws, (2) checking these predictions through the collection of empirical data, and (3) modifying the theory—constructs and laws—on the basis of the empirical results. Positive results serve to strengthen the laws or clarify the meaning of the constructs; negative evidence results in rejection or revision of the theory.

The primary goal in construct validity studies is to provide clearer definitions of psychological constructs. The validation process proceeds by the accumulation of evidence. Five general data collection methods were discussed: (1) intratest measures—e.g., content validity, homogeneity; (2) intertest measures—e.g., factor analysis; (3) criterion-related validity studies; (4) studies involving experimental manipulation; and (5) generalizability studies—e.g., the multitrait-multimethod matrix.

An example of the process of construct validation, Barron's development and validation of the Ego-strength Scale, was given. The role of construct validity in psychological theory was emphasized throughout the discussion.

Suggestions for further reading

Bechtoldt, H. P. Construct validity: a critique. *American Psychologist*, 1959, 14, 619–629. A criticism of construct validity from the point of view of logical positivism.

Campbell, D. T. Recommendations for APA test standards regarding construct trait or discriminant validity. *American Psychologist*, 1960, 15, 546–553. Campbell proposes that tests be evaluated not only in terms of what their scores correlate with but also in terms of the variables with which test scores do not correlate.

Campbell, D. T., & D. W. Fiske. Convergent and discriminant validation by the multitrait-multimethod matrix. *Psychological Bulletin*, 1959, 56, 81–105. Presentation of a method of test validation that differentiates between relationships attributable to traits and those attributable to methods of measuring the traits.

Cronbach, L. J., & P. E. Meehl. Construct validity and psychological tests. *Psychological Bulletin*, 1955, 52, 281–302. The classic paper describing the concept of construct validity.

Ebel, R. L. Obtaining and reporting evidence on content validity. *Educational and Psychological Measurement*, 1956, 16, 269–282. A discussion of the types of evidence used to determine the content validity of a test.

Ebel, R. L. Must all tests be valid? *American Psychologist*, 1961, 16, 640–647. Ebel raises the question as to whether validity is a necessary concept or whether knowledge of reliability and what the test covers is sufficient.

Kerlinger, F. M. *Foundations of behavioral research*. New York: Holt, Rinehart and Winston, Inc., 1965. Chap. 25 briefly discusses construct validity in nontechnical terms.

Loevinger, J. Objective tests as instruments of psychological theory. *Psychological Reports*, 1957, Monograph supplement 9. An extensive and involved discussion of the roles that psychological tests play in specifying concepts which might be used in building psychological theory.

Royce J. R. Factors as theoretical constructs. *American Psychologist*, 1963, 18, 522–528. A discussion of the reality of factors as defined by factor analysis and their role as theoretical constructs.

Scores and norms

Chapter 7

INTRODUCTION

After a test is administered, each individual's responses are compared with a predetermined key to obtain his score on the test. Usually this score is expressed as the number of items agreeing with the keyed responses. For tests with definable correct responses, such as achievement and ability tests, the keyed responses are the correct answers; for tests with no "correct" responses, such as interest and personality inventories, the keyed responses are the predominant choices of a particular criterion group. Sometimes other scores are used—e.g., the number of errors, the number of correct responses minus some proportion of the incorrect responses, the time taken to complete the test, or a rating on some scale of quality. These scores, obtained directly from the test, are called *raw scores*.

A raw score takes on meaning only in its relation to the performance of a relevant group of comparable individuals. To illustrate, suppose that a test consisting of 100 items requiring the multiplication of two one-digit numbers is administered to a class of fourth-grade students. Using as the (raw) score the number of items answered correctly, Johnny scores 75. Is this a high, average, or low score? Without knowing how other students in the class performed and without knowing whether they scored higher or lower than Johnny, we cannot ascribe much meaning to his score. But, by comparing Johnny's score to the scores of other class members, we can determine Johnny's ranking in the class and thus interpret his score.

Interpretation of an individual's test score, then, proceeds by a comparison of his performance to the performance of some reference group, called a *norm group.* Tables showing the performance of a group or various groups on a test are called *norm tables* or, more simply, *norms*. The norms used to interpret a given score will depend on the person being tested and the purpose for which the testing is done. In all cases, the individual's scores will be compared to a group of people who are, in some way, similar to him, either by possessing certain characteristics in common or by being his prospective competitors.

The interpretation of test scores by use of norm groups emphasizes an important aspect of psychological measurement, i.e., that *psychological measurement is relative rather than absolute.* As mentioned above, there are few situations in psychological measurement where absolute standards have been developed. In the example cited there is, in one sense, the possibility of an absolute standard. Because there are only 100 possible permutations of two one-digit numbers we could say that Johnny knew 75 percent of the material. And, as the total universe of potential items is circumscribed, and in this case all items were included on the test, we have, in effect, an absolute standard of comparison. But to determine if 75 percent is a good, average, or poor performance for a child of his age, education, and training in multiplication, we would have to know how other children of similar age, education, and training in multiplication performed. In other words, we would have to compare his performance to a norm group of his peers.

In other instances we are interested in an individual's relative performance on a number of tests. We might like to know, for example, whether a student scored higher on the verbal or quantitative section of an aptitude test; whether his interests are more similar to those of accountants, engineers, or lawyers; or whether his knowledge of word meanings is superior to his comprehension of the meaning of sentences and paragraphs. In these circumstances one must first obtain some index of performance, in comparison to a relevant norm group, on each test separately and then compare scores of the various tests. So, even when the primary interest is in intraindividual comparisons, the individual's test scores must be compared to those of other people.[1]

A second essential element for interpreting test scores is sufficient validity data. Unless validity data are available, unless there is adequate evidence as to what the test measures or predicts, then a person's score, even when compared to a norm group, tells us nothing more than his ranking in the group. In the absence of validity data there is no way to know what the test measures and thus no meaningful way to interpret scores on the test. Though this point may seem obvious it is frequently overlooked. Too often test users assume that test scores provide useful information because (1) the test title infers that the test measures some important characteristic and (2) norm data are available. But unless there

---

[1]When an individual's score is interpreted by comparing his performance with that of a relevant norm group, the measurement is called *normative;* when the scores have meaning only in relation to a preference hierarchy within a particular individual (such as tests where the individual has to choose between alternatives, both of which are scored but on different scales), the measurement is called *ipsative.* This distinction will be considered further in Chapter 12.

are adequate validity data, unless there is evidence that the test measures a particular trait or is related to some criterion, attributing meaning to test scores on the basis of norm data alone is gratuitous.

To summarize, *there are two essentials for meaningful test interpretation: (1) validity data indicating what trait the test measures or what criteria it predicts and (2) adequate normative data. Accurate interpretation of test scores is impossible without both types of information.*

NORMS

A norm group provides a basis of comparison by showing the test performance of a standard group. Norm data are usually presented in the form of a table, a *norm table*, that shows the proportion of the norm group obtaining each test score or scoring within various ranges. For any test there are a number of different groups that could potentially be used as norm groups. So, in developing norms, the first question becomes: What are the meaningful groups to use?

Looking at the problem from the test developer's viewpoint, the question becomes: With what groups is the test designed to be used? The norm groups should be chosen to represent these groups. If the test is designed to assess high school seniors' aptitude for college work, the norm groups should consist of high school seniors considering college. If the test is designed to measure the personality characteristics of adult women, the basic norm group would consist of a cross-section of adult women. If the test is designed to measure the reading readiness of kindergarten students, the norm group should consist of kindergarten students who have not begun reading instruction. If the test has more than one purpose, or is designed for use with various groups (as most tests are), more than one norm group will be needed.

The test user looks at the norms from a slightly different vantage point. Because he is using the test with a particular group and for a specific purpose, his primary question is: Which of the available norm groups is most appropriate? Here again, as with the test developer, several norm groups may be directly relevant. For example, when counseling a high school student regarding his plans to study engineering in college, if the relevant norm data are available, the counselor may compare the student's scholastic aptitude scores to (1) high school students planning to attend college, (2) high school students planning to study engineering, (3) students at the several universities the student is thinking of attending, and (4) students enrolled in engineering curricula in the universities the student is thinking of attending.

Considerations in building and evaluating norm groups

The test developer, user, or reviewer must consider several factors when constructing or evaluating norm groups. The first requirement is that *the nature of the norm groups be clearly defined.* The general specifications of the norm groups will be dictated by the purposes and uses of the test, but within this range there is a wide variety of potential norm groups. Therefore a concise, yet clear, description of the nature and characteristics of the group is necessary. A statement that the norm group is composed of "5000 college freshmen" will not suffice; rather a statement of the following nature is needed:

> The norm group consists of entering freshmen, male and female, enrolled in liberal arts curricula at land-grant universities.

This statement would represent a minimum statement—it would be desirable to further spell out the defining characteristics of the group—What exactly is an "entering freshman"? What curricula are subsumed under the label "liberal arts"? What constitutes the population of land-grant universities and what are the characteristics of these universities?

If the norm group is composed of people in a particular job or occupation, the title of the job should be listed, its code in the *Dictionary of Occupational Titles* given or the job duties detailed, and the type of business or industry, the geographic location, years of experience of the workers, and other relevant information included. For achievement tests, relevant information would include the grade level and age of the students, the type of school, the average intellectual ability of the students, and their experience in the subject matter area being tested.

A corollary consideration is whether various subgroups of the population perform differentially on the test. If the subgroups do exhibit different levels or ranges of performance, then separate norm groups should be constructed for each subgroup. For example, men perform better than women on tests of mechanical aptitude and, conversely, women score higher than men on clerical aptitude tests. Both types of tests, therefore, generally provide separate normative data for men and women. Other variables that frequently are related to test performance and thus may constitute the basis of separate norm groups include age, education, socioeconomic status, intelligence, occupation, geographic region, and the amount of special training.

In most instances the norm group is composed of a sample drawn from the relevant population rather than the entire population. Thus the second requirement is that *the norm group be a representative sample of the population.* If a test is designed for use with third-grade students, the norm group should be representative of third graders—it should include proportionate numbers of urban and rural students, students of various races, students from both high and low socioeconomic areas, students from various areas of the country, and so forth. Failure to provide a representative sample will, of course, bias the norm data and make interpretation of scores difficult. Since data are often easier to obtain from certain subgroups of the population (e.g., it is easier to get data from high socioeconomic status suburban schools than from ghetto schools and easier to collect a sample of college students than 18-year-olds who are working), the possibility of biased sampling is ever present.

Implicit in the previous paragraph is the requirement that the sampling procedure be clearly defined. Thus, to return to our previous example, the description of the sampling, and thus the norm group, might be:

> The norm group consisted of 5000 entering freshmen tested in the first week of classes in September 1968; 250 students (125 male and 125 female) were randomly selected from students enrolled in liberal arts curricula at each of 20 land-grant universities; universities were randomly selected from among all land-grant institutions.

As with the description of the population, the more precise and comprehensive the description the better.

The absolute size of the norm group is of less importance than the representativeness of the sampling of the parent population. Certainly a minimum-sized group is necessary for stability but a smaller, better-selected group is always more desirable than larger, vaguely-defined norm groups. It is impossible to specify exactly how large any particular norm group should be. Because the stability of the data is inversely proportional to the size of the (norm) group, the larger the groups the more consistent the results. For any standardized test it is not unreasonable to expect several hundred cases in each sampling cell, depending on the degree of precision needed; other tests will require samples of various size. (For a discussion of the relation between sample size and stability of sample statistics see Hays, 1963, or Edwards, 1969.)

A final consideration is *the recency of the norms*. With rapid changes in education and job requirements, norms that were developed a number of years ago may no longer be relevant. Because complex materials are now being introduced at lower grade levels, the present-day student has been exposed to more and different materials than his counterparts of previous years. Job requirements have changed radically and, consequently, so have the skills of the workers. Norms should periodically be updated and old norms looked upon with appropriate scepticism.

Local norms

The test user, when considering the various norm groups available, may find that none fits his purposes precisely. Or he may want to utilize a more restrictive group than the norm groups given in the test manual which are, of necessity, usually rather broad in scope. For instance, the classroom teacher may want to compare the performance of each of her students not only to the national norms given in the manual but also to other students in her class or in the local school system. In each of these situations, one solution would be to construct *local norms*.

The advantage of the local norm group is, of course, that it allows comparisons between a person's scores and those of his immediate associates. As each class, school, company, or group is in some ways unique, so will its members differ in some, possibly important, ways from the members of the norm groups listed in the manual. Therefore the test performance of the local group may be different from the national norm groups, and reliance on the latter might lead to improper inferences. For example, in any individual school the students in a particular grade or class will not have had educational experiences equivalent to those of students in the national norm group. The local students also will probably differ from the national norm group on factors that are related to school achievement—factors such as the educational and socioeconomic background of their families. When such differences obtain between the local and national norm groups, the local group may well represent a better standard of comparison.

The test user has still one further option—he can use both local and national norms. This approach will, of course, extract the maximal amount of information from the test scores.

TYPES OF SCORES

The first step in the interpretation of test scores is to express the raw scores on another scale, one that provides a basis for interpreting an individual's score. In this section we will consider five classes of scores: content scales, percentiles, standard scores, developmental scales, and ratios and quotients. These scales vary in the assumptions made about the nature of the underlying measurement scale. For example, percentiles are essentially rankings and thus assume an ordinal measurement scale; standard scores are based on a standard unit, the standard deviation, and thus assume an interval scale; the various quotients assume, at least implicitly, a ratio scale. In our discussion of each scale type we will consider the rationale of the scale, consider its advantages and disadvantages, discuss the varieties of scores falling within the category, and illustrate how each type is computed.

Content scales

Content scales compare an individual's performance to a standard defined by the content of the test. In essence, they compare an individual's performance to some ideal performance; in this sense, they represent the closest approximation to an absolute scoring scale available in educational and psychological testing. Because the idea of perfect performance cannot be meaningfully defined for typical performance measures, content scales are only applicable to tests of maximal performance. They are used infrequently—only with achievement tests.

The simplest type of content scale would be the percentage correct, that is:

$$\text{Percentage correct} = \frac{\text{items correct}}{\text{total items}} \times 100\% \qquad (7.1)$$

This score, obviously, tells what proportion of the test items the individual answered correctly and, because of its computational ease and superficial meaningfulness, has a certain appeal. Reflection, however, indicates that scores derived in this manner are highly dependent on the properties of the test items. A score of 85 percent, for example, would be interpreted differently if the test items were quite difficult or exceedingly simple. Interpretation is further complicated by the fact that, except in certain special cases where items are differentially weighted according to their difficulties, two persons can obtain the same score by answering questions of varying difficulty. For example, on a 100-item test one person might obtain a score of 60 percent by answering the 60 easiest items, while another might obtain the same score by answering some easy and some difficult items. In this situation one could argue that, even though the scores of the two individuals were equal, their knowledge was not equivalent.

Ebel (1962) has proposed that more use be made of what he calls *content standard test scores*. The term "content" implies that the scores are based directly on the tasks that make up the content of the test, i.e., on the level of performance or skills the student exhibits. This emphasis, which is characteristic of all content scales, contrasts with the usual procedure that compares the student's performance, not to the content of the test, but rather to the performance of other individuals. By "standard," Ebel means both that the scores are expressed on a common scale (the percent of the maximal possible score) and, more importantly, that the process of test construction, administration, and scoring are standardized (cf. Chapter 1). Ebel's point is not that content scores should be substituted for normative scores, but that content and normative scores should be utilized in conjunction with each other.

Obviously the crucial step in constructing any content scale is to clearly specify and unambiguously delineate the content domain sampled by the test. Given these specifications, evidence on how well the test meets the specifications (its content validity) and knowledge of the psychometric properties of the test items (e.g., their difficulty, reliability), one could interpret scores in terms of content. Alternatively, the interpretation process could start with the total score on the test. By specifying the types of items answered correctly or incorrectly by the typical person attaining each of several score levels, an individual's score can be interpreted in terms of the skills or difficulty of the problem solved that typify persons at his score level.

The major advantage of content scores is, of course, that they are interpreted in terms of content—in terms of the level of performance (difficulty) or skills that the individual has mastered. Thus content scores give a direct indication of the present level of skill and mastery, rather than a relative ranking within some group. For most purposes focusing on the development of the individual (e.g., schooling), this is exactly the type of evidence that is most relevant. The major disadvantage is that content and difficulty cannot be specified as unambiguously as the model might suggest. Except for relatively limited tasks (e.g., the multiplication of two-digit numbers) specification of the content universe is exceedingly complex. Also, the difficulty gradient in most tests is such that students do not pass all items up to a given level of difficulty, and then fail the remainder, the more difficult items; rather they miss some easier items and pass some harder ones. Therefore, interpreting test scores by saying that a student has mastered the subject matter to a given level of difficulty is an approximation, not a definitive statement.[2]

Percentiles

The most widely-used method of expressing test scores is the *percentile rank*. The percentile rank of a given score can be defined as *the percentage of persons in the appropriate reference (norm) group who obtain lower scores*. The percentile rank thus indicates the percentage of people in the norm group whose scores fall below a given score. When applied to an individual's score, the percentile rank gives the person's rank in the norm group, expressed in terms of percentages. Thus a percentile rank of 78 indicates that 78 percent of the people in the norm group scored lower than the score in question. Or, if a raw score of 26 on a test is equivalent to a percentile rank of 5, then 5 percent of the people in the norm group will have obtained scores lower than 26.

The steps in Table 7.1 show the procedures for computing percentile ranks and points.[3] The data are the scores of one class of entering freshmen women in a college of liberal arts at a midwestern university. The test score used is the composite score on a scholastic aptitude test. The numbers of the procedural steps correspond to the numbers of the columns in the table.

GRAPHIC PROCEDURES.   Percentile ranks and points can also be obtained using graphic procedures. For example, we could plot the *CP* values (Step 4) on a graph (see Figure 7.1) and obtain a curve, called an *ogive*. From this curve

---

[2]Difficulty, too, is a normative, not an absolute, measure. That is, the difficulty of an item is defined by proportion of people in a given population who pass (or fail) the item. In another population a different proportion of people would probably pass the item and, consequently, a different difficulty would be assigned to an item. Therefore, interpretation of items in terms of difficulty of content mastered is still a relativistic interpretation.

[3]The table shows only one method of computing percentile ranks. (For other methods see e.g., Ebel, 1965, Chap. 8; Ghiselli, 1964, Chap. 4; Cronbach, 1960, Chap. 4.)

TABLE 7.1 Computation of percentile ranks and points

Percentile ranks

(1) Prepare a frequency (F) distribution of the scores. (See Chapter 1 Appendix for details.)

(2) Find the cumulative frequency (CF), the number of persons scoring lower than the score in question, by summing the frequencies (F) of each score below the score in question. E.g., the CF for a score of 20 equals the number of people scoring 19 or below, or $3 + 0 + 1$ or 4.

(3) A percentile rank is the proportion of people scoring below a given score. As test scores are discrete when theoretically we have a continuous scale (see page 15), we correct for discontinuity by finding the cumulative frequency to the mid-point (CF_{mp}) of the score interval by adding one-half the number of scores in the interval to CF, or

$$CF_{mp} = CF + .5f_i$$

where $f_i =$ frequency of the particular score.

E.g., for a score of 20, $CF_{mp} = 4 + (.5 \times 5) = 6.5$

(4) Find the cumulative proportion (CP) by dividing CF_{mp} by N, the total number of cases. In this example, divide by 177. For a score of 20:

$$CP = \frac{CF_{mp}}{N} = \frac{6.5}{177} = .037$$

(5) To find the percentile ranks multiply CP by 100.

	(1)	(2)	(3)	(4)	(5)
Raw score	F	CF	CF_{mp}	CP	Percentile rank
33	0	177	177.0	1.000	100
32	4	173	175.0	.989	99
31	7	166	169.5	.958	96
30	17	149	157.5	.890	89
29	22	127	138.0	.780	78
28	18	109	118.0	.667	67
27	28	81	95.0	.537	54
26	15	66	73.5	.415	42
25	22	44	55.0	.311	31
24	14	30	37.0	.209	21
23	8	22	26.0	.147	15
22	6	16	19.0	.107	11
21	7	9	12.5	.071	7
20	5	4	6.5	.037	4
19	3	1	2.5	.014	1
18	0	1	1.0	.006	1
17	1	0	0.5	.003	1
	177				

Table 7.1 (continued)

Percentile points

A *percentile point* is the point on the raw score scale corresponding to a given division of the proportions of cases. For example, the percentile point corresponding to a percentile rank of 80 is that point on the raw score scale that divides the top 20 percent of the distribution from the remaining 80 percent. To find this point, note that:

Raw score	CP
30	.890
29	.780

and, by interpolation percentile point 80 equals:

$$PP_{80} = 29.0 + \frac{(.800 - .780)}{(.890 - .780)} = 29.0 + \frac{(.020)}{(.110)}$$

$$= 29.0 + .18 = 29.2$$

or, a raw score of 29.2 is equivalent to a percentile point of 80. Other percentile points can be found in an analogous manner.

we could read percentile points directly or, if we were using grouped data (class intervals greater than one unit), we could obtain equivalent percentile ranks for each score point by interpolating from the graph.

PERCENTILE POINTS. In computing percentile ranks we found the proportion of individuals who scored lower than a given test score. In other words, the

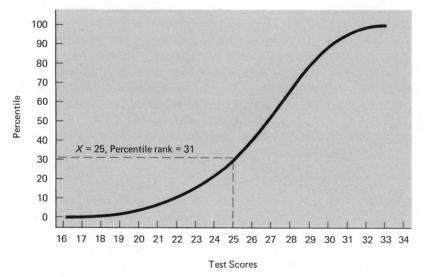

Figure 7.1 Graphic method of determining percentile points.

direction of movement was from test scores to the distribution of people. Sometimes, however, the question is what test score divides the distribution into certain proportions. For example, we may wish to know what is the minimum score needed to be in the top 20 percent of the distribution. Essentially we are trying to find the test score corresponding to a percentile rank of 80. This can be done by finding the cumulative proportion associated with each raw score, then interpolating to find the point of the score scale corresponding to the appropriate percentile rank. (See example in Table 7.1.) The point on the score scale corresponding to the desired percentile rank is called a *percentile point*, or frequently a *percentile*.

DECILES. Percentile points divide the score distribution into 100 equal parts. In many circumstances, however, such fine distinctions are not needed and dividing the distribution into a smaller number of segments—e.g., fourths, fifths, or tenths—may be sufficient. Of these divisions, tenths are most frequently used, and the score points dividing the distribution into tenths are referred to as *deciles*. As deciles divide the distribution into ten equal segments by cutting at the 10th, 20th . . . 90th percentile points, computing deciles is the same as computing the 10th, 20th . . . 90th percentile points. In essence, deciles provide a ten-step ranking scale, with each step containing 10 percent of the scores.

EVALUATION OF PERCENTILES. One advantage of using percentiles is the ease with which they can be understood—knowing a person's relative ranking in a relevant comparison group is, to most persons, a simple, direct, and meaningful index of performance. Also, for many purposes, ranking of individuals within a group is sufficient precision, and thus more complex transformations are not needed.

Percentile ranks also have two major limitations. First, they are ranks and thus constitute measurement on an ordinal scale, which does not guarantee equal sized units, and so they cannot legitimately be added, subtracted, multiplied, or divided. This may not be a serious limitation to the person interpreting a test but can be a serious liability to anyone doing research utilizing test scores. A second characteristic of percentiles is of more concern to the test user. As percentiles ranks have a rectangular distribution and test scores generally approximate the normal curve, the units on the two scales are not directly comparable. Rather small raw score differences near the center of the distribution produce relatively large percentile differences; conversely, large raw score differences at the extremes of the distribution produce only small percentile differences. (See Figure 7.2.) Unless these relations between raw scores and percentile ranks are kept in mind, differences between percentile ranks can easily be misinterpreted—in particular, seemingly large differences in percentile ranks near the center of the distribution tend to be overinterpreted.

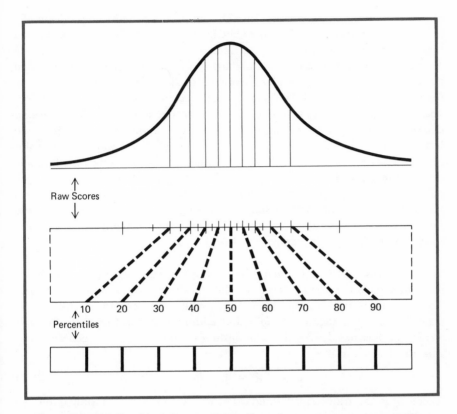

Figure 7.2 Relationship between distribution of raw scores and percentile ranks.

Standard scores

Percentile scores, being ranks, represent measurement on an ordinal scale. For several reasons, but particularly when further statistical analyses are to be made of test scores, it would be valuable to have scores expressed on an interval scale— i.e., to have a scoring scale whose units were all of equal size. There is a class of scores, called *standard scores*, that possess this property. The basic unit of all standard score systems is the standard deviation; hence the label "standard scores."

Any standard score is basically *the deviation of a raw score from the mean, expressed in standard deviation units:*

$$z = \frac{X - \bar{X}}{s} \tag{7.2}$$

where z = a standard score, X = a specified raw score, and $\bar{X}$ = the mean and s = the standard deviation of the raw score distribution. When transmuting raw scores into standard scores (z) we change from a scale having a mean of $\overline{X}$ and a standard deviation of s into a scale having a mean of 0, a standard deviation of one unit, and whose unit of measurement is the standard deviation.

Several properties of such a standard score system should be noted. First, the absolute value of the standard score will indicate the distance of the score from the mean of the distribution. Second, scores above the mean will have positive signs, and scores below the mean, negative signs. Third, because standard scores are expressed on an interval scale, they unquestionably can be subjected to the common arithmetic manipulations. Fourth, because the transformation of raw scores to standard scores was linear, the shape of the distribution of standard scores will be similar to that of the raw scores—i.e., if the raw score distribution was approximately normal so will be the distribution of z scores; if the raw score distribution was skewed, so will be the distribution of z scores. Finally, if the distribution of raw scores approaches normality the range of z scores will be from approximately -3 to $+3$.

$\mathcal{Z}$ SCORES. Although z scores have the advantage of being on an interval scale, they have the disadvantage of involving decimals and negative numbers. To avoid these difficulties z scores are usually transformed to still another scale, taking advantage of the fact that adding a constant or multiplying by a constant does not destroy the relationships within the scale. In general terms, this transformation is:

$$\mathcal{Z} = A + Bz \qquad (7.3)$$

where $\mathcal{Z}$ is the transformed standard score, A and B are constants, and z is defined in Formula (7.2) above. The distribution of scores on this new scale will have a mean of A and a standard deviation of B, but the relationships between scores will be the same as if they were expressed as z scores.

Although any value of A and B can be used, the recommended procedure (APA, 1966) is to set the mean (A) equal to 50 and the standard deviation (B) equal to 10, thus:

$$\mathcal{Z} = 50 + 10z \qquad (7.4)$$

This transformation is designed to eliminate decimals and negative numbers and to express scores on a scale having, in a normal distribution, a range of approximately 60 points (20–80). Other transformations can, of course, be made using any mean and standard deviation that are appropriate and desirable.

An example of the computation of $\mathcal{Z}$ scores is given in Table 7.2. The basic data are the same as those in Table 7.1.

NORMALIZED STANDARD SCORES. One disadvantage of the standard score system described above is that the shape of the distributions of $\mathcal{Z}$ scores and raw scores will be the same. If the distribution of standard scores were normal in

TABLE 7.2 Computation of standard scores

(1) Compute the mean ($\overline{X}$) and standard deviation (s) for the score distribution. (See Chapter 1 Appendix for details.)
Computations from the data in the Table show $\overline{X} = 26.36$ with $s = 3.09$ points.
(2) For each raw score, find $x = X - \overline{X}$, the deviation from the mean.
(3) Find $z = x/s$ for each score. This step converts the raw scores to a scale with the standard deviation as the unit of measurement. Each score is now expressed as a number of s units from the mean
(4) To get rid of negative numbers and decimals, z scores are usually transformed to another scale with an arbitrary $\overline{X}$ and s. The recommended procedure is to set $X = 50$ and $s = 10$. To transform the scores use the formula: $Z = 50 + 10z$. For example, for a raw score of 27: $Z = 50 + 10\ (.2) = 52$, and for a raw score of 19: $Z = 50 + 10\ (-2.4) = 26$.

Raw score	(2) $x = X - \overline{X}$	(3) $z = x/s$	(4) $Z =$
32	5.64	1.83	68
31	4.64	1.50	65
30	3.64	1.18	62
29	2.64	0.85	58
28	1.64	0.53	55
27	0.64	0.21	52
26	−0.36	−0.12	49
25	−1.36	−0.44	46
24	−2.36	−0.76	42
23	−3.36	−1.09	39
22	−4.36	−1.41	36
21	−5.36	−1.73	33
20	−6.36	−2.06	29
19	−7.36	−2.38	26
18	−8.36	−2.71	23
17	−9.36	−3.03	20

shape, rather than following the distribution of obtained scores, we would not only have an interval scale but also a scale where an individual's standard score could be converted directly into a percentile ranking. A transformation to a normal distribution can be made using the table of Areas of the Normal Curve (see Appendix), by making use of the fact that in a normal distribution there is a specifiable relationship between standard scores (z scores) and the areas within the curve (i.e., the proportion of cases falling between any two points). This latter transformation is an *area transformation*, in contrast to the linear transformation of raw scores to z or Z scores.

An example of the computation of normalized standard scores is shown in Table 7.3. The steps listed illustrate the computation of normalized standard scores, designated here as NSS. The basic data are those used in Tables 7.1 and 7.2. The procedure forces the scores into a normal distribution. In order to do this there must be some basis for assuming that scores on the characteristic

TABLE 7.3 Computation of normalized standard scores

(1) For each raw score find the cumulative proportion (*CP*) according to the procedures described in Table 7.1.

(2) Enter the Table of Areas of the Normal Curve (see Appendix) and find the *z* score comparable to *CP*. For scores above the median (*CP* $\geq$ .500) use the column labeled "Area of Larger Proportion," for scores below the median (*CP* $\leq$ .500) use the column "Area of Smaller Proportion." The step gives you the *z* score that cuts the distribution into the desired areas.

(3) As with non-normalized standard scores, normalized standard scores are usually transformed to another scale. Again the recommended procedure is to set $\overline{X} = 50$ and $s = 10$ giving:

$$NSS = 50 + 10z$$

Raw score	(1) CP	(2) z	(3) NSS = 50 + 10z
32	.989	2.29	73
31	.958	1.73	67
30	.890	1.23	62
29	.780	0.77	58
28	.667	0.43	54
27	.537	0.09	51
26	.415	−0.21	48
25	.311	−0.49	45
24	.209	−0.81	42
23	.147	−1.05	40
22	.107	−1.24	38
21	.071	−1.47	35
20	.037	−1.79	32
19	.014	−2.20	28
18	.006	−2.51	25
17	.003	−2.75	22

(4) Comparable percentiles can be obtained by multiplying $CP \times 100$ or through use of the Table of Areas of the Normal Curve.

being measured are, in fact, normally distributed. If the scores cannot be assumed to be normally distributed, forcing them into a normal distribution will only distort the nature of the distribution. Normalized standard scores are thus computed when an obtained distribution of scores approaches a normal distribution but, because of sampling errors, remains slightly different. Such a situation frequently occurs in standardization of tests on large, heterogeneous samples.

As with all standard score scales, any arbitrary mean and standard deviation can be used. The recommended procedure is to use a mean of 50 and standard deviation of 10. However, normalized standard scores with other bases can be used if the situation warrants. Because normalized standard scores and linearly transformed standard scores (Z scores) are often reported on scales with the same constants ($\overline{X} = 50$, $s = 10$), they can easily be confused. If the distribution of raw scores is normal, both sets of transformed scores will have the same values; the farther the distribution of raw scores deviates from normality, the greater the discrepancy in the two sets of derived scores.

T SCORES. When normalized standard scores are reported on a transformed scale which uses a mean of 50 and a standard deviation of 10, they are frequently called T scores. This usage causes some confusion as T scores were originally defined (McCall, 1922) with reference to a particular norm group and not in a generic sense. Moreover, some persons use the T-score label when referring to unnormalized standard score systems which use the 50–10 base. However, as used today, the T-score designation generally applies to any normalized standard score system with $\overline{X} = 50$ and $s = 10$.

STANINES. One well-known variety of standard score is the *stanine*. The stanine scale is a nine-unit standard score scale, with score values ranging from 1–9, with 5 as the mean and a standard deviation of two units. Each score category on the scale is one-half standard deviation wide except for the two extreme categories. The exact relations are shown in Figure 7.3. The stanine system, utilizing one-digit standard scores, has certain advantages—stanines, for example, can be punched into a single column of a data processing card. Like any other system that reduces the score range by grouping, it sacrifices precision for simplicity.

INTERPRETATION OF STANDARD SCORES. Interpretation of standard scores is by reference to standard deviation units. A z score of 1.00, a Z of 60, and a normalized standard[4] score of 60 all indicate a score one standard deviation above the mean of the distribution. Similarly, a z of -1.50, a Z of 35, and a

---

[4]Unless otherwise noted, any standard score used in examples will be on a scale with $\overline{X}$ = 50 and s = 10.

normalized standard score of 35 all represent a score one and one-half standard deviations below the mean. Thus, standard scores indicate the relative position of a score, expressed as a deviation of x standard deviations from the mean.

For a person unfamiliar with the concept of the standard deviation, such an interpretation will, at best, be vague. However, when using normalized standard scores or when the distribution of unnormalized standard scores approaches a normal distribution, standard scores can, with reference to the normal curve, be directly converted into percentile rankings. A standard score of 60 can thus be interpreted not only as being one standard deviation above the mean but also as being equivalent to a percentile rank of 84; a standard score of 35 will not only be one and one-half standard deviations below the mean, it can also be said to be equivalent to a percentile rank of 7. These relationships between standard scores and percentile ranks, being functions of the score distributions and not test content, will hold regardless of the nature and content of the test. Thus, normalized standard scores (or z scores when the distribution approaches normality) have the computational advantages of an interval scale and the interpretive ease of percentiles.

EVALUATION OF STANDARD SCORES. Standard score systems express test scores on an interval scale rather than on an ordinal scale. As interval scales, they have the mathematical advantages inherent in such scales and thus are valuable when further statistical analyses are necessary, for example, when several scores are to be combined into one composite measure. Also, because all standard scores are based on a common unit of measurement, scores from different tests can be directly compared if they were derived from the same norm group. In addition, normalized standard scores permit reference to a standard distribution (the normal curve) and direct conversion to percentiles, thus simplifying interpretation.

Development of standard scores involves more computational labor than percentiles, but in an era of electronic calculating machines and computers this is no great disadvantage. These scores are also less familiar than percentiles and are thereby harder for the layman to understand. Confusion can also be introduced into the interpretation by the utilization of different arbitrary means and standard deviations and by the fact that unnormalized and normalized standard scores are frequently not carefully distinguished, scores being referred to only as standard scores. Therefore, the test user must always ascertain the values of the constants (mean and standard score) used in the particular test[5] under consideration, and whether the scores are normalized or represent only a linear transformation of the raw scores. Finally, normalizing standard scores forces the

[5]For example, the following standard score scales are used on well-known tests: Stanford-Binet (mean 100, standard deviation 16), Wechsler scales (100, 15), Army General Classification Test (100, 20), Wechsler subtests (10, 3), College Board Scholastic Aptitude Test (500, 100), and Graduate Record Exam (500, 100).

scores into a normal distribution. This procedure is justified to smooth out sampling errors; if it distorts the essential shape of the distribution, however, it may only produce added complications rather than increase precision.

The relationship of percentiles, z scores, $\hat{z}$ scores, and several other commonly used types of scores is shown in Figure 7.3. This figure shows the relationships when the distribution of raw scores is normal; naturally, the relationships would be different in distributions with marked deviations from normality.

Developmental scales

Another class of scoring scales is based on the fact that certain abilities, skills, and characteristics develop in a systematic manner—for example, a child's ability to solve complex intellectual tasks increases with age, and knowledge in most fields of academic study will increase with additional years of schooling.

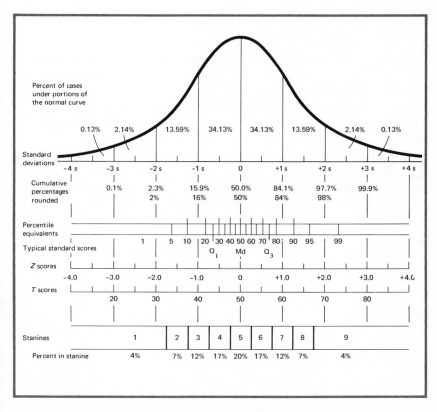

Figure 7.3 Relationship of several common scoring scales. (Adapted from H. G. Seashore. Methods of expressing test scores. New York: The Psychological Corporation, Test Service Bulletin no. 48, 1955.)

Because these abilities do increase systematically, scoring scales can be developed that compare an individual's performance with that of the average person of various developmental levels. On these scales, the individual is assigned a score that indicates the developmental level that his performance typifies. As might be expected, these developmental scales are generally of two types—age scales and grade scales.

AGE SCALES.   Alfred Binet, when developing the first individual intelligence test around the turn of the century, conceived of the idea of measuring mental growth by comparing a child's performance with that of the average child of various age levels. To construct such a scale required the identification of intellectual tasks or items that discriminated between children of various ages, i.e., items that varied systematically with age. When Binet found an item that could be successfully completed by the majority of children at a given age, but not by children at younger ages, this item was included on the test. For example, if the majority of eight-year-olds can answer the items: "What is nine times nine?" and "What is Egypt?" but fewer than half of the seven-year-olds can answer these items, then these items could be considered typical of the intellectual performance of eight-year-old children and included on a test as items at the eight-year-old level. By collecting a number of items that were appropriate for each age level, Binet developed a scale to assess the level of mental development of children. The score a child receives is the age level of the normative sample that his performance best typifies. These scores on the Binet test are referred to as *mental ages*.

All age scales are developed by using essentially the same reasoning and procedures. Because age scales assign a score to an individual by comparing his performance to the average child of various ages, they are interpreted by comparing a child's performance to children of a given age. For example, if a child can correctly answer the items commonly answered by ten-year-olds, but fails most of the items at higher age levels, his age score would be ten. Note that the fundamental assumption of age scales is that the ability, skill, or characteristic being tested increases systematically with age and that the two essential elements are: (1) a series of tasks or items that discriminate between persons of different ages and (2) a norm group composed of a representative sample of persons of different ages which provides the basis for assigning an item to a particular age group. A hypothetical example of the assignment of items to age levels is given in Figure 7.4.

For skills that vary systematically (especially at a constant rate) with age, the age scores are straightforward and easy to interpret; if the characteristic does not vary systematically, age scales are inappropriate. When the rate of change varies from year to year, inequalities in unit size are produced, thus complicating interpretation. For example, development of most intellectual abilities proceeds rapidly, and at a fairly constant rate, throughout childhood, but the rate of

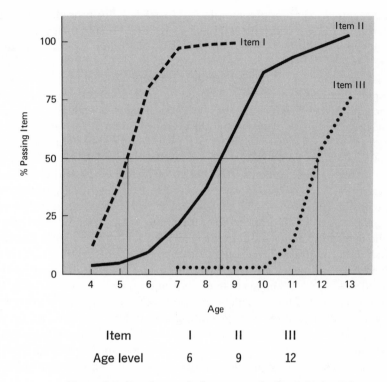

Item	I	II	III
Age level	6	9	12

Figure 7.4 Development of an age scale: item placement.

growth decelerates during adolescence. Therefore, the amount of increase in, say, reading comprehension will be less between the ages of 17 and 18 than between ages 7 and 8, thereby producing scale units of unequal size.

Furthermore, as performance on many variables will be affected by relevant education, training, or general life experiences, what is "normal" for a given age under certain circumstances may not be "normal" performance for the same age level under different circumstances. For all of these reasons, age scales are most appropriately used with younger children growing up in rather "typical" surroundings; for adults and children from restricted or atypical environments, age scores will be less meaningful.

GRADE SCALES. An analogous type of score is the grade score. Grade scales, rather than comparing an individual's performance to persons of different ages, compare his performance with that of the average student in various grades. Thus if Jeremy's grade score on an arithmetic test is 3–5, we can interpret his performance as being comparable to the average student in the fifth month of the third grade. (Because growth continues throughout the year, grade scores are usually reported in grades plus months within grade.) The procedures for selecting items, building a test, and assigning scores are directly analogous to those used on age scales with the exception, of course, that grade levels are substituted for age levels.

Like age scores, grade scores are appropriate only when the characteristic being measured varies systematically between grade levels. Moreover, one must assume equivalence of educational experiences. That is, a student's score cannot be interpreted as being equivalent to the average student in a given grade unless his educational experiences have, in fact, been comparable to the average student of that grade. To illustrate, suppose we have a mathematics test designed for junior high school students that consists of 75 items—50 arithmetic and 25 algebra items. Suppose also that the average score for eighth-grade students is 40, for ninth-grade students 50, and that algebra is not taught until the ninth grade. Albert, an eighth-grade student, takes the test and obtains a raw score of 50—the average score for ninth-grade students. Does this score mean he knows as much mathematics as the average ninth grader? Not necessarily. He probably obtained his score by being extremely accurate on the items that he studied, the arithmetic items, while the average ninth-grade student obtained a score of 50 by answering some of the arithmetic and some of the algebra items correctly. In other words, Albert and the average ninth-grade student both obtained the same scores but by answering different items correctly. Albert's knowledge of mathematics could not, as a common misinterpretation of grade scores might lead you to believe, be considered equivalent to the average ninth-grade student because he has not studied algebra.

Because of this problem in interpreting grade scores, many experts recommend using *percentile ranks within grades* rather than grade scores. This approach compares an individual's score, not to the average student in various grades, but to other students within the same grade. Scores are expressed as relative rankings (percentile ranks) within a particular grade level—in our example, Albert's score might be reported as falling at the 95th percentile rank for eighth-grade students. Here again the comparison is meaningful only if the student's educational experiences are comparable to those of students in the normative group.

Besides being highly dependent on the materials taught at various grade levels, grade scores also depend on the composition of the normative group. If the policy of a school is to retain children in a grade when their performance does not meet certain minimal standards and to advance them when their development clearly surpasses their classmates, any grade will include some students who are older and others who are younger than the children who have advanced from grade to grade according to normal promotional policies. To control for such diversity, some test publishers use *modal age grade norms*, i.e., norms developed on samples that include only students who are in the grade typical of their age level. Students who are accelerated or retarded a year or more are thus eliminated from the norm groups, thereby providing a better estimate of the performance of the typical child in a given grade.

When interpreting grade scores, therefore, one must take into account not only the appropriateness of the content but also any sectioning and promotion policies that differentiate the class under study from the norm group.

EVALUATION OF DEVELOPMENTAL SCALES. Although the advantages and disadvantages of developmental scales have already been indicated, they will be briefly reviewed here. Their primary advantages are: (1) they report scores in understandable units, in terms of age or grade equivalents; thus (2) they provide a direct comparison with the performance of a student's peers; and (3) they would seem to provide a meaningful basis for intraindividual comparisons and study of growth over time. Their main disadvantages are: (1) they are appropriate only when the characteristic measured changes systematically with age, thus being limited mainly to use with younger children; (2) they are greatly influenced by the composition and previous education, training, and experiences of the norm group used in their development; (3) inequalities in unit size at various ages are frequently present; and (4) extrapolations from one level to another are very risky. In short, the presumed advantages of such scores may be more apparent than real.

Ratios and quotients

We now turn to the several attempts to develop scales that involve the ratio of two separate scores. Probably the best known of these is the *intelligence quotient*, or *IQ*. But not infrequently, especially in achievement testing, one runs across quantities labeled educational quotients or accomplishment quotients, or bearing some similar name.

INTELLIGENCE QUOTIENTS. Binet constructed his intelligence test so that scores were expressed on an age scale. When his test was translated and introduced in the United States, some psychometricians felt that the mental age did not give a complete picture of mental development. They pointed out that a mental age of 10 would have differing implications if it were obtained by a child of 8, a child of 10, or one of 15, and consequently suggested that the rate of mental development should be measured as well as the level of development (i.e., the mental age). The intelligence quotient was developed as an index of the rate of intellectual development, and was defined as the ratio of the child's mental age to his chronological age:

$$IQ = \frac{\text{mental age}}{\text{chronological age}} \times 100 \qquad (7.5)$$

(Multiplication by a factor of 100 eliminates decimal places.) It can readily be seen from formula (7.5) that a child whose intellectual development is average for his age (i.e., whose mental age equals his chronological age) will obtain an IQ of 100, children whose mental development is more rapid than average will obtain scores over 100, and those whose development is slower than average will obtain IQ's below 100. Furthermore, the greater the rate of development deviates from the average, the farther the IQ will fall from 100.

An IQ computed in this manner, the ratio of mental age to chronological age, is known as a *ratio IQ*. Because of the problems associated with nonequivalent standard deviations (Terman and Merrill, 1937) and the fact that intellectual growth does not increase linearly with increasing age, the ratio IQ is no longer used on the major intelligence tests and is only of historical interest. Instead, standard scores based on a representative sample of the population at each level are used. These scores, called *deviation IQ's*, have a mean of 100 and a standard deviation of 15 (Wechsler scales) or 16 (Stanford-Binet) points at each age level.

ACHIEVEMENT QUOTIENTS.   The IQ attempts to measure the rate of general intellectual development; in educational testing one sometimes encounters measures that purportedly indicate the rate of educational development or achievement. These indices are all ratios which use as their numerator some measure of achievement and as the denominator chronological age, a measure of intellectual ability or grade placement. The logic of such ratios is similar to the logic of the ratio IQ, to compare the person's actual achievement to his expected achievement (as estimated from his age, grade, or intelligence). As the numerator (the measure of achievement) in such formulas usually is a grade score, the quotient will have all the disadvantages inherent in grade scores. Quotients that involve the comparison of achievement test scores to intelligence test scores suffer also from (1) the fact that the ratio of two unreliable scores will be even less reliable than either individual measure and (2) the assumption that achievement is determined solely by intellectual ability, which is the assumption of the ratio, is unwarranted. Therefore, ratios based on the comparison of achievement test scores to age or grade placement should be interpreted only with extreme caution; ratios of achievement to intellectual development can best be ignored.

METHODS OF PRESENTING NORMATIVE DATA

In the earlier portions of this chapter we have discussed the considerations involved in constructing and selecting an appropriate norm group and the characteristics of various scales used to aid in interpreting test scores. We now turn to the methods of summarizing and presenting normative data, with our discussion focusing on three methods—conversion tables, profiles, and expectancy tables.

Conversion tables

The simplest and most basic technique is the *conversion table* or, as it is sometimes called, the *norm table*. A conversion table is simply a schedule showing the raw scores and equivalent derived scores—be they percentiles, standard scores, or any other type of score—for a particular norm group. The conversion table enables the test user to convert a raw score to a derived score or find the raw score equivalent of a given derived score; hence the label "conversion table." The essential elements of a conversion table are (1) a list of raw scores, (2) a corresponding list of derived scores, and (3) a description of the norm group.

An example of a conversion table is shown in Table 7.4, which is derived from the data in Tables 7.1 and 7.2 and gives the percentile rank and standard score equivalents of the composite score on a college aptitude test for a group of freshmen women in a liberal arts curriculum. Thus, if a student's raw score were 27, her percentile rank would be 54 and her standard score 52. We could interpret her score by saying that, compared to freshmen women in the liberal arts college curriculum at this university, she was .2 standard deviations above

TABLE 7.4 Example of a conversion table. Percentile rank and standard score equivalents on a college aptitude test

Raw score	Percentile rank	Standard score
32	99	68
31	96	65
30	89	62
29	78	58
28	67	55
27	54	52
26	42	49
25	31	46
24	21	42
23	15	39
22	11	36
21	7	33
20	4	29
19	1	26
18	1	23
17	1	20

$N = 177$ freshmen women in liberal arts at a midwestern university.

the mean (standard score = 52) or that her score exceeded 54 percent of the students (percentile rank = 54) in the curricula.

There are several aspects of this interpretation that are worth emphasizing. First, the comparison was made to a particular norm group, in this case freshmen women in liberal arts curriculum at a particular university. To compare her performance with that of other groups would require other norm tables. Second, scores were expressed both as percentiles and as standard scores. Depending on its function, any conversion table may list only one or several types of derived scores. Third, the conversion table, as it stands, gives only the student's relative performance within the norm group; it gives no direct evidence of validity or of the outcomes that might be associated with a particular test score. If the test predicts some relevant outcome, we can make some inferences from her scores. For example, if the test predicts college grades, we can infer that the higher her ranking (test score) the higher the grades she will probably attain.

Conversely, *if there is no validity evidence relating the test scores to some relevant outcome, the data in the conversion table will tell only the student's relative ranking within the group—and nothing more.* This latter point cannot be overstressed. Too often the availability of normative data is taken as a license to offer added meaning to test scores, i.e., to interpret performance on the test as indicative of probable high performance on some criterion. Without validity data, conversion tables only translate the raw score into another type of score. With relevant validity data, however, conversion tables provide a means for making interpretations more meaningful. Even with validity data, criterion performance can be inferred only from normative data; there is no direct link—that is, raw scores are converted to relative performance measures, not expressed in outcome terms. There is, as we shall see later, no reason why normative data cannot be expressed in terms of outcome and a conversion table used to directly convert raw scores to a measure of expected outcome.

COMPLEX CONVERSION TABLES. Frequently data from several subtests or scales or from the various tests in a single battery are presented in one conversion table. When interpreting such data one caution is paramount—unless the scores on all tests are based on the same norm group they are not directly comparable, because score will be based on different samples of people. If the data are all based on a common norm group, as they should be, this type of conversion table provides a method for directly comparing the performance of an individual on various subtests or the tests within the test battery.

Table 7.5 is an illustration of a conversion table that simultaneously presents the normative data for several subtests. In Table 7.5 the derived scores are given in the marginal columns and the raw scores for different subtests are given in the body of the table.

Another alternative procedure uses a conversion table to show the performance of several distinct norm groups on a single test. An example of such a

TABLE 7.5   Example of a conversion table showing norms for several subtests

Scale score	English	Math	Social Studies	Natural Science	Composite
35		99			
34		95		99	
33		90	99	96	
32		84	97	91	99
31		76	93	83	97
30		66	86	75	92
29	99	56	79	65	84
28	97	46	72	55	74
27	93	36	62	45	62
26	87	28	54	34	50
25	79	22	45	25	39
24	69	18	35	19	29
23	59	14	27	15	21
22	48	11	21	11	14
21	37	8	16	8	9
20	28	6	12	6	6
19	20	4	8	5	4
18	14	3	6	3	2
17	9	2	5	2	2
16	5	1	3	2	1
15	3		3	1	
14	2		2		
13	1		1		

Table shows the percentile equivalents on the four subtests (plus composite) of the American College Testing Program (ACT). Sample was 2087 entering freshmen at a midwestern university.

table is shown in Table 7.6. This table not only gives derived scores for several groups, allowing the test user to compare an individual's scores to several relevant groups simultaneously, but also allows comparisons to be made of the performance of diverse groups as groups. That is, by observing the derived score equivalents of various raw scores we can infer which norm group is "tougher." For example, in Table 7.6, College D is the "toughest" norm group, since a given raw score will have a lower percentile equivalent in College D than in any other group. Conversely, College C is the "easiest" norm group as the percentile equivalents are generally highest. (College D is an engineering program, College C a nontechnical curriculum enrolling women primarily.) Or, to view the results

TABLE 7.6 Example of a conversion table showing the performance of several norm groups on the same test

Score	A	B	College C	D	E
36		99		99	
35	99	98		97	
34	96	94	99	92	99
33	94	88	98	86	97
32	90	81	96	77	94
31	82	74	95	67	90
30	72	66	92	57	84
29	62	58	87	45	75
28	55	52	82	35	65
27	50	44	76	26	59
26	43	36	67	17	52
25	35	29	59	11	44
24	28	24	53	8	36
23	20	18	45	5	29
22	14	13	38	3	24
21	11	11	30	2	19
20	8	7	24	1	14
19	6	4	17		10
18	4	3	13		7
17	3	2	9		4
16	1	1	5		2
15			3		1
14			2		
13			1		
N	177	486	340	528	307

Table presents percentile equivalents of ACT mathematics test scores for five colleges within the same university. (See text for explanation.)

in a different manner, a raw score of 28 will be equivalent to a percentile rank of 82 in College C, 65 in College E, 55 in College A, 52 in College B, and 35 in College D. These findings, of course, reflect the differences in mathematics background and ability of students who elect to enter the various colleges. As such, the conversion table not only provides useful normative data, but it also indicates the characteristics (in this example, mathematics ability) of the students in the various norm groups.

To directly compare various groups the scores must have been obtained under equivalent conditions. If, for example, scores on a scholastic aptitude test were obtained from one group when the test was administered as a selection test and for another group when the testing was structured as a standardization project, the motivation of the two groups might differ, and the results would not be comparable. Similarly, if a personality inventory were administered to one group as a counseling aid and another as a basis for determining suitability for military service, the motivation for dissimulation would probably vary between the two samples. Any differences in sampling biases in the various groups will further complicate the comparisons.

Profiles

When considering several scores conjointly, a method that would clearly display the results of the various tests simultaneously would be desirable. The *test profile*, a graphic method of presenting the results of a series of tests, serves just this need. Basically a profile is a graph on which a series of test scores are plotted. All scores are plotted on the same scale using norms derived from a common group. The individual's score on each test (or subtest) is entered at the appropriate score level for each test (or subtest). The profile shows at a glance the configuration of the individual's scores on the various tests, indicating the relative position of his several scores. A typical test profile is shown in Figure 7.5.

Several rules must be followed to prevent a misrepresentation by the profile. First, the norm group used should be identical for each test included on the profile. If diverse norm groups are used for the various tests, the scores, being based on different groups, will not be directly comparable. Second, all scores must be plotted on the same scale—that is, all scores should be expressed as percentiles, all as a particular type of standard score, or all as age scores. Corollary to this second point is the need for assigning dimensions to the profile that do not exaggerate small differences nor compress large differences. This latter problem can be minimized if a third rule is followed—to build into the profile some index of error. Because all tests are to some extent unreliable, and differences between test scores are even more unreliable, insignificant differences between scores are prone to be overinterpreted. One interesting attempt to minimize the danger of overinterpretation (used by the Psychological Corporation on their Differential Aptitude Tests) is to construct the profile so that a difference of a certain measurable distance on the profile represents a significant difference between two scores; the user thus can quickly ascertain which pairs of scores differ significantly. An alternative approach (used by the Cooperative Test Division) is to report scores as *bands* rather than as exact scores, the differences between scores being significant only if the bands do not overlap. In this approach a percentile rank would be reported not as 66, but as a band of percentile ranks, say 62–70. Or a standard score might be reported not as 36, but as a range 34–38. The essential operation is to build in some margin of error, a margin (usually) based on the standard error of measurement. The band approach also guards against too precise interpretation of scores by forcing the user to think of scores as ranges rather than points.

MINNESOTA COUNSELING INVENTORY
PROFILE SHEET

11-12

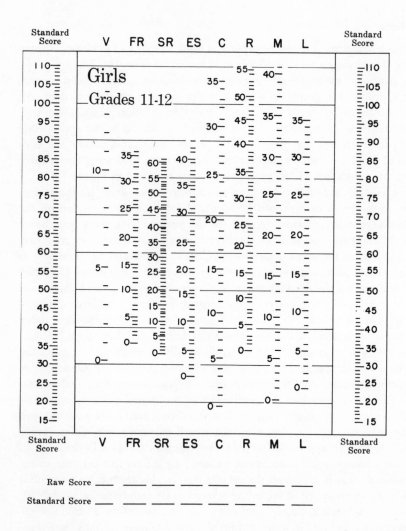

Figure 7.5 Illustration of a test profile. Reproduced by permission. Copyright
© 1957 by The Psychological Corporation, New York, N. Y. All rights reserved.

NORMAL PERCENTILE CHARTS. One of the best ways of presenting test profiles, a method that both guards against overinterpretation and simplifies interpretation, is by use of *normal percentile charts*, which are profiles where the scores are reported in percentile ranks but the dimensions of the scale are drawn to correspond to a standard score (z) scale. That is, the distances on the score (vertical) axis are equal to z-scale units but corresponding percentile ranks are placed along this scale. In other words, percentile ranks are superimposed on a standard score scale. This procedure is based on the fact that, in a normal distribution, there is constant relationship between z scores (deviations from the mean in standard deviation units) and areas included within the normal curve (percentile ranks). Review of Table 7.3 should clarify the relationship. The normal percentile chart provides the advantages of both percentiles and standard scores, more accurately reflects the relationship of raw scores to percentiles (see discussion, earlier in chapter), and minimizes the chances of misinterpreting differences between percentiles. An example of a normal percentile chart is illustrated in Figure 7.6.

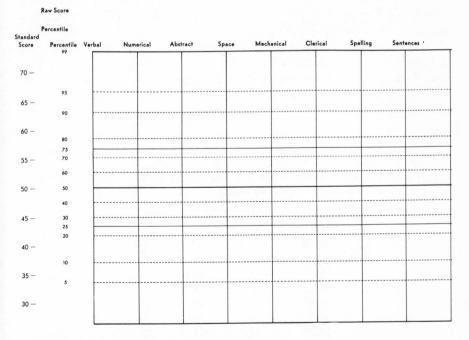

Figure 7.6 Illustration of a normal percentile chart. The profile form is derived from Differential Aptitude Tests (The Psychological Corporation). Note that the vertical axis is scaled in standard score units with percentile ranks superimposed on this scale. Reproduced by permission. Copyright © 1961, 1963 by The Psychological Corporation, New York, N. Y. All rights reserved.

Expectancy tables

Conversion tables and profiles present normative data with only implicit reference to validity. That is, if the test has some degree of validity then one can infer that higher test or derived scores connote greater chances of obtaining a higher criterion score. (In the rare cases where the validity coefficient is negative then low scores on the predictor go with high criterion scores.) For ease of interpretation it would be desirable to have a method of presenting test scores that directly showed the relationship between the test scores and criterion scores for the normative group.

Expectancy tables are a method of combining normative and validity data so that the relationship between test scores and criterion scores is shown directly. Basically an *expectancy table* shows the percentage of people with a given predictor score or range of predictor scores who obtain various criterion scores. An example of an expectancy table with one predictor is Table 7.7, which shows the chances, in 100, of a person with a given test score attaining a particular grade average. (Grade-point averages were calculated using A = 4, B = 3, C = 2, D = 1 and F = 0.) This table allows a prediction of the students' chances of obtaining various grade-point averages to be made, i.e., we can say that 89 out of 100 students with test scores of 28 will obtain at least a C average and 34 out of 100 will attain a B average or higher. Thus we have more relevant information than if we compared the student to a norm group and found that his score was at the, say, 79th percentile rank. In short, expectancy tables skip the intermediate step of derived scores and endow scores with meaning in outcome (criterion) terms.

TABLE 7.7 Expectancy table for predicting first quarter college grades from a college aptitude test

Test raw score	Grade-point average		
	≥ 3.0	≥ 2.0	< 2.0
32–	93	99+	1
30–31	58	97	3
28–29	34	89	11
26–27	19	75	25
24–25	14	63	37
22–23	5	52	48
20–21	4	49	51
18–19	2	44	56
16–17	3	36	64

A more complex expectancy table, in which two variables are jointly used to predict grade-point average, is shown in Table 7.8. The data in Table 7.8 are the same as those presented in Table 7.7 except high school rank serves as an added predictor. To interpret an individual's score we find the cell at the intersection of the raw corresponding to his test score and the column corresponding to his high school rank; the figures in the cell at the intersection of this row and column indicate the probabilities of obtaining various criterion scores. Thus we find that 92 out of 100 students with a test score of 28 and a high school rank in the third 10 percent obtained at least a C average, and 16 out of 100 attained a B average or higher. Again we can directly interpret predictor scores in terms of outcome measures.

Construction of an expectancy table is a relatively simple matter. First, predictor scores and criterion scores must be divided into categories. Then the frequency of each combination of predictor and criterion scores is determined. These frequencies are next converted to percentages or proportions and a table is constructed. (An illustration of this method is given in Table 7.9.) Expectancy tables can also be constructed using regression equations, a procedure that gives a smoother distribution of scores than using the empirical distribution. (For further details on the construction of expectancy tables see Wesman, 1966).

EVALUATION OF EXPECTANCY TABLES. The major advantage of expectancy tables is that they combine normative and validity data and thus enable

TABLE 7.8 Expectancy table for predicting first quarter college grades from a college aptitude test and high school rank

Test raw	High school rank (in tenths)						
score	First	Second	Third	Fourth	Fifth	Sixth	Seventh –Tenth
30–	82–98–2	26–93–7					
28–29	52–94–6	21–89–11	16–92–8	30–80–20	7–47–53		
26–37	37–93–7	18–81–19	9–65–35	5–66–34	17–52–48	*–36–64	
24–25	35–93–7	19–70–30	4–61–39	13–49–51	3–37–63	*–40–60	8–16–84
22–23	17–95–5	7–63–37	4–61–39	3–41–59	3–40–60	*–32–68	6–25–75
20–21	22–78–22	4–67–33	5–50–50	3–43–57	5–52–48	*–36–64	*–45–55
18–19			*–31–69	*–38–62	6–45–55	8–41–69	*–33–67
–17					*–20–80		4–26–74

The numbers within the cells represent the chance in 100 of attaining at least a 3.0, at least a 2.0 and below a 2.0 grade-point average, respectively. Where a cell is blank, there were too few cases for a stable estimate to be made; an asterisk (*) indicates less than one chance in 100. The probabilities are based on observed frequencies, unsmoothed by theoretical consideration, thus show some reversals in trends.

TABLE 7.9 Construction of an expectancy table

(1) The input data are the predictor (test) and outcome (criterion) scores for a given sample. In our example we will use the data in Table 5.1, that used in all the validity illustrations.

(2) Both predictor and outcome data must be classified into categories. This is generally done so as to get meaningful categories that contain enough cases to permit stable estimates. We will divide the outcome data into two categories—rated successful and unsuccessful, i.e., score 1–3 and 4–8 — and the predictor scores into 7 levels: 0–2, 3, 4, 5, 6, 7 and 8–10. This latter division, insures with one exception, that there will be 10 cases at each level (A larger number of cases in each cell would be desirable; however, with a total sample of 100 cases, larger groups are infeasible).

(3) Within each predictor level score, the frequency of each outcome is then determined. This will result in a table of the form:

		Outcome		
		1–3	4–8	Σ
	0–2	9	0	9
	3	9	2	11
	4	9	3	12
Test	5	9	11	20
scores	6	5	13	18
	7	1	14	15
	8–10	0	15	15
	Σ	42	58	100

(4) Within each predictor level, find the proportion of cases having each outcome. For example, for test score = 3, 9/11 or 82 percent of the cases have an outcome score in the range 1–3 and 2/11 or 18 percent are in the 4–8 range. Repeat for each predictor score level.

(5) Construct the final form of the expectancy table using as the cell entries the chances in 100 (i.e., the percentage of cases) that a given test score is associated with a given outcome. For our example the table would be:

Table 7.9 (continued)

Chances (in 100) of being rated successful as a function of predictor test scores		
	Job rating	
	Successful	Unsuccessful
Test score	(4–8)	(1–3)
8–10	100	0
7	93	7
6	72	28
5	55	45
4	25	75
3	18	82
0–2	0	100

test scores to be directly interpreted in terms of expected outcomes rather than as a rank in a group. In many circumstances this type of interpretation is more meaningful than a ranking interpretation. For example, the prospective college student is generally more interested in knowing his chances of attaining a B or a C average at a particular college than knowing his rank on the test compared to that of other prospective students. Knowing that his score places him at the 55th percentile does not tell him whether the probabilities indicate almost certain academic success, a 50–50 chance of success, or probable failure.

Expectancy tables, however, have several disadvantages. In order to present the data in tabular form, both predictor and criterion data must be put into classes, and grouping continuous data into classes always sacrifices some precision. Also, unless the sample is very large, some cells will contain only a few cases and thus provide unstable estimates. Even with a large number of cases, categorizing the scores may do some violence to the data because, unless there are exact and meaningful cutting points, any classification system will be somewhat arbitrary. (In Tables 7.7 and 7.8, the 2.0 grade-point average was selected because it was the minimum average that allowed the student to stay in school.) Finally, whenever the number of predictors exceeds two, presentation becomes complicated, requiring more than one table to present the data.

Expectancy tables also illustrate clearly a dilemma that plagues psychological testing—how to apply group data to the individual. The figures within the cells of an expectancy table show the probability that a given criterion performance will occur given certain predictor scores. These data are derived from the performance of a group of people and are directly interpretable when dealing with groups. For example, if a particular combination of predictor scores (i.e., a cell in the expectancy table) indicates that the probability of success on the job is .63, then an employer can expect that 63 percent of the applicants that he hires who have this particular combination of predictor scores will be successful —assuming, of course, that the criterion for success does not change. It is when this score is interpreted for an individual, however, that difficulties are encountered. The chances of success are .63 for the class; however, any individual will either succeed or fail, i.e., for an individual the probability is either 1.00 (succeed) or 0.00 (fail). To say that an individual has a 63 percent chance of success is logically meaningless. When interpreting data from expectancy tables to an individual, then, it must be stressed that the predictions are group averages and that these data give only an estimate of the success of a group of people obtaining similar predictor scores.[6]

FOUR PROBLEMS

In this final section we shall briefly consider several special problems that arise in connection with normative data and translating scores into different scales. First we re-examine the sources of error that enter into normative data. Then we consider the relationship of validity data to normative data. Third, we look at the problem of equating scores from various tests. And, finally, we consider change scores.

Errors in scores

Throughout the book, including at several points in the current chapter, we have emphasized and re-emphasized that scores on psychological and educational tests contain some error of measurement. Now we raise the question still another time in an attempt to summarize much of the previous discussion and indicate how error in test scores will affect the interpretations made from normative data. In doing so we will consider three sources of error: (1) errors due to unreliability, (2) errors due to invalidity, and (3) errors attributable to improper generalization.

UNRELIABILITY.   Our discussion of the conversion of raw scores to various derived scores assumed that a given raw score could be transformed into an equivalent derived score, i.e., we discussed the transformations as if test scores were precise indicators. However, it was pointed out that as psychological tests

---

[6]You will recall that a somewhat analogous situation obtains when criterion scores are predicted through the use of a regression equation. In the regression situation, the predicted criterion score 'is the average score made by all persons with the particular predictor score, and the error is the extent to which an individual's score deviates from the group average.

never exhibit perfect reliability, test scores should be treated as ranges or bands rather than as exact points. Many test publishers, being aware of this problem, have developed conversion tables or profiles that utilize a band approach to score interpretation. Some publishers have even extended this concept to the interpretation of differences between subtest scores. Even if the test publisher has not used this approach, the reader should by now be sensitized to providing his own band interpretation to test scores. If exact scores are used, it should be with the understanding that such scores are not precise indicators but rather the best estimate that we have of the person's "true" score. That is, to say that a certain score is equivalent to a percentile rank of 55 does not mean 55 is the person's exact rank, rather it should be interpreted as the best available estimate of his rank.

INVALIDITY. An equally important source of interpretive errors is often overlooked—the invalidity of test scores or, more precisely, the lack of validity evidence. As has been pointed out previously, without evidence as to what is measured or predicted by test scores, normative data tell nothing more than the individual's relative ranking within the normative group. Yet the very fact that normative data are available, regardless of the presence or absence of validity data, provides a subtle temptation to interpret test scores *as if validity data were available.* If a test is labeled as a measure of mathematical aptitude, and if normative data are available, it is only too easy to interpret scores on the test as if they predicted success in activities involving mathematics. Or, if the test is labeled as a measure of introversion, and there are normative data available, it is very easy to say that a person scoring high on the test is an introvert.

Probably no other error occurs more frequently in the interpretation of psychological test data than to infer meaning of test scores from the title of the test and normative data, neglecting the fact that validity data supporting the interpretation is either nonexistent or fragmentary. But to summarize what should now be obvious: *normative data are not sufficient for accurate test interpretation; one needs both normative and validity data.*

GENERALIZABILITY. It frequently happens that none of the available norm groups have exactly the same characteristics as the individuals whose test scores are being interpreted. To the extent that the individuals differ from the norm group, errors of faulty generalization may be introduced into the test interpretation. Sometimes this problem can be overcome by developing local norms and conducting local validity studies; at other times—as when dealing with a single individual—such a procedure is not feasible. Although a value cannot be assigned to the probability of making an erroneous generalization from a noncomparable norm group, the test user should constantly be aware of the possibility of such faulty generalizations.

Validity data as normative data

In the previous section we emphasized the need for both normative and validity data before accurate test interpretations could be made. Of the various scoring systems discussed in the chapter, only expectancy tables and content scores provided direct links between raw scores and criterion behaviors. The other types of scores require a chain of inference from derived scores through raw scores to validity data before interpretations in criterion terms can be made. It would thus seem that in order to simplify test interpretation, conversion tables should be prepared whenever possible for direct translation of test performance (raw scores) into behaviorally defined outcome (criterion) categories.

Criterion scores could be derived and reported in various manners—there would be no need to restrict presentation to the expectancy table format. For example, one can easily conceive of a conversion table similar to Table 7.4, but instead of raw scores being converted to percentile ranks and standard scores, they would be converted directly into an outcome measure, say, predicted grade average. The mode of deriving the scores, and thus the exact nature of the score, could follow any of the validity procedures described in Chapter 5. If the use of criterion norms were to become a standard practice, the gratuitous attribution of meaning to unvalidated test scores would necessarily decrease.

Equating scores

Test users frequently encounter a situation similar to the following:

> Jimmy Jones applies to Midwest State College and Prestige University. As part of the application procedure to Prestige U. he then takes the XYZ College Aptitude Test. He also submits his scores on the XYZ Test to Midwest State. Unfortunately Midwest State requires the ABC College Aptitude Test and holds his application until he takes the ABC Test. Jimmy may well ask why scores on the XYZ Test cannot be substituted for scores on the ABC Test, because both tests purportedly measure aptitude for college. (Or the admissions office at Midwest State may be willing to accept his scores on the XYZ Test if they can determine the meaning of scores on the XYZ Test in terms of the ABC Test, with which they are familiar.)

The basic problem in this situation is that of equating the two test scores, to place them on a common scale.

One fundamental distinction is whether the tests are actually equivalent or merely comparable (Wesman, 1958). Scores on tests can be considered comparable if they represent the same standing in a given population; that is, if scores are based on the same norm group, they are comparable. However, to be considered equivalent, the items on the tests must represent the same content domain—that is, the tests must be interchangeable in regards to content. It is at just this point that most attempts to equate test scores get hung up, as tests having the same purpose or falling into the same general class do not necessarily measure the identical content areas nor do they utilize equivalent norm groups.[7]

EQUATING METHODS.   Suppose, however, that two tests have an adequate degree of equivalence so that developing and equating procedure appears justified. How would we go about it? One common procedure is the equipercentile method. In this technique both tests are administered to the same normative sample, the raw scores on both tests are translated into percentile ranks; then, using the percentile ranks as pivot points, a table of equivalent raw scores can be prepared. That is, if a raw score of 55 on Test ABC is the 90th percentile rank, and a raw score of 36 on Test XYZ is also at the 90th percentile, the scores of 55 and 36 can be considered equal. To return to our example, if Jimmy Jones submitted a score of 36 on Test XYZ to Midwest State, the admissions officer could convert this score to a 55 on Test ABC and thereby know the meaning of Jimmy's score. The precision of the conversion will, of course, be dependent on the standard deviations and reliabilities of the individual tests and their intercorrelation.

An alternative procedure, one that in some ways sidesteps the equivalence problem, equates the tests in terms of criterion measures. That is, rather than use equal percentile ranks as the pivot point, equal outcomes (in the example, we might use equal college grade averages) are used as the basis of equating the tests with criterion measures. This approach sidesteps the content equivalence problem since, in a prediction situation, by definition, identical predicted criterion scores imply equivalent test scores and, implicitly, equivalent degrees of the relevant trait.

Change scores

All of the scoring systems discussed were oriented toward scores obtained at a single point in time. In order to measure changes in the individual it would be necessary to test the individual at several points in time, obtain derived scores for each testing, and then compare the derived scores and make inferences about the person's growth. For example, if the same standardized achievement battery is administered every December in a school, and if Johnny obtained a grade score of 3.5 in December of 1967 and a grade score of 3.8 in December of 1968, we could say that his growth during the year—being only .3 year units—

[7]For example, there is constant pressure to equate scores on the Wechsler Intelligence Scales with the Stanford-Binet and scores on the American College Testing Program Test with the College Board's Scholastic Aptitude Test. But because the content of these tests is not equivalent (see Chapter 11), only comparability, but not equivalence, can be obtained. (See e.g., Anghoff, 1964.)

was less than expected. But as was pointed out earlier (Chapter 4) such interpretations are filled with danger. However, because of the lack of scores that directly measure change and norms that show the expected change in any time period, the test user generally must rely on such a procedure.

Perhaps with the increasing emphasis on the study of change, a more adequate conceptualization of change scores and a sophisticated system of change scores will be developed. Such improvements are drastically needed, especially in education, where the fundamental goal of the process is change.

Summary

In order to interpret test performance, an individual's scores must be compared to some standard. In educational and psychological testing, this standard is usually the performance of a specified representative group of individuals who resemble the individual on certain relevant characteristics. This group is called a norm group and their performance constitutes the norms. If unambiguous interpretations are to be made from normative data, the dimensions of the norm group must be clearly defined, the particular sample of persons chosen to constitute the norm group must be selected without bias, and the norms must be of recent origin. If the normative data provided by the test publisher, or available from other sources, are not sufficient, local norms may be constructed.

Scores derived directly from test performance, the raw scores, are generally transformed to another scale to aid the interpretation process. Five general classes of scores were discussed—content scales, percentiles, standard scores, developmental scales, and ratios. *Content scales* derive their meaning from an exacting specification of the content or skills tapped by the test. Thus they relate the individual's performance directly to the content domain, in contrast to the other varieties of scores discussed which relate the individual's performance to that of other persons. *Percentile* ranks indicate the person's ranking in the norm group in percentage terms. Because percentiles represent an ordinal scale (and for many purposes an interval scale would be desirable) raw scores are often transformed to standard scores which measure on an interval scale. *Standard score* scales express scores in terms of the deviation from the sample mean in standard deviation units. The basic unit of measurement in these scales is, therefore, the standard deviation; hence, the label standard scores. Standard scores may be obtained by linear transformations or through area transformations. The latter type are called normalized standard scores. *Developmental scales* interpret performance by comparing the individual's score to that of the average or typical person of a given developmental level. The two most common developmental scales are age scales and grade scales. *Ratio scores* are the quotient of two variables. The most well-known example is the ratio intelligence quotient (IQ).

Normative data may be presented in various formats. *Conversion tables* show raw scores and comparable derived scores for one or more norm groups in tabular form. *Profiles* present the performance of a single norm group on several tests, subtest, or scales in a graphic fashion. *Expectancy tables* show normative data in outcome terms by giving the expected criterion performance of individuals having certain test scores or combinations of test scores. Thus expectancy tables combine normative and validity data.

Four specific problems in interpreting test scores were also briefly discussed: (1) the problem of errors introduced by unreliability, invalidity, or using norm groups that are not completely relevant; (2) the tendency to interpret normative data as if it were validity data; (3) the problem of equating scores from various tests; and (4) the appropriate method of deriving change scores.

The basic philosophy of this chapter can be summarized by saying that meaningful interpretation of test scores cannot occur unless two kinds of data are available: (1) validity data indicating what trait the test measures or what criteria it predicts and (2) adequate normative data.

Suggestions for further reading

Bauernfeind, R. H. Are sex norms necessary? *Journal of Counseling Psychology*, 1956, 3, 57–62. This article addresses the question: When are separate norm groups needed and when can groups with distinctive demographic characteristics be combined for normative purposes?

Davis, J. A. Nonapparent limitations of normative data. *Personnel and Guidance Journal*, 1959, 37, 656–659. A nontechnical discussion of some of the limitations of normative data that often result in misleading and inappropriate interpretations of test scores.

Ebel, R. L. Content standard test scores. *Educational and Psychological Measurement*, 1962, 22, 15–25. A discussion of how to derive test scores that can be interpreted in terms of content mastered.

Lindquist, E. F. Equating scores on nonparallel tests. *Journal of Educational Measurement*, 1964, 1, 5–9. An illustration of the problems involved in attempting to equate scores on two widely used college admissions tests.

Lyman, H. B. *Test scores and what they mean.* Englewood Cliffs, N. J.: Prentice-Hall, Inc., 1963. A classification and discussion of the variety of test scores in current use.

Schrader, W. B. A taxonomy of expectancy tables. *Journal of Educational Measurement*, 1965, 2, 29–35. A classification and discussion of the various approaches to constructing expectancy tables.

Seashore, H. G. *Methods of expressing test scores.* New York: The Psychological Corporation, Test Service Bulletin No. 48, 1955. A comparison of the various types of test scores with particular reference to their comparability when scores are distributed normally.

Wesman, A. G. *Double-entry expectancy tables.* New York: The Psychological Corporation, Test Service Bulletin No. 56, 1966. The construction and use of complex expectancy tables.

Combining test scores

Chapter 8

INTRODUCTION

In previous chapters we have, with a few exceptions, discussed only one test or one score at a time; we have presented the basic concepts of psychological measurement using single test scores as examples. In practice, however, one seldom deals with only a single test score. Generally scores are combined to arrive at a composite score or prediction. At least three varieties of combinations are frequently encountered: (1) individual test items are combined into a scale, subtest,[1] or test; (2) scores on several subtests or scales are combined into a composite score, and (3) scores on various tests are combined to yield a composite prediction. Although these three problems involve different components, from individual items to total tests, the logic and statistical methods involved in the combinations are basically similar.

Combining items

Every test is composed of a number of independent items. Various subgroups of these items may be combined to form scales or subtests, or there may be no internal divisions and all the items contribute to one overall test score. The score on any

[1]The term *subtest* will be used to refer to a self-contained section of a test, that is, a sequence of items all of which contribute to a common score and are not scored on any other subtest. On a test with time limits, each subtest generally will be separately timed. All of the items on the subtest generally will be of the same format. A *scale* will refer to any group of items that contribute to a common score. The items on a scale can occur successively or, as usually is the case, may be scattered throughout the test, among items on other scales. Subtests will usually be found on tests of maximal performance, and scales on measures of typical performance.

subsection or the test proper will be the composite of the scores on the individual items.[2] Most frequently, the scale scores are unweighted composites, that is, all items are given equivalent (usually unit) weights:

$$X_c = I_1 + I_2 + \cdots + I_i + \cdots + I_n \tag{8.1}$$

where X_c is the composite score and I_1 through I_n are the scores on the n individual items comprising the test. It is also possible to weight the individual items differentially:

$$X_c = a_1 I_1 + a_2 I_2 + \cdots + a_i I_i \cdots + a_n I_n \tag{8.2}$$

where a_1 to a_n are the weights assigned to each item. Unless he has some specific interest in the individual items, the test user generally will work with only the composite score (X_c).

The empirical data show that the validity of an unweighted composite usually closely approximates the validity of a weighted composite when the composite is based on a large number of elements, as is the case for items constituting a test, thus test items generally are not differentially weighted.

Combining subtests

Many tests are composed of several subtests or scales, each of which yields a score; these scores may or may not be combined into a composite score. For example, the Guilford-Zimmerman Temperament Survey has ten scales measuring such traits as general activity level, objectivity-subjectivity, and masculinity-femininity. A score is obtained on each scale but there is no overall or total score. The male form of the Strong Vocational Interest Blank reports scores for approximately 50 occupations and, like the Guilford-Zimmerman, has no total score. On the other hand there are a number of tests that provide both subtest and composite scores. The Wechsler Adult Intelligence Scale (WAIS) is a good example. The WAIS is composed of 11 independent subtests. Six of these subtests (Vocabulary, Information, Arithmetic, Comprehension, Similarities, and Digit Span) comprise a Verbal Scale, and the sum of the scores on these six subtests is transformed into a Verbal IQ. The other five scales (Digit Symbol, Picture Completion, Block Design, Picture Arrangement, and Object Assembly) comprise a Performance Scale, and a Performance IQ is computed in an analogous manner. A Full Scale IQ is derived from performance on all 11 subtests.

As is the case when individual items are combined into a composite score, when subtests are combined into a composite, the primary consideration is to determine the optimal weighting for each subtest score.

[2] In addition to scored items, a test or subtest may also contain items that are not scored, e.g., "warm-up" items, experimental items or buffer items.

Combining tests

Frequently several tests or predictors[3] are utilized simultaneously. For example, when deciding among applicants, the admissions officer of a college will frequently consider high school grades, scores on college aptitude and achievement tests, accomplishment in nonacademic areas, and recommendations of teachers and counselors. Counselors in the U. S. Employment Service, when counseling adults about job placement frequently administer the General Aptitude Test Battery, a battery consisting of 12 tests, measuring nine factors, that are predictive of success in various occupations.

In both of these situations the test user is faced with the problem of making sense of the results of the several tests. In order to arrive at the decision he needs to make, he must, in some manner, combine the test scores, taking into account not only the data that confirm each other, but also the contradictions in the data. In other words, he must find a pattern that permits the data to be summarized.

Three basic questions

In any situation where test scores are to be combined, three interrelated questions must be answered. First, what methods may appropriately be used to combine the scores? Second, what is the optimal method of combining the scores? And third, how much and what kind of data (scores) are needed to produce an optimal combination?

The answer to the first question will depend primarily on the purpose of combining the test scores—on the decision that has to be made. If the desired outcome requires that the individuals in the sample be ranked in order of competence, one technique will be appropriate; if the outcome requires only that individuals be placed in broad groups, a different technique is needed; if the grouping is known and the question is which variables best differentiate the groups, still another method may be used. In short, the type of problem will be the primary determinant of the appropriateness of the method.

Although certain characteristics of the data (e.g., whether they are expressed on an ordinal or interval scale) may influence the choice of a method, in general types of data and method are independent. That is, the same set of data may be combined by different methods and/or for different purposes. For example, a combination of aptitude, achievement, and interest test data could be used, even for the same individual, in a selection battery, to choose among several jobs

[3]When discussing techniques that combine scores for predictive purposes we will use the terms test and predictor interchangeably. A predictor may be a test, as defined in Chapter 1, or any other quantifiable variable, e.g., years of education, age, occupational level, number of previous jobs.

(placement) and for long-range vocational counseling. Because these three problems ask different questions and thereby require different answers, the method of combining scores might well be different in each situation. Yet all methods would utilize the same set of data.

The second question is essentially the validity question. Generally we are looking for the combination of tests that yields the highest criterion-related validity and thus will evaluate the composite by the standards of criterion-related validity (see Chapter 5). In situations where criterion-related validity is not the appropriate concern, (e.g., as in factor analytic studies) evaluation will, of course, be made in terms of the relevant variety of validity.

The third question is closely related to the other two, especially the second. In situations where a combination of tests is being used to predict a criterion, we start with the single best predictor and keep adding predictors to the composite as long as the validity of the new combination is higher than that of the previous combination. If a test is added to the composite and the validity of the composite does not increase, the test has provided us with no new information and can be eliminated. Because we are interested in tests that add some increment to predictive accuracy, we are concerned with *incremental validity* (Sechrest, 1963). If a test contributes some unique variance to the combination, it may increase predictive accuracy and thus have incremental validity; if it does not add to predictive accuracy, it is tapping essentially the same traits or characteristics as the predictors already being used and thus tells us nothing that we do not already know. One important task, then, is to select variables that will demonstrate incremental validity, i.e., ones that tap unique components.

A parallel concern is the number of variables needed before a composite attains optimal predictive accuracy. Empirical studies show that when combining test scores into a composite predictor the point of diminishing returns generally occurs quite rapidly. Rarely does the inclusion of more than three or four variables increase the predictive accuracy in any practically significant amount.

METHODS OF COMBINING TEST SCORES

In this section we will consider the various ways that scale, subtest, and test scores may be combined into a composite measure. In discussing the various methods we generally will not differentiate between combining subtest scores and combining test scores (which themselves are composites of item and/or subtest scores) because the logic of the method remains the same regardless of the unit of analysis. We will present the logic of each method, describe the appropriate purposes and uses for the method, and indicate some of its advantages and limitations. Whenever feasible, an example based on actual data will be included.

To provide a framework for the discussion that follows, we present some of the dimensions along which the techniques vary. (1) As mentioned above, the scores contributing to the composite can be given equal weight or they may be differentially weighted. Differential weighting may be made on some rational basis, to produce an optimal weighting according to the particular criterion of optimality, or it might merely be fortuitous, reflecting some empirical characteristic of the data. (2) Some of the methods assign individuals to classes or categories while others utilize continuous measurement. The measurement mode may vary between the input and output sides or may be the same on both sides. (3) The method of combination may be either statistical, rational, or intuitive. That is, the combination may be made according to a statistical model or on the basis of the psychologist's judgment. (4) The variables used may be either objective, e.g., test scores or demographic information, or subjective, e.g., ratings or attributed characteristics. If the data are to be combined statistically, even the subjective data must be assigned numerical values; if the mode of combination is intuitive, such quantification is not essential. (5) Some of the methods assume that a low score in one area can be compensated for by an excess of another ability or skill; other methods are noncompensatory, eliminating persons who fall below a cutting score on any test. (6) The addition of the tests to the composite may be simultaneous or sequential—that is, all variables may be analyzed simultaneously or the analysis may proceed in stages. Some methods can operate in either fashion. (7) Some of the methods are predictive, having as their goal the optimal prediction of some criterion. Other techniques are descriptive, serving only to summarize the data from diverse measures.

With these dimensions in mind, we now turn to a discussion of six major methods of combining test scores—clinical judgment, rational methods, multiple cutoff, multiple regression, discriminant analysis, and factor analysis—and several lesser known but interesting methods.

Clinical judgment

Probably the most frequently used method is for the test user to make some intuitive combination of the test scores. The high school counselor, when discussing college plans with a student, generally does not make statistical predictions of the student's chances of success in each college being considered. Rather he will consider the student's high school grades, scores on college admissions tests, other people's opinions about the student, and his knowledge of the various colleges and make some general summary statement or prediction such as: "State University may be a little rough, but Northwest College offers the same program and you'll have a better chance of succeeding there." Or a clinical psychologist, reflecting on scores on various scales of a personality inventory, might conclude: "The patient is very depressed, emotionally unstable, anxious, and tends to act out his problems. Yet, as he has highly developed superego controls, I don't think that he will commit suicide." In both examples, the psychologist weighed the various factors and arrived at a conclusion or prediction.

The distinguishing characteristic of the clinical approach is that it is an individualized intuitive process. Regardless of the type of data used as input—be it objective, subjective, or a combination of both—the psychologist considers the diverse data and arrives at what, to him, seems to be the meaning of the data. The results of his deliberations may be a global statement (This man is dishonest), a specific prediction (He will cheat on the final exam), or a series of if-then statements (If he feels that he cannot obtain an A any other way, then he will cheat. If the probability of being caught is low, then he will cheat). He may also attach some degree of confidence to his judgment. The form of the judgment and its specificity will be determined by the purposes of the judgment and the willingness of the psychologist to be specific in his predictions.

How the psychologist combines data clinically has been extensively studied (see, e.g. Meehl 1954, 1957; Holt, 1958; Hoffman, 1960; Goldberg, 1968) but the parameters are still not completely defined. However, the process goes somewhat as follows: When a psychologist looks at a test profile he undoubtedly considers several elements: the highest score or scores, the lowest scores, the general elevation of the profile (Are the scores generally high or low?), the scatter (Do the scores tend to cluster at one level, or are some high and some low?), the shape of the profile, and so forth. He also takes into account what he considers the unique features of the scores or combinations of scores, other characteristics of the individual that he thinks may influence the scores, and situational and environmental factors. He then combines the various data, differentially weighing the factors according to what he thinks is their relative importance. This weighing is, of course, not explicit and precise like a mathematical formula but rather an implicit, perhaps even unconscious, phenomenon. Yet the net result is a prediction from the data.

VALIDITY. The usefulness of clinical prediction, as with the usefulness of any other technique, must be evaluated by determining its validity. That is, the number of correct decisions made using the clinical approach must be compared with the number of correct decisions made using other approaches. Unless the approach can produce more correct decisions, make the same number of correct decisions more efficiently, or make different types of predictions than will other methods, it is no more valuable. The usefulness of clinical prediction will be discussed in detail after a consideration of other types of methods for combining test scores. Suffice to say here that the evidence for the superiority of clinical judgment over statistical methods is far from overwhelming.

EVALUATION OF THE CLINICAL APPROACH. Advocates of the clinical approach stress its several presumed advantages. First, it allows for consideration of unique and/or configural patterns of scores. Because most of the statistical techniques involve linear combinations of variables, or at best only simple configurations, the clinician would argue that they are limited in usefulness; only human judgment is capable of discriminating such configurations. To really understand and predict human behavior one must take into account the highly configural nature of the interactions between variables. Second, as statistical analyses are normative, they do not indicate how to handle atypical patterns. Because each individual is unique and atypical, normative statistical techniques are never completely applicable to any individual. Hence sophisticated clinical analyses are needed. Third, even if normative data are generally applicable in a particular situation, statistical predictions must be overridden in certain circumstances. For example, Meehl (1954) gives an example of the highly predictable movie-going behavior of an individual being disrupted by his sustaining a broken leg. The clinician would argue that he, being aware of this overriding factor (the broken leg) could take it into account and reverse the prediction, while the statistical formula has no provision for incorporating this new bit of data. In short, clinical prediction could be expected to be of value when there are unique or novel patterns, when some special factor influences the prediction, and when the probabilities of occurrence (base rates) of one or more variables are very low.

In response, the statistically oriented psychologist would argue that the assumption of complex configural patterns has not been verified by available data, that the clinician's supposed ability to identify overriding causes is often misused, and that following the base rates or statistical predictions will lead to the maximum hit rate. They view the clinician as operating like an inefficient computer, one that assigns less than optimum weights to the predictor variables. The weight of the evidence, at least as it pertains to the prediction of specific outcomes or behaviors, tends to support the statistician rather than the clinician.

Rational methods

A second approach utilizes rational bases for combining test scores. The simplest approach would be to sum the scores of the individual variables (e.g., items, subtests, tests) to arrive at a composite score:

$$X_c = X_1 + X_2 \cdots + X_i \cdots + X_n \tag{8.3}$$

where X_c is the composite score and $X_1 \ldots X_i \ldots X_n$ are the scores on the n variables making up the composite. Although Equation (8.3) might appear to weight all variables equally, in fact the weight given to each variable will be proportional to its standard deviation—the test with the largest s being weighted heaviest and those with a smaller s receiving less weight. To weight each subtest equally requires that the standard deviations of all tests be equal. This can be accomplished by changing all scores to standard scores and then combining them:

$$z_c = z_1 + z_2 \cdots + z_i \cdots + z_n \tag{8.4}$$

where $z_1 \ldots z_i \ldots z_n$ are the scores on each test expressed in standard score form. Other rational weighting methods could also be used. For example, we could weight the scores according to their reliabilities or according to the standard error of measurement. All of these methods involve purely rational weighting based on some *a priori* conception of the ideal weighting procedure.

VALIDITY. As is true with clinical combinations, the ultimate test is the validity of the predictions made using alternative weighting methods. The empirical evidence indicates that when a small number of predictors are involved, differential weighting based on empirical relationships between variables generally results in more valid predictions and thus is to be preferred over rational weighting systems. With a large number of predictors, however, the validity of simple unit weighting generally approaches that of differential weighting and thus may be substituted, with little loss of precision, for the more complex differential weighting techniques. The prime example is the weighting of items comprising a test. Because a test generally includes a relatively large number of items, it is generally not necessary to use other than simple unit weights—score one point for a keyed response and zero for other responses—for item scores. In fact, several tests that formerly used differential item weighting systems have moved to a unit weight system. For example, the Strong Vocational Interest Blank, in its latest revision, has changed from a -4 to $+4$ weighting system to a $-1, 0, +1$ weighting format (Strong and Campbell, 1966).

In summary, unless there is some compelling reason for using one of the rational weighting systems, elements in a composite will generally be given unit weights or will be differentially weighted by a technique, such as multiple regression (see below), that takes into account empirical relationships among variables. The former approach will generally be used to weight items, the latter for weighting tests in a prediction equation.

Multiple cutoff

In the discussion of criterion-related validity (Chapter 5), methods of determining an optimal cutting score were discussed. The cutting score was set so as to maximize the probability that a person scoring higher than the cutting score would succeed on the criterion task, and one whose score fell below the cutting score would fail. The cutting score served as the selection point, persons scoring above the line being accepted and those scoring below it being rejected. Although, when dealing with psychological traits, discrimination is generally probabilistic and imprecise, when considering other characteristics such as physical abilities, one can conceive of cutting points that represent minimum standards—standards that a person must attain if he is to succeed on the criterion task. For example, near-normal hearing is necessary if a person is to function effectively as a telephone switchboard operator; jet pilots must be of a certain stature if they are to fit in the cockpit and be able to reach the important controls; a fire watcher in a National Forest lookout tower must have acute vision, otherwise he could not spot a fire.

THE PARADIGM.   With either probabilistic or deterministic discrimination, it is possible to develop cutting scores on two or more predictors operating jointly. The paradigm for this procedure, using two predictors, is shown in Figure 8.1. If the individual's scores are above the cutting score on both variables, he is acceptable; if his score on *either* variable falls below the cutting score on that variable, he is not acceptable. This paradigm can be generalized to any number of predictors (dimensions) but, regardless of the number of predictors, if the person's score falls below the cutting line on *any* variable, he is rejected; to be accepted, he must exceed the cutting score on *all* variables.

Several points about the multiple-cutoff model should be noted:

1. The model is noncompensatory. That is, a poor performance (score) on one variable cannot be compensated for by superior performance on another variable. Even if a person obtained exceedingly high scores on all tests except one, and fell below the cutting score on that one, he would be eliminated. Therefore, this model is appropriately used only when there is evidence that the variables are, in fact, noncompensatory. If compensation between predictors does occur, and the multiple-cutoff model is used, many errors in classification

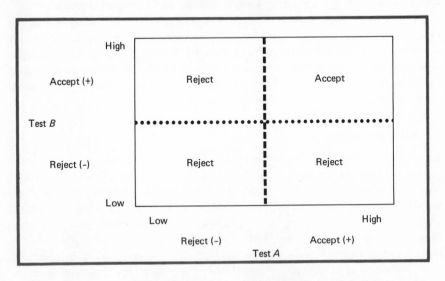

Figure 8.1 The multiple-cutoff paradigm. The marginal categories show the decision (accept or reject) on each test considered individually; scores on both variables run along some continuum from low to high; the broken line indicates the cutting score on Test *A*, the dotted line the cutting score on Test *B*; the cells of the table show the decision based on both tests acting as joint predictors.

will be made. These errors will consist of eliminating some individuals who could have succeeded and selecting some who will fail.

2. The model is most relevant when discrete cutting lines differentiate persons having the necessary requirements from those who lack the relevant skills; in these circumstances, setting the cutting line consists of identifying the point of this minimum amount of ability. If the model is used with probabilistic data, where there is no definite cutting point, the cutting scores will be set to maximize certain outcomes. In this latter situation, cutting scores on the several variables will be manipulated simultaneously to obtain the desired outcomes; in the former case, cutting scores can be determined for each variable independently.

3. The decision made is either to accept or reject. That is, the individual is placed in one of two categories—those meeting the minimum requirements and those who do not meet the minimum standards. (More complex or numerous categories can be used. To clarify exposition, however, the discussion will be restricted to the two category case.) Thus we obtain a pool of acceptable candidates; if we wish to rank the people within this pool, or otherwise distinguish between them, we must use an additional analysis.

DETERMINING VALIDITY. The validity of predictions made using the multiple-cutoff paradigm is evaluated by determining the number of correct decisions (placements) made. As is the case with single predictors, the evaluative criterion may be either total correct decisions or positive hits. The number of correct decisions must also be compared to the base rates and to other techniques to determine if multiple cutoff is the optimal strategy. As with all techniques involving multiple predictors, one is also interested in the point at which adding additional predictors does not increase the validity of the composite.

AN EXAMPLE. An example of the development and evaluation of a multiple-cutoff prediction strategy is shown in Table 8.1. This example uses two predictors, neither of which has a distinct cutting point. Thus the example shows how cutting lines on two variables can be set jointly so as to maximize the number of correct decisions.

SUCCESSIVE HURDLES. The discussion of the multiple-cutoff method assumed that the scores on all the predictors were obtained concurrently. In practice, however, the predictor data are often collected sequentially. With sequential administration of predictors, all applicants do not take all tests; instead, only applicants who pass one test go on to the next one in the sequence, the rest of the group being eliminated. Because successful applicants must pass a series of tests, or surmount a series of hurdles, the method is often referred to as "successive hurdles."

TABLE 8.1   An example of the multiple-cutoff method

(1) PROBLEM. To determine the optimal combination of cutting scores on two variables—rank in high school class (HSR) and an achievement test on high school mathematics (MATH)—to select students for a college of engineering.

SAMPLE. 660 freshmen engineering students in a midwestern university.

CRITERION. Grade-point average (GPA) during the freshman year. This measure was dichotomized at GPA = 2.00, the minimal GPA needed for continuation in the program. Students obtaining a GPA $\geq$ 2.00 were considered acceptable, those with GPA < 2.00 were unacceptable.

VALIDITY. The total number of correct decisions (total hits) was used as a validity index.

(2) DATA. The basic data are listed in the table below. The first figure in each cell is the number of students with GPA < 2.00, the second figure is the number with GPA $\geq$ 2.00. The scores have been grouped into classes. Note that a HSR = 1 is the highest score and that greater values indicate a lower class rank.

HSR	MATH 0–24	25–29	30–34	35–39	40–44	45–49	50–54	55–65	Σ
1–5	*	0–2	1–4	2–10	2–11	1–16	0–23	1–28	7–94
6–10	*	1–5	1–3	1–17	2–22	0–28	1–25	0–12	6–112
11–15	0–2	1–0	2–7	1–13	4–17	1–12	3–7	1–5	13–63
16–20	1–2	2–2	2–10	2–12	6–13	6–9	0–4	1–6	20–58
21–25	1–2	2–2	3–5	5–5	5–13	4–12	2–10	*	22–49
26–30	3–1	2–3	2–13	5–5	2–6	1–4	2–4	0–1	17–37
31–35	3–3	2–2	8–5	4–6	3–1	1–3	0–6	*	21–26
36–40	3–2	2–2	0–5	5–2	1–1	2–3	*	*	13-15
41–45	2–0	1–3	5–3	2–3	3–4	2–1	*	*	15–14
46–50	2–3	3–0	1–2	2–1	2–2	*	*	*	10–8
51–60	7–4	1–0	2–1	*	1–0	*	0–1	*	11–6
61–99	12–3	6–0	1–1	*	*	*	*	*	19–4
Σ	34–22	23–21	28–59	29–74	31–90	18–88	8–80	3–52	174–486 = 660

*No cases in cell.

(3) ANALYSIS. To determine the optimal cutting score—ignoring the problem of the number of places available in the class—required considering the number of correct decisions made using a particular pair of cutting lines. If we choose, for example, the cutting lines HSR $\leq$ 35 and MATH $\geq$ 30:

Table 8.1 (continued)

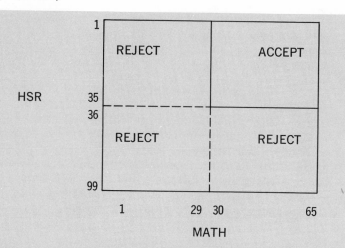

we would find that use of these cutting lines would result in 499 correct decisions—413 persons who were accepted and succeeded plus 86 rejects who would have failed.

Varying the cutting lines in analogous fashion we find:

CUTTING SCORE		ACCEPT		REJECT		TOTAL
		GPA		GPA		
MATH	HSR	<2.00	≥2.00	<2.00	≥2.00	HITS
30	35	88–413		86–73		499
30	40	96–424		78–62		502
30	45	108–435		66–51		501
30	50	113–440		61–46		501
30	60	116–442		58–44		500
25	35	98–429		76–57		505
25	40	108–442		66–44		508
25	45	121–456		53–30		509
25	50	129–461		45–25		506
25	60	133–463		41–23		504

(4) INTERPRETATION. The optimal selection procedure would be to require a combination of a MATH score of 25 or higher and an HSR of 45 or less. Using these cutting scores, 509 correct decisions would be made, an improvement of 23 (about 5 percent) over the base rates. The selection ratio, using these cutting scores, would be .87, or almost 9 of 10 applicants would be accepted. The fact that only a small increase in predictive accuracy was found can be

Table 8.1 (continued)

> attributed, at least in part to (1) the large degree of self-selection occurring among students entering the curricula and (2) by utilizing grades for the freshman year, students who dropped out during the year—who are generally of lower ability than those who persist—are not included in the data.
>
> Because no great improvement in hit rate was attained, and refusing admission to a student who might succeed is certainly less desirable than admitting a student who later fails, one might well conclude that no cutting lines should be set, and the admissions policies be left unchanged.
>
> (5) ADDENDUM.   It can be shown that the same maximum hit rate can be attained using HSR alone, and thus MATH adds nothing to predictive efficiency. The student who wishes to confirm the last statement can work out the problem for himself.

To illustrate the method, consider the case of a company recruiter trying to hire college graduates to work as production engineers in an automobile manufacturing plant. His first requirement may be that the applicants have a major in Mechanical Engineering. This is the first hurdle. Only mechanical engineering students can go on to the next step; all other applicants are eliminated, regardless of their interest in or aptitude for the job. As a second step, or hurdle, the applicant has an on-campus interview with the recruiter. Those that obtain a favorable rating from the interviewer can go on to the next step, and those with unfavorable ratings are eliminated. Let us suppose that the next step is a test battery. Only those persons who passed the recruiters' scrutiny take the tests. Again, some applicants pass and others fail, further reducing the pool. As a final hurdle, those who succeeded on the test battery have an interview with their prospective supervisor at the job site. Those that receive an acceptable rating are offered positions, the others must look elsewhere. Only those persons who passed all hurdles were offered a job; those that failed at any single point in the sequence were eliminated. This sequence is illustrated in Figure 8.2.

If the sequential selection procedure is to have the maximum value, the most valid predictor should be used first, followed by the next most valid predictor, and so on. The last step would utilize the least valid predictor. At this point, the predictor may be little better than chance, but since the pool of surviving applicants is the best pool possible, given the validity of the predictors, the validity of the entire sequence will be only slightly affected by the use of a poorer predictor at this point.

In practice, the order of presentation of the predictors is usually determined by practical and economic considerations. Because it is more economical to send one recruiter to a university to interview 50 students than to send these 50 students to the company plant for interviews, the on-campus interview is usually

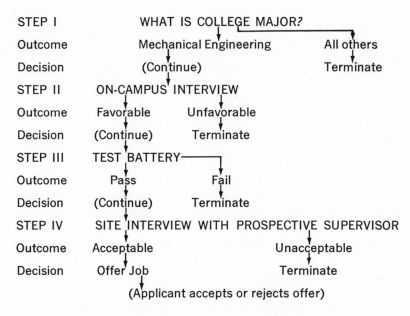

Figure 8.2 An example of a sequential selection strategy.

conducted before the plant interview, regardless of the validity of the two inter-views. Similarly, relatively simple selection methods, such as the application blank and screening tests, are often administered early in an employment pro-cedure because they are rapid, inexpensive ways to reduce the pool of appli-cants. The more costly and time consuming (though not necessarily more valid) selection methods occur later in the sequence and are applied to a smaller group of applicants, i.e., those that have survived the first hurdles. The total cost of the selection procedure is thus minimized.

EVALUATION OF THE MULTIPLE-CUTOFF METHOD.   The primary advantage of the multiple-cutoff method is, of course, its applicability to situations where precise minimum or cutting scores can be established on certain crucial vari-ables. By its noncompensatory nature the model assures that a person's ex-ceedingly good performance on one variable does not overshadow, or com-pensate for, his deficiencies in other areas. The model is appropriate for se-quential selection strategies and when the variables combine in a nonlinear manner. The model is also highly compatible with a decision-making accuracy approach to validity. Finally, the computation ease and ready interpretability are desirable features.

The model also has several disadvantages. By using classes rather than con-tinuous measurement, some precision is sacrificed. Unless there are definable, absolute cutting scores, some people whose scores fall just below the cutting lines, and who would have succeeded through utilization of a compensatory skill or ability, will be eliminated. Also, the technique provides a pool of acceptable candidates, not a rank ordering; to select from the pool those persons with the greatest probability of success requires further analyses using different techniques.

Multiple regression

The multiple-cutoff method assumed that there was no compensation between predictors. However, in most situations involving psychological variables some degree of compensation does occur. One student may study long hours to compensate for his lesser ability or weaker background in a course while another student, possessing a facile mind and retentive memory, studies hardly at all; two workers attain the same production level, one by working rapidly and producing a relatively large number of both acceptable and defective units, the other works by working slowly but rarely spoiling a unit; one football receiver uses his speed to get free, another compensates for his lack of speed by excellent fakes. In all of these situations, a relatively high degree of one skill or ability compensates for a relative weakness in another relevant area.

THE PARADIGM. In situations where compensation is the rule, a procedure other than multiple cutoff can be used; multiple regression is the most frequently used model. Multiple regression is similar to the regression procedure described in Chapter 5 except that more than one predictor is used.

The basic logic of multiple regression can best be illustrated by the regression equation. A *multiple-regression equation* takes the form:

$$Y' = a + b_1 X_1 + b_2 X_2 + \cdots + b_i X_i \cdots + b_n X_n \qquad (8.5)$$

where Y' is the predicted criterion score, X_1 through X_n are the scores on the n predictor variables, and a and b_1 through b_n are weighting constants.[4] Each predictor (X_i) receives a weight (b_i) that is proportional to its contribution to predictive accuracy. This additive nature of the equation establishes the compensatory nature of the analysis.

To better illustrate the compensatory nature of the model, consider the case where there are only two predictors, both positively correlated with the criterion measure. In this situation the regression equation will have the form:

$$Y' = a + b_I X_I + b_{II} X_{II} \qquad (8.5a)$$

Because a, b_I, and b_{II} are all constants, the only values that can change are X_I and X_{II}. Various combinations of scores on X_I and X_{II} will produce the same

---

[4] Equation (8.5) and our discussions and examples will use raw scores in the regression equation. Analogous equations could be written in standard score format.

predicted criterion score (Y'). At one extreme would be a person who scored high on Test I and relatively low on Test II; at the other extreme would be a person who scored low on Test I but high on Test II. The same predicted criterion score could also be obtained by a person scoring in the middle ranges on both tests.

Figure 8.3 shows the multiple-regression model in a two-predictor problem. The exact placement and slope of the line indicating a given predicted criterion score will depend on the relative contributions of each predictor variable to predictive accuracy. The compensatory nature of the model should be obvious from Figure 8.3. Analogous figures could be conceived for any number of predictors.

The computational details of the multiple-regression analysis, being quite complex, will not be discussed in detail here; instead only general statements describing the procedure will be made. The reader who is interested in the details of multiple-regression analysis should consult a statistics textbook (e.g., Dubois, 1957; Edwards, 1969; and Hays, 1963).

The input data are the means and standard deviations of the predictors and criterion and a correlation matrix—a table showing the correlations between all pairs of variables. The analysis proper consists of solving a series of simultaneous equations, a task which nowadays is usually done by a computer. The analysis weights the predictors so that the combination of weighted test scores that pre-

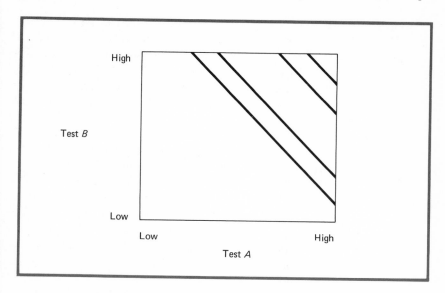

Figure 8.3 The multiple regression paradigm. The lines within the figure are lines of equal predicted criterion scores, i.e., every point on a given line represents an equivalent predicted score; the closer the line to the upper right hand corner, the higher the predicted score.

dicts the criterion with the least amount of error is obtained. The output has two components of prime interest: (1) the regression equation [see formula (8.5)] which indicates the weighting of the various tests and can thus be used for predictive purposes and (2) a *multiple-correlation coefficient*, R, which indicates the correlation between the various predictors, considered jointly, and the criterion measure.

Several aspects of the analysis merit special mention: (1) As the analysis is based on a linear model, it is appropriate only when the relationship between predictors and the criterion is linear. (2) Theoretically, any number of variables can be used as predictors; in practice, the number is limited by the available data and computational facilities. (3) The method allows computation of error estimates for both R and the weighting factors (beta weights); thus the statistical significance of the multiple correlation and its components can be determined. The ability to determine the significance of the contribution of any variable allows variables that contribute no significant variance to be eliminated and the regression equation to be based on only those variables which add to predictive accuracy. (4) In general, variables that will contribute to predictive accuracy, and thus will be included in the regression equation, are those having high correlations with the criterion and low correlations with the other predictors. These are the variables which predict some significant, unique component of the criterion behavior.

VALIDITY. Validity in the multiple-regression model can be viewed from two angles: the validity of the overall prediction and the validity of each component predictor. The former, the validity of the composite, is indicated by the magnitude of the multiple-correlation coefficient, R. The interpretation of this coefficient is analogous to the interpretation of a validity coefficient derived from a single predictor (see Chapter 5). The validity of each individual predictor can be evaluated by determining its incremental validity, that is, by asking if this predictor contributes any unique variance, and if it increases predictive accuracy over and above the level of accuracy attained without including it in the multiple correlation. If a predictor does not significantly increase R it can be eliminated. Using this criterion of validity, variables that are correlated with the criterion may well not be included in the prediction (regression) equation because they measure a trait or characteristic tapped by another variable already included in the equation, and thus contribute no additional information. In practice, two to four predictors generally are sufficient to reach maximal predictive accuracy.

AN EXAMPLE. An example of a multiple-regression analysis is shown in Table 8.2. The problem considered is that of predicting college grades from high school performance and test scores. The analysis was made by a *stepwise* procedure, i.e., the best predictor was included first; then the predictor, which, in combination with the best predictor, increased R the greatest amount was added; the third predictor included was the one, which in combination with the first two, added the greatest amount to R; and so on. The analysis was terminated when an additional variable no longer significantly increased the multiple-correlation coefficient. The computational steps are not shown, only the summary data—R and the regression equation—at each step. Inspection of Table 8.2 will show that several of the points mentioned previously hold, e.g., the variables included in the regression equation are those that have high correlations with the criterion and low correlations with the previously added variables; not all predictors are added to the prediction equation. As the data in Table 8.2 are the same as those in Table 8.1, the differences in the two approaches can be seen by comparing the two tables.

EVALUATION OF THE MULTIPLE-REGRESSION METHOD. Probably the greatest advantage of the multiple-regression method is that it allows a predicted criterion score to be derived for any individual. By substituting the person's test scores in the regression equation, his predicted criterion score can be obtained. Individuals can thus be ranked according to their predicted criterion performance. Another advantage is that, because of the compensatory nature of the model, various combinations of ability patterns are acceptable. Also an index of predictive accuracy R (or R^2), is available along with an estimate of prediction error (the standard error of estimate). The selection of the variables to be included in the regression equation from among all possible predictors is also objective, being determined by the significance of the beta weights for each variable.

The disadvantages are several. The computational labor is tedious, an objection that is mitigated by the availability of computers and other calculating devices. Second, the availability of a predicted criterion score may give an aura of exact predictability when the predicted criterion score is actually a best estimate, the mean of the distribution of criterion scores for all individuals having the same predictor scores. However, one can compute the standard error of estimate of a multiple-correlation coefficient (R) in a manner analogous to that used with r. And, third, the model is inappropriate when compensation among abilities cannot be assumed; when a minimal level of one ability is, in fact, necessary; and when predictor scores are not related to the criterion in a linear manner.

Discriminant analysis

In both the multiple-cutoff and multiple-regression models, scores on a number of predictors were combined to predict some criterion performance. That is, the orientation was toward a selection problem where the basic question was: "Which individuals will perform better?" However, another question can be

TABLE 8.2　Example of a multiple-regression problem

(1) PROBLEM. Scores on seven tests—two scholastic aptitude tests (ACT, MSAT), a test of reading speed (RDG SP) and comprehension (RDG COMP), an English test (ENGL), and a math test (MATH)—plus the student's rank in his high school class (HSR) were used to predict grade-point average (GPA) during the freshman year. The sample consisted of 660 freshmen in the College of Engineering at a midwestern university.

ANALYSIS. Analysis was done on a computer using a step-wise multiple-regression procedure which adds the predictors one at a time, in order of their contribution to the multiple correlation.

(2) THE INPUT DATA. The input data consisted of the means and standard deviation on all variables plus the matrix of intercorrelations among the variables. These data were:

Variable	$\bar{X}$	s	GPA	HSR	ACT	MSAT	RDG SP	RDG COMP	ENGL	MATH
GPA	2.317	.625	1.000							
HSR	21.4	17.0	−.544	1.000						
ACT	26.1	3.3	.444	−.621	1.000					
MSAT	52.2	12.4	.384	−.553	.760	1.000				
RDG SP	40.4	9.2	.237	−.313	.497	.456	1.000			
RDG COMP	28.5	9.3	.327	−.431	.675	.661	.844	1.000		
ENGL	186.3	28.5	.390	−.589	.705	.741	.468	.594	1.000	
MATH	40.5	10.9	.471	−.592	.681	.598	.374	.481	.591	1.000

Note that HSR is scaled so that a score of 1 is the highest possible score, and 100 the lowest; thus HSR correlated negatively with other variables. GPA is on a scale where A = 4, B = 3, etc.

(3) STEP I. The first step selected the single best predictor. This predictor was HSR and its validity was .544:

$$R_{\text{GPA,HSR}} = .544$$

Table 8.2 (continued)

The regression equation, using only HSR would be:

$$GPA' = 2.74523 - .01998 \,(HSR)$$

where GPA' is the predicted GPA. Note also, that the important fact is the magnitude of the correlation between HSR and GPA, not the sign of the correlation.

(4) STEP II. The second step selected the variable, which in combination with HSR, gave the highest value of R. This predictor was MATH and the multiple correlation was:

$$R_{GPA,HSR+MATH} = .574$$

and the regression equation would be:

$$GPA' = 2.10372 - .01499 \,(HSR) + .01321 \,(MATH)$$

(5) STEP III. The next step selected the variable, that in combination with HSR and MATH gave the highest R. This variable was ACT and the multiple R was:

$$R_{GPA,HSR+MATH+ACT} = .577$$

and the regression equation would be:

$$GPA' = 1.79550 - .01408 \,(HSR) + .01115 \,(MATH) + .01423 \,(ACT)$$

(6) STEPS IV–VII. These steps added the remaining variables in order, but as none of the variables increased R more than .01, they were not added to the regression equation.
(7) SUMMARY. The results can be summarized by showing R, R^2, and the increase in R produced by each additional variable.

Step	Variables	R	R^2	Increase in R
(I)	HSR	.544	.296	.544
(II)	MATH	.574	.330	.030
(III)	ACT	.577	.333	.003
(IV–VII)	RDG COMP, RDG SP, MSAT, ENGL	.578	.334	.001

The analysis showed that the asymptote of predictive accuracy was reached using three of the seven variables and that using only two variables resulted in essentially as accurate prediction as using three predictors.

asked: "What group does the individual most closely resemble?" Instead of a selection problem we now have a type of classification or placement problem. One method of attacking this problem is *discriminant analysis*. (Several alternative designations—e.g., discriminant function analysis, multiple discriminant analysis —are used interchangeably with the term discriminant analysis.)

THE PARADIGM.   In the previous paragraph the basic question of discriminant analysis was phrased in terms of comparing an individual to a group. Actually that question presupposes another question: "What variables differentiate the groups?" That is, before one can say which of several groups an individual most closely resembles, he must first know what variables differentiate the groups. In other words, the first step is to construct an index to assess the degree of similarity between the groups.

To illustrate, suppose that we have a group of college freshmen who are enrolled in various curricula—engineering, business, physical sciences, social sciences, and the humanities—and we wish to develop an index that can be used in counseling undecided students, i.e., an index that will indicate the curricular group that a student most closely resembles. One method would be to collect a variety of data on each group—their abilities, interests, personal characteristics, etc.—and run a discriminant analysis to determine (1) if the groups were, in fact, different and (2) which variables contribute to the difference, i.e., which variables best discriminate between the groups. If a combination of variables (a discriminant function) can be found which differentiates the groups, it can be applied to assess the similarity of any individual to each of the curricular groups.

Discriminant analysis, to recapitulate, is directed to two problems: (1) determining the combination of variables that best differentiates between defined groups and, (2) once the function that differentiates the group is known, classifying individuals in terms of their similarity to the various groups. In order to accomplish these ends, the analysis attempts to establish the function (combination of variables) that will maximize the differences between groups while minimizing the differences within groups. In terms of variance (or scatter) the analysis can be viewed as attempting to maximize between groups variance and minimize within groups variance. The ideal situation would have subgroups that are distinctly different from each other, but which were each composed of a homogeneous subgroup of persons. In practice, of course, such ideal separation does not occur; rather, the groups overlap in varying degrees.

Although discriminant analysis is not limited to any set number of groups or variables, the logic of the position can best be illustrated using two groups and two variables. Figure 8.4 shows four possible relations between the groups. In section (a) we have very good discrimination between the groups, there being no overlap between the groups on either Test I or Test II. Classification errors would be at a minimum, the only question being the disposition of persons whose scores fall in the range between the groups. Section (b) shows the case where one test (I) discriminates very well and the other (II) not at all. Classification error would be minimal in this situation. In diagram (c) there is overlap on both variables but still fairly good discrimination between groups. Classification

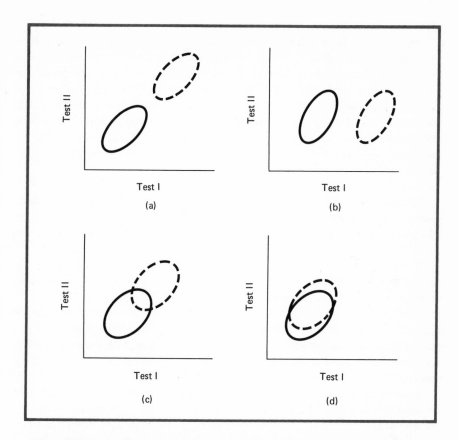

Figure 8.4 The discriminant analysis paradigm: (a) very good discrimination on both variables; (b) very good discrimination on Test I; no discrimination on Test II; (c) some, but not complete, discrimination on both tests; (d) no discrimination on either test; almost complete overlap. [Note: the ellipses represent the distribution of scores within a group.]

would be made on the basis of a combination of the scores on the two variables with relatively few errors. Finally, diagram (d) shows almost complete overlap between the two groups. In this situation, neither variable differentiates the groups, and accurate classification, even on the basis of the two variables, would be impossible.

It should be mentioned that discriminant analysis can readily fit the selection paradigm. The necessary condition is that the groups represent classifications on the criterion measure, e.g., successful carpenters and unsuccessful carpenters, or graduates and dropouts. A discriminant analysis could be performed and if, for example, the applicant resembled successful carpenters rather than unsuccessful ones, he would be hired.

VALIDITY. The validity of the discriminant analysis will be evaluated in various ways, depending upon which of the two aspects of the problem is being investigated. When considering if the two groups can be differentiated, the appropriate index of validity will be the proportion of the variance that is accounted for by the variables making up the discriminant function. The greater the proportion of variance accounted for, the higher the validity. When considered the alternative question, that of the similarity of the individual to the group, the appropriate index is the proportion of correct classifications made— the hit rate.

AN EXAMPLE. Because of the complexity of the rationale and computational procedures of discriminant analysis, no example will be given here. The reader who is interested in an example can consult Cooley & Lohnes (1962, Chapter 6).

EVALUATION OF DISCRIMINANT ANALYSIS. One major advantage of discriminant analysis is that it answers a different type of question, i.e., the question of the similarity of an individual to a group. Moreover, a person can be compared to a number of groups simultaneously. Discriminant analysis not only indicates the variables that differentiate the groups, but also provides a practical aid for classification. By casting the criterion variables in terms of categories of success, it can also be utilized in the selection paradigm. A primary disadvantage would seem to be its computational complexity, which makes it more suitable for research projects and large scale personnel programs than for the occasional user. Because discriminant analysis is a recent development, not enough data have become available to make definitive comparisons between it and other methods.

Factor analysis

Most of the techniques discussed earlier in this chapter combined test scores for prediction or classification purposes, while factor analysis combines scores for other purposes: to reduce the number of variables, summarize a mass of data, or build an index. Whereas the other methods combined heterogeneous measures to improve predictive or classification accuracy, factor analysis combines homogeneous measures with the goal of having one variable, the factor, replace several diverse measures. Thus its usefulness is primarily as a theoretical or explanatory tool, as a method of index construction, rather than as a practical decision-making aid.

THE PARADIGM. Since our previous discussion of factor analysis focused on homogeneity, we will review the general logic of factor analysis and illustrate its application to the problem of combining test scores. Factor analysis, it will be recalled, is a technique for determining the minimum number of constructs (factors) necessary to account for the interrelations (correlations) among a set of variables. Its goal is to find clusters of variables that measure the same factor and fall into a common class. This clustering process reduces the number of explanatory concepts in the system.

When dealing with test (or scale or subtest) scores, the input data for a factor analysis would consist of scores of i individuals on t tests. These data are converted to a correlation matrix showing the correlations between the t tests. The correlation matrix is then factor analyzed by one of a variety of methods (see, e.g., Harman, 1967; Guilford, 1954; or Kerlinger, 1965), the details of which need not concern us here. The factor analysis transforms the correlation matrix into a factor matrix, a matrix giving the correlations between the test scores and the underlying factor scores. That is, the correlation matrix, which has as many columns and rows as there are tests (i.e., is a $t \times t$ matrix) is transformed into a factor matrix having as many rows as tests and as many columns as factors (i.e., a $t \times f$ matrix, where f is the number of factors). Because the number of factors will be less than the number of tests ($f < t$), the factor matrix will be smaller than the correlation matrix.

The factor analysis also provides other information: (1) the minimum number of factors needed to account for the correlations among the tests; (2) the *factor loadings*—the relative weight of each factor in determining the performance on each test; (The factor loadings are essentially the correlations between the test and the factor.) and (3) the *communality*, or the total amount of variance in the test scores accounted for by common factors. A common factor, you will recall, is a factor that two or more variables share in common.

In summary, factor analysis answers the questions: How many factors account for the performance of the test? What are these factors? And, how much variance in each test is accounted for by the common factors? Factor analysis is similar to the other techniques discussed in that it combines scores to arrive at a type of composite; it differs in that the purpose of the combination is not to increase predictive accuracy, but rather to purify explanatory concepts.

AN EXAMPLE.   An example of a factor analysis is shown in Table 8.3. This example has been chosen for illustrative purposes and presents a highly simplified, perhaps unrealistic, example—actual data being much more complex, involving more tests with the factors probably not so clearly evident. However, for illustrative purposes, the clarity and simplicity are virtues.

EVALUATION OF FACTOR ANALYSIS.   Because we have not discussed factor analysis in detail, and a thorough evaluation of its concepts and procedures would require detailed knowledge of the procedures involved, we shall make only general comments on the advantages and disadvantages of the method. Certainly one advantage of factor analysis is its reduction of diverse measures to a smaller number of purer measures. In any situation where psychological con-

TABLE 8.3 Example of a factor analysis

(1) PROBLEM. To factor analyze the correlations between six tests to find (a) the number of factors accounting for performance on the tests, (b) the loadings of each test on each factor, (c) the proportion of variance in each test accounted for by the common factors, and (d) the nature of the factors.

(2) DATA. Suppose we have the following correlation matrix:

	V	R	S	N	AS	AT
V	—	.72	.63	.09	.09	.00
R	.72	—	.57	.15	.16	.09
S	.63	.57	—	.14	.15	.09
N	.09	.15	.14	—	.57	.63
AS	.09	.16	.15	.57	—	.72
AT	.00	.09	.09	.63	.72	—

Inspection of the data reveals that there are two clusters of tests —one composed of tests V, R, and S; the other composed of tests N, AS, and AT.

(3) ANALYSIS. If the correlation matrix (above) is subjected to a factor analysis using Thurstone's centroid method (1947), with rotation, the following factor matrix will be obtained:

TESTS	A	B	C	h^2
V	.86	.00	.03	.74
R	.83	.09	.11	.71
S	.75	.10	—.09	.57
N	.10	.75	—.09	.57
AS	.09	.83	.11	.71
AT	.00	.86	.03	.74

The figures within the table represent the *factor loadings*, the correlation between test and factor scores. Thus the figure .86 in the upper left corner is the loading of Test V on Factor A. The far right column, labeled h^2, gives the *communalities*, or common factor variance. The communality for Test R was obtained $h^2 = (.83)^2 + (.09)^2 + (.11)^2 = .71$; communalities for the other tests were similarly obtained.

(4) INTERPRETATION. The answers to our original questions would be:

    (a) *Number of factors*. Two clear factors emerged, A and B; C representing essentially zero correlations is not an interpretable factor.

Table 8.3 (continued)

> (b) *Factor loadings*. These are shown in the factor matrix. Tests V, R, and S load significantly on Factor A; tests N, AS, and AT load on Factor B.
>
> (c) *Communalities*. These are shown in the right hand column. Four of the tests—V, R, AS, and AT—have over 70 percent of their variance explained by the common factors. The other two have over half of their variance attributable to the common factors.
>
> (d) *Nature of the factors*. This cannot be determined without-knowing the composition of the tests. Given that V is a vocabulary test, R a reading test, S a test of synonyms, N a test of numerical reasoning, and AS and AT arithmetic tests, it would be evident that Factor A was a *verbal* factor and Factor B a *numerical* factor.
>
> ---
>
> [Note of caution. This example is based on fictitious data given by Kerlinger (1965, Chapter 36). Factor analyses of actual data would be more complex, probably involve additional tests, and would not present such clear-cut, readily interpretable results.]

structs are utilized, these constructs must be clearly defined; factor analysis is one step toward better definition. By reducing the number of constructs, through showing that one factor accounts for the scores on several tests, it aids the cause of parsimony and, hopefully, reduces the proliferation of tests. By showing that various tests measure the same concept, and providing evidence on the degree of interrelation of the concepts (factors), it also clarifies the results of psychological research. In situations where relatively pure measures of a given trait or construct (i.e., homogeneous tests) are required, factor analysis of the items would seem to be an essential step in the test construction process. Finally, although factor analytic procedures are not completely objective, they are reproducible by other investigators.

Several criticisms of factor analysis are often heard. One common criticism is that nothing comes out of a factor analysis that doesn't go into it, that is, a factor will not be found unless a test measuring that factor is included in the input data. Although this is undoubtedly a valid criticism of factor analysis, it also pertains to any other type of analysis, a fact that critics of factor analysis sometimes overlook. Second, because there are various methods of factor analysis, one may get different results depending on the computational method used. Probably the most fundamental question here is whether to assume that factors themselves can be correlated (oblique) or must be independent (orthogonal). This question can be resolved only by determining which procedure provides the most explanatory power. A third problem centers around the existential status of factors. If one adopts the framework that factors are only summarizing variables, no problems arise. However, many writers seem to assume that because a factor can be identified it must therefore exist in some real or independent sense. Some writers even go as far as to attribute causal powers to factors. Such attributions pose serious philosophic problems. For further discussion of the "reality" and scientific status of factors see Royce (1963), Guilford (1961), and Overall (1964). Finally, there is the labeling problem. Because labeling a factor is a subjective matter and the results of a factor analysis are frequently not clear cut, the proper label for the factor is not always evident. In these circumstances, different names (or misleading ones) can be assigned to factors, thus masking the meaning of the data.

We should also mention that factor analysis can be applied to data other than test (or item) scores. For example, a factor analysis could be conducted on people, rather than over tests, thus grouping individuals by their similarities rather than producing groupings of tests (Cattell, 1952).

Other methods of combining scores

In this section we will present the basic ideas of several methods of combining scores which are not in as widespread use as techniques discussed above. Since each method represents a distinct point of view or is of particular value in certain circumstances, they are worthy of some, albeit brief, mention.

CONFIGURAL SCORING.   Configural scoring refers to combining scores in ways that consider patterns of responses rather than only simple linear additive combinations. The approach can be applied either to item responses or test scores; we will, however, restrict the usage to combinations of item scores, using the category profile analysis to refer to attempts to combine test (or scale or sub-test) scores configurally.

A classical example of configural scoring is the paradox presented by Meehl (1950). Suppose that two true-false items are used to distinguish between schizophrenic and normal subjects. Both items are administered to 50 schizophrenics and 50 normals and the response pattern shown in the upper portion of Table 8.4 obtained. As can be seen, half of each group responded true (T) and half false (F) to each item and each item considered individually has zero validity. We would predict, therefore, that when the items are considered jointly, the validity would also be zero. However, suppose that all normals answered both items in the same way—either TT or FF—and all schizophrenics were inconsistent in their responses, i.e., responded TF or FT. If this situation obtained, and the two items were scored configurally, the configuration would have perfect validity, normal and schizophrenic subjects being discriminated without error. This result is shown in the bottom half of Table 8.4.

TABLE 8.4   An example of configural scoring

When the items are scored individually the following results obtain:

	ITEM A				ITEM B	
Response		Schiz.	Normal	Response		Schiz.	Normal
	T	25	25		T	25	25
	F	25	25		F	25	25

When the responses to Items A and B are considered jointly, the following results occur:

		Schiz.	Normal
Response	TT or FF	0	50
Pattern	TF or FT	50	0

Because of the possibility of such dramatic increases in validity through configural scoring, and the predisposition to believe that human behavior is complexly and configurally determined, a fair amount of empirical work has been done in the area of configural scoring. Unfortunately little success has been obtained, simpler scoring techniques generally being found to be as valid as configural scoring. These results can be at least partially attributed, no doubt, to the fact that using large numbers of items compensates for interactions among items and the fact that, in many cases, the combinations tried have had no firm theoretical base.

PROFILE ANALYSIS.   Earlier in the chapter, in discussing clinical combinations, we mentioned the intuitive profile analyses performed by the clinician when interpreting test profiles. In addition to these subjective combinations, a number of objective techniques have been developed. For example, Cronbach and Gleser (1953) have developed a general distance function (D^2) which measures the absolute difference in scores between two test profiles. The technique considers only the magnitude of differences between profiles; it does not consider other, perhaps relevant, dimensions of the profile—for example, the shape of the profile.

Other profile analysis techniques are based on various characteristics of the test profile. One approach, which has been widely used with the Minnesota Multiphasic Personality Inventory (MMPI), is to consider "high point" codes. This approach ranks the various scale scores in order of magnitude and classifies the persons on the basis of their (one or two) highest scores. The modal characteristics of persons having this high point code are attributed to any individual obtaining this high point code. Although utilizing a simple ordinal classification method, studies (e.g., Meehl, 1959) have shown this method to be as valid as more complicated profile analysis techniques.

MODERATOR VARIABLES.   A third approach utilizes *moderator variables*, i.e., variables that identify subgroups of persons who are differentially predictable. Thus, if a different pattern of scores is predictive for males and females, then sex is serving as a moderator variable in the situation. Or, if different patterns of scores predict academic success for Negro and white children, then race is serving as a moderator variable in the school situation.

A good example of the empirical development of moderator variables are Ghiselli's studies of predictability (Ghiselli, 1956, 1960a, 1960b, 1963). The general model is as follows: First, following traditional regression procedures for several predictors, a predicted criterion score was obtained for each individual in the sample. Then each person's predicted criterion score was compared to his actual criterion score and a discrepancy score (difference between predicted and obtained criterion scores) obtained. If the absolute value of this discrepancy score is small, the individual is predictable; if its absolute value is large, the individual is unpredictable. The next step is to find a variable that correlates with the discrepancy score. This variable, which is the moderator variable, is usually developed by empirical procedures such as item analysis. The moderator variable is then used to identify predictable and unpredictable persons in future samples. If the predictive battery is applied only to people classified as predictable by the moderator variable, then the validity of the selection procedure can be increased. This increased predictive accuracy is obtained at the cost of a reduction in sample size, unpredictable people being eliminated from further consideration. Ghiselli has found that this technique, based on the assumption of a general trait of predictability, is useful in an industrial selection situation, and other investigators (e.g., Frederiksen & Melville, 1954; Frederiksen & Gilbert, 1960; Saunders, 1956) have found it to be useful in academic situations. Unfortunately, a number of other investigators, including the author (Brown & Scott, 1966) have not replicated the findings. Thus the final verdict as to the usefulness of the technique is not yet in.

Modifications of the moderator approach can also be applied to other problems. For example, the technique can be utilized to determine which of two tests or test batteries is most predictive for an individual, thereby increasing validity while eliminating the necessity of administering the same test to all persons. (See, e.g., Brown & Scott, 1967; Ghiselli, 1960b.)

OTHER MULTIVARIATE TECHNIQUES.   One of the blessings wrought by computers is the feasibility of using statistical techniques whose complex computational procedures previously rendered them inapplicable. In the testing area the availability of computers, besides making analyses like factor analysis and multiple regression less time consuming, has opened the possibility of using other multivariate analyses, analyses that consider several independent (predictor) variables and several dependent (criterion) variables jointly. That is, rather than restrict the studies to problems that relate several predictors to one criterion measure, it is becoming more feasible to study the relation of several predictors to several criterion measures. Because the idea of a single criterion is an oversimplification, with multiple criteria generally being necessary and desirable, such analyses are an improvement over simpler models. For example, we might wish to study the relationship of children's intelligence, family background, achievement in specific subject matter areas, social skills, emotional development, and nonclassroom accomplishments to their academic performance, leadership behavior, and reputation among their peers in such a manner that all outcome variables are considered simultaneously. Or we might want to study the pattern of study techniques characterizing students enrolled in different curricula, where we know that students in different curricula have differing abilities, interests, values, and personality characteristics. Such studies are amenable to multivariate analyses.

Because of the relative newness of such techniques, and their theoretical and computational complexity, they have not yet been widely used in psychological and educational testing. Nor will they be discussed further here. The mathematically sophisticated reader who is interested in pursuing this area should consult sources such as Anderson (1958), Cooley & Lohnes (1962) or Wilks (1962).

COMPARISON OF METHODS

Before discussing the various methods of combining test scores, we listed seven dimensions along which the techniques varied (p. 202). Three of these dimensions—the situations in which each technique is most appropriately used, the requirements of the input and output data, and the validity of the methods—will now be utilized as a basis for comparing the methods.

Comparison along some of the other dimensions are so obvious that they need only brief mention here. For example, it should be evident that clinical judgment is the only technique involving intuitive combinations of data, that the rational methods combine scores according to some rationally developed scheme, and that the other methods—multiple cutoff, multiple regression, discriminant function, and factor analysis—all use statistically based weighting. It should also be evident that, unless a particular fortuitous set of circumstances obtain, only certain rational combinations will give equal weight to all variables; all other techniques employ differential weighting.

Areas of use

In our earlier discussion the methods of combining scores were dichotomized into predictive and descriptive uses, that is, the goal might be either to predict some criterion behavior more accurately or to summarize diverse data in order to make some general descriptive statements. Predictive uses can be broken down further into two classes: selection and classification problems.

In the *selection* situation, tests are usually combined by either the multiple-cutoff or multiple-regression methods, the particular method chosen being a function of the type of input data and whether the desired outcome is a ranking or a pool of applicants. Generally the multiple-regression model should be used unless (1) the input data are not on a continous scale, (2) noncompensatory traits are used as predictors, or (3) the relation between predictors and criterion is not linear. If any of these three conditions holds, the multiple-cutoff method is more appropriate. Discriminant analysis and clinical judgment can also be structured to function in the selection situation. Rational combinations can also be used as a basis for selection, but as they will almost certainly be less valid than combinations based on differential weighting, they will rarely be used.

Two further points should also be noted. First, in many situations, a sequential selection strategy is more efficient or less costly than other strategies and so is the preferred approach. The successive hurdles variation of the multiple-cutoff method was designed for just such situations. Combinations based on clinical judgment can, of course, also be readily adapted to sequential strategies. The stepwise multiple-regression procedure, although allowing predictors to be added to the regression equation sequentially, requires all predictive data to be collected prior to the start of the analysis, and so does not fit a sequential strategy.

Second, a combination of methods can be, and often is, used. For example, the first stage in a selection procedure may be an interview. Here the interviewer reaches a decision on the basis of his clinical judgment which, in turn, is derived from a variety of impressions that he has of the applicant. The next step may be a test battery where a decision is made from scores combined by multiple-regression or multiple-cutoff procedures, and so on. Thus several different techniques may be used sequentially—a different technique being utilized at each stage in the process.

Discriminant analysis is clearly suited for the *classification* situation because it provides an indication of the person's similarity to several groups, in this case persons profitting from different treatment conditions. Clinical judgment, of course, can be applied to the classification problem. The multiple-regression model can also be adapted to the classification problem by developing separate regression lines for each treatment condition. Figure 8.5 illustrates this procedure with two groups. The two lines, labeled A and B, are the regression lines which show the predicted criterion score under treatment A and B, respectively. If the individual's combined test scores (that is to say, his predicted criterion score) fall to the left of the point of intersection of the two regression lines, he is assigned to treatment condition A; if his scores fall to the right of the intersection, he is assigned to treatment B. In other words, each individual is assigned to a treatment group so as to maximize his criterion scores. For example, suppose Treatment A were a regular physics course, Treatment B an honors physics

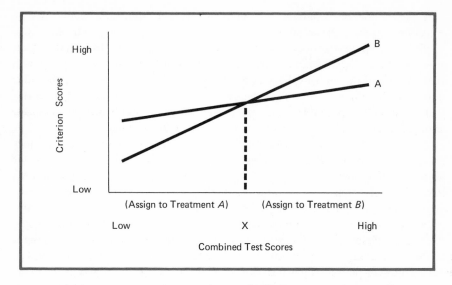

Figure 8.5 Multiple regression applied to the classification problem.

course, and the test scores were a combination of scores on a scholastic aptitude test and grades in mathematics courses. Then, students having higher aptitude and better grades in mathematics courses (above the level designated by the X in Figure 8.5) would be assigned to the honors course and other students would be assigned to the regular course.

All of the methods presented provide *descriptive* information because all, in some way, combine diverse data to arrive at an overall summary score or prediction. In addition, the weightings given to each variable in the composite, or the order in which the variables are added to the composite, gives an idea of the relative importance of each variable. However, factor analysis and discriminant analysis provide the clearest examples of methods that provide descriptive information. Factor analysis serves this function by summarizing the results of various tests and identifying the underlying factors, the hypothetical constructs that account for performance on a variety of tests. Discriminant analysis, by identifying the variables that differentiate the various groups and describing how the groups differ, gives a clearer idea of the nature of the groups.

Data characteristics

The methods also differ in the type of data acceptable as input and the mode of data output. And, as the type of data available will influence the choice of analytic method, the data requirements of each method will be briefly reviewed. First, we consider input data. The clinical method, because of its flexibility (or lack of rigor, one might say) accepts any type of input data—subjective or objective, qualitative or quantitative, discrete or continuous. All the other methods require predictor data to be expressed quantitatively. Even data which are subjectively based, such as ratings, must be scaled in some manner prior to analysis. All of the statistically based methods, with the exception of the multiple-cutoff method, assume that the predictor data is on a continuous scale; multiple cutoff is adaptable to discrete classes. Thus, in practically all instances, data expressed on a continuous quantitative scale are needed.

The output mode also varies. Again, the clinical method allows any manner of output, the only restriction being the ability of the clinician to express his judgment in a particular mode. Multiple-cutoff methods partition the subjects into select/reject classes. The other methods provide a ranking along a continuous scale—multiple regression giving a predicted criterion score; factor analysis, a correlation between the tests and factor scores; and discriminant analysis, the degree of similarity of an individual to a group. Of course, in discriminant analysis and multiple regression, if one is willing to divide the output scores at some point (or points) along the scale, the output can be expressed as membership in a class. For example, when multiple regression is used to predict grades or job performance, a point on the criterion scale may be designated as the minimal acceptable criterion performance; this score divides individuals into two classes: acceptable and unacceptable performers. Or, in discriminant analysis, a point along the discriminant function may be chosen so that persons whose scores fall in one range are classified as being in one group while those in another range fall in another group.

Finally, it should be reiterated that all methods except factor analysis are concerned primarily with the performance (test scores) of individuals and the goal is to make predictions about, or give descriptions of, individuals or groups. Factor analysis, in contrast, uses tests as the unit of analysis. Although the data utilized in a factor analysis is based on the test performance of individuals, the primary concern involves characteristics of tests—that is, the interest is in the factors being tapped by the tests and the tests' loading on these factors. Using these data to describe characteristics of persons is one step removed from the actual factor analysis. However, it is possible (as was pointed out earlier) to factor analyze people rather than tests, and thus to group persons in terms of their similarity.

Validity

The value of any test, as has been repeatedly stressed throughout the book, is indicated by its validity. Thus it would be inappropriate to leave the discussion of combining test scores without further consideration of the validity of the various methods of combining test scores. In the framework of combinations of test scores, there are three viewpoints of validity: (1) the validity of the composite function, (2) the validity of the individual elements comprising the composite, and (3) the comparative validity of the various methods. In the discussion that follows, we assume that all necessary experimental controls have been instituted in the validity studies and that the empirical results have been cross-validated. Thus we can speak of validity in general terms, rather than validity resulting from a particular set of fortuitous conditions.

VALIDITY OF THE COMPOSITE. Because the purpose in combining several test scores is to increase validity, the minimal essential requirement is that the validity of the composite should be significantly greater than the validity of any single element (test, predictor) contributing to the composite. If the validity of the composite is not higher than that of the most valid element, then building a composite has been a fruitless exercise. As a corollary, we could also state that a test should not be added to the composite unless it adds to predictive accuracy, that is, unless it has incremental validity. Thus any composite will not utilize all possible predictors but will only include those predictors that contribute unique information. Obviously the composite should also improve on the base rates or on the predictive efficiency of the previous selection method.

The statistic used to evaluate validity will depend upon the combination method used. In multiple regression, the value of R (or R^2) will be the appropriate index of validity. In the multiple-cutoff model, or when multiple regression is used in a classification problem, the hit rate will be the validity index. Alternatively, a measure of average criterion performance may be used with both the multiple-regression and multiple-cutoff models. When discriminant analysis is used to differentiate between groups, the percent of variance accounted for is the best index; when used to classify individuals, the proportion of correct classifications (hit rate) will be an appropriate index. Since factor analysis is used to reduce the number of variables, the proportion of variance accounted for by the common factors will provide an index of validity (factorial validity). In clinical and rational combinations, the appropriate index will depend on the purpose of the combination.

VALIDITY OF COMPONENTS. The validity of the component elements of the composite can be assessed in several ways. At the simplest level one can look at the correlation between a single predictor and the criterion or the hit rate attained using only that particular test. However, these approaches assume that each predictor is being used in isolation, when in fact it is being used as part of a composite. An appropriate index, therefore, will be one that assesses the contribution of the individual test to the predictive efficiency of the composite. In short, we are interested in the incremental validity of the predictor, i.e., the ability of the predictor to contribute unique information.

To illustrate, consider the multiple-regression model. Using a stepwise model (as in the example in Table 8.2), we first select the variable that, by itself, is the best single predictor of the criterion. The validity of this test as a part of the composite is identical to its validity when used in isolation as the sole predictor. Next, we select the predictor, which in combination with the first, gives the best multiple prediction—the highest R. The incremental validity of this predictor is represented by the increase in R, or alternatively R^2, that is obtained by adding it to the best predictor. This value will not be the same as the validity of this predictor when it stands alone. Rather, it is a function of the test's validity as a predictor of the criterion (zero-order validity) and its intercorrelation with the first predictor. We then add, as the third predictor, the variable which, in combination with the first two, results in the greatest increase in R. Again its contribution is measured in terms of the increase in R, or R^2. And so on, until addition of more predictors results in no further significant increase in R.

This method of evaluation could be applied in an analogous fashion to the multiple-cutoff situation. The only difference would be that validity would be evaluated by the increase in the hit rate rather than the increase in the multiple-correlation coefficient.

Some people object to the notion of incremental validity, claiming that it gives a misleading picture of the contribution of predictors added after the first predictor. In support of their position they cite as an example a test that has a relatively high validity when used as the only predictor, but which correlates highly with the first predictor and thus adds little to the multiple prediction. They feel that interpreting the contribution of this predictor in incremental terms does not truly represent the test's validity, as it implies that the test is less valid than it really is. In the opinion of the author this criticism does not hold water because validity is situation-specific, and in this particular situation the validity of the composite is the prime concern; thus the contribution of any predictor must be evaluated in terms of its contribution to the composite, i.e., in terms of its incremental validity. A more damaging criticism of incremental validity is the fact that the contribution of the first predictor is usually assessed by comparing its validity (R or hit rate) to chance (or zero validity) when, in actuality, it should be evaluated by determining its improvement over the base rate validity. Thus, rather than underestimate the contribution of subsequently added predictors, incremental validity will tend to overestimate the contribution of the first component test.

COMPARATIVE VALIDITY. Because the different models are based on different assumptions, are typically used in different situations, and express their results in different terms, little data is available to compare two or more techniques directly as applied to the same problem. There are, however, two situations where comparisons are of some interest: the comparison of multiple-cutoff and multiple-regression models in the selection situation, and the comparison of clinical and actuarial prediction.

Consider first the comparison of cutoff and regression methods. Although in many instances it would appear that both methods may be equally useful, the empirical results support the generalization that the method whose assumptions best fit the realities of the situation will yield the higher validity. If compensation between predictor variables does occur, and there is a linear relation between predictors and the criterion, the multiple-regression model will be more valid. If some degree of noncompensation is present, or if the relation between predictor and criterion variables is other than linear, then the cutoff model will be more valid. In other words, if both models can appropriately be used, the regression model is generally preferable, being more valid.

Another problem that has resulted in a great amount of study by psychologists is the comparison of clinical and statistical, or actuarial, prediction. The latter includes all models based on a statistical combination of test scores. The controversy over the relative merits of these two approaches was given its original impetus by a book by Meehl (1954) *Clinical Versus Statistical Prediction.* In this book, Meehl surveyed the available evidence and concluded that, although clinical predictions may have certain unique functions, in those situations where both clinical and statistical predictions have been made, statistical prediction has always been equally accurate or more so than clinical predictions.

In the years following publication of the book there have been a number of articles in the psychological journals concerning the clinical-actuarial issue. Some have emphasized the philosophy and logic of the two approaches, concluding that the two types of prediction are appropriate in different situations. For example, clinical prediction is claimed to be appropriate when an "open ended" prediction needs to be made, and actuarial prediction is appropriate for predicting specific observable criteria. Other studies have compared clinical and actuarial predictions in various situations—academic performance, job performance, psychiatric diagnosis, response to various treatments, and so forth. The weight of the evidence is that when a specific circumscribed outcome is to be predicted, the actuarial approach is usually as good as, if not better than, the clinical prediction. This is not unexpected, because the statistical techniques are designed to minimize prediction error and weight each predictor optimally. The best that an individual making his clinical predictions can hope for, unless he can identify a relevant variable not considered in the equation, is to duplicate the optimal weighing of the formula. However, even if the clinician could identify a new variable, this variable could then be incorporated into a new statistical prediction formula, thus regaining the advantage for the formula.

TWO FINAL POINTS.   Two further points should be emphasized. First, all combinations should, of course, be cross-validated. The need for cross-validation is particularly crucial when combining several measures because the measurement errors involved in each measure may cumulate, rather than cancel each other out; consequently, the composite measure (or prediction) will contain large amounts of measurement error. Because of this error, multiple-correlation coefficients (and other multiple measures) are subject to large shrinkage (i.e., decrease in magnitude) upon cross-validation. The cross-validated R, consequently, is a more accurate estimate of the true degree of relationship, than the non-cross-validated measure.

Utility must also be considered in addition to validity. Because use of additional predictors will, undoubtedly, increase both direct and indirect costs, and as the increment in predictive accuracy generally drops off rapidly with additional predictors, the costs associated with obtaining additional predictor data may well overbalance any benefits attained by using an additional predictor. The use of fewer predictors may thus result in lower validity but higher utility.

Summary

In most situations scores on more than one test are available or test scores are used concurrently with other data. Therefore, there is a need for objective methods of combining scores on several variables—either to make a prediction or provide a description of the individual. This chapter discussed the methods for combining test scores and focused on several issues—the logic and assumptions of the various methods, the type of data that serve as input and output, the situations in which each method may be appropriately used, and the validity of the methods. Wherever feasible, an example of the application of the technique was presented.

Although a distinction can be made between combining items to form a test, combining subtest or scale scores, and combining scores on several tests, the majority of the methods can be applied, with only minor modifications, to each of these three areas. The discussion in the chapter concentrated on the latter two situations.

Six methods of combining test scores were presented in detail. (1) In the *clinical judgment* method the clinician considers all the available evidence and, through some intuitive and not wholly explicit process, arrives at a conclusion. Although the method is exceedingly flexible—accepting any type of input data and being able to express conclusions in any desired form—it suffers from lack of objectivity and reproducibility. (2) *Rational methods* use objective data and combine them according to a predetermined weighting scheme. As differential weighting systems, which take into account the peculiarities of a given set of data, generally prove more valid than rational weightings, these methods are of limited usefulness. (3) The *multiple-cutoff* method sets a definite cutting line, i.e., minimum acceptable standard, on each variable and categorizes subjects as to whether they surpassed the cutting line on all variables or failed to meet the cutting criterion on at least one variable. It is a noncompensatory model which provides a pool of acceptable candidates. A variation of the method, referred to as successive hurdles, follows the same logic but considers predictors in sequential steps. (4) The *multiple-regression* model assumes a linear relation between the predictors and criterion and allows compensation between predictors. The process weights the various tests in terms of their contribution to prediction and provides both a regression equation, which indicates the weight given to each variable, and a multiple-correlation coefficient, R, which reflects the correlation between the composite and the criterion. (5) *Discriminant analysis* is a technique for determining which variables differentiate predefined groups. It can also be used to specify which of several groups a given individual most closely resembles and so is helpful with classification problems. (6) The final method, *factor analysis*, is somewhat different in philosophy than the others, having as its goal the identification of factors underlying performance on a series of tests. It serves both to clarify the meaning of test scores and to reduce the number of explanatory variables needed.

Several other techniques—configural scoring, profile analysis, moderator variables, and other multivariate techniques—were also briefly mentioned.

It was emphasized that the method of analysis utilized should be determined primarily by the characteristics of the data and the structure of the problem, but where several methods are equally appropriate, that the choice between methods should be made on the basis of their comparative validity. As illustrations of two such situations it was pointed out that, in general, multiple regression will be more valid than multiple cutoff, and actuarial prediction will be more valid than clinical judgments. It was also emphasized that the validity of a component element in a composite should be evaluated by its contribution to the composite, its *incremental validity*, rather than the validity it would show if it were the sole predictor.

Suggestions for further reading

Brown, F. G., & L. Wolins. An empirical evaluation of the American College Testing Program. *Personnel and Guidance Journal*, 1965, 43, 451–456. An illustrative study showing how test scores and other data can be combined to predict a practical criterion.

Cronbach, L. J., & G. C. Gleser. Assessing similarity between profiles. *Psychological Bulletin*, 1953, 50, 456–473. A discussion of methods for determining the similarity between test score profiles and the presentation of a method they devised.

Drake, L. E., & E. R. Oetting. An MMPI pattern and a suppressor variable predictive of academic achievement. *Journal of Counseling Psychology*, 1957, 4, 245–247. A study illustrating how use of a configuration of test scores can improve prediction over use of a simple combination.

Meehl, P. E. *Clinical versus statistical prediction*. Minneapolis: University of Minnesota Press, 1954. The classic statement on this problem; a review of previous evidence and a formulation of the problem.

Meehl, P. E. A comparison of clinicians with five statistical methods of identifying psychotic MMPI profiles. *Journal of Counseling Psychology*, 1959, 6, 102–109. An empirical study comparing a number of methods for classifying personality inventory profiles.

Meehl, P. E., & A. Rosen. Antecedent probability and the efficiency of psychometric signs, patterns, or cutting scores. *Psychological Bulletin*, 1955, 52, 194–216. The authors point out that the usefulness of a classification technique will depend on the frequency with which the phenomenon being predicted occurs in the population; they also consider the different types of decisions that might be made.

Sawyer, J. Measurement *and* prediction, clinical *and* statistical. *Psychological Bulletin*, 1966, 66, 178–200. A reformulation of the clinical versus statistical problem pointing out that the measurement data, as well as the predictive model, may be either clinical or statistically based.

Sechrest, L. Incremental validity. *Educational and Psychological Measurement*, 1963, 23, 153–158. The author points out that a test should be evaluated in terms of the amount of unique information it provides, not in terms of its zero-order correlation with a criterion.

Selecting and evaluating tests

Chapter 9

INTRODUCTION

In the previous chapters we have discussed the basic requirements of good tests. These characteristics and requirements have been treated individually and somewhat abstractly. For the majority of persons, however, the problem of greatest concern will not be that of constructing tests or conducting validity studies, but rather of being able to choose and evaluate tests when the need arises. This chapter will focus on the problems of test selection and evaluation and thus will be, in part, a review and summary of the material in previous chapters. In addition, it will serve as an introduction to the remainder of the book, where specific types of tests will be discussed, by pointing out the types of questions that should be asked in evaluating any test.

There are two separate but related problems to be considered. The first is selecting from among the myriad of published tests the one or more tests that best fit one's purposes. The second problem is to evaluate a given test which has, on some basis, been chosen for consideration. Since the evaluation of any given test presupposes that it has been selected because it has met certain, at least vaguely defined, requirements, we will first discuss the process of selecting a test from all possible tests.

SELECTING A TEST

In most situations where a test might prove useful a first step is to select one or a small number of tests from among those available which, on the basis of certain general guidelines, appear potentially to meet the requirements. That is, we have certain general requirements in mind (e.g., type of test and age or educational level of the test takers) and the task is to identify tests that meet these requirements. After the search has been narrowed to a few potential tests we can evaluate each test in this pool and select the one that seems to best meet our requirements.

General considerations

There are several general considerations that can serve to narrow the field of potential tests. These include the purpose of the testing, the characteristics of the group being tested, practical limitations, and the availability of persons who can interpret the tests. Delimitation within these areas will serve to reduce the potential pool of tests to a manageable number, allowing detailed review of the best prospects.

PURPOSE   The most important question is: What (trait) is to be measured and for what purpose? If we are interested in measuring mathematics achievement, we can immediately eliminate all other types of tests; if concerned with vocational interests, we can limit our further search to vocational interest inventories; and so on. Even if we cannot specify an exact type of test, we can often delimit the general area, or several areas, and thus direct our further search into these areas.

Besides being able to define the area (achievement, interest, personality, etc.) one should also know the purpose of the testing. Is the test to be used for selection, as a diagnostic device, for research studies, or for some other purpose? Specifying the purpose aids delimitation primarily through indicating the format and type and variety of scores that the test must supply. If, for example, an English grammar test is needed for placement of students in various sections of an English course, a test with comprehensive coverage of content would be required but one summary score would suffice. However, if an English grammar test is to be used for diagnostic purposes, one would need a test that covers, in some detail, various areas of grammar and provides separate scores for each subarea.

GROUP TESTED   A second basic consideration is the nature of the group tested. Are we testing adults or children? Groups having atypical educational or cultural backgrounds? People with handicaps or special abilities? Because tests are developed and are appropriately used for only certain age, educational, and cultural groups, knowledge of the characteristics of the group being tested will further limit the number of possible tests. Thus, while knowing that we need an English grammar test for diagnostic testing limits our search, the additional requirement that the test be appropriate for junior high students will further limit the field of potential tests.

The particular characteristics of the persons being tested that will be relevant in any particular situation will, of course, depend on the unique qualities of the situation and the purpose of the testing. The characteristics that may be important in any testing situation are, in general, those that are to be considered in forming norm groups—for example, age, education, socio-economic background, intelligence, and level of particular skills such as reading ability. Whenever test performance will vary as a function of one of these characteristics, that characteristic should be considered when selecting the test.

PRACTICAL CONSIDERATIONS. Frequently there are practical limitations that must be taken into account when selecting a test. One common consideration is *time*. Usually we are not able or willing to devote unlimited time to testing. For example, an employment manager may use a screening test only if it can be administered in less than a half hour; an instructor may require a test that can be given within the class hour; a college admissions testing program may feel that a half-day is the maximum time that students can be asked to devote to testing. Probably the most common limitation is the need for tests given in public schools to conform to the school class schedule. This limitation implies that the test must be able to be administered within one class period, or a multiple of a class period, or must have subtests that can be given in a single period.

A second practical consideration is *cost*. Most users of tests operate within a budget and thus must choose a test that fits their budget. A school system may have $3.00 per pupil budgeted for testing and thus must select tests that can be obtained for that price. In determining costs it must be remembered that the cost of testing includes not just the test booklets and answer sheets but also such costs as scoring and reporting. Certain cost-saving methods are available, however. If a test has a separate answer sheet, the test booklets can be reused and the costs spread over several years. Or if staggered testing sessions can be arranged (i.e., the test given to one group at one time and another group at a different time) a smaller number of test booklets may suffice.

For a complete cost analysis one must also take into account indirect costs—time to prepare the test materials, examiner time, time for interpreting and reporting test scores, etc. Only if these factors are included can a complete analysis of costs of the testing program be obtained.

A third area of practical considerations is that of *administrative problems*. In order for a test to be given there must be staff who can administer the test and appropriate physical facilities must be available. No doubt one reason for the popularity of paper-and-pencil tests is that many of them can be administered by the educated layman with only minimal training and in facilities such as the ordinary classroom. Other tests, such as individual intelligence tests and personality tests, often require specially trained administrators. Other tests require special apparatus and special rooms or areas for administration. Need for highly trained administrators, individual administration, and special apparatus not only limit the applicability of tests but also increase costs.

The importance of these practical considerations should be put in perspective. Rather than being considered hard and fast determinants, they should be looked upon as flexible guidelines. Certainly, in the choice of tests, practical considerations are of much less importance than the technical quality of the test. Also, practical limitations are sometimes more apparent than real. For example, we mentioned above how the cost of test supplies could be reduced by buying tests with separate answer sheets and reusable booklets and by staggered testing schedules. Of all the considerations involved in selecting tests, practical ones are least important and most flexible.

INTERPRETATION.   An aspect of staffing that is often overlooked is the need for staff that are competent to interpret the results of tests that have been given. Too frequently people seem to assume that because a test can be administered by almost any educated layman it also can be interpreted by almost anyone. This is not the case, however, even with the least complex test. Test interpretation is more than reporting scores to an individual. For effective interpretation one must know thoroughly the strengths and limitations of the test, the background of the testee, the situation in which he took the test, and the consequences that the interpretation will have on and for the person. One must also possess skills for communicating the results and meanings of test scores to the test taker or to other persons (teachers, etc.) who will make use of the results. (For a discussion of the problems of test interpretation see Goldman, 1961.)

There is no doubt that misinterpretation of test results by untrained and incompetent persons is one of the main reasons for the dissatisfaction with psychological testing expressed by many persons. Probably the most common error is to overinterpret test results by generalizing beyond the validity and normative data, claiming that the test measures traits that it does not measure and attributing a higher degree of accuracy to the test scores than the reliability and validity evidence warrants. On the other hand, there have been numerous incidents where tests were administered, the results filed, and never used because no one was available to interpret the results—again a misuse of tests. The moral is clear. Tests should not be administered unless there are competent persons available to interpret them.

FACE VALIDITY.   You will recall that a test has face validity when the test items appear to measure the trait actually being measured. In some instances, as when tests are used for research purposes, face validity may be of only minor importance. In other situations, particularly when tests are used for making decisions about individuals, such as in selection for a job or educational opportunities, face validity may be crucial because it affects the test taker's motivation and reaction to the test. If there is reason to believe that the test taker's performance will be affected, then, if at all possible, a test with high face validity should be selected.

What tests are available

Given that we know the purpose of the testing, the type of scores needed, the composition of the group to be tested, and that we have recognized any practical limitations, the next step is to identify the tests, out of the hundreds of available tests, that meet these minimum requirements. Here one can start with any of several sources—reference books, textbooks on psychological measurement, publishers' catalogs, journals—or one can consult with experts. The most efficient place to start the search will, in most instances, be with one of the standard reference books.

REFERENCE BOOKS. There are two basic reference books, both edited by Oscar K. Buros. One, *Tests in Print* (1961) is, as its subtitle indicates, a comprehensive bibliography of tests used in education, psychology, and industry. This book is both a classified index to and supplement to the other major reference, the *Mental Measurements Yearbook*. The major objective of *Tests in Print* is to provide a comprehensive bibliography of tests published and currently available in English-speaking countries.

Although some confidential and restricted tests, such as the College Entrance Examination Board's Scholastic Aptitude Test, are included, the great majority of the over 2100 listings in *Tests in Print* are tests that are published and widely available to qualified users. The tests listed cover all areas—personality, intelligence, achievement, interests, etc.—and are listed by type, thus allowing the test user to focus his search. For each test there is an entry that includes the title of the test, the examinees and level that the tests were designed for (e.g., grades 4–6), the author, publisher, publication date, an indication of any parts or subtests, the number of scores and what they represent, and any special comments (e.g., "new form available annually," "for research use only"). In addition, the entry contains cross-references to other categories the test is listed in within *Tests in Print* and cross-references to the *Mental Measurements Yearbook*. An additional feature is a listing of out-of-print tests. These listings contain only the name of the test and a brief comment on where to find further information.

The main use of *Tests in Print* is, of course, to determine whether any published tests are available in a given category. Thus it is an excellent starting point. Its major weakness is that it is solely a listing, providing only minimal information. One will always have to consult further sources for more detailed information about the test. Also, a reference of this nature becomes dated unless revised versions are published periodically.

The other major reference, also edited by Buros, is the *Mental Measurements Yearbook*. Actually this is not an annual publication but rather a series with volumes issued every several years—the fifth edition having been published in 1959, the sixth edition in 1965, and the seventh edition now in preparation. The *Yearbooks* have three major objectives: (1) to provide a readily available, comprehensive, up-to-date bibliography of tests and sources of information about test construction, validation, and use; (2) to encourage more sophisticated and higher quality critical evaluations and appraisals of tests and testing practices; and (3) to encourage authors and publishers to put fewer, but better, tests on the market. The first purpose has been accomplished by the information provided within the *Yearbooks* and the second at least partially attained by the high critical standards of the *Yearbook* reviews. The third goal has, unfortunately, not been accomplished.

In many ways the *Yearbooks* are the test users' bible. The entry for each test (1219 tests in the sixth edition) includes certain basic data—the test title; author, publisher and publication date; groups for which the test is intended; part scores, levels, forms; method of scoring; cost; time, both working time and total administration time; pages; and an indication if reliability and validity data are available. (See Figure 9.1.) There is also a list of published articles that refer to the test and cross-references to the test in other editions of the *Yearbook*. Separate from the test listing is a section of reviews of books about testing, a directory of periodicals that publish articles on testing and measurement, a directory and index of test publishers, and several indices (by test name, title, classification).

Although the descriptive and index material are of value, the heart of each *Yearbook* is the critical review of tests. Although not every test is reviewed, the more important, widely used, and new and revised tests are reviewed.[1] The almost 800 reviews in the sixth edition vary in length from several paragraphs to several pages. By and large, they are written by leaders in the field of measurement and are frankly critical and evaluative. When several reviews are made of a single test, as is the case for about half of the tests reviewed, the reviews are usually written from different perspectives. Thus a test measuring comprehension of French might be reviewed by a psychologist who would focus on the technical merits of the test and by a French teacher who would concern himself with the adequacy of the content and coverage of the test.

For comprehensiveness and critical evaluations there is no single source to match the *Yearbooks*. Not only does the descriptive information enable the user to determine if the test meets his requirements, but the reviews also provide expert opinions on the merits and limitations of the test. All test users should become familiar with this reference.

---

[1] A system of cross-referencing allows readers to quickly locate other reviews of the test in previous issues of the *Yearbook*.

origin and not of a kind likely to be useful to an American user. A reference is made to the use of the test in the measurement of mental deterioration. Two references in French are given to deterioration studies.

Until the publishers produce evidence that this test is equal or superior to the many non-verbal tests published in the United States, it has little to commend it for use in guidance situations. The fact that it is a test of a single item type may make it useful for certain factor analytic studies.

[455]

★Deeside Non-Verbal Reasoning Test: English-Welsh Bilingual Version. Ages 10–12; 1961–63; 2 forms: test 1 ('61), test 2 ('63), (16 pages) ; separate mimeographed manuals for test 1 ['61, 17 pages], test 2 ['63, 19 pages] ; distribution restricted to directors of education; 25s. per 25 tests; 7s. 6d. per manual; postage and purchase tax extra; 37–38(60) minutes; W. G. Emmett; George G. Harrap & Co. Ltd. *

[456]

*Doppelt Mathematical Reasoning Test. Grades 16–17 and employees; 1954–63; IBM; Form A ('54, 4 pages) ; manual ('58, 10 pages) ; bulletin of information ('63, 36 pages) ; revised procedures for testing center operation ('63, 8 pages) ; distribution restricted and test administered at specified licensed university centers; scoring and reporting handled by the local center; examination fee to centers: $1 per examinee; fees to examinees are determined locally and include reporting of scores to the examinee and to 3 institutions or companies designated at the time of testing; additional score reports may be secured from the publisher at a fee of $1 each; 50(60). minutes; Jerome E. Doppelt; Psychological Corporation. *

REFERENCES

1. SCHWARTZ, MILTON M., AND CLARK, F. EUGENE. "Prediction of Success in Graduate School at Rutgers University." J Ed Res 53:109–11 N '59. * (PA 35:1223)
2. ROEMMICH, HERMAN. "The Doppelt Mathematical Reasoning Test as a Selection Device for Graduate Engineering Students." Ed & Psychol Meas 21:1009–10 w '61. *

W. V. CLEMANS, Director, Test Department, Science Research Associates, Inc., Chicago, Illinois.

The *Doppelt Mathematical Reasoning Test* contains 50 problems that differ from the usual pattern for multiple choice questions in that there are no stems. The task facing the examinee is defined once for the entire set ín the directions which state:

Each problem in this test consists of five mathematical figures or expressions. Four of these have something in common which is not shared by the remaining one. You are to choose the *one* figure or expression which does *not* belong with the other four and mark the letter corresponding to your choice in the proper place on the answer sheet.

None of the problems involves mathematics beyond the usual secondary school level. The

test can be easily administered to large groups or to individuals.

The manual states that the test "was designed primarily as an aid in the selection of students for graduate work" and that it "may also be useful in the classification and assignment of college graduates applying for positions in industry which require mathematical reasoning."

Correlations of the DMRT with faculty ratings or grades for three groups of 41, 57, and 109 graduate students taking mathematics suggest that the test may have some value for selecting graduate students. The coefficients obtained were .52, .71, and .43, respectively. Similar coefficients are reported for 28 graduate students in chemistry and 26 undergraduates in a psychometrics course, but a coefficient of only .32 was found for 29 medical students. This latter finding is hardly significant, but is the only coefficient reported for a criterion group whose course work is not primarily quantitative. The Psychological Corporation supplies summaries of five studies reported by independent investigators that tend to corroborate the claim that the test relates to measures of success in graduate study in mathematics or statistics. Apparently no systematic approach has been made to determining how valuable the test is for graduate students in other areas. Validity data for industrial criteria have not yet been supplied.

In the norms section of the manual percentile equivalents are given for five small student samples ranging in size from 102 to 145 students selected from 15 colleges and universities. The groups consisted of senior psychology students, medical students, psychology majors, education majors, and graduate students taking courses in statistics. Percentile equivalents are also given for a group of 388 engineers from one industrial organization.

Reliability coefficients were computed for each of the six groups using the odd-even approach and the Spearman-Brown formula. The coefficients range from .78 to .85. The author points out that the lowest values were found for the most homogeneous groups. He fails to point out, however, that the three groups yielding the highest reliability coefficients (all .85) not only had the largest standard deviations but also the lowest means. This phenomenon suggests to this reviewer that the higher values may have been due to speeded-

Figure 9.1 A page from *The Sixth Mental Measurements Yearbook*, O. K. Buros, Ed. (Highland Park, N.J.: The Gryphon Press, 1965), p. 456.

TEXTBOOKS. Many textbooks on psychological and educational testing provide descriptions and evaluations of various tests. Depending on the purpose of the text, the coverage may be superficial or detailed, comprehensive or limited. A number of texts (e.g., those by Anastasi, 1968; Cronbach, 1960; Thorndike and Hagen, 1961; Adams, 1965; Berdie et al., 1963; Super and Crites, 1962) discuss many of the most widely used tests and are valuable sources to consult when choosing and evaluating tests. In contrast to the *Mental Measurements Yearbooks*, textbooks are more limited in coverage (i.e., they do not try to cover all tests) but are likely to provide more information regarding the rationale, construction, and structure of a given test.

JOURNALS. A third source of information is psychological and educational journals. A few journals (for example, *Journal of Educational Measurement* and *Journal of Counseling Psychology*) periodically publish test reviews, and it may be that the test being considered has been reviewed in one of these journals. Several other publications (for example, the *Review of Educational Research* and the *Annual Review of Psychology*) devote issues or chapters to reviews of testing and measurement. Studies using tests are published in a large number of journals (e.g., *Journal of Applied Psychology, Journal of Consulting Psychology, Journal of Counseling Psychology, Personnel and Guidance Journal, Journal of Educational Measurement, Educational and Psychological Measurement, Personnel Psychology, Measurement and Evaluation in Guidance*). One can search for studies using the tests under consideration and/or studies of similar problems to see what tests have been used and with what success. The main disadvantage of journals as information sources is, of course, that the information is diffused throughout many issues of many journals.

We should also mention that several journals—particularly *Psychometrika* and *Educational and Psychological Measurement*—publish articles on the more technical aspects of measurement.

EXPERTS. A fourth source of information, expert judgment, should be briefly mentioned. Most colleges and universities and many public school systems have staffs responsible for testing programs within the institution and/or instructors of psychological and educational measurement. In addition, there are psychologists who work for public or private agencies, are personnel men in business and industry, or are in private practice, who know about tests and testing. These persons generally can give suggestions on appropriate tests, direct the test user to appropriate information sources, or suggest persons or agencies that will help with the testing problem.

TEST PUBLISHERS. For further, more detailed information about a test one must consult test publishers.[2] All publishers print catalogs listing the tests that

---

[2]As noted above, a list of test publishers may be found in the *Mental Measurements Yearbook*.

they publish and giving certain basic information about them. Of more value, however, is the fact that publishers also provide *specimen sets* of most tests. A specimen set, which can be obtained for a minimal fee, consists of a copy of the test, the answer sheet, scoring key, technical and interpretive manuals, and other relevant aids. The provision of these materials allows the potential user to evaluate the content, format, administration, and technical quality of the test.

CONDUCTING THE SEARCH.   Probably the most efficient procedure is to start with *Tests in Print* and the *Mental Measurements Yearbooks*. Journals and textbooks can provide further information, evidence that can also be used in the final evaluation of the tests selected for detailed evaluation. By this point, the field of potential tests should have been narrowed to a small number, possibly only one or two, that meet the general requirements discussed above. Before making a final selection, however, the test user will want to obtain specimen sets of those tests that have survived his preliminary screening and use them as a basis of a detailed study.

However, it is possible that no available test will meet even the general requirements. In this case a decision must be made as to the next course of action. One alternative is not to use a test but to turn to another method to provide the relevant data. If it is conceivable that even the general guidelines may have been too rigid, then certain of the requirements might be changed, or at least relaxed, thus allowing use of a test that previously had seemed unusable. A third possibility is to construct a test that will meet the original requirements. Because test construction is both time consuming and expensive when done correctly, the specially constructed test is probably the least feasible alternative.

EVALUATING A TEST

Let us assume, however, that several tests appear to meet the general requirements. The task then becomes to evaluate these surviving tests and select the one, from among the possible tests, that appears to be most promising. These evaluations are usually made using the materials in the speciman set—the content and coverage of the test can be ascertained by studying the individual items; the test takers' task from the test, answer sheet, and administrative directions; the technical adequacy from the test manual.

The *test manual* is the basic source of information about the construction and standardization of the test. It should contain detailed information regarding the procedures used in selecting and constructing the test items, directions for administration and scoring, normative data, reliability and validity data, and other information to aid in the interpretation of the scores obtained from the test.[3] In short, the test manual should provide all the data necessary to evaluate

---

[3]A test may have a number of manuals covering various dimensions, e.g., one for administration and scoring; a second, technical manual covering reliability and validity data; and a third, interpretive manual.

the administrative and psychometric aspects of the test. Obtaining and studying the test manual is probably the most important step in choosing and evaluating a test.

Two considerations

When evaluating any test two overriding considerations must constantly be kept in mind. First, one must adopt a sceptical and critical attitude, especially regarding the psychometric characteristics—consistency, validity, scores, and norms. Certainly some minimal amount of evidence is needed in order to make an adequate evaluation of a test, but beyond this one must always be on guard not to be overwhelmed by sheer amounts of data. Constantly ask: How was this data collected? Were the proper experimental conditions and controls maintained? What do these data mean? In short, consistently and rigorously hold to the standards and principles discussed in previous chapters.

The second major consideration is that the test will be used in a specific situation, with a specific group of persons, for a specific purpose. Thus we are always looking for the test that is most appropriate for a particular purpose. This may, or may not, be a test that has proven valuable for other, even related, purposes or in other presumably similar stituations. Even though there are certain areas that are relevant in the evaluation of any test, there are also certain specific requirements that must be met if a test is to be useful in a particular situation. In other words, there is no test that will serve best in all situations. There is a test-situation interaction: a well constructed test with seemingly wide applicability may be inappropriate in a given situation, while a test of more limited scope may be ideal. Therefore, one must always consider the specific, unique aspects of the situation in which the test will be used.

Formats for evaluating tests

As with the various proposals for techniques of studying, singing styles, and batting stances, there is no one format or procedure for evaluating a test. An individual who consistently evaluates tests will, in time, develop his own format and procedure, emphasizing the characteristics of tests that he thinks most important. There are, however, common elements that must be included in any test evaluation.

STANDARDS FOR EDUCATIONAL AND PSYCHOLOGICAL TESTS.   There have been several attempts to systematically designate standards for evaluating tests. The most recent and comprehensive of these is the *Standards for Educational and Psychological Tests and Manuals* (APA, 1966). The pamphlet, prepared by a joint committee of three major professional organizations concerned with testing—the American Psychological Association, the American Educational Research

C1. The manual should report the validity of the test for each type of inference for which it is recommended. If its validity for some suggested interpretation has not been investigated, that fact should be made clear. ESSENTIAL

C1.1. Statements in the manual about validity should refer to the validity of particular interpretations or of particular types of decision. ESSENTIAL

[Comment: It is incorrect to use the unqualified phrase "the validity of the test." No test is valid for all purposes or in all situations or for all groups of individuals. Any study of test validity is pertinent to only a few of the possible uses of or inferences from the test scores.

If the test is likely to be used incorrectly for certain areas of decision, the manual should include specific warnings. For example, the manual for a writing skills test states that the test apparently is not sufficiently difficult to discriminate among students "at colleges that have selective admissions."]

C1.2. Wherever interpretation of subscores, score differences, or profiles is suggested, the evidence in the manual justifying such interpretation should be made explicit. ESSENTIAL (Also see B4.4.)

[Comment: One aptitude test manual indicates the difficulties involved in computing the statistical significance of differences between scores in a profile. In an effort to cope with this problem a convenient method of approximating the significance of plotted differences is provided. Cautions and limitations of this type of profile interpretation are suggested.]

C1.21. If the manual for an inventory suggests that the user consider responses to separate items as a basis for personality assessment, it should either present evidence supporting this use or call attention to the absence of such data. The manual should warn the reader that inferences based on responses to single items are subject to extreme error, hence should be used only to direct further inquiry, as, perhaps, in a counseling interview. ESSENTIAL

C2. Item-test correlations should not be presented in the manual as evidence of criterion-related validity, and they should be referred to as item-discrimination indices, not as item-validity coefficients. ESSENTIAL

[Comment: It is, of course, possible to make good use of item-test correlations in reasoning about construct validity. However, such correlations are not, in themselves, indicators of test validity; they are measures of internal consistency.]

Content Validity

C3. If a test performance is to be interpreted as a sample of performance or a definition of performance in some universe of situations, the manual should indicate clearly what universe is represented and how adequate is the sampling. ESSENTIAL

[Comment: Some consideration should be given to the adequacy of sampling from both the appropriate universe of content and the universe of behaviors that the items are intended to represent. For example, the manual of a test of achievement in American history might not only describe the item types used and the coverage of the subject matter, but also should describe to what extent responding to the test items serves as an adequate sample of the examinee's attainment of such skills as critical reading of historical material, including evaluation of evidence, analysis of cause and effect relationships, and whatever other behaviors are considered to be "achievement in American history."]

C3.1. When experts have been asked to judge whether items are an appropriate

Figure 9.2 An excerpt from the *Standards for Educational and Psychological Tests and Manuals.* (Washington, D.C.: American Psychological Association, 1966.

Association, and the National Council on Measurement in Education—was designed as a guide to test users and producers in evaluating whether a given test manual carries "information sufficient to enable any qualified user to make sound judgments regarding the usefulness and interpretation of the test" (p. 2). In other words, does the material presented with the test (usually in the test manual) enable the user to make an evaluation of the potential usefulness of the test?

The *Standards* cover six areas—dissemination of information (provision of manuals and other aids), interpretation, validity, reliability, administration and scoring, and scales and norms. Within each section are a number of general principles (standards) and subprinciples. These standards are classified on three levels: essential, very desirable, and desirable. The essential recommendations, of course, represent the minimum amount of information that should be presented about the test. Along with the recommendations are appropriate explanatory comments and examples. (See Figure 9.2.) The *Standards* is an excellent reference for use in evaluating a test; every test user should own, study, and constantly use this reference.

A SUGGESTED FORMAT.   Following is a format, in outline form, that the author has found useful in evaluating tests. This guide, as any other, should be treated as a minimum guide, as a series of essential questions. In any particular test evaluation other questions may also be asked; what these additional questions are will depend on the type of test, the use to which it will be put, and the composition of the group tested. For example, if a test is longer or more comprehensive than necessary for the particular purpose the prospective user might want to know the answers to such questions as: Is there any way the test can be split so that certain sections can be eliminated? What effect will this split have on the validity of the test? Will the scores obtained from the revised test be comparable to those obtained using the entire battery?

The evaluation covers various areas, utilizing information obtained from various sources. The general information (author, publisher, etc.) and the practical features of time and cost are probably already known from the references sources consulted in narrowing the search for a test. This information can be confirmed, and missing data supplied, from the test manual. Next we study the test itself, focusing on the format and layout and on the content and coverage of the individual items. Here some reference will have to be made to the manual, and other sources, as when determining the rationale and method of selecting items. After study of the test items, we turn to the psychometric characteristics of the test—its reliability, validity, scores, and norms. Data for these sections will come primarily from the test manual, which will also provide the information regarding administration and scoring. Finally, we take into account any other information, from the test publisher's material or outside sources, that may be relevant to our evaluation.

Suggested format

1. General Information
   Title:
   Author:
   Publisher:
   Publication date:
   Forms and levels: (Equivalent forms available?)
   Manual and other technical aids:
2. Purposes and Uses
   Purpose as stated by author:
   Other purposes/uses implied by author:
   Other purposes/uses reported in literature:
3. Practical Considerations
   Direct costs: (booklets, answer sheets, scoring, etc.)
   Indirect costs:
   Time: (working time, total administrative time)
4. Format and Layout
   General editorial quality: (printing, paper, format, readability, etc.)
   Arrangement of items and subsections/parts:
   Appeal to layman (face validity):
   Test takers' ease of comprehension and response:
5. Items and Their Coverage
   Basis of item selection:
   Coverage: (especially, over- and underrepresented areas)
   General quality of items: (complexity, ambiguity, control of response
      sets, etc.)
   Variety of item formats:
   Item difficulty:
6. Consistency
   Evidence (amount and quality) on various types of consistency:
      equivalence:
      stability:
      equivalence and stability:
      internal consistency:
   Factors influencing reliability and magnitude of their effect:
   Reliability of subtest scores: (if applicable)
   Reliability of difference scores: (if applicable)
   Standard error of measurement: (total, subtest/scales)
   Consistency for different groups of subjects:
7. Validity
   Evidence (amount and quality) of:
      content validity:

construct validity:

criterion-related validity: (note especially criteria; incremental validity)

What traits does test measure: (construct validity, homogeneity, discriminant validity)

Validity of subtest/part scores:

Confidence in predictive ability for groups, for individuals:

Generalizability of validity data to other groups, situations:

8. Scores and Norms

Norm groups: (how many? clearly defined? size? sampling? recency? broken down by appropriate classes?)

Will local norms be needed?

Scales used to report scores:

Any interpretative aids available?

Information on subtest scores:

9. Administration and Scoring

Individual or group administration:

Qualifications for test administrator:

Apparatus, equipment needed for administration:

Instructions for administration: (for administrator, for test taker, to control response biases)

Timing, amount and ease:

How scored? (hand, machine: ease of scoring)

Directions for scoring: (Scoring objective? If scoring subjective, what evidence for agreement between scorers? What scoring aids? Who can score test?)

10. Other Information

Comments by reviewers/users:

Test part of series or battery:

Any auxilliary services available/provided: (research, scoring)

The decision

Once the evaluation of the test, or tests, has been completed, the user must make a decision. If he has been evaluating only one test, he must decide whether it looks promising enough to put into use. If he has been evaluating several tests he must choose between them, or possibly reject them all. Reaching this decision is a rational, evaluative process similar to that involved in determining the content validity of the test. No single index, simple or complex, is available. The test user must weight the advantages and limitations of the test or tests in question, make a decision, and then proceed on the basis of that decision.

The evaluative procedure does not end at this point. Because each testing situation is in some ways unique, it is impossible to predict with absolute certainty that the test chosen will, in fact, work. A tryout in an actual situation is essential. Preferably, a preliminary tryout should be conducted before the test is put into widespread or routine use. Ideally, a tryout will involve use of several tests with a sample of persons from the population that will be used later, with the final test selection being based on the results of the tryout. If a tryout is not feasible, a test should be adopted tentatively and its value kept under constant review and evaluation. In all circumstances, the value of a test will not be determined finally until validity data, based on studies made of the test in the actual situation where it is used, are available.

Summary

The process of selecting and evaluating tests is a systematic, rational process consisting of the following steps:

1. Outline your general considerations: the purpose of the testing, characteristics of the group being tested, practical and interpretive limitations.

2. Determine what tests are available.

3. Obtain information about the tests and evaluations by previous users from tests, journals, and reference books. Using this data, select the several most promising tests.

4. Obtain samples (specimen sets) of these tests.

5. Do your own detailed evaluation of the tests, keeping in mind the unique requirements of your particular situation. On the basis of this evaluation, make your selection of the test to be used.

6. If possible, conduct an experimental tryout.

7. Put the test into use. Obtain periodic evaluations of its effectiveness.

The need for holding to rigorous critical standards of evaluation and for continual evaluation cannot be overstressed. If, at any point in the procedure, the test fails to meet your standards its use should be discontinued and other tests or procedures substituted.

Suggestions for further reading

Buros, O. K. (Ed.) *The sixth mental measurements yearbook.* Highland Park, N. J.: Gryphon Press, 1965. The most recent edition of the test users "bible" which contains basic information and critical reviews of published tests; every test user should be familiar with the organization and contents of this book.

Katz, M. (Ed.) Locating information on educational measurement: sources and references. Princeton, New Jersey: Educational Testing Service, 1965. Evaluation and Advisory Service Series, No. 1. A pamphlet listing the various sources which provide information on psychological tests.

Standards for educational and psychological tests and manuals. Washington, D. C.: American Psychological Association, 1966. A pamphlet developed by professional organizations concerned with testing which provides minimum standards for the provision of information regarding the construction procedures and technical quality of psychological and educational tests.

The measurement of achievement

Chapter 10

INTRODUCTION

In the previous chapters we have discussed the basic principles of psychological and educational measurement, the essential characteristics of a measurement instrument, and the bases for interpreting test scores. The following chapters will apply these principles and concepts to the measurement of achievement, aptitudes and abilities, and personality characteristics. As in the previous chapters, the emphasis will be on basic principles; specific tests will be introduced only to exemplify or support the general principles. This approach has been adopted in hopes that the reader will learn principles applicable to the evaluation of any test he might encounter, rather than learn only a series of facts about particular tests.

We will begin by considering the category of test that is most familiar to the majority of persons—the achievement test.

PRINCIPLES OF ACHIEVEMENT TESTING

You have all taken any number of tests that are considered measures of achievement. For example, classroom examinations, which you have been exposed to throughout your school career, clearly fall within the category of achievement tests. So do the test batteries that you took during your elementary and secondary school days, which measured your mastery of certain basic school subjects—arithmetic and mathematics, spelling, history, natural sciences, reading, and so forth. You can not only give examples of achievement tests but can probably also specify the types of items included on such tests: questions measuring knowledge of specific facts, problems involving the manipulation of numbers and formulas, questions based on information contained in a reading passage, items requiring application of your knowledge to new situations, and, at least on classroom examinations, essay questions.

A question remains, however: How can an achievement test be differentiated from other types of tests? Probably the first response of most people would be that achievement tests measure what the person has learned. This is obviously true, but a little reflection will show that all educational and psychological tests measure what the individual has learned. One could take another tack and say that achievement tests assess mastery of academic subjects. Yet the test that you took to obtain a driver's license was obviously an achievement test. Or we might try to define achievement tests by the type of items included on the test or the processes used in responding to the items—recall of facts, reasoning, problem solving, and so forth. Yet anyone looking at two unlabeled tests, one measuring achievement and another scholastic aptitude, would be hard put to correctly classify them.

Finally one might try to distinguish achievement tests by their uses. If a test is designed to evaluate the effectiveness of teaching or learning, it is an achievement test; if the goal is to predict future performance, it is classified as an aptitude test. For the most part, this is a critical distinction. However, there are instances where achievement tests are used as the basis of predicting future performance because past performance is frequently the best predictor of future performance.

In this book a test will be classified as an achievement test if (1) it measures learning that has occurred as a result of experiences in a relatively controlled learning situation, such as classroom or training program, and (2) when the frame of reference is the present or past, that is, to the current state of knowledge or what has been learned.

Three assumptions

Adopting this view of achievement implies certain basic assumptions. The first is that the skill and content domains covered by the test can be specified and defined in behavioral terms. Although some educators feel that certain important aims of education cannot be specified behaviorally (e.g., a positive attitude towards learning, aesthetic appreciation), as tests measure behavior, educational goals must be expressed in behavioral terms; otherwise they cannot be measured. All this requirement really means is that the skills, responses, methods of attacking problems, and other behaviors must be specified in a manner that is readily communicable to other persons. As a corollary, the *important* goals must be differentiated from the peripheral or incidental goals. Because any test will be limited by time and length considerations, only certain outcomes can be measured; the dimensions measured should be the most important ones.

A second assumption is that the test does, in fact, measure these important behaviors rather than irrelevant considerations. This is an assumption of the validity of the test; an assumption which can be given empirical confirmation. To cite another example, if the knowledge necessary to correctly answer the test items could have been obtained outside the classroom, and the goal of the test is to measure what the student has learned within a particular class, then the test will not be measuring what it is supposed to be measuring.

The third assumption is that the test takers have had equal exposure, or equal opportunities for exposure, to the material being tested. This assumption is generally well met on the typical classroom examination, since the material covered by the test has generally been specified by the teacher, the student knows what sources are to be covered, and all persons taking the exam have had approximately equal exposure to the relevant material.

The problem of unequal educational experiences becomes more crucial when dealing with standardized achievement tests. Because standardized tests are designed for administration in a variety of settings, of necessity they cover subject material that is widely taught. To the extent that the subject matter taught in any particular school differs from that assumed by the test, the students in the school will not have had equivalent experiences to the norm group. Thus their scores are not directly comparable to the norm group.

To consider an example with current social significance, if a test standardized on middle-class and upper-middle-class children is administered to children from a disadvantaged area, the normative data is again inappropriate, as the experience of the two groups has not been comparable. The scores of the children from the disadvantaged area, when compared to the norm group, will show how they compare to their more privileged age-mates; they will not tell how their scores rank in comparison to persons whose educational experiences have been more similar to their own.

Types of achievement tests

Various dimensions could be used to classify the varieties of achievement tests. One obvious basis of classification is by *content*—some achievement tests measure knowledge of spelling, others arithmetic, others the history of the United States, still others the construction and use of percentile norms, and so forth. The content area can be defined very broadly (for example, American History) or in narrow terms (e.g., the economic causes of the Civil War); or one could consider content in hierarchical terms, from broad general content areas to very specific subtopics. The standard references (e.g., *Tests in Print*, the *Mental Measurements Yearbooks*), as well as many publishers' catalogs, utilize content classifications, enabling the test user interested in a particular content or subject area to readily locate the available tests.

Achievement tests can be viewed as serving three general functions: survey, diagnostic, and readiness. An achievement test acts as a survey when it provides an estimate of the overall level of performance in a content area. *Survey tests*, therefore, sample a wide range of content and generally yield only one score. The typical classroom final examination is an illustration of a survey test. A *diagnostic test*, in contrast, attempts to assess relative strengths and weaknesses in important component skill or content dimensions. Thus a diagnostic test must be divided into subtests and scores provided for each important component element. For example, a diagnostic test in reading might include subtests covering word recognition, word comprehension, vocabulary, rate of reading, story comprehension, identification of sounds, and syllabication[1]. By studying the pattern of scores, the psychologist can determine the areas in which the individual needs remedial work. A *readiness test* indicates whether the individual possesses the essential skills needed to learn the material at the next higher level of complexity. By its emphasis on prerequisite skills, a readiness test resembles a diagnostic test; in its use to predict further performance the readiness test, in a sense, serves as an aptitude measure. The most common example of a readiness measure are reading readiness tests, administered at the end of kindergarten or beginning of first grade to determine if the child has learned the skills necessary to start formal instruction in reading.

Although most achievement tests are paper-and-pencil tests, some are performance tests, requiring the student to demonstrate his skill through an actual performance by constructing something, performing a physical feat, or producing an artistic composition. Paper-and-pencil tests are further divisible into two general classes, recall and recognition. On *recognition tests* all possible answers are included with the question and the task is to choose between alternatives; on a *recall* test, the student must construct an answer. Multiple-choice and true-false items illustrate the former, essay and completion items the latter.

A distinction can be made between standardized achievement tests and classroom, or teacher-made, tests. *A standardized test* constructed by a test publisher, using the skills of curriculum experts and test construction experts, is designed for use in a wide variety of situations (schools). Thus its content will necessarily be broad, that is, it will include content typically covered in many schools, be based on the content presented in widely used textbooks, and the opinions of curriculum experts as to what are the important knowledge, principles, approaches, and constructs in the field. Norms will generally be national in scope. The *teacher-made test*, in contrast, will be constructed by the classroom teacher, or possibly by a committee of teachers in the same school or school system. Rarely will test construction experts be used, and pretesting items will

---

[1]These subtest titles are from the (Triggs) Diagnostic Reading Tests, lower level, grades 4–8.

generally not be possible. The content area will be more circumscribed, being based on the curriculum of a particular class or school system, and, as it represents a narrower domain, will be covered in more detail. Scores will be interpreted with reference to the student's immediate competitors—his classmates.

Standardized tests are useful when the purpose of the testing is to compare the students' performance in different content areas; when one wants to compare an individual student, a class, or a school system to a wider segment of the population; when comparing classes or schools with each other; and when measuring growth over a period of years. Teacher-made tests are used when the emphasis is on determining if specific curriculum goals have been met and when comparing students to their immediate peers, such as when assigning grades.

Uses of achievement tests

Throughout our discussion we have mentioned a variety of uses for achievement tests; the reader can probably supply a number of other possible uses. Any given test will generally serve several functions simultaneously and, in the case of standardized tests, the same test may serve diverse functions for various users. Before turning to a more detailed discussion of standardized and teacher-made achievement tests, it would be well to review the uses of achievement tests.

STUDENT USES.   Probably the single most important use of any achievement test, but particularly of teacher-made tests, is to provide *feedback to students* regarding the effectiveness of their learning. Because effective learning does not occur without knowledge of results, without the student knowing whether his responses were correct or incorrect, feedback is necessary. To be most effective, this feedback should be continual, should occur as immediately as possible, and should be made in terms of specific responses—i.e., the student should obtain knowledge of the accuracy of each individual response.

One often encounters the view that tests *motivate students to study*. To accomplish this purpose, tests are frequently used to show the student how much he does *not* know and thus supposedly to stimulate him to study. Or the threat of a test may be used to insure that the students will study and thus presumably learn—hopefully the basic concepts of the course but often only the material the students know will occur on the examination. The student may also learn other things when examinations are used primarily as a threat—fear of failure, test anxiety, dislike of school, or a feeling that the correct answer on a test is the most important goal of education. But data from learning experiments would lead to the conclusion that a test would most effectively serve as a stimulus to study when it functions as a reinforcer, when it shows the students that they can learn the material. Tests can serve as a stimulus for learning, not when used as a threat, but rather when used for their feedback and reinforcement value.

Diagnostic and counseling uses of achievement tests are also primarily for the benefit of the individual student. When achievement tests are used for *diagnostic purposes*, making a diagnosis is valuable only if it identifies the probable source of the student's difficulty and indicates the possible courses of remedial action. A diagnostic reading test is administered, not to determine the causes of a student's poor reading, but as a basis for planning a remedial program that will increase his reading skill.

There are times when achievement tests may be useful in the *counseling* process. For example, the discrepancy between a student's aptitude and achievement test scores may give some insights into his interests, study habits, or motivations. In academic counseling, achievement test data can indicate gaps in the student's knowledge and aid in program planning. Finally, because past performance is often the best single indicator of future performance, achievement tests can be utilized as aptitude measures to predict future academic success.

INSTRUCTOR USES.   An achievement test should not only furnish feedback to the learner but should also provide *feedback to the instructor*, so that he can ascertain how well his objectives have been met and how effective his teaching has been. By studying the accuracy of response to each item, the types of incorrect responses made, and the distribution of various erroneous responses among different subgroups of students, the teacher can identify the gaps in students' knowledge and can point out their misconceptions. Hopefully, the analysis will also provide clues as to which aspects of the teaching led to incomplete learning, thus providing a basis for modifying teaching behavior to insure more effective learning. The analysis, of course, also indicates which material must be reviewed because it was not learned on the original presentation.

Because teacher-made tests are designed to measure the attainment of the objectives of a particular course or unit, they are almost always a better basis for *assigning grades* than are standardized tests. Using an achievement test as the primary basis for grading assumes that the material on the test represents the desired outcomes of instruction. Therefore, the content and format of the examination must reflect these outcomes. Unfortunately, as many critics of "objective" (i.e., multiple-choice, true-false) items have pointed out, this is often not the case.

The teacher can use achievement tests in several other ways. Administering a *pretest* (i.e., a test given before the material has been covered in class) can serve as a diagnostic device. By identifying the knowledge and skills that the students already possess and the areas of lack of knowledge, the curriculum and teaching can be tailored to fit the needs of a particular individual or class. The teacher could also use an achievement test as a *check on students' studying*—for example, give a quiz to determine if, in fact, students have read a required assignment. Such a test need only cover the major points of the assignment and may be very brief. Or a teacher can use an achievement test to *stimulate discussion* by administering the test and using the students' responses, or difficulties with the items, as the base of discussion.

ADMINISTRATIVE USES. Achievement tests frequently are used as *selection* tools as, for example, when scores on the achievement sections of the Graduate Record Exam are used to select students for graduate work. Civil service examinations are used to determine whether an applicant has the requisite job skills. When an achievement test is used as a selection device one assumes that (1) the skills measured by the achievement test are, in fact, necessary skills for adequate performance and (2) past achievement is a good predictor of future performance.

In educational settings, achievement tests may be used to place students in courses. For example, when entering college you may have taken an achievement test in a language that you had previously studied and, on the basis of your test performance, been assigned to a particular level or section of the language course. If a given subject is taught in different ways or at different rates, an achievement test might be used to determine the section of the course that each student should enter. In industrial and business settings, achievement tests may be used to determine which of several positions best fits an individual's skills. In each of these samples, the function of the test is to aid in making *placement or classification* decisions.

Achievement tests are also used to determine whether a person has attained a standard, usually a minimal standard, to engage in some specific activity. For example, driver's license examinations are achievement tests designed to establish that the applicant has the requisite skills to drive an automobile on public streets and highways. The written portion of the test establishes the applicant's knowledge of traffic laws; the performance part (driving test) establishes his ability to actually drive the car in traffic. Other examples of using achievement tests as a *performance standard* would include examinations for professional licenses (e.g., medical specialties, professional engineering, or CPA); examinations given at the end of a training program in business and industry; preliminary exams for the doctorate; and examinations for credit or for testing out of a course.

EVALUATION OF INSTRUCTION. Probably no other area is so filled with danger, or provides so many examples of the misuse of test scores, as the use of achievement tests to evaluate the effectiveness of teachers or a particular curriculum or teaching method, or to compare schools. Because achievement tests do measure students' knowledge, and because a basic objective of education is the acquisition of knowledge, achievement tests do play an important part in the evaluation of instruction (and of teachers and teaching methods). The problem is that this evaluation process is not as simple or straightforward as some people seem to believe.

Drawing definitive conclusions from studies which compare various in-structional methods is very difficult, even when great care has been taken in designing an experiment (see, e.g., Gage, 1963; Campbell & Stanley, 1963). Drawing inferences from fortuitous collections of data, such as results of district wide testing programs, is almost always not a valid procedure.

CLASSROOM TESTS

All students are familiar with the ubiquitous teacher-made test. In fact, by the time you have read this far you have probably taken at least one, or possibly even several, tests over the material in this book. The distinguishing features of these tests were that they were constructed by the course instructor and covered only the material taught in this particular course or a unit within the course. These tests probably have never been, nor ever will be, given to any other class; individual items, however, may have appeared on examinations during previous terms and others may appear in future tests. The primary purpose of the examination was probably for assigning grades, although possibly if you are in an exceptional course, the major purpose was to provide feedback to you and the instructor regarding the progress of your learning. This same examination process is repeated in thousands of classrooms, from first grade through graduate school, every day. In fact, it is rare when examinations are not a routine part of a course.

Because the typical classroom examination is administered only once in a particular form, and then to a particular class under a singular set of cir-cumstances, the methods of constructing and evaluating teacher-made tests are somewhat different from the methods of constructing and evaluating standardized tests.

The discussion of the classroom tests will proceed in stages that parallel the process the teacher goes through in constructing and analyzing the test. Our presentation will be illustrative and evaluative; a detailed discussion of the process of building good test items must be reserved for other books (see, e.g., Brown, 1970; Ebel, 1965; or Wood, 1960).

Planning the classroom test

The nature of the test, and even the decision to test at all, should follow from the instructor's philosophy of education and his goals and objectives for the par-ticular course. These basic philosophic views will determine not only the nature of the testing, but also the frequency and timing of examinations. If the instruc-tor feels that the sole purpose of testing in the classroom is for the assignment of grades, he will give a final test and, at most, several other tests, usually at the end of a unit. If, however, he feels that the primary purpose of classroom testing is to facilitate learning, then his tests will no doubt be more frequent and spaced to maximize their impact on learning.

The instructor's educational objectives for the course will also determine the content and format of his exams. If his objectives are to teach basic vocabulary and facts, his test can consist, say, of purely factual items plus definitions; if the main objective is to teach a particular computational skill, the exam should consist of applications of that skill; if the goal is to have the student integrate a variety of material and arrive at a reasoned evaluation or conclusion, the examination must allow the student to demonstrate his ability to integrate the material, hence it will probably be an essay test. Of course, in most circumstances, there will be several objectives and a comprehensive examination will have to assess several distinct types of performance.

The first step in building a classroom test, therefore, is for the instructor to specify the goals, objectives, and desired outcomes of the course. (This specification should, of course, occur when the instructor plans the course, not when he starts to build an examination.) As has been repeatedly emphasized, these goals must be stated in behavioral terms, in terms that clearly specify the type of behavior that the student is expected to exhibit. It is not enough to indicate that students are expected "to understand percentiles"; rather, the goals should be expressed, e.g., "the student is expected to demonstrate his understanding of percentile ranks by computing percentile ranks from a set of raw scores and by drawing valid conclusions about a person's ranking knowing his percentile rank." Without such clearly specified objectives, there is no logical way to know what should be included on the test.

THE TEST PLAN.   Given a set of goals and objectives expressed in behavioral terms, the instructor can proceed to the process of constructing the examination. Here the teacher, as test constructor, will be concerned with two basic dimensions—the coverage of content and the skills that the student is expected to display.

In a classroom examination, the content coverage is usually fairly well specified as definite reading assignments and the material covered in the class periods can be used as an operational definition of the content universe. Suppose, for example, that the test is to cover the varieties of scores used on psychological tests. The content universe might be defined as the reading assignments on scores—e.g., "Chapter 7 of this text plus any material discussed in the class periods devoted to test scores."

Given this content domain, the instructor will also specify the several skills he considers worth testing. Using the previous example, the instructor may be interested in assessing the student's ability to (1) define the various types of scores, (2) compute the various scores from a set of raw data, and (3) interpret the various types of scores. The exact skills tested on any examination will, of course, be determined by the nature of the material covered and the instructor's

ideas about the important skills. Although the relevant skills can be classified
in various manners, skills which are frequently measured on classroom tests
include knowledge, comprehension, application, analysis, synthesis, and evaluation (Bloom, 1956).

The dual considerations of content and skills provide a convenient format for
constructing a *test plan*. An example of such a plan is given in Table 10.1, using
as an illustration the hypothetical test over test scores. Along the vertical axis we
have listed the major content areas to be covered—in this instance, seven major
topics. On any given test, the number and specificity of content categories will
depend upon the logical breakdown of the content material and the length of the
test; however, in a classroom test the number of categories will usually range
from about 5 to 12. Along the horizontal axis are listed the three skills to be
measured—definitions, computation and interpretation. The test plan thus
provides a convenient outline of the content and skills to be covered, an outline
that insures that the relevant aspects of the material will be considered when
constructing test items.

The test plan is generally elaborated one further step by the assignment of
weights to each content and skill category. These weights indicate the relative
emphasis to be given to each topic and skill and, consequently, tell what proportion of the test is to be devoted to each type of item. One way of approaching the
weighting question is to assign weights to content and skill areas independently.
In the example in Table 10.1 the four content areas and the three skill categories
are differentially weighted. These weights represent the judgment of the test
constructor (teacher) as to the relative emphases to be given each category; a
different test constructor might, of course, assign different emphases (weights).

TABLE 10.1   An example of a test plan: test on types of test scores

		Skills		
Content areas		Defini- tions (30%)	Compu- tation (50%)	Interpre- tation (20%)
Need for derived scores	10%	3% (1–2 items)	5% (2–3)	2% (1)
Content scores	10%	3% (1–2)	5% (2–3)	2% (1)
Percentiles	20%	6% (3)	10% (5)	4% (2)
Standard scores	20%	6% (3)	10% (5)	4% (2)
Developmental scores	10%	3% (1–2)	5% (2–3)	2% (1)
Ratios and quotients	10%	3% (1–2)	5% (2–3)	2% (1)
Comparison of types of scores	20%	6% (3)	10% (5)	4% (1)

Weighting of the marginal categories does not directly indicate the emphasis to be given to any content-skill cell; that is, it does not tell how many items of any particular type are to be included on the test. However, by multiplying the row weightings by the column weightings for all content by skill combinations we obtain an approximate picture of the composition of the test. We say "approximate" because some cells may not be meaningful, e.g., what would a computation problem involving the need for derived scores entail? Or, for other reasons, the instructor may wish to shift emphases in particular areas.

If the test is comprised of items all given equal score weight, the figures in the cells can be directly translated into the number of items required. For example, in Table 10.1, the number of items that would be devoted to each content-skill category on a 50-item objective test, where each item receives unit weight, are indicated in parentheses. If the test items were assigned differential weights, the percentages would indicate the relative weight to be given each cell. Thus items dealing with the computation of percentiles would comprise 10 percent of the test; this might be one problem or several problems totaling 10 percent of the score (i.e., five points on a 50-point test).

In summary, the test plan not only indicates the topics and skills to be covered by the test, it also indicates the relative emphases to be given to each content, skill and content-skill category. To the extent that the test, when constructed, accurately mirrors these emphases it will have content validity.

ITEM FORMAT.   The next task facing the test constructor is to determine the format of the test items. Should the items measure only recognition or should they require the student to recall the correct answer? Should the test consist of numerous short items or a smaller number of broader, more comprehensive items? If recognition items are to comprise the test, should they be multiple-choice or true-false items? If several different types of items are to be included, what is the optimal mixture of item types? These are the types of issues that the test constructor must decide.

The answers to these questions are partially determined by the skills to be assessed and the nature of the content domain. If, for example, the test is designed to measure the ability to marshall arguments to support a point of view, the item format will, almost necessarily, be that of an essay examination. In other instances the test constructor will have his choice among several alternative formats. For example, on a test designed to measure students' ability to identify state capitals, items might be presented as multiple-choice items:

The capital of New York state is:

(a) Albany (b) Buffalo (c) New York City (d) Rochester

as true-false items:

The capital of New York state is Albany. (True or False?)

or as completion items:

The capital of New York state is _____.

or in other formats.

The major choice regarding item format usually is between utilizing a large number of specific items or a smaller number of fairly broad items. In other words, a choice between multiple-choice (or true-false, short answer, or other relatively objective items) on one hand and essay questions on the other. The former procedure has the advantage of allowing more representative sampling of content by permitting questions from each relevant content area to appear on the exam. The essay format concentrates coverage into certain areas, rather than providing representative coverage of content areas, but covers these areas in greater depth. Therefore, from a strictly sampling point of view the former procedure is to be preferred. However, as the formats also differ on a variety of other dimensions—e.g., skills tapped, ease of contruction, testing time, scoring ease, and bias—in choosing between the two formats, the test constructor should realize that he will always be scarificing one set of goals for another.

OTHER CONSIDERATIONS. Before beginning construction of the test items, the teacher must decide on the *time limit* and *length of the test*. Because the purpose of a classroom test almost always is to determine the extent of students' knowledge rather than speed of response, the time limit should be set so that all, or almost all, of the students can finish the test within the time limit. The amount of time needed will, of course, vary with the number, difficulty, and length of the items, the age of the students, and many other variables. College students can typically answer about 50 multiple-choice questions per hour; high school and elementary students need longer time limits. The time to be devoted to essay questions will depend primarily on the completeness of the response desired. The author has found that college students need a minimum of an half hour for a minimally adequate response to almost any essay question and that even more time is frequently desirable. Younger children, though providing shorter answers, take longer to write and compose their answers. The teacher's experience with the length of time his students take to answer essay questions in the degree of completeness he deems desirable is the best guide when setting time limits.

The teacher must also decide on the *difficulty* of the items to be included on the test. The desired level of difficulty will depend on the purpose of testing and the uses to be made of the test scores. If, for example, the purpose of the exam is to check on whether students have read some assigned material, then relatively simple questions (ones that anyone having read the material can easily answer but people who have not read the material cannot answer) will suffice. If the purpose of the examination is to discriminate between individuals, as when attempting to stretch out the distribution in order to assign grades, items of medium difficulty (50–60 percent correct responses) are optimal. If the purpose is to find which students do not understand the material, again easy items will do. If there are certain essential items, items that cover points the teacher feels must be covered by the examination, these items should be included on the test regardless of their difficulty.[2] Also, in any test it is well to begin with several relatively easy "warm-up" items, those that allow the students to get in the swing of the test and build their confidence.

The instructor must also decide whether the students are to be instructed to guess when uncertain and whether a *correction for guessing* should be made (see p. 273). Finally, although most examinations are administered with the student unable to use any aids, the teacher may want to consider *open-book* and *take-home examinations*. In the view of their proponents, take-home and open-book tests better reflect the realities of the nonacademic world; opponents argue that the student will often have to make decisions under time pressures and on the basis of incomplete information, and that the typically classroom examination better represents this situation. Although neither type is appropriate to all situations, both certainly could be more frequently utilized in the classroom.

Varieties of items

The teacher's next step is to construct the items that will be included on the test. In this section we will discuss some of the item types that the classroom teacher may use and will indicate their basic assumptions, mode of construction, common variations, and advantages and limitations. Because most academic courses involve primarily symbolic (i.e., verbal and mathematical) concepts, we will concentrate on items measuring these areas.

Several frequently used types of items (e.g., multiple-choice, matching) require the student to recognize the correct response from several presented alternatives or identify a given bit of information as being correct or incorrect (true-false items). These items, called *recognition* items, assume that a student's knowledge of the subject matter can be adequately tapped by his ability to discriminate between correct and incorrect response alternatives. They do not require the student to reproduce any material; his task is to recognize the appropriateness of a given alternative. Other items, called *recall* items, require the student to actually reproduce the correct response. Examples of this class include short answer and completion items, essay questions, and mathematics and physics problems. A third general class of items includes those where the student must perform a feat such as playing a musical instrument, baking a cake, painting a picture, or running the 100-yard dash. These items are, not surprisingly, called *performance* items.

---

[2] It should be re-emphasized that difficulty is not an immutable quantity; the phrasing of the item, as well as the composition of the class, can affect the difficulty of an item. That is, various items covering the same content may vary in difficulty because of the structure and wording of the items.

Advocates of recall items stress that, because research generally shows recall to be a more difficult task than recognition, recall items present a more stringent, and thus better, test. They would also point out that most "real life" situations require the construction or production of a response, not a choice among a finite set of clearly labeled alternatives. Advocates of recognition items would stress the technical superiority of recognition items (e.g., their higher reliability) and the fact that it has not been clearly demonstrated that use of recall items results in superior learning or better retention. Advocates of both positions would probably admit that students will use differing study habits depending on the type of item included in the test.

The controversy is confounded by the failure to make a clear distinction between learning and testing. If the purpose of the testing is other than as a learning exercise, say to assign grades or for selection or placement, the critical consideration is not how the student may most effectively be brought to the desired level of accomplishment but whether the test gives a valid picture of his present level of achievement. Viewed in this manner, if a recognition measure is highly correlated with a recall measure of the same material, or with some desired outcome of the course, it is a valid measure of achievement. Thus, if a recognition test requiring the student to spot errors in sentence contruction is highly correlated with the student's ability to construct good English sentences, as measured by more direct methods, then the recognition examination can be substituted for actually writing sentences when the goal of the testing is to make an estimate of his present level of ability. Note that we did not say that the ability to construct good sentences can be developed by identifying errors in other people's sentences; it may be that this ability can be developed only by having the student write sentences. What we are saying is that the results of the learning process, however it occurred, can be measured by either technique.

But now let us turn to a brief discussion of several of the more common item types.

MULTIPLE-CHOICE. A multiple-choice item consists of a stem, which may be either a question or an incomplete statement, and a set—usually four or five—of alternatives. The student's task is to select the alternative that correctly answers the question posed by the stem or complete the statement begun in the stem.

For example:

If two tests rank the people in a given population in the same order, the tests are said to be:

(a) comparable
(b) equivalent
(c) homogeneous
(d) reliable

The stem of the item must present the problem in complete enough detail so that there is no ambiguity as to the nature of the problem; the alternatives provide the basis for inferring whether the student possesses the desired knowledge.

Distractors on multiple-choice items often are chosen to represent the most frequent incorrect responses. One empirical method of obtaining distractors would be to have a sample of students respond to a recall form of the item and determine which wrong answers are most prevalent; these responses would be incorporated as distractors. Other methods of selecting distractors include use of common misconceptions, logical alternatives, and distractors that maximize item validity. (See Ebel, 1965; Cronbach and Merwin, 1955.)

Although multiple-choice items have been criticized for testing only factual material, if properly designed, they can be used to test various skills. For example, mathematical and statistical problems are readily adaptable to the multiple-choice format:

> The mean on a test is 20 and the standard deviation is 5 points. Mike scores 13; his Z score is:
> (a) 14
> (b) 26
> (c) 36
> (d) 65.

This format requires the student to go through the same sequence of steps as if the item were presented in the typical problem format; the only difference is that he selects as the response to the item, the alternative that corresponds to his solution of the problem.

Many other examples could be given (see, e.g., *Multiple-Choice Questions: A Close Look*, Educational Testing Service, Princeton, N.J., 1963), but the point is clear—multiple-choice questions can be used to test skills other than simple recognition of facts (see Figure 10.1, pp.284-286).

Multiple-choice questions are adaptable to most content areas. And, because a large number of multiple-choice items can be administered in a relatively short period, representative sampling of content and skill areas is possible. Scoring of multiple-choice items is rapid and objective, and the results are conducive to item analysis procedures, thus providing data that can be used to improve the test as well as provide feedback to the teacher and student. One presumed disadvantage is the limited applicability of multiple-choice items, but this is usually the result of shoddy test construction procedures (it is easier to write factual items than ones testing more complex skills); it is not an inherent limitation of the item format. Good multiple-choice items are, without doubt, difficult and time consuming to construct; therefore the time saved in scoring the test is generally balanced by the added time needed to construct the items.

Several variations of the traditional multiple-choice format are sometimes encountered. One procedure bases a series of multiple-choice items on one reading passage, diagram, chart, table, or other set of stimulus materials. This variation permits one set of stimulus material to be extensively probed, but might, as a consequence, sacrifice some representativeness of sampling. Another frequently encountered variation allows the student to select none, one, or up to all alternatives as being correct. This procedure, in essence, changes the multiple-choice item into a series of true-false items and has the advantages and disadvantages of the true-false format.

TRUE-FALSE. In the true-false format a declarative statement is presented, e.g.,

The mean is a measure of the dispersion of a set of test scores.

or

If an intelligence test could be developed, each item of which represented an equivalent amount of intellectual ability, the test would measure on an interval scale.

and the student indicates whether the item is true or false (or some other comparable dichotomy as yes-no, correct-incorrect). In essence, he must make an absolute judgment of the veracity of the statement. If any part of the statement is incorrect, the item is false.

Because true-false items are largely restricted to unambiguous factual material their usefulness is limited. They are most appropriate with younger children (who are not as alert to the subtleties of language) and when only a superficial estimate is needed, for example, to check whether students have read an assignment. True-false items are easily scored and relatively easy to construct, certainly much easier than multiple-choice items.

Several alternative formats are sometimes used with true-false items. One requires the student to indicate whether a statement is true or false and then correct the statement if it is false. The major disadvantage of this procedure is that a false item can be corrected in many ways, including a variety of trivial ways, e.g.,

Item: Percentile ranks fall in a normal distribution. T or F.
Response: False
Correction: Percentile ranks do *not* fall in a normal distribution.
Intended correction: Percentile ranks fall in a rectangular distribution.

thus forcing the teacher to make decisions regarding the acceptability of any specific correction.

An alternative format requires the student to respond true or false and indicate his confidence in his choice along some continuum of confidence. By weighting responses in proportion to the confidence the student expresses in his response (positive weight if the item is answered correctly and negative weight if answered incorrectly), the range of scores is increased. Whether this procedure results in more valid and reliable items, however, is open to question.

MATCHING.　Matching items consist of two parallel lists, one consisting of a series of stimulus words or phrases and the other containing a series of responses. The student's task is to match the appropriate response with each stimulus. A typical matching item might be:

DIRECTIONS: The following items all refer to consistency of measurement. For each statement in the left column choose the method from the right column which is most appropriate. Each response alternative may be used once, more than once, or not at all.

1. Method used to determine the consistency of this test.
2. Method whose results are most affected by the speededness of the test.
3. Method used to determine the degree of intercorrelation among items on the test.
4. Method used to determine if students' values change with college experience.

A. Stability
B. Equivalence
C. Stability and equivalence
D. Split-half
E. Internal consistency

Note that the items could be administered as four separate multiple-choice items, each item having an identical set of response alternatives; thus, in essence, a matching item is a series of multiple-choice items, covering a homogeneous content domain, with the same set of responses serving for all items.

Because matching items are essentially multiple-choice items, they have many of the same advantages, limitations and uses as multiple-choice items. The major considerations in determining whether to use a matching format are: (1) whether there are a series of items of homogeneous content and (2) the degree of emphasis to be given the content area covered by the matching item. The use of a matching item will necessarily involve devoting four or five items to a single content category; unless this great an emphasis is desired on a single topic, disproportionate weighting will occur.

SHORT ANSWER AND COMPLETION.　All of the item types discussed thus far have required only recognition of the correct response. In most situations, the same material can also be tested using a short answer or completion format, a format that requires the student to supply the correct response. For example, the multiple-choice item illustrated on page 265 could also be administered as a completion item:

If two tests rank the people in a given population in the same order, the tests are said to be (*comparable*).

or as a short answer item:

> Two tests may be said to be comparable when (*they rank the people in a given population in the same order*).

The distinction made between a short answer and completion item is mainly the length of response—the completion item requires the student to provide a response that is a word or two in length, the short answer item requires him to answer in a sentence or two.

Because short answer and completion items generally cover the same ground as objective recognition items (e.g., multiple-choice, matching, true-false), and there is no definitive evidence that either recognition or recall items are definitely superior, the format to be used depends upon the preferences, item writing skills, and educational philosophy of the instructor. This format is also appropriate for younger children (e.g., in elementary schools) who are less likely to be confused with the mechanisms of responding than on a multiple-choice item. Also, it is easier and less time consuming to compose a short answer or completion item than to build a good multiple-choice item covering the same topic.

The major disadvantage of the format involves scoring—not only will scoring take longer than for recognition items, but it will almost certainly require some decision making on the part of the scorer and thus increase unreliability. For example, in the item "Reliability can be defined as _____," it is obvious that there are a large number of possible responses and shades of responses that will be wholly or partially correct. When scoring this item the teacher would have to decide which responses were acceptable and how much credit would be allowed for each variation. Scoring will be easiest and most objective when the teacher prepares a chart of acceptable responses (a scoring key) prior to scoring the test.

One obvious variation of the short answer item is the definition item. Definitions are usually presented as a list of words preceded by directions as to the required length and specificity of the definition. Or, the student may be asked to indicate the importance, describe, compare, or identify persons, places, events, or objects. In mathematics, the student may be asked to provide formulas.

ESSAY. At some not clearly specifiable point, a short answer item shades into an essay question. The distinction between the two types of items, however, is not solely in terms of their length; it also involves the function the item performs. While a short answer item is best suited to tap knowledge of factual material or the ability to identify and define concepts, structures, persons, or events, an essay question provides a basis for evaluating the student's ability to organize ideas, integrate and evaluate material, as well as for indicating his knowledge of the relevant factual material. Responses to essay questions may also reflect attitudes, creativity and verbal fluency—factors that may or may not be relevant to the purposes of the testing.

A typical essay question might be phrased somewhat as follows:

Define reliability verbally and by presenting a formula. Identify and differentiate between the various measures of reliability indicating their paradigm, the influencing error sources, and their appropriate uses.

The primary advantage of the essay question is that it assesses certain skills—e.g., organization, integration, evaluation—which cannot be tested as effectively by other item formats. Because of the semistructured format, the answer can be approached from several equally valid angles, thus yielding a flexibility not found in other formats. As with other recall items, faking and guessing are minimized. The length of response allows the student to treat a question in some depth. Although the oft-cited advantage of essay items, the ease of item construction, may be more apparent than real, certainly it is easier to write a test composed solely of essay questions than one composed of multiple-choice items.

The disadvantages of the essay format become readily apparent when scoring begins. To read and grade even a few essay items is a time consuming task. Because each response will be different, equating scores of students using different information and approaching problems from the different angles becomes considerable. The evidence is overwhelming that the reliability of grading essay questions—from grader to grader, time to time, or question to question—is often unsatisfactory, even when scoring standards and procedures are well specified. And, as mentioned previously, essay examinations do not provide as accurate sampling of the content domain as does the same amount of time devoted to multiple choice or other "objective" items.

One variation of the essay question uses a composition (e.g., a poem, test manual, journal article) as a stimulus for an evaluative essay. Viewed in this manner, a book review or term paper would be a variation of an essay item.

PROBLEMS. The content of certain subjects, particularly in mathematics and the physical sciences, lends itself to test items expressed as problems. Here the item poses a problem for the student. Usually the solution involves identifying the basic question asked and the relevant parameters and data, setting up an equation or computational procedure, then solving for the correct answer:

On the GW Test of Conservative Thinking, Herbert scores 35. The group mean is 45 and the standard deviation is 5 points. If scores are transformed to a standard score system (Z scores) using a mean of 50 and a standard deviation of 10, Herbert will obtain a Z score of _____.

In this example the problem is defined (to find the Z score equivalent of a given raw score) but the student must set up the formula from his knowledge of the definition of standard scores:

$$Z = 50 + 10\left(\frac{X - \bar{X}}{s}\right) = 50 + 10\left(\frac{35 - 45}{5}\right) = 50 + 10(-2) = 30$$

and then solve the equation. The reader can think of many other examples of potential problems.

The problem format is obviously well suited to testing computational skills and ability to apply knowledge to new situations. Memory of formulas and other factual information may be an integral part of the item or these tools may be provided within the test or by using an open-book procedure. Construction of problem items is generally quite easy because there are a large variety of possible items and the skills to be measured are well specified. Scoring can be objective if attainment of the correct answer is the sole consideration; if, however, partial credit is to be awarded for the correct procedure marred by incorrect computations, a subjective element enters into the scoring.

In certain areas an appropriate test may have the student perform or demonstrate some skill. For example, in a typing class the best test may be a test of speed and/or accuracy of typing; in instrumental music, the ability to sight-read and perform a passage; in physical education, to bowl a line or run the 100-yard dash. In an English composition class, an appropriate test may be the writing of a theme—a task that is highly similar to the essay question in format, process, and scoring. In a botany class, the student may be asked to demonstrate his knowledge by collecting specimens. The variety of available test formats is limited, in short, only by the subject matter and the teacher's ingenuity.

Administering and scoring the test

Ideally, more items will have been built than are to be included on the test, enabling the teacher to select the items from the pool which (1) are the best written, (2) test the most important concepts, and (3) produce a distribution of content and skills that closely parallels the test plan. More realistically, the teacher will probably write items until he has the necessary number of adequate ones, roughly representing the content and skill distribution visualized in the test plan.

The next step is to collate the items for presentation to the class. The most common procedure, undoubtedly, is to duplicate the test questions so that each student will have his own copy of the test, but other procedures may be used. For example, the teacher might read the questions; however, this is a clumsy procedure, used only with young children and other persons with limited reading skills. Or the items might be projected on a screen, a procedure which places definite time restrictions on responding but is an excellent method of presenting certain types of identification items, e.g., identifying sites on a map, the artist or characteristics of a painting, or the parts of the body. Or in a science class, the teacher might set up displays and base the questions (which will usually be printed on a separate sheet) on these displays. Or in a highly automated system, items might be presented by computers and students respond directly on the computer console.

ADMINISTRATION. There are several essential requirements in the administration of a classroom test. First are the directions, which initially occur several days or weeks prior to the test when the teacher informs the students of the purpose of the test, the content domain covered by the test, the format the test will take, its length, and the date it will be given. The test proper should contain explicit directions as to the time limit, how and where to respond, the scoring weight assigned each item, and procedures to adopt when uncertain as to the correct response. For recall items, directions should indicate the length of response desired. If the item format changes within the test, this fact should be noted by a new set of directions. Of course, with mature students, or when a test is similar to previous tests in the course, formal directions may be minimal. In any situation, however, the teacher should check that students are not confused by the directions and are responding correctly.

Second, the testing room environment should be conducive to optimal performance. Generally this means only a quiet, well lighted and ventilated room, free from interruptions and distractions, with students seated far enough apart so as not to interfere with each other's performance. When special equipment is used (e.g., projectors, displays), the room should be arranged so that each student can see, hear, or have access to the materials.

Third, provision should be made for handling special problems and emergencies. If, for example, a student has a hearing problem he should be seated so that he can hear all important material. The teacher should also have plans in mind for handling unforeseen interruptions—illness, defective tests, fire drills—with a minimum of confusion. In such emergency situations, as with many aspects of test administration, no set of rules can be given; one has to rely on the sound judgment of the test administrator.

SCORING. The exact scoring procedures will depend on the type of items but in all cases will involve comparing each student's responses to a scoring key. Recall items must be individually scored by the teacher; for recognition items, scoring may be done either by hand—that is, by a visual checking against the key—or by electronic scoring machines. Scoring by the machines is, of course, faster and more error free but requires special answer sheets. The use of separate answer sheets, whether for electronic scoring or hand scoring, increases the complexity of the responding procedure and thus may hinder or confuse younger children.

The teacher must also assign weights to each item, a decision that should be made prior to the administration of the exam. For true-false, multiple-choice, matching, and most completion and short-answer items, the weight generally will be one point for each correct response. Problems, essays, and some short-answer items may have several points assigned to each item. If the teacher wants to award partial credit on these items, as he probably will, he must clearly specify the bases on which partial credit will be awarded.

The total points assigned for correct responses will generally be used as the (total) test score. In some circumstances, however, the teacher may want to apply a *correction for guessing*. These corrections subtract a portion of the wrong responses from the correct responses. The general formula to correct for guessing is:

$$\text{Corrected Score} = R - \frac{W}{N - 1} \tag{10.1}$$

where R is the number of correct responses, W the number of incorrect responses, and N the number of response alternatives per item. Thus, with true-false items the formula would be:

$$\text{Corrected Score} = R - W \tag{10.1a}$$

as there are only two possible alternatives, true and false; for multiple-choice items with four alternatives the formula would be:

$$\text{Corrected Score} = R - \frac{W}{3} \tag{10.1b}$$

These formulas assume that the student responds randomly when unsure of the correct response—a highly tenuous assumption in most cases.

Whether correction for guessing is a worthwhile expenditure of effort is a debatable point (see, e.g., Ebel, 1965; Davis, 1951, 1964). Proponents argue that correcting for guessing produces scores which better reflect the student's true achievement level and discourages the habit of wild guessing. Opponents of correcting scores argue that the ranking of students will be approximately the same whether or not scores are corrected,[3] that guessing patterns are not random as assumed by the correction formulas, that the probability of obtaining a high score by guessing is exceedingly small, that applying the correction makes scoring more cumbersome, and that making rational guesses under conditions of uncertainty may be a habit worth cultivating. It would seem that the burden of proof would fall upon proponents of correcting for guessing; in this author's opinion, as yet they have not made a compelling case.

Analyzing the test

After the test has been administered and scored, the teacher may want to analyze the test scores to see how effective a measuring instrument he has constructed. Although in practice only a few conscientious teachers make systematic analyses of their tests, the feedback provided by such analyses will undoubtedly help the teacher improve his test construction skills and provide information regarding the effectiveness of his teaching and the learning of the students.

---

[3]When every person responds to every item the correlation between corrected and uncorrected scores will, of course, be 1.00.

Analyses proceed on two levels: (total) test scores and individual items. When analyzing test scores we will be concerned with the distribution of the test scores, and their validity and reliability. At the individual item level we will be concerned with the difficulty of the items, the attractiveness of the various alternatives, and the discrimination power of the items.

THE DISTRIBUTION OF SCORES. A computation that is almost universally made is to determine the distribution of scores obtained by the students taking the examination. Usually this distribution is prepared before assigning grades. However, if we also compute a measure of the central tendency of the scores (either the mean or median), which indicates the *difficulty* of the test, and plot the distribution of scores, valuable information will be provided regarding the effectiveness of the test.

A normal distribution, with the majority of scores falling in the middle ranges and fewer scores falling toward the extremes, provides good discrimination between students at either end of the distribution and generally will be the optimal distribution when grades are assigned. If the distribution is negatively skewed, with many students obtaining high scores and few obtaining low scores, the test is quite easy. This distribution would not be very useful when assigning grades because there is poor discrimination in the upper score segments even though the test does discriminate between students with lesser degrees of knowledge. If the purpose of the testing were to check on an assignment or to insure that students have mastered the basic material so that more advanced topics might be introduced, such a distribution would be expected. If the distribution is positively skewed, with few persons obtaining high scores, again the test would be of limited usefulness for grading, as it is apparently very difficult. However, if the data represented a pretest over unstudied material, it would have the predicted distribution.

The mean (or median) indicates the absolute difficulty of the test. For tests designed to discriminate between students, a mean score slightly higher than 50 percent of the maximum possible score is optimal (with an approximately normal distribution). For mastery tests, an average score near the maximum would be desired. In all circumstances, discrepancies between the expected and actual average scores may provide useful information for evaluating the test.

CONSISTENCY. Because the typical classroom examination has only one form and will be administered only once, reliability methods that require equivalent forms or repeated administrations generally can not be used. Therefore, the teacher is left with two alternative methods of obtaining a consistency estimate—split-half and internal consistency.[4] When using the split-half method,

---

[4]The application of split-half and internal consistency analyses is straightforward when the test items each have unit weight. If the items are differentially weighted, alterations in the procedures for computing reliability must be made.

an odd-even split will generally suffice, since the classroom test will typically be a power test with the items positioned essentially at random. Of course, correction by the Spearman-Brown formula must occur to take into account the length of the test.

The other available approach is to use a measure of internal consistency. This approach, it will be remembered, assumed that all test items measure the same general trait or factor. Although the skills measured in the typical classroom exam are generally positively intercorrelated, whether they are so highly intercorrelated that they measure one factor is problematical. Thus the assumptions of the internal consistency formula are only approximated.

VALIDITY.   In achievement testing, as has been repeatedly stressed, content validity is the primary procedure for establishing validity. So, too, with classroom examinations. The basic procedure is to compare the skills and content covered by the items with the test plan. If the items cover the material given in the plan, and cover important rather than trivial material, then the test has content validity. This process, of course, assumes that the test plan is a fair reflection of the content domain and the instructional goals—a consideration that was discussed previously.

Sometimes the validity of a classroom test can be supported by other evidence. Some of the sources are external to the class; for example, when courses occur in a sequence, the relationship between scores on a final examination in one course and success in the following course could be determined. Or scores on classroom tests could be correlated with standardized achievement tests covering the same general content area. If external measures are unavailable, data from sources within the class can be used. For example, if test scores do not parallel the teacher's judgment of the students' expected performance—e.g., if the pupils she judges to be best prepared score low and the poorer students score high—the validity of the test might be called into question. (These results might, of course, also reflect upon the teacher's judgmental ability.) The scores on any single examination could be related to scores on other exams or other assignments, e.g., term papers and reports. We might even be interested in comparing test results and the students' judgment of their learning. All of these data sources provide, albeit somewhat biased,[5] evidence of the validity of the test.

Item analysis

We now turn to the question of the quality of the individual items comprising the test, a question that is answered by data from item analyses. Although item analyses are usually applied to recognition items, particularly multiple-choice

[5]For example, where the criterion measure involves teachers' judgments, criterion contamination may operate, because the teacher probably knows the students' test scores and grades in previous courses.

items, with certain modifications they can be applied to other types of items, even essay questions. In the following discussion we will use the multiple-choice format as an illustration and consider only simple methods of item analysis— methods which are feasible for classroom tests. These methods do, however, illustrate the general logic of item analysis. The reader who wishes to study item analysis in more detail should read Brown (1970), Davis (1951), Ebel (1965), or Wood (1960).

PROCEDURE.   In conducting an item analysis the basic procedure is to compare the responses of a high scoring and a low scoring group. In doing this, we want to obtain enough respondents in each group to obtain a stable estimate of the relevant statistics but not so many as to make the data analysis task overwhelming. The classroom teacher will generally be faced with the former problem rather than the latter.

The first step in the process is to rank the tests in order of total scores. Then divide the tests into subgroups. It has been shown that when the distribution is normal, the optimal procedure is to use the upper and lower 27 percent of scores (ignoring the middle 46 percent) as the basis for computing item statistics. With very large classes the teacher may want to use this split or an approximation to it. With smaller groups (less than 100) an appropriate procedure is to divide the group at the median and compare responses of the upper and lower halves. This split increases stability (by having statistics based on the largest possible sample) and provides a more rigorous test of item discrimination (by including all scores, not just extreme groups).

The next step is to tally the number of responses to each alternative of each item for each subgroup. These data, for five items, are shown in Table 10.2. These data are the responses of the upper and lower 30 students in a class of 60 students. The upper half of each table shows the frequencies of choice of each alternative; the lower half shows these data as proportions.

ITEM DIFFICULTY.   One measure of interest is the difficulty of the item, the proportion of persons who choose the correct (keyed) response. This index can vary in value from 1.00, when everyone answers the item correctly, to .00, when all individuals choose an incorrect alternative. As was mentioned previously, discrimination among members of the sample is maximized when difficulty levels center around .50–.60, that is, when approximately one-half of the group correctly answer the item. For other purposes other difficulty levels are desired—for example, a warm-up item should be answered correctly by 90 percent or more of the students.

When dealing with only two groups, as with the data in Table 10.2, an estimate of item difficulty can be made by averaging the difficulty levels of the two groups:

$$\text{Difficulty} = \frac{P_{\text{high}} + P_{\text{low}}}{2} \qquad (10.2)$$

that is, the difficulty of the item is the average proportion passing the item. Formula 10.2 assumes that the difficulty level for the middle group, if there is one, falls halfway between the difficulty level for the two extreme groups. Applying this computational method to the items in Table 10.2 we find that

TABLE 10.2 Examples of item analysis data

ITEM		A*	B	C	D
1. The primary criterion used in	N High	30	0	0	0
selecting items for the Binet	N Low	24	2	4	0
test was the item's:	P High	1.00	.00	.00	.00
(a) ability to discriminate	P Low	.80	.07	.13	.00
between children of					
different ages		Difficulty		.90	
(b) correlation with total		Discrimination		.20	
score on the test					
(c) ability to measure one of					
the basic intellectual					
factors					
(d) correlation with grades					
received in school					
subjects					

ITEM		A	B	C	D*
2. Which of the following is *not* a					
difference between aptitude	N High	3	3	2	22
and achievement tests?	N Low	7	8	6	9
(a) their time reference—	P High	.10	.10	.07	.73
past, present, or future	P Low	.23	.27	.20	.30
(b) the specificity of the					
content area covered by		Difficulty		.52	
the test		Discrimination		.43	
(c) the uses to which test					
results are put					
(d) the type, form and con-					
tent of the test items					

ITEM		A	B*	C	D
3. The IQ's on the common					
individual intelligence tests,	N High	10	19	0	1
such as the Stanford-Binet	N Low	17	12	0	1
and Wechsler, are:	P High	.33	.64	.00	.03
(a) the ratio of mental age	P Low	.57	.40	.00	.03
to chronological age					
(b) a form of normalized		Difficulty		.52	
standard score		Discrimination		.24	
(c) a special variety of					
percentiles					
(d) an age score with a					
transformed mean					

Table 10.2 (continued)

4. If the distribution of raw scores on a test were approximately normal, the greatest difference in raw scores would be between percentiles:

	A*	B	C	D
N High	17	2	3	8
N Low	2	12	8	8
P High	.57	.07	.10	.36
P Low	.06	.40	.27	.27

   (a)　1 and 5
   (b)　51 and 55
   (c)　91 and 95
   (d)　It would be equal in all cases listed above.

Difficulty　.32
Discrimination .51

5. The major weakness of grade-point average as a criterion of academic success in college is that GPA is:

	A*	B	C	D
N High	16	0	2	12
N Low	18	3	3	6
P High	.53	.00	.07	.40
P Low	.60	.10	.10	.20

   (a)　only one of many possible indices of success
   (b)　unstable from quarter to quarter
   (c)　based on ratings, not objective measures
   (d)　based on different courses for different people

Difficulty　.56
Discrimination −.07

---

*Correct alternative. Difficulty and discrimination indices are defined in text.

item 1 is quite easy (difficulty = .90), item 4 is relatively difficult (difficulty = .32), and the other three items are answered correctly by about half of the students. Item 4 may be difficult (or item 1 easy) because of a peculiarity of the structure of the item or because the material covered by the item was not learned by the students; only further analyses can indicate which explanation is most likely.

ITEM DISCRIMINATION. A second fundamental index is the discriminating power of the item, the ability of the item to differentiate between subgroups of students. Ideally, we would have an index of item validity which showed the relation of item responses to an extratest criterion measure; in practice, such external measures are not generally available. Thus the discriminating power of the item is computed by comparing individual item responses to the total score on the test, because the total score provides the best estimate of the students' overall knowledge of the content domain. Note that when comparing the response on an individual item to the (total) test score, we are assuming that all the test items are measuring the same skill or set of skills. Although this assumption may seem unjustified, the empirical data usually support this generalization. (For a discussion of this issue see Ebel, 1968 and Horn, 1966.)

Many indices of item discrimination have been developed, ranging from simple to exceedingly complex models. Because of computational ease, and the fact that the more complex methods are not demonstrably better than the simpler ones, the teacher will probably want to use a simple method. Thus in Table 10.2, we have used the difference in proportion of correct response between the high and low groups as an index of discrimination:

$$\text{Discrimination} = P_{high} - P_{low} \qquad (10.3)$$

The value of this discrimination index can range from $+1.00$ to -1.00. A value of $+1.00$ would occur if all the persons in the high group answered the item correctly and all the low group choose an incorrect response; a value of -1.00 would occur if all the subjects in the low group obtained the correct response and none of the high group were correct. A value of 0.00, which indicates no discrimination between the groups, occurs when both groups have the same proportion of correct responses.

What constitutes an acceptable value for the discrimination index is an open question although, obviously, the higher the positive value the better.[6] Items with indices of $+.40$ or higher are certainly good items; items with indices of .20 or higher contribute to discrimination but probably can be improved; items with lower indices contribute little to discrimination; and items with negative indices discriminate, but in the wrong direction. Using these standards, items 2 and 4 in Table 10.2 would be considered good items, items 1 and 3 discriminate in the correct direction but probably could be improved, and item 5 discriminates negatively. As is the case with difficulty indices, the data tell only the extent of discrimination; they do not tell why the item functions as it does.

The previous discussion has assumed that, in order to be considered a good item, the item should discriminate. If the purpose of the item is to contribute to maximizing individual differences, this is undeniably true. However, if the item is to serve other purposes—say as a warm-up item or to check if students have mastered certain basic material—discrimination power may be a minor, or even irrelevant, consideration. In both of the examples cited, item difficulty would be a more crucial index of the effectiveness of the item.

EFFECTIVENESS OF DISTRACTORS.   The pattern of responses to each alternative to each item often indicates why the item functions as it does and suggests

---

[6]One could, of course, accept only items that attained a given level of statistical significance. However, as statistical confidence levels are related to sample size, with small classes (a) the results from any one class will be unstable and (b) statistically significant differences may not occur. The most feasible procedure for the clasroom teacher is to reuse items that discriminate on successive examinations; in essence, to cross-validate items in several classes.

ways the item can be improved. Consider the examples in Table 10.2. Item 1 was very easy and thus the distractors (incorrect alternatives) had little attractiveness. Item 2 presents a different pattern. Although the item was relatively easy for the high group, it was difficult for the low group. Note also that the responses of the low group, as well as the incorrect responses of the high group, are spread evenly across all alternatives. This pattern indicates that all alternatives were pulling their weight and were feasible alternatives for a person who did not know the correct response. These data, combined with the values of the difficulty and discrimination indices, show item 2 to be an excellent item. In contrast, item 3 had only two alternatives that drew any support worth mention [(a) and (b)] and thus the choice for the students was between only two, not four, alternatives. The item discriminated somewhat, but could be improved by strengthening alternatives (c) and (d). Items 4 and 5 present interesting patterns. Item 4, although difficult, discriminated well. Note that most persons in the high group who chose the incorrect response, and many of the low group, chose alternative (d); however, the most common incorrect response for the low group was (b). Examining the item content shows that persons in the low groups tended to get the relationship between percentiles and raw scores reversed [i.e., they selected (b)]. Item 5 discriminated negatively, primarily because many of the high group members chose alternative (d) rather than (a), the response keyed correct. Consideration of item 5 shows that (d) is a possible correct response, as GPA's *will* be based on different courses for different persons, raising a question as to their comparability. In this item, the more knowledgeable students have been misled.

Evaluation of classroom tests

What, then, can we say in summary regarding classroom tests? Certainly it should be clear that effective instruction can not occur without periodic evaluation and feedback, that is, without some sort of testing. The question is the frequency and form of the testing. Because the goals of instruction for any class will ultimately be determined by the classroom teacher, using as a guide the goals of the school system, classroom tests are a necessary part of education.

Technically, classroom tests do not meet all of the requirements set out in earlier chapters. They are standardized to the extent that they consist of a common set of items that are administered to all members of a particular group under identical conditions. Scores are compared to a common norm group—the class—but are rarely expressed on other than ordinal scales. The reliability of classroom tests is usually not computed and, in one sense, is superfluous because only one test is available and will be used regardless of its reliability. Validity is determined primarily by content validity, any evidence of empirical validity being derived from sources internal to the test.

One particular issue that has caused a considerable amount of debate is the relative merits of multiple-choice (and other objective items) versus essay examinations. The resolution would seem to depend on the recognition that the two tests formats are complementary, not opposed. Essay tests will be most appropriate with small classes, when time pressures are minimal or nonexistent, when the subject matter is to be covered in depth, and when the skills to be tested include organization, integration, evaluation, or creativity; multiple-choice items will be used with large classes, for broad sampling of content, with time pressures, and when testing of recognition skills is sufficient. The time the essay format saves during test construction will be more than compensated for by the scoring time needed; conversely, multiple-choice items take much longer to construct but are rapidly scored. The main disadvantages of essay items are the scoring time and unreliability and the limited coverage of topics; multiple-choice questions suffer from being relatively highly structured and testing recognition, not recall.

The status of classroom examinations is contradictory. Even groups that vigorously attack other types of testing generally concede that the measurement of classroom achievement is an essential educational process. Yet, few teachers, either in their college preparation or while practicing their art, take the necessary time to build better tests, analyze the test after it is given, fully utilize the test as a learning tool, or increase their test building skills. Hopefully those of you who plan to become teachers will take the time.

STANDARDIZED ACHIEVEMENT TESTS

In education, there frequently is need for information which can be obtained only from broad-scale and standardized samples of student performance: the measurement of educational growth from year to year; the comparison of different curricula or teaching methods; measurement of retention of skills over long time intervals; placement of students having differing educational backgrounds. Accurate information relating to these problems can not be obtained through use of *ad hoc* teacher-built tests; hence, the need for standardized achievement tests.

Rather than spell out the differences between standardized achievement tests and classroom tests, we shall discuss the construction of standardized achievement tests, letting the reader compare and contrast the two types of tests.

Construction

Once the need for a particular standardized test has been recognized, the preliminary stages of test construction are handled by advisory committees consisting of educators and representatives of the test publisher. This committee establishes general guidelines for the test such as: What content and skills should be covered? What relative emphasis should be given content and skills? What is the appropriate age range? What is the length of the test? What is the relationship between this test and other tests in the battery and/or on the market? If a test battery is to be constructed, what tests should be included? Is a survey or a diagnostic instrument needed? Which of the various approaches to the subject matter will be stressed? What test format should be used? How many scores or subtests are needed? And so on, through many more questions. The answers form the general plans and guidelines for the test.

The actual construction of the test is usually managed by subject matter experts working in conjunction with test construction experts employed by the test publisher. Although the procedural steps will vary depending on the nature of the test (and other matters, such as whether the test is new or a revision and whether the test is part of a battery), a typical sequence would be: planning the test, writing the items, pretesting the items, assembling the test, determining the technical adequacy of the test, and developing normative and interpretive material (Educational Testing Service, 1965).

PLANNING.   One obvious difference between standardized and classroom tests is that the former, having been planned by more than one person, will reflect a compromise among points of view rather than the preferences and biases of only one person—the classroom teacher. Therefore, the standardized test will include content which is widely accepted as being basic to an area and which is presented in the frequently used sources. Also, because the test will be applied to diverse and heterogeneous groups and probably will be administered only once a year in any class, the content domain sampled will be broader than on a classroom test and no single subtopic will be covered in depth.

The planners of a standardized test also may have a problem of articulation. Because most tests will be parts of a battery of achievement tests and will be designed for a particular grade level or range of grades, the test must fit appropriately into the sequence and battery. Furthermore, as the test will probably be expected to serve several functions simultaneously, diverse and perhaps contradictory characteristics may have to be built into the test.

Given these boundary conditions, the engineering of the test plan is very similar to that of a classroom test. The test constructors will generally use some form of the content-skills grid; however, they will use more dimensions and define these dimensions more specifically than will the teacher building a classroom examination. In short, the process is the same, the difference being in the formality and thoroughness of the specifications.

ITEM WRITING.   Items are written by subject matter specialists or professional item writers, reviewed by test and subject matter specialists, edited, revised and rewritten, reviewed again, and so on until an acceptable form of the item is attained. In addition, proposed items are reviewed by curricular experts other than those who wrote the items. Note especially that item writing is done by, and items are independently reviewed by, subject matter experts; the test specialists serve as technical advisers, not determiners of content. Thus the test reflects the content educators think important and not, as is sometimes charged, that which psychometricians feel is important.

It should also be noted that, although the classroom teacher has recourse to a variety of item formats, items on standardized achievement tests will be almost exclusively recognition items. The reasons are several: more adequate sampling of content; ease, speed, and accuracy of scoring; and higher reliability. Because multiple-choice items proffer more advantages and fewer limitations than other types of objective items, they are most widely used. The item writing task thus usually becomes one of writing multiple-choice items. Because of the importance of standardized tests, and the resources devoted to developing these tests, exceedingly sophisticated forms of multiple-choice items have been developed (see e.g., Figure 10.1 and Educational Testing Service, 1963).

Many more items will be written than the number that will appear on the final forms of the test, often three or four times as many. The required number of items will then be selected from this pool of items, using pretest data to identify items displaying the desired characteristics. When more than one form of the test is being constructed, the need will be for enough good items to fill the several forms plus enough additional items so that the forms can be equated in content, difficulty, reliability, and along other relevant dimensions.

ITEM TRYOUT. Although experienced item writers can identify and eliminate items with obvious faults, there is no assurance that any given item will perform as expected when administered to groups of students. Thus, before the final form of a test is compiled, preliminary forms are administered to samples of students, and the relevant item statistics computed. On the basis of these data some items are eliminated from further consideration, others are revised, and others are deemed acceptable as they stand.

ASSEMBLING THE TEST. The crucial aspect in assembling the final forms of the test is to balance all the relevant considerations to produce a test with the desired characteristics. For example, the various content and skill categories should be represented in the proportions outlined in the test plan. The number of items must be appropriate for the time limit. The test must be of the proper difficulty level and a wide distribution of scores be obtained. If several different item formats are included, they must appear in proper proportion. Moreover, these same considerations must be applied to each form of the test and the various forms must be equated to each other—an extremely delicate process.

Finally, the test is again reviewed by subject matter and test construction specialists. After they have made any necessary modifications the test is printed.

Figure 10.1 Examples of sophisticated multiple-choice items. From *Multiple-Choice Questions: A Close Look*. Copyright © 1963 by Educational Testing Service. All rights reserved. Reprinted by permission.

Courtesy of the Metropolitan Museum of Art, Gift of John D. Rockefeller, Jr., 1932.

In which of the following centuries was the piece of sculpture shown above most probably produced?

(A) The fifth century B.C.
(B) The fourteenth century A.D.
(C) The sixteenth century A.D.
(D) The eighteenth century A.D.
(E) The twentieth century A.D.

Figure 10.1 (continued)

Question 17

One method of obtaining "artificial gravity" in a space station is to have the station rotating about axis AA' as it revolves around Earth.

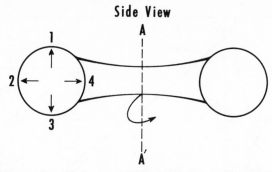

Side View

The inhabitants of the space station would call which direction "down"?
(A) Direction 1
(B) Direction 2
(C) Direction 3
(D) Direction 4
(E) Any one of the four, depending on speed of rotation

Question 22

The question below is followed by two statements, labeled (1) and (2), in which certain data are given. In this question you do not actually have to compute an answer, but rather you have to decide whether the data given in the statements are sufficient for answering the question. Using the data given in the statements plus your knowledge of mathematics and everyday facts (such as the number of days in July), you are to select answer

(A) if statement (1) ALONE is sufficient but statement (2) alone is not sufficient to answer the question asked,
(B) if statement (2) ALONE is sufficient but statement (1) alone is not sufficient to answer the question asked,
(C) if both statements (1) and (2) TOGETHER are sufficient to answer the question asked, but NEITHER statement ALONE is sufficient,
(D) if EACH statement is sufficient by itself to answer the question asked,
(E) if statements (1) and (2) TOGETHER are NOT sufficient to answer the question asked and additional data specific to the problem are needed.

If x is a whole number, is it a two-digit number?
  (1) x^2 is a three-digit number.
  (2) 10x is a three-digit number.

Figure 10.1 (continued)

Question 2

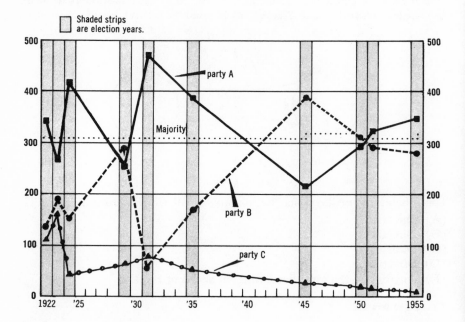

The graph above represents the political composition from 1922 to 1955 of which of the following?

(A) German Bundestag
(B) French National Assembly
(C) Italian Chamber of Deputies
(D) British House of Commons

TECHNICAL ADEQUACY. Because students' response to the completed test may differ from their response to the pretests, analyses of completed forms of the test are vital to insure that students can finish within the time limits and that a reasonable distribution of scores is obtained. The consistency of the test scores must be determined, particularly the equivalent forms reliability. The validity of the test—always content validity but often also criterion-related—must be established. Varied normative data must be collected. Although the process of test development is designed to insure that the completed test will be adequate in these respects, empirical tests are needed to confirm the effectiveness of the test construction process (see below).

INTERPRETIVE DATA. The final step in test development is the provision of useful interpretive data and aids. One essential aid is a technical manual containing information on the definition of the content-skills domain, the basis of item selection, item statistics, normative data, validity and reliability data, and any other information necessary for determining the meaning of the test scores. Adequate nomative data is especially cruicial. A wide variety of norm tables should be presented, using methods that are precise yet readily understandable by test users: teachers, administrators, parents. To help accomplish this end the test publisher will usually provide, in addition to the technical manual, a variety of interpretive aids, e.g., explanatory pamphlets, student report forms, and profiles. Though these tasks may appear rather pedestrian in comparison to the sophisticated statistical analyses of the psychometrician, the quality and understandability of the interpretive aids probably have as much, if not more, influence on the adequacy of test usage than any other element.

Technical characteristics

Before illustrating the major types of standardized achievement tests, we will review the basic technical considerations in evaluating tests—consistency, validity, and norms—as they apply to standardized achievement tests. Our purpose in this section will be only to set certain general guidelines, to provide a framework for evaluation. In evaluating a particular test used for a specific purpose, certain unique considerations and bases for evaluation will, of course, need to be taken into account. (For other discussions see, e.g., Educational Testing Service, 1961; Ebel, 1956; Englehart, 1964.)

CONSISTENCY. In our previous discussions (Chapters 3 and 4) we mentioned five methods of estimating consistency. Three of these indices—stability, stability and equivalence, and homogeneity—have only limited usefulness with standardized achievement tests. It might seem that if we were interested in retention of knowledge over relatively long time periods, as we will be in many educational situations, a test exhibiting a high degree of stability would be desirable. However, as differential learning and forgetting will occur in the interval between testings, a test that was sensitive to minor changes in knowledge would be unstable (i.e., the coefficient of stability would be low); but this instability would be true variability, not error variance. The value of stability estimates are thus limited. Measures of stability and equivalence will, consequently, also be of limited value.

The typical achievement test is designed to measure a variety of abilities and skills, not just one. Although these characteristics may be positively correlated and, indeed, the test construction process has insured that the test items (or subsamples of items) will be intercorrelated positively, the level of relationship is not such that the test can be considered homogeneous in the strict sense of the term. For both the rational and empirical reasons, measures of homogeneity will not be applicable.[7] An obvious exception is subtests of diagnostic batteries, where the goal is to identify the basic components of a skill or ability; here homogeneity may be a relevant consideration.

Elimination of stability and homogeneity measures restricts the class of preferred procedures to two: measures of equivalence and split-half measures. The former method, being based on two distinct samples of performance, is obviously a broader yet more stringent measure and is thus to be preferred. And, as many achievement batteries have at least two published forms, evidence of equivalent forms reliability is generally obtainable.

Although the factors influencing the magnitude of a reliability coefficient will not be reviewed in detail here (see Chapter 3), two factors deserve special mention. The magnitude of a reliablity coefficient, it will be recalled, depends upon the composition of the group taking the test and, in particular, the breadth of the distribution of scores; the more heterogeneous the distribution of scores, the higher the potential r_{tt}. As a standardized achievement test is generally applicable at several grade levels, and as inclusion of several grade levels in the sample used to determine reliability will undoubtedly increase the heterogeneity of the scores and consequently increase the potential magnitude of r_{tt}, reliability estimates based on such samples will be inflated. A more stringent, accurate, and useful estimate is the reliability within a given grade level. Second, if the test is speeded and/or a relatively large proportion of the students do not finish within the time limits, the reliability estimate (particularly when computed by the split-halves method) will be spuriously inflated.

VALIDITY.   Because the behavior of inherent interest is identical with the behavior manifested on the test items, and since the test items sample the behavioral domain, the appropriate validity index is a measure of the adequacy of sampling—to wit, content validity. When attempting to establish the content validity of any achievement test, two considerations are particularly relevant. (1) To determine content validity requires that the content domain be clearly specified. Although in the process of test construction, the test developers specify the content domain clearly and in detail, this definition is not always transmitted, through the test manual or other devices, to the test user. However, if the test user (or a test reviewer or any other interested party) is to evaluate the content validity of a test, this specification must be made public. (2) Any individual user will, of course, define the content universe differently than did the test developers. Therefore, the test will be more or less appropriate for his particular purposes, depending on the congruence of the two definitions of the content domains. The test user will have to make a judgment of this congruence, of the appropriateness of the test for his purposes. This judgment will be a situation-specific estimate of the content validity of the test.

---

[7]Empirical evidence indicates that items on classroom examinations generally intercorrelate positively. However, as there is no presumption that such tests are homogeneous, in the sense discussed previously, indices of homogeneity would appear logically inappropriate.

When standardized achievement tests are used for purposes other than determining the status of an individual's knowledge in a given area, their validity may be determined by methods other then content validity. For example, when a standardized achievement test is used for placement, the proportion of correct placements or the increase in average criterion performance might be used as a validity index; when used as a diagnostic tool, a possible index would be the correlation with diagnoses made using other methods.

There is an aspect of construct validity which appears to be germane; that is, discriminant validity. If an achievement test is to be considered an accurate measure of achievement, it should measure only achievement and not related variables. Close inspection of standardized achievement tests would show that many are saturated with other factors, usually reading comprehension or general intelligence, and thus fail the test of discriminant validity.

NORMS.   Scores on standardized achievement tests may be interpreted by either norm-referenced or criterion-referenced standards (Glaser, 1963). When measurement is *norm-referenced*, an individual's performance is interpreted by comparing his performance to that of other persons who are, in some relevant way, similar to him. This is the traditional approach, where scores are reported as a standing within a group. Because groups possessing various characteristics will exhibit different score distributions, various norm groups are needed. When testing achievement, these groups will usually represent various grade levels, geographic areas, types and sizes of schools, or other similar dimensions.

Norm-referenced scores, however, provide no direct indication of the individual's degree of proficiency in the subject matter. Therefore, it may be desirable to provide *criterion-referenced* norms, allowing scores to be interpreted as the amount of proficiency or skill the individual exhibits in the content area (cf. Ebel, 1962). In other words, the score would describe what the student could do, i.e., his degree of proficiency at a given point in time, not how he compares to other students. Although criterion-referenced scores have not been widely used, there is increasing demand (Glaser, 1963; Gagné, 1967; Ebel, 1962) for such scores.

Survey tests

The most frequently used standardized achievement tests are survey tests which, you will recall, emphasize broad sampling of the content domain. And, as the purpose of a survey test is to provide an indication of the student's overall command of a given content area, a single summary score is usually the only score reported. Although a survey test may stand by itself, often it is part of a battery of achievement tests.

In selecting or evaluating a survey test, several considerations are preeminent. First, the test items should be a representative sample of a defined content universe; that is, the test should have content validity. A prior requisite, of course, is that the content universe be clearly and unambiguously specified. On survey tests the content universe, of necessity, will be quite broad, but this requirement does not preclude a clear specification of the domain.

In defining the content domain, test constructors have taken one of two approaches: they have emphasized either (1) factual content and knowledge of subject matter or (2) general skills that are assumed to be transferable to several subject matter areas. The two approaches are not mutually exclusive; rather, they represent different emphases. In certain areas, for example mathematics, it would be difficult to separate the two approaches since content and skills are confounded in any problem. On the other hand, a chemistry exam that stressed factual knowledge and one that emphasized the processes used in attacking chemical problems would be very different examinations.

Some survey batteries have taken the former approach, providing tests covering the more traditional subject matter areas. Others, like the Iowa Tests of Basic Skills, have attempted to assess broad fundamental skills, (e.g., vocabulary, reading, language, work-study skills, and arithmetic). A clear example of the skills approach is the Work-Study Skills portion of the Iowa Tests of Basic Skills, which contains problems involving the skills of map reading, reading graphs and tables, and the use of reference materials; skills which can be applied in a variety of subject matter areas.

If a test battery, rather than a single test, is the focus of concern, two additional po nts become important: (1) how adequately the battery, as a whole, samples the pertinent content areas, and (2) the interrelationships between tests within the battery. In the former case the question is whether the battery covers the important aspects of the curriculum. To use a facetious example, an achievement battery for elementary school children which did not cover basic arithmetic operations would obviously be incomplete. In the latter case, the concern is that the tests within the battery are not highly intercorrelated and, thus, in fact, are measuring the same thing.[8]

A second requirement is that the test measure achievement, not some other ability. This requirement may be harder to attain than might be expected. The broad skills that determine performance on survey tests also permeate other tests and to the extent that they, rather than content factors, determine the score obtained, an achievement test will be indistinguishable from an aptitude test.

---

[8]The question of the expected and acceptable range of intercorrelations is complex. The empirical evidence is that scores on tests within a battery will be positively intercorrelated(with higher intercorrelations found with younger children). Because the tests are all paper-and-pencil tests, measure skills learned in school, and have a high verbal content, it would be unrealistic to expect correlations to approach zero. But any substantial positive correlations should be carefully scrutinized.

However, specific irrelevant factors that influence scores—for example, reading comprehension or test-taking skills—can and should be minimized. Also, unless there is some overwhelming argument to do otherwise, a survey test should be a power test, because the primary objective is to measure the students' proficiency and the complexity and difficulty of the problems they can solve, not the speed with which they can recall the response.

Another desirable characteristic of survey tests is that they measure not only the student's current status but also provide a basis for measuring growth. Because tests are designed primarily to assess current status rather than for measuring growth, this requirement is generally met by providing an integrated series of test batteries, each battery covering several grade levels. Although a battery may not include the same tests at each grade level, since different skills and topics are emphasized at each grade level, there will be some overlap from one level to another, providing some basis for measuring growth.

The Sequential Tests of Educational Progress (STEP) illustrate how an integrated test battery can operate. The STEP battery is published at four levels (for grades 4–6, 7–9, 10–12, and 13–14), and at each level the same six tests are represented: Reading Comprehension, Writing, Mathematics, Science, Social Studies, and Listening Comprehension. The tests are quite reliable and are available in equivalent forms. All of these factors combine to permit meaningful statements about growth to be made. For example, a comparison might be made between a student's Reading Comprehension score obtained in fifth grade and his Reading Comprehension score as a high school junior. In addition, STEP has a special score scale that permits direct comparisons to be made between two scores on the same test; that is, the two reading comprehension scores can be expressed on the identical scale.

IMPLICATION FOR TEST CONSTRUCTION. The considerations discussed in the preceding paragraphs, when coupled with the requirements of an adequate test discussed in previous chapters, lead to several implications for constructing survey achievement tests: (1) More than one form of the test should be available. If repeated measurements are to be used—for example, to measure growth over a period of time—equivalent forms are needed to prevent any effects due to retesting with the same items. (2) Each level of the test should cover only a few grades, probably no more than three. Because the basic skills emphasized and the materials taught vary widely between grades, and students' skills change rapidly, especially at younger ages, attempts to make one level of a test serve a wide age (grade) range usually result in the test difficulty being inappropriate at one or both ends of the range. (3) As the topics covered in any grade will change over time, and the pool of knowledge is constantly increasing, a test must be periodically revised if it is not to become dated. (4) Scores should be expressed in meaningful units. In schools following traditional grade level organizational practices, this score preferably should be percentiles within grades. For non-graded schools and other special circumstances, none of the common scores seem particularly appropriate. Here again, content scores would seem desirable. (5) Normative data from a wide variety of groups, having distinctive characteristics, should be available.

In general, standardized achievement tests meet these requirements quite well. There are a number of tests and test batteries published that cover a variety of content and skills, that have been published in equivalent forms and at different age levels, that are periodically revised, that are reliable and provide a variety of normative data. The main issue with such tests is not their technical adequacy but rather with the importance of the material tested, i.e., do standardized achievement tests measure the most important skills or do they just measure a smattering of mundane and lower-level skills?

EXAMPLES.   Some examples of survey tests and batteries are given in the following list. This listing is not intended to be exhaustive nor to constitute a recommendation for these particular tests; rather it is to illustrate the variety of survey tests available. We will make no attempt to evaluate individual tests here, since a thorough evaluation would be too space consuming (besides being rather artificial) and would represent the author's evaluation of the test for a hypothetical use and population. It is suggested, rather, that the reader obtain a copy of one or more standardized achievement tests and their manuals, and make his own evaluation for a situation where he might conceivably use the test. After you make your evaluation, compare it to one in another source—say, the *Mental Measurements Yearbook*. Such a process will be of greater value than any artificial evaluation that could be made here.

California Achievement Tests (California Test Bureau, 1957 with 1963 norms).
Grade 1—college sophomore; five levels; 1½–3 hours; equivalent forms.
Major areas covered: Reading (vocabulary, comprehension), Arithmetic (reasoning, fundamentals), Language (mechanics, spelling).
Purpose: to measure educational attainment and diagnose difficulties in basic skill areas.

Comprehensive Tests of Basic Skills (California Test Bureau, 1968).
Grades 2.5–12, four overlapping levels; 3+ hours; equivalent forms.
Areas: Reading (vocabulary, comprehension), Language (mechanics, expression, spelling), Arithmetic (computation, concepts, applications), Study Skills.
Emphasis on basic skills, concepts, relationships, and abstractions.

Iowa Tests of Educational Development (Science Research Associates, Inc., 1962).
Grades 9–12; Two full school days.

Areas: Understanding of Basic Social Concepts, Background in the Natural Sciences, Correctness and Appropriateness of Expression, Ability to do Quantitative Thinking, Ability to Interpret Reading Materials in Social Studies, Ability to Interpret Reading Materials in Natural Sciences, Ability to Interpret Literary Materials, General Vocabulary, Uses of Sources of Information.

Measures "broad and generalized intellectual skills and abilities"; what student can do, not what he knows; content not restricted to high school curriculum.

Iowa Tests of Basic Skills (Houghton-Mifflin Company, 1964).
Grades 3–9; equivalent forms; 6+ hours.
Areas: Vocabulary, Reading Comprehension, Language (spelling, mechanics, usage), Work Study Skills, Arithmetic Skills (concepts, problem solving).
Generalized skills approach (similar to ITED).

Metropolitan Achievement Tests (Harcourt, Brace & World, Inc., 1958–62).
Grades 1–12; six levels, equivalent forms; 2–5+ hours.
Areas: Vary with level; Intermediate (5–6) and Advanced (7–9) Levels, for example, cover Word Knowledge, Reading, Spelling, Language, Language Study Skills, Arithmetic Computation, Arithmetic Problem Solving and Concepts, Social Studies Information, Social Studies Skills, Science.
Note there are separate tests of concepts and information.

SRA Achievement Series (Science Research Associates, Inc., restandardized, 1963–67).

Grades 1–9; four levels, equivalent forms.
Areas: Reading (vocabulary, comprehension) and Arithmetic (reasoning, concepts, computation) included at all levels; Language Arts (mechanics, usage, spelling) grades 2–9; Social Studies, Science and Work Study Skills (optional) on grade 4–9 multilevel form.
Has optional test of Modern Math Understanding.

Sequential Tests of Educational Progress (Cooperative Test Bureau, ETS, 1956–57).
Grade 4–college sophomore; four levels; parallel forms; 70 minutes per test.
Areas: Reading, Writing, Listening, Mathematics, Science, Social Studies.
Listening test requires students to answer questions based on orally presented materials.

Stanford Achievement Tests (Harcourt, Brace & World, Inc., 1964)
Grades 1.5–12; six overlapping levels; equivalent forms; up to 5+ hours.

Areas vary with level: Reading, Language Arts, and Arithmetic (or Mathematics) included at all levels; Science and Social Studies in grades 4–12. On most levels major areas are broken down into specific tests—e.g., on Primary level II (grades 2.5–3.9) there are separate tests of Word Reading and Paragraph Meaning and of Arithmetic Computation and Arithmetic Concepts.

High school battery (9–12) has supplemental tests in Arts and Humanities, Business and Economics and Technical Comprehension.

Cooperative Achievement Tests (Cooperative Test Bureau, ETS).

Grades 7 up; not an integrated battery.

Areas: Tests are available in English, Mathematics (nine tests—e.g., Geometry, three levels of Algebra, Calculus), Science (five areas), Tests of the Physical Science Study Committee, Social Studies (seven tests—e.g., American History, World History, American Government), Topical Tests in American History (eight tests on specific topical areas), Foreign Language Tests (five languages).

College Entrance Examination Board Achievement Tests (CEEB)

A series of one-hour achievement tests taken only in conjunction with the Scholastic Aptitude Tests (see Chapter 11). Tests are available in approximately 15 areas—e.g., English Composition, Literature, French, American History and Social Studies, Biology, Physics.

Advanced Placement Examinations (CEEB)

Tests designed to allow colleges to grant advanced placement and/or credit for work covered prior to college entrance. Tests are three hours long, and include both essay and objective sections. Currently there are tests in 11 areas: American History, Biology, Chemistry, English, European History, French, German, Latin, Math (Calculus), Physics and Spanish. Modern languages include listening comprehension tests.

College Level Examination Program (CEEB)

A series of objective (1½ hour) tests to establish credit for nonregular academic experiences (e.g., independent study) or to establish competency (e.g., in the transition between colleges). There are general examinations in five areas (English Composition, Humanities, Natural Sciences, Social Sciences, Mathematics); subject examinations are available in approximately 20 areas (e.g., American Government, Statistics, General Chemistry, Analysis and Interpretation of Literature) with tests in other areas being developed.

Some further examples of items from standardized achievement tests are shown in Figure 10.2. Although a representative sample of items obviously cannot be presented in so limited a space, the examples should give the reader a feeling for the types of items found in achievement tests. Here again there is no substitute for detailed studying of the actual test materials.

Figure 10.2 Examples of items from standardized achievement tests.

A. Items from a grade school level battery (Stanford Achievement Test, Intermediate I, grades 4-5)

Test 2. Paragraph Meaning

Paragraph Meaning

DIRECTIONS: Read each paragraph below. Decide which of the numbered words or phrases below the paragraph is *best* for each blank. Look at the answer spaces at the right or on your answer sheet (if you have one). Fill in the space which has the same number as the word(s) you have chosen.

SAMPLES

The singing birds entertain us. We like to __A__ their __B__ .

A 1 touch   3 hear   1 2 3 4
   2 see   4 feel   A ○ ○ ● ○

B 5 songs   7 flight   5 6 7 8
   6 colors   8 tricks   B ○ ○ ○ ○

Jumbo had been a circus elephant all his life. He had started working for the circus when he was very ____.

  1 young   3 happy   1 2 3 4
  2 large   4 old

Test 5. Language

Language   *Usage*

DIRECTIONS: Read each sentence below. Decide which, *if either*, of the two choices in each sentence is correct in *standard written English*. Look at the answer spaces at the right or on your answer sheet (if you have one). If the choice numbered 1 is correct, fill in the space under the 1. If the choice numbered 2 is correct, fill in the space under the 2. If neither choice 1 nor choice 2 is correct, fill in the space under the N. ("N" stands for "neither.")

SAMPLES

                                                   1 2 N

A Joe 1 set in the chair............. A ○ ● ○
     2 sat

                                                   1 2 N

B Sally 1 ain't here. .... B ○ ○ ○
      2 aren't

Figure 10.2 (continued)

Part D. Dictionary Skills

Language   *Dictionary Skills*

DIRECTIONS: This is a test of your ability to use a dictionary. In this test two words (in boxes) are shown as they might appear in a dictionary, with four dictionary definitions given for each word. Below the box for each word are five questions. In the first two questions, the given word is used in a sentence. Read each sentence, then decide which dictionary definition *best* defines the word as it is being used in the sentence. Look at the answer spaces at the right or on your answer sheet (if you have one). Fill in the space which has the same *number* as the definition you have chosen. Three other questions are asked about each word. For each of these, decide which answer is *best* and mark the space which has the same *letter* as the answer you have chosen.

SAMPLES

> **check** (chek)   1. *n.* A pattern in squares of different colors.   2. *v.* To prove true or right.   3. *n.* A mark showing that something has been examined or compared.   4. *v.* To hold back or control.

G Miss Jones made a **check** beside each example.

G 1 ○ 2 ○ 3 ● 4 ○

H The word **check** in the sentence above is —

    a a noun   b a verb   c an adjective   d an adverb

H a ○ b ○ c ○ d ○

Test 7. Arithmetic Concepts

Arithmetic Concepts

DIRECTIONS: Read each question. Decide which of the answers given below is correct. Look at the answer spaces at the right or on your answer sheet (if you have one). Fill in the space which has the same letter as the answer you have chosen.

SAMPLE

A A dime is worth how many cents?

    a **2**   c **10**

    b **5**   d **25**

A a ○ b ○ c ● d ○

Figure 10.2 (continued)

Test 9. Part B. Study Skills

Social Studies   *Study Skills*

DIRECTIONS: Look at each graph or map and read the questions that go with it. Find the *best* answer to each question. Then look at the answer spaces at the right or on your answer sheet (if you have one). Fill in the space which has the same number as the answer you have chosen.

Use the graph below in answering questions 25–29

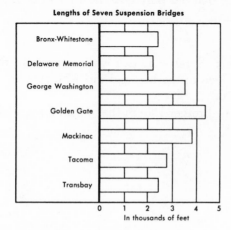

Lengths of Seven Suspension Bridges

Which of the following bridges is the longest?

    1 George Washington   3 Tacoma   1 2 3 4
    2 Mackinac   4 Transbay

If you drove at the same speed over each of these bridges, which bridge could you cross the quickest?

    5 Golden Gate
    6 Transbay
    7 Delaware Memorial   5 6 7 8
    8 Bronx-Whitestone

The length of the George Washington Bridge is closest to that of what other bridge?

    1 Golden Gate Bridge
    2 Delaware Memorial Bridge
    3 Tacoma Bridge   1 2 3 4
    4 Mackinac Bridge

How many bridges are over 2000 feet in length?

    5 four   7 seven   5 6 7 8
    6 three   8 six

What is the length in feet of the Mackinac Bridge?

    1 3000   3 3800   1 2 3 4
    2 4000   4 380

Figure 10.2 (continued)

B. *Items from a junior high school level battery (Iowa Tests of Basic Skills, grade 7)*

Usage   *Indicate the line that contains a mistake in the use of words.*

44. 1) Miss Penny scolded Bob because he had not did his homework.
    2) The old rowboat gave us nothing but trouble from the start.
    3) If you go near that old billy goat, he'll try to butt you
       with his horns.
    4) (No mistakes)

45. 1) Hurry up, Jack. Surely you can work faster than that.
    2) Prizes were given to the boy and girl who caught
       the biggest fish.
    3) Harry, let your brother ride in the wagon for a while.
    4) (No mistakes)

Arithmetic Concepts

87. Which set of three numerals can be arranged to
    represent the largest number?
    1) 1, 0, 9   3) 3, 8, 8
    2) 2, 5, 8   4) 4, 2, 6

88. Which of these addition exercises can be explained
    by the picture below?
    1) $\frac{1}{4} + \frac{1}{2} = \frac{3}{4}$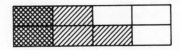
    2) $\frac{1}{4} + \frac{3}{8} = \frac{5}{8}$
    3) $\frac{3}{4} + \frac{1}{2} = \frac{5}{4}$
    4) $\frac{1}{2} + \frac{1}{8} = \frac{5}{8}$

Test items on pages 298 and 299, copyright © 1964 by the State University of
Iowa. Reproduced by permission of Houghton Mifflin Company, publishers.

Figure 10.2 (continued)

Reading Graphs and Tables

The pupils in Grade 7 at Lee School started a program to improve their reading speed. Tests were given three times each year for two years. The graph below shows the results for five of the pupils and for the class as a whole.

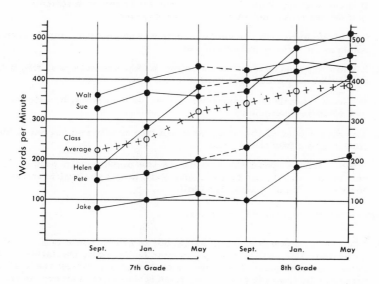

41. **Who was the fastest reader at the end of the eighth grade?**
    1) Walt   3) Helen
    2) Sue   4) Pete

42. **Who made the greatest improvement during the seventh grade?**
    1) Helen   3) Walt
    2) Jake   4) Sue

43. **Which pupil gained approximately 110 words per minute while in the eighth grade?**
    1) Walt   3) Pete
    2) Helen   4) Jake

Figure 10.2 (continued)

C. Items from a test designed for high school seniors

English Composition Test

No sentence has more than one kind of error. Some sentences have no errors. Read each sentence carefully; then on your answer sheet blacken space

A If the sentence contains *faulty diction;*
B if the sentence is *wordy;*
C if the sentence contains *clichés* or *inappropriate metaphors;*
D if the sentence contains *faulty grammar* or *sentence structure;*
E if the sentence contains *none* of these errors.

7. One of the sources of the king's income was an entire monopoly of the whole manufacture and sale of salt.

8. His mother mentioned that he will go to kindergarten next fall, but she will be very much surprised if he liked it.

9. While the chemist was experimenting in his laboratory, he detected a new cleansing compound.

10. The razor's edge of the wind cut at his face cruelly and tugged at his clothes like a frightened child.

11. White pelicans spend the summer in the northwestern part of the continent and migrate in a diagonal path across the prairie states to their winter habitat along the Gulf.

European History and World Cultures Test

16. "To princes power is given on earth, but to priests power is given also in heaven. The former have power over bodies only, the latter have power also over souls. Therefore, to that degree by which the soul is more worthy than the body, by so much is the priesthood more worthy than the kingdom. Single rulers have single provinces, and single kings have single kingdoms; but Peter rules them all."

Which of the following subscribed to the point of view above?

(A) Henry II of England
(B) Innocent III
(C) The Apostle Peter
(D) Leo I
(E) Louis XIV of France

17. "All life is pain, pain caused by selfish desire, pain which can be relieved only by renouncing our desires and achieving complete forgetfulness of ourselves. This common fate of mankind makes brothers of men."

The quotation above expresses the basic idea of

(A) Buddhism
(B) Confucianism
(C) Islam
(D) Shintoism
(E) Taoism

Figure 10.2 (continued)

Questions based on graphs, charts, or cartoons require you to use your historical knowledge in interpreting data. Question 18 is based on the following table.

ANNUAL PRODUCTION OF STEEL
(In Thousands of Metric Tons)

Year				
1865	225	13	97	41
1870	286	68	169	83
1875	723	396	370	258
1880	1,320	1,267	660	388
1885	2,020	1,739	1,202	533
1890	3,637	4,346	2,161	566
1895	3,444	6,212	3,941	899
1900	5,130	10,382	6,645	1,565
1905	5,983	20,354	10,066	2,110
1910	6,374	26,512	13,698	3,506

18. Reading from left to right, the column headings should be

 (A) Great Britain, United States, Germany, and France
 (B) Italy, Great Britain, Russia, and Germany
 (C) Germany, Great Britain, Russia, and France
 (D) Great Britain, United States, France, and Germany
 (E) Germany, Russia, Great Britain, and United States

Math Test, Level 1

1. **Which of the following is an expression for $\sqrt{-49} - \sqrt{-25}$ in the form a + bi, where a and b are real?**
 (A) $0 + (\sqrt{24})i$ (B) $0 + (\sqrt{74})i$ (C) $0 + 24i$ (D) $0 + 2i$
 (E) $2 + 0i$

2. **If x + 2 = y, what is the value of $|x - y| + |y - x|$?**
 (A) −4 (B) 0 (C) 2 (D) 4
 (E) It cannot be determined from the information given.

3. **Two rectangular solids have the dimensions 4, 6, h, and 8, 2, (2h − 1), respectively. Their volumes are equal when h =**
 (A) $\dfrac{1}{8}$ (B) $\dfrac{4}{5}$ (C) 1 (D) 2 (E) 4

4. **If f(x) = 5x + 6, then f(x) < 16 if and only if**
 (A) x < 2 (B) x > 2 (C) x = 2 (D) −2 < x < 2
 (E) x is any real number

5. **If x is the measure of an acute angle such that $\tan x = \dfrac{k}{3}$, then $\sin x =$**
 (A) $\dfrac{k}{3 + k}$ (B) $\dfrac{3}{\sqrt{9 - k^2}}$ (C) $\dfrac{k}{\sqrt{9 - k^2}}$ (D) $\dfrac{3}{\sqrt{9 + k^2}}$

 (E) $\dfrac{k}{\sqrt{9 + k^2}}$

Figure 10.2 (continued)

6. The circle in Figure 1 has center at O. If PQ and QR are secants and if x = 40, what is y?

   (A) 10
   (B) 20
   (C) 30
   (D) 40
   (E) It cannot be determined from the information given.

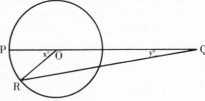

Physics Test

Ability to interpret experimental data

17. A tuning fork vibrating at 500 vibrations per second in a certain gas produces waves in the gas whose successive rarefactions are 3.00 feet apart. The speed of sound in the gas could be calculated

    (A) only if the density of the gas were also known
    (B) only if the temperature of the gas were also known
    (C) only if both the density and the temperature of the gas were also known
    (D) only if the amplitude of the oscillation were also known
    (E) with no further information

Questions 18-21:

Figure 2

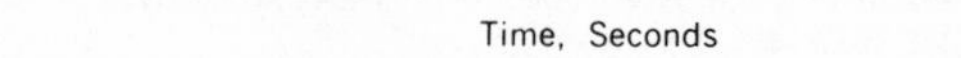

Velocity, Meters per Second

Time, Seconds

The graph in Figure 2 shows the velocity of a car as a function of time while the car moves along a straight track.

18. During the 7th second, the car is moving with constant

    (A) speed
    (B) velocity
    (C) acceleration
    (D) momentum
    (E) kinetic energy

19. During the first 3 seconds, the car has an average acceleration of about

    (A) $-\dfrac{8}{3}$ m/sec^2 (D) $\dfrac{4}{3}$ m/sec^2

    (B) $-\dfrac{4}{3}$ m/sec^2 (E) $\dfrac{8}{3}$ m/sec^2

    (C) 0 m/sec^2

Other types of standardized achievement tests

Survey batteries are the most widely used standardized achievement tests; however, a variety of other types are also available. Some of these, such as readiness measures and advanced placement examinations, are used solely in educational settings. Others, such as diagnostic and proficiency tests, may find uses both within and without the educational system.

DIAGNOSTIC TESTS. In the teaching of any subject or skill, one encounters students who have difficulty learning. Some students have trouble with many or all aspects of the material while others seemingly falter over only one or two aspects of the material. However, if the learning is of a basic academic skill, particularly reading or mathematics, the difficulties may affect learning in all academic areas. The particular stumbling blocks may be apparent or hidden; diagnostic tests have been developed for the latter case to pinpoint the (hidden) causes of the student's difficulty.

A diagnostic test, therefore, must cover the component abilities necessary for successful performance of the activity. Before tests can be built to measure these component abilities the abilities must, of course, be identified. The identification of these components will be both an empirical or a logical undertaking. In either case, several implications pertain: (1) The skill must be such that dividing the gross performance into components does not destroy the nature of the total act; if it does, any partitioning of the skill will be arbitrary and the test results will be of limited usefulness. (2) The test will necessarily be composed of several subtests or scales, each measuring a single component. The common procedure is to utilize subtests, each designed to measure a single component. However, it might be argued that the scale approach (or some other more holistic approach) would retain the integrity of the performance better than would the subtest approach and thus should be used whenever feasible. (3) The various subtests should be homogeneous or should measure combinations of skills that are, in some respects, inseparable. (4) The test battery should be inclusive; if certain fundamental skills are not measured by a subtest then it will be impossible to ascertain the exact cause of the individual's difficulty. (5) Finally, the subtest scores should have implications for remedial work; that is, the appropriate form of remedial treatment should follow directly from the pattern of scores.

Diagnostic tests are most common in reading and arithmetic, primarily because both are fundamental educational skills that can be broken down into component skills. For example, one reading test (the Diagnostic Reading Scales) has four major scores—word recognition, oral reading, silent reading, and auditory comprehension—plus supplementary measures of rate of silent reading and phonics. Another (the Diagnostic Reading Tests, grades 4–8) measures word recognition, comprehension, vocabulary, rate of reading, story comprehension, and both oral and silent word attack skills. Although these two tests may not measure the basic components of reading, in the ideal sense discussed above, use of subtests provides a more thorough understanding of a student's reading skills than do survey measures of reading speed and comprehension.

READINESS MEASURES. Readiness tests, like diagnostic tests, are generally concerned with fundamental skills, particularly reading. The basic question to be answered by readiness tests is: "Does the student possess the necessary skills to succeed in a particular educational task?" In other words, is he ready to start to study a particular skill. A readiness test is really a predictive or prognostic device. Hence its validity is determined by its effectiveness in separating students who are, from those who are not, ready for instruction in the relevant area.

The first step in test construction task, thus, is to identify the various skills that are predictive of success. In some instances, they may be general intellectual or physical abilities; for example, before a child can learn to read, his visual discrimination must be developed to a level where he can distinguish among printed letters. In other instances, the indication may be possession of an appropriate fund of knowledge. For example, knowledge of addition is fundamental to learning multiplication; one must understand algebraic equations before he can learn to balance chemical equations. One can also conceive of attitudes and predispositions toward learning and attacking problems as being essential aspects of readiness.

Readiness tests, however, are usually encountered at the preschool and kindergarten age levels, where the interest is in determining readiness to begin formal educational programs, particularly instruction in reading. Because readiness tests are designed for use with children who have not yet learned to read, they will, necessarily, involve other than verbal material. Thus reading readiness tests usually consist of pictorial and symbolic materials administered with oral directions; the directions instruct the child to mark or otherwise indicate one of the objects pictured. Some items from a typical reading readiness test are shown in Figure 10.3.

One word of caution should be interjected regarding the use of readiness measures. Because these tests are typically administered to children whose test-taking skills are undeveloped, whose attention span is short, and whose emotional behavior is often erratic, the test results may well present a misleading picture of the child. Thus decisions about the child's readiness should never be based solely on tests; rather, the test results should be supplemented with other information, e.g., observations by teachers and parents.

PROFICIENCY TESTS. Although achievement tests are generally associated with educational programs, they are also used in business, industrial, military, and professional settings. An obvious example is tests given in training programs. These tests generally are comparable to classroom examinations but, in situations where the training program is repeated continuously and involves large numbers of persons, as in military training situations, the tests used may well

A. Student marks the object mentioned in a statement (story) read by the teacher (e. g, "Mary took her dog for a walk") Designed to measure simple sentence recall and listening discrimination.

B. Student marks picture of word that starts with same sound as stimulus picture (i.e., fish and finger start with same sound). Measures discrimination of sounds.

Figure 10.3 Examples of items from a readiness test. From the communication skills section of "Instructional and Assessment Materials for First Graders" (prepared for Board of Education of the City of New York by the Educational Testing Service). Reprinted by permission of the Board of Education, City of New York.

be standardized. Achievement tests are also used for selection and placement in business and industry, as, for example, when a typing test is used as a screening device in hiring office workers. Achievement tests are also used as a basis for promotion in many civil service and military positions.

An interesting use of achievement tests is for licensing or certification in certain professions, e.g., medicine, law, accounting, and engineering. Generally the examination is only one hurdle in the licensing procedure, which also includes education and experience requirements. The basic assumption when using achievement tests for certification is, of course, that there are certain skills or knowledge that an individual must possess if he is to successfully engage in a given occupation or practice a particular profession. The achievement test serves as a mechanism for determining whether the individual possesses these competencies. Depending on the particular circumstances (e.g., what occupation, whether the governing board is local or national, the availability of other measures) the examination may be informal and *ad hoc*, like the classroom examination, or a thoroughly standardized test, or, most commonly, something in between.

ADVANCED PLACEMENT EXAMINATIONS. The educational analog of the vocational proficiency test is, in many ways, the advanced placement examination. These examinations are designed to establish the student's competency (proficiency) in a given content domain, allowing him to be placed at an advanced level of a course, rather than repeating material that he has already mastered. These examinations are typically administered at the college level and cover materials presented in universally taught courses. In essence, they are a standardized course examination.

The best known advanced placement examinations are those administered by the Committee on Advanced Placement of the College Entrance Examination Board. A related program is the College Level Examination Program, also sponsored by the College Board (see list, pp. 294-295).

Both the Advanced Placement and College Level Examination Programs have been developed in recognition of the diversity in both institutions of higher education and the background and preparation of college students. By providing means for a student to exhibit competence in a subject matter area or field, other than by the traditional means of taking courses, they provide for flexibility in educational planning, allowing the student to progress at a rate that parallels his abilities. They also provide a vehicle for granting credit for experiences obtained outside the classroom. By combining the test development skills of a test publisher with local standards for interpreting scores, the advantages of standardization and adaption to local requirements are both present in one instrument.

MEASURES OF EDUCATIONAL OUTPUT. One final utilization of standardized achievement measures should be mentioned—to assess the achievement level of broad samples of students, as a measure of educational outputs (Astin & Panos,

1969). One example of this approach is the international study of achievement in mathematics (Husén, 1967). In this study, a standardized paper-and-pencil mathematics achievement examination was administered to students in 12 countries to assess their proficiency in mathematics. A variety of other data (on the characteristics of the schools, students, and teaching methods) were also collected in an attempt to identify the factors that determined the level of mathematic achievement in the various countries.

Another illustration is the proposed National Assessment of Educational Progress (Tyler, Merwin & Ebel, 1966). This program will involve the administration of achievement tests to a representative sample of American children and adults. Because the assessment is concerned with the performance of groups rather than individuals, each individual will take only parts of the test battery. Although analysis will be made of certain variables (e.g., geographic region, size of school) to determine the environmental factors that most effect achievement, the major purpose of the assessment is to ascertain the level of achievement in various areas by American students of various age levels. Although this may seem like a desirable, or at least innocuous, goal and, in fact, it may seem surprising that few such surveys have been conducted in the past, the project has encountered surprisingly strong opposition, mainly from persons who feel that the results will be used to set standards for education.

Issues in achievement testing

Standardized achievement tests have been criticized from several quarters and for a variety of reasons. (See, e.g., Hoffman, 1961, 1962; Black, 1963.) One set of criticisms revolves around the fact that the published standardized achievement batteries rely almost exclusively on multiple-choice items. Critics point out that not only do multiple-choice items fail to measure certain important skills, but that the item format also has certain imperfections (e.g., the items are likely to be ambiguous and to penalize students with greater knowledge of exceptions to laws and rules). The conclusion of many of these critics seems to be that multiple-choice questions should be replaced by a better type of item. The nature of this new type is often not clear; presumably it would be some form of an essay item. Hence, this issue reduces to another form of the recognition-recall debate, which will not be repeated here.

There are, however, two points that must be emphasized. For one, it would be infeasible to conduct a large scale testing program using essay items because of the grading problems (time, money, and scorer unreliability). Even if scoring problems could be overcome, the content sampling issue would have to be resolved. Two approaches are possible: (1) allow the student a choice among alternative essay questions, or (2) have all students answer the same questions and assume that the students who know all about the subject will not be penalized and those who do not will be justly penalized. The former approach, of course, introduces problems of equating scores on diverse items; the latter takes a rather unrealistic and simple-minded view of learning, expecting students to know everything about all aspects of a subject.

Secondly, there is the learning-testing distinction mentioned earlier. Because the results of learning can be assessed by methods different from the learning method, if the goal of testing is to obtain an indication of the amount learned, there is no logical reason why the test must involve the same procedures as the learning process. Critics who point out that the multiple-choice approach cannot produce certain desired learnings may be correct; however, it does not follow that the results of some of these learning experiences cannot be assessed with objective tests.

A second set of issues revolves around the questions of whether standardized tests determine the curricula and whether teachers teach to tests. The latter view presumes that students' test results will be available to the teacher's superiors (e.g., principals, superintendents, school boards) and that teachers will be evaluated in terms of their students' performance. Thus, to make themselves look good, teachers will teach to the test, stressing the materials that they know (or presume) will be covered on the test and neglecting other equally important materials. Thus, test scores will reflect the teacher's ability to outguess the test, rather than the students' true achievement. Although some teachers, no doubt, try to teach toward tests, the incidence of such behavior is unknown but probably overestimated. In addition, the evidence from coaching studies (see p. 59) would indicate that such attempts to influence scores are likely to be unsuccessful.

Note also that this view assumes that the test measures outcomes other than the important outcomes of education. In fact, one sometimes hears that standardized tests are worthless because they measure what test publishers are interested in, not what educators say are the important outcomes. Such arguments only betray the ignorance of their proponents because, as was mentioned earlier, the content of achievement batteries is determined by subject matter experts, not by psychologists and test specialists. Although test publishers may claim that their tests reflect classroom practices, it is uncertain whether they reflect or lead classroom practices. If they lead they do, in effect, determine curricula. The overriding issue is not whether tests lead or follow classroom practices but whether the test content reflects important educational outcomes. If it does, the issue tends to dissolve.

Still another aspect of the testing-curricula relationship is the proper use of achievement batteries in evaluating teachers, instructional methods, curricula, and school systems. Because so many of the studies using achievement batteries in such evaluations have involved faulty design, the teachers and other educators justifiably have negative attitudes toward such evaluations. The point that we would stress, however, is that such evaluations, when conducted according to the principles of good experimental design and used in conjunction with other relevant evidence, can provide an important source of data for evaluating educational programs, a source that should not be overlooked. However, ad hoc comparisons of fortuitously collected data are generally of little, if any, positive value and may be detrimental.

A third issue in achievement testing is just beginning to arise (see Gagné, 1967; Glaser, 1963). Most of the tests that we have discussed, and the models for reliability and validity, are based on an individual difference or discrimination model. That is, the tests are built to maximize differences between individuals, to discriminate between individuals. Hence, an item or test that does not discriminate between individuals is discarded. An opposing view feels that this model may be inappropriate. This view holds that the function of achievement tests is to indicate whether the student has mastered certain important knowledge, skills, abilities, and principles. Thus, if the purpose of a unit of instruction is to teach students the proper uses of "who" and "whom," the test should indicate whether they have learned this distinction. Items would be chosen to represent the variety of situations where the two words might be used—a procedure similar to the traditional model. But, in this view, if every student obtained 100 percent accuracy on the test it would only show that all students had mastered the material and that the teaching had been effective. The fact that the test did not discriminate among students with differing degrees of knowledge would be unimportant and irrelevant.

This view, of course, assumes that there are basic units of knowledge to be learned, that these units can be identified, and that items can be constructed to measure these units—assumptions that would also hold for tests contructed in the traditional manner. It differs from the traditional model by denying that the criterion of discrimination between students has any relevance. The emphasis, in short, is on mastery, not individual differences.

Evaluation of standardized achievement tests

Of all the classes of psychological and educational tests, standardized achievement measures have, by and large, attained higher standards of consistency, validity, and normative data than any other variety of test. This is not to say that all standardized achievement measures are satisfactory; far from it. Rather, there are a number of standardized achievement tests on the market, particuarly survey tests, that are highly reliable ($r_{tt} > .90$), have content and predictive validity, and which provide normative data from representative samples of the population. Thus a potential user has a high probability of finding a carefully constructed and technically satisfactory achievement test.

Yet there are several ways in which standardized achievement tests could be improved. Consider first normative data. Although the task of collecting normative data is somewhat easier on achievement tests, because of the "captive" nature of the population being sampled (persons attending school), these data are likely to underrepresent lower socioeconomic and disadvantaged groups. And as the education of these children will probably be inferior to those of their more privileged contemporaries, the normative data may be inappropriate for these groups. Then, too, normative data is usually norm-referenced rather than content-referenced; the latter, we have repeatedly stressed, have certain definite advantages in educational settings. And, third, normative data are usually presented for national samples or samples designated in some gross manner (by geographic region, size of school), necessitating the construction of local norms.

One might also hope for more diversity in approaches to measuring achievement. Most standardized achievement tests are composed primarily of objective items presented in a paper-and-pencil format. Furthermore, all students take the same items in the same sequence. These factors have two consequences: (1) skills that are not tapped by objective items will not be measured; (2) the flexibility in adapting a test to an individual is severely limited.

The use of other than objective items remains a problem because of the difficulties in scoring nonobjective items. Although there are a number of research projects being conducted attempting to objectify the scoring of essay examinations (see, e.g., Coffman, 1966), and even to use computers to grade nonobjective items (Page, 1967), even if scoring could be objectified, the time and costs of scoring essay examinations would probably make their use infeasible in large scale testing programs. Unless a new form of item is developed that allows the testing of skills not tapped by objective items, and which does not have the scoring problems of essay items, evaluation of these skills will have to use techniques other than standardized tests.

The other problem, that of adapting the test to the individual, appears closer to solution. One approach is to use that used by the College Level Exams,

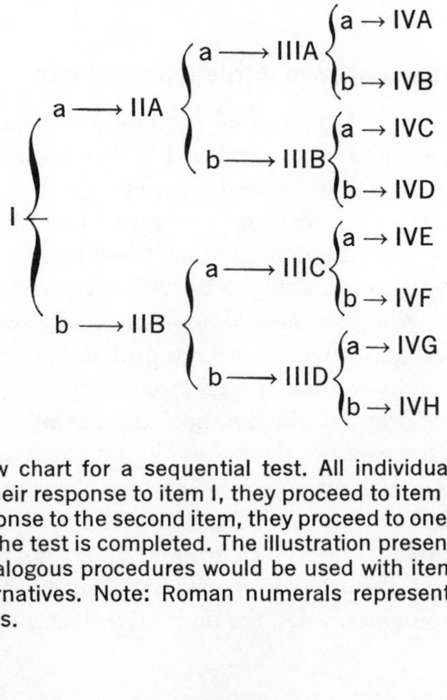

Figure 10.4 Flow chart for a sequential test. All individuals attempt item I. Depending on their response to item I, they proceed to item IIA or IIB. Depending on their response to the second item, they proceed to one of four third items; and so on until the test is completed. The illustration presents an item with two alternatives. Analogous procedures would be used with items having different number of alternatives. Note: Roman numerals represent items, lower-case letters responses.

to design tests that can be used to evaluate nontraditional learning experiences. Another approach is to use *sequential testing* methods. In this approach the answer an individual gives to one item determines which of several items will be presented next in sequence. Thus, for example, if we start with an item of a particular difficulty level, persons passing this first item would be directed to an item at the next highest difficulty level while persons failing the item would be directed to another item of the same difficulty or even an easier item, depending on their response to the first item. (See Figure 10.4.) In this way, the person's level of competence can be established with a minimum number of questions. The salient features of this approach are: (1) the response to one item determines which item appears next, (2) there must be a logical framework for sequencing items, e.g., by their difficulty, (3) different individuals will go through different sequences of items, and (4) performance is evaluated primarily in content-referenced terms. The procedure is similar to that used in a programmed textbook using branching methods. Although sequential tests have been presented in paper-and-pencil format, they are ideally suited for presentation by computer. It seems a safe bet to assume that more computer-based sequential tests will be developed in coming years.

Summary

Achievement tests may be defined as tests that measure learning that has occurred under relatively controlled learning conditions (such as the classroom) and which measure the students' present state of knowledge and/or what he has learned. When constructing an achievement test one assumes that the skill and content domain covered by the test can be specified, that the test items sample this domain, and that all persons taking the test will have had equal opportunities to learn the material. Thus, the essential steps in test construction are to define, in behavioral terms, the outcomes expected from the learning experience and to build items that sample these outcomes.

Achievement tests have various uses: to provide feedback to students regarding their learning, to motivate students, to provide diagnosis and counseling, to give feedback for the instructor, to assign grades, to use as a pretest, to check on studying, to stimulate discussion, selection, placement, and classification, to use as a performance standard, and to evaluate instructional programs.

There are two major classes of achievement tests: teacher-made or classroom tests and standardized tests. The classroom test is constructed by the teacher and stresses local goals. The process of constructing (from test planning through item writing), administering, scoring, and interpreting classroom tests was discussed in detail. So were the advantages and disadvantages of certain common item types: multiple-choice, true-false, matching, short answer and completion, essay, and problems. Simple item analysis procedures for determining the difficulty, discrimination power, and attractiveness of alternatives of items were discussed.

Standardized achievement tests are constructed by test publishers, with the aid of curriculum experts, and are designed for use in a wide variety of situations and schools. Hence they are, necessarily, broader in scope than classroom tests and stress content that is widely taught. The construction of standardized achievement tests was discussed and several varieties of standardized achievement tests were illustrated: survey tests, diagnostic tests, readiness measures, proficiency tests, advanced placement examinations, and measures of educational output.

Some of the points stressed throughout the chapter were: (1) the need for careful planning of the test, including specification of the desired learning outcomes in behavioral terms; (2) the differences in construction procedures, coverage, and use of classroom and standardized tests; (3) that content validity is generally the appropriate method of establishing the validity of achievement tests and that content validity is of two natures—how well the test items sample the universe as defined by the test constructor and how well the test items sample the domain as defined by the test user; (4) the difference in philosophy between norm-referenced and content-referenced scores; (5) the advantages and limitations and skills tapped by various test and item formats: and (6) the variety of uses for achievement tests.

Suggestions for further reading

Brown, F. G. *Measuring achievement in the classroom.* Hinsdale, Ill.: The Dryden Press Inc., 1970. A short introduction to the construction of achievement tests and other methods of assessing academic performance in classroom settings.

Dressel, P. L., and associates. *Evaluation in higher education.* Boston: Houghton Mifflin Company, 1961. A discussion of evaluation problems particular to higher education; includes both general problems and evaluation in specific content areas.

Ebel, R. L. *Measuring educational achievement.* Englewood Cliffs, N. J.: Prentice-Hall Inc., 1965. A thorough discussion of the construction and uses of classroom tests by a leading expert in the field.

Educational Testing Service. *Multiple-choice questions: a close look.* Princeton, N. J. 1963. An illustration of some of the complex types of multiple-choice items that have been developed; an answer to critics of multiple-choice tests.

Hoffman, B. *The tyranny of testing.* New York: P. F. Collier, Inc., 1964 (originally published in 1962). An indictment of objective tests and testers.

Thorndike, R. *Educational measurement* (rev. ed.) Washington, D. C.: The American Council on Education, 1969. A revision of the standard source on the construction, analysis, and uses of tests in education.

Tyler, R. W., J. C. Merwin, & R. L. Ebel. Symposium: A national assessment of educational progress. *The Journal of Educational Measurement*, 1966, 3, 1–17. The purposes, plans for and problems in conducting a national assessment of the achievement of American children and young adults.

Wittrock, M. C., & D. E. Wiley (Eds.). *Problems in evaluation of instruction.* New York: Holt, Rinehart and Winston, Inc., 1970. A collection of papers of various aspects of evaluation, with evaluation considered in a very broad sense.

The measurement of aptitudes and abilities

Chapter 11

INTRODUCTION

Although most of us have had more exposure to achievement tests than any other type of test, if asked to give an example of a psychological test, the average person would probably cite an intelligence or aptitude test. "IQ tests" and "tests that tell you what you can do" have become known as the psychologist's stock in trade. Some people appear to believe that these tests have almost magical power, bestowing on the psychologist the ability to predict educational and vocational success unerringly; to others they are biased and pseudoscientific indicators. Our goal in this chapter will be to present a balanced view of the advantages and limitations of aptitude measures.

Aptitude, achievement, and ability

The learnings tapped by an aptitide measure reflect the individual's total life experience. But, whereas an achievement test focuses on what has been learned, an aptitude test focuses on what can be learned in the future, this distinction being the hallmark of the definition of aptitude. Most definitions of aptitude include a phrase stating that *aptitude tests indicate the ability to acquire certain behaviors or skills given appropriate opportunity* (see e.g., English & English 1958; Drever, 1964; Michael, 1960). Thus aptitudes are important, not necessarily in themselves, but because they indicate the probability that certain other behaviors can or will be acquired or learned. What is to be learned may vary from a complex intellectual skill, like a foreign language or calculus, to simple motor or physical acts. Thus the definition of aptitude encompasses the ability to learn a variety of skills or behaviors, the common thread being not the type of skills learned but the ability to learn.

To clarify our terminology, we might include a third concept—*ability indicates the power to perform a task; aptitude, the power to learn to perform a task.* In other words, ability refers to a current state, aptitude to a future state. In this respect, ability is similar to achievement. However, ability and achievement differ in that achievement tests usually measure the outcomes of specific learning experiences, while ability tests measure the results of more general or broad learning experiences. All three concepts involve measurement of maximal performance.

Some basic assumptions

When measuring aptitudes the tester adopts a *trait-and-factor view* of human abilities. That is, human abilities are conceptualized as being organized and expressed through combinations of intercorrelated behaviors and responses. To say that someone has mathematical aptitude is, in essence, to say that he possesses a set of (intercorrelated) skills, abilities, and characteristics that enables him to learn mathematics. These skills, abilities, and characteristics *are* the aptitude. An aptitude is thus a construct, a summarizing term, and not an entity. The trait-and-factor approach is also normative in the sense that an individual's aptitude is compared to that of other persons rather than to an absolute standard. To say that Johnny has high aptitude for mathematics means that he can learn it faster, with less effort, or to a greater level of complexity than the majority of his peers; to say that George has no aptitude for mathematics does not mean that he cannot learn any of this skill, but only that it will be more difficult for him than for most other persons.

If a trait (aptitude) is to predict future performance, it must be relatively stable over time. This emphasis on stability has led many people to conclude that aptitudes are inherited characteristics that do not change throughout life. (Note such common expressions as: a God-given talent, a natural athlete, born with ability.) There is no doubt that aptitudes do have genetic bases; there is also no doubt, however, that aptitudes reflect prior learning and the interaction between genetic potentials and environmental (learning) effects. The apparent stability of aptitude measures, therefore, does not indicate that aptitudes are determined solely by genetic factors but rather that they are a reflection of the consistency of most individual's life patterns. Given the proper set of circumstances, aptitudes can be drastically influenced by environmental and situational characteristics (see, e.g., Anastasi, 1958; Bloom, 1964; Hunt, 1961; Vernon, 1961).

A third assumption is that aptitudes account for a significant portion of the variance in criterion performance. An individual's performance on a given task is not determined solely by situational forces but is also a function of the characteristics of the individual—his aptitudes. This is not to say that characteristics of the individual are the *only* important determiners of performance (as studies that utilize only psychological variables as predictors often seem to assume) but rather that the contribution of personal characteristics is not negligible. In all situations, performance will be determined by the individual's aptitudes, environmental factors, and the interaction of the two. The importance of any single component will, of course, depend on the particular situation. When individuals do not vary widely in their relevant traits (aptitudes), performance differences will be determined primarily by environmental characteristics; when the group is heterogeneous and the situation remains quite stable, individual differences become more important. The psychologist's task is to study the relative contribution of each variable in particular situations and to formulate general laws that relate trait and environmental conditions to performance.

Our definition stated that aptitudes assess the ability to learn, *given* the opportunity to learn. Hence when we say that Johnny has an aptitude for art, we are acutally predicting that Johnny will become a better than average artist if given proper training; there is no reason to believe that he will develop his ability without the relevant training. Thus, our prediction from an aptitude test is that a certain combination of abilities and skills (the aptitude) coupled with appropriate training will lead to a certain behavior.

Although the statement "aptitude plus training equals accomplishment" appears straightforward and simple, it actually is highly complex. For example, what do we mean by appropriate training? Is the same training appropriate for all individuals? Or is there an interaction between training and personal characteristics? Will the same training program produce different effects if introduced at different points in the individual's development? To what extent does the person's aptitude score reflect the results of previous relevant training? If the person fails to perform at the expected level is this to be taken as evidence, ipso facto, of the inappropriateness or failure of the training?

Or consider that elusive characteristic called "motivation." Aptitude tests, being tests of maximal performance, assume the test taker is motivated to make a maximal score; if not, the meaning of the score is ambiguous. Also, because aptitude indicates the ability to learn a skill with training, we must assume that the student is motivated during training; if not, we cannot say whether the training failed for lack of aptitude or lack of motivation. Finally, given the aptitude and training, the individual must be motivated to perform.

The process of defining an aptitude and understanding its operation thus involves the collection of various types of evidence; it is, in essence, an exercise in construct validity.

Theories of intellectual structure

Aptitude testing presupposes, as mentioned above, a trait-and-factor approach to the structure of abilities. We assume, then, that intellectual functioning can be described by a number of basic dimensions (traits or factors) and the person's standing on each dimension. More precisely, we need to know (1) the number of traits needed to (completely) describe a person, (2) the nature of these traits, (3) the relationships between these traits, and (4) the person's score on a measure (test) of each trait.

The development of a theory of intellectual structure has occupied the attention of a number of psychologists. Their attack has been both empirical and theoretical, but generally has been closely connected with intelligence testing and has utilized factor analysis as the primary analytic technique. Although research on the structure of the intellect has been proceeding throughout the twentieth century, there is still considerable controversy as to the validity of the proposed models. To give a flavor of the various approaches, précis of several historically interesting and currently fashionable models are presented below.

GENERAL INTELLIGENCE THEORIES. The simplest approach is to postulate a unitary ability, i.e., a single general capacity. This view holds that although intelligence may be expressed in diverse fashions or may be directed toward a variety of activities, basically it is a single ability. Any test that provides a single score (IQ) is, at least in a broad sense, representing a uni-factor theory. However, because the empirical data frequently suggest that a more complex model is needed, the uni-factor approach is considered too simplistic by most present-day theorists.

One type of general intelligence model is that of Spearman, who was the first person to propose a theory of intellectual structure based on statistical analyses of data from psychological tests. Spearman proposed a two-factor theory. The first factor was a general capacity or mental energy factor, which was basically a reasoning factor. In addition to this general factor (labeled *g*), each test measured skills that were specific to that particular test; hence, the second component was specific intelligences (see Figure 11.1a). Thus, although assigning primary importance to the general factor, the theory does recognize that other specific factors (and even other general factors) must be considered. The implication for measuring intelligence, however, is that the best test would be one saturated with general intelligence.

GROUP FACTORS. The approach that is accepted by the largest number of American theorists is one of group factors. This approach, which assumes that the fundamental dimensions can be represented by a relatively small number of fairly broad common factors (see Figure 11.1b), arose out of the work of Thorndike, Kelley, and Thurstone. Particularly Thurstone, with his concept of primary mental abilities, has publicized the group factor view. Although the exact abilities (group factors) found in any specific study depend upon several variables (e.g., the tests used, the nature of the sample tested, and the method of

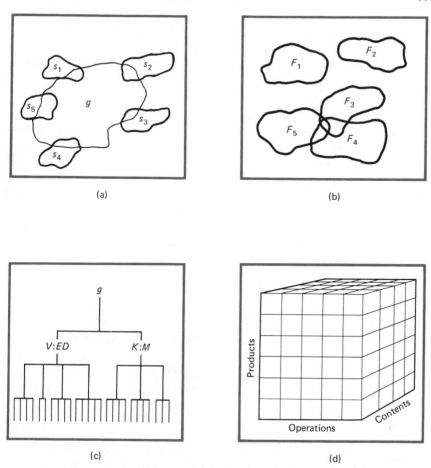

Figure 11.1 Models of intellectual structure: (a) Spearman's model; (b) a group factor model; (c) a hierarchical model (after Vernon, 1950); (d) Guilford's model (from *The Nature of Human Intelligence*, McGraw Hill, Inc., 1967).

analysis), the following factors have appeared with some regularity and have been confirmed by several investigators:

Space: the ability to visualize geometric patterns in space
Perceptual speed: quick and accurate noting of details
Number: quickness and accuracy in simple arithmetic computations
Verbal comprehension: knowledge of the meaning and relationship of words
Word fluency: ability to use many words
Rote memory: immediate recall of rote materials
Induction: ability to extract rules.

To measure intellectual ability, therefore, one would administer a battery composed of tests which individually measured one of the group factors. If the tests in the battery do, in fact, measure the primary mental abilities, *any* complex intellectual task or skill can be represented by a weighted composite of the relevant group factors.

HIERARCHICAL THEORIES. The basic idea of this approach is that intellectual structure can be conceived of as a hierarchy, extending from one or more broad general factors (general intelligence?) through group factors to more and more specific factors. For example, Vernon (1950) has proposed a model (see Figure 11.1c) where general ability (*g*) is at the apex of the hierarchy. This general factor is subdivided into two major group factors—a verbal-educational (V:ED) factor and a practical-mechanical (K:M) one. Each of these categories is further subdivided into group factors and then into more and more specific factors. For example, at the third level of the hierarchy, which represents minor group factors, we might find a spatial factor similar to Thurstone's group factor. At the next lower level, this factor might be further subdivided into three more specific factors: for example, (1) the ability to comprehend spatial relations using the body as a point of reference, (2) the ability to mentally manipulate a series of visual objects through a sequence of motions, and (3) the ability to make left-right discriminations. (cf. Michael et al., 1957). The hierarchical approach represents an intuitively satisfying collation of data and, since tests can be constructed to represent any level in the hierarchy, it is a useful tool for guiding test construction.

GUILFORD'S THREE-DIMENSIONAL MODEL. The most recent theory is Guilford's (1956, 1959, 1967) three-dimensional model. (Figure 11.1d). Guilford conceives of intellectual functioning as having three dimensions: operations, contents, and products. Operations are the processes involved in intellectual behavior—in Guilford's system, cognition, memory, divergent thinking, convergent thinking, or evaluation. The contents of these operations may be figural, symbolic, semantic, or behavioral. And, third, the products may be units, classes, relations, systems, transformations, or implications. Thus, the model contains 120 cells (5 operations $\times$ 4 contents $\times$ 6 products), each of which represents a distinct factor that is measured by a separate test. For example, in Guilford's scheme, the well-known verbal comprehension factor (vocabulary) becomes the ability to cognize semantic units. From the theorist's viewpoint, Guilford's precisely defined and integrated model has much to recommend it, including the advantage of being able to specify in advance the nature of currently unmeasured intellectual abilities.

The various models presented are both conceptual and heuristic devices. Because their comparative validity has not been determined, whichever model a particular investigator adopts will generally be a function of his individual preferences. The most widely used individual intelligence measures (the Stanford-Binet and Wechsler scales) are based on a general intelligence model. The group factor theory is most clearly shown in the multifactor batteries such as the *Primary Mental Abilities* and the *Differential Aptitude Tests*. No test is explicitly derived from a hierarchical theory, and Guilford's model is too new to be the basis of any widely used test.

It should be emphasized that not all test constructors have based their work on a particular theory of intellectual structure. In fact, the dominant approach has been an empirical one of attempting to predict a specific criterion with the maximal accuracy. Thus tests of scholastic aptitude have been developed, not in accord with a prevailing theory of intellectual structure, but by including skills that previous research has shown to be predictive of academic success. Most tests of dexterities and physical skills were developed, not to reflect a given theory, but rather to measure the components shown by job analyses to be important in the performance of certain types of jobs. In other words, empirical, rather than theoretical considerations, were pre-eminent.

With these general considerations in mind, we now turn to a discussion of the various categories of aptitude measures. As usual, our coverage of available tests will not attempt to be comprehensive and exhaustive. Rather we will discuss tests that exemplify the various approaches and types of aptitude measures.

MEASURES OF GENERAL INTELLECTUAL ABILITY

Throughout the twentieth century, attempts to measure intellectual ability, or intelligence, have played a pre-eminent role in psychological testing (Goslin 1963). In earlier years, the idea of general intelligence held forth; during the last three decades, with a few exceptions, attention has focused on intellectual abilities (in the plural). However, measures of general intellectual ability are still widely used and, in spite of their theoretical deficiencies, have shown practical utility (McNemar, 1964).

Intelligence, like so many other terms in psychology, is intuitively meaningful to most people but difficult to define precisely. Of the many definitions proposed, several appear repeatedly: the ability to learn, adaptability to new situations, (abstract) reasoning ability, and facility in the use of symbols. Some writers broaden the definition to include other than purely intellectual capacities—for example, Thorndike's use of the terms *abstract*, *mechanical*, and *social intelligence* and Vernon's distinction between *verbal-educational* and *concrete-mechanical* intelligences. Other writers and many test developers prefer the well-known operational definition: intelligence is what an intelligence test measures. This latter definition, rather than being a tautology, emphasizes that an intelligence test is a signal, that it points to the nature of the domain being measured, and thus the test and testing procedure defines the concept being measured.

Rather than becoming bogged down at this point in arguments about the definition of the term "intelligence," let us look at how intelligence is measured by various tests.

Stanford-Binet Intelligence Scale

The Stanford-Binet Intelligence Scale is the healthiest surviving descendent of Binet's original scale. Binet developed his test to identify slow learners in Paris schools. Using a definition of intelligent behavior that stressed the ability to take and maintain a definite direction or set, the capacity to adapt in order to obtain a given end, and the power of self-criticism, he developed a test which was first published in 1905 and later revised in 1908 and 1911. Although the test departed from then current practices along many dimensions, three aspects were of greatest import: (1) the use of complex molar tasks as test items, (2) the use of an age standard,[1] and (3) the attempt to measure general mental development rather than separate mental faculties.

The test became popular and several attempts were made to translate it and adapt it for American usage. The adaptation that caught on in the United States was Terman's version, first published in 1916, which has become known as the Stanford-Binet. Terman's test was an extension and improvement on Binet's scale and, in many respects, uses Binet's scale only as a point of departure. The 1916 version was important for several reasons. It was the first test to provide detailed administrative and scoring instructions, recognizing that variations along these dimensions could produce wide differences in scores. Second, the concept of the IQ was introduced. Third, the need for securing a representative sample of subjects for standardizing the test was recognized. (For a detailed discussion of the development of the Stanford-Binet see Terman & Merrill, 1937, 1960, or Goodenough 1949.)

The 1937 revision did not attempt to measure anything different from the 1916 form but only to do a better job of measurement. Two forms of the test were constructed—Form L and Form M. The test covered the age range 2 years to adult and was standardized on over 3000 children (age $1\frac{1}{2}$–18). Selection of items was based on three criteria: (1) the item measured behavior considered intelligent, (2) the percentage of children passing the item increased rapidly with age, and (3) the mean mental age (MA) of children passing and failing the item differed significantly. The test was very heavily loaded with verbal materials to the exclusion of items measuring other types of intellectual functioning and the administrative procedure was time-consuming. But compared to the earlier form of the Stanford-Binet and other available intelligence tests, the 1937 revision did sample a wider range of abilities, covered a wider age range, and provided more detailed instructions for administration and scoring.

[1]The concept of the mental age was first introduced on the 1908 revision.

THE 1960 REVISION. When making a decision regarding the desirability of revising an existing test, a test constructor must consider the advantages of a revision—e.g., elimination of obsolete materials, utilization of new techniques of test construction, incorporation of changes shown to be desirable by use of the test. He must then weigh these against the disadvantages of such a revision—e.g., the time and cost of the revision, and the rendering irrelevant of much of the normative, validity, and experimental data about the test (Anastasi 1968, Terman & Merrill 1960). When faced with this question, the authors of the Stanford-Binet opted for a revision consisting of an updating of materials and rechecking of item effectiveness rather than a complete restandardization of the test. The result was publication of single scale, Form LM, that incorporated the best items from Forms L and M of the 1937 revision.

Rather than administer the test items to an entirely new standardization sample—an expensive and time-consuming project—the data for the revision were based on the responses of approximately 4500 persons (age 2½–18) who had taken Form L or M between 1950 and 1954. Although this sample was not representative of American school children and was drawn from only six states, care was taken to avoid obviously selective factors (e.g., tests administered in clinics to children referred for learning or adjustment problems were not used).

Several analyses were run on each item. First, the present level of difficulty of each item was computed so that items which had become easier or more difficult could be reassigned to an appropriate age level (e.g., the identification of certain objects, particularly a telephone and stove, was more difficult because the models pictured had become obsolete). Second, the percentages of children passing each item at successive age levels was determined, and new growth curves developed and compared to the 1937 results. The correlation between each item and the total score was computed as an index of internal consistency. Item analyses were conducted for several regional and socioeconomic classes to insure that the items did not discriminate unfairly against certain children. (For example, it was felt that an item asking what to do if late for school might be unfair to children who rode a school bus, and an item about birthday parties might be unfair to children from lower socioeconomic classes; analyses showed neither item to be unfair.) Some items, which otherwise were adequate, were slightly modified so as to present the object or person pictured in more up-to-date form. A number of other special analyses were also performed (see Terman & Merrill, 1960, for details).

Items[2] on Form LM are grouped into 20 age levels. At the youngest age levels, from ages II through V, there is a separate test for each six-month level. From ages V through XIV there is one set of subtests for each year. In addition,

---

[2]We will use the terms item and subtest interchangeably when discussing the Stanford-Binet as some of the tasks (e.g., vocabulary) contain several questions, are arranged as subtests, and are administered at several age levels, while others consist of one or several closely related questions, appear at only one age level, and thus are more similar to individual test items.

there is an Average Adult level plus three levels of Superior Adults. At each level, except Average Adult, there are six subtests plus an alternate subtest; the Average Adult level consists of eight subtests plus one alternate. A given subtest may appear at only one age level or occur at several age levels, different levels of proficiency being required for passing at different age levels. For example, the Vocabulary subtest appears at age levels VI, VIII, X, XII, XIV, plus the four adult levels. At age VI, successfully defining six words constitutes success; at the Superior Adult III level, 30 of 45 words must be correctly defined in order to pass the subtest.

The composition of the test can best be appreciated by actual study of the test kit. To give a flavor of the items, the following list briefly describes the items that appear at four age levels. Some of the distinct features of the test can be noted from this sample of items. Note that at Age II the test items involve sensory-motor skills, the ability to follow directions, and identification of objects and parts of the body; verbal and language skills play a minor role. By Age VI the tests are heavily weighted with verbal skills (Vocabulary, Analogies, Differences) and discriminations (Differences, Mutilated Pictures), and numerical concepts begin to appear. Age X again emphasizes verbal skills, but many of the items now involve abstract concepts rather than relying on concrete experience (as at Age VI). By the Average Adult level the test materials are almost entirely verbal and symbolic with heavy emphasis on abstract conceptualizations.

AGE II

1. Three-hole Form Board. Placing three geometric objects in form board.
2. Delayed Response. Identifying placement of hidden object after 10-second delay.
3. Identifying Parts of the Body. Point out features on paper doll.
4. Block Building Tower. Build four-block tower by imitating examiner's procedure.
5. Picture Vocabulary. Naming common objects from pictures.
6. Word Combinations. Spontaneous combination of two words.

AGE VI

1. Vocabulary. Correctly define six words on 45-word list.
2. Differences. Telling difference between two objects.
3. Mutilated Pictures. Pointing out missing part of pictured object.
4. Number Concepts. Counting number of blocks in a pile.
5. Opposite Analogies II. Items of form "Summer is hot; winter is _____."
6. Maze Tracing. Finding shortest path in simple maze.

AGE X

1. Vocabulary. Correctly define 11 words on same list.
2. Block Counting. Counting number of cubes in three-dimensional picture, some cubes hidden.

3. Abstract Words I. Definition of abstract adverbs.
4. Finding Reasons I. Giving reasons for laws or preferences.
5. Word Naming. Naming as many words as possible in one minute.
6. Repeating six digits. Repeat six digits in order.

AVERAGE ADULT
1. Vocabulary. 20 words correct.
2. Ingenuity I. Algebraic word problems involving mental manipulation of volumes.
3. Differences between Abstract Words. Differentiate between two related abstract words.
4. Arithmetical Reasoning. Word problems involving simple computations.
5. Proverbs I. Giving meaning of proverbs.
6. Orientation: Direction II. Finding orientation after a verbal series of changes in directions.
7. Essential Differences. Give principle difference between two related concepts.
8. Abstract Words III. Meanings of abstract adverbs.

The Stanford-Binet is individually administered and, because of the complexity of the testing procedures, requires a trained examiner. Testing begins at the age level where "the child is likely to succeed, but not without some effort" (Terman and Merrill, 1960, p. 59). Typically, this will be the age level immediately lower than the child's chronological age. The testing proceeds until every set of items from the highest age level where all items are completed successfully (called the *basal age*) through the lowest age where all items are failed (called the *ceiling or maximal age*) have been administered.

SCORING. The correctness of each response is determined by comparing it with an extensive list of correct response variations given in the test manual. Scoring is on an all-or-none basis, a given item either being passed or failed with partial credit not permissible. Scores are translated into an age scale by assigning a certain number of months' credit to each correct answer. These credits, when added to the basal age, give the mental age of the subject. The procedure is illustrated in Table 11.1.

Because of problems with equating the distribution of IQ's at various age levels and the nonlinearity of the mental growth curve, the 1960 revision incorporated a deviation IQ system to replace the ratio IQ used on previous forms. Without going into the technicalities of the procedures followed in establishing this IQ scale (see Terman & Merrill, 1960, or Pinneau, 1961, for details), suffice it to say that the IQ's reported on Form LM are standard scores with a mean of 100 and a standard deviation of 16 points.

The psychologist thus has two distinct, though related, ways of interpreting performance on the Binet. The mental age gives an indication of the present level

TABLE 11.1 Computation of a Mental Age and Intelligence Quotient on the Stanford-Binet

Year level	Number of tests passed	Month's credit per test	Mental Age credits Years	Months
III–6	6	(basal age)	3	6
IV	5	1	—	5
IV–6	5	1	—	5
V	4	1	—	4
VI	2	2	—	4
VII	1	2	—	2
VIII	0	(ceiling age)	—	0
			3 yrs.	26 months

Mental Age = 5 years, 2 months (5–2)

If the child's chronological age were 4 years, 8 months (4–8), his IQ (found from tables in manual) would be 111.

of the subject's intellectual development; the IQ gives an indication of the relative rate of intellectual development compared to his agemates. Although both mental age and IQ are normative scores, being based on the performance of a standard sample of children, a mental age score can also be interpreted in terms of the type and complexity of task that the child can perform; hence, it can be interpreted as a content score.

CONSISTENCY AND VALIDITY. Although reliability data on Form LM is scanty, data from extensive studies of Form L and M (McNemar, 1942) indicated that the coefficient of equivalence was generally .90 or higher with samples of children aged 5 or older, even when these reliability coefficients were obtained using samples that were homogeneous in age. These levels of reliability can be translated into a standard error of measure of approximately 5 IQ points. In general, reliability was higher for older than for younger children and for children having lower rather than higher IQ's. The method of item selection, requiring an item to correlate with the total score, assured that the test would be homogeneous. Coefficients of stability are remarkably high (see discussion of the stability of the IQ below).

If we adopt a strict definition, the content validity of the Binet cannot be established, because the universe of "intelligent behaviors" is not delimited by the authors. However, they state that intelligent behavior is exhibited in the solution of problems such as analogies, opposites, vocabulary, comprehension, similarities and differences, absurdities, completion of verbal and pictorial materials, and memory for rote and meaningful materials. Thus there is an implicit definition of the content universe sampled, one which is heavily weighted with verbal reasoning abilities.

The Binet can more appropriately be viewed as serving as a sign rather than as a sample of intelligent behavior; construct validity thus becomes the central issue. Here several lines of evidence are relevant. First, the item selection criteria (age differentiation, internal consistency) serve both to select items for the test and to define the construct of intelligence. Second, factor analyses (e.g., McNemar, 1942; Jones, 1949) have shown that performance on the Stanford-Binet reflects a general factor, verbal reasoning, but that other abilities (e.g., memory, perceptual) have some influence on performance at certain age levels. That a general factor should be found is not surprising when one considers that one selection criterion for items was their relation to the total score on the test. Third, criterion-related validity studies have shown that Stanford-Binet IQ's correlate positively with a variety of measures of academic accomplishment (e.g., grades, years of education, teacher's ratings, and achievement test scores) and that the correlations are usually slightly higher for verbal areas (e.g., English, history, and reading) than in mathematics and science areas.

In short, the Stanford-Binet is a reliable measure of the intellectual ability, particularly verbal abilities, of school-aged children. In fact, because of its technical quality plus its historical position, the Stanford-Binet has come to serve as *the* standard for measuring intelligence, the standard against which all other purported measures of intelligence must be calibrated. Thus the strengths and limitations of the Stanford-Binet approach to measuring intelligence are, to a considerable extent, reflected in many other instruments.

Wechsler scales

The Stanford-Binet has certain drawbacks as a measure of adult intelligence. Because the items were developed for children they are frequently inappropriate for adults or are detrimental to the maintenance of motivation. Then, too, use of the mental age concept (and thus age scales) is of questionable utility with adults. And, third, the available normative data were collected on children, not adults. For these and several other reasons, David Wechsler developed a scale for measuring adult intelligence. His original scale, the Wechsler-Bellevue Intelligence Scale, was first published in 1939; in 1955 this scale was modified and restandardized as the Wechsler Adult Intelligence Scale (or WAIS).

WECHSLER'S APPROACH. Several considerations played a predominant role in shaping Wechsler's tests. One was the necessity of having the test content and scoring procedures selected for their appropriateness for adults and the normative data based on adult samples. Second, by defining intelligence as "the aggregate or global capacity of the individual to act purposefully, to think rationally and to deal effectively with his environment" (Wechsler, 1958, p. 7), Wechsler adopts a general intelligence approach. This view is supported by the statement that the subtests are "different measures of intelligence, not measures of different kinds of intelligence" (Wechsler, 1958, p. 64); in other words, the subtests measure different ways that intelligence may manifest itself. Yet, somewhat paradoxically, Wechsler also stresses the use of the test as a diagnostic instrument, using patterns of subest scores as the basis for making inferences about the individual's intellectual and emotional status. Third, although the IQ is viewed as "a comprehensive statement about the person's over-all intellectual functioning ability" (Wechsler, 1958, p. 156), and as an index of his relative brightness compared to his age peers, Wechsler stresses that intelligence is not the mere sum of abilities tapped by the various subtests. Rather, it is the configuration of abilities plus motivational and personality factors that produce intelligent behavior.

THE WAIS. The WAIS consists of eleven subtests. Six of the tests are grouped together to form a Verbal Scale. The other five tests comprise the Performance Scale. All 11 tests make up the Full Scale. The 11 tests are described in the following list.

VERBAL SCALE

Information: 29 items which measure the range of the examinee's knowledge, retention of learned materials, and assess the examinee's cultural background. Items are of the form "Where does wool come from?" and "Who wrote *Paradise Lost?*"

Comprehension: 14 items measuring judgment and "common sense." Includes translation of proverbs and items of form "Why should children be warned against playing with matches?"

Arithmetic: 14 items testing concentration, arithmetic ability, and problem-solving skill. All items have time limits and are simple word problems, e.g., "If I have $15 and earn $8 more, how much money do I now have?"

Similarities: 13 items measuring logical thinking and conceptual ability; a good measure of general intelligence. Items are of the form "In what way are a car and a boat alike?"

Digit Span: Tests attention and immediate memory by items requiring examinee to repeat series of digits either forward or backwards.

Vocabulary: 40 words of varying difficulty. Is the best single index of Full-Scale IQ; indicates range of knowledge and cultural background.

PERFORMANCE SCALE

Digit Symbol: Measures flexibility and ability for new learning through a task requiring the substitution of symbols for numbers. Speeded.

Picture Completion: 21 items that require examinee to tell what is missing in a picture of a common object. Measures perceptual ability, particularly ability to differentiate essential from unessential details.

Block Design: Examinee reproduces designs with colored blocks. Measures ability to analyze and organize. Good test for observing problem-solving strategy as well as distorted perception and visual-motor co-ordination. Generally considered best single performance test. Time limits.

Picture Arrangement: Requires examinee to arrange a group of pictures (similar to comic strip panels) to tell a coherent story. Measures ability to comprehend a total situtation. Bonus points for rapid solutions.

Object Assembly: Task is to assemble pieces of a puzzle to form a common object. Speeded. Tests perceptual ability and persistence.

Within each subtest, items are arranged in approximate order of difficulty. Items in a given subtest are administered sequentially, testing being discontinued after a prescribed number of consecutive failures, at which point administration of the next subtest is begun. Some of the items have time limits and others are untimed. As with the Stanford-Binet, the WAIS is individually administered and requires a trained examiner.

Items are scored by comparing the subject's response to a list of acceptable response variations given in the manual (see Figure 2.3).

Points are assigned on the basis of correctness and on several tests, speed of response; on some tests, differing numbers of points are awarded depending on the quality of the response. Thus, in contrast to the age scale approach of the Binet, the WAIS is a *point scale* (as are the other Wechsler scales). The raw scores on each subtest are then converted into a standard score ($\overline{X} = 10$ points and $s = 3$ points). The subtest standard scores are next summed and converted into three IQ scores: a Verbal IQ, a Performance IQ, and a Full-Scale IQ. Because Wechsler was concerned with the fact that test performance deteriorated with age, IQ's are computed separately for several age groups[3]; hence, the IQ indicates an individual's relative standing within a group of his age peers. The IQ's are deviation IQ's with $\overline{X} = 100$ and $s = 15$ (cf. the Stanford-Binet IQ) derived from a normative sample which, in essence, was a cross-section of the U.S. adult population.

[3]IQ conversion tables are presented in the manual for the following age levels: 16–17, 18–19, 20–24, 25–34, 35–44, 45–54, 55–64, 65–69, 70–74, and 75 and over (Wechsler, 1955).

CONSISTENCY AND VALIDITY. The data presented by Wechsler (1955) show that the Verbal, Performance, and Full-Scale IQ's are all highly reliable ($r_{tt} \geq .93$).

When the WAIS is used as a diagnostic instrument, the questions of subtest reliability and the reliability of subtest difference scores become important. The distribution of standard errors of differences between pairs of subtest scores had a median of three points, leading Wechsler to conclude that "Differences as large as five points may be unusual enough to be noteworthy" (Wechsler, 1955, p. 18). In other words, unless two subtest scores differ by five or more points, the difference may not be statistically meaningful and thus must be interpreted with caution. Unfortunately, Wechsler (1958) and other clinicians who use the WAIS as a diagnostic instrument have ignored this advice and have interpreted differences of much smaller magnitude as being meaningful differences.

Items were selected for inclusion on the Wechsler scales by studying previous tests to determine what sorts of items best measured intelligent behavior, from clinical experience, and by trying out experimental items on groups of known characteristics. Wechsler has also presented a detailed justification of including each subtest as a measure of intelligence (Wechsler, 1955). Such procedures support the content and construct validity of the measures. Although the exact magnitude depends on the group tested, a correlation of .80–.85 between WAIS and Stanford-Binet IQ's is about the maximum found. WAIS scores have also been correlated with a variety of educational, job, and miscellaneous criteria.

One might also ask whether the division of the test into Verbal and Performance scales is justified by the empirical evidence. Several types of evidence are relevant here. First, the Verbal and Performance IQ's correlated .77, .77 and .81 in three reliability samples. Second, although scores on the verbal subtests generally correlate higher with the Verbal IQ than with Performance IQ (and vice versa for performance subtests), the difference in correlations are generally low; the median being less than .10. The performance tests, with the exception of Object Assembly, correlate about as high with Verbal IQ as with Performance IQ. The third line of evidence, factor analysis data, is more complex. A general factor, best labeled a general reasoning factor, is typically found; however, two other factors usually also appear—a verbal comprehension factor and a nonverbal or performance factor—and a memory factor is sometimes found. To summarize, although there is some support for separate Verbal and Performance scales, the evidence is far from overwhelming. To consider the WAIS as a measure of general intelligence would not be incompatible with the empirical data.

OTHER WECHSLER SCALES. In spite of the fact that original rationale for constructing the Wechsler-Bellevue, and later the WAIS, was to provide a measure of intellectual ability particularly appropriate for adults, two tests for children have since been constructed as outgrowths of the adult scales. The first of these, the Wechsler Intelligence Scale for Children (WISC) is an extension, to lower age levels, of the Wechsler-Bellevue. The format of the WISC is similar to the adult scales—only one WISC subtest (Mazes) does not appear on the adult form—as many of the WISC scales were constructed by adding easier items to the adult scale and eliminating some of the more difficult items. Of particular interest is the relationship between WISC and Stanford-Binet scores. Here two facts emerge: (1) the tests are quite highly intercorrelated, the modal correlation found in various studies being in the .80's and (2) the range of IQ's appears to be greater on the Binet than the WISC, with brighter children tending to obtain higher IQ's on the Binet than the WISC and duller children scoring higher on the WISC.

In 1967 another Wechsler scale, the Preschool and Primary Scale of Intelligence (WPPSI) was published. This test is designed for use at ages 4–6½, when the child is beginning his formal schooling and accurate measures of intelligence may play an important part in many critical educational decisions. The format and subtests are quite similar to the WAIS and WISC, but certain changes have been made (e.g., including more nonverbal tasks) to make the test appropriate for preschoolers.

Other measures of general intelligence

The Stanford-Binet and Wechsler scales represent only several of the myriad of intelligence tests, albeit they are probably the most important intelligence tests. The remaining intelligence measures can be classified into four categories: group tests, nonverbal or performance measures, tests designed for very young children (i.e., infants and preschoolers), and culture-fair measures. The first three classes will be discussed below; the fourth (culture-fair measures) will be considered later in the chapter.

GROUP TESTS.   Group intelligence tests are typically composed of several types of items: vocabulary, general information, arithmetic, and reasoning items. In particular, group intelligence tests are often heavily weighted with vocabulary items, either in the traditional form or variations such as selecting the correct word for use in a sentence or an analogies items. The widespread use of vocabulary items reflects the empirical finding that vocabulary is the best single index of intelligence. General information items (e.g., "The capital city of France is:...." "The population of the United States is:....") are included to estimate the individual's range of knowledge. Arithmetic items generally involve only simple computation and, certainly, no more complexity than basic algebra. Reasoning items may be verbal or nonverbal analogies, number series (i.e., "What is the next number in the sequence 1..2..4..7..11..?"), or other similar items. By and large, group tests include the item types that have proven to be the most valid indices of intellectual ability. The fact that these item types (i.e., vocabulary, general information, arithmetic, and reasoning) are the most valid indices no doubt reflects the high premium placed on verbal and symbolic tasks in our culture.

Group tests share certain common features. Group administration permits more efficient testing of large numbers of persons and, because of the less complex procedures, a group test generally does not require a highly trained professional administrator. On the other hand, the format usually requires that the test be administered with a time limit, that direct observation of test-taking behavior is not feasible, and that certain persons—e.g., young children and other persons who cannot read—cannot be tested. Group tests are usually paper-and-pencil tests with items cast in the multiple-choice format.

Although group intelligence tests were originally designed to be economical substitutes for individual tests, and still are widely used in just this manner, they have assumed an existence of their own. For example, a variety of group intelligence tests, the scholastic aptitude test, is designed to predict academic success; that these tests measure general intelligence is only a secondary consideration, though their high correlation with individual intelligence measures will evidence the fact that they do measure intelligence. Group intelligence measures are also used for industrial and business screening. These tests are generally short (often only 15–30 minutes working time), are constructed along traditional lines, and include items covering the common components of intellectual ability. Because of their short length, there may be problems in content sampling and in attaining an adequate level of reliability, a wide range of item difficulty, and a wide enough distribution of scores to enable meaningful discriminations to be made among individuals.

PERFORMANCE TESTS.   All of the intelligence tests discussed thus far have been composed wholly or primarily of verbal items and all have relied on verbal directions. But there are several groups for whom verbal testing materials may present problems—persons being tested in other than their native language, the very young, the severely mentally retarded, and those with visual or auditory handicaps. When testing these groups there is need for performance items that measure the ability to conceptualize, categorize, and do abstract thinking but which do not rely on verbal stimulus materials, response modes and/or directions.

Performance tests consist of a variety of items, some of the most common of which are:

Form Boards: The examinee must place cut-out objects in the corresponding hole on a board, usually within a time limit.
Block Designs: The examinee reproduces a design using multicolored cubes (c.f. the Wechsler subtest).

Mazes: The examinee traces the shortest path through mazes of varying difficulty.

Object Assembly or Puzzles: Examinees must fit pieces together to make an object (c.f. Wechsler and Binet subtests) or complete a puzzle.

Scores on these tests usually correlate positively with scores on verbal measures of intelligence, but the magnitude of the correlation is generally not so high that scores on the two types of tests can be substituted for each other.

The use of nonverbal and performance tests has been decreasing in recent years because, with increasing educational opportunities and decreasing immigration, verbally loaded tests can be appropriately administered to a greater proportion of the population. Then, too, since verbal and performance tests appear to measure somewhat different abilities (and in our culture measures of verbal ability have proved to be more useful than measures of other intellectual abilities), whenever there is a choice between verbal and nonverbal tests the verbal measure is usually preferred.

PRESCHOOL AND INFANT TESTS. The testing of infants (children less than 18 months old) and preschool children (ages 18 months to 5 years) presents enough special problems to merit separate consideration. One obvious reason for the discontinuity between preschool and other tests is that the typical child does not learn to read or write until he is in first grade and about 6 years old; therefore, tests requiring any reading skills are obviously inappropriate for preschool children (and even of questionable appropriateness in the primary grades). Furthermore, prior to school entrance most children are not practiced in manipulating marking devices in response to directions; hence, even the relatively simple task of indicating one of several objects by marking, which is the response format used on many tests at the primary level, may be beyond their grasp. Thus preschool tests are often performance tests or, if they involve verbal materials, require the child to respond orally to orally presented questions.

The typical preschool test includes some or all of the following item types: perceptual and motor skills (e.g., block designs, copying patterns or structures, and form boards), simple discriminations (identifying which object in a series is different, telling how it differs), recognition of incongruities (indicating what is missing or out of place in a picture), naming parts of the body or common objects and/or indicating their function, following simple directions, and tests of immediate memory (e.g., repeating words or digits, noticing what object in a group has been removed during a short period when the stimuli has been covered from the subject's view). Infant tests typically involve assessment of gross and fine motor control, coordinated movements, ability to communicate in language and by other modalities (e.g., through gestures or facial expressions), and social responsiveness. (See e.g., Anastasi, 1968, Chapter 10.)

Most infant and preschool tests explicitly or implicitly utilize a developmental approach by including items and measuring skills and abilities that typify children at various developmental stages. The developmental approach places tremendous importance upon obtaining satisfactory normative data since, if the norm group is not representative, any conclusions drawn about meaning of an individual's scores will be in error. Obtaining a representative sample of preschool children or infants is not an easy task because no single source, such as public schools, is available from which a representative sample of children can be drawn. Normative samples are thus often composed of volunteers or drawn from special groups (e.g., children from a particular clinic), sources that are likely to be biased in terms of parent's socioeconomic and educational level.

The age of the examinees interposes certain administrative problems. With infants it may be necessary to observe and rate their spontaneous behavior or use a semistructured testing situation, rather than to rely solely on responses elicited by specific items. Young children also have short attention spans, tire easily, might be shy or refuse to interact with the examiner, might prefer to play with the test materials rather than continue with the test, are easily upset, and might otherwise exhibit erratic behavior. Because they have limited conceptions of time, speeded items are generally inappropriate. In addition, scoring of infant and preschool tests is often not completely objective, frequently being based on ratings derived from behavioral observations. These factors serve (1) to underscore the need for trained and perceptive examiners and (2) to decrease reliability. This lower reliability of infant and preschool tests is well documented by the empirical data, particularly for infant tests.

Because infant and preschool tests generally adopt a developmental approach, an age differentiation criterion can be applied as one approach to determining validity. A second approach would be to relate scores on infant and preschool tests to scores on established intelligence tests taken at later ages. The data from numerous studies show the correlation between scores on infant tests and adolescent or adult intelligence to be essentially zero.[4] However, correlations between scores on the Stanford-Binet (or its derivative tests, e.g., the Cattell Infant Intelligence Scale) obtained during preschool years correlate as high as .55–.75 with adolescent Stanford-Binet IQ's.

Three empirical questions

The research literature relating to intelligence test scores is voluminous. Rather than attempt a summary, we will look very briefly at three major issues in the measurement of intelligence—the nature of mental growth curve, the stability of

[4]Most studies have attempted to predict adolescent or adult IQ from an infant test administered at a particular point in time. Recently, several investigators have improved predictive accuracy by using the trend of infant IQ scores. However, the absolute level of consistency remains low.

the IQ, and the relationship of intelligence test scores to several socially relevant variables. The reader who desires a more comprehensive discussion of issues in intelligence measurement should consult references such as Anastasi (1968), Bayley (1955, 1968), Bloom (1964), Guilford (1967), Hunt (1961), Pinneau (1961), Tyler (1965), or Vernon (1961).

THE MENTAL GROWTH CURVE. If one plots a measure of intellectual development against chronological age, from birth to adolescence, using a random sample of subjects, he will obtain an S-shaped curve (see Figure 11.2a).[5] Several features of the curve are worthy of note. First, there is a period of relatively rapid growth during early childhood followed by a slower rate in the adolescent and early adult years. This relation holds regardless if we measure the absolute or relative increase. Second, the curve is essentially linear during the childhood years. Third, mental development reaches an asymptote in the early adult years, stays near this level until middle age or later, and then begins to decline. (See also Figure 11.2b.)

Figure 11.2a is a summary curve representing the average performance of a group of persons on a measure of general intelligence such as the Binet or Wechsler. The rate of growth, however, varies from function to function and from person to person. For example, research (Wechsler, 1958) has shown that performance on certain tests, especially highly speeded ones, declines at an earlier age than do scores on other subtests. (See Figure 11.2b.) The shape of the curve also varies from individual to individual, with some persons being "late bloomers" (starting slow and developing late) while others seem to be "early wilters." Or, to use another example, persons of higher intelligence levels, those who are more highly educated, and those working in occupations requiring intellectual skills tend to maintain or even increase their ability throughout a longer period of life. Thus there is no single mental growth curve, but rather many curves, each depending on the function and individual tested.

STABILITY OF THE IQ. Another set of questions centers on the stability of intelligence test scores: How stable is the IQ? How many points change in IQ can be expected on retesting? What factors can produce changes in the IQ? What is the relative magnitude of changes produced by the various factors? At what age level is change most likely to occur? Are changes systematic or random? Do certain aspects of intelligence fluctuate more, or more readily, than others? Are the scores of certain types of individuals more stable than others? The perceptive reader will recognize that all of these questions presume that intelligence is, in some degree, unstable. The basic question, consequently, is: Under what conditions and to what extent do intelligence scores vary?

[5]The exact shape of the curve will depend on the particular units used to scale mental development. The curve depicted in Figure 11.2 used a scaling procedure recommended by Guilford (1967).

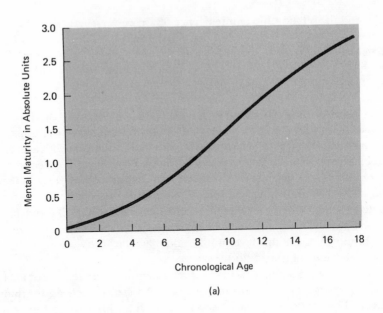

(a)

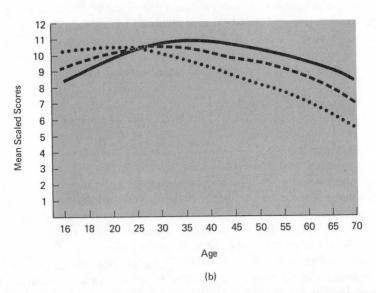

(b)

Figure 11.2 Mental growth curves: (a) mental growth during childhood (after Guilford, 1967, and Thurstone & Ackerson, 1929); (b) scores on three WAIS subtests during adult years. (Adapted from D. Wechsler, *The Measurement and Appraisal of Adult Intelligence*, 1957. Permission granted by The Williams & Wilkins Company, acting for the copyright owner).

Although the earlier literature stressed the stability of the IQ, it is now recognized that the apparent stability reflected the fact that most people experience relatively constant environmental conditions. As a consequence, environmental factors do not have a chance to fully demonstrate their effects. And, as would be expected, the greatest fluctuations in IQ's occur with the greatest change in environmental conditions, this environmental stability leads to stability in intelligence test scores. Moreover, the cumulative nature of intellectual development and measurement tends to produce artifacts that insure a high correlation between successive IQ measures (Anderson, 1940). However, other data have shown that marked changes (both improvement and decrements of 20 IQ points or more) in IQ do occur under certain conditions.

What factors, then, produce greater than chance changes in the IQ? Some of the factors that may decrease intelligence are obvious—injury or illness, particularly if it effects the brain or central nervous system, and severe emotional trauma. Others are less obvious but reasonable; for example, spending long periods of time in extremely restricted or deprived environments may result in decreased intellectual performance. Similarly, spending one's entire life, or even one's earliest (preschool) years, in a restricted environment certainly limits intellectual development. Conversely, removal of an emotional block or the provision of an especially stimulating environment or educational experiences, can lead to increased effectiveness on intellectual tasks.

The relationship between intelligence and experience can also be viewed in a slightly different manner (see, e.g., Jensen, 1968, 1969). Assume that the environment must provide a certain minimal amount of stimulation if normal intellectual growth is to occur, that is, if the individual is to develop his intelligence maximally within the limits set by his genetic characteristics. If this threshold of stimulation is reached, the person's intellectual development will proceed normally and consistently unless, of course, something occurs that reduces the effective environmental stimulation to below the threshold; at this point normal development will be retarded. Similarly, if the stimulation threshold is not reached during early years, mental development will be arrested. Because mental growth is most rapid in early childhood, and because all learning depends on previous learning, changes in environmental conditions will be optimally effective at this time; thus the stress on the importance of adequate intellectual stimulation in the earliest years (Bloom, 1964; Hunt, 1961). Because most persons grow up in environments where the effective stimulation level is above the threshold and do not experience major changes in environmental conditions, their mental development will be consistent and not restricted. However, moving to or from a severely restricted environment can produce noticeable changes in the effectiveness of intellectual functioning, changes that will be reflected in the IQ.

Two further points should be briefly noted. First, the low correlations observed between measures of infant and adult intelligence are attributable to the unreliability of infant tests and to the fact that different skills are measured when testing infants and testing adults, as well as the effects of environmental conditions. To cite only the most obvious difference, adult tests are highly saturated with verbal material while infant tests emphasize sensori-motor development. Second, our discussion has considered intelligence as a unitary ability, as being described by a single general factor. However, Cattell and his colleagues (Cattell, 1963, 1968; Horn, 1967) have suggested that intelligence be viewed as consisting of two general factors: fluid intelligence and crystallized intelligence. Crystallized intelligence has a heavy cultural component and is best measured by those subtests that traditionally compose intelligence tests: vocabulary, numerical skills, and general and specific information. Fluid intelligence involves more perceptual and performance skills. Because the relative contributions of fluid and crystallized intelligence to intellectual performance vary from person to person and because fluid and crystallized intelligence have different growth curves (fluid intelligence begins to decline at an earlier age), the stability of intellectual performance will also depend on the role fluid and crystallized components play in the behavior measured.

INTELLIGENCE AS A PREDICTOR.   Another area that has been the subject of a large amount of research is the relationship between intelligence and other socially relevant criteria, i.e., the ability of intelligence scores to predict nontest behaviors. The Binet test, you will recall, was originally developed to differentiate slow learners from other children—in essence, to predict academic success. Since Binet's time innumerable studies have been conducted relating intelligence measures to a variety of educational outcomes—e.g., years of schooling, grades, achievement test scores, prizes and awards. (See, e.g., Goslin, 1963.) Considering the diversity of tests, samples and criteria used, the results of these studies have been amazingly consistent; the correlations between scores on general intelligence tests and measures of academic success generally fall in the .40–.70 range. The correlations are generally higher when the criteria is based on a standardized measure of achievement rather than teachers' judgments and when the criterion courses are more academic or verbal in content (e.g., mathematics or English, in contrast to music or art). With younger children, general intelligence measures predict as well or better than tests of specific abilities.

The relationship of intelligence test scores to occupational achievement is also a controversial area. On one hand there are studies, such as the famous Army studies (Harrell & Harrell, 1945), which have shown that occupations can be ranked in terms of the intellectual ability of persons working within these occupations. Then, too, it is well documented that occupational membership is closely related to educational attainment and that educational attainment can be predicted from intelligence test scores. On the other hand, there are studies (e.g., Thorndike & Hagen, 1959; Hoyt 1965) that seem to show little relationship between ability and achievement (academic and occupational success), at least when relative success is predicted *within* an occupational group. Perhaps the best reconciliation of the present knowledge is that many occupations may have minimal intellectual requirements, but that given an individual who possesses these minimal intellectual requirements, his performance in a particular occupation will be determined by factors and abilities other than intellectual ability.

Evaluation of general intelligence tests

Any evaluation of general intelligence tests is essentially an evaluation of the construct of general intelligence. There is no doubt that general intelligence tests sample a certain constellation of abilities (e.g., vocabulary, fund of general information, numerical ability) and measure these abilities with high reliability. Furthermore, the technical requirements of standardization, objectivity, and adequate normative data are met on many general intelligence measures, particularly on tests like the Stanford-Binet and Wechsler scales. The fundamental question, then, is whether the concept of general intelligence is a viable one.

There would, at first blush, appear to be many reasons for rejecting the notion of general intelligence. The tests themselves are composed of several different types of items. Then, too, factor analyses of both general intelligence tests and batteries of tests of intellectual abilities have confirmed the existence of a number of distinct intellectual abilities. True, these abilities tend to be positively intercorrelated, but not to the extent that one would subsume them all under one general ability. A slightly different type of study has shown that at different age levels, performance on general intelligence tests is a function of different sets of abilities; again an argument against the general intelligence view. Why, then, do psychologists persist in building general intelligence tests and insist on using a single score, usually the IQ, to summarize an individual's intellectual abilities? One reason, no doubt, is historical tradition; the early tests used this approach and their descendents have followed in their footsteps. But this is hardly a sufficient reason. Probably more important is the fact that general intelligence tests have proven useful in predicting a variety of educational and other socially relevant criteria. Furthermore, as we shall see later in the discussion of multiaptitude batteries, in the majority of situations prediction using multiple abilities has proven no more effective than predicting from a single index of general intelligence.

The debate over the concept of general intelligence illustrates the distinction between basic research on the structure of abilities and application of knowledge gained to the technology of test construction. It would be hard to argue against the view that intellectual ability is best conceived of as a number of intelligences or, if you will, a number of quite distinct intellectual abilities. However, although test constructors have been able to develop tests measuring these abilities, the tests do not produce greater predictive efficiency than do general intelligence measures. As general intelligence tests are more familiar to test users, more efficient, simpler to interpret, and as valid as multiaptitude batteries, many persons prefer to use general intelligence tests even though they realize the theoretical limitations of such measures.

MULTIAPTITUDE BATTERIES

Many psychologists cite evidence from factor analytic studies, including factor analyses of the Stanford-Binet and Wechsler, as indicating that the general intelligence approach is too simplistic. Also educational and industrial psychologists concerned with differential placement and classification and counselors concerned with differential abilities want information on various abilities, not merely scores on a single ability. All of these people support the development and use of multiaptitude batteries.

The adoption of a multiaptitude approach has several implications for the test construction process. First a test battery, not just a single test, must be constructed. If one conceives of intellectual structure as consisting of relatively broad and more or less independent factors or abilities, and if intellectual ability is to be measured with any degree of completeness, then a number of indepent dent tests will have to be built. Specifically, the test battery must contain at leasas many tests as there are abilities to be measured. A second, or perhaps corollary, implication is that each test or subtest will measure one, and only one, ability.

A closely related issue is whether to use only measures of pure factors or whether the tests can be comprised of items measuring several closely related abilities. Test batteries taking the former approach can legitimately be referred to as multifactor tests; tests taking the latter approach are more properly called multiaptitude tests. As there is some evidence to suggest that the structure of abilities may not be the same at different age levels, the test constructor must also determine the optimal division of age levels. As intraindividual comparisons will be made, high reliability and small standard errors of measurement *must* be attained; but this requirement must be balanced against the possibility of producing an inordinately long battery. The test constructor must, of course, also make decisions regarding all other relevant parameters—e.g., item difficulty, timing, response modes, and the nature of the normative groups.

As the tests within a multiaptitude battery will, hopefully, be predictive of relevant and important criteria, the question of the proper method of combining the test scores arises. In theory, every criterion can be predicted from a particular combination of factors (test scores); the empirical question is to determine the optimal weighting of the factors. Application of the multiple-regression model allows the appropriate weights to be assigned to each predictor. Thus the same basic set of predictors (test or factor scores) can be used to predict every criterion, but the various components will be differentially weighted when predicting various criteria.

The Differential Aptitude Tests

As our primary example of a multiaptitude battery we have chosen the Differential Aptitude Tests (DAT) published by the Psychological Corporation. The development of the DAT was guided by certain general principles. Two of the most important were that the test battery should measure multiple abilities rather than general ability and that the test should be useful in educational and vocational guidance. In addition, the tests in the battery were to be independent. But, rather than measuring factorially defined constructs, the DAT measures constructs that are considered independent traits by counselors and other test users. Because the test constructors felt that the level of ability an individual possesses is usually the critical consideration, not his speed of response, the tests are power tests. A singular exception is the Clerical Speed and Accuracy Test.

The differential aptitude approach directly implies two other guiding principles: that the test battery yield a profile of ability scores and that the provision of adequate norms is a *sine qua non* of the test construction process. The three remaining principles derive from the intended use of the tests in the public schools: that the test materials be practical, that the tests be easy to administer, and that alternate forms be made available.

In reviewing the guiding philosophy of the DAT, one can see the interplay of theoretical and practical demands and the necessity of tempering a purely psychometric approach with the requirements for developing an instrument that provides meaningful scores to the student and his counselor. In constructing the DAT the authors have satisfied the essential psychometric requirements (e.g., of reliability and normative data) but have never lost sight of the needs of the test user.

THE TESTS. The DAT battery consists of eight separately administered tests. Three of the tests—Verbal Reasoning (VR), Numerical Ability (NA), and Abstract Reasoning (AR)—measure general intellectual abilities. Since the test authors realized that no clear distinction between ability and achievement can be drawn but, that if tests are to be used as aptitude measures, a common core of experience must be tapped, items on VR and NA use materials commonly taught in elementary schools in this country. VR utilizes a special form of analogies item which requires the student to base his answer on reasoning rather than mere associations. (See Figure 11.3 for illustrations of DAT items.) NA uses computation items rather than word problems to avoid contamination from irrelevant abilities. The authors propose adding the VR and NA scores to obtain an index of scholastic aptitude and, consequently, use this combination (VR + NA) as a ninth score on the battery. The AR items tap the ability to perceive and apply a general operating principle through a series of diagrams.

Figure 11.3 Sample problems from the Differential Aptitude Tests. (For Verbal Reasoning, Numerical Ability, Abstract Reasoning, Clerical Speed and Accuracy: Reproduced by permission. Copyright 1947, © 1961 by The Psychological Corporation, New York, N. Y. All rights reserved. For Mechanical Reasoning, Space Relations, Language Usage: Reproduced by permission. Copyright 1947, © 1961, 1962 by The Psychological Corporation, New York, N. Y. All rights reserved.)

Verbal Reasoning

Pick out the combination of (numbered and lettered) words which will make a true and sensible sentence.

EXAMPLE X.   .....is to water as eat is to.....

| 1. continue | 2. drink | 3. foot | 4. girl |
| A. drive | B. enemy | C. food | D. industry |

Numerical Ability

Select the correct answer.

EXAMPLE X

Add	13	A	14
	12	B	25
	—	C	16
		D	59
		E	none of these

EXAMPLE Y

Subtract	30	A	15
	20	B	26
	—	C	16
		D	8
		E	none of these

Abstract Reasoning

Select the answer figure that completes the series begun in the Problem Figures.

PROBLEM FIGURES   ANSWER FIGURES

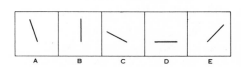

Space Relations

Decide which figure can be made from the pattern at the left.

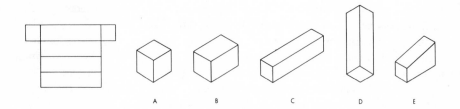

Figure 11.3 (continued)

Mechanical Reasoning

Answer the question about the picture.

This test consists of a number of pictures and questions about those pictures. Look at Example X on this page to see just what to do. Example X shows a picture of two men carrying a machine part on a board and asks, "Which man has the heavier load? If equal, mark C." Man "B" has the heavier load because the weight is closer to him than to man "A," so on the separate Answer Sheet you would fill in the space under B, like this ───→ A B C

Now look at Example Y. The question asks, "Which weighs more? If equal, mark C." As the scale is perfectly balanced, "A" and "B" must weigh the same, so you would blacken the space under C on your separate Answer Sheet, like this → A B C

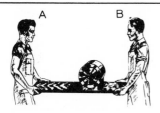

X

Which man has the heavier load?

(If equal, mark C.)

Speed and Accuracy

Mark the blank on the answer sheet corresponding to the underlined combination on the Test Items.

TEST ITEMS				
V. <u>AB</u>	AC	AD	AE	AF
W. aA	aB	BA	Ba	<u>Bb</u>
X. A7	7A	B7	<u>7B</u>	AB
Y. Aa	Ba	<u>bA</u>	BA	bB
Z. 3A	3B	<u>33</u>	B3	BB

SAMPLE OF ANSWER SHEET

	AC	AE	AF	AB	AD
V	:::::	:::::	:::::	▬	.:::::
	BA	Ba	Bb	aA	aB
W	:::::	:::::	▬	:::::	:::::
	7B	B7	AB	7A	A7
X	▬	:::::	:::::	:::::	:::::
	Aa	bA	bB	Ba	BA
Y	:::::	▬	:::::	:::::	:::::
	BB	3B	B3	3A	33
Z	:::::	:::::	::::::	:::::	▬

Language Usage

I. Spelling. Indicate whether the word is spelled correctly or incorrectly.

EXAMPLES

W. man

X. gurl

Y. catt

Z. dog

SAMPLE OF
ANSWER SHEET

	RIGHT	WRONG
W	▮	⁝⁝
X	⁝⁝	▮
Y	⁝⁝	▮
Z	▮	⁝⁝
	RIGHT	WRONG

Figure 11.3 (continued)

II. Grammar. Indicate which part of the sentence contains an error.

EXAMPLE   SAMPLE OF ANSWER SHEET

Ain't we / going to the / office / next week / at all.

A   B   C   D   E

The other five DAT tests are more specific in content and function. There of the tests—Clerical Speed and Accuracy (CSA), Mechanical Reasoning (MR), and Space Relations (SR)—would seem to be most valuable in vocational counseling. CSA is the sole test in the battery placing primary emphasis on speed, measuring speed of performing a simple perceptual task. MR measures comprehension of mechanical and physical principles expressed in familiar situations. SR measures the ability to visualize and mentally manipulate concrete materials. The other two tests, Language Usage I: Spelling, and II: Grammar, are both achievement tests. The authors justify their inclusion in the battery because "they represent basic skills which are necessary in so many academic and vocational pursuits" (Bennett, Seashore & Wesman, 1966, pp. 1–9).

Because of the stress on differential ability, the authors recommend administering the entire battery of eight tests so that the pattern of scores can be considered when counseling the student.

CONSISTENCY.   On a multiaptitude battery such as the DAT, consistency of measurement can be assessed in several ways. Data from various sex and grade (8–12) groups show that the corrected split-half reliabilities of all subtests[6] exceed .85, and that the reliabilities are all over .90 if only students in grades 10–12 are used. No long-term stability data are yet available for the new forms, but data from previous forms showed r's of .58–.87 over the period of three years (from grades 9 to 12), with VR and LU I and II showing the greatest consistency. The equivalent forms reliability of the new forms, L and M, is not reported in the manual; a strange oversight considering the completeness of the consistency, validity, and normative data reported in the manual.

Because the pattern of test scores is the basis of interpretation, the intercorrelations between scores become of paramount importance. The data presented in the manual show (for various samples) that the intercorrelations range from .16–.75, with the largest number falling in .51 and .69 range. The outstanding feature of the data matrix is the low correlation of CSA with the other tests. (Note that it also is the only speeded test in the battery.) Although the test authors conclude, "In general, the coefficients demonstrate that the abilities measured by the separate tests are sufficiently different to warrant the inclusion

[6]As CSA is speeded, equivalent forms reliability coefficients were used instead of split-half estimates.

of all the tests in the series." (Bennett et al., 1966, p. 7-1), hard-nosed psychometricians may arrive at a different conclusion after scrutinizing the same data.

VALIDITY. An abundance of validity data is available for the DAT, approximately 60 pages in the test manual being devoted to it. The bulk of the data presented involves prediction of grades in specific high school courses. Although any attempt to summarize these data will necessarily involve oversimplification, several trends are apparent: (1) Grades in the common high school courses are best predicted by three of the eight tests—VR, NA, and Grammar—and by the VR + NA composite. (2) VR + NA is usually the best predictor of grades. In the core areas—English, Mathematics, Science, Social Studies, History, and Languages—the median validity coefficients generally are in the .50s. (3) By and large, grades in courses are best predicted by the corresponding test. For example, the VR and Grammar tests are the best single predictors of English grades, NA is the best predictor of mathematics grades, and Grammar is the best predictor of success in language courses. (4) In less academic courses, such as art and industrial arts, there is some, but far from overwhelming, support for the differential validity of the DAT tests. (5) When results are considered school-by-school, there is a wide range of validity coefficients. For example, the validity of the VR + NA composite ranged from .18 to .86 when predicting English grades and from .00 to .78 when predicting mathematics grades in various schools. These data illustrate the situation-specific nature of validity data and reinforce the need for evaluating the validity of a test in each specific situation. (6) Finally, the validity coefficients are slightly higher for girls than for boys, a trend that has been observed in a variety of situations (Seashore, 1962).

Other types of validity data are less prevalent. Some data are presented which show that prediction of eleventh-grade course grades from eighth-grade DAT scores was only slightly less accurate than the accuracy of predicting eighth-grade grades from the same DAT scores. Evidence is also presented showing that DAT scores are highly correlated (frequently as high as .70–.80) with scores on achievement test batteries administered either concurrently with or after the DAT. Note, however, that these correlations are with achievement test scores, not with amount learned; there is no direct evidence that DAT scores predict learning. Finally, several large scale follow-up studies indicate that students who obtain different amounts of post-high school education and/or enter different occupations can be discriminated on the basis of their (high school) DAT scores; however, the difference appears to be as much a function of the level of DAT scores as the pattern of scores.

SCORE INTERPRETATION. In many ways, the DAT procedures are a model for the interpretation of test scores. Normative data are presented for large representative samples of high school students, separate norm tables being available for each grade and sex grouping. On CSA, a highly speeded test, there are even separate norms, depending on what type of answer sheets were utilized. Raw scores are translated into percentile ranges to emphasize the fact that each score contains some measurement error and caution the user against overinterpretation. Normal percentile charts are used to present the test scores graphically. Furthermore, these profiles are printed so that a difference of one inch between two subtest scores represents a significant difference in scores, again simplifying the interpretation process. Finally, the test authors stress the value of collecting local validiy data and suggest use of expectancy tables to present normative-validity data.

EVALUATION.   The DAT is a well-constructed test of abilities that predict academic success and which counselors feel have significance for vocational and educational guidance. The test construction process illustrates a blending and balancing of practical and theoretical concerns. Administration and scoring procedures are simple and straightforward, and reliability estimates are adequate. Validity data are abundant and, although most of it concerns prediction of academic grades, it is in this area that the test will find greatest use. Normative and interpretive data are very good.

Only one concern clouds the picture. The DAT is a multiaptitude battery and the justification for such batteries is that the component tests will measure independent traits and will be differential predictive. Neither of these facets has been firmly established by the available data. Thus, although the DAT is a well-constructed battery and a good general predictor, it (like other multiaptitude batteries) does not live up to its promise as a differential predictor.

Other multiaptitude batteries

In many ways the DAT typifies the approach to and problems encountered in development of a multiaptitude battery. However, there are several other batteries which, because of their special features, deserve at least brief mention. These include the SRA[7] Primary Mental Abilities (PMA), the Flanagan Aptitude Classification Tests (FACT), and the General Aptitude Test Battery (GATB). The reader who desires more information on these or other multiaptitude batteries should consult Buros, 1965; Super, 1958; or Super and Crites, 1962.

SRA PRIMARY MENTAL ABILITIES.   The PMA is important historically as it developed directly out of Thurstone's pioneering research on the factorial structure of abilities and was the first multifactor battery. Thurstone spent several decades attempting to understand the nature and structure of abilities,

---

[7]SRA stands for the name of a particular test publisher, Science Research Associates.

using the same general method in most studies: administer a large number of tests (often 50 or more) to a large number of subjects, compute the intercorrelation between each pair of tests, and factor analyze. He interpreted his results as indicating that a small number of "primary" factors (see p. 221) accounted for a large proportion of variability in performance, regardless of the age or ability level of the subjects.

Based on this research, Thurstone developed a series of test batteries. The current revision of the series includes five levels covering the kindergarten through high school range. Each level includes tests of four or five primary abilities. The reviews of the PMA (e.g., Super, 1958) have often been quite critical, citing the battery's technical inadequacies in several areas. Perhaps the lesson to be drawn from the PMA is that results of basic research cannot be routinely translated into a workable test; there are problems of consistency, validity, and normative data to be overcome. Or, as Super has more picturesquely phrased it, "The pioneer who blazes the trail and builds the first log cabin does not necessarily build a good house for the city that later develops around the site of his cabin" (Super, 1958, p. 90).

FLANAGAN APTITUDE CLASSIFICATION TESTS. Both the DAT and PMA were designed for school-aged children and emphasize those abilities that underlie academic performance. The FACT, in contrast, was explicitly designed to tap abilities that are important in successful occupational performance. Systematic job analyses were conducted to identify elements common to a number of jobs and related to successful job performance. Tests were then constructed to measure 21 job elements, using content that was directly relevant to the occupational world. For example, the *Inspection* test requires the subject to compare pictures of small parts and identify ones having imperfections. (See Figure 11.4.) Note that the skill tested, the rapid and accurate perception of details, is also tested on the DAT and the PMA, but the test content is now vocational. Or, to use another example, the *Assembly* test consists of a picture of a number of disassembled parts followed by a series of pictures of completed parts; the subject's task is to choose the completed object which can be made from the disassembled parts. On other tests in the battery (e.g., Arithmetic, Vocabulary) the content is not specifically vocational. The critical questions concerning the FACT are, however: (1) Does the use of vocationally relevant materials produce a more valid battery? and (2) Do the tests show differential validity? Although the rationale of the test and the author's experience lend credence to the test's claims for validity, until more empirical data are available one must return a Scottish verdict—"not proven."

THE GENERAL APTITUDE TEST BATTERY. In contrast to the multiaptitude batteries discussed previously, the GATB, which was developed by the U.S. Employment Service (USES) for use by employment counselors in State Em-

A. Inspection

Task is to identify parts having flaws — that is, ones that do not match first part in row.

SAMPLE PROBLEMS

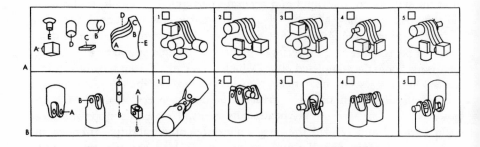

B. Assembly

Task is to indicate which completed part can be made by assembling component parts.

PRACTICE PROBLEMS

Figure 11.4 Examples of items on FACT inspection and assembly tests. Sample and practice items from Inspections and Assembly sections of FACT, copyright 1953, John C. Flanagan. Reprinted by permission of the publisher, Science Research Associates, Inc.

ployment Service offices, includes several performance measures. Two of the nine factors measured by the test—Finger Dexterity and Manual Dexterity—utilize performance tests; the other seven factors (Intelligence, Verbal Aptitude, Numerical Aptitude, Spatial Aptitude, Form Perception, Clerical Perception, and Motor Coordination) use the conventional paper-and-pencil format.

The GATB has several distinctive features besides utilization of performance measures. For one, it is designed for use with job applicants as a basis for job placement and referral. Also, an extensive program of research, including longitudinal studies, is being carried out by the USES to increase the pool of validity and interpretive data. The paradigm used in the majority of these studies involves identifying the aptitudes needed to perform a given occupation and establishing the minimum scores on tests of these critical aptitudes needed for successful job performance. This approach implies the use of a multiple cutoff strategy for selection and validation; an approach that some testing experts feel to be less desirable than a multiple regression strategy (cf. Chapter 8).

Evaluation of multiaptitude batteries

Multiaptitude tests, like any other class of tests, vary widely among themselves; thus any overall evaluation will be subject to numerous qualifications. However, consideration of several fundamental questions can serve to put the tests in perspective. First, are multiaptitude tests based on any explicit rationale? Multiaptitude tests derive from a specific theory—that human performance can be described by a relatively small number of basic abilities. Many of the tests are based on a further assumption: that the appropriate strategy for identifying these fundamental traits is factor analysis. Thus multiaptitude tests are based on a specific defined rationale. Two, are the desired technical standards of test construction attained? Although there are wide differences among the tests, it is clear that highly adequate levels of consistency and sufficient normative data can be obtained (see, e.g., the DAT). Third, do the multiaptitude tests cover a wide range of abilities? Although the batteries discussed covered from four to twenty-odd abilities, their coverage was generally limited to academically related abilities that could be tested by a paper-and-pencil format. One might hope for broader coverage of skills and more ingenious formats.

Fourth, do the tests measure "pure" factors? Because some of the most important abilities may be factorially complex and abilities tend to correlate positively within the population, the test constructor may be faced with a choice between measuring pure, and possibly trivial, factors and measuring less pure, more complex, and more meaningful factors. Most test constructors have opted for the latter alternative. Finally, do the tests demonstrate differential validity? In many ways this is the central issue; yet it is here that support for the multiaptitude approach is the weakest. While the empirical evidence shows that single tests within multiaptitude batteries, or combinations of tests, can predict specific academic outcomes, there is little strong evidence that the tests are differential predictive—either in terms of different tests predicting different criteria or of increasing predictive efficiency by using profiles of scores. The validity of multiaptitude tests in predicting vocational criteria is less well established. In short, multiaptitude tests, even when well constructed and when technically sound, have not demonstrated their ability to accomplish their stated goal—that of being differential predictive.

MEASURES OF SPECIAL ABILITIES

General intelligence tests and multiaptitude batteries both attempt comprehensive measurement—the general intelligence test by providing an estimate of an individual's overall level of intellectual performance, and the multiple aptitude battery by assessing performance on the basic intellectual abilities. In this section we will discuss several classes of tests that are more limited in purpose or scope.

Scholastic aptitude tests

Scholastic aptitude tests, as their name implies, are designed to predict performance in academic situations. They differ from general intelligence measures primarily by having a more limited focus, that of predicting academic performance. However, both general intelligence tests and multiaptitude batteries predict academic success, and as basic intellectual skills are important determiners of success in most educational settings, it would be surprising if the content of scholastic aptitude tests differed markedly from that of general intelligence and multiaptitude tests. And, in fact, they are so similar that even an expert would have difficulty categorizing many tests as being either general intelligence measures or scholastic aptitude tests. Yet because of their distinctive features, scholastic aptitude tests can be considered separately from general intelligence tests.

BASIC FEATURES. The fact that scholastic aptitude tests are designed to predict academic accomplishment has several important implications. First, validity will be determined by how well the test predicts relevant academic criteria. That is, the relevant model for evaluation is criterion-related validity; content and construct validity are essentially irrelevant. The emphasis on criterion-related validity leads to the second implication: the content of a scholastic aptitude test is unlimited, and any content which predicts scholastic performance is acceptable. Thus critics who argue against the use of multiple-choice items on scholastic aptitude tests are missing the point. If multiple-choice items predict academic performance (as in fact they do) then they are proper items for inclusion on a scholastic aptitude test. This is not to say, however, that the criteria of academic success against which the tests are validated are without weaknesses, but this is another question. The standard of effectiveness of the test is how well it predicts the stipulated criterion, no more and no less.

What, then, are the criteria that are used to validate scholastic aptitude tests? The most obvious and widely used are grades—in specific courses or grade averages. But other criteria are also possible, e.g., scores on achievement tests, teachers' ratings, completion of an education program, prizes or awards won, or rate of learning. For various reasons, however, validation studies have generally utilized obvious criteria such as grades. Consequently the tests often predict a particular type of educational accomplishment, grade-getting ability.

Although the content of scholastic aptitude tests is basically unlimited, in point of fact content is generally quite standardized, with only a few item types appearing with any regularity. Among the most widely used item types are: vocabulary or a variation such as analogies or sentence completion (selecting the proper word to complete a sentence); reading comprehension (where the student reads a paragraph and then answers questions based upon the information contained in the paragraph); numerical ability, tested through straight computation and/or word problems; tests of abstract reasoning (such as number series problems or nonverbal analogies); general information items; and tests of tool skills such as use of the dictionary, map reading, and the interpretation of tables and graphs. The exact content will, of course, vary with the age level of the students. For example, in the primary grades, before children have acquired any fluency in reading, vocabulary will be tested by picture vocabulary items, but at older ages more complex item forms, such as analogies, can be introduced. Similarly, items measuring skill in using the dictionary and reading simple maps may be included at the elementary level, while at the high school and college levels students will be required to interpret complex tables and graphs.

Because the educational system is cumulative, with present and future learning being based on past learning, and since past performance is the best predictor of future performance, it would be surprising if scholastic aptitude tests were not heavily loaded with material based on previous school learnings. And they are. However, to avoid being too closely tied to specific learnings and educational experiences, the tests concentrate on skills and materials which are widely taught, and which transfer to a wide variety of situations. Furthermore, whenever possible items are constructed so that the student must apply his repertoire of knowledge and skills to new situations. Specific information, if needed, is provided in the item content. For example, a reading comprehension item, even though it covers a topic new to the student, can test his ability to extract salient features from what he has read. Or a graph interpretation item, though presenting a student with data he has never previously encountered, can test his ability to interpret graphs. Previous learning may thus play a role in test performance by influencing problem-solving strategy as well as being reflected in knowledge of specific factual material.

Because the specific content must vary from grade level to grade level, most standardized scholastic aptitude tests are part of a series consisting of separate tests at various age levels. The pragmatic problem is to decide how many age levels to include, where to divide the levels, and what sort of articulation must occur between age levels. The age-level problem is also reflected in the norms; the test constructor must obtain representative samples of students at each grade level. Because each level of the test will be used in several adjacent grades and periodic testing will probably occur, provision of equivalent forms at each level is highly desirable.

Finally, scholastic aptitude tests will be power tests. On a power test, you will recall, the test taker has sufficient time to attempt a series of items which are arranged in order of increasing difficulty. Scores thus reflect the complexity or difficulty of the items the student can correctly answer. Since the important dimension of academic performance is the complexity of the material that can be mastered, rather than speed of responding, validity will be higher when a power test is used as a predictor.

EXAMPLES. The preceding paragraphs, plus the discussion of general intelligence tests, should give the reader a good idea of the format and content of scholastic aptitude tests. Rather than single out a particular test for detailed comment, we will indicate (see list below) only the characteristics, levels, and content of a number of the widely used scholastic aptitude tests and illustrate (in Figure 11.5) some of the variety of items that appear on these tests. If the reader would check the manuals of these tests he would find, by and large, that the tests are valid predictors of academic criteria, that directions and administration procedures are well specified, that scoring is objective, that the tests are quite reliable (frequently $r \geq .90$ within a given grade), and that normative data based on a large and quite representative samples are provided. In short, a number of good scholastic aptitude tests are available. The user's choice between available batteries will thus usually be based on the appropriateness of a given test in his particular situation and practical considerations such as length, availability of scoring services, and cost.

Academic Promise Tests (Psychological Corporation).
Grades 6–9.
Scores or sections: Verbal, Nonverbal, Total (V + NV).
Similar to 4 sections (VR, NR, AR, LU) of DAT.

California Test of Mental Maturity (California Test Bureau).
Kindergarten–college/adult; eight levels; both long ($1\frac{1}{2}$ hours) and short (40 min) forms available. Patterned after Stanford-Binet (see text).
Scores or sections: Language, Nonlanguage, Total (L + NL).

Differential Aptitude Tests (Psychological Corporation).
  Grades 8–12, adult; one level.
  Scores or sections: eight tests (see text).

Henmon-Nelson Tests of Mental Ability (Houghton-Mifflin Company).
  Grade 3–college graduate; four levels.
  Scores or sections: Verbal, Quantitative, Total (V + Q).
  Items arranged in omnibus-cycle form by difficulty.

Kuhlmann-Anderson Measure of Academic Potential (Psychological Corporation).
  Kindergarten–college freshman; eight levels.
  Scores or sections: Verbal (grades 7–13), Quantitative (7–13), Total (all levels).
  Overlapping levels for grades 3 up.

Lorge-Thorndike Intelligence Tests (Houghton-Mifflin Company).
  Kindergarten–college freshman; six levels.
  Scores or sections: Verbal (4–13), Nonverbal (all levels).

Ohio State University Psychological Test (Wilbur L. Layton).
  Grade 9–college freshman; one level; untimed.
  Scores or sections: Vocabulary, Analogies, Reading Comprehension.
  Heavy verbal emphasis; short form (Minnesota Scholastic Aptitude Test) has been developed.

Otis-Lennon Mental Ability Test (Harcourt, Brace & World).
  Kindergarten–college freshman; six levels.
  Scores or sections: Total.

School and College Ability Tests (Cooperative Test Division, ETS).
  Grade 4–college sophomore; four levels.
  Scores or sections: Verbal, Mathematical, Total (V + M).
  Series II; Series I (grade 4–college senior) still available; several forms restricted circulation for use in college admissions.

Tests of Educational Ability (Science Research Associates, Inc.)
  Grades 4–12; three levels.
  Scores or sections: Language Skills, Reasoning Skills, Quantitative Skills.

Short Tests of Educational Ability.
  Kindergarten–grade 12; five levels.
  Scores or sections: vary with level, 3–4 per level.
  K–3 pictorial materials only.

American College Testing Program (ACT).
  College admissions; one level.
  Scores or sections: English Usage, Mathematics Usage, Social Studies

Reading, Natural Sciences Reading, Composite.
Emphasis on developed skills.

Scholastic Aptitude Test (College Entrance Examination Board).
College admissions; one level.
Scores or sections: Verbal, Mathematics.
A preliminary *SAT* available for practice; also achievement tests.

ETS Special Aptitude Exams (ETS).
Admissions.
Scores or sections: vary.
Various tests—not one battery, e.g., Secondary School Admissions Test, Test of English as a Foreign Language, Graduate Record Examinations, Admissions Test for Graduate Study in Business, Law School Admissions Test, National Teachers Examination.

COLLEGE ADMISSIONS TESTS.   One particular type of scholastic aptitude test, the college admissions test, has been the center of so much attention and debate in both the popular press and professional literature (see, e.g., Black, 1963; Hoffman, 1962; Lavin, 1965) that it is worthy of special comment. These tests—of which there are two major national batteries, the College Entrance Examination Board's Scholastic Aptitude Test (SAT) and the American College Testing Program battery (ACT)—are designed to aid college and university admissions officers in evaluating the qualifications (i.e., probability of academic success) of applicants for admission.

Although the ACT and SAT are both college admissions tests, they differ in both content and format. The ACT battery is composed of four tests (English Usage, Mathematics Usage, Social Studies Reading, and Natural Science Reading), each of which provides a score. In addition, the average of the four test scores is reported as a composite score. The tests in the ACT battery are achievement oriented, emphasizing the ability to apply developed skills. For example, the Social Studies and Natural Sciences tests place primary emphasis on the ability to interpret reading paragraphs, and the English items are all in the context of a reading selection.

The College Board program, in contrast, makes a clearer separation between its aptitude and achievement tests. The SAT is the measure of scholastic aptitude and provides two scores: a Verbal score and a Mathematical score. No composite score is obtained. As with the ACT, all items are in a multiple-choice format. The Verbal section consists of antonym, sentence completion, analogy, reading comprehension, and general understanding (information) items; the Mathematical section includes word and computational problems in algebra, geometry and basic arithmetic processes, the interpretation of graphs and charts, and logical reasoning items. In addition to the SAT, a series of hour-long achievement tests covering various subjects, and in some areas levels within subjects,

Figure 11.5 Examples of scholastic aptitude test items.

A. Items from elementary level test

1. Identify the picture that is not like the other three.

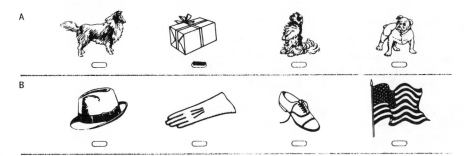

2. Select the picture that is related to the third picture in the same way that the second is related to the first. (Picture Analogies)

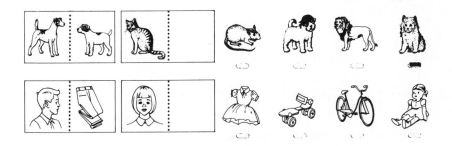

3. Picture vocabulary. Identify object teacher refers to — e.g., "Mark the thing we drink from." "Find the picture that shows two boys running."

Figure 11.5 (continued)

B. Sample items from a junior high level test

Practice Examples

*Sample
Answer Spaces*

Eye is to **see** as **ear** is to –

   head   hear   talk   nose   cheek

The right answer is choice **b** "hear" so a mark
has been made in the answer space under **b** in
answer row **X** of the Sample Answer Spaces.

X   a b c d e   ○ ● ○ ○ ○

A boy bought 3 pencils at 5¢ each. How much did
the 3 pencils cost?

   5¢   10¢   20¢   25¢   none of these

The right answer, of course, is 15¢. Since this
answer is not given, choice **k** "none of these" is
correct. See how the answer space under **k** in
row **Y** has been marked.

Y   f g h j k   ○ ○ ○ ○ ●

○ is to ○   as   ☐ is to –

 ☐   ☐   ○   ○   ▭

Z   a b c d e   ● ○ ○ ○ ○

The right answer is choice **a** so the answer space
under **a** in row **Z** has been marked.

C. Sample items from a college admissions test

Verbal: Sentence completion and analogies

23. The Indo-European group of languages is a relatively junior member
of the Old World linguistic family, evolving at a time when such
languages as Sumerian and those in the Hamitic and Semitic groups
were of respectable ------.

   (A) origin
   (B) antiquity
   (C) usage
   (D) size
   (E) fluency

24. Though he was romantic and sensual in his aesthetic philosophy, his
life was one of ------.

   (A) disillusionment
   (B) abandonment
   (C) creativity
   (D) naïveté
   (E) austerity

Figure 11.5 (continued)

25. Plato's insistence on the all-pervading domination of the state, exaggerated though it be, is exaggerated on the actual lines of Greek practice, and ------ the ------ between their point of view and our idea of individual dignity.

    (A) evades . . inconsistency
    (B) prevents . . relationship
    (C) minimizes . . incongruity
    (D) indicates . . antithesis
    (E) resolves . . dispute

    In each of the following questions, a related pair of words or phrases is followed by five lettered pairs of words or phrases. Select the lettered pair which best expresses a relationship similar to that expressed in the original pair.

26. KNIFE:INCISION :: (A) bulldozer:excavation   (B) tool:operation
    (C) pencil:calculation   (D) hose:irrigation   (E) plow:agriculture

27. TORCH:LIBERTY :: (A) tray:waiter   (B) scales:justice
    (C) candle:poverty   (D) bars:punishment   (E) lever:power

28. ADVERTISEMENT:PURCHASE :: (A) defense:conquest
    (B) attitude:conviction   (C) electioneering:vote
    (D) offer:force   (E) attempt:achievement

29. UNIFY:ONE :: (A) qualify:numerous   (B) nullify:invalid
    (C) simplify:valuable   (D) multiply:positive   (E) identify:anonymous

30. TESTIMONY:OATH :: (A) future:prediction
    (B) advertisement:quality   (C) decision:judgment
    (D) product:guarantee   (E) confidence:promise

Verbal: Reading comprehension

     The essential trick of the Renaissance pastoral poem, which was felt to imply a beautiful relation between rich and poor, was to make simple people express strong feelings in learned and fashionable language. From seeing elements of the two sorts of people combined
(5) like this the reader thought better of both; the best parts of each were used. The effect was in some degree to combine in the reader or the author the merits of the two sorts; he was made to mirror in himself more completely the effective elements of the society in which he lived. This was not a process that had to be explained in the course
(10) of writing pastoral poems; it was already shown in the clash between style and subject, and to make the clash work in the right way the writer had to keep up a firm pretense that he was unconscious of it.
     The usual process for putting further meanings into the pastoral situation was to insist that the shepherds were rulers of sheep and

Figure 11.5 (continued)

(15) so compare them to politicians or bishops or what not; this piled the heroic convention onto the pastoral one since the hero was another symbol of his whole society. Such a pretense, no doubt, made the characters unreal, but not the feelings expressed or even the situation (as opposed to the setting) described. The same pretense is often valuable in modern writing.

53. Which of the following is LEAST likely to be found in a Renaissance pastoral?

   (A) Serious intent
   (B) The heroic convention
   (C) Symbolism
   (D) Elegance of expression
   (E) Accurate depiction of social structures

54. In lines 17-19 the author finds it necessary to oppose the situation to the setting because

   (A) in pastoral poetry a possibly real situation is conveyed by unreal characters in unreal scenes
   (B) setting and situation are natural opposites
   (C) the addition of the heroic convention makes the pastoral setting an absurd situation
   (D) situation and setting are the same in modern writing
   (E) in pastoral poetry the pretense makes the setting even more real than the situation

55. The author would say that of the following the LEAST artificial element in pastoral poetry is the

   (A) heroic convention
   (B) characterization
   (C) level of language
   (D) underlying emotion
   (E) pastoral convention

Mathematical

79. If $x(x - y) = 0$, which of the following is a correct conclusion?

   (A) $x = 0$ (B) Either $x = 0$ or $x = y$
   (C) $x = y$ (D) $x^2 = y$ (E) Both $x = 0$ and $x - y = 0$

80. The area of one circle is nine times that of another. The circumference of the larger circle is how many times that of the smaller?

   (A) 3   (B) $4\frac{1}{2}$ (C) 6   (D) 9   (E) 18

81. A number n equals $\frac{3}{2}$ the average of the three numbers 7, 9, and t. What is t in terms of n?

   (A) $\frac{2n}{3} - 16$ (B) $\frac{4n}{3} - 16$ (C) $2n - 16$

   (D) $\frac{9n}{2} - 16$ (E) $\frac{n}{2} + 8$

Figure 11.5 (continued)

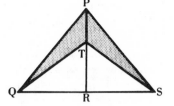

82. Triangle QTS above has base QS of 15 inches. If altitude RT is extended 4 inches to P, what is the area of QTSP?

    (A) 30 sq. in   (B) 60 sq. in.   (C) 90 sq. in.   (D) 120 sq. in.
    (E) 150 sq. in.

83. What is the average of the first 25 positive whole numbers?

    (A) 12   (B) 12.5   (C) 13   (D) 13.5   (E) 26

84. The houses on the east side of a street are numbered with the consecutive even integers from 256 to 834, inclusive. How many houses are there on the east side of the street?

    (A) 287   (B) 288   (C) 289   (D) 290   (E) 291

Items in part C reprinted with permission from the College Entrance Examination Board, New York, from *A Description of the College Board Scholastic Aptitude Test, 1967.*

is available in CEEB series. The student selects and takes two or three of the achievement tests.

One criticism of college admissions tests concerns the duplication of effort involved when students have to take both the ACT and the SAT because of different requirements of colleges. Why, many people ask, cannot one test be substituted for the other? Or, phrasing this question in more technical terms, can scores on the ACT and the SAT be equated? While it is possible, of course, to equate scores on the ACT and SAT statistically, doing so will provide only comparable scores; the two tests cannot be considered equivalent because they cover different content areas. And, because they measure different content areas (and probably vary in difficulty) one or the other of the tests may be more appropriate for a given college or university.

A second criticism states that many important abilities are not tapped because of the multiple-choice format. This is no doubt true, but neither thoughtful psychologists nor test publishers claim that the tests measure all the important abilities; rather they stress that test scores should be used only in conjunction with other evidence —e.g., grades, teachers' recommendations, evidence of special skills and abilities—when making decisions about students. A related criticism holds that opportunities for high education are too dependent on scoring well on college admissions tests, since colleges place undue emphasis on test scores. Individual schools vary widely in the reliance they place on tests from (1) allowing test scores to determine admissions to (2) virtually ignoring test scores. However, we would again emphasize that if test use is based on the results of validity studies, undue reliance on test scores (or, for that matter, any other piece of information) will be minimized.

Finally, college admissions tests have been said to be unfair to persons from atypical, disadvantaged, and culturally limited backgrounds. Although individuals from these groups may, in fact, be penalized, the available data indicate that the tests predict as well for minority group students as for middle-class students. However, these results may reflect the fact that minority group students suffer the same handicaps in the college situations as they do on the test. That is, because the same skills and abilities are needed for successful performance in college as are needed to obtain a high score on the test, the tests (although possibly biased) still predict success.

EVALUATION.   It may seem nitpicking to consider scholastic aptitude tests as distinct from group tests of intelligence. But because intelligence tests and scholastic aptitude tests are based on different philosophies (i.e., the measurement of a general human trait versus prediction of academic success), rely on different types of validation (i.e., construct versus criterion-related validity) and utilize different norm groups (i.e., general population versus college freshmen), they can be separated in theory, if not in fact. The main criticism leveled at scholastic aptitudes tests is that they do not cover all the relevant educational skills and thus predict only a limited range of educational outcomes. This criticism cannot be denied, but since the tests are designed to predict academic criteria, limitations of the test reflect shortcomings in criteria and point up the need for developing alternative criteria.

Creativity

An area of intense current interest is creativity (see, e.g., Getzels & Jackson, 1962; Barron 1963; MacKinnon, 1962; Taylor & Barron, 1963; Torrance, 1962; and Guilford, 1967). Some of the interest has been generated because of the importance of creativity in certain occupations (e.g., artists, research scientists), other interest has been directed toward the study of creativity as a basic intellectual ability, and yet other interest toward creativity as a problem-solving method. Research strategy has been of two general types: some studies have concentrated on the personal characteristics and background experiences that typify creative persons, while others have attempted to directly study the creative process.

Defining the construct of "creativity" or "creative behavior" is an exercise in convergent and discriminant validity. Not only must the various skills and functions that are proposed as manifestations of creativity be intercorrelated (convergent validity), but they also must be distinct from other abilities, particularly intelligence (discriminant validity). There is general agreement that in order for a behavior to be indicative of creativity or a test classed as a measure of creativity, responses must be produced rather than selected from among available alternatives. Operationally, the subject is required to think divergently or produce a number of responses to a specified stimulus situation; for example, he might be asked to indicate all the possible uses of a brick. A second essential element of creative behavior is that the responses produced be, in some sense, original.[8] Although some writers appear to accept all original responses as being of equal value, most writers insist that some limitation in regard to relevance be placed on responses to eliminate obviously absurd responses. There is also some disagreement as to the role personality and motivational variables should play in the definition. As a working definition to guide test construction, creativity is viewed as the ability to think divergently, to produce a large number and variety of original (but not irrational) responses to a stipulated stimulus situation.

TESTS OF CREATIVITY.   The search for characteristics that identify creative persons and pleas for identification and training of creative talent have far outstripped the development of tests for measuring creativity. However, several tests have been developed and, in addition, parts of established tests (e.g., Word Fluency measures) are sometimes considered to be indices of creativity. Some of the tests developed from Guilford's structure of the intellect model, particularly those that measure aspects of divergent thinking, can be classed as tests of creativity. Examples include Guilford's tests of

Word Fluency: rapid listing of words containing a given letter
Ideational Fluency: naming things or objects that belong in the same class
Associational Fluency: producing synonyms
Alternative Uses: listing possible uses for an object, other than its normal uses
Consequences: listing the various possible consequences of a given act

Note that these tests all require verbal responses. Other tests in the model require *figural* responses, for example,

Making Objects: drawing objects utilizing a specified set of stimulus designs;

while others, though requiring pictorial responses, are primarily conceptual tasks, for example,

Match Problems: based on an illustrated design made of matchsticks, the subject must remove a certain number of matchsticks to produce a new design.

Each of these tests measure a specific cell in Guilford's model and, although sharing class membership along certain dimensions, are thus essentially independent abilities.

[8]Barron has noted that a response can be original in at least two ways: (a) it can be original in a normative sense, not occuring frequently under usual circumstances or (b) it may be original to an individual, occurring for the first time in his experience. Creativity tests are concerned with the former variety of originality.

In contrast to Guilford's tests, which were an outgrowth of a research program, Torrance has developed creativity tests in an educational context. As a consequence, the tests measure creativity as it might be complexly expressed in a natural setting (a school) rather than emphasizing factorial purity. Nevertheless, there is a high degree of similarity between the two tests.

The *Torrance Tests of Creative Thinking* consists of ten subtests divided into two major sections, are structured as games or activities rather than as tests, and are presumed to be applicable from kindergarten through graduate school, although certain modifications have to be made for younger children, e.g., individual administration below the fourth-grade level. *Thinking Creatively with Words* consists of seven activities. The first three are based on a single sketch, the subject's task being to list the questions he would ask to find out what is happening in the picture, guess the possible causes of the action in the sketch, and guess the possible consequences of the action pictured. Other activities require suggesting improvements for a toy, suggesting unusual uses for a common object, asking questions about the same common object, and guessing the consequences of a stipulated improbable action. All tests are speeded and scoring is on three dimensions: fluency (number of relevant responses), flexibility (variety of response classes), and originality. *Thinking Creatively with Pictures* consists of three tests: a Picture Construction activity which requires the subject to utilize a colored shape in constructing an original picture, a Picture Completion test which requires the subject to sketch objects using pairs of specified irregular lines, and a test where the subject constructs designs, either from pairs of parallel lines or circles, depending on the form of the test used. The Figural tests are scored on the basis of fluency, flexibility, originality, and elaboration.

EVALUATION. Certain problems are apparent on creativity tests. For example, both the Torrance and Guilford tests place a premium on speed of production. Scoring, of course, cannot be completely objective: however, data show that the use of trained scorers and a scoring manual can produce acceptable levels of scorer reliability. Still, the reliability of most creativity tests are lower than desirable, especially if individual scores are to be reported. Normative data are generally quite limited. Guilford's procedures, of course, insure that his tests will have both factorial and discriminant validity. However, as he has worked primarily within his model, correlations with other tests and socially relevant criteria are generally lacking. The Torrance tests, in contrast, have been related to a variety of criteria but the research has lacked the systematic nature of Guilford's. Consequently, no clear pattern of validity results has emerged.

A question concerning creativity that is not restricted to any one test involves the relationship between creativity and intelligence. Many people have been led to believe that intelligence and creativity are unrelated. What, in fact, seems to obtain is that creativity and intelligence are positively correlated in the general population; however, within a given intelligence range, intelligence as traditionally measured and creativity are essentially uncorrelated. Furthermore, studies have shown that within a given intelligence range, students who score relatively high on creativity measures but lower on intelligence tests perform as well on many academic tasks as individuals who score high on intelligence tests and lower on creativity. In certain situations the high creativity groups excel; in others, the high intelligence groups excel. These studies show not that intelligence and creativity are uncorrelated (as they have sometimes been interpreted), but that the same performance can be attained *by utilizing different abilities*—a not unsurprising result.

Culture-fair tests

The problem of cultural influences on test performance has been studied for many years. Originally, investigators attempted to develop tests that would eliminate all effects of culture and presumably measure the individual's inherent abilities and personality traits. However, it soon became apparent that because the cultural environment operates upon an individual and interacts with hereditary factors from the moment of birth (or even before), any attempt to develop a *culture-free* test was doomed to failure. Consequently, the emphasis in test construction has shifted to the development of *culture-fair tests*, i.e., those which, while not eliminating cultural effects, attempt to control certain critical variables, thus making the test equally fair to all persons.

To accomplish this end, procedures must be developed to control the influence of parameters which are important determiners of test performance but vary widely between cultures.[9] An obvious example is language. Not only would a test written in one language be inappropriate for a person who does not speak that language fluently; but also words and phrasing have different connotations in different cultures. Therefore a direct translation of a test from one language to another will not necessarily produce comparable tests. Another important dimension is speed. In our culture, responding rapidly is stressed, and thus most persons will attempt to complete a test within the time limits. In other cultures, and indeed within certain American subcultures, speed of performance is not highly valued. Use of a speeded test with these groups would produce ambiguous results. A third relevant facet is the role of competitiveness and the motivation to do one's best. In this country most children and adults attempt to do their best (i.e., have maximal performance motivation) even without explicit directions to do so. Yet, in cultures or subcultures where competition is not stressed, one cannot expect the test taker to have similar motivation. A fourth

[9]These statements could equally well be applied to characteristics that vary between subcultures within a given population. For convenience we will use only the term cultural differences; the reader should keep in mind that we are referring to cultural and/or subcultural differences.

dimension of concern is the relative emphasis given to different content areas in different cultures. Even if several subjects are taught in various cultures, it cannot be assumed that they are given the same relative emphasis or have the same importance in all cultures.

VALIDATION STRATEGIES. Regardless of the approach used in constructing a culture-fair test, its effectiveness will be determined by accumulating validity evidence. That is, unless it can be demonstrated that the test is fair and equally valid for various cultural groups, it cannot be said to have attained its purpose.

One possible strategy is implicit in the ordinary use of tests: develop, use, and validate the test in one culture. Unless the test happens to be applied to a different cultural group, no problems arise. If a test is needed to do a similar job in a different culture, a new test is constructed within that culture, perhaps, but not necessarily, being guided by the original test. Such a strategy obviously sidesteps the basic issue.

A second possible strategy is to develop a test in one culture and then validate it in other cultures. If the test proves valid in a variety of situations in a variety of cultures, it can be considered a culture-fair measure. To expect a test to be valid in all cultures is undoubtedly expecting too much; yet some generalizability across cultures is necessary. This strategy has frequently been applied. For example, many tests have been translated into foreign languages and used in foreign countries (see, e.g., Lonner, 1968). Needless to say, tests are usually more valid in the culture they were developed in than in other cultures where they happen to be applied.

One disadvantage of this second approach is that it does not, in any explicit manner, consider the impact of culture-related variables during the test construction process. A third strategy focuses on the item selection process by first identifying skills and content areas common to many cultures and including on the test only items that measure these universal elements. The effectiveness of the test construction procedure is subsequently checked by validation studies in a variety of cultures. The fundamental step in this procedure is the identification of skills and relationships which are common to a number of cultures. This requirement restricts the pool of potential items to certain classes of stimuli, e.g., characteristics of human beings and nonverbal tasks such as relationships between geometric objects and designs. But even these items may be heavily culturally loaded.

EXAMPLES OF CULTURE-FAIR TESTS. Variations on the Goodenough Draw-a-Man Test, a widely used measure of children's intelligence, have frequently been used in cross-cultural studies. As the task is straightforward, drawing a figure of a man (or woman), and involves content and skills which seem to be universal, the test would seem to be quite appropriate for cross-cultural studies. Yet data from cross-cultural studies show that scores on the test vary between cultural groups with higher scores occurring in cultures stressing skill in representational art.

Other tests that have been used in cross-cultural studies (e.g., Cattell's Culture-Fair Intelligence Test, the Leiter International Performance Scale, and Raven's Progressive Matrices) emphasize abstract reasoning, primarily through items which measure relationships among geometric and other nonverbal stimuli. For example, Raven's *Progressive Matrices Test*, which was designed to measure Spearman's *g* factor, consists of a matrices of varying degrees of difficulty from which one section has been removed (see Figure 11.6). The test taker must choose, from among 6–8 alternatives, the element that completes the

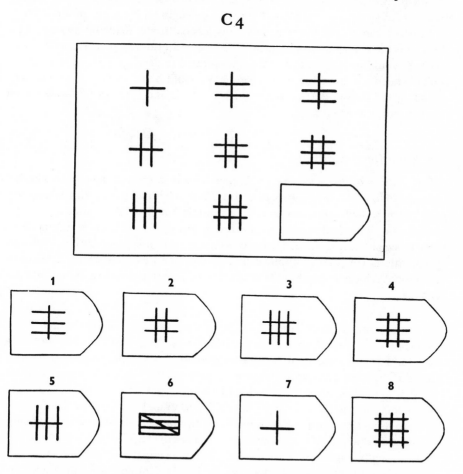

Figure 11.6 Example of item from Raven's Progressive Matrices Test. Reproduced from *Standard Progressive Matrices* by permission of J.C. Raven, author, and H.K. Lewis, (London) and the Psychogical Corporation of New York, Publishers.

design. Again, the relationship rather than the design is the important feature. However, data show that scores on the test vary as a function of several culturally relevant variables.

FUTURE DIRECTIONS. Whereas psychologists have long abandoned the search for culture-free tests, many psychologists now feel that even the quest for a culture-fair test is illusory. If one eliminated all culturally-relevant effects, he would be left with trivia. Furthermore, he would be unable to predict any socially meaningful criteria because criteria themselves are culturally laden. Consequently, as the social usefulness of a test increases so, too, does its loading on culturally relevant variables. Thus we are caught on the horns of a dilemma. To further complicate matters, seemingly less culturally loaded materials, such as nonverbal items, have often proven to be as culturally loaded as verbal items. Thus it would seem that, rather than attempting to develop additional or better culture-fair tests, the research strategy now should be to concentrate on understanding the factors that produce different levels and types of performance in various cultural groups.

Vocational aptitudes

Most of the tests discussed in this chapter have measured intellectual ability or aptitude. However, the concept of aptitude is much broader, covering vocational and occupational aptitudes as well. Certainly intellectual aptitudes, such as verbal and numerical reasoning, are important determiners of vocational success, especially in the professions and occupations requiring extensive academic preparation. Yet there is another class of aptitude measures which focuses on vocational skills and emphasizes prediction of vocational rather than academic criteria.

CHARACTERISTICS OF VOCATIONAL APTITUDE TESTS. Several characteristics distinguish vocational aptitude tests from their more academically oriented cousins. For one, the item content represents job components more closely than do items on scholastic aptitude tests. For example, while vocabulary may be a good sign of academic aptitude, rarely does actual course work include vocabulary exercises; in contrast, the ability to visualize objects or diagrams as they are rotated in space or the ability to manipulate small parts, as well as being a basis of test items, may be an essential component of a job. In other words, the tests frequently approximate *job samples*. Because occupational performance, and even component elements of jobs, may be highly complex, any single test designed to predict job performance will necessarily be factorially complex. On the other hand, if one chooses to try to develop factorially pure measures of specific skills, he will have to construct a large number of tests, as the evidence

(Fleishman, 1967) indicates that vocational skills, particularly motor and manipulative skills, are quite independent.

While scholastic aptitude tests measure mental and conceptual skills, vocational aptitudes include both conceptual skills and motor and manipulative abilities. Consequently, although a large number of vocational aptitude tests retain a paper-and-pencil format for administrative and scoring ease, they are not restricted to this format. Furthermore, many of the tests base scores on response speed, either because speed is an essential element in successful job performance or because the basic task is so simple that the only meaningful way to discriminate between individuals is in terms of speed of response.

EXAMPLES OF VOCATIONAL APTITUDE TESTS. A number of vocational aptitude tests use a paper-and-pencil format. An example is the *Bennett Mechanical Comprehension Test*, the test from which the DAT Mechanical Comprehension section was derived. This test measures the subject's ability to understand physical principles as they are expressed in practical situations (see Figure 11.3). Studies have shown that scores on the Bennett are unrelated to intelligence in homogeneous groups, that scores are relatively unaffected by training in physics, that there are large sex differences, and that scores on the tests predict success in a variety of training programs and on a variety of jobs—e.g., mechanics, machine operators, foremen, inspectors, machine testers, and toolmakers (Super & Crites, 1962, pp. 242–256).

Another vocationally relevant ability which can be assessed by paper-and-pencil tests is spatial visualization—the ability to visualize two- and three-dimensional objects as they are rotated, manipulated, or changed in some manner. For example, the *Minnesota Paper Form Board* presents a stimulus consisting of several geometric pieces and requires the test taker to select, from among several alternatives, the geometric design that can be made by assembling the pieces. Note that this version requires the individual to mentally, rather than physically, manipulate the pieces of the object.

A quite different ability that also can be assessed by paper-and-pencil tests is clerical aptitude. Tests of this ability (e.g., *The Minnesota Clerical Test* and the *Clerical Speed and Accuracy* section of the DAT) might equally well be called tests of perceptual speed and accuracy because they assess the person's ability to note details quickly and accurately. The typical format requires the subject to compare pairs of names or numbers and indicate whether the two elements are identical or differ in any respect. Clerical tests are probably the best example of a pure speed test, as the skill tested is so simple that almost anyone could attain 100 percent accuracy given sufficient time; however, people differ widely in the speed with which they can perform the task.

Other vocational aptitude tests, particularly those measuring manipulative and dexterity skills, involve performance tests. As an illustration we will use the *Purdue Pegboard*, a test designed to measure two types of dexterity: arm-and-hand

and finger dexterity. The test apparatus consists of a $1 \times 1\frac{1}{2}$ foot board with two parallel rows of holes drilled down the center and a set of shallow trays at one end. The trays contain metal pins, collars, and washers. The test consists of four separately timed portions: one, placing pins in the holes one at a time with the right hand; two, the same task only using the left hand; three, using both hands simultaneously; and fourth, assembling pin-washer-collar-washer combinations using both hands. Other tests of manipulative abilities involve tasks such as placing cutouts into a form board and manipulating objects with a tweezers or other tools.

VALIDITY. Any general statements about the validity of vocational aptitude tests must be qualified as, as might be expected, validity coefficients are highly situation-specific (Ghiselli, 1966; Super and Crites, 1962). It is clear, however, that validity coefficients of vocational aptitude tests used to predict vocational criteria are generally lower than those for intelligence or scholastic aptitude tests predicting academic criteria. It is also clear that prediction generally is better when the criterion is performance in a training program rather than on-the-job performance.

Because scores on many vocational aptitude tests often correlate with other relevant variables (such as intelligence and education), the relative contribution of vocational aptitude measures to predictive efficiency should be assessed in terms of their incremental validity; however, this procedure frequently is not used. Similarly, studies using multivariate prediction models and the use of moderator variables are only now beginning to appear. Harking back to Dunnette's warning that the ideas of *the* criterion and an overall measure of job success may be gross oversimplifications (Dunnette, 1966), studies should attempt to predict specific job behaviors. Finally, in business and industrial situations where personnel decisions often are on an accept-reject basis and the contribution of a worker potentially can be assessed in dollar terms, it is surprising to find so little validity data expressed as decision-making accuracy or utility indices.

The situation is further complicated by the fact that scores on many vocational aptitude tests vary as a function of the maturity and experience of the subject and practice on the test. Even though two persons may have the same test score, one person's score may represent the limit to which his ability may develop, while the other score may represent a still developing ability. These scores would, of course, have different implications, especially in the predictive situation. Again we have an illustration of the necessity for interpreting test scores in the context of their relationship to other variables.

Musical and artistic abilities

Our final class of aptitude measures includes tests of musical and artistic ability. These seemingly disparate types can be considered together because many of the same problems are encountered in both areas. For example, in both music and art one can clearly distinguish between appreciation and performance. It is one thing to be able to paint a picture, throw a pot, or cast a statue; it is another to be able to understand and appreciate a work of art. The two skills are not necessarily highly intercorrelated—many persons can evaluate the merit of a work of art but are themselves able to produce only stereotyped works. Consequently, tests of the two skills must be quite different. Similarly, music appreciation and the ability to play an instrument (or sing) are distinct abilities.

A second common element is the difficulty in predicting successful performance in artistic and musical activities. These difficulties take several forms. For one, even experts often disagree dramatically when rating the quality of a given performance or the merit of a particular musical or artistic work. Then, too, in the musical and artistic fields, more so than in many other occupations, "success" seems to be a function of a particularly fortuitous combination of ability, training, hard work, personality factors, the availability of opportunities to perform, the correspondence of one's performing style to the current mood, and "breaks."

Appreciation tests are best exemplified in the artistic areas. The format of most tests is quite similar: the test taker is presented with representations of two works of art—one a work of proven and judged merit, the other the same or similar object in slightly modified form—and is asked to choose the work which is aesthetically superior. Aesthetic sensitivity is measured by the extent to which the examinee can select the appropriate response. Test scores discriminate between relevant groups (e.g., artists and art teachers obtain higher scores than do other persons), but these differences may result from either selection practices and/or training in art.

Tests of both musical and artistic performance skills generally assess component skills rather than attempting to measure complex skills. Thus, for example, the *Seashore Measures of Musical Talents* measures components skills such as pitch, rhythm, timbre, loudness discrimination, and tonal memory. In the pitch test the subject indicates which of two tones is higher (or lower) in pitch; the rhythm test requires the subject to compare two rhythm patterns and to judge if they are similar or different. Performance tests in art typically require the examinee to produce drawings under restricted conditions (e.g., using a set of irregular lines as part of a picture). Scoring has the handicap of requiring quality ratings, which may introduce reliability problems.

Tests of artistic and musical skill would seem to be prime candidates for a threshold approach to interpretation. That is, if the examinee scores low, indicating lack of the necessary skills, his chances for attaining success are virtually nonexistent. For example, a person who has trouble discriminating between tones will never learn to play the violin. However, because of the myriad of factors that determine artistic or musical success, performance above the threshold level would not be a guarantee of success but only an indication that the person has the minimal level of ability necessary.

Summary

Aptitude tests indicate the ability to acquire a particular behavior or skill with appropriate training or opportunity. That is, they stress the prediction of future performance. The performance predicted may be very broad (such as learning a foreign language), or quite specific. Abilities refer to the present level of proficiency in a given skill. Aptitudes and abilities are not inherited characteristics of the individual, although they are influenced by genetic factors, but rather reflect constellation of learned behaviors and skills.

Several attempts have been made to organize our knowledge about aptitudes and abilities into a theory of intellectual structure. These approaches, which usually are based on data derived from factor analyses, can be classified into four general models: (1) General intelligence theories, which postulate a pervasive general capacity or mental energy factor. Intelligence tests yielding an overall IQ reflect this model. (2) Group factor models, which suggest that intellectual structure can best be described by a small number of fairly broad factors. Multiaptitude batteries illustrate this model. (3) Hierarchical models which arrange abilities on a series of levels according to their generality or specificity. (4) Guilford's model, which considers three dimensions of intellectual functioning: operations, contents, and products.

The concept that has been most studied and translated into specific tests is general intelligence. Although there is disagreement regarding the definition of the construct of intelligence, there is fairly general agreement regarding the types of items and tasks that can be used to measure intelligent behavior. These tasks were illustrated by an extensive discussion of the Stanford-Binet Intelligence Scale and the Wechsler scales. Also considered were several other approaches to the measurement of intelligence: group tests, performance tests, and infant and preschool tests. The research findings on three basic questions—the mental growth curve, the stability of the IQ, and the use of intelligence tests as predictors —were briefly considered. The data support the conclusion that general intelligence tests have proven useful in a variety of situations, even though some of their basic assumptions are contradictory to certain empirical facts.

Another broad class of aptitude measures that was discussed were the multiaptitude batteries, tests which attempt to measure a number of important abilities within the framework of a single battery. Although heavily influenced by the factor analysts, these batteries generally do not measure pure factors. The basic philosophy behind multiaptitude batteries is: (1) that human abilities can be described by a small number of fairly broad traits; (2) that tests can be devised to measure these basic abilities and aptitudes; and (3) that any criteria can be predicted using a properly weighted combination of scores on the various tests within the battery. The multiaptitude approach was illustrated by the Differential Aptitude Tests. Although multiaptitude tests have numerous advantages, they have been less than successful in accomplishing their goal of differential prediction.

We then discussed several other classes of aptitude tests: (1) scholastic aptitude tests, which are closely related to group intelligence tests but focus on the prediction of academic criteria; (2) measures of creativity; (3) culture-fair tests, which attempt to minimize the influence of culturally related variables on test performance; (4) measures of vocational aptitudes, such as mechanical comprehension, spatial visualization, and clerical aptitude; and (5) attempts to measure musical and artistic abilities.

Suggestions for further reading

Bloom, B. S. *Stability and change in human characteristics*. New York: John Wiley and Sons, Inc., 1964. A comprehensive review of the evidence regarding the development and stability of human traits and the variables which influence stability.

Ghiselli, E. E. *The validity of occupational aptitude tests*. New York: John Wiley & Sons, Inc., 1966. A summarization of the evidence of the effectiveness with which occupational criteria can be predicted by psychological tests.

Goslin, D. A. *The search for ability*. New York: Russell Sage Foundation, 1963 (Wiley Science Edition, 1966). The history and current status of standardized ability testing with emphasis on the social consequences of testing.

Guilford, J. P. Three faces of intellect. *American Psychologist*, 14, 1959, 469–479. An introduction to Guilford's structure-of-the-intellect model.

Horn, J. L. Intelligence—Why it grows, why it declines. *Trans-Action*, November 1967, 23–31. A readable introduction to Cattell's theory of fluid and crystallized intelligence.

Jensen, A. R. How much can we boost IQ and scholastic achievement? *Harvard Educational Review*, 1969, 39, 1–123. A consideration of the genetic and environmental determinants of IQ and scholastic achievement with implications for compensatory educational programs.

McNemar, Q. Lost: our intelligence. Why? *American Psychologist*, 1964, 19, 871–882. A discussion of the meaning of intelligence and the effectiveness of general intelligence and multiaptitude tests.

The measurement of personality characteristics

Chapter 12

INTRODUCTION

More than other areas of psychological and educational testing, personality measurement is characterized by a variety of approaches. One reason is that "personality" encompasses a broad and heterogeneous area and includes a plethora of concepts and constructs (see, e.g., Hall & Lindzey 1957). Additionally, the personality domain has been the subject of much theorizing, with different theories leading to different approaches to both the definition and measurement of the central concepts. Nevertheless, three distinct approaches to personality measurement can be identified—self-report techniques, projective methods, and situational methods.

SELF-REPORT TECHNIQUES. One widely used method of measuring personality characteristics is to have the individual describe or characterize himself. The individual may be presented with a list of adjectives and asked to check the ones that describe his personality; he may be asked to respond to a series of descriptive statements, indicating whether or not they describe him; he may be asked to report his reactions to situations, or to indicate his attitudes, interests, or values. The common element in these situations, and all self-report techniques, is that the individual provides a description or report of his own behavior and/or reactions.

The basic assumption behind this approach is quite simple—the individual is in the best position to observe, describe, and report upon his own behavior. Even if an observer could follow you around 24 hours of each day he still would not be privy to all aspects of your life; he could not know your attitudes or reactions to certain events, your thoughts and reasons for taking certain actions, although he could ask you about them or infer them from your overt behavior. In short, only you can observe yourself in all situations; thus you can base your report on the widest possible range of observations.

A corollary of the assumption, that the person will report his behavior in an unbiased manner, rests on less solid ground. Most personality theories, in fact, imply that the person will, without doubt, present a biased picture of himself. Thus, when constructing and scoring self-report techniques, it becomes necessary either to eliminate the opportunity to present a biased report or to identify the degree to which such tendencies operate. In fact (as we shall see in much greater detail below), much of the effort in developing personality tests and much of the controversy over the value of personality measures is directed at this issue.

Of the many possible stimulus situations that could be used to elicit the person's description of himself, the most widely used method is the *personality inventory*. An inventory consists of a relatively large number of statements, such as:

I frequently get headaches.
I enjoy competitive games.
New and different experiences excite me.
People often expect too much of me.

The test taker responds true (or agree, or some other variation) if the item describes or characterizes him, false (or disagree, etc.) if the statement does not describe him. Because all test takers respond to the same set of questions, an inventory can be likened to a standardized interview. Although some writers stress the fact that there are no "correct" (in the absolute sense) answers as being a fundamental characteristic of the inventory approach, we will use the term more in the dictionary sense, that of an inventory being a detailed listing of objects or events, thus stressing the broad coverage and multi-item format.

Self-report techniques are often referred to as *objective tests*. If we follow our usage of objectivity as referring to the recording of responses and the scoring procedures, self-report techniques are, in fact, objective measures; however, if, in addition, we consider that responses to the items are not unbiased, that they reflect personal needs and characteristics, a subjective or projective element clearly enters into the test (Meehl, 1945).

PROJECTIVE METHODS. Projective techniques (or projective methods) present the test taker with ambiguous stimuli and ask him to interpret or impose some structure upon it. This methodology follows from the *projective hypothesis* which states that an individual, when confronted with an ambiguous situation, will impose a structure that reflects his particular personality organization. Thus by knowing how a person interprets ambiguous stimuli, we can infer something about his personality structure.

An example of a projective technique that is familiar to most persons having even a nodding acquaintance with psychological testing is the Rorschach Method, or Ink Blot test. The Rorschach consists of a series of designs that resemble ink blots; the test takers task is to tell what he sees in the blots. Here, obviously, are stimuli that have no inherent meaning, and therefore any meaning attributed to the pictures must be supplied by the subject, the meaning he projects into the blots. Another well known and widely used variety of projective method is illustrated by the Thematic Apperception Test (TAT). The TAT consists of a series of pictures showing persons engaged in various activities; the testee's job is to construct a story describing the characters and action. A third approach is the sentence completion test, wherein incomplete sentences serve as stimuli and the response task is to complete the sentence.

SITUATIONAL METHODS. A third general class of personality assessment methods is held together by the common requirements that the individual be placed in a situation that calls for some action or reaction, his behavior be observed and/or recorded, and a rating made of certain personality characteristics that are displayed. For example, several persons might be brought together around a table and instructed to devise a plan and organization for an advertising campaign. By observing how the individuals interact with each other, present their ideas, how their ideas are accepted by other members of the group, who is elected to leadership positions, how they handle their assignments, and other relevant behaviors, an observer could rate the persons along several personality dimensions (e.g., leadership, sociability, effectiveness of expression, dominance, and cooperativeness).

A widely used, or perhaps we should say overused, situational method is the *interview*. Although we usually think of one person interviewing another, it is possible to have several interviewers (as in a press conference or selection boards) and/or several candidates being interviewed simultaneously by one interviewer. The interview procedure itself can vary from a highly structured sequence of questions to an open-ended encounter that follows the interests of the participants. So, too, the ratings or evaluation which result from an interview may be anything from quantitative ratings on well-defined dimensions to global and qualitative evaluations.

Some problems peculiar to personality measurement

In most respects the measurement of maximal performance is quite straightforward. The tester and test taker both usually know how the test scores will be used and the meaning that will be attached to various performance levels. The structure of the testing situation is such that trying one's best is the accepted set, and the items have answers that are either definitely correct or incorrect (although the test taker may not know which ones are correct and which are incorrect). In contrast, when measuring typical performance the purpose of the testing and the interpretation to be placed on scores is frequently hazy to the test taker, the appropriate motivation or set for taking the test may be unclear and, as there are no "correct" responses, the meaning of any response, let alone the item, may be ambiguous.

WHAT IS MEASURED? Aptitude and ability testing assumed a trait model, and the purpose of the measurement was to establish an individual's scale position for each trait measured. An analogous approach can be used in personality measurement. As each individual's pattern of trait scores will differ from every other individual, each individual has, in a sense, a unique personality structure. (Cf. Allport, 1955, and note that it is the pattern of traits, not the traits *per se*, that vary between individuals; a trait that was manifested in only one individual would be difficult, if not impossible, to identify.) If, however, we cluster individuals on the basis of the similarity of their trait patterns we have the start of a *typology*, with "types" being defined by the similarity of their scores on various traits. However, a few theorists propose that the model for personality assessment should be a true typology, involving mutually exclusive types, rather than a typology that is, in essence, a multidimensional trait model.

Another frequently voiced objection to the trait approach is that the model is too static to adequately represent the dynamic configuration that is personality. While there is no doubt that personality is a dynamic concept, and that any measurement procedure will necessarily "freeze" personality at a given point, it is difficult to ascertain exactly what dynamic measurement of personality traits would entail. If by dynamic is meant changing over time, then repeated testings combined sequentially (similar to combining frames to produce movement in a motion picture) can represent the dynamic nature of personality. If by "dynamic" is meant some complex configuration that can be ascertained only by an intuitive combination of elements, we do have a different type of measurement, but one that is less precise and more susceptible to error.

On self-report inventories another sort of question can be raised. If a person responds "yes" to the item "I frequently have headaches," how shall we interpret his response? We can, of course, accept the statement at face value as an accurate report; but can we really know what the response means without knowledge of how the test taker defined the terms "frequently" and "headache"? Or should we accept the response only as the second best source of information about the individual, the best source being direct observation? Adoption of this view implies acceptance of the response as an indicator of the true state of affairs, albeit an estimate one step removed from direct observation. Or should we view the response as an interesting bit of verbal behavior, in and of itself, and determine the meaning of the response by empirical studies (Meehl, 1945)? In this view, the truth of the response is irrelevant; the important aspect is what the individual says about himself and the behavioral correlates of making such a statement. This third viewpoint is espoused by persons supporting the empirical keying of personality inventories. In this approach the interpretation of any response is determined solely by what the response signifies, by what it points to, by its empirical correlates.

DOES THE MEASUREMENT PROCESS AFFECT THE INDIVIDUAL? One feature that distinguishes psychological and educational measurement from physical measurement is the degree to which the measurement process may affect the object or person being measured. Although the measurement process may affect the physical object or event being measured, this influence generally is of little consequence. But when measuring psychological characteristics of individuals, we must be concerned with the effects that the measurement process might have on the behavior of the individual being tested.

When measuring maximal performance, it is recognized that the test may affect the test taker's behavior, but this effect frequently does not occur during the testing situation. There are exceptions, however, as when a student experiences failure in the early part of a test and consequently gives up and does not try on the remaining items. (It is precisely for this reason that it was suggested that tests begin with several easy items.) But typically, given a set for maximal performance at the beginning of a test, an individual will hold the set throughout the test with any effects of the testing experience occurring at another time.

Tests of typical performance appear to be more susceptible to changes produced by the testing situation, effects that may be manifested during the testing situation. It is not uncommon for a counselee who has just taken a test to tell the counselor "You know, when I started to think about my interests when taking that interest inventory, I decided that I really don't like engineering after all." But of more direct interest are the effects manifested during the testing process that influence the test taker's responses. Some people, when confronted with items that force them to think about themselves, become defensive and mask their true personalities; others are unwilling to say other than pleasant and socially desirable things about themselves; others are forced to consider aspects of their personalities that they had never before confronted.

If these test-taking reactions carry over outside the testing situation, the person has literally been changed by the testing; if they are manifested only on the test and do not carry over outside the test, the validity of the test becomes questionable. In either instance, the test has produced a change in the individual.

RESPONSE SETS AND STYLES. When testing maximal performance the only possible way to distort scores is not to respond or to deliberately select wrong answers and thereby lower the score. On tests of typical performance, however, the situation is more complex. For example, the test taker may alter his responses so that the test will picture him in a more or less desirable light than would honest responding. Or the test taker might attempt to distort the responses to present a particular picture of himself—for example, as being aggressive, sociable, having the interests of physicians, or being very religious. Such conscious and unconscious attempts to respond to test items so as to present a particular picture of oneself are referred to as *response sets*.

When the test taker adopts a particular response set he is imitating the responses of a person with the particular characteristics he is trying to emulate. Because personality items frequently are ambiguous or subtle (in the sense that their keying is not obvious), this may be a more difficult task than distorting achievement test scores by selecting obviously incorrect responses. Yet the evidence is overwhelming that test takers do adopt response sets and that these sets do affect their scores. (See, e.g., Rorer 1965; Longstaff, 1948; Edwards, 1957; Berg, 1967; Jackson & Messick, 1958.) The test constructor must thus devise means of identifying and/or controlling this tendency to dissimulate.

To illustrate a response set, we will consider the variable of *social desirability*. Edwards (1957, 1967) has shown that personality items can be ranked with high reliability along a dimension that indicates whether the statement is considered socially desirable or undesirable. For example, the statement "I am an intelligent and creative person" would almost certainly be judged as highly desirable, while the statement "I often have temper tantrums when something doesn't go my way" would almost certainly be rated as socially undesirable.

Edwards' contention was that many people respond to items on personality inventories, not solely in terms of their actual behavior and characteristics, but also in terms of the social desirability of the items. When confronted with the item, "I have strange and peculiar thoughts", the test taker's response will be determined by whether he has what he considers to be strange and peculiar thoughts *and* by the perceived social desirability of the item, in this case its extreme undesirability. As would be expected, items that are rated as being socially desirable are endorsed with greater frequency than items rated as being socially undesirable; in fact, there is a very high positive correlation between the social desirability rating of an item and the probability of its being endorsed.

Research data from studies of social desirability have been given widely divergent interpretations: that the major source of variance in certain personality test scores can be attributed to the social desirability response set (Edwards, 1957, 1959); that the effects ascribed to social desirability are really a manifestation of an acquiescence response style (Couch & Keniston, 1960); or that the results cannot be unambiguously interpreted (Block, 1965). Part of the reason for the confusion, no doubt, is that the studies of response sets have, too often, concerned themselves only with test-taking behavior and not with extra-test variables (see McGee, 1962).

In addition to content-dependent response sets, various content-independent response tendencies, or *response styles*, have been postulated. Examples of response styles include the tendency to select some response when unsure of the correct response (guessing), the tendency to agree with a statement when having no informed basis for agreeing or disagreeing (acquiescence), and the tendency to avoid extreme categories on multicategory ratings (central tendency). Note that an essential condition for manifestation of a response style is that the test taker has no rational choice between responses—either because the item is ambiguous, meaningless, or too difficult. In these situations, it is postulated, the test taker will respond not at random but in accord with a particular response style. Note also that response styles may operate on tests of maximal performance as well as tests of typical performance; for example, most students, when unsure of the correct response to true-false items, consistently choose "true."

Since Cronbach first voiced concern over the effects of response tendencies (1946, 1950), there has been a plethora of research studies. Like the studies of response sets, different investigators have reached widely divergent conclusions (compare, e.g., Jackson & Messick, 1958, and Rorer, 1965). In a recent review Rorer (1965) concluded that, when forced to guess, test takers do not respond randomly; that even in these situations, response styles usually explain no more than 20 percent of the variance in scores; that there is no reason to believe that respondents are forced to rely on response styles on objective personality, interest, and attitude inventories; that response styles are easily alterable; and that these styles may be test-specific. Nevertheless, the search for viable response styles goes on, and test constructors must be aware of the possible effects of response styles.

ITEM SAMPLING.   One final problem should be briefly noted—that of obtaining a large and representative sampling of items. In measuring achievement, abilities, and aptitudes, the content universe is relatively well defined and items can be scaled in terms of difficulty. By sampling items from various content areas and at varying difficulty levels, a test can be constructed (using relatively few items) that will accurately estimate how the individual would perform in the universe being sampled.

In measuring typical performance the situation is more complex. The traits being measured are broad, frequently heterogeneous, and often not clearly defined. The variety of possible stimuli is exceedingly large. (E.g., Edwards & Walsh, 1963, report a pool of 3000 personality items; there are over 18,000 adjectives in the English language to describe personality.) As people seem to respond to the nuances of personality items, minor differences in content and wording often produce large differences in response rates; and, because behavior is multiply determined, to sort out the effects of any given variable, as distinct from the actions and interactions of other variables, requires a large number of items. The designation "typical performance" also implies that the behavior measured occurs in a wide variety of situations. Thus the number of items on a personality test frequently is much greater than on a test of maximal performance; in fact, most personality inventories consist of several hundred items.

SELF-REPORT INVENTORIES

The common element in all self-report techniques is that the test taker serves as the observer and reporter of his behaviors, attitudes, or feelings. However, several other characteristics also typify self-report techniques: the measuring instrument is usually an inventory, the format is paper-and-pencil, several traits are measured simultaneously by different scales, scoring is normative, and appropriate procedures must be built into the test to control the action of response sets and styles.

Scale construction strategies

As the interpretation of any score depends upon the manner in which the scale was constructed, and because several distinct approaches to scale construction are used in self-report inventories, we will begin our discussion with a consideration of the various strategies of scale construction. In particular, we will consider three approaches: rational (or a priori) methods, empirical keying, and homogeneous keying. After we have discussed the various strategies, we will illustrate how they have been applied in the construction of extant personality inventories.

LOGICAL KEYING.   One approach to scale construction, which was used on most earlier instruments, is to assign items to scales on theoretical or rational bases. In practice, this means that once the test constructor has decided on the trait to be measured, he writes items that *appear* to measure that trait. For example, a scale measuring "introversion" would probably be composed of items like the following:

I blush easily.
At a party I introduce myself to people that I do not know.
I prefer small parties with friends to large affairs.
Reading is one of my favorite activities.

Keying of the items would be on rational bases only. Although there might not be universal agreement regarding the keying of any single item, the scale construction procedure favors items whose keying is quite obvious.

The construction of a personality inventory often begins by writing items that appear to bear a logical relationship to the trait being measured. But this approach must be treated only as a beginning because items that *appear* to measure a given trait may not, in fact, measure that trait. Also, a test composed only of items bearing an obvious relation to the trait being measured, when administered to anyone other than a very naïve testee, would be exceedingly prone to distortion and dissimulation.

EMPIRICAL KEYING.   In a second approach, items are selected on the basis of their empirical relationship with a criterion measure. The first step in this procedure is to select a (criterion) group that displays the characteristic or trait to be measured. Suppose, for example, we were interested in the trait of leadership (assuming that leadership is, in fact, a trait). We would first ask the question: Can we identify a group of persons who display leadership ability?[1] One possible approach would be to define leaders (i.e., define the criterion group) as people who have been elected to offices in certain organizations. Thus, if we were dealing with a high school population, we might define our criterion group as including class officers, student council representatives, captains of athletic teams, and presidents of major clubs and organizations.

The next question to answer is: What characteristics differentiate the leaders from other students? To answer this question requires at least two things: a pool of stimuli (items) and a comparison group composed of persons who are not leaders. To collect a pool of items we might consult textbooks on studies of leadership behavior, ask peers or other judges to list qualities they think describe leaders, review tests measuring leadership and related traits, and from these sources write or select a large pool of potential items. As nonleaders we might include participants in athletics and clubs or a cross-section of the student body, excluding those students designated as leaders. We would then administer the items to both groups.

Suppose that we follow the procedure described and obtain the following hypothetical results:

| | Proportion responding "true" | | |
Item	Leaders	Others	Difference
I would rather give directions than follow another person's directions.	.75	.37	.38
People often ask my advice.	.36	.32	.04
In my leisure time I like to listen to classical music.	.28	.07	.21
I frequently have headaches.	.09	.12	−.03

Which items distinguish the leaders from other persons? Although there are differences between the two groups on all four items, only the first and third items show relatively large differences; these two items thus would be included

---

[1]Note that, although we refer to the trait being measured as "leadership ability," we are interested in the individual's typical performance as a leader — how he habitually reacts when in a position of leadership, not his maximal performance—does he know how a leader should react?

on the leadership scale and the second and fourth items discarded. Note also that, although the results for the first and fourth items might have been predicted from logical considerations, we would have expected the second item to show a difference; yet because there was no difference, the item would be eliminated. Conversely, although there are no logical grounds for expecting leaders to prefer classical music more than other persons, they do, and thus this item would be included on the scale.

By using these procedures with a large number of items, a scale can be developed. The method of item selection guarantees that the scale will have concurrent validity—as the items selected for the scale discriminate between the groups, consequently a combination of these items will also differentiate the groups. By repeating the procedure using the same pool of items but different criterion groups, a multiscale test can be developed, each scale measuring a particular criterion or trait.

Two aspects of the procedure deserve especial mention. First, because items are keyed to a particular criterion group, the nature of the criterion group will be reflected in the scale. In our example leaders were defined as persons holding certain offices. But is this an adequate definition of leadership? Does election to an office really constitute leadership? Granted that the persons selected are leaders, is the group representative of all leaders? If a different definition of leadership is used, or if the criterion group does not adequately reflect the stipulated definition, the scale will not be completely appropriate. Thus, whenever using an empirically keyed scale, score interpretations will always be relative to the original criterion group.

A related concern is the generalizability of the scale. The test construction procedure has guaranteed that the scale will have concurrent validity. But will it predict criteria other than membership in the criterion group? Does the test make any theoretical sense? Such questions can be answered only by further study of the test. While the first question is a straightforward empirical question, the second is more complicated. Because the items were chosen on empirical bases, their theoretical meaning was an irrelevant issue. Yet if we wish to build a psychological theory, or use the test results in confirmation of a theory, we have to be able to make theoretical sense out of empirical results. An important consideration then becomes how to integrate seemingly meaningless results (e.g., the fact that leaders like classical music) into the theoretical network. We have, in short, an exercise in construct validity.

HOMOGENEOUS KEYING. A third strategy for scale development is based on the assumption that, in order for a scale to reflect a psychologically meaningful variable, the scale must be homogeneous. Items not correlating highly with the other scale items are thus eliminated because they are considered to be measuring a different trait or construct; only those items that are highly correlated with other items in the scale are retained.

The scale development process proceeds as follows: A large number of items are administered to an appropriate standardization group—usually a representative sample of the population in which the test will be used. The intercorrelations among items are factor analyzed or subjected to some other analytic procedure that clusters the items into homogeneous groups. These homogeneous item groupings form the basis of a scale. The content of the items comprising the scale gives meaning, and a name or label, to the scale. It is assumed that the analytic procedure will identify the dimensions that are measurable; if a proposed construct is not represented by a cluster of items, the construct is presumed not to exist.

The process of homogeneous keying results in unidimensional scales which have some contruct validity. Whether the scales have any criterion-related validity is another question, a question that can be answered only by empirical data. Although many people who prefer homogeneous keying feel the method insures that scales will measure important dimensions, more empirically oriented test users and researchers demand further empirical proof of the scales' validity. So, too, those with preferences for homogeneous keying will demand that the empiricist explain the meaning of their scales. In short, the difference between empirical and homogeneous keying is in method, in data preferences, and in research style.

COMBINING STRATEGIES.   The logical, empirical, and homogeneous keying methods represent the three major approaches to the construction of scales for self-report personality inventories. Combinations of strategies are, of course, possible. Although the rational approach is no doubt the weakest, all approaches use rational methods when selecting items in the earliest stages of test construction; that is, items are placed in the pool of potential items only if there is some rational reason for doing so. It has also been suggested that the optimal test construction strategy is a combination of empirical and homogeneous keying. In this approach, homogeneous scales would first be constructed by factor analysis or other clustering techniques. The homogeneous keys would then be validated against empirical criteria and those items that did not demonstrate empirical validity would be eliminated. The final scale would thus be homogeneous and empirically valid, thereby, hopefully, being both practically and theoretically useful.

The Strong Vocational Interest Blank: an empirically keyed interest inventory

That men and women who work in different occupations have different abilities, aptitudes, interests, attitudes, and personality characteristics is a well-documented fact. The study of vocational interests is the study of one aspect of this area—the preferences, likes, and dislikes of persons in various occupational and vocational groups. Because the measurement of vocational interests illustrates many of the problems in personality measurement, it will be used as a jumping-off point for our discussion.

APPROACHES TO THE MEASUREMENT OF INTERESTS. Before beginning the construction of an instrument for measuring vocational interests, the test constructor must make at least three fundamental decisions. First, he must select the general approach to interest measurement that he will follow. Second, he must decide whether to measure interest in specific occupations or in broad vocational areas. And third, if he chooses the inventory approach, he must decide between empirical and homogeneous keying. Let us consider each question briefly.

Vocational interests can be measured in at least four different ways (Super & Crites, 1962). One approach would be to study *stated interests* by asking each individual to name the occupations he was interested in and to use his response as the measure of interest. If a student said he was interested in becoming a pharmacist, the statement would be taken as a measure of his interests. Or we might consider his *manifest interests* by observing how the person actually spends his time. Thus, if a student stated that his interest was in mathematics but spent countless hours collecting rock specimens, even to the extent of neglecting to do his mathematics, his manifest interest would be in geology. A third approach, called *tested interests*, attempts to derive an objective indication of interests by standardized achievement tests, the assumption being that a person who is interested in a given area will learn and retain more information about that area, i.e., one who knows more about physics than history would be said to have more interest in physics than in history. A fourth approach asks the test taker to express his liking or preference for a wide variety of activities that bear some relation to vocational interests. That is, we take an inventory of his vocationally and occupationally relevant preferences; hence, the label *inventoried interests*. Almost all of the instruments that have been developed to measure vocational interests fall within this fourth category.

A second decision is whether to measure interests in specific occupations or in broad vocational areas. If one opts for the former approach, the inventory would have scales measuring interest in, say, medicine, law, real estate sales, military careers, psychology, elementary school teaching, and other occupations. Using the latter approach would result in scales that covered broad vocational areas—e.g., scientific, mechanical, artistic, sales, or linguistic interests. In other words, we can adopt a rather broad-gauged or narrow-gauged approach.

A third dimension that distinguishes between various interest inventories is the method of scale construction. Therefore, the third decision is between keying methods. The approach may be logical, with items assigned to scales solely on a rational, a priori basis; empirical, with items assigned to scales on the basis of their observed relationship to some criterion; or homogeneous, with items assigned to scales on the basis of their intercorrelations. Again, each of these various approaches has been applied to the development of interest inventories with the empirical method appearing to predominate at this time.

GENERAL DESCRIPTION. The first form of the SVIB appeared in 1927 and the latest revision was published in 1969. The inventory has both men's and women's forms. Because research has shown that vocational interests of most persons do not stabilize until age 20–25, the test is primarily for adults; the manual recommends that the test not be given to persons under 17 unless they are relatively mature (Strong & Campbell, 1966, p. 2).

The men's form (1969 revision) consists of 399 items divided into the following eight sections.

Part I. *Occupations* (100 items; indicate if Like, are Indifferent to, or Dislike)
Sample items: Actor, Advertising Man, Military Officer
Part II. *School Subjects* (36 items; L-I-D)
Sample items: Algebra, Art, Philosophy
Part III. *Amusements* (49 items; L-I-D)
Sample items: Golf, Playing the piano, Jazz concerts
Part IV. *Activities* (48 items; L-I-D)
Sample items: Adjusting a carburetor, Making a speech, Methodical work
Part V. *Types of People* (47 items; L-I-D)
Sample items: Optimists, Babies, Nonconformists
Part VI. *Order of Preference of Activities* (four sets of ten activities; select three that Like Most and three that Like Least in each set of ten)
Sample items: Discover an improvement in the design of a machine, Sell the machine, Teach others the use of the machine
Part VII. *Preferences between Two Items* (40 pairs; mark preference between two)
Sample items: Airline pilot—Airline ticket agent, Deal with things—Deal with people, A few close friends—Many acquaintances
Part VIII. *Your Abilities and Characteristics* (39 items; mainly yes–?–no)
Sample items: Win friends easily, Plan my work in detail, Discuss my ideals with others

On the majority of the items, the testee responds by indicating whether he likes, is indifferent to, or dislikes a particular activity; however, some items require a ranking of several stimuli. The inventory is untimed, with the median time for completing the blank being approximately 30 minutes.

Because of the large number of items and scales, scoring is usually done by private scoring agencies using electronic scoring machines. Four types of scales are scored: occupational scales, nonoccupational scales, administrative indices, and basic interest scales. The approximately 50 *occupational scales*[2] compare individuals to specific occupational groups—e.g., Dentist, Personnel Director, Artist, Lawyer. The *nonoccupational scales* measure variables such as academic

PROFILE— **STRONG VOCATIONAL INTEREST BLANK** —FOR MEN (Form T399)

Reprinted from the 1969 Supplement to the Manual for the Strong Vocational Interest Blanks, copyrighted by the Board of Trustees of the Leland Stanford Junior University and published by Stanford University Press

BASIC INTEREST SCALES

SCALE	STD. SCORE	PLOTTED SCORE
PUBLIC SPEAKING		
LAW/POLITICS		
BUSINESS MANAGEMENT		
SALES		
MERCHANDISING		
OFFICE PRACTICES		
MILITARY ACTIVITIES		
TECHNICAL SUPERVISION		
MATHEMATICS		
SCIENCE		
MECHANICAL		
NATURE		
AGRICULTURE		
ADVENTURE		
RECREATIONAL LEADERSHIP		
MEDICAL SERVICE		
SOCIAL SERVICE		
RELIGIOUS ACTIVITIES		
TEACHING		
MUSIC		
ART		
WRITING		

DOUBLE LINE = AVERAGE SCORE FOR 650 52-YEAR-OLD MEN.   SINGLE LINE = AVERAGE SCORE FOR SAME MEN WHEN 16 YEARS OLD.

OCCUPATIONAL SCALES

OCCUPATION	STD. SCORE		OCCUPATION	STD. SCORE
I DENTIST		VI	LIBRARIAN	38
OSTEOPATH			ARTIST	47
VETERINARIAN			MUSICIAN PERFORMER	46
PHYSICIAN			MUSIC TEACHER	36
PSYCHIATRIST		VII	C.P.A. OWNER	42
PSYCHOLOGIST		VIII	SENIOR C.P.A.	40
BIOLOGIST			ACCOUNTANT	36
II ARCHITECT			OFFICEWORKER	24
MATHEMATICIAN			PURCHASING AGENT	25
PHYSICIST			BANKER	28
CHEMIST			PHARMACIST	26
ENGINEER			FUNERAL DIRECTOR	20
III PRODUCTION		IX	SALES MANAGER	36
ARMY OFFICER			REAL ESTATE SALESMAN	32
AIR FORCE OFFICER			LIFE INS. SALESMAN	28
IV CARPENTER		X	ADVERTISING MAN	42
FOREST SERVICE MAN			LAWYER	43
FARMER			AUTHOR-JOURNALIST	50
MATH-SCIENCE TEACHER		XI	PRESIDENT-MFG.	43
PRINTER				

SUPP. OCCUPATIONAL SCALES

CREDIT MANAGER	
CHAMBER OF COM. EXEC.	
PHYSICAL THERAPIST	
COMPUTER PROGRAMMER	
BUSINESS ED. TEACHER	
COMMUNITY REC. ADMIN.	

OCCUPATION	
POLICEMAN	
V PERSONNEL DIRECTOR	
PUBLIC ADMINISTRATOR	
REHABILITATION COUNS.	
YMCA STAFF MEMBER	
SOCIAL WORKER	
SOCIAL SCIENCE TEACHER	
SCHOOL SUPERINTENDENT	
MINISTER	

NON-OCCUPATIONAL SCALES
AACH   AR   DIV   MFII   MO   OIE   OL   SL

ADMINISTRATIVE INDICES
TR   UNP   FC   LP   IP   DP

Figure 12.1 The Strong Vocational Interest Blank Profile: Male form.

[2]Because various test scoring agencies use different equipment, they may require different answer sheets. They also score slightly different sets of scales. Thus there is no one universal profile for the SVIB, hence the statement that approximately 50 scales are scored.

achievement, masculinity-femininity, and diversity of interest. The *administrative indices* include the number of "unpopular" responses, the percentage of "Like" responses and similar data. The *basic interest scales*, which first appeared in 1969, are clusters of homogeneous items covering a single content area—e.g., Sales, Science, Teaching, Writing. Because our focus, at this point, is on scale development using empirical keying, we will restrict our discussion to the occupational keys. Also, as the procedures were identical on both forms, we will refer only to the Men's form of the test.

The most common use of the SVIB is for counseling high school and college students regarding their vocational plans. Although it may seem absurd that a student should have to take an interest test to find out his interests, with limited work experiences and the consequent misperceptions of jobs, plus the inability to view ourselves objectively, an inventory can often clarify interests or attitudes. Although the SVIB is utilized for selection and placement, both in academic and business settings, the fact that it can be faked (see, e.g., Longstaff, 1948) would seem to dictate caution when using the test in this manner.

SCALE DEVELOPMENT. Occupational scales on the SVIB were developed by comparing the interests of men working in a given occupation to those of men-in-general; thus, scores provide a measure of the similarity of a person's interests to those of men in various occupations. The procedure for developing scales was strictly empirical. The first step was to select criterion groups. Although the exact bases for selection varied somewhat between scales, in general the criterion group for each occupation was composed of about 300 men aged 25 to 55, who had been employed in the occupation at least three years (thus insuring that they were at least minimally successful on their job) and who indicated that they liked their work. Second, the item pool was administered to the criterion groups and their responses were compared to the responses of a group of men-in-general, a group that represented occupations that college graduates usually enter.[3] If an item differentiated between men-in-general and men in the occupation, it was included on the scale for that occupation. On earlier forms of the SVIB, responses were weighted (from $+4$ to -4) in proportion to their discrimination power; in the latest revision weights have been restricted to $+1, 0$ and -1 since studies showed that unit weighting produced as valid scales and, of course, simplified scoring.

After a scale was developed by item analyses procedures, the responses of the criterion group and men-in-general were scored on the resultant occupational key to insure that the scale did, indeed, differentiate the two groups. If the groups were separated satisfactorily, norms and scores were established. The standard score system used is a linear transformation (with $\overline{X} = 50$, $s = 10$)

[3]For a description of the men-in-general group, or the occupational (criterion) groups see the test manual (Strong & Campbell, 1966).

and uses the criterion group as the "norming" group. Thus, a score of 50 is the mean of the distribution of scores of persons in an occupation, a score of 60 is one standard deviation above the occupational mean, and so on. The men-in-general group, though used in selecting the items for a scale, plays no direct role in norming.

The question may well be raised as to how effective this scale development procedure was; that is, to what extent can men-in-general and men employed in a given occupation be separated? The occupational and men-in-general groups overlap (Tilton, 1937) from 15 to 52 percent, with a median overlap of 31 percent. Occupations that draw persons with distinctive personal characteristics, and which have relatively few practitioners, can be differentiated better than the more popular occupations.

As mentioned previously, the composition of the criterion groups, in effect, defines the dimension being measured. The criterion groups used on the SVIB varied in size, method of selection, and how well they represented the profession. Although some samples were of recent origin (e.g., the computer programmer scale is based on 500 men tested in 1965), many of the criterion groups are based on small, old, and nonrepresentative groups. Although at first blush this may seem to invalidate the test, Campbell (1965, 1966) has shown that occupational interest patterns have not changed as much over the years as one might believe. Then, too, scales can be (and are) continually revised using better occupational samples.

Finally, the perceptive reader may have already deduced that there is no reason that the scale development procedure cannot be extended to the problem of differentiating specialties within occupations. And, in fact, *specialty scales* have been developed for at least two occupations—psychology and medicine— by contrasting the responses of men in different specialty areas of the occupation with those of the average practitioner of the occupation (note: *not* men-in-general). Thus, for example, it is possible to differentiate between industrial, clinical, counseling, and experimental psychologists.

THE PROFILE. As an aid to interpretation, SVIB scores are usually presented as a profile (see Figure 12.1). The occupational scales are grouped according to their intercorrelations, with the scales that are highly intercorrelated (generally > .60) being grouped together.

To further simplify interpretation, each scale score range has been given a letter equivalent, ranging from A (standard scores $\geq$ 45) through C (standard scores < 30). Persons scoring in the A and B+ range have interests similar to persons successfully engaged in the occupation; a C rating indicates interests dissimilar to persons in the occupation; and scores in the B range represent some interest in common, but not to the degree shown by an A rating.

Not only must the scores in particular occupations be considered, but also the pattern of scores. The pattern is important for many reasons: (1) Not all occupations are represented by scales. Thus to obtain an indication of a person's interest in a nonrepresented area, the score pattern in related areas must be considered. (2) Because there are various ways of performing an occupation and various jobs within occupations, the pattern of scores may give a clue to the specialty or type of position to be considered. (3) A preponderance of high scores in the several occupations comprising a group reinforces the suggestion that the person's interests are in that area. (4) Low scores, or reject patterns, indicate areas where the individual's interests are definitely dissimilar to persons currently employed in the field. (5) The relative scatter of the scale scores— whether scores cluster at about the same level or fall throughout the score range—gives an indication of the relative strengths of the various interests. (For further discussion of the interpretation of SVIB profiles, with case studies, see Strong & Campbell 1966; Darley & Hagenah, 1955; or Layton, 1958.)

EMPIRICAL RESULTS. Having discussed the theory of measurement utilized in constructing the SVIB and having described the instrument that resulted from the application of this approach, the question of the empirical concomitants of SVIB scores remains. To completely survey the literature on the SVIB would require an entire book (see, e.g., Darley & Hagenah, 1955; Layton, 1960), so we will only skim the available evidence, indicating some of the types of questions that have been asked and some of the answers that have been given.

How stable are SVIB scale scores? They are consistent over short periods—a median r of .91 being found for a two-week interval—and remarkably consistent over longer periods. In what must surely rate as one of the longest term retest studies, Strong (1955) found a median r of .67 over a 22-year interval! If we ask at what age interests tend to stabilize, the answer is usually at around 20 (Darley & Hagenah, 1955; Strong & Campbell, 1966).

What is the relationship between interests and other psychological characteristics? Although there is some relation between interests and ability, studies which relate these two variables show only moderately positive correlations (rarely over .30). Similarly, studies of the relationship between interests and personality measures have shown some consistent patterns, but the magnitude of the correlations is always low. Nor have interest scores been found to correlate highly with academic or vocational success or satisfaction.

What, then, do SVIB scores predict? Although the statistics of Stong's widely quoted conclusion, that the odds are 3.5 to 1.0 that a person will enter an occupation that he had an A score in, have been questioned (Brown, 1961), the trend of the data supports the generalization that persons do tend to select, enter, and remain in occupations that are compatible with their interests as measured by the SVIB (Strong, 1943, 1955; Layton, 1960). There also is some evidence (Berdie, 1955; Kelly & Fiske, 1951) that the SVIB can significantly add to predictive ability in academic situations. However, McArthur (1954) showed that while SVIB scores predicted occupational choice for college men from public high schools, stated interests were better predictors for men from private high schools. Apparently, the role that interests play in determining vocational choice depends on the background of the person.

Can the interests of nonprofessional men be measured? The SVIB measures only interests of men in professional, semiprofessional, and business occupations. For many years little success was obtained in measuring the interests of nonprofessional men. However, recently Clark and his associates (Clark, 1961), working with Navy enlisted men's specialties, have developed an inventory measuring interests in occupations other than professions.

Can the interests of women be measured? The interests of women, like those of nonprofessional men, have proven harder to measure than those of professional men. One reason is that a large proportion of women have interests that are family centered and only a small proportion of women pursue careers in professional occupations. Although there is a women's form of the test, the number of scales is about half the number of the men's form. Also, research on women's interests is limited and the meaning of much of the available data is not clear. (See Lewis, 1968, for a summary.)

The Minnesota Multiphasic Personality Inventory: an empirically keyed personality inventory

Just as work on group intelligence tests and interest inventories began around the time of World War I, so did the development of personality inventories. The grandfather of present day inventories, the Woodworth Personal Data Sheet, was developed to spot emotionally unstable soldiers during World War I. During the period between World War I and World War II a number of personality inventories were developed, the best known of which were the Bernreuter Personality Inventory and the Bell Adjustment Inventory, both still being used. The inventories of this era were, by and large, keyed by a priori methods, measured only one or a few dimensions, and lacked empirical validity evidence.

The major landmark in the development of self-report personality inventories, however, was the Minnesota Multiphasic Personality Inventory (MMPI), first published in 1942. The MMPI incorporated the best features of the previous inventories, added some twists of its own, and has significantly influenced the course of personality measurement and research since its publication. Let us see, therefore, what is unique about this instrument.

DEVELOPMENT OF THE MMPI. The authors of the MMPI hoped to develop a new kind of personality inventory—"an objective instrument for the "multiphasic assessment of personality by means of a profile of scales" (Hathaway, 1960, p. vii). By "multiphasic" they meant an instrument that would measure many facets of personality simultaneously, in contrast to the single (or few) trait tests available at that time. Furthermore, they hoped to include only empirically developed scales.

The basic procedure used was empirical keying. The criterion groups were composed of persons classified into one of the then prevalent psychiatric diagnostic categories—hysterics, hypochondriacs, schizophrenics, etc.—and were carefully selected so as to represent unambiguous manifestations of the classification group being studied. The responses of the criterion group were compared to the responses of "normals" to select those items that differentiated between normals and the diagnostic group. Both validation and cross-validation samples were used. Although the basic "normal" group consisted of hospital visitors (who proved to be a good cross-section of the population), other normal groups were also used to test the discriminating power of the items—college students, a group of WPA workers (used to control on urban and socioeconomic factors), and a group of patients hospitalized for physical rather than mental complaints. The last group illustrates the value of using various normal samples. An item might differentiate between normals and a criterion (psychiatric) group but really be discriminating only between hospitalized and nonhospitalized persons; however, if the item also discriminated between persons hospitalized for mental and for physical complaints, it could be assumed to be tapping an essential aspect of the psychiatric disorder.

The basic item pool consisted of a wide variety of descriptive statements taken from other inventories, textbook descriptions, psychiatric case writeups, medical records, and self-descriptions. Typical items are of the form:

I frequently find myself worrying about something.
At times I feel like smashing something.
I am happy most of the time.
I cry easily.
I am afraid when I look down from a high place.
What others think of me does not bother me.[4]

Subjects were asked to respond Yes, No, or Cannot Say (?) as to whether the statement described them.

The process of developing and purifying the scales, which varied somewhat for each scale, will not be described in detail here. (For a detailed description see Dahlstrom & Welsh, 1960 or Welsh & Dahlstrom, 1956.) Suffice it to say that the technique involved comparing the response frequencies of the criterion groups with those of the various normal groups. Eight diagnostic scales were developed—the criterion groups, and thus the scale name: hypochondriasis (Hs), depression (D), hysteria (Hy), psychopathic deviate (Pd), paranoia (Pa), psychasthenia (Pa), schizophrenia (Sc), and hypomania (Ma). As each scale was developed independently, some items are scored on more than one scale.

[4]Items reproduced by permission. Copyright 1943 by the University of Minnesota. Published by the Psychological Corporation, New York, N.Y. All rights reserved.

VALIDITY SCALES. One of the major innovations of the MMPI was the development of scales to identify various test-taking attitudes. These scales are called *validity scales* because deviant scores on these scales invalidate the rest of the scale scores or at least question their validity. One of the indices, the *?* or Cannot Say scale is not really a scale but simply a count of the number of omitted items. If a large number of items is omitted the test may be discarded or the test taker may be asked to complete the test; a small number of omissions is generally neglected and the test scored as usual. Actually, the problem of omissions is relatively minor because the distribution of *?* score is highly skewed with a mode of zero and a median of close to zero.

On personality inventories, some persons will try to present themselves in the best possible light. To identify these people a scale of 15 items, called the *Lie* (*L*) scale is included on the MMPI. These items are virtues that few mortals possess, at least in the degree indicated by the items. Persons who answer many of the items in the keyed direction either are trying to present a good impression or are very moral, in the conventional and straight-laced sense. The items are quite obvious to any one with much sophistication.

Just as there are situations where a person might want to present a good impression, there are situations where a person might want to appear more disturbed or give a poorer impression, e.g., to increase the probability of being accepted into therapy, or to avoid an onerous assignment. These persons can sometimes be detected by their scores on the *F scale*, a scale consisting of items that are infrequently answered in one direction. However, high scores can also be obtained by people who do not understand the testing process, by answering randomly, and by people who are truly disturbed. Thus no simple interpretation of the *F scale* is possible, and its scores have to be considered in conjunction with other data.

The fourth validity index, the *K scale*, consists of items that are susceptible to distortion or faking. The scale was developed in an attempt to reconcile MMPI scores with psychiatric diagnoses for several subsets of individuals whose MMPI scores did not typify their behavior (see Meehl & Hathaway, 1946, for scale construction details). Persons scoring high on the *K scale* tend to be defensive and deny personal inadequacies and problems of self-control; low scores indicate a willingness to say bad or sick things about oneself. Thus a low score may be indicative of faking "bad" (but also seems to be a good prognostic sign for psychotherapeutic success) while high scores may represent faking "good." Correcting certain of the diagnostic scales with the *K* score increases the validity of the diagnostic scales; thus *K* corrected scores are used on certain of the clinical scales.

One further method of identifying possible invalidated scores should be mentioned. As the items comprising each scale were selected because they discriminated between the criterion (diagnostic) group and normals, some of the items will not bear any logical relationship to the label of the scale. For example, the item, "I often feel as if things were not real," could readily be identified as being on the *Sc scale*, while the item, "I enjoy children," would not seem to bear any obvious relation to schizophrenia (as distinct from other diagnostic categories). The former items can be considered obvious and the latter, subtle items. For each diagnostic scale, two subscales thus can be constructed—one of obvious items and the other of subtle items—the test scored on both subscales, and any differences noted. Such a procedure has been followed with some of the MMPI scales, providing another method of detecting dissimulation.

THE INVENTORY. The inventory consists of 550 items to which the test taker responds true or false, depending upon whether the item is or is not characteristic of him. Although the MMPI can be administered in card form (each item being printed on a separate card with the subject sorting the cards into piles), the usual format has the items listed in a booklet with responses made on a separate answer sheet. No time limit is used and, as the reading level of the items is very low, an average adult should have no trouble in completing the MMPI in less than an hour.

The inventory is typically scored on the validity scales (L, F, K), the eight clinical scales discussed previously, plus several other scales: most frequently masculinity-femininity (Mf) and social introversion-extraversion (Si). Scores are converted to a T *score* scale, a standard score scale with $\overline{X} = 50$ and $s = 10$; the basic norm group being the Minnesota normal group. (See Figure 12.2.)

Reliability estimates for the MMPI scales, as for most personality measures, are of relatively low magnitude in comparison to the reliabilities attained by measures of maximal performance. Scale retest reliabilities fall in the .60–.90 range over short periods (a month or less) with normal subjects. The reliabilities decrease over longer time periods but do not seem to be noticeably lower for deviant groups. Although the MMPI scales were not designed to be homogeneous scales, internal consistency estimates of .90 and higher have been obtained for several of the scales. (A summary of the consistency data can be found in Appendix K of Dahlstrom & Welsh, 1960.)

INTERPRETATION OF MMPI SCORES. Even though the diagnostic scales were constructed by rigorously adhering to empirical procedures, it soon became apparent that the test would not be a highly accurate diagnostic sorting device. It was equally apparent that using the test solely as a shortcut to establishing a diagnosis was a tremendous waste of information. The item pool of the MMPI was too rich to be used for so limited a purpose. Thus the inventory, and the item pool itself, have been used for a variety of other practical and theoretical purposes in personality assessment and research.[5]

[5]For example, over 200 scales have been (empirically) developed from the item pool measuring such diverse traits as anxiety, ego strength, academic achievement, originality, pharisaic virtue, and ulcer personality.

Furthermore, it became apparent that to make maximum use of the information provided by the MMPI, scores would have to be interpreted, not by treating each scale individually, but in terms of patterns of scores. But to interpret scores configurally requires certain rules and procedures for arranging and summarizing the pattern of scores. To accomplish this end, and also because the scales had obtained surplus meaning over their original diagnostic label, each scale was given a number according to its order on the profile. The MMPI profile could then be coded as a sequence of numerals corresponding to the various scale scores. Several alternative coding systems are available, the distinction between them being primarily in the complexity of the symbolization used. One simple system uses only the two highest scale scores to form the code; thus, a profile with the highest score on scale 4 (Pd) and the second highest score on scale 9 (Ma) would be classified "49." Slightly more complex systems may use a combination of the three highest scales and the lowest scale; e.g., a code might be 498-2. Highly complex systems use various symbols to indicate the rank ordering of scale scores, the absolute level of scores, and the scores that differ by only one point. A description of the various coding systems can be found in Dahlstrom & Welsh (1960). (It is interesting to note that coding of profiles uses all three levels of measurement—the original scale scores are on an interval scale, the rank ordering of scales represents ordinal measurement, and the use of profile types in interpretation is nominal measurement.) Coding permits objective classification of MMPI profiles—by similarity of profile codes—and thereby enables one to search for behavior patterns that typify a particular profile code, thus providing a basis for interpreting scores on the test.

It would not be unfair to say that many of the major advances in the objective interpretation of personality test scores have resulted directly from attempts to interpret the MMPI. One of the first approaches to interpretation was the Atlas approach (Hathaway & Meehl, 1951). The *MMPI Atlas* consists of a collection of MMPI profiles, arranged by profile code, with each profile followed by a brief narrative description of the characteristics of the person whose profile was presented. The test user, when confronted with a profile needing interpretation, could look in the *Atlas* for examples of profiles with similar coding, read the personality descriptions, and get a flavor of the behavior characterizing persons having that particular profile pattern. The *Atlas* approach suffers, however, from the limitations that anecdotal approaches to knowledge have. As a source of hypotheses about expected behaviors, however, it is a valuable interpretive aid.

As use of the MMPI expanded, a folklore of interpretation clues developed, based on patterns of profile scores. Thus a profile with scales 1 and 2 the highest scores was said to indicate a neurotic pattern with depression and probably pain and/or somatic complaints; if scale 8 was significantly higher than scale 7, the indication was that the person was psychotic rather than neurotic; the relation of scores on scales 3 and 4 was said to indicate the amount of libidinal energy; and so on. Some of these folklore interpretations were supported by hard

The Minnesota Multiphasic Personality Inventory

Starke R. Hathaway and J. Charnley McKinley   Scorer's Initials_____

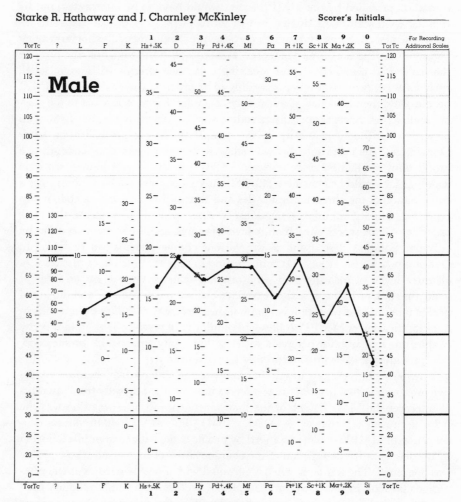

Figure 12.2 The Minnesota Multiphasic Personality Inventory Profile. Reproduced by permission. Copyright 1948 by The Psychological Corporation, New York, N. Y. All rights reserved.

data, others were the distillation of intensive clinical experience, and others probably represented severe cases of selective retention. Because of their unsystematic nature, these proposed interpretations lacked many of the requisites for being acceptable scientific knowledge.

What was needed were more systematic data regarding the characteristics of persons obtaining certain patterns of MMPI scores; or, as Meehl phrased it, what was needed was a good cookbook (Meehl, 1956). A good cookbook (or codebook, as they came to be known) would be empirically derived; would be based on a representative, or at least specifiable, population; and would summarize the characteristics of persons having a given MMPI profile that differentiated them from others. Because there are many possible MMPI patterns, and data must be available for a number of people having the same profile in order to insure stable results, the development of a cookbook requires tremendously large samples. However, several cookbooks have been developed (e.g., Drake & Oetting, 1959; Marks & Seeman, 1963). The codebooks represent the most advanced step in objectifying the interpretation of personality test scores; whether any individual clinicians will consider them as a step in the right direction will depend upon whether he believes that interpretation of personality test scores can be an objective, even mechanical, procedure or whether it must be an intuitive matter.

SOME RESEARCH QUESTIONS AND RESULTS.   As with the Strong, the research on the MMPI is so voluminous that it would be impossible to summarize in a few pages. (Dahlstrom & Welsh, 1960, for example, have devoted an entire book to an attempt to summarize the MMPI literature.) So we will only select several illustrations of the type of research questions that have been investigated.

One question that can be asked is: Which of the available methods of summarizing and interpreting MMPI profiles is most valid? This question is often raised in conjunction with the clinical versus statistical prediction issue. The most comprehensive studies (e.g., Goldberg, 1965; Meehl, 1959) have shown that: (1) actuarial methods are more accurate than clinical judgment and (2) the simpler actuarial methods are generally as accurate as the more complex, configural models.

A second set of research studies revolve around the question of the process clinicians go through in interpreting profiles and making diagnoses. This area of investigation was sparked by the writings of Sarbin (1944) and Meehl (1954). The types of questions raised include: What cues do clinicians use in making interpretations? How much information must be presented before the clinician can make a stable and/or valid judgment? How accurate are clinicians in their judgment? Can clinicians be trained to be more accurate or make better use of the available cues? Although the research designs utilized to study this problem have been very sophisticated, the results of the studies have been disappointing if one expected judges to agree among themselves, to be accurate predictors or at least to become more accurate with training, or that judges would make use of complex configural clues. One could summarize the evidence, somewhat irreverently, by stating that clinicians tend to use rather simple-minded approaches and, when it comes to simple-minded approaches, the computer and statistical formula are better than the human brain (Goldberg, 1968).

A third group of studies have centered on the question of what the MMPI scales measure. One approach is factor analysis, either of scale scores (e.g., Welsh, 1956; Kassebaum, Couch & Slater, 1959) or items within the scales (e.g., Comrey, 1957). Welsh pointed out that factor analyses of MMPI scales have typically found two major factors. The first is an anxiety or general emotional disturbance factor and the second appears to be a denial, repression, and lack of self-insight factor. Other researchers have attempted to interpret these general factors in terms of response sets but cannot seem to agree on what the set is, some feeling that it is social desirability, others feeling that it is acquiescence. Still others (e.g., Rorer, 1965; Block, 1965) feel that the variance in MMPI scores is primarily "true" variance, representing substantive differences between individuals, rather than response set components.

CONTRIBUTIONS OF THE MMPI. The MMPI is one of the most widely used, if not the most widely used, self-report inventory. It is used as a diagnostic aid, as a screening device, as a counseling and psychotherapeutic tool, and as a research instrument. It is used for decision making and descriptive purposes. Its wide usage attests to the fact that many psychologists consider it to be both valid and useful in both clinical and research settings. But the MMPI is also important for its influence on the development of objective personality assessment procedures—more so than any other test. What then are its major contributions?

For one, the MMPI demonstrated that personality measurement could be an objective, empirically based procedure. Previously, personality measures had used a priori scoring keys or, at best, used statistical criteria based on item distribution properties. The MMPI, in contrast, built scales by empirical methods. Second, the MMPI incorporated validity scales to control distortion. Although several previous tests had made passes at validity keys, the MMPI was the first to incorporate validity scales as an integral part of the testing and interpretation procedure. Third, research on the MMPI demonstrated that not only could the process of test construction be empirical and objective, but also could the test interpretation process. The development of coding systems, atlases, configural scoring rules, and cookbooks all represented attempts to objectify the interpretation process. Fourth, and by no means least, the MMPI has provided a large item pool that has been used for development of further scales and in research projects of various sorts. Particularly important is the fact that new scales could be developed from the item pool without changing the stimulus situation for the test taker, thus increasing the comparability of results obtained in different settings. That is, the test taker responds to the same pool of items, arranged in the same order (i.e., the same test) regardless of how many scales are scored. But, by scoring the test on various keys, different sets of scores can be obtained.

Other empirically keyed instruments

We have discussed the Strong Vocational Interest Blank and the Minnesota Multiphasic Personality Inventory at length to illustrate the process of constructing, validating, and interpreting an empirically keyed inventory. We will now briefly discuss two empirically keyed instruments that differ from the SVIB and MMPI in some crucial respect. Again our coverage will be illustrative rather than comprehensive; the reader who wishes a complete list or review of personality inventories must look elsewhere (e.g., Buros, 1965).

THE CALIFORNIA PSYCHOLOGICAL INVENTORY. One of the most frequently heard complaints about the MMPI concerns its "pathological" nature. In many senses, the California Psychological Inventory (CPI) can be considered as an MMPI for normal persons.

The CPI consists of 480 statements, an appreciable minority of which overlap with MMPI items, which are presented in a format similar to the MMPI In contrast to the MMPI, however, the 18 CPI scales are designed to measure dimensions of normal personality—e.g., dominance, sociability, tolerance, achievement via independence, and flexibility. These 18 scales are grouped (not entirely empirically) into four categories: measures of poise, ascendancy, and self-assurance; measures of socialization, maturity, and responsibility; measures of achievement potential and intellectual efficiency; and measures of intellectual and interest modes.

The majority of the scales, though not all the scales, were developed by empirical methods. Thus, for example, the Dominance scale was validated (1) by testing its ability to differentiate between groups of students rated as "most" and "least" dominant by teachers and/or principals and (2) by correlating dominance scores with the ratings of dominance by peers or psychologists. In short, scales were validated against "real life" social criteria so that the scales would measure important and socially relevant personality dimensions. This, then, is the important aspect of the CPI—the fact that it illustrates that empirical keying procedures can be applied to measuring "normal" personality as well as to measuring traits of a more extreme or pathological nature.

KUDER OCCUPATIONAL INTEREST SURVEY. This inventory is a recent addition to the list of interest inventories developed by G. F. Kuder who, along with E. K. Strong, has been the major contributor to the field of interest measurement. Although the Occupational Interest Survey (OIS) more closely parallels the SVIB than do Kuder's earlier inventories (see the discussion of the "Kuder Preference Record—Vocational" below), it differs from the SVIB in several respects. First, items are presented in a triad format, the test taker's job being to select the activity that he most prefers and the one he least prefers from among the three alternative statements. This procedure is essentially forced-choice and lets one triad do the work of three separate items. For example, the triad:

a. watch a baseball game
b. play in a baseball game
c. teach children to play baseball

could also be presented as three separate items, the test taker indicating his liking or disliking of each activity separately (as on the SVIB), or the alternatives could be paried (a versus b, a versus c, and b versus c) and the test taker required to select one alternative in each pair.

Second, the OIS is scored on a somewhat different set of occupational scales than the SVIB, although there is some overlap between occupations scored on the two inventories. The fact that the same occupations appear on both inventories should not, however, be taken as an indication that occupational scales with the same label measure the same things, as Zytowski (1968) has shown that the correlations between supposedly comparable scales are often low. In addition, the OIS can be scored on scales representing educational majors as well as occupational groups.

The basic difference between the OIS and the SVIB is in the derivation of scale scores. Both inventories use empirical keys based on the similarity of an individual's responses to those of men in an occupational group. However, scores on the OIS represent the correlation between the individual's interests and the interests of men in various occupations (Kuder, 1963, 1966). The comparison of the individual to the criterion group is thus direct on the OIS, avoiding the problems associated with selecting an appropriate men-in-general group. Although extensive research has not yet been published, Kuder claims that this procedure significantly reduces classification errors.

Many other empirically-keyed personality inventories could be discussed but, by and large, as they represent variations on the inventories already discussed—perhaps being designed for a different age level or to measure a different set of traits—rather than illustrating fundamentally different approaches to personality measurement, we will turn to another approach to personality measurement: homogeneously keyed inventories.

Homogeneous keying of inventories

The inventories discussed thus far in this chapter have all been criterion-centered; that is, the sole requirement for an item to be retained on the scale being that it predicted the criterion measure. Formal personality theory played little, if any, role in item selection, and the homogeneity of the resultant scale was an irrelevant consideration. In fact, because most criterion measures are heterogeneous, one could almost be assured that the resultant scale would be heterogeneous.

But, as was mentioned previously, one can take other approaches to scale development. One attack sets homogeneity as the prime requirement of any scale and, consequently, the test construction process is designed to insure that the completed scale will be homogeneous. The dimensions that the test is to measure may be well specified before the test construction process starts or the factors (scales) may be allowed to emerge from the empirical data. The item selection procedure can vary from clustering intercorrelated items through intricate factor analytic designs. In all instances, however, the goal is to develop a scale that is homogeneous.

To illustrate, consider the hypothetical example of constructing a scale to measure interest in intellectual activities. The first step would be to collect or write a group of items that, on a priori grounds, appeared to measure intellectual propensities. These items would then be administered to a representative sample of individuals, responses recorded, and item intercorrelations computed. Items that did not correlate highly with the other items or the total scale score would be eliminated. If the item scores were factor analyzed, items not loading on the major factor would be eliminated. The entire process would be repeated on another sample to cross-validate the items statistics. In this way, a pure or homogeneous scale could be developed.

The actual scale development process would, of course, vary from the ideal paradigm presented in the previous paragraph. For example, if the factor analysis indicated that the items measured more than one factor, the test constructor would have to decide whether to include scales for the several factors or retain only items measuring the factor of prime concern. If several scales were being developed simultaneously, procedures used must both insure that each individual scale is homogeneous and that the several scales are not highly intercorrelated.

This method of scale development assumes that the most meaningful constructs are reflected by homogeneous dimensions. Criterion-related validity, while not irrelevant, is a secondary consideration. As, at least theoretically, the prediction of any complex criterion can be accomplished by appropriate weighting of the various homogeneous scores, the homogeneous scale approach proffers the advantages of the empirically keyed instrument (criterion-related validity) plus the advantage of measuring along homogeneous, and therefore presumably more meaningful, dimensions (construct validity).

KUDER PREFERENCE RECORD—VOCATIONAL. Just as the SVIB is the classic example of an empirically keyed interest inventory, the Kuder-Vocational is the prototype of an homogeneously keyed interest inventory. Like the other Kuder inventories, the item format is the triadical, the test consisting of 168 triads. Unlike the SVIB and Kuder OIS, which assess interest in specific occupations, the Kuder-Vocational, as its title implies, measures interest in broad vocational areas. Thus it is appropriately used in situations where the concern is with identifying broad areas of interest, rather than choosing a specific occupation.

The process of scale construction proceeded as follows. After an item pool had been developed, a priori item keys were constructed using purely logical considerations. Thus, for example, all items that appeared to measure literary interests were included on one scale, all items denoting scientific interests on another, and so on.[6] The items were then administered to an experimental sample and items that did not correlate with the total score on the a priori key were eliminated. By this procedure, the scoring keys were made more homogeneous. (That this procedure worked is evidenced by the fact that Kuder-Richardson coefficients for the scales range from .85 upward in various samples.) These analyses resulted in the scrapping of some a priori scales and the restructuring of others. Analogous procedures were used to add scales to later editions of the test. The present form of the test consists of ten scales: Outdoor, Mechanical, Computational, Scientific, Persuasive, Artistic, Literary, Musical, Social Service, and Clerical.

Because responding to the inventory items requires a choice between alternatives and because alternative responses are scored on different scales, any response will increase the score on one scale but consequently limit the maximal possible score on another scale (the scale on which the nonchosen alternative is scored). Or, viewed from a different angle, the sum of the raw scores, barring omissions, will be the same for each person. Therefore, scores on the Kuder-Vocational are *ipsative*, not normative.

How are ipsative scores to be interpreted? Consider two individuals, Jim and Bill, who score at the 80th and 60th percentile, respectively, on the Mechanical scale of the Kuder-Vocational. Can we say that Jim has stronger mechanical interests than Bill? Not unambiguously, because Bill's score on the Mechanical scale may have been attenuated because there were a number of areas wherein he had strong interests while Jim, lacking interest in any area but mechanics, obtained an inflated score on the Mechanical scale. That is, the scoring procedure on the Kuder (or on any ipsative scale) ranks interests in terms of their relative strength within the individual but gives no indication of the absolute strength of any interest. Thus a person with intensive interests in several areas will have his intense interests cancel each other out, and if an individual who is generally indifferent has stronger interest in one area, the score in this area will be spuriously inflated.

Furthermore, the fact that Jim scores at the 80th percentile on the Mechanical scale and the 95th percentile on the Clerical scale does not allow us to unambiguously state that he has stronger interests in clerical work than in mechanical

---

[6]When scoring a particular scale one must consider those items (triads) where one (of the three) alternatives is relevant to that scale. Thus, items that are relevant for (i.e., will be scored on) the scientific scale are those items where one of the alternatives measures scientific interest. Conversely, as each triad has statements representing three different interest areas, each item (triad) will appear on three scoring scales.

areas, because this interpretation is clouded by the general interest level of (American) males in mechanical and clerical areas. Since the average male probably has stronger interests in mechanical than clerical activities, the same percentile rank on the two scales would not indicate comparable levels of interest, and a lower percentile ranking on the mechanical scale may actually represent more intense interests than a higher rank on the clerical scale. (For a further discussion of the problem of interpreting ipsative scores, see Bauernfeind, 1962, or Katz, 1962.)

Thus, in spite of the fact that the scale development procedures on the Kuder Vocational make logical sense and produce homogeneous scales, and the percentile reporting of scores is seemingly straightforward, the ipsativity of the test makes meaningful interpretations difficult.

Other self-report inventories

Of the three major approaches to the construction of personality inventories— rational, empirical and homogeneous—two have been illustrated and the other (rational) was rejected as an incomplete (and thus unacceptable) strategy. In this section we will discuss four inventories whose special characteristics make them worthy of special comment: a test designed to control a major response set; a test that includes both empirical and homogeneous keys; and two tests that are based on typologies.

EDWARDS PERSONAL PREFERENCE SCHEDULE.   The Edwards Personal Preference Schedule (EPPS) is a self-report personality inventory, consisting of 225 items in forced-choice format scored on 15 scales corresponding to Murray's need categories (see Figure 12.3). Whether the EPPS, in fact, adequately measures the dimensions that it supposedly taps is an open question (see reviews in Buros, 1965, by Radcliffe and Stricker), but one that is of secondary importance for our purposes. Of primary importance is the fact that the EPPS was designed to control the effects of one of the major response sets—social desirability.

Edwards, it will be recalled, showed that there was a high correlation between the rated social desirability of an item and the probability of endorsement of that item. This finding cast doubt on the validity of all self-report inventories, for it opened the possibility that test takers were responding not solely to the content of the test item, but also to its social desirability. Thus scores on, say, the MMPI might as readily be interpreted as measures of the test taker's willingness to say socially undesirable things about himself as measures of the traits the inventories presumed to measure. The test constructor, consequently, must decide how to control for this possiblity, and insure that scores reflect trait differences rather than differences attributable to the social desirability variable.

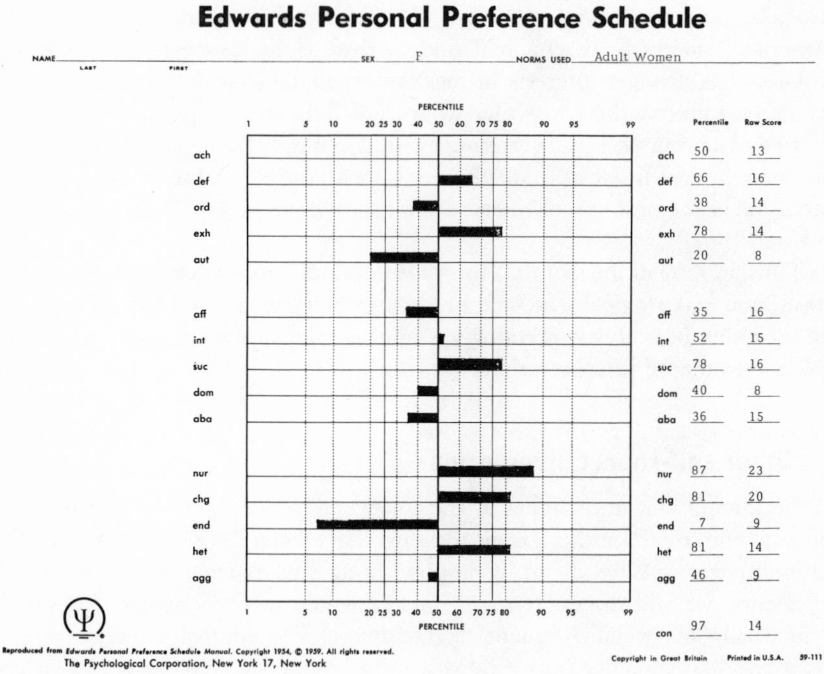

Edwards Personal Preference Schedule

Figure 12.3 The Edwards Personal Preference Schedule Profile. Reproduced by permission. Copyright 1954, © 1959 by The Psychological Corporation, New York, N. Y. All rights reserved.

Edwards reasoned that the best way to control social desirability was to force the test taker to choose between two equally desirable (or undesirable) alternatives, each of which measured different traits. By pairing alternatives having the same rated social desirability but measuring different traits, the test taker must respond on the basis of item content, because both statements in the pair are equally desirable or undesirable. Thus confronted with the choice between two equally desirable alternatives, e.g.,

I like to help my friends when they are in trouble.
I like to do my very best in whatever I undertake.

or two equally undesirable alternatives, e.g.,

I feel depressed when I fail at something.
I feel nervous when giving a talk before a group.[7]

[7]Items reproduced by permission. Copyright 1953 by The Psychological Corporation, New York, N.Y. All rights reserved.

the test taker will respond primarily on the basis of content. Of course, on any particular item, one statement may be more socially desirable for a given individual than the other, but averaging over all items on the test the effects of social desirability should cancel out.

How well did he succeed in attaining his goal? The preponderance of evidence seems to indicate that although the influence of social desirability is much less on the EPPS than on the typical personality inventory, its influence has by no means been completely eliminated.

Two other important consequences of Edwards' attempt to control social desirability by use of a forced-choice format should be mentioned. First, utilization of the forced-choice format necessarily resulted in ipsative scores, thereby introducing complications into both the interpretation and statistical analyses of the scores. And, second, concentration on controlling the effects of the social desirability variable evidently resulted in less care being devoted to item selection, the only apparent criterion for inclusion being the logical relation of the item content to one of Murray's need categories. Thus it appears that in test construction, as in other endeavors, when one attempts to maximize one value he frequently sacrifices another.

MINNESOTA VOCATIONAL INTEREST INVENTORY.   In the discussion of interest research, we mentioned that one of the difficult tasks in interest measurement has been to develop scales that measured the interests of nonprofessional men. However, Clark and his associates (Clark, 1961) working with Navy enlisted men were able to develop such an inventory, the Minnesota Vocational Interest Inventory (MVII). The MVII, as it finally evolved, consists of 158 triadical items, e.g.:

Repair electrical wiring.
Fix a clogged drain.
Check for errors in a copy of a report.[8]

with the test taker indicating which of the three activities he likes best and which of the three he would most dislike. Thus the item format is similar to the Kuder inventories.

Although there are a number of notable features about the MVII, the one that is most relevant to our discussion is the fact that the MVII has two sets of scoring scales—Occupational Scales and Homogeneous Scales. The Occupational Scales were developed by empirical keying methods similar to those used on the SVIB. The basic procedure was to contrast the responses of men in a particular occupation (e.g., baker, printer, carpenter, painter, truck driver, machinist, and electrician) with the responses of tradesmen-in-general. Note

[8]Items reproduced by permission. Copyright © 1965 by The Psychological Corporation, New York, N.Y. All rights reserved.

that the basic comparison group, tradesmen-in-general, is different from the men-in-general group used on the SVIB, which was composed of men in professional occupations, but that in both cases the item selection procedures were similar and the comparison group was composed of persons working in occupations at the same occupational level as the occupations being keyed.

The MVII also may be scored on a number of Homogeneous or Area Scales. Here the procedure for keying responses was similar to that for other homogeneous scales, items that were intercorrelated being placed on the same scale. Nine homogeneous scales were developed, as indicated in Figure 12.4. Although one might expect that the homogeneous keys and the occupational keys would be quite independent, the empirical data (Clark, 1961) show that each homogeneous key is highly correlated with at least one occupational scale. For example, the Mechanical homogeneous key correlates high positively with the occupational keys for Truck Mechanic, Sheet Metal Worker, and Plumber, and high negatively with Retail Sales Clerk, Stock Clerk, Tabulating Machine Operator, and several other occupational keys.

TWO TYPOLOGIES. Most of the inventories discussed have not been outgrowths of specific personality theories. Partially, no doubt, this situation obtains because both empirical and homogeneous keying are heavily dependent on the nature of the data, and what the data show often is not exactly what the theorist expects. On the other hand, tests that are developed rationally to fit a theory, using a priori methods of test construction, suffer from obvious defects and thus may be scientifically unacceptable. The appropriate congruence of empirical and theoretical efforts apparently has not yet been reached. But to illustrate theory-based personality measures, we will mention two tests that are offshoots of specific personality theories. Furthermore, both of the tests represent a particular type of theory, a typology, that differs from the usual trait approach.

One of the inventories, the Allport-Vernon-Lindzey *Study of Values*, is a well-known and widely used instrument. The Study of Values measures theoretical, economic, aesthetic, social, political, and religious values, one scale for each type in Spranger's typology. Item selection was based on internal consistency criteria. The designation Study of Values implies that an evaluative component, not just an interest dimension, is being assessed. Consistent with the evaluative emphasis, the several item formats used all require the test taker to choose between or rank several alternative values. This forced-choice procedure, of course, produces ipsative measurement requiring scores to be interpreted intra-individually.

The other inventory that springs from a formal typology is the *Myers-Briggs Type Indicator*. This inventory is modeled after the Jungian typology and classifies persons along four supposedly dichotomous dimensions: extraversion-introversion, sensation-intuition, thinking-feeling, and judgment-perception. The items' content centers around preferences, habitual behaviors, and value judg-

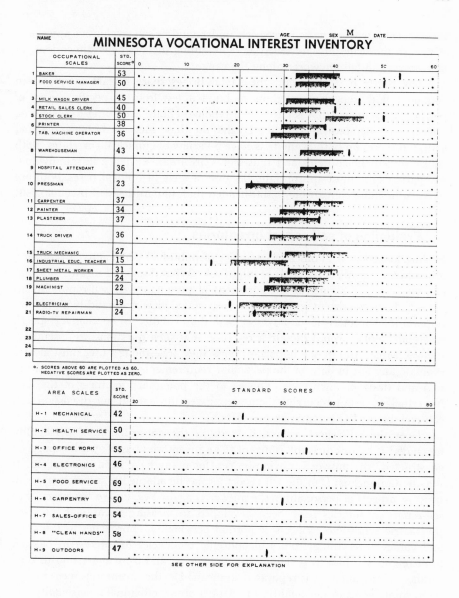

Figure 12.4 The Minnesota Vocational Interest Inventory Profile. Reproduced by permission. Copyright © 1965 by The Psychological Corporation, New York, N. Y. All rights reserved.

ments. In effect, the test is trying to get at the person's approach to thinking and structuring experience. For example, the judgment-perception scale attempts to determine whether the person's approach to his experiences is basically judgmental and evaluative or a more perceptive, understanding, nonevaluative approach. Although the scales are presented as representing dichotomous dimensions, in fact, scores can fall anywhere along the range.

The Study of Values and the Myers-Briggs share certain attributes in common. Both represent attempts to build a test from a specific theory of personality, a theory that is basically a typology. Both, according to reviewers, have failed to demonstrate conclusively that they have succeeded in their original goal, but scores on both of the tests have a variety of empirical correlates. Both utilize forced-choice items and thus scores are ipsative; hence intraindividual comparisons are most appropriate. Because of their theoretical bases, both are likely to be more compatible to soft-headed than to hard-headed psychologists.

Evaluation of self-report inventories

Having looked at a number of examples of published personality inventories, albeit in too cursory a fashion, we might ask "What does it all mean?", "What can we conclude about the measurement of personality by self-report inventories?" To be consistent with the previously stated view that validity is the most important characteristic of any test and that validity is, in many respects, situation-specific, would dictate a response that such questions are essentially unanswerable. And in one important sense they are—the test user must always evaluate any test in light of the particular requirements of the particular situation and draw his own conclusion as to the potential usefulness of the test. Nevertheless, certain recurring themes appeared throughout our discussion and can now be used to summarize this section.

Does the self-report approach work in the construction of personality measures? If by this question is meant: Can inventories based on self-reports be constructed? the answer is obviously Yes, for many have been constructed. If the question means: Can the self-report format be adapted to a wide variety of traits or aspects of personality? the answer is again Yes, for we have seen that self-report inventories have been developed to measure vocational interests, psychiatric syndromes, aspects of normal personality, approaches to thinking, and values—everything from schizophrenic tendencies to interest in baking, from religious values to psychopathic tendencies, and from aggression to nurturance. If the question is rephrased to mean: Do the inventories measure the basic components of personality, the depths of an individual's personality? no answer can be given. Instead, one must ask, what is meant by "basic components?" If, like some factor analysts, one means well-documented factors, then the answer is Yes; if, like some personality theorists, you mean some intangible underlying motivating agent, then the answer is "probably not."

Do self-report personality inventories attain the desired standards of consistency and validity? Certainly the evidence shows that the consistency of personality measures, be it stability, equivalence, or even internal consistency measures, is generally lower than that of other types of measures. But is this a function of the phenomenon we are dealing with or the mode of measurement? There is evidence that well-constructed inventories can meet even the most rigorous standards of internal consistency and stability (e.g., Strong's 18-year follow-up). Validity is another question. In most cases the appropriate method of establishing validity is construct validity, which can neither be established overnight nor summarized in a single index. Certainly there is an abundance of evidence showing that scores on personality inventories relate to a variety of other variables; but in the large majority of the instances the relationships are disappointingly low—too low to be used as definite validity evidence.

What is the relationship between personality measurement and personality theory? With several notable exceptions, tests developed to reflect the prime variables in a particular theory have not been epitomes of good test construction methodology, and conversely, the most rigorous test construction methods have been adopted by persons whose philosophic viewpoint approached dust-bowl empiricism. Personality inventories have, of course, been used to test concepts in and deductions from personality theory, but too often the tests used have been accepted uncritically, developed on an ad hoc basis, or used for purposes for which they were not designed. In short, the relation between formal personality theory and practice of personality measurement is slight.

Have empirical correlates of personality inventory scores been established? If anything is certain in personality measurement it is that scores on the widely used personality inventories have been, or will be, correlated with practically any variable imaginable. For example, the *Sixth Mental Measurements Yearbook* lists 1400 studies utilizing the MMPI, over 600 for the SVIB, and over 500 for the Kuder-Vocational; and the Edwards PPS had well over 300 references in the first ten years after its publication. So there is no doubt that there is a plethora of data; the problem is to make any sense out of the data. Because much of the data is situation-specific, collected on particular samples in a particular place at a particular time for a particular purpose, rather than as part of systematic attempts to understand the meaning of a particular test or test score, the data are almost impossible to comprehend. One can only admire the attempts made to summarize the data on particular tests—attempts like those of Dahlstrom and Welsh (1960) for the MMPI, Darley & Hagenah (1955) for the SVIB, Super & Crites (1962) for a variety of tests, and some of Buros' reviewers.

What impact do response sets, response styles, and faking have on inventory scores? In spite of concentrated research and attempts at control, it is clear that the effects of these variables have not been completely eliminated from any of the extant inventories. Although the identification of the direction and amount of possible dissimulation (as in the MMPI validity scales), and incorporation of these data into the test interpretation process is a desirable step, adoption of a test format that would eliminate their effects would be an even more desirable solution. The most systematic attempt to accomplish this end (Edwards' work) has been only partially successful. Furthermore, because much of the research on these variables has involved only intratest measures and not extratest variables, it is impossible to definitely ascertain whether their effects are test-specific or represent broader personality traits. But without doubt, response sets and styles do influence test scores, and faking of personality inventories is possible.

Is empirical or homogeneous keying a better approach to construction of self-report inventories? To answer this question, of course, requires another question: more effective for what purpose? There is no question but that empirically keyed tests (e.g., the MMPI and SVIB) are more widely used, receive stronger support from the research literature, and have had a greater impact on personality assessment. These conclusions hold in spite of the fact that the homogeneous keyed instruments, theoretically, should possess the advantages of an empirically keyed instrument plus the advantage of providing homogeneous, and hence hopefully more readily interpretable, scores. The reasons for the failure of the homogeneously keyed instruments is unclear; but one possible reason is that the existing inventories do not tap all the relevant factors. Ideally, of course, the instrument should include items that are *both* empirically and homogeneously keyed, not in the sense of the parallel scales on the MVII, but in the sense that the items included on a scale have surmounted both an empirical and a homogeneous selection hurdle.

Are various item formats differentially effective? For the most part, constructors of items for self-report personality inventories have not been noticeably creative, relying primarily on two basic item formats: (1) a statement that is to be agreed or disagreed with and (2) a forced-choice between two or more alternatives. Although the latter approach has certain benefits in controlling irrelevant variables, it also leads to ipsative scores and thus to problems in analyzing and interpreting scores. Lacking any persuasive argument based on differential reliability and/or validity, there may be some slight advantage for the simpler, former approach. One would hope, however, that test constructors might show more ingenuity in attempting to develop new item formats. To cite only one example of what might be done, Goldberg has been experimenting with an item format that requires the respondent to indicate whether he has engaged in an activity in the past (say, climbing a mountain or "telling off" a teacher), what his subjective reaction to the experience was (did he like it or dislike it), and what is the probability that he will engage in the activity in the future. This format not only provides a large quantity of response data from a single stimulus item but also allows for the analysis of response patterns.[9]

[9]For example, what is indicated when the response pattern is: I have done this, I like it, but I will not do it in the future? Or if the pattern is: I have done this, I didn't like it, but I will do it again? Or if one group of persons responds: I have done it, I liked it, and I'll do it again, and another large segment responds to the item: I haven't done it, I wouldn't like it, and I won't do it in the future? Ascertaining the meaning of such patterns would present an intriguing research problem. (L. R. Goldberg, personal communication, 1968).

Finally, for what practical purposes can self-report inventories be used? Because of the openness of self-report inventories to faking and other varieties of dissimulation, they can legitimately be used and interpreted only when it is assured that the test taker is treating the test as a measure of typical, not maximal, performance. The empirical data certainly support the use of the Strong in vocational counseling, and, if used with caution, possibly in educational and vocational placement. The more traditional personality inventories exhibit such low relationships with real-life criteria that their use for purposes other than hypothesis building, and to make statements about the general characteristics of groups, seems quite tenuous.

PROJECTIVE METHODS

Self-report personality inventories fall within the same psychometric tradition as achievement and ability tests, emphasizing objectivity and standardization so as to achieve acceptable levels of consistency and validity. In many ways, the testing procedures and methodology duplicate those of achievement and aptitude testing, differing only in content and consequently the appropriate criteria used to validate the scores. Although psychological theory played a part in the construction of these tests, theory was usually subordinate to the technical psychometric requirements. Projective methods, in contrast, have been more closely related to theory than other varieties of tests, being associated with the dynamic theories of personality, in particular psychoanalysis.

WHAT DEFINES A PROJECTIVE METHOD? The term projection, when applied to projective methods, is used in a very general sense to denote the process by which the characteristics of the individual (his personality structure) influence the ways in which he perceives, organizes, and interprets his environment. The implication for test construction is obvious—to study personality, one should present an individual with a set of new and/or ambiguous stimuli, observe how he reacts to structure the situation, and from his responses make inferences concerning his personality structure. The crucial requirements are that the stimulus situation lack definite structure and that the test taker be given wide latitude in his mode of response, because unduly restricting his response options would, in effect, be structuring the task.

Not all authors would agree that the ambiguity of the stimulus and the leeway in responding are the essential features of projective methods. Lindzey (1961), for example, after surveying the various definitions of projective techniques, concluded that the hallmarks of projective techniques were their sensitivity to unconscious or latent aspects of personality, the multiplicity of responses permitted the subject, that several personality dimensions are measured simultaneously, the subject's unawareness of the purpose of the testing,[10] and the richness of the response data elicited. In addition, certain other characteristics frequently occur but are not of prime importance: the ambiguity of the stimulus, the use of holistic analyses, the evocation of fantasy responses, and the fact that there are no correct or incorrect responses.

Rather than haggle further over a universal definition, we will describe several projective methods; after reading these descriptions the reader can decide for himself which dimensions are fundamental and which are only typical.

The Rorschach method

No other psychological test is as well known, has intrigued the layman as much, or caused as much division of opinion among psychologists as the Rorschach method.

The test itself consists of ten cards, each of which contains an amorphous design resembling a blot formed by folding a piece of paper containing a still wet drop of ink. All of the designs are symmetrical and printed on a white background; half are in shades of gray and black, others are gray plus color, still others are completely chromatic with no grays. (Figure 12.5 shows a design similar to a Rorschach card.)

The use of "inkblots" as stimuli illustrates an important aspect of projective testing: the unimportance of item content. The only requirement of the stimulus is that it be unstructured but capable of having a structure imposed upon it. The inkblots are, of course, essentially meaningless; yet because they resemble and suggest real objects, they are capable of being structured, allowing the subject to project meaning onto them. Thus they are ideally suited to serve as stimuli, even though they have no inherent meaning.

The administration of the Rorschach typically occurs in two stages. During the first stage the administrator presents the cards, one at a time and in a set order. The subject is instructed to report what he sees in the blots, i.e., what the blots resemble or suggest to him. The second stage of the administration is an inquiry. In this stage the subject goes through the cards, in sequence, a second time, commenting upon the features of the blots which caused him to make a particular response. Whereas the administrator seldom comments during the first stage, he may actively question the subject during the inquiry. The test is, obviously, administered individually.

---

[10]Awareness of the purposes of the testing is, of course, a relative rather than an absolute condition. When we say that a person is unaware of the purposes of the testing, we generally mean, not that he is completely unaware of the purposes of the test, but rather that he does not know what scores will be obtained or exactly how they will be used. In this connection we might mention Kelly's (1958) classical distinction: an objective test is a test where the test taker tries to guess what the examiner is thinking, and a projective test is a test where the examiner tried to guess what the test taker is thinking.

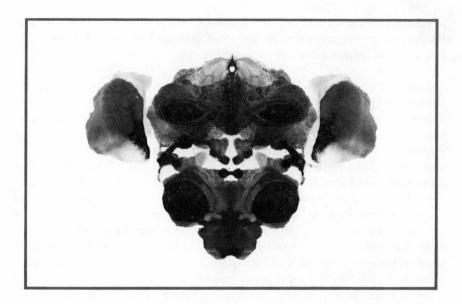

Figure 12.5 An inkblot similar to those used in the Rorschach method.

SCORING AND INTERPRETATION. There are several distinct approaches to scoring the Rorschach. In general, all the systems agree that certain dimensions, e.g., location, determinant, and content, should be scored but disagree on the exact scoring techniques—the relative emphases to be given each score category and the other dimensions scored. *Location* refers to the portion of the blot used as the basis of the response and can vary from use of the whole blot, through use of a major detail or segment of the blot, to use of a minor detail of the blot, or even use of white background space. *Determinants* refer to which aspect of the blot determined the response: the shape or form, shading or texture, coloring, and whether movement was perceived. *Content*, of course, refers to the category the percept falls into—e.g., a human, details of humans, an animal, a plant. Every response is scored on all three dimensions: location, determinant, content.

These scores, plus other data (e.g., total number of responses, reaction times, various ratios between scores, whether the responses were popular or original) are combined into a *psychogram*. From this point, interpretation becomes a highly individualized matter—some clinicians relying of actuarial patterns and signs, others proceeding on a completely intuitive basis; some emphasizing the pattern of scores, others emphasizing individual responses; some paying particular attention to content, others paying little attention to the content. It is at this point, consequently, that the Rorschach loses its objectivity. Although actuarial validity data concerning particular scores could be developed, these have not become popular because of certain statistical problems (Cronbach,

1949b), e.g., different numbers of responses are given by different subjects, and because many Rorschach users feel that statistical treatment destroys the dynamic and holistic nature of the interpretation.

VALIDITY. Although the literature is replete with studies utilizing the Rorschach (over 3000 studies being listed in the *Sixth Mental Measurements Yearbook*), the validity of the method is often questioned, with opinions ranging from the view that its validity is beyond question to the view that it is a worthless instrument. The reasons for these differences of opinion are numerous. The statistical problems with the scores, for one, render much of the validity data meaningless or at least inconclusive. Then, too, because control of all relevant variables is next to impossible in studying personality, results of studies are open to various interpretations. Third, as the test is supposed to measure unconscious motivating factors, and criterion measures reflecting these factors are not available, direct validity evidence is often not feasible. Conversely, studies of the relationship between Rorschach scores and objective criterion measures are often considered trivial by the depth psychologists. Fourth, although the test is supposed to reflect basic personality structure, changes in the testing situation can affect the subject's responses (Masling 1960). And, fifth, when Rorschach scores are correlated with other variables, the correlations usually do not approach .00 or 1.00, thus leaving them open to various interpretations. (This fifth point, particularly, and the others to a lesser extent, also are relevant to validity studies in other domains.)

One final point should be emphasized because it reflects a widespread confusion. Because interpretations of Rorschach scores are highly individualized, most studies validate not solely the Rorschach, but a particular examiner's interpretation of the Rorschach. That is, the test and examiner are confounded and simple validation of the test is impossible. For example, if Dr. Chiaroscuro looks at Rorschach psychograms of students at Waterman College and, on the bases of the psychograms identifies the students' need for intensive counseling, any study that relates his diagnoses to an independent criterion will be, in essence, validating Dr. Chiaroscuro's intepretation of the Rorschach, not just the test. What validity should be attributed to the examiner and what to the test is an unanswerable question in this design. To validate Rorschach scores one would, of course, have to relate psychogram scores to the criterion directly, without the examiner's interpretation.

MODIFICATIONS. As would be expected with an instrument as popular as the Rorschach, there have been various modifications of the method. Some of these have been designed to permit group administration, while others have attempted to make the scoring more objective. The major modification is the *Holtzman Inkblot Test* (Holtzman, 1959, 1961). Holtzman's test differs from the Rorschach in several ways: (1) there are 45 cards rather than ten, (2) the subject is allowed only one response per card, (3) scoring is restricted to a small number of important dimensions—location, form appropriateness, form definiteness, color, shading, and movement energy level—although provision is made for scoring other dimensions, (4) quantitative scoring weights are used, and (5) several forms of the test have been developed. These changes result in reliable scores, avoid many of the statistical problems inherent in the Rorschach, and simplify administration, while retaining many desirable projective features of the original test.

The Thematic Apperception Test

On a continuum measuring degree of structure of personality measures, the self-report inventories would fall at the high structure end and the projective methods at the unstructured end. But projectives vary among themselves in degree of structure. While the Rorschach presented the test taker with a highly ambiguous stimulus situation and permitted wide latitude in response, the *Thematic Apperception Test* (or TAT) presents the subject with a more structured stimulus and response situation, yet does not approach the restraints imposed by the usual self-report technique.

THE TEST. The TAT consists of a set of 20 cards, 19 of which picture scenes varying in content and ambiguity, but typically of people engaged in some activity, and one blank card. (Figure 12.6 illustrates the type of card used.) The cards are presented to the subject, one at a time, and he is requested to make up a story about the card, including details such as: what is happening, who are the people involved, what actions have preceded the scene, what will happen, what are the actors thinking and feeling. The examiner plays a relatively passive role, giving the initial instructions and recording the responses.

The basic rationale of the test depends heavily on the mechanism of identification, the assumption being that the test taker will identify with one of the characters in the scene, particularly the hero or central actor. As the stimuli on the TAT are more realistic, involving people pursuing various activities, the test has more face validity and more apparent relevance to the life of the test taker than does the Rorschach, thus permitting identification to occur.

As with the Rorschach, there are several scoring systems. The original system proposed by the test's developer emphasized the analysis of the needs of the hero and the environmental press that impinged upon him—an emphasis that followed directly from his theory of personality (H. A. Murray, 1938). Many of the other scoring systems are variations of Murray's approach, differing in the role of structural (noncontent) variables, the unit of analysis used, and the degree of inference required. In general, the various scoring and interpretation systems place great reliance on the analysis of the thematic content of the stories, with structural properties and objective indices playing a relatively minor role.

Figure 12.6 A card similar to those used on the Thematic Apperception Test.

The exact content of the test (i.e., cards used) varies somewhat with the age
and sex of the subject; thus, while not providing equivalent forms, some flexibility is possible in adapting the test to the subject. Special sets of cards have
also been developed for use with various groups—for example, Negroes (the
Thompson modification) and children (the Children's Apperception Test).

Other sets have been developed to measure particular personality variables, such as McClelland's use (McClelland et al., 1953) of modified TAT cards for the study of achievement motivation.

VALIDITY.   Determination of the validity of the TAT is a difficult task. The first question one has to answer is whether the stories actually represent manifestations of an individual's personality or whether they are merely stereotypic reactions to the situations pictured. Even if we can assume that the stories do represent true manifestations of the subject's personality, can we assume that he identifies with the hero, that the hero's problems and reactions and press acting upon him are reflections of the testee's situation? Then, too, lack of agreement on a single scoring and interpretation system complicates the task. And as the test is proposed not as a diagnostic or classification technique, but rather to provide a general description of the content of personality, the ubiquitous criterion problem looms large. Hence, scientifically acceptable validity data remain difficult to find.

Other projective methods

While the Rorschach and TAT are the two most popular projective techniques, a number of other approaches are also used. The one with the longest history is the *word association technique*. The typical procedure in word association tests is for the examiner to read a list of words, one at a time, the subject responding with the first word that comes into his mind. The ideal stimulus words are ones that permit a wide variety of associations, some of which have diagnostic significance.

Although most interpretive techniques stress content analysis, empirically keying methods can readily be applied to word association tests. For example, to build a scale to identify depressed individuals, one would key responses that occurred more (or less) frequently in protocols of depressed persons than in an appropriate normal sample.

Another well-known projective method is the *sentence completion test*. These tests typically consist of sentence stems, the subject's task being to complete the sentence in his own words. Like word association tests, the ideal stems are those that can be completed in several ways and which deal with diagnostically relevant topics. Scoring usually is quite subjective, stressing content analysis, but can be objectified. Sentence completion tests are easily administered and scored, are quite flexible, but, more so than most projective techniques, do not disguise their purpose from the test taker.

A third type of projective method, *figure drawings*, have been used for the assessment of both mental ability and personality dynamics. The simplest form of this technique requires the test taker to draw a person; more complex versions require the subject to draw (or paint) several persons or to draw a person in relation to other objects. Scoring and interpretation, though more objective than on most projective techniques, are far from standardized; however, most systems rely upon the characteristics of product (the drawing), the method of attack, comments the individual makes to explain his approach or product, and the examiner's inquiry about the drawing. A major advantage of the method is that, because the test content is a universally relevant subject matter, the technique is equally applicable in almost any cultural group.

Finally, several projective methods can be subsumed under the label *expressive methods:* role-playing techniques and psychodrama, where the subjects act out a particular role or part; play techniques, in which a child is presented with a variety of objects and asked to play with them in a particular manner. There are also other categories of projectives; picture completion and arrangement tests, where the examinee constructs a story, either by completing or arranging pictorial or cartoon-like materials; reproduction techniques, such as the Bender-Gestalt, that require the subject to remember and reproduce designs; tests involving manipulation and interpretation of designs; and so on. In short, almost any unstructured situation can be used as stimulus material for a projective method.

Evaluation of projective methods

Is the widespread, though presumably decreasing (Thelen et al., 1968), use of projective methods justified by the validity evidence? Do projectives accomplish their stated aims? Is any information provided by projectives that is not obtainable by other methods? Are there particular situations where projective methods are the most useful techniques? Can projective methods be faked?

Before considering these validity questions, one might ask a prior question: are projective methods tests? A test , you will recall, was defined as a systematic procedure for measuring a sample of an individual's behavior. For the current purposes, the crucial phrase is "systematic procedure"; systematic referring to content, administration, and scoring. By and large, the content of projective techniques is as standardized as that of other tests. The administrative procedure, though more flexible than standardized aptitude and achievement tests and self-report personality inventories, is comparable to the procedures used on individual intelligence tests. Furthermore, on most projective methods, the administrative procedure is, in principle, capable of being standardized. However, when it comes to scoring procedures, trouble arises. With a couple of notable exceptions (e.g., Holtzman's Inkblot Test), scoring procedures are either unstandardized and/or there is disagreement between several alternative scoring systems. Hence, adhering to a literal interpretation of the definition, projective methods do not qualify as tests.[11]

---

[11] The APA *Standards*, in fact, even recommend that self-report personality measures be referred to as inventories or questionnaires rather than tests. (Principle B1.11).

The lack of standardized scoring procedures produces other important consequences. Without quantifiable scores, consistency estimates cannot be made. Without objective scoring, adequate normative data cannot be provided; and a weakness of almost all projective methods is the lack of adequate normative data, without which interpretation of scores must be idiographic rather than normative or nomothetic.

As in most aspects of personality measurement, the basic concern is construct validity, and here we encounter an inpenetrable barrier. For if projective techniques measure basic aspects of personality, the individual's innermost drives and motivations (and if these facets are, by definition, unconscious and thus inaccessible to observation and measurement), then one can never have a direct test of the validity of a projective method. Several indirect lines of evidence can, however, be brought to bear. For example, if a projective method (or any other personality test) measures "basic" traits, scores should be relatively unaffected by ephemeral conditions associated with the particular test administrator, the conditions of test administration, slight changes in the stimulus materials or responding mode, or transient states of the test taker. Yet all of these factors influence response to projective techniques. Also, dissimulation is possible on projective methods. Thus, whatever projectives measure, it is not pervasive immutable aspects of personality structure.

What sort of evidence do projectives provide that is not available from other methods of measuring personality? One presumed advantage of projective measures was the richness of responses generated, and, consequently, the variety of dimensions tapped. In surveying the literature one would be hard put to find a variable that is measured by a projective technique which has not also been measured by more objective methods. The question then becomes, do projectives assess these variables more validly or efficiently; and here no definitive evidence is available nor will there likely be any until the scoring problems of projectives are overcome.

Thus, can we conclude anything about the value of projectives? Judged by the standards of classical psychometric and testing theory, projective methods would be rated as unacceptable, as instruments that should be drummed out of the arsenal of psychological tests. Yet many clinicians apparently find them useful. Can so many people be wrong? Possibly. But one can defend the alternative view that classical testing theory is limited, that it is only one among several possible approaches to knowing what another person is like, and that projectives constitute one of these other classes. One also cannot ignore the fact that, while other methods divorce the test from the interpreter, interpretation of projective methods involves an examiner-test interaction, opening the possibility that different dynamics may be involved. For example, the testing procedure might provide the examiner with clues to the examinee's personality, clues that he could not obtain in any other way. Yet the question of the validity of these clues is open to scientific test and often projectives have failed the test.

SITUATIONAL METHODS

Self-report and projective methods are in a sense artificial because they measure reactions in a contrived testing situation. And, although the testing situation possesses certain definite advantages—for example, control of the effects of irrelevant variables by standardizing conditions—it is still a special situation, one step removed from real life. Thus, interpretations made on the basis of behaviors exhibited on a test are open to the criticism that the subject's behavior might have been different in a real life situation. We can vitiate this argument by establishing a relationship between test scores and external criteria; however, the failure to find a relationship between a test-defined variable and an external criterion measure always has at least two explanations: (1) there is, in fact, no relationship between the two variables, or (2) the test does not measure the variable it is designed to measure.

The necessity for the testing situation to be as natural as possible would seem particularly critical when typical performance is measured. Ideally we would stuby the behavior a person typically exhibits, not his reports of how he does or would behave. To illustrate, suppose that we want to obtain an indication of how effective a workman will be as foreman or supervisor. One approach would be to administer a test in which the items present a variety of supervisory problems. There are at least two distinct ways in which this approach might be invalidated: (1) the workman might respond to the test as a measure of maximal performance, choosing the responses that he knows represent acceptable supervisory practices, rather than selecting the alternative that describes his most probable behavior, or (2) either because his experience offers no basis for choice, or because he unconsciously distorts his responses, those responses will not indicate how he would act if given the job of supervisor. In neither case would we obtain an indication of his most probable typical behavior. An alternative way to measure his supervisory ability would be to have him serve as supervisor for a period of time, either on the job or in a simulated job situation, with a trained observer rating his behavior, that is, to conduct a situational test.

Dimensions of situational methods

Situational methods can be differentiated along a number of (bipolar) dimensions. First, and most important, is whether the assessment situation is natural or contrived. The subject's performance in a natural situation may be observed and rated or the rating be made in a specially designed, and thus somewhat artificial, testing situation. Ratings of football players on the basis of their game performance is an example *par excellence* of a natural situation; ratings based on performance in a leaderless group discussion represent the artificial or contrived setting.

A second dimension involves the subject's awareness that he is being observed and/or rated. In natural situations, he may or may not be aware that he is being rated; in contrived situations, almost without exception, he will be aware of the rating process. Of course, the fundamental question is not whether the subject is aware of being observed and rated; the basic question is whether this awareness affects his behavior, and thereby precludes obtaining measures of typical performance. Although one might argue that, as we are constantly being rated (e.g., on our job performance, as a student, and by family and friends), any additional observation should have little effect. But most persons, knowing they are being observed, will try harder and will put their best foot forward. Therefore, when the person knows he is being observed and rated, the test results may yield evidence of maximal behavior rather than solely of typical behavior.

Situational methods also vary in scope and procedure. The assessment process may cover several days or a rating may be made on the basis of a few minutes performance. The test may be devised to provide a global assessment, a complete personality description, or a rating made on a single trait or aspect of personality. The test may be applied to several individuals simultaneously, in some cases performance being a group effort, or each individual may be tested separately.

Finally, there is the question of the appropriate performance measure (test score). Although there is no reason why objective performance measures cannot be used for many situational tests—and when measuring maximal performance they are particularly appropriate—in most cases test scores are ratings by a trained observer. The rater will observe the individual's approach to the problem, his interactions with other individuals in the test situation, the output, and, on the basis of these observations, will rate the individual on the relevant dimensions.

Examples of situational tests

Situational tests are generally both expensive and time consuming. The only one that is used to any extent is the simplest and least costly, the interview. The other examples that we will discuss have not received widespread use, generally being restricted to special situations.

THE INTERVIEW.[12]   The interview is one of the most widely used, if not the most widely used, assessment technique. Most persons have probably been interviewed many times—as part of the application procedure for a school or

---

[12]In our discussion we will consider only interviews that are used for assessment and evaluative purposes. Interviews with other purposes—e.g., counseling and therapeutic interviews—will not be discussed here.

college, when applying for a job, or when joining a club or organization. Although an interview generally consists of one person interviewing another, there are a number of possible variations of this traditional procedure. One, the *panel intesview*, involves confrontation of one person by a panel of interviewers. This procedure has the obvious advantage of decreasing the repetition that would occur if each member of the panel interviewed the candidate individually. Another variation is the *stress interview*, where the interviewer subjects the interviewee to considerable stress by constant probing, asking personal and embarrassing questions, trying to confuse him, and by other similar techniques, the purpose being to see how the subject reacts under stressful conditions, a presumably more valid test than a nonstressful situation.

In evaluating interviews several questions are of prime importance: Can reliable ratings be obtained from an interview? Is any information obtained from interviews that cannot be obtained in other manners? What is the predictive validity of interview data?

It is well known that various interviewers will arrive at widely divergent conclusions after interviewing the same candidate. One reason for this unreliability is the lack of standardization—not only do different interviewers cover different topics but they also look for different qualities in an individual. The reliability of interview judgments can be increased by structuring the interview so that the same topics are covered by all interviewers and the traits to be rated and the rating procedure are clearly specified. Even when given reliable ratings, we encounter a second question—does the interview provide information that cannot be obtained in other manners? As factual information and estimates of personality traits can be collected more economically in other ways (e.g., by application blanks and self-report inventories, respectively), the maximal payoff will be attained by concentrating on social behavior and bits of information which would particularly qualify or disqualify the person (e.g., speech problems, unique abilities or accomplishments).

Finally, predictive validity. Here the evidence shows that interview ratings decrease validity as often as they increase it. The reason for this finding being that interviewers overemphasize particular traits they think important (cf. the discussion of clinical judgment in Chapter 8. Still interviews continue to play a major role in assessment procedures; apparently because almost everyone feels that he is an excellent judge of other people.

INDIRECT TESTS. Some of the methods might best be described as indirect tests; "indirect" because the test serves primarily as a vehicle for observing the behavior of the subject and not as an end in itself. A common example is the *leaderless group discussion*. In this technique a group of persons are brought together and asked to discuss some, usually controversial, topic. In other situations, the test may be to devise a plan of operations (e.g., a sales campaign), to construct some object or device, or to solve a problem or overcome some difficulty (e.g., how to cross some natural obstacle, such as a stream or canyon, using only selected materials). Although success in completing the task may be scored, the focus is usually on characteristics displayed in attacking the problem—such as perseverance, leadership, and other interpersonal traits.

A basic assumption of indirect tests is that observations based on performance in more life-like situations will lead to more valid scores. Yet the perceptive subject will almost certainly realize the artificiality of the situation, will be able to deduce the traits that are being rated, and thereby alter his performance in these areas. Indirect tests, therefore, often become maximal rather than typical performance measures.

OSS ASSESSMENT. One of the most intensive assessments ever conducted was done by the OSS during World War II (The OSS Assessment Staff, 1948). In order to select personnel for OSS assignments, a three-day assessment procedure was developed. Groups of candidates were brought to an assessment center and subjected to a wide vairety of assessment techniques: paper-and-pencil tests of intellectual and personality characteristics, stress and other interviews, problem-solving exercises, numerous ingenious indirect situational tests. Performance in these tasks were rated by the Assessment staff (which included psychologists, physicians, and military officers) and ratings were also obtained from peers. On the basis of these ratings, a formulation of the personality structure of each individual was developed and a prognosis of his success on OSS assignments was made. Because of the nature of the criterion, a systematic validity study was precluded. However, some reviewers (e.g., Vernon, 1964) have concluded that the validity of such intensive assessments do not justify the time and effort expended in the assessment, and that the same data can be obtained by simpler and less costly assessment procedures.

IN-BASKET TEST. An interesting example of a contemporary attempt to make a global assessment of a candidate's job performance is the In-basket Test (Frederiksen et al., 1957), which attempts to simulate the job conditions for an occupation (variations of the test have been constructed for several occupations, including school administrators and military officers). The person being rated is provided with a variety of materials (e.g., organizational charts, technical reports, surveys, and memoranda) that he can study to obtain background knowledge of the situation. He is then presented with materials that might be found in his "in-basket" and is asked to take action on these matters. For example, a school administrator might have to decide whether to hire (or fire) a particular teacher, how to handle a complaint regarding damage done by school children during the lunch hour, plan a campaign for passage of a school bond issue, decide on the adoption of new texts, plan how to handle teachers' demands for higher salaries, and so on. He can handle each problem by making a decision, requesting further information, deferring action until a later date, assigning the job to a subordinate, or in any other manner that he could use on the job. Decisions will be made on the basis of his repertoire of job skills, taking into consideration the characteristics of the particular situation as described in the background materials. Scoring is on a variety of dimensions, involving both the handling and outcome, and stresses general styles or patterns of handling administrative tasks. The nature of the In-basket test makes it suitable as a training device as well as a selection test.

Evaluation of situational tests

One obvious disadvantage of situational tests is their cost: they involve relatively large amounts of both the candidates' and raters' time, can be applied to only one or a few candidates simultaneously, require trained judges to observe and rate performance, and often require expensive materials. The fundamental question is not, however, the absolute cost but whether their advantages justify the additional costs. We would probably have to conclude that the answer to this question is No, that any increase in validity does not overbalance the additional costs. This conclusion would hold even considering that the techniques are generally employed in the selection of personnel (e.g., military officers, school superintendents, and OSS agents) where a mistake in judgment can involve great costs, and thus a costly selection device might well repay its costs. On the other hand, one must consider that these techniques may be used in training as well as assessment situations.

Another weakness of situational techniques is that they generally rely on ratings for scores, and ratings are not as reliable or valid as objective test scores. In many cases, the weaknesses of ratings derive from the fact that the dimensions on which the individual is being rated are not well defined and the rating procedures are not clearly specified; consequently, disagreement among raters is to be expected. Even when the dimensions are clearly defined and the rating procedure is standardized, there are a number of errors that plague ratings: (1) the *halo effect*, the tendency to bias ratings on all characteristics to conform with one's general opinion of the person being rated; (2) the tendency of some raters to be over-tolerant and thus generally rate persons too high—the *error of leniency*—and, in contrast, the tendency of other raters to be exceedingly harsh in their ratings, and (3) the *error of central tendency*, the tendency to avoid extreme categories in ratings. (See Guilford, 1954, Chapter 11, for an excellent discussion of rating procedures and problems.)

Finally, there are the joint problems of synthesizing and expressing the results of the assessment. Because situational tests generally involve measurement along more than one dimension, scores must be combined to produce an integrated picture of the individual. But if the end product of this combination is a global personality description, direct predictions of specific behaviors may not be possible. If, on the other hand, the data are expressed as a series of specific predictions, an integrated picture will not be available, and generalizing beyond the original predictions to other predictions may be difficult. In either instance, there is the additional problem of the appropriate method of combining the various scores to arrive at a summary (cf. Chapter 8). The problem of combining scores is further complicated by the fact that the component data often have undesirable statistical properties (e.g., they are unreliable, have a limited range of values, or are expressed on an ordinal scale). In short, many of the difficult and unsolved problems in psychological measurement pertain to the problem of synthesizing data from situational tests.

ISSUES IN PERSONALITY MEASUREMENT

Having reviewed some examples of the major approaches to measuring personality, we will now consider some of the important issues in personality measurement. The term *issues* (defined as points in question) was deliberately chosen because, in personality measurement even more than in other areas of educational and psychological testing, many fundamental questions remain without definite answers. Although most of the issues concern technical points, significant social issues are also raised by personality measurement, and, in the long run, the development of personality testing may be more influenced by these social and political issues than by the more mundane technical issues.

Technical and theoretical issues

Throughout the chapter we have referred to particular tests, or approaches to test construction, that did not meet some of the technical standards for consistency, validity, and normative data outlined earlier in the book (and in the APA *Standards*). At this point it would be well to review and evaluate the current status of personality testing in regards to some of the more important questions.

STANDARDIZATION.   One of the stipulated requirements of a psychological test was that it be standardized (in content, administrative procedures, and scoring). Although the content of some personality measures may be varied slightly to suit the needs of a particular individual or situation, by and large, content is quite well standardized. The only noticeable exceptions are some of the situational tests, e.g., interviews and leaderless group discussions. Similarly, administrative procedures are generally standarized. It is in scoring procedures that many personality measures lack standardization. Projective methods, in particular, seem prone to using unstandardized and subjective scoring methods. While some persons may argue that standardizing scoring procedures will destroy the flexibility of the method, the loss by not standardizing scoring procedures—that of being able to interpret scores normatively—would seem to be of greater consequence than the loss of flexibility.

NORMS. Even among the measures having standardized scoring procedures, a common weakness of personality measures is the lack of adequate normative data. Part of the problem stems from disagreement over what constitutes an appropriate norm group for a personality test. Should it be a sample of the general population? Include only persons of the same sex? Same age? Same education or socioeconomic level? On most personality tests general population norms are desirable. The readily available populations, such as students and military inductees, are not representative of the general population; nor can they be used to define a meaningful normative group. This is in contrast to the situation which obtains in achievement and aptitude testing, where these captive populations often are the normative group of interest.

CONSISTENCY. The trend of the research data is that scores on personality measures are generally less stable than scores on measures of maximal performance. Whether these results are primarily attributable to the measurement procedures or the traits being measured is an unsettled question. As few personality test constructors even attempt to develop equivalent forms, the ability to draw equivalent samples of items in the personality domains remains essentially untested. Although empirically keyed scales are generally factorially complex, homogeneous personality scales have been developed. Studies also indicate that scores on personality measures are relatively susceptible to even slight variations in the conditions of the test administration, the wording of the items, and to short-term fluctuations within the individual. In summary, personality measures are generally less consistent than would be desirable if the test results are to be interpreted for individuals; the question is how consistency can be improved without radically changing the nature of the tests.

DISSIMULATION. The evidence is clear that responses on personality tests reflect both item content and response biases. This is true of projective and situational tests, as well as self-report techniques. What, then, can be done to minimize the effects of these variables? At least three approaches are possible. First, structure the testing situation so that the test taker has no motivation to try to dissemble. Second, include some dissimulation indices on the test to assess the degree of bias. And, third, establish empirical relations between test scores and extratest criteria so that the meaning of the score can be determined independently of the dynamics determining the score.

CRITERIA. In personality measurement the universe sampled is generally not well defined (i.e., the test serves as a sign) nor are external criteria readily apparent. In some cases, particularly with projectives and other depth techniques, the variable being measured is defined so as to preclude meaningful external criteria. Thus in personality measurement, the usual approach to validation is construct validity and even here, because of the hazy definitions of some variables, one often has to make broad leaps of faith to accept certain criterion measures as valid reflections of the underlying construct. What, for example, is an appropriate criterion measure for a measure of flexibility?

THE UNIT OF ANALYSIS.   Closely related to the criterion problem is the issue of the appropriate unit of analysis. Self-report techniques measure several relatively independent dimensions or traits and, in so doing, are criticized by the advocates of holistic analyses. The latter claim that attempts to analyze personality piece by piece necessarily will fragment and destroy the phenomena being studied. In reply, the proponents of the trait approach insist that scientific measurement can occur only when the dimensions are treated individually. Although there is no logical reason why measurement cannot occur at both levels (after all, gross and microscopic anatomy are both respectable subjects), psychologists usually defend one or the other approach, not a synthesis. The question could be rephrased: what is the appropriate point to combine scores? In answer to this question, the trait camp would say that scores on individual traits should first be collected and then synthesized into an overall view, while the holistic camp would emphasize synthesis, with more specific reactions to be deduced from the general personality picture.

COMPARATIVE VALIDITY.   The question of comparative validity has at least three aspects: (1) How does the validity of personality measures compare with the validity of achievement and aptitude tests? (2) Which of the general approaches to personality measurement is most valid? And (3) within a given approach, which specific technique is most valid? Of course, as validity is situation-specific, any answer to these questions will reflect the trends of the evidence rather than give a definitive answer applicable in all situations.

The first question has several answers. Looking at the absolute magnitude of validity coefficients, one would conclude that validity is generally lower for personality tests than other types of measurement. Yet, because different situations and criteria are involved, one cannot conclude that personality measurement is inherently less valid than the measurement of aptitudes and achievement. If we look at the incremental validity of personality measures, we find that there are few situations where the addition of personality variables significantly increases predictive accuracy over measures of maximal performance. However, the situations where tests are typically used as predictors (e.g., academic success and job performance) are ones that are heavily weighted with intellectual and skill components.

The author's conclusion in regard to the second question should be obvious from the amount of space devoted to the three major approaches. However, one could argue that this conclusion was reached only because the author adopted the traditional psychometric criteria of validity. Granted, but until alternative methods of assessing the effectiveness of measurement procedure are developed, these are the only acceptable standards available. Finally, in spite of the theoretical advantages of homogeneous keying, the hard evidence supports empirical keying as the better method of keying self-report inventories.

PSYCHOLOGICAL THEORY.   Although there is a close relationship between personality measurement and theories about methodology, there is not a close relationship between personality measurement and substantive personality theory. Some of the tests described have had their roots in a particular theory (e.g., the Edwards and TAT in Murray's need-press theory, the Rorschach in psychoanalytic theory, and the Myers-Briggs in Jungian theory), but personality tests in general—and empirically keyed self-report techniques in particular— have had only fleeting connections with theory. When convenient, various investigators have used particular scales to measure constructs in their theory or model, but systematic attempts to build tests measuring the basic theoretical constructs or attempts to build a theory of personality around a particular test are few and far between.

Social issues

Although there has been some reaction against ability and aptitude tests— mainly on the grounds that they reflect "middle-class" values and educations and thus discriminate against persons from culturally disadvantaged backgrounds and other atypical individuals—the majority of persons, experts and laymen alike, consider these tests, when used properly, to be an impartial method of assessing competence.

In the realm of personality testing, however, there has been a reaction against the idea of testing itself. In particular, asking an individual questions about certain subjects—usually his political and religious beliefs and his sexual attitudes and behavior—is felt to invade the individual's privacy. Another view is that use of personality measures, particularly in personnel decisions, rewards conformity and penalizes individuality; again an unwarranted use of tests.

As in many controversies the issues are complex, and no simple prescription or decree will ameliorate the situation. For one, the invasion of privacy is often confused with the improper use of tests. Misuse of personality measures is relatively common, in spite of attempts at control by a formal code of ethics (APA, 1963) and by standards controlling the distribution of tests (APA, 1966).

A first type of misuse occurs when persons untrained in the use of a particular technique nevertheless use it in applied psychological work. A second common type of misuse involves applying a test in a situation where its validity has not been demonstrated. Whether such practices are unethical or stupid, or both, is a moot point. The major concern is that the use of unvalidated measures and the administration of tests by unqualified persons may result in decisions that may be harmful to the individual who takes the test.

But assuming that some (at least presumptive) validity data is available, we can return to the question of whether personality measurement *does* invade privacy. And here the issue becomes a legal as well as a psychological one for, in our society, the question of what constitute the limits of privacy will ultimately be determined by legal and legislative action.[13] Legal rulings are necessary as, although we all supply personal information in many situations (such as in financial affairs), persons differ in what they consider a reasonable request. Where one person may feel that a certain request may be unreasonable and even constitute an invasion of his privacy, the same request may seem reasonable, or even innocuous, to another person. The question is where to draw the line between reasonable and unreasonable requests.

One approach to deciding where to set the limits would be to stipulate certain categories of requests (e.g., information about sexual and religious activities and attitudes) as being invasions of privacy in all circumstances. The main disadvantage of this approach, from the social scientists' view, is that these sensitive areas are frequently the ones that provide the most meaningful data. Another approach would be to allow questions about these areas to be raised only in certain situations, e.g., as part of medical treatment or examination. Such an approach would discount empirical validity as being a meaningful concept. A third approach is to restrict use of personality measures to certain professions or to persons possessing certain qualifications (e.g., psychiatrists and licensed psychologists); here we ignore the differing competencies of persons within the same occupation and introduce the question of which professional group should control personality assessment. Thus any arbitrary restrictions will not be wholly effective.

Perhaps the key to the issue is found in the fact that people often react negatively to personality measurement because they do not understand how the test will be used. In short, the test is threatening because it represents an unknown quantity; if the purposes and uses of the test become known, their objections often vanish. For example, most counselors have had the experience of a student adamantly rejecting interest or personality tests but who, after having the purposes and uses of the tests explained to him, has no further objections. The moral for the test user is obvious.

The issues discussed in the previous paragraph also have direct relevance for the legal aspects of the privacy issue. For if, and only if, the test taker understands the nature of the test and how the results will be used can he make an informed decision as to the value of the test for himself and whether he wishes to submit to the testing. Then he can decide whether the test will invade his

---

[13]Bills placing restrictions on the use of psychological tests have been introduced into Congress.

privacy and give (or withold) his *informed consent* to the testing.[14] If he gives his informed consent to the testing he is, in essence, saying that he feels the testing will not invade his privacy. Hence, the concept of informed consent is central to the entire issue.

Summary

This chapter considered the problems of developing and interpreting measures of personality characteristics or, more generally, measures of typical performance. The focus was on three major approaches to personality measurement— self-report techniques, projective methods, and situational methods.

The measurement of personality characteristics raises some issues that were of lesser import in other areas of psychological testing: the question of exactly what is being measured; whether the measurement process affects the individual and thus influences his responding; the extent to which attempts to influence responding in a certain direction (response sets) and content-independent response habits (response styles) influence scores; and whether personality measures adequately sample the domain being measured.

The fundamental assumption of self-report techniques is that the individual himself is in the best position to observe and report upon his behavior; hence the individual's self-reports are used as the response data. Self-report techniques usually use the inventory format with keying being either logical (based on the rational associations between items), empirical (based on the relationship between an item response and an extratest criterion), or homogeneous (based on interrelations among items). Because self-report techniques are open to response bias, procedures for identifying and controlling these biases have been built into many inventories.

The Strong Vocational Interest Blank and the Minnesota Multiphasic Personality Inventory were discussed in detail to illustrate the process of constructing empirically keyed personality inventories. The role of the MMPI in the history of personality assessment was stressed. Examples were also presented of other empirically keyed self-report inventories, of inventories that have been developed by homogeneous keying, and instruments that were constructed for specific purposes (e.g., the Edwards Personal Preference Schedule being constructed to control the influence of the social desirability variable). It was concluded that self-report techniques, being more objective than other approaches to personality measurement, had certain advantages over other approaches. In addition, empirical keying seems to have been more effective than either rational or homogeneous keying.

---

[14]For further discussion see *Privacy and Behavioral Research* (1967), Ruebhausen & Brim (1966), and the November 1966 issue of the *American Psychologist*.

Projective methods present the subject with an ambiguous stimuli and require that he structure the situation in some manner. The manner in which he projects structure on the situation is used as the basis for making inferences about his personality structure. Typical projective methods discussed include the Rorschach Inkblots and the Thematic Apperception Test. It was concluded that the major defect of most projective methods was their lack of objective scoring and interpretation procedures.

Situational tests place the test taker in a problem situation and observe and rate his behavior and reactions. Although some of the problem situations are contrived, in general situational tests provide a more realistic, life-like situation than do self-report inventories or projective methods. However, they are also expensive, time-consuming, and often must rely on ratings (which have certain disadvantages as scores).

Some of the technical and social issues in personality measurement were also discussed including the misuse of tests and the invasion-of-privacy issue.

Suggestions for further reading

Cattell, R. B. What is "objective" in "objective personality tests"? *Journal of Counseling Psychology*, 1958, 5, 285–289. A clarification of the various meanings of "objective" as used in personality measurement.

Clark, K. E. *Vocational interests of nonprofessional men.* Minneapolis: University of Minnesota Press, 1961. As well as discussing the construction of the MVII, this small book considers many of the technical problems in personality measurement (e.g., item weighting, homogeneous versus empirical keys) and their relation to test construction.

Edwards, A. L. *The social desirability variable in personality assessment.* New York: The Dryden Press, Inc., 1957. A short presentation of the evidence of the existence of a social desirability response set and its effect on responses to personality inventories.

Kerlinger, F. N. *Foundations of behavioral research.* New York: Holt, Rinehart and Winston, Inc., 1965. Chap. 28, Observation of behavior. A brief introduction to some of the problems in, and approaches to, observing and rating behavior.

Lindzey, G. *Projective techniques and cross-cultural research.* New York: Appleton-Century-Crofts, 1961. Chaps. 2–5 discuss some of the basic issues in projective methodology: the definition of a projective method, varieties of techniques used, their theoretical basis, and some general considerations in using and interpreting projectives.

Meehl, P. E. The dynamics of "structured" personality tests. *Journal of Clinical Psychology*, 1945, 1, 296–303. The classic description of the variables determining responding on self-report inventories.

Meehl, P. E. Wanted—a good cookbook. *American Psychologist*, 1956, 11, 263–272. Consideration of the need for, and development of, objective codebooks for interpreting personality test results.

Mischel, W. *Personality and assessment.* New York: John Wiley & Sons, Inc., 1968. Personality assessment considered in relationship to personality theory and empirical studies of personality.

Problems and trends

Chapter 13

Having described the process of test construction, the basic concepts of testing, and the varieties and uses of tests, we will now consider some of the major problems and trends in the utilization of psychological and educational tests. As a framework for this discussion, we will first summarize some of the most important principles presented in the previous chapters.

GENERAL PRINCIPLES

A test can be defined as a systematic procedure for measuring a sample of an individual's behavior. Systematic procedures insure that irrelevant variables will be controlled and that all persons will take the test under equivalent conditions. Because a test is a measuring instrument, testing procedures must fulfill certain requirements regarding the establishment of scale units; most psychological tests approximate an interval scale. Since only a sample, not all, relevant behavior is measured, any statements made about the individual's total repertoire of behavior or about the existence of underlying traits are necessarily inferential.

Notice also that a test measures only developed skills and characteristics at a given point in time. An individual's test score will be a function of his inherited characteristics, his learning and life experiences prior to the test, and the conditions of the testing session. Although, in order to interpret test scores, the assumption is often made that (at least within broad limits) the testees have had comparable prior experiences and exposure to the test materials, this assumption cannot be verified from the test itself. Therefore, while scores from a single testing

428

session may provide useful predictive data, an understanding of the developmental processes that resulted in the individuals' obtaining a particular score requires repeated testing and extratest sources of information.

Tests serve three functions—as predictors, as samples, and as signs. A test functions as a predictor when it predicts some qualitatively different, extratest behavior, as when a scholastic aptitude test is used to predict college grades. A test can be conceptualized as a sample when it attempts to represent (sample) a clearly defined universe of content or behavior; classroom examinations are a clear illustration of this function. A test serves as a sign when it points out the nature of the (still incompletely defined) behavioral universe being sampled— for example, an intelligence test defining the nature of intelligent behavior. These three functions parallel the notions of criterion-related, content, and construct validity. Furthermore, they roughly parallel the three major types of tests—with aptitude tests serving as predictors, achievement tests as samples, and personality tests as signs.

A mathematical model has been developed to represent the reliability, homogeneity, and validity of psychological tests. This model is an individual differences model and is based on the concepts of a true score, which can be further subdivided into a relevant (valid) component and an irrelevant component, and error. A number of procedures and formulas for computing the various forms of the reliability coefficient (stability, equivalence, internal consistency), for relating reliability to validity, and for determining validity have been developed.

The central concept in testing is validity, which can be defined as the extent to which the test measures the trait it is supposed to measure or does the job it was designed to do (e.g., predict a given behavior or outcome). There are three major types of validity: content, criterion-related, and construct validity. As validity is situation-specific, a distinction can be made between the validity of a test in a particular situation (its usefulness) and the validity of the test as measuring some psychologically meaningful variable. The majority of the studies in the literature are concerned with criterion-related validity of particular tests in particular situations. Unfortunately, these studies often neglect certain vital information: (1) the base rates, (2) the incremental validity of each test, and (3) the utility of the testing procedure. The main thesis of this book is that a test is valid to the extent that the number of correct decisions made using the test is an improvement over the base rates and/or utilization of alternative techniques; in other words, incremental validity, broadly conceived, is the basic index of the effectiveness of a test.

The interpretation of test scores requires a combination of validity and normative data; a mere indication of where an individual's score falls within a particular norm group is rarely, if ever, valuable without supporting validity data. That is, normative data expressed in outcome terms, such as through expectancy tables, is generally more meaningful than other kinds of normative data. Although most normative data is expressed as norm-referenced scores—where an individual's performance is compared to that of a group of his peers—scores can also, under some conditions, be expressed in criterion-referenced terms, by comparing an individual's performance to some absolute or ideal standard.

PROBLEMS

It should be apparent that testing is not without its problems. At various places in the book the deficiencies of current practices and procedures have been mentioned; the reader undoubtedly has questioned other assumptions or procedures. The problems discussed below are particularly critical or pervasive; other more specific problems could as easily have been included.

PRACTICAL PROBLEMS. The standards for the distribution of testing materials and the suggested qualifications of test users do not completely prevent unqualified persons from gaining access to tests and possibly misusing them when making decisions about individuals or evaluating the effectiveness of a program. Because these standards are without legal force or other sanctions, except in cases involving flagrant violations, it might appear that test sales and usage should be legally controlled as, for example, pharmaceuticals are controlled. However, an effective control mechanism, which does not unduly restrict qualified users, has not yet been developed. There is no doubt, though, that more stringent controls over the distribution and use of tests can and should be instituted.

Another problem is that, in many important areas, the supply of standardized tests is limited or nonexistent. For example, it is only during the past several years that tests of creativity have appeared; testing of writing skill is still in a relatively primitive stage; and tests of organizational ability, logical thinking, critical thinking, motivation (academic and otherwise), and many personality characteristics are virtually nonexistent. In many areas there are only one or two, even minimally acceptable, tests. Furthermore, most standardized tests are limited to the paper-and-pencil, multiple-choice format. Thus, in both content and format, the testing arsenal is limited and could well be expanded.

On the other hand, no effective way to remove out-of-date and invalid (or unvalidated) tests from the market has been developed. As long as enough persons buy a test to make publication profitable, these tests continue to be published. Oscar Buros, when instituting the *Mental Measurements Yearbooks*, hoped that publication of critical reviews of tests would aid in removing the abundance of poor tests from the market; this effort, he feels, has not succeeded (Buros, 1968). Ideally, test users would be sufficiently well trained so that they could identify the deficiencies in these tests and, by not purchasing the tests, make their publication unprofitable, thereby forcing the publisher to revise the test or withdraw it from circulation. Unfortunately such an ideal has not been realized; in fact, getting prospective teachers, counselors, personnel men, and other potential test users to take courses in educational and psychological measurement is, in itself, somewhat of a problem.

FACTORS INFLUENCING TEST SCORES. Probably the most neglected area of testing research is the study of the effects of environmental, situational, and personal variables on test performance. Too often test scores are naïvely interpreted as precise indices of immutable psychological traits. But studies have shown conclusively that test performance is a function of numerous variables. (See, e.g., Bloom, 1964; Edwards, 1957; Guilford, 1967; Hunt, 1961; Masling, 1960; Rosenthal & Jacobson, 1968.) Thus, if tests scores are to be interpreted accurately, the effects of any extraneous variable on test performance must be thoroughly understood. Knowledge of the effects of nontest variables is particularly critical when test scores serve as the basis of theoretical constructs.

VALIDITY PROBLEMS. As validity is the central concept in psychological testing, any problems in the conceptualization and/or application of validity studies will be especially crucial. The failure to consider base rates in determining validity has been discussed in detail. Criterion problems, both conceptual and practical, have already been mentioned in Chapter 5, as has the fact that the several possible validity indices may not agree with each other. The fundamental problem, however, is that the concept of validity is an amalgam of practical and theoretical considerations and never completely separates the two (see, e.g., Ebel, 1961; Loevinger, 1957). Furthermore, the 40-odd types of validity proposed in the literature defy the neat tripartite classification described in the *Standards for Educational and Psychological Tests*.

A second problem is the level of predictive accuracy attained by present tests. For example, when predicting academic performance from scholastic aptitude test scores, validity coefficients generally cluster around .50–60 (Fishman & Pasanella, 1960; Lavin, 1965). Utilization of multiple predictors (e.g., aptitude tests in combination with personality measures) usually increases predictive accuracy only slightly. Furthermore, this level of predictive accuracy has been essentially constant over the past several decades, even when new tests or analytic methods have been introduced. Although there are certain dangers associated with a high level of predictive accuracy (see Goslin, 1963; Young, 1961), the present tests and methods, which account for less than half of the criterion variability, are far from optimal. Athough new analytic models (e.g., moderators and Dunnette's validation model) show promise of improving predictive accuracy, there are not enough data available to draw a definitive conclusion. Since validity data are situation-specific, application of results obtained in one situation to another, presumably comparable, situation always involves some risk. Procedures which allow for grouping similar situations (Dunnette,

1963; Ghiselli, 1963) reduce this risk and increase the probability that the validity data will generalize. Then, too, as validity evidence is based on the performance of groups of individuals, the meaning of individual scores is always somewhat ambiguous.

The question of the optimal method to combine (predictor) scores, so as to increase validity, is still open. Although actuarial methods have generally proven to be more accurate than clinical methods, in many circumstances—for example, when a personality description rather than a specific prediction is the desired outcome—actuarial methods are not generally applicable. (Codebooks are obvious exceptions.) A set of standard rules and procedures for deriving descriptions and classifications would be helpful. Also needed is the further development and adaptation of powerful methods for comparing an individual to a group, rather than ranking individuals along continua (e.g., discriminant analysis); multivariate techniques which establish the relationship between several predictors and several criterion measures simultaneously; and techniques for differential prediction and placement (Cronbach & Gleser, 1957; Horst, 1954).

THE MODEL. The traditional model used for conceptualizing test scores, you will recall, is an individual differences model. As long as the purpose of the testing is to discriminate between individuals, the model is appropriate. If, however, the testing focus is on something other than individual differences— say, on how well the individuals have learned a particular set of materials—the traditional model may not be directly relevant.

Several aspects of consistency of measurement are illustrative of the type of problems and limitations encountered. Typical reliability measures consider variation over only several of the relevant dimensions; consistency over time and forms is recognized, consistency over situations and persons is not. Thus a broader concept of reliability may be needed. Then, too, the classical reliability model, with its emphasis on score stability, encounters problems when dealing with change scores. Not only are there several alternative definitions of homogeneity—it is classed as a type of internal consistency reliability by some writers, as an aspect of construct validity by others, as an aspect of both reliability and validity by still others, and even as a distinct property of tests—there is also disagreement as to whether, and under what circumstances, homogeneity is a necessary or desirable property of tests. Here, again, clarification is needed.

The model, even though being an individual differences model, is concerned with the average or typical person. Thus all individuals are treated similarly and no provision is made for the atypical person. For example, the weights associated with each test in the multiple regression equation are identical for all individuals. However, in some circumstances the optimal procedure may necessitate differentially weighting the various predictors for each individual. In other words, the general model could be improved by incorporating procedures which

(1) identify atypical persons, persons for which the model is not applicable, and (2) take into account individual characteristics through differential weighting or other procedures.

One can also question the practice of using tests (and other measures) to predict future performance. Here the concern is not with the accuracy of prediction, an issue previously discussed, but with the idea of prediction. The reason for predicting is, of course, to maximize the fit between the individual and the treatment applied, e.g., to insure that those persons chosen to enter a college are the ones who are most likely to profit from attending that college. But, if as some people have argued, the very act of predicting may influence the outcome—that the test scores might be part of a self-fulfilling prophecy—then persons who are predicted to succeed, by virtue of the prediction, have a higher probability of success.[1] Such predictions will apparently be valid, but their validity will be spurious and illusory. At a different level, one must be concerned with the possible side effects of excessive reliance on prediction and preselection—e.g., creation of an artificial elite based on test-taking ability, loss of motivation and hope, rewarding potential rather than performance.

SOCIAL CONSEQUENCES. The topic of the previous paragraph was really the (possible) social consequences of testing. Although testing—by identifying and optimally utilizing talent—generally is beneficial, it may also have some undesirable side effects. There is no doubt that tests are fairer and more accurate indices of ability than many other procedures that have been used as selection devices (e.g., skin color, who one's parents are, wealth, social or political influence), still they may be biased or perpetuate certain undesirable practices and attitudes.

Ebel (1964), for example, has identified four possible consequences of educational testing, consequences that critics of testing have implied might result from testing programs. The four are: (1) Testing "may place an indelible stamp of intellectual status—superior, mediocre or inferior—on a child" and consequently determine his adult social status, influence his self-esteem, or decrease his motivation (if scores are low); (2) testing may lead to a narrow conception of ability or to the pursuit of a single goal, thus reducing the diversity of talent in society; (3) testing places test publishers in the position of determining educational content; and (4) testing encourages inflexible, impersonal, and mechanical methods of appraisal and thereby reduces human freedom. Although Ebel refutes these arguments, and points out some of the dangers of not testing, he also points out that little discussion of these issues is based on hard data as such data, although needed, are not available.

[1]See, e.g., Rosenthal & Jacobson, 1968, or Young, 1961, for a discussion of expectancies and performance.

Finally, there is the issue of the invasion of privacy (for a discussion of this issue, see Chapter 12). Even if a test is valid and provides useful information, but does so at the cost of invading an individual's privacy, the advantages of testing must be demonstrated to outweigh the disadvantages if the tests are to be used. Sometimes unobtrusive measures of public behavior (Webb et al., 1966) can be substituted for psychological tests, avoiding the possibility of asking questions that might be considered as probing into personal matters.

TRENDS

In the course of the book we have paid scant attention to the history of testing and measurement, feeling that in a limited space it was more important to present the basic principles and procedures and illustrate the applications of testing rather than to discuss the stages in their development.[2] At this point, however, we will take the perhaps foolhardy step of predicting some of the trends that might be expected in educational and psychological testing in the coming years.

The first prediction is somewhat paradoxical: there will be increasing use of tests but, concurrently, there will be increased questioning of the use of tests. To predict an increasing use of tests is a safe bet: the larger labor force, the increase in the number of students in all types of educational programs, the diversity of educational programs, the emphases on utilizing individual talents and individualizing instruction, the demonstrated effectiveness of tests, the wide variety of tests available, governmental recognition and support of testing programs, and many other factors, all insure that more use will be made of tests (and other sources of information) in making decisions about and with individuals. On the other hand, the current emphasis on human rights and the negative reactions, in some quarters, to our increasingly mechanized and impersonal society will probably lead to attacks on tests and other methods which attempt to describe and classify persons objectively. Ideally, these two counter-trends would merge, resulting in the use of tests only where they can be demonstrated to be fair and valid and assist the development and utilization of individual talents.

A second trend will be a relative increase in the use of achievement tests and a decrease in the use of aptitude tests. The distinction between achievement and aptitude measures has been unclear. In addition, aptitudes have been saddled with some connotations (e.g., immutability and genetic determination) which increase the probability that scores will be misinterpreted. Recent studies have shown that aptitude measures are more susceptible to the influence of other

[2]Discussions of the history of testing can be found in Goslin, 1963, and Goodenough, 1949, and traced through the papers in the volume edited by Anastasi (1966).

variables than had previously been suspected. And evidence indicates that, in most situations, predictions made from achievement measures are as accurate as those made from aptitude measures. These factors undercut much of the justification for using aptitude measures; and, when combined with an emphasis on educational achievement and demonstrated competency—which requires achievement, ability, and proficiency measures—should change the relative emphases on aptitude and achievement testing.

Similarly, less use will probably be made of personality measures, especially in situations involving personnel or educational decisions. This change will result from two separate forces: (1) the validity of personality measures as decision-making aids has not been demonstrated by hard research data, and (2) the questions of invasion of privacy that arise in connection with the use of personality measures will probably limit their use somewhat. Personality measures will continue to be used extensively in counseling and research, perhaps with increasing frequency.

Third, many new types of tests will appear. Some of these will be excursions into content areas not previously tapped by psychological tests, e.g., some of the tests in the various cells of Guilford's structure of the intellect model. Equally as noticeable will be changes in the format of tests. Rather than being limited to paper-and-pencil formats, as are most currently available standardized tests, test materials can now be presented by television, tape recordings, or computers. The latter will probably be the single most important influence on further testing. Computers have been used for the rapid scoring and "norming" of standardized tests, making national testing programs feasible; in building model item and test score distributions which can be used to study the assumptions of psychometric theory; in making possible the application of complex methods of combining and analyzing test scores; and for many other purposes.

But perhaps the most important effect will be a shift in emphasis, on achievement tests, from norm-referenced to criterion-referenced scores. As computer-assisted instruction and its cousin, programed learning, have promoted individualized instruction and given promise of enabling more students to attain a wider range of educational skills, so, too, the testing emphasis may shift from measuring achievement differences between students (the individual differences or norm-referenced approach) to measuring how much an individual has learned compared to what the teacher and/or course is attempting to teach (the absolute or criterion-referenced approach).

New test formats are possible through use of the computer; for example, the computer is an ideal instrument for administering a sequential test. On this type of test, instead of all students taking the identical items in the same order, the next item each testee attempts is determined by his response to the previous item (see Figure 10.4), the particular sequence being chosen to maximize discrimination and/or follow logically from the item content. Potentially, sequential tests allow for both more efficient testing and for the individualization of testing.

A fourth trend will be the reconceptualization of some of the basic ideas in psychological testing. Some of these reformulations will arise out of the realization that present conceptions are limited (e.g., Cattell's and Cronbach's reconceptualization of reliability, the notion of construct validity); others in an attempt to explain research data (e.g., Cattell's notion of fluid and crystallized intelligence); others when it becomes apparent that the present models do not satisfactorily handle certain practical problems (e.g., the problems with change scores); and still others because increasing statistical sophistication and the availability of computers for data analyses allow for more complex analyses than were previously feasible (e.g., certain types of factor analyses and the moderator model). These factors, combined with more critical looks at the goals and functions of testing, and with the increasing interaction of testing with experimental psychology, should lead to the reformulation of many old concepts and persistent problems.

Fifth, there will be increasing concern with the social consequences of testing. No longer will a psychologist be able to administer a test, make decisions on the basis of the test scores, and not worry about the consequences to the individual or society. As this problem has been discussed several places previously, it need not be repeated here. However, it should be emphasized that the concern with social consequences will be broad—involving not only philosophic questions such as the optimal utilization of talent within society and the issue of invasion of privacy, but also an increased concern with such practical problems as evaluating the effectiveness of educational programs and processes.

A FINAL WORD

In this book we have tried to accomplish several things: to present the basic concepts of measurement as they apply to psychological and educational testing, to indicate how educational and psychological tests are developed and used, to identify factors which influence test performance and show how these factors operate, and to illustrate the variety of psychological and educational tests. But, more importantly, we have attempted to develop a critical attitude so that, when confronted with the need to select or interpret a test, you will approach the task with deliberate caution, carefully weighing the multitude of factors which must be considered. No book can completely prepare you for this task; it can only be developed by continual study of tests, test manuals, journal articles and books about testing, and by direct experience in the development, validation, and use of educational and psychological tests. This book, then, is but a beginning.

Finally, in a discussion which has focused on the methods of educational and psychological testing, it is easy to overlook an important point—it is not the *test* which is of prime importance but the *individuals* who take the tests. Their test scores will influence decisions which may alter the course of their lives. Therefore, when using and interpreting tests, our foremost concern must be with the effects of the testing on the individual. Keeping this fact in mind will be the greatest single deterrent to misuse of tests.

Suggestions for further reading

Anastasi, A. (Ed.). *Testing problems in perspective.* Washington, D. C.: American Council on Education, 1966. A selection of papers from the annual conferences on testing problems sponsored by the Educational Testing Service; shows the historical development of testing over a 25-year period.

Ebel, R. L. The social consequences of educational testing. *Proceedings of the 1963 Invitational Conference on Testing Problems.* Princeton, New Jersey: Educational Testing Service, 1964. (pp. 130–143). An analysis of the major issues in educational testing; considers the harmful consequences that critics attribute to tests, the benefits of using tests, and the dangers of not using them.

Goslin, D. A. Standardized ability tests and testing. *Science,* 1968, 159, 851–855. Consideration of some of the major issues and criticisms in the use of tests; written for a general audience.

Thorndike, R. L. Educational decisions and human assessment. *Teachers College Record,* 1964, 66, 103–112. A nontechnical discussion of some of the problems and advantages in using tests and other measurement methods as aids in making educational decision.

Appendix

AREAS OF THE NORMAL CURVE WITH COMPARABLE PERCENTILE RANKS AND STANDARD SCORES

Consider a normal distribution of scores with the area within the curve equal to 1.0000 units:

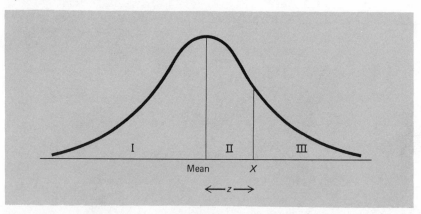

Under these circumstances certain constant relationships hold; the most important of these for psychological testing are tabled below.

Column A lists the normal deviate (z), the deviation of an obtained score (X) from the mean in standard deviation units, i.e.:

$$z = \frac{X - \text{Mean}}{s} = \frac{x}{s}$$

z, of course, can be either positive or negative depending upon whether the obtained score falls above or below the mean.

Column B indicates the proportion of area of the curve that falls between the mean and the corresponding z (i.e., area II in the figure).

Column C indicates the proportion of the area in the larger section when the distribution is divided at point z (i.e., areas I + II in the figure). When z is positive, this will be the proportion of the area falling below point z; when z is negative, this will be the proportion falling above point z.

Column D gives the area in the smaller section (i.e., area III in the figure); this area equals (1 − the value in column C).

Column E is the percentile rank associated with z when z is positive.

Column F gives the corresponding percentile rank when z is negative.

Column G gives the standard score, Z, (where $Z = 50 + 10z$) when z is positive.

Column H gives Z for the corresponding negative value of z (−z).

(A)	(B)	(C)	(D)	(E)	(F)	(G)	(H)
	Area mean	Area larger	Area smaller	Percentile		Z	
z	to z	portion	portion	+z	− z	+z	− z
0.00	.0000	.5000	.5000	50	50	50	50
0.05	.0199	.5199	.4801	52	48		
0.10	.0398	.5398	.4602	54	46	51	49
0.15	.0596	.5596	.4404	56	44		
0.20	.0793	.5793	.4207	58	42	52	48
0.25	.0987	.5987	.4013	60	40		
0.30	.1179	.6179	.3821	62	38	53	47
0.35	.1368	.6368	.3632	64	36		
0.40	.1554	.6554	.3446	66	34	54	46
0.45	.1736	.6736	.3264	67	33		
0.50	.1915	.6915	.3085	69	31	55	45
0.55	.2088	.7088	.2912	71	29		
0.60	.2257	.7257	.2743	73	27	56	44
0.65	.2422	.7422	.2578	74	26		
0.70	.2580	.7580	.2420	76	24	57	43
0.75	.2734	.7734	.2266	77	23		
0.80	.2881	.7881	.2119	79	21	58	42
0.85	.3023	.8023	.1977	80	20		
0.90	.3159	.8159	.1841	82	18	59	41
0.95	.3289	.8289	.1711	83	17		
1.00	.3413	.8413	.1587	84	16	60	40
1.05	.3531	.8531	.1469	85	15		
1.10	.3643	.8643	.1357	86	14	61	39

(A)	(B)	(C)	(D)	(E)	(F)	(G)	(H)
	Area mean	Area larger	Area smaller	Percentile		Z	
z	to z	portion	portion	+z	− z	+ z	− z
1.15	.3749	.8749	.1251	87	13		
1.20	.3849	.8849	.1151	88	12	62	38
1.25	.3944	.8944	.1056	89	11		
1.30	.4032	.9032	.0968	90	10	63	37
1.35	.4115	.9115	.0885	91	9		
1.40	.4192	.9192	.0808	92	8	64	36
1.45	.4265	.9265	.0735	93	7		
1.50	.4332	.9332	.0668	93	7	65	35
1.55	.4394	.9394	.0606	94	6		
1.60	.4452	.9452	.0548	95	5	66	34
1.65	.4505	.9505	.0495	95	5		
1.70	.4554	.9554	.0446	96	4	67	33
1.75	.4599	.9599	.0401	96	4		
1.80	.4641	.9641	.0359	96	4	68	32
1.85	.4678	.9678	.0322	97	3		
1.90	.4713	.9713	.0287	97	3	69	31
1.95	.4744	.9744	.0256	97	3		
2.00	.4772	.9772	.0228	98	2	70	30
2.05	.4798	.9798	.0202	98	2		
2.10	.4821	.9821	.0179	98	2	71	29
2.15	.4842	.9842	.0158	98	2		
2.20	.4861	.9861	.0139	99	1	72	28
2.25	.4878	.9878	.0122	99	1		
2.30	.4893	.9893	.0107	99	1	73	27
2.35	.4906	.9906	.0094	99	1		
2.40	.4918	.9918	.0082	99	1	74	26
2.45	.4929	.9929	.0071	99	1		
2.50	.4938	.9938	.0062	99	1	75	25
2.55	.4946	.9946	.0054	99.5	0.5		
2.60	.4953	.9953	.0047	99.5	0.5	76	24
2.65	.4960	.9960	.0040	99.6	0.4		
2.70	.4965	.9965	.0035	99.6	0.4	77	23
2.75	.4970	.9970	.0030	99.7	0.3		
2.80	.4974	.9974	.0026	99.7	0.3	78	22
2.85	.4978	.9978	.0022	99.8	0.2		
2.90	.4981	.9981	.0019	99.8	0.2	79	21
2.95	.4984	.9984	.0016	99.8	0.2		
3.00	.4987	.9987	.0013	99.9	0.1	80	20

References

Adams, G. S. *Measurement and evaluation in education, psychology and guidance*. New York: Holt, Rinehart and Winston, Inc., 1965.

Allport, G. W. *Becoming: basic considerations for a psychology of personality*. New Haven, Conn.: Yale University Press, 1955.

American Psychological Association. Technical recommendations for psychological tests and diagnostic techniques. Washington, D. C.: American Psychological Association, 1954.

American Psychological Association. Ethical standards of psychologists. *American Psychologist*, 1963, 18, 56–60.

American Psychological Association. Standards for educational and psychological tests and manuals. Washington, D. C.: American Psychological Association, 1966.

Anastasi, A. The concept of validity in the interpretation of test scores. *Educational and Psychological Measurement*, 1950, 10, 67–78.

Anastasi, A. Heredity, environment and the question "How." *Psychological Review*, 1958, 65, 197–208.

Anastasi, A. *Differential psychology*. (3rd ed.) New York: Crowell-Collier and Macmillan, 1960.

Anastasi, A. (Ed.) *Testing problems in perspective*. Washington, D. C.: The American Council on Education, 1966.

Anastasi, A. *Psychological testing*. (3rd ed.) New York: Crowell-Collier and Macmillan, 1968.

Anderson, J. E. The prediction of terminal intelligence from infant and preschool tests. Thirty-ninth Yearbook, National Society for the Study of Education, 1940, Part I, 385–403.

Anderson, T. W. *An introduction to multivariate statistical analysis*. New York: John Wiley & Sons, Inc., 1958.

Angoff, W. H. Technical problems of obtaining equivalent scores on tests. *Journal of Educational Measurement*, 1964, 1, 11–13.

Astin, A. V. Standards of measurement. *Scientific American*, 1968, 218(6), 50–62.

Astin, A. W. Criterion-centered research. *Educational and Psychological Measurement*, 1964, 24, 807–822.

Astin, A. W., & R. J. Panos. The evaluation of educational programs. In R. L. Thorndike (Ed.) *Educational measurement*. American Council on Education, 1969.

Balma, M. J. The concept of synthetic validity. *Personnel Psychology*, 1959, 12, 395–396.

Barron, F. *Creativity and psychological health*. Princeton, N.J.: D. Van Nostrand Company, Inc., 1963.

Bauernfeind, R. H. Are sex norms necessary? *Journal of Counseling Psychology*, 1956, 3, 57–62.

Bauernfeind, R. H. The matter of "ipsative" scores. *Personnel and Guidance Journal*, 1962, 41, 210–217.

Bayley, N. On the growth of intelligence. *American Psychologist*, 1955, 10, 805–818.

Bayley, N. Behavioral correlates of mental growth: birth to thirty years. *American Psychologist*, 1968, 23, 1–17.

Bechtoldt, H. Construct validity: a critique. *American Psychologist*, 1959, 14, 619–629.

Bennett, G. K., H. G. Seashore, & A. G. Wesman. *Manual for the Differential Aptitude Tests*. (4th ed.) New York: The Psychological Corporation, 1966.

Berdie, R. F. Aptitude, interest and personality tests: a longitudinal comparison. *Journal of Applied Psychology*, 1955, 39, 103-114.

Berdie, R. F., et al. *Testing in guidance and counseling*. New York: McGraw-Hill, Inc., 1963.

Bereiter, C. Some persisting dilemmas in the measurement of change. In C. W. Harris (Ed.), *Problems in measuring change*. Madison, Wis.: University of Wisconsin Press, 1963.

Berg, I. A. (Ed.) *Response set in personality assessment*. Chicago: Aldine Publishing Co., 1967.

Black, H. *They shall not pass*. New York: William Morrow & Company, Inc., 1963.

Block, J. *The challenge of response sets: unconfounding meaning, acquiescence, and social desirability in the MMPI*. New York: Appleton-Century-Crofts, 1965.

Bloom, B. S., et al. *Taxonomy of educational objectives, handbook I: cognitive domain*. New York: David McKay Company, Inc., 1956.

Bloom, B. S. *Stability and change in human characteristics*. New York: John Wiley & Sons, Inc., 1964.

Brogden, H. E. On the interpretation of the correlation coefficient as a measure of predictive efficiency. *Journal of Educational Psychology*, 1946, 37, 65–76.

Brown, F. G. A note on expectancy ratios, base rates, and the SVIB. *Journal of Counseling Psychology*, 1961, 8, 368–369.

Brown, F. G. *Measuring achievement in the classroom*. Hinsdale, Ill.: The Dryden Press, 1970.

Brown, F. G., & D. A. Scott. The unpredictability of predictability. *Journal of Educational Measurement*, 1966, 3, 297–301.

Brown, F. G., & D. A. Scott. Differential predictability in college admissions testing. *Journal of Educational Measurement*, 1967, 4, 163–166.

Brown, F. G., & L. Wolins. An empirical evaluation of the American College Testing Program. *Personnel and Guidance Journal*, 1965, 43, 451–456.

Buros, O. (Ed.) *The fifth mental measurements yearbook*. Highland Park, N. J.: Gryphon Press, 1959.

Buros, O. (Ed.) *Tests in print*. Highland Park, N. J.: Gryphon Press, 1961.

Buros, O. (Ed.) *The sixth mental measurements yearbook*. Highland Park, N. J.: Gryphon Press, 1965.

Buros, O. The story behind the Mental Measurements Yearbooks. *Measurement and Evaluation in Guidance*, 1968, 1, 86–95.

Campbell, D. P. Stability of interests within an occupation over 30 years. *Journal of Applied Psychology*, 1966, 50, 51–56.

Campbell, D. P. The stability of vocational interests within occupations over long time spans. *Personnel and Guidance Journal*, 1966, 44, 1012–1019.

Campbell, D. T. Recommendations for APA test standards regarding construct, trait, and discriminant validity. *American Psychologist*, 1960, 15, 546–553.

Campbell, D. T., & D. W. Fiske. Convergent and discriminant validation by the multitrait-multimethod matrix. *Psychological Bulletin*, 1959, 56, 81–105.

Campbell, D. T., & J. C. Stanley. Experimental and quasi-experimental designs for research on teaching. In N. L. Gage (Ed.), *Handbook of research on teaching*. Skokie, Ill.: Rand McNally & Company, 1963.

Cattell, R. B. The three basic factor analytic research designs—their interrelations and derivatives. *Psychological Bulletin*, 1952, 49, 300–304.

Cattell, R. B. What is "objective" in "objective personality tests"? *Journal of Counseling Psychology*, 1958, 5, 285–289.

Cattell, R. B. Theory of fluid and crystallized intelligence: a critical experiment. *Journal of Educational Psychology*, 1963, 54, 1–22.

Cattell, R. B. Validity and reliability: a proposed more basic set of concepts. *Journal of Educational Psychology*, 1964, 55, 1–22.

Cattell, R. B. *The scientific analysis of personality*. London: Penguin Books, Inc., 1965.

Cattell, R. B. Are I.Q. tests intelligent? *Psychology Today*, March 1968, 56–62.

Clark, K. E. *The vocational interests of nonprofessional men*. Minneapolis: University of Minnesota Press, 1961.

Coffman, W. E. On the validity of essay tests of achievement. *Journal of Educational Measurement*, 1966, 3, 151–156.

College Entrance Examination Board. Effects of coaching on Scholastic Aptitude Test scores. New York: College Entrance Examination Board, 1965.

College Entrance Examination Board. A description of the College Board Scholastic Aptitude Test. 1967–1968. Princeton, N. J.: College Entrance Examination Board, 1967.

Comrey, A. L. A factor analysis of items on the MMPI hypochondriasis scale. *Educational and Psychological Measurement*, 1957, 17, 568–577.

Cooley, W. W., & P. R. Lohnes. *Multivariate procedures for the behavioral sciences*. New York: John Wiley & Sons, Inc., 1962.

Couch, A., & K. Keniston. Yeasayers and naysayers: agreeing response set as a personality variable. *Journal of Abnormal and Social Psychology*, 1960, 60, 151–174.

Cronbach, L. J. Response sets and test validity. *Educational and Psychological Measurement*, 1946, 6, 475–494.

Cronbach, L. J. *Essentials of psychological testing*. New York: Harper & Row, Publishers, 1949.

Cronbach, L. J. Statistical methods applied to Rorschach scores: a review. *Psychological Bulletin*, 1949, 46, 393–429.

Cronbach, L. J. Further evidence on response sets and test design. *Educational and Psychological Measurement*, 1950, 10, 3–31.

Cronbach, L. J. Coefficient Alpha and the internal structure of tests. *Psychometrika*, 1951, 16, 297–334.

Cronbach, L. J. *Essentials of psychological testing.* (2nd ed.) New York: Harper & Row, Publishers, 1960.

Cronbach, L. J. Validity. In R. L. Thorndike (Ed.), *Educational measurement.* (rev. ed.) Washington, D. C.: American Council on Education, 1969.

Cronbach, L. J., & G. C. Gleser. Assessing similarity between profiles. *Psychological Bulletin*, 1953, 50, 456–473.

Cronbach, L. J., & G. C. Gleser. *Psychological tests and personnel decisions.* Urbana, Ill.: University of Illinois Press, 1957.

Cronbach, L. J., & G. C. Gleser. *Psychological tests and personnel decisions.* (2nd ed.) Urbana, Ill.: University of Illinois Press, 1965.

Cronbach, L. J., N. Rajaratnam, & G. C. Gleser. Theory of generalizability: a liberalization of reliability theory. *British Journal of Statistical Psychology*, 1963, 16 (2), 137–163.

Cronbach, L. J., & P. E. Meehl. Construct validity in psychological tests. *Psychological Bulletin*, 1955, 52, 281–302.

Cronbach, L. J., & J. C. Merwin. A model for studying the validity of multiple-choice items. *Educational and Psychological Measurement*, 1955, 15, 337–352.

Cureton, E. E. Validity, reliability, and baloney. *Educational and Psychological Measurement*, 1950, 10, 94–96.

Dahlstrom, W. G., & G. S. Welsh. *An MMPI Handbook: a guide to use in clinical practice and research.* Minneapolis: University of Minnesota Press, 1960.

Darley, J. G., & T. Hagenah. *Vocational interest measurement: theory and practice.* Minneapolis: University of Minnesota Press, 1955.

Davis, F. B. Item selection techniques. Chap. 9 in E. F. Lindquist (Ed.), *Educational measurement.* Washington: American Council on Education, 1951.

Davis, F. B. *Educational measurements and their interpretation.* Belmont, Cal.: Wadsworth Publishing Co., 1964.

Davis, J. A. Non-apparent limitations of normative data. *Personnel and Guidance Journal*, 1959, 37, 656–659.

Doppelt, J. E. How accurate is a test score? Test Service Bulletin No. 50. New York: The Psychological Corporation, 1956.

Drake, L. E., & E. R. Oetting. An MMPI pattern and a suppressor variable predictive of academic achievement. *Journal of Counseling Psychology*, 1957, 4, 245–247.

Drake, L. E. & E. R. Oetting. *An MMPI codebook for counselors.* Minneapolis: University of Minnesota Press, 1959.

Dressel, P. L., & associates. *Evaluation in higher education.* Boston: Houghton Mifflin Company, 1961.

Drever, J. *A dictionary of psychology.* (rev. ed.) Baltimore: Penguin Books, Inc., 1964.

DuBois, P. H. *Multivariate correlational analysis.* New York: Harper & Row, Publishers, 1957.

Dunnette, M. D. A modified model for test validation and selection research. *Journal of Applied Psychology*, 1963, 47, 317–323.

Dunnette, M. D. *Personnel selection and placement*. Belmont, Cal.: Wadsworth Publishing Co., 1966.

Ebel, R. L. Obtaining and reporting evidence on content validity. *Educational and Psychological Measurement*, 1956, 16, 269–282.

Ebel, R. L. Must all tests be valid? *American Psychologist*, 1961, 16, 640–647.

Ebel, R. L. Content standard test scores. *Educational and Psychological Measurement*, 1962, 22, 15–25.

Ebel, R. L. The social consequences of educational testing. Proceedings of the 1963 Invitational Conference on Testing Problems, Educational Testing Service, 1964. Pp. 130–143.

Ebel, R. L. *Measuring educational achievement*. Englewood Cliffs, N. J.: Prentice-Hall, Inc., 1965.

Ebel, R. L. The value of internal consistency in classroom examinations. *Journal of Educational Measurement*, 1968, 5, 71–73.

Educational Testing Service. Making the classroom test: a guide for teachers. Princeton, N. J.: Educational and Advisory Service Series, No. 4, 1961.

Educational Testing Service. *Multiple-choice questions: a close look*. Princeton, N. J.: Educational Testing Service, 1963.

Educational Testing Service. *ETS builds a test*. Princeton, N. J.: Educational Testing Service, 1965.

Edwards, A. L. *The social desirability variable in personality assessment*. New York: Holt, Rinehart and Winston, Inc., 1957.

Edwards, A. L. Social desirability and personality test construction. In B. M. Bass & I. A. Berg (Eds.), *Objective approaches to personality assessment*. Princeton, N.J.: D. Van Nostrand Company, Inc., 1959. Pp. 100–118.

Edwards, A. L. The social desirability variable: a review of the evidence. In I. A. Berg (Ed.), *Response set in personality assessment*. Chicago: Aldine Publishing Co., 1967. Pp. 48–70.

Edwards, A. L. *Statistical anaylsis*. (3rd ed.) New York: Holt, Rinehart and Winston, Inc., 1969.

Edwards, A. L., & J. A. Walsh. Relationships between various psychometric properties of personality items. *Educational and Psychological Measurement*, 1963, 23, 227–238.

Englehart, M. D. What to look for in a review of an achievement test. *Personnel and Guidance Journal*, 1964, 42, 616–619.

English, H. B., & A. C. English. *A comprehensive dictionary of psychological and psychoanalytical terms*. New York: David McKay Company, Inc., 1958.

Faller, J. E. Precision measurement of the acceleration of gravity. *Science*, 1967, 158, 60–67.

Fishman, J. A., & A. K. Pasanella. College admission-selection studies. *Review of Educational Research*, 1960, 30, 298–310.

Fleishman, E. A. Individual differences and motor learning. Chap. 8, pp. 165–191, in R. M. Gagné (Ed.), *Learning and individual differences*. Columbus, Ohio: Charles E. Merrill Books, Inc., 1967.

Frederiksen, N., et al. The in-basket test. *Psychological Monographs*, 1957, 71 (9).

Frederiksen, N., & A. C. F. Gilbert. Replication of a study of differential predictability. *Educational and Psychological Measurement*, 1960, 20, 759–767.

Frederiksen, N., & S. D. Melville. Differential predictability in the use of test scores. *Educational and Psychological Measurement*, 1954, 14, 647–656.

Gage, N. L. (Ed.) *Handbook of research on teaching*. Skokie, Ill.: Rand McNally & Company, 1963.

Gagné, R. Instructional variables and learning outcomes. Paper presented at a symposium on Problems in the Evaluation of Instruction, University of California, Los Angeles, 1967.

Getzels, J. W., & P. W. Jackson. *Creativity and intelligence: explorations with gifted students*. New York: John Wiley & Sons, Inc., 1962.

Ghiselli, E. E. Differentiation of individuals in terms of their predictability. *Journal of Applied Psychology*, 1956, 40, 374–377.

Ghiselli, E. E. The prediction of predictability. *Educational and Psychological Measurement*, 1960, 20, 3–8.

Ghiselli, E. E. Differentiation of tests in terms of the accuracy with which they predict for a given individual. *Educational and Psychological Measurement*, 1960, 20, 675–684.

Ghiselli, E. E. Moderating effects and differential reliability and validity. *Journal of Applied Psychology*, 1963, 47, 81–86.

Ghiselli, E. E. *Theory of psychological measurement*. New York: McGraw-Hill, Inc., 1964.

Ghiselli, E. E. *The validity of occupational aptitude tests*. New York: John Wiley & Sons, Inc., 1966.

Glaser, R. Instructional technology and the measurement of learning outcomes: some questions. *American Psychologist*, 1963, 18, 519–521.

Gleser, G. C., L. J. Cronbach, & N. Rajaratnam. Generalizability of scores influenced by multiple sources of variance. *Psychometrika*, 1965, 30, 395–418.

Goldberg, L. R. Diagnosticians versus diagnostic signs: the diagnosis of psychosis versus neurosis from the MMPI. *Psychological Monographs*, 1965, 79 (9).

Goldberg, L. R. Simple models or simple processes? Some research on clinical judgments. *American Psychologist*, 1968, 23, 483–495.

Goldman, L. *Using tests in counseling*. New York: Appleton-Century-Crofts, 1961.

Goodenough, F. L. *Mental testing: its history, principles, and applications*. New York: Holt, Rinehart and Winston, Inc., 1949.

Goslin, D. A. *The search for ability: standardized testing in social perspective*. New York: Russell Sage Foundation, 1963.

Goslin, D. A. Standardized ability tests and testing. *Science*, 1968, 159, 851–855.

Guilford, J. P. *Psychometric methods*. (2nd ed.) New York: McGraw-Hill, Inc., 1954.

Guilford, J. P. The structure of intellect. *Psychological Bulletin*, 1956, 53, 267–293.

Guilford, J. P. Three faces of intellect. *American Psychologist*, 1959, 14, 469–479.

Guilford, J. P. Factorial angles to psychology. *Psychological Review*, 1961, 68, 1–20.

Guilford, J. P. *The nature of human intelligence*. New York: McGraw-Hill, Inc., 1967.

Gulliksen, H. *Theory of mental tests*. New York: John Wiley & Sons, Inc., 1950.

Guttman, L. A basis for analysing test-retest reliability. *Psychometrika*, 1945, 10, 255–282.

Hall, C. S., & G. Lindzey. *Theories of personality*. New York: John Wiley & Sons, Inc., 1957.

Harman, H. H. *Modern factor analysis*. Chicago: University of Chicago Press, 1967.

Harrell, T. W., & M. S. Harrell. Army General Classification Test scores for civilian occupations. *Educational and Psychological Measurement*, 1945, 5, 229–239.

Harris, C. W. (Ed.) *Problems in measuring change*. Madison, Wis.: University of Wisconsin Press, 1963.

Hathaway, S. R. Foreword to W. G. Dahlstrom & G. S. Welsh. *An MMPI Handbook: a guide to use in clinical practice and research*. Minneapolis: University of Minnesota Press, 1960.

Hathaway, S. R., & P. E. Meehl. *An atlas for the clinical use of the MMPI*. Minneapolis: University of Minnesota Press, 1951.

Hays, W. L. *Statistics for psychologists*. New York: Holt, Rinehart and Winston, Inc. 1963.

Helmstadter, G. C. *Principles of psychological measurement*. New York: Appleton-Century-Crofts. 1964.

Hoffman, B. The tyranny of multiple-choice tests. *Harper's Magazine*, March 1961, 37–44.

Hoffman, B. *The tyranny of testing*. New York: Crowell-Collier and Macmillan, Inc., 1962.

Hoffman, P. J. The paramorphic representation of clinical judgment. *Psychological Bulletin*, 1960, 57, 116–131.

Holt, R. R. Clinical and statistical prediction: a reformulation and some new data. *Journal of Abnormal and Social Psychology*, 1958, 56, 1–12.

Holtzman, W. H. Objective scoring of projective techniques. In B. M. Bass & I. A. Berg (Eds.), *Objective approaches to personality assessment*. Princeton, N.J.: D. Van Nostrand Company, Inc., 1959. Pp. 119–145.

Holtzman, W. H. *Inkblot perception and personality*. Chap. 2, Development of the Holtzman technique. Austin, Tex.: University of Texas Press, 1961.

Horn, J. L. Some characteristics of classroom examinations. *Journal of Educational Measurement*, 1966, 3, 293–295.

Horn, J. L. Intelligence—why it grows, why it declines. *Trans-Action*, November 1967, 23–31.

Horst, P. A. A technique for the development of a differential prediction battery. *Psychological Monographs*, 1954, 68 (9).

Horst, P. A. *Psychological measurement and prediction*. Belmont, Cal.: Wadsworth Publishing Co., 1966.

Hoyt, D. P. The relationship between college grades and adult achievement. A review of the literature. *ACT Research Reports*, September 1965, No. 7.

Hunt, J. McV. *Intelligence and experience*. New York: The Ronald Press Company, 1961.

Husén, T. (Ed.) *International study of achievement in mathematics*. (2 vols.) New York: John Wiley & Sons, Inc., 1967.

Jackson, D. N., & S. Messick. Content and style in personality assessment. *Psychological Bulletin*, 1958, 55, 243–252.

Jensen, A. R. Social class and verbal learning. In M. Deutsch, I. Katz, & A. R.

Jensen (Eds.), *Social class, race, and psychological development.* New York: Holt, Rinehart and Winston, Inc., 1968. Pp. 115–174.

Jensen, A. R. How much can we boost IQ and scholastic achievement? *Harvard Educational Review,* 1969, 39, 1–123.

Jessor, R., & K. R. Hammond. Construct validity and the Taylor Anxiety Scale. *Psychological Bulletin,* 1957, 54, 161–170.

Jones, L. V. A factor analysis of the Stanford-Binet at four age levels. *Psychometrika,* 1949, 14, 299–331.

Kassebaum, G. G., A. S. Couch, & P. E. Slater. The factorial dimensions of the MMPI. *Journal of Consulting Psychology,* 1959, 23, 226–236.

Katz, M. Interpreting Kuder Preference Record-Vocational scores: ipsative or normative? Paper presented at 1962 convention of American Personnel and Guidance Association.

Keats, J. A. Test theory. In P. R. Farnsworth, (Ed.), *Annual review of psychology.* Palo Alto, Cal.: Annual Reviews, Inc., 1967, 18, 217–238.

Kelly, G. A. The theory and technique of assessment. *Annual review of psychology,* 1958, 9, 323–352.

Kelly, E. L., & D. W. Fiske. *The prediction of performance in clinical psychology.* Ann Arbor, Mich.: University of Michigan Press, 1951.

Kerlinger, F. N. *Foundations of behavioral research.* New York: Holt, Rinehart, and Winston, Inc., 1965.

Kuder, G. F. A rationale for evaluating interests. *Educational and Psychological Measurement,* 1963, 23, 3–12.

Kuder, G. F. The Occupational Interest Survey. *Personnel and Guidance Journal,* 1966, 45, 72–77.

Kuder, G. F., & M. W. Richardson. The theory of estimation of test reliability. *Psychometrika,* 1937, 2, 151–160.

Lavin, D. E. *The prediction of academic performance.* New York: Russell Sage Foundation, 1965.

Layton, W. L. Minnesota studies in student personnel work, No. 8, Counseling use of the Strong Vocational Interest Blank. Minneapolis: University of Minnesota Press, 1958.

Layton, W. L. Minnesota studies in student personnel work, No. 10, The Strong Vocational Interest Blank: research and uses. Minneapolis: University of Minnesota Press, 1960.

Lewis, E. C. *Developing woman's potential.* Ames, Iowa: Iowa State University Press, 1968.

Lindquist, E. F. Equating scores on non-parallel tests. *Journal of Educational Measurement,* 1964, 1, 5–10.

Lindzey, G. *Projective techniques and cross-cultural research.* New York: Appleton-Century-Crofts, 1961.

Loevinger, J. A systematic approach to the construction and evaluation of tests of ability. *Psychological Monographs,* 61(4), 1947.

Loevinger, J. Objective tests as instruments of psychological theory. *Psychological Reports,* Monograph Supplement 9, 1957, 3, 635–694.

Longstaff, H. P. Fakability of the Strong Interest Blank and the Kuder Preference Record. *Journal of Applied Psychology,* 1948, 32, 360–369.

Lonner, W. J. The SVIB visits German, Austrian, and Swiss psychologists. *American Psychologist*, 1968, 23, 164–179.

Lord, F. M. Do tests of the same length have the same standard error of measurement? *Educational and Psychological Measurement*, 1957, 17, 510–521.

Lord, F. M., & M. R. Novick. *Statistical theories of mental test scores*. Reading, Mass.: Addison-Wesley Publishing Company, Inc., 1968.

Lorge, I. The fundamental nature of measurement. In E. F. Lindquist (Ed.), *Educational measurement*. Washington, D. C.: American Council on Education, 1951. Pp. 533–559.

Lumsden, J. The construction of unidimensional tests. *Psychological Bulletin*, 1961, 58, 122–131.

Lyman, H. B. *Test scores and what they mean*. Englewood Cliffs, N. J.: Prentice-Hall, Inc., 1963.

MacKinney, A. C. The assessment of performance change: an inductive example. *Organizational Behavior and Human Performance*, 1967, 2, 56–72.

MacKinnon, D. W. The nature and nuture of creative talent. *American Psychologist*, 1962, 17, 484–495.

McArthur, C. Long-term validity of the Strong Interest Test in two subcultures. *Journal of applied Psychology*, 1954, 38, 346–353.

McCall, W. A. *How to measure in education*. New York: Crowell-Collier and Macmillan, 1922.

McClelland, D. C., J. W. Atkinson, R. A. Clark, & E. L. Lowell. *The achievement motive*. New York: Appleton-Century-Crofts, 1953.

McGee, R. K. Response style as a personality variable: by what criterion? *Psychological Bulletin*, 1962, 59, 284–295.

McHugh, R. B. The interval estimation of a true score. *Psychological Bulletin*, 1957, 54, 73–78.

McNemar, Q. *The revision of the Stanford-Binet Scale: an analysis of the standardization data*. Boston: Houghton Mifflin Company, 1942.

McNemar, Q. Lost: our intelligence. Why? *American Psychologist*, 1964, 19, 871–882.

Magnusson, D. *Test theory*. Reading, Mass.: Addison-Wesley Publishing Company, Inc., 1966.

Marks, P. A., & W. Seeman. *The actuarial description of abnormal personality—an atlas for use with the MMPI*. Baltimore: The Williams & Wilkins Company, 1963.

Masling, J. The influence of situational and interpersonal variables in projective testing. *Psychological Bulletin*, 1960, 56, 65–85.

Meehl, P. E. The dynamics of "structured" personality tests. *Journal of Clinical Psychology*, 1945, 1, 296–303.

Meehl, P. E. Configural scoring. *Journal of Consulting Psychology*, 1950, 14, 165–171.

Meehl, P. E. *Clinical versus statistical prediction: a theoretical analysis and a review of the evidence*. Minneapolis: University of Minnesota Press, 1954.

Meehl, P. E. Wanted—a good cookbook. *American Psychologist*, 1956, 11, 263–272.

Meehl, P. E. When shall we use our heads instead of the formula? *Journal of counseling Psychology*, 1957, 4, 268–273.

Meehl, P. E. A comparison of clinicians with five statistical methods of identifying psychotic MMPI profiles. *Journal of Counseling Psychology*, 1959, 6, 102–109.

Meehl, P. E., & S. R. Hathaway. The K factor as a suppressor variable in the MMPI. *Journal of Applied Psychology*, 1946, 30, 525–564.

Meehl, P. E., & A. Rosen. Antecedent probability and the efficiency of psychometric signs, patterns, or cutting scores. *Psychological Bulletin*, 1955, 52, 194–216.

Michael, W. B., et al. The description of spatial-visualization abilities. *Educational and Psychological Measurement*, 1957, 17, 185–199.

Michael, W. B. Aptitudes. In C. W. Harris (Ed.), *Encyclopedia of Educational Research*. (3rd ed.) New York: Crowell-Collier and Macmillan, 1960. Pp. 59–63.

Mischel, W. *Personality and assessment*. New York: John Wiley & Sons, Inc., 1968.

Mosier, C. I. Batteries and profiles. In E. F. Lindquist (Ed.), *Educational measurement*. Washington, D. C.: American Council on Education, 1951. Pp. 764–808.

Murray, H. A. *Explorations in personality*. New York: Oxford University Press, 1938.

The OSS Assessment Staff. *Assessment of men*. New York: Holt, Rinehart and Winston, Inc., 1948.

Overall, J. E. Note on the scientific status of factors. *Psychological Bulletin*, 1964, 61, 270–276.

Page, E. B. Grading essays by computer: progress report. Proceedings of the 1966 Invitational Conference on Testing Problems. Princeton, N. J.: Educational Testing Service, 1967. Pp. 87–100.

Pinneau, S. R. *Changes in intelligence quotient from infancy to maturity*. Boston: Houghton Mifflin Company, 1961.

Privacy and behavioral research. Executive Office of the President, Office of Science and Technology. Washington, D. C.: U. S. Government Printing Office, 1967.

Rasch, G. An item analysis which takes individual differences into account. *British Journal of Mathematical and Statistical Psychology*, 1966, 19(1), 49–57.

Richardson, M. W., & G. F. Kuder. The calculation of test reliability coefficients based on the method of rational equivalence. *Journal of Educational Psychology*, 1939, 30, 681–687.

Rorer, A. R. The great response-style myth. *Psychological Bulletin*, 1965, 63, 129–156.

Rosenthal, R., & L. Jacobson. *Pygmalion in the classroom. Teacher expectation and pupils' intellectual development*. New York: Holt, Rinehart and Winston, Inc., 1968.

Royce, J. R. Factors as theoretical constructs. *American Psychologist*, 1963, 18, 522–528.

Ruebhausen, O. M., & O. G. Brim, Jr. Privacy and behavioral research. *American Psychologist*, 1966, 21, 423–437.

Sarason, S. B., K. S. Davidson, F. F. Lighthall, R. R. Waite, & B. K. Ruebush. *Anxiety in elementary school children*. New York: John Wiley & Sons, Inc., 1960.

Sarbin, T. R. The logic of prediction in psychology. *Psychological Review*, 1944, 51, 210–228.

Saunders, D. R. Moderator variables in prediction. *Educational and Psychological Measurement*, 1956, 16, 209–222.

Sawyer, J. Measurement *and* prediction, clinical *and* statistical. *Psychological Bulletin*, 1966, 66, 178–200.

Schrader, W. B. A taxonomy of expectancy tables. *Journal of Educational Measurement*, 1965, 2, 29–35.

Seashore, H. G. Methods of expressing test scores. Test Service Bulletin No. 48. New York: The Psychological Corporation, 1955.

Seashore, H. G. Women are more predictable than men. *Journal of Counseling Psychology*, 1962, 9, 261–270.

Sechrest, L. Incremental validity: a recommendation. *Educational and Psychological Measurement*, 1963, 23, 153–158.

Smedslund, J. Concrete reasoning: a study of intellectual development. *Monographs of the Society for Research in Child Development*, 1964, 29 (2, Serial No. 93), 3–39.

Stanley, J. C. Reliability. In R. L. Thorndike (Ed.), *Educational Measurement* (rev. ed.) Washington, D. C.: American Council on Education, 1969.

Stevens, S. S. Mathematics, measurement, and psychophysics. In S. S. Stevens (Ed.), *Handbook of experimental psychology*. New York: John Wiley & Sons, Inc., 1951. Pp. 1–49.

Strong, E. K. *Vocational interests of men and women*. Stanford, Cal.: Stanford University Press, 1943.

Strong, E. K. *Vocational interests 18 years after college*. Minneapolis: University of Minnesota Press, 1955.

Strong, E. K., & D. P. Campbell. *Manual for Strong Vocational Interest Blanks*. Stanford, Cal.: Stanford University Press, 1966.

Super, D. E. *The use of multifactor tests in guidance*. Washington: American Personnel and Guidance Association, 1958.

Super, D. E., & J. O. Crites. *Appraising vocational fitness*. New York: Harper & Row, Publishers, 1962.

Taylor, C. W., & F. Barron. *Scientific creativity: its recognition and development*. New York: John Wiley & Sons, Inc., 1963.

Taylor, H. C., & J. T. Russell. The relationship of validity coefficients to the practical effectiveness of tests in selection: discussion and tables. *Journal of Applied Psychology*, 1939, 23, 565–578.

Terman, L. M., & M. A. Merrill. *Measuring intelligence*. Boston: Houghton Mifflin Company, 1937.

Terman, L. M., & M. A. Merrill. *Stanford-Binet Intelligence Scale: manual for the third revision, form L-M*. Boston: Houghton Mifflin Company, 1960.

Thelen, M. H., et al. Attitudes of academic clinical psychologists toward projective techniques. *American Psychologist*, 1968, 23, 517–521.

Thorndike, R. L. Reliability. In E. F. Lindquist (Ed.), *Educational measurement*. Washington, D. C.: American Council on Education, 1951. Pp. 560-620.

Thorndike, R. L. Educational decisions and human assessment. *Teachers College Record*, 1964, 66, 103–112.

Thorndike, R. L. (Ed.) *Educational measurement*. (rev. ed.) Washington, D. C.: American Council on Education, 1969.

Thorndike, R. L., & E. P. Hagen. *Ten thousand careers*. New York: John Wiley & Sons, Inc., 1959.

Thorndike, R. L., & E. P. Hagen. *Measurement and evaluation in psychology and education*. (2nd ed.) New York: John Wiley & Sons, Inc., 1961

Thurstone, L. L. *Multiple-factor analysis*. Chicago: University of Chicago Press, 1947.

Thurstone, L. L. & L. Ackerson. The mental growth curve for the Binet tests. *Journal of Educational Psychology*, 1929, 20, 569–583.

Tilton, J. W. The measurement of overlapping. *Journal of Educational Psychology*, 1937, 28, 656–662.

Torrance, E. P. *Guiding creative talent.* Englewood Cliffs, N. J.: Prentice-Hall, Inc., 1962.

Tyler, L. *The psychology of human differences.* (3rd ed.) New York: Appleton-Century-Crofts, 1965.

Tyler, R. W., J. C. Merwin, & R. L. Ebel. Symposium: a national assessment of educational progress. *Journal of Educational Measurement,* 1966, 3, 1–17.

Vernon, P. E. *The structure of human abilities.* London: Methuen & Co., Ltd., 1950.

Vernon, P. E. *The measurement of abilities.* (2nd ed.) London: Methuen & Co., Ltd., 1961.

Vernon, P. E. *Personality assessment: a critical survey.* London: Methuen & Co., Ltd., 1964.

Webb, E. J., et al. *Unobtrusive measures: nonreactive research in the social sciences.* Skokie, Ill.: Rand McNally & Company, 1966.

Wechsler, D. *Manual for the Wechsler Adult Intelligence Scale.* New York: The Psychological Corporation, 1955.

Wechsler, D. *The measurement and appraisal of adult intelligence.* Baltimore: The Williams & Wilkins Company, 1958.

Weitz, J. Criteria for criteria. *American Psychologist,* 1961, 16, 228–231.

Welsh, G. S. Factor dimensions A and R. In G. S. Welsh & W. G. Dahlstrom, *Basic readings on the MMPI in psychology and medicine.* Minneapolis: University of Minnesota Press, 1956. Pp. 264–281.

Welsh, G. S., & W. G. Dahlstrom (Eds..) *Basic readings on the MMPI in psychology and medicine.* Minneapolis: University of Minnesota Press, 1956.

Wesman, A. G. Reliability and confidence. Test Service Bulletin No. 44. New York: The Psychological Corporation, 1952.

Wesman, A. G. Double-entry expectancy tables. Test Service Bulletin No. 56. New York: The Psychological Corporation, 1966.

Wilks, S. S. *Mathematical statistics.* New York: John Wiley & Sons, Inc., 1962.

Wittrock, M. C., & D. E. Wiley. *Problems in evaluation of instruction.* New York: Holt, Rinehart and Winston, Inc., 1970.

Wood, D. A. *Test construction: development and interpretation of achievement tests.* Columbus, Ohio: Charles E. Merrill Books, Inc., 1960.

Wright, B. D. Sample-free test calibration and person measurement. *Proceedings of the 1967 Invitational Conference on Testing Problems.* Princeton, N.J.: Educational Testing Service, 1968. Pp. 85–101.

Young, M. *The rise of the meritocracy.* Baltimore: Penguin Books, Inc., 1961.

Zytowski, D. G. Relationships of equivalent scales on three interest inventories. *Personnel and Guidance Journal,* 1968, 47, 44–49.

Author Index

Subject Index